A FIELD GUIDE TO BIRDS OF RUSSIA AND
ADJACENT TERRITORIES

PUBLISHER'S NOTE

In 1991, seven years after *A Field Guide to Birds of the USSR* was first published, the Soviet Union ceased to exist as a political and geographical entity. Although we have revised the title of this volume to reflect the drawing of new boundaries, it is impossible to rewrite the entire text. This does not, however, detract from the guide's usefulness to both ornithologists and bird watchers.

A FIELD GUIDE TO

Birds of Russia and Adjacent Territories

V. E. FLINT, R. L. BOEHME, Y. V. KOSTIN,
A. A. KUZNETSOV

ILLUSTRATED BY Y. V. KOSTIN

TRANSLATED FROM THE RUSSIAN BY
NATALIA BOURSO-LELAND

ORNITHOLOGICAL ADVISOR,
JAMES BAIRD

PRINCETON UNIVERSITY PRESS

Copyright © 1984 by Princeton University Press
Published by Princeton University Press, 41 William Street,
Princeton, New Jersey 08540
In the United Kingdom: Princeton University Press,
Chichester, West Sussex

Originally published as *A Field Guide to Birds of the USSR*

ISBN 0-691-08244-8
ISBN 0-691-02430-8, pbk.
First Princeton Paperback printing, 1989

Library of Congress Cataloging-in-Publication Data
will be found on the last printed page of this book

This book has been composed in Linotron Baskerville

Princeton University Press books are printed on acid-free paper
and meet the guidelines for permanence and durability of the
Committee on Production Guidelines for Book Longevity of the
Council on Library Resources

Printed in the United States of America

10 9 8 7 6 5

Color plates printed by Princeton Polychrome Press

CONTENTS

LIST OF FIGURES   vii

TRANSLATOR'S FOREWORD   ix

INTRODUCTION TO ENGLISH-LANGUAGE EDITION   xv

A FIELD GUIDE TO BIRDS OF RUSSIA AND ADJACENT TERRITORIES   1

BIBLIOGRAPHY   309

INDEX OF ENGLISH NAMES   311

CROSS-REFERENCE LIST *by Peter Alden*   315

INDEX OF GENERA   345

INDEX OF RUSSIAN NAMES   348

LIST OF FIGURES

Biotic Zones of the USSR   xvi

Fig. 1   Chart of a Bird   xxxii

Fig. 2   Bird Measurements   xxxii

Fig. 3   Bird Crests   xxxiii

Fig. 4   Types of Feet   xxxiv

Fig. 5   Types of Feet   xxxiv

Fig. 6   Tail Types   xxxv

Fig. 7   Flock Formations   xxxv

Fig. 8   Bird Bands of Various Ornithological Stations   xxxvi

Fig. 9   Egg Shapes   xxxvi

Fig. 10   Posture of Birds on Water   4

Fig. 11   A Grebe's Nest   6

Fig. 12   Bill of Horned Grebe and Black-necked Grebe   7

Fig. 13   Bill of Northern Fulmar and Large *Larus* Gull   9

Fig. 14   Eastern White Pelican in Flight   11

Fig. 15   Short-legged Waterbirds in Flight   14

Fig. 16   Gray Heron at Its Nest   15

Fig. 17   Great Egret Chick   17

Fig. 18   White Stork at Its Nest   24

Fig. 19   Long-legged Waterbirds in Flight   25

Fig. 20   Swans, Geese, and Shelducks in Flight   27

Fig. 21   Dabbling Ducks and Sawbills in Flight   36

Fig. 22   Mallard Duckling   37

Fig. 23   Bill of Female Common Eider and King Eider   42

Fig. 24   Rear Toe of Dabbling Duck and Pochard   45

Fig. 25   Diving Ducks and Sea Ducks in Flight   49

Fig. 26   Bill of Merganser and Dabbling Duck   53

Fig. 27   Feet of Raptors   56

Fig. 28   Raptors in Flight   58

Fig. 29   Black Kite Nestling   59

Fig. 30   Regurgitated Pellets of Undigested Materials   64

Fig. 31   Raptors in Flight   66

Fig. 32   Nostrils of Juvenile Lesser Spotted Eagle and Steppe Eagle   68

Fig. 33   Nest of Greater Spotted Eagle   69

Fig. 34   Bill of Peregrine Falcon and Northern Goshawk   75

Fig. 35   Gyrfalcon Nest on a Precipice   77

Fig. 36   Raptors in Flight   78

Fig. 37   Footprints of Large Birds   81

Fig. 38   Northern Black Grouse Chick   82

Fig. 39   Scats of Game Birds   83

Fig. 40   Gallinaceous Birds in Flight   86

Fig. 41   Crane's Nest   93

Fig. 42   Spotted Crake Chick   99

Fig. 43   Shorebirds in Flight   105

Fig. 44   Shorebird Feet   115

Fig. 45   Black-tailed Godwit Chick   126

Fig. 46   Tail Feathers of Great Snipe   133

Fig. 47   Tail Feathers of Snipe   134

Fig. 48   Bird Footprints   136

Fig. 49   Tail of Adult Long-tailed Jaeger and Parasitic Jaeger   138

Fig. 50   Gull Chick   139

Fig. 51   Marsh Terns in Flight (Summer)   149

Fig. 52   Murre Chick   155

Fig. 53   Alcids in Water   161

Fig. 54   Pallas's Sandgrouse and Black-bellied Sandgrouse in Flight   163

Fig. 55   Pigeons in Flight   165

Fig. 56   Wing of Oriental Cuckoo and Eurasian Cuckoo   170

Fig. 57   Snowy Owl Nestling   172

Fig. 58   Flight Silhouettes of Typical Nightjar and Owl   176

Fig. 59   Tail of European Nightjar and Gray Nightjar   180

Fig. 60   Birds in Flight   184

Fig. 61   Fir and Pine Cones: Seed Removal by Woodpecker and Crossbill   188

Fig. 62   Feet of Tree Pipit, Meadow Pipit, and Northern Skylark   201

Fig. 63   Bill of Shrike and Thrush   207
Fig. 64   Beetle Impaled on Thorn by
   Shrike   208
Fig. 65   Passerine Nests   213
Fig. 66   Passerine Nests   215
Fig. 67   Wings of Chiffchaff and

   Arctic Warbler   236
Fig. 68   Sparrow Nestling   295
Fig. 69   Nests of Spanish Sparrow   296
Fig. 70   Corvids in Flight   301
Fig. 71   Nest of Black-billed Magpie   306

TRANSLATOR'S FOREWORD

PUBLISHED in 1968, the original Russian edition of *Birds of the USSR* was soon out of print and hard to find even in the bookstalls of Moscow. Although a limited number of books were exported, it has also been difficult to obtain in North America. For bird-watching groups who ventured into the USSR in pursuit of local specialties, little nontechnical information for regions east and south of the Urals has been available in the English language (although European field guides were used for regions west of the Urals, and Japanese guides helped with parts of the Soviet Far East). The present English-language edition is a translation of the first popular Russian field guide, which was originally written as part of a series of books on flora and fauna of the USSR.

Amateur bird watching in the USSR emerged only in the mid to late 1960s, when it slowly grew as a hobby of interest to Russians. Since ornithology is carefully studied as a science only by specialists, and is most often a hobby for those who work in related fields of the natural sciences, there are very few counterparts to the sophisticated western amateur birder.

Russians traditionally have a great love of nature, and are often knowledgeable "practical naturalists." They are familiar with many species of mushrooms, barks, and berries that are put up for the winter as tonics and delicacies. Various combinations of roots, leaves, and flowers are popularly used both in cosmetics and in folk medicine. In the countryside, villagers still often depend on hunting for animals and birds as a source of fresh meat. With the increase of nature reserves and the need to enforce conservation measures in order to protect a number of rapidly diminishing species of flora and fauna, local attitudes of Soviet citizens had to change. A game bird might have been a source of dinner at one time, but now people are asked to protect and appreciate it as a creature valuable to the balance of nature. Since conservation education programs have been established in many regions, public awareness has grown and numerous publications are devoted to nature protection. Some newspapers and journals now carry regular columns with birdwatching information.

The present edition includes updated information and revisions provided by the senior author, Dr. Vladimir E. Flint, to the translator over the course of several trips to Moscow and by correspondence. Some suggestions made by Princeton University Press and its reviewers for making this field guide more useful to English-speaking bird watchers have been incorporated with the approval and assistance of the senior author. Bird sizes, range and distribution information, several maps, a few species descriptions, indexes, and the introduction to the English-language edition are new. Some information included under "Field Marks" and a number of range maps have been updated. In several cases, taxonomic nomenclature has been revised and updated with the approval of the senior author.

Since I am not an ornithologist, it has been my great good fortune to have convinced James Baird, Director of the Conservation Department of the Massachusetts Audubon Society, to review my translation for general accuracy. It should be emphasized that Mr. Baird's task was not to cast a critical scientific eye on the work of Messrs. Flint, Boehme, et al., but simply to ensure that the biological language, a specialized tongue in all countries, had the same authentic ring in English as it does in the original Russian. Despite efforts to translate the material into the best possible Anglo-American ornithological usage, some terms—such as those describing uniquely Russian habitats or vegetation—are impossible to translate satisfactorily.

English-language names of birds have been the responsibility of Peter C. Alden of the Massachusetts Audubon Society, and taxonomic preferences have been agreed upon with the senior author (see Cross-reference Index).

I have used System 1 (or the Popular System) with some minor modifications for transliteration of proper names of birds from the Russian. The system is described in *The Transliteration of Modern Russian for English-language Publications*, by J. Thomas Shaw (Madison: University of Wisconsin Press, 1967).

Spellings of proper geographical names have been taken from *Webster's New Geographical Dictionary* (Springfield, Mass.: G. & C. Merriam Co., 1977). Some of these proper names do not coincide with System 1 transliteration (Lake Baikal instead of Baykal, for example). In these cases, the more common dictionary spelling (Lake Baikal) prevailed.

In the text, Red Data Book refers strictly to the Red Data Book of the USSR, as distinct from that published by the International Council for Bird Preservation (ICBP Bird Red Data Book), which covers the entire world. The ICBP Red Data Book lists only fourteen species from the USSR.

Definitions of some geographic terms not usually appearing in the same sense in English-language publication have been here paraphrased from the official Great Soviet Encyclopedia and the Short Soviet Geographical Encyclopedia.

West Asia refers mostly to non-Soviet territory (Perednaya Aziya). It is the southwestern part of the main continental mass of Asia from the Bosporus, Mediterranean, and Red Sea lands of Asia to the uplands of the Iranian Plateau, and consists of two main portions: southern lowlands—southwest Asia in the strict sense, that is, the Levant

(Lebanon and Syria), Israel, Jordan, Iraq, Arabia, and the various adjoining political entities; and the northern uplands, embraced by the term Asia Minor—the Anatolian Plateau (Turkey), Armenian Plateau (Transcaucasia: Armenia, southern Georgia), and the Iranian Plateau (Iran and Afghanistan to the Indus River).

Central Asia refers to the Soviet republics of Kazakhstan, Uzbekistan, Kirgizia, Tajikistan, and Turkmenistan.

The Soviet Far East is the region beginning near the city of Khabarovsk and including areas east of the Amur and Ussuri Rivers, as well as the Kamchatka Peninsula, Sakhalin, and the Kuril Islands.

Briefly, it is useful to recall that there are fifteen republics in the USSR. The Russian Soviet Federated Socialist Republic (RSFSR), commonly referred to as "Russia" in the West, is the largest republic in the Soviet Union, and includes Leningrad and Moscow, and stretches across Siberia to the Pacific. Other union republics are Moldavia, Belorussia, and the Ukraine; Estonia, Latvia, and Lithuania in the Baltic; three Transcaucasus republics—Armenia, Georgia, and Azerbaijan; and five Central Asian republics—Kazakhstan, Uzbekistan, Kirgizia, Tajikistan, and Turkmenistan. In this publication, the authors often separate out Kazakhstan (due to its size) when referring to that republic, as well as referring to "the rest" of Central Asia.

An oblast, okrug, and krai are smaller than a republic and are further administrative subdivisions.

NOTES ON BIRDING IN THE USSR FOR TRAVELLERS

There are a number of obstacles to successful field ornithology for the visitor to the USSR: the roads don't always go where the birds are; and random exploration is not permitted. The first holds no terror for anyone in good health who has birded beyond the "developed" world; in fact, the absence of roads often means the presence of undisturbed habitat and may be counted more a blessing than a curse. The second obstacle, however, is more troublesome. The very essence of bird watching is courting the unpredictable: exploring likely looking habitats off the beaten path or simply waiting in a promised spot before sunrise for some avian activity to begin. The tight, highly structured tourist itineraries generally available through Intourist, the Soviet travel agency, are not compatible with effective or enjoyable bird watching. This travel agency prepares routes that do not always coincide with places where the most interesting birds can be seen. Once in place, changing these fixed routes can be rather complicated, if not impossible. Birders should try to join an organized birding tour to Russia, if possible.

Second, most tourists have little knowledge of the geography and natural history of the Soviet Union prior to their arrival. Though there are areas in the north and east that are sparsely settled, virgin land is not often found near large cities. A significant amount of land is occupied by farming or industry, containing only a few common species of birds. Some tourist routes include (if requested) reserves where nature has been well preserved and where there is a wealth of birds living in complete protection. One should be prepared for the fact that many regions of Siberia, the far north, the Ussuri region, and Central Asia are not yet prepared to receive tourists. This will often hamper or preclude the possibility of becoming acquainted with some of the more interesting birds found in these areas.

And finally, as in any other country of the world, there are many widespread species of birds in the Soviet Union that can be seen nearly everywhere. But there are also rare or localized species that are well known because of the work of professional ornithologists over a period of years. It is unlikely that the ordinary tourist will have an opportunity to see many, if any, rare birds during the period of a short visit. What follows are some suggestions on how to get around these and other obstacles to a successful birding tour of the USSR.

If birding is to be the main objective of a visit to the Soviet Union, it is vital to do some research about the avifauna, and then plan an itinerary consisting of places that have good birding potential, such as mountains, wetlands, deserts, and regions with Russian endemics and northern Asian specialties that do not occur in western Europe or Alaska; and places that are likely to be accessible to foreign visitors, that is near major roads and population centers. Many mountain and waterside spots, for instance, have tourist facilities and can readily be visited. In many of the larger cities west of the Urals, it is possible to rent cars from Intourist and plan a driving itinerary. Although exact routes and timing must be specified well in advance, this option still allows more elbow-room for the avid bird watcher than any group excursion. It is also possible to stay at state-operated camp sites rather than hotels, again allowing more time in the field.

There are also a number of Intourist-approved hiking itineraries traversing routes that seem promising ornithologically. One route in the western Caucasus, for example, begins at the reserve at Teberda (where there is a good hotel and some excellent coniferous forest), traverses the Klukhorsky Pass at 2,781 meters, and descends to Sukhumi on the Black Sea coast. As Dr. Flint notes in his introduction, the Russian highlands hold some of the most interesting birds, and on such a high Caucasus trek, one should be able to see specialties such as Kruper's Nuthatch, Guldenstadt's Redstart, Radde's Accentor, Red-fronted Serin, Lammergeier and Caucasian Snowcock, as well as interesting mammals such as the maral, tur, and chamois. Foreigners are generally not allowed to hike on their own or to join Russian or

East European groups, but West European hiking groups often advertise such excursions.

If a group tour with Americans or Europeans is preferred, sign up for a natural history tour rather than a general-interest program, since the general program will provide little opportunity for serious bird watching. The migration months of April to May and August to September are the best times to travel for birding.

The Soviet government has established an impressive system of over 120 large nature reserves (*zapovedniki*) comprising over 20 million acres, as well as over 37 million acres of sanctuaries (*zakazniki*) where nature protection is less strict and public use somewhat broader. Some of the zapovedniki are staffed by highly knowledgeable scientists and naturalists, and contain rare plants, animals, and/or fine examples of habitat. Overall administration of the reserves and sanctuaries is divided between the Department of Nature Reserves and Hunting (Ministry of Agriculture in Moscow); regional branches of the Academy of Sciences of the USSR; some universities; local administrations of hunting and forestry; and various committees for the preservation of nature. Few have any facilities for visitors, and most are not normally open to foreign tourists, since they are operating scientific establishments. However, visits to some may be possible by prior arrangement. A list of zapovedniki, entitled "Nature and Game Reserves of the USSR," with locations, brief floral and faunal descriptions, and addresses of administrations, is available from the U.S. Department of Commerce. Write to the Clearing House for Federal Scientific and Technical Information, Springfield, VA 22151.

Finally, it may be worth noting that visitors who can accommodate themselves to the particularities of the organization of Soviet travel will find their experience far more rewarding than will those who are less flexible.

ACKNOWLEDGMENTS

Due to many years of work in private cultural exchange, it has been an enormous satisfaction to have been involved in the production of this English-language edition with Princeton University Press, and particularly with the support and thoughtful guidance of Edward Tenner, Science Editor.

Peter C. Alden of the Massachusetts Audubon Society is responsible for the preparation of the Latin and English indexes that greatly enhance the usefulness of this publication. Comments and questions on nomenclature may be addressed to the Massachusetts Audubon Society, Lincoln, MA 01773

I would like to thank Christopher Leahy of the Massachusetts Audubon Society for his important assistance and advice in writing the foreword. My appreciation goes also to Yuri Raskin for invaluable assistance and advice in translation; to Doreen Ross and Veronica Worth for help in organization and preparation of the typescript, and to Tamara Bourso for considerable typing and organizational assistance; also to Claudine Nacamuli for her patient and endless typing and corrections. I am also grateful to Margaret Case, my copy editor at Princeton University Press, for valued help. Prof. David Sloane of Tufts University kindly advised me on the system of transliteration used, and made suggestions for modification of the standard system. My deepest gratitude goes to Betsy Moyer for her caring and painstaking reading of the proofs.

I would like to acknowledge the invaluable aid of the International Affairs staff of the U.S. Fish and Wildlife Service and the Science Section of the U.S. Embassy in Moscow. Their assistance was made possible through the USA-USSR Environmental Agreement, Area 5— Protection of Nature and the Organization of Preserves.

The hard work and dedication of Dr. Vladimir I. Flint must be noted, as well as the invaluable cooperation of his Russian colleagues, Dr. Rurik Boehme and Prof. Alexander Kuznetsov. I am also grateful to Dr. Vladimir Jacobi and Dr. Stanislav Lipin for invaluable advice.

Again, I must express a great indebtedness to James Baird for his kind and tireless help and advice in editing of my translation. It would never have been possible without his assistance, and I remain grateful for his encouragement, wisdom, and friendship.

Natalia Bourso-Leland
1981

INTRODUCTION TO THE
ENGLISH-LANGUAGE EDITION

THE Soviet Union is an enormous country. It occupies 22 million square kilometers and nearly one-sixth of the earth's land mass. The distance between its eastern and western boundaries is nearly 12,000 kilometers. Its northern and eastern regions are washed by many seas and oceans; along its southern borders stretch high mountain ranges. It is not surprising, therefore, that the wildlife of the Soviet Union varies greatly: on the lands of this country, one can find desert and tundra, massive taiga and regions of steppe, mountains, and valleys of enormous rivers. Naturally, a significant portion of the environment is occupied by agricultural or industrial endeavor.

In conjunction with the diversity of physical environment, there is a great variety in the bird fauna of the Soviet Union. About 750 species of birds have been recorded. The early surveys of Russian birdlife were carried out by European and Russian ornithologists in the 1800s. Most areas from the Mediterranean to western and Central Asia and Siberia were explored, and extensive series of specimens were collected. It was discovered that several dozen species do not nest anywhere except in the Soviet Union. Most of these "unique" species breed in Siberia, and are of particular interest to scientists and bird watchers alike.

Interest in the study of birds and bird watching has risen greatly in recent decades among nonprofessional amateur ornithologists. Tourist travel from the United States and Western Europe to the USSR has also risen considerably. Millions of people travel to the Soviet Union to acquaint themselves with life in this country, with its monuments, and with its natural environment. And for many, it is also interesting to become acquainted with its birds.

In order to make it easier to find interesting birds and to provide some advance warning about possible disappointments, we would like to outline a very brief description of the different regions of the Soviet Union, to describe their environments and bird faunas, and to make some practical suggestions, particularly with regard to the optimal periods for seeing them.

GENERAL OVERVIEW OF NATURAL HISTORY IN THE USSR

In width, the territories of the Soviet Union span several geographical zones, which are characterized by specific land-relief, climate, and faunal elements. The islands of the Arctic Ocean, Novaya Zemla, Franz Josef Land, Northern Land, the Novosibirsk Islands, Wrangel

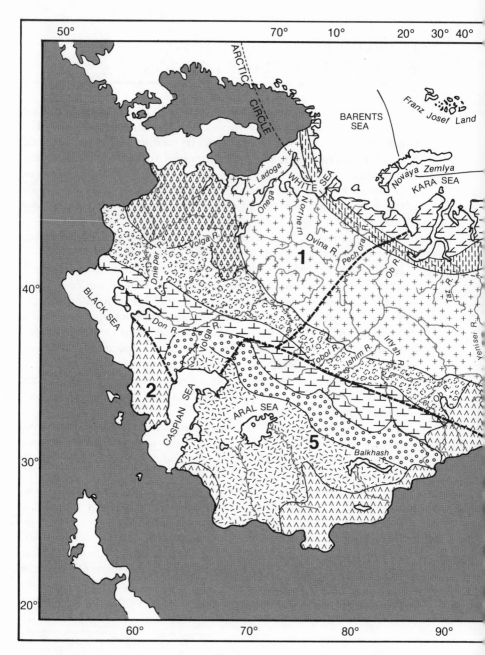

BIOTIC ZONES OF THE USSR

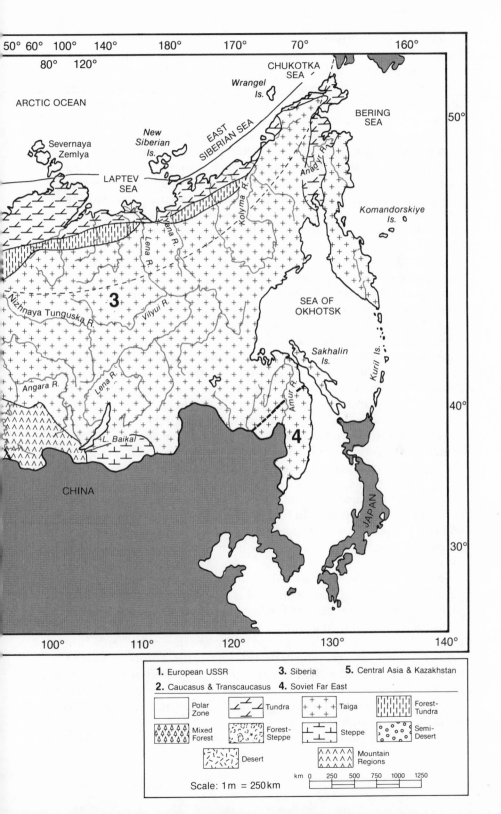

50° 60° 100° 140°   180°   170°   70°   160°
     80°   120°

CHUKOTKA
SEA

ARCTIC OCEAN

Wrangel Is.

New Siberian Is.

BERING
SEA

Severnaya
Zemlya

EAST SIBERIAN SEA

50°

LAPTEV
SEA

Komandorskiye Is.

Nizhnaya Tunguska R.

Lena R.

Yana R.

Kolyma R.

Anadyr R.

3

Vilyui R.

SEA OF
OKHOTSK

Angara R.

Lena R.

Sakhalin Is.

Kuril Is.

40°

Amur R.

4

L. Baikal

CHINA

JAPAN

30°

100°   110°   120°   130°   140°

---

1. European USSR   **3.** Siberia   **5.** Central Asia & Kazakhstan

2. Caucasus & Transcaucasus   **4.** Soviet Far East

Polar Zone

Tundra

Taiga

Forest-Tundra

Mixed Forest

Forest-Steppe

Steppe

Semi-Desert

Desert

Mountain Regions

km 0   250 500 750 1000 1250

Scale: 1m = 250km

Island, and some others are in the so-called polar ice region, or the region of arctic desert. Vegetation is almost nonexistent here, and is generally restricted to lichens or mosses. Much of the area consists of rocky ground. Further south, along all the continental seashores of the Arctic Ocean, there is a broad zone of tundra, where boreal vegetation is only represented in dwarf forms such as creeping willow and dwarf birches. Grassy-like cover exists, but consists mostly of mosses and sedges. South of the Arctic Circle, genuine boreal vegetation, primarily larch, first appears along river valleys, then along other water bodies. Regions of boreal forest alternate with open tundra spaces, and this type of landscape is called forest-tundra. Moving farther south, the regions of coniferous forest become larger and more varied, and begin to include fir (including silver fir) and pine (including Siberian pine). Here, forest-steppe changes over into the next geographical zone, the taiga. In land mass, this region of the taiga is larger than all the other zones. This is where the huge mountain ranges of Siberia are located—where, except on the highest mountain peaks, the mountainsides are covered with thick and nearly impenetrable virgin coniferous forests.

On about the fifty-fifth parallel, the coniferous forests of the taiga zones begin to give way to deciduous forests. In the western regions of European USSR, as one moves southward, the taiga becomes mixed forest, and after that broad-leaved; whereas to the east, the taiga is replaced by forest-steppe. In this mixed forest, fir and pine mix with birch, aspen, alder, and other deciduous species. In the region where broad-leaved trees predominate, a mixture of oak, maple, and linden begins. In the forest-steppe zones of western Siberia and Kazakhstan, the vegetation changes as one moves southward from the boreal forest to open steppe. Here, regions of meadow and steppe alternate with isolated boreal massifs and small patches of woodland that are primarily made up of birches. In contrast to arctic, tundra, forest-tundra, and taiga regions, forest-steppe has been used by man since ancient times, and its natural resources have been considerably transformed by agriculture.

South of the forest region borders, approximately on the fifty-third parallel, the open plains begin; this is the region of steppe. Here various grasses dominate; and further south, there is a great predominance of wormwood. Of the grasses, the most characteristic are speargrass and sheep's fescue. The steppe zones, like the forest-steppe, are primarily used for agriculture, particularly in the European part of the USSR, where untouched virgin regions are protected today only in isolated areas and most of the land is covered with wheat and other crops. Thus the steppes of Europe and Asia have met the same fate as the American prairies.

As we move south, the climate becomes drier; grasses and lush vegetation slowly begin to give way to more drought-resistant plants. Among these drought-resistant forms, biyurgun[1] occupies a considerable area. This is the region of semi-desert. Farming is not possible here without irrigation, and thus the overall natural flora and fauna have changed very little in the last centuries. At the same time, semi-desert is particularly good for sheep herding, and this has left a considerable mark on the environment by selective foraging and over-grazing.

Semi-desert zones give way to the region of genuine desert. Desert here is divided into two types, sand and clay. Argillaceous (clay) deserts, as a rule, are flat, and the predominating vegetation is wormwood and camel briar.[2] Shrub growth exists only in regions of ancient systems of irrigation that are currently being rebuilt. Sandy deserts have a relief that is either wavelike or hilly, where timber vegetation begins again. Sand desert vegetation is primarily represented by psammophilic forms, such as saxal trees, which have a highly developed root system. In some regions there are patches of bare, wind-blown sand that form a fantastic network of wavelike sand dunes. Until recently, deserts have not been used by man because of the extreme severity of their climate. But where there are natural or artificial sources of water, and thus oases, farming is intensive. Mastery of the deserts is planned for the near future by means of irrigation and the building of canals. A number of canals, including the Kara Kum Canal, have already been built and are currently in use. The appearance of water in the desert will create some significant changes in all of the natural environment of these zones, and will dramatically change the flora and fauna.

The southern regions of the Soviet Union are locked in by mighty mountain ranges—the Caucasus, Kopet-Dag, Pamir, Tien-shan, Altai, Sayan, Khamar-daban, and Khingan. As a rule, mountains (in all but the driest of temperate zone areas) are altitudinally zoned with vegetative belts. At the foot of the mountains there is steppe or steppe-like vegetation; further up there is a region of broad-leaved and coniferous forests changing over into alpine meadows; and further up, the nival zone with perpetual snows and glaciers. Many of the middle-elevation mountain ranges are intensively used for farming and industry, and are heavily populated; whereas the higher regions are sparsely populated. The Caucasus and Ural mountains are heavily populated in areas that are most accessible.

Latitudinal zones of the flora and fauna are disrupted by large inland bodies of water, such as the Caspian and Aral seas and large

[1] *Translator's note*: There is no exact English equivalent for this spiny desert plant, *Anabasis salsa*.

[2] *Translator's note*: There is no exact English equivalent for this forage plant, *Alkagi gagnebin*.

artificial reservoirs; disruptions also occur along valleys of large rivers, which usually flow in a longitudinal direction (Volga, Ob, Yenisei, Lena, Indigirka, Kolyma, and others). Here the vegetative forms are often found outside the limits of their usual geographical zones. The same is true of the faunal world, and is particularly true of birds.

Basic Bird Complexes

As in any other part of the world, some species of birds in the Soviet Union have a very broad range, inhabiting several types of habitat, whereas other birds are tied very closely to a particular habitat during the nesting period.

Birds of the Arctic Zones. The variety of birds found in the arctic tundra is limited, though many occur in great numbers and hold considerable interest. Primary species include Barnacle and Greater White-fronted Geese, the Long-tailed Duck, Common Eider, Curlew Sandpiper, Red Knot, Purple Sandpiper, Gray Plover, Ruddy Turnstone and other shorebirds; the Red-throated Loon, and Snowy Owl; and Ivory, Sabine's, Glaucous, and other gulls. Rookeries of nesting seabirds are found along rocky precipices of island shores. Primary species include Marbled and Kittlitz's Murrelets, the Black Guillemot, Black-legged Kittiwake, and, in some regions, Dovekie. The passerines are characteristically poorly represented, and only the Snow Bunting and Lapland Longspur nest here. Without exception, all of these birds migrate to warmer latitudes for the winter.

Birds of the Tundra Zones. The bird fauna of the continental tundra is significantly richer than that of the islands in the Arctic Ocean, although the number of species of birds living in the tundra is still not very large. Of all the tundra species, there is the greatest variety among the shorebirds. There are sections, for instance, of swampy valley tundra along the lower Indigirka River, where it is possible to observe up to thirty species of nesting shorebirds! Widespread Siberian tundra shorebirds include the Dunlin, Pectoral Sandpiper, and Temminck's Stint. In some areas the Rufous-necked Stint, Sharp-tailed and Curlew Sandpipers, Sanderling and Western Sandpiper are common. The Spoon-billed and Baird's Sandpipers, and Long-toed Stint have very small breeding ranges. The Gray and Red-necked Phalaropes, Gray and both Golden Plovers, and the Long-billed Dowitcher breed in a number of localities. Among the waterfowl, this area is a major breeding area for Bewick's Swan; Red-breasted, Brent, Lesser White-fronted, and Bean Geese; King, Steller's and Spectacled Eiders; Northern Pintail, and Greater Scaup. Specialized predators of the tundra include the Long-tailed, Parasitic, and Pomarine Jaegers. Black-throated, Red-throated, and Yellow-billed Loons are often seen near shore. Willow and Rock Ptarmigan are permanent residents here. Among the gulls there are several areas with colonies of the exquisite Ross's Gull. Passerines are not well represented. Besides the Lapland Longspur and the Snow Bunting, the tundra is the summer home of the Red-throated Pipit, Common Redpoll, Bluethroat, Yellow Wagtail, Willow Leaf-Warbler, Little Bunting, and several others. Of the raptors, the Common and Rough-legged Buzzards are characteristic; more rare are the Peregrine Falcon and Gyrfalcon. In years when the lemming population is high, the Snowy Owl nests. Nesting cranes include the Siberian White Crane and Sandhill Crane.

Birds of Forest-Tundra Zones. The bird fauna of the forest-tundra combines a few members of the tundra fauna with birds that are characteristic of the taiga zones to the south. The number of species of shorebirds is less, particularly among the sandpipers, with no Gray Plover, Long-billed Dowitcher, or Bewick's Swan nesting in this area. Passerines predominate in forest-tundra, and the following are numerous: Naumann's Thrush, Dusky Leaf-Warbler, other warblers, Little and Rustic Buntings, Pallas's and Northern Reed-Buntings, Siberian Tit, Siberian Accentor, crossbills, and the Pine Rosefinch. On the lakes, Bewick's Swans are replaced by the Whooper Swan. There is a greater variety of ducks, including Green-winged Teal, Eurasian Wigeon, Northern Shoveler, Tufted Pochard, White-winged and Black Scoters. Many birds typical of the tundra will nest in forest-tundra in hospitable years; even such rarities as the Ross's Gull and sometimes the Siberian White Crane. As a rule, forest-tundra has a less conspicuously visible avifauna than the tundra.

Birds of the Taiga Zones. Among the birds typical of the vast coniferous forests known as taiga are the grouse, which include Western and Black-billed Capercaillies, Northern Hazel Grouse, and Siberian Spruce Grouse. A large variety of owls occurs, though individuals are rarely encountered. Owls of the taiga include Northern Eagle-Owl, Great Gray, Ural, and Boreal Owls, Northern Pygmy-Owl, and Northern Hawk-Owl. Interspersed in the forest are swampy regions where the Eurasian Crane, gulls, grebes, and rails nest. Characteristic passerines include the Siberian Jay, Eurasian Nutcracker, crossbills, Pine Rosefinch, Northern Bullfinch, and several species of tits, flycatchers, and thrushes. The diversity of thrushes is particularly interesting, as these fine songsters include the Orange-flanked Bush-Robin, Siberian, Black-throated and Scaly Thrushes, and White-throated Rock-Thrush. Among the woodpeckers of the taiga are the Northern Three-toed, Black, and Lesser Spotted Woodpeckers. Raptors that inhabit the taiga include the Golden Eagle, Northern Goshawk, Northern Sparrowhawk (in the west), and Besra Sparrowhawk (in the east); whereas along river valleys the White-tailed Sea-Eagle and Osprey hunt for fish.

Birds of the Amur and Soviet Far East taiga are to be found nowhere else but in the taiga zone. These species reflect the nearness of the fauna of southeastern Asia. In the Soviet Far East, broad-leaf vegetation typical of maritime eastern China and Korea follows the river valleys and mixes with the coniferous taiga forests, resulting in a great wealth and variety in the bird population. In virtually the same region it is possible to see both true inhabitants of dark coniferous taiga, such as the Black-billed Capercaillie, Siberian Spruce Grouse, Three-toed and Black Woodpeckers, Great Gray and Ural Owls, alongside birds of a more tropical nature, such as the Broad-billed Roller, Asian Paradise-Flycatcher, Blue-and-white and Narcissus Flycatchers, Ashy Minivet, Chestnut-flanked White-eye, Indian Cuckoo, Hodgson's Hawk-Cuckoo, and Black-capped Kingfisher.

It should also be noted that the southeast region of the taiga zone is extremely rich in bunting species. Nesters include Chestnut-eared, Tristram's, Black-faced, Yellow-throated, Yellow-browed, Japanese Gray, and Pine Buntings, plus one of the rarest birds in the USSR—the Jankowski's Bunting.

The taiga has many resident species such as the grouse, woodpeckers, owls, and a number of passerines such as the Siberian Jay, Eurasian Nutcracker, Eurasian Nuthatch, and tits. But in some years of food shortages, these normally sedentary species are forced to erupt elsewhere.

Birds of Mixed and Broad-leaved Forests. The bird fauna of the mixed and broad-leaved forests exceeds the taiga in the number of species (with the exception of the taiga of the east). It should be noted that mixed and broad-leaved forests are currently being significantly transformed as a result of agricultural endeavors, and have, to a significant degree, lost their original appearance. It therefore follows that the bird fauna has changed, as well. In addition, the region is made even more diverse by the influence of southern species, boreal species, and species partial to second growth and hedgerows. Those species most closely associated with this area are the Eurasian Green and Gray-headed Green Woodpeckers, Eurasian Roller, and many of the species of warblers. Among the larger birds, one can still find grouse, some raptors (Common Buzzard, Eurasian Honey-Buzzard, and others), and ducks in the area of the mixed and broad-leaved forests. Thus, this region that was once entirely forested has been penetrated by a large number of birds connected with meadow and partly steppe vegetation, and today is a region that has a diverse avifauna.

A great number of the bird species breeding in mixed and deciduous forests migrate south for the winter, although some, especially those residing primarily in taiga, are nonmigratory. In the autumn, some species that breed further north retreat southward to this area for the winter: Common and Rough-legged Buzzards, Snowy Owl, redpolls, Bohemian Waxwing, Northern Bullfinch, Eurasian Siskin, and Eurasian Goldfinch.

Birds of the Forest-Steppe Zones. The bird fauna of the forest-steppe, as might be expected, is a mixture of species from the forests to the north and the plains tó the south, and has few unique features. In the more open habitats of forest-steppe zones, the most conspicuous birds are larks and raptors: Northern Skylark, Black and White-winged Larks, Pallid and Montagu's Harriers, Eurasian and Lesser Kestrels, European Pratincole, and Red-footed Falcon. In wooded areas, birds from the mixed and deciduous forests are more characteristic. These include grouse, Willow Ptarmigan, Eurasian Cuckoo, several species of buntings (Yellowhammer and Pine Bunting), Eurasian Crow, Eurasian Rook, European Golden Oriole, plus several species of warblers, thrushes, and pipits.

Near the numerous salt- and fresh-water lakes of the forest-steppe zone, one can find many species of ducks; predominating are Northern and Tufted Pochards, Mallard, Green-winged Teal, Garganey, Northern Shoveler (Ruddy and Common Shelducks locally), Great Crested and Black-necked Grebes, Common Coot, Spotted Crake (shy), Common Gallinule, Water Rail, Common Redshank, Bar-tailed Godwit, Eurasian Curlew, Black Tern, White-winged Black Tern, Black-headed Gull, Eurasian Bittern, and Marsh Harrier. Of the passerines, the most characteristic are Great Reed Warbler and the Bearded Reedling.

Birds of the forest-steppe are primarily migratory. Only a few species remain for the winter—grouse, Willow Ptarmigan, and crows; several species of thrushes and larks winter along roadsides, although they are not numerous. A number of more northerly breeding species also find suitable wintering habitat in forest-steppe, such as the Rough-legged Buzzard, Snowy Owl, Snow Bunting, and Lapland Longspur.

It is worth repeating that the natural landscape of the forest-steppe zones has been significantly transformed by recent human activities.

Birds of the Steppe Zones. The vast steppes have also been significantly changed by human inhabitants and their machines. A large portion of the original grasslands has been replaced by agricultural areas. These changes, which take the form of irrigation, villages, and windbreaks, have resulted in the appearance of many species that are uncharacteristic of the region in its earlier natural state, but that are closely tied to human activities. Such species are the Eurasian Rook, Tree and House Sparrows, Barn Swallow, Northern Starling, and other man-following species.

The most characteristic and typical non-passerines of the steppe are Great and Little Bustards, Demoiselle Crane, Sociable Lapwing, Black-winged and European Pratincoles, Steppe Eagle, Pallid Harrier, Lesser Kestrel, and Saker Falcon. The passerines are strongly represented by larks and pipits. Common species are the Black and White-winged Larks, Northern Skylark, Lesser and Greater Short-toed Larks, Mongolian and Calandra Larks, and Richard's, Tawny, and Godlewski's Pipits. Although the typical steppe landscape appears uninteresting, it has a fairly diverse avifauna.

Birds of Semi-Desert Zones. The bird fauna of the semi-desert, which is located between regions of steppe and desert, has a mixed, intermediate character. On the whole, it is closer to the avifauna of the steppe, featuring such species as the Steppe Eagle, Demoiselle Crane, Great and Little Bustards, European Pratincole, Northern Skylark, Calandra, White-winged and Mongolian Larks, and numerous varieties of pipits. Semi-desert also attracts species rarely seen to the north of this zone, such as Long-legged Buzzard, Black-winged Stilt, Black-capped Avocet, and Crested Lark.

In semi-desert, there is a wealth of southern species and many water birds. Water birds of note include the Red-crested Pochard, White-headed Duck, Ruddy and Common Shelducks, Dalmatian and Eastern White Pelicans, and Greater Flamingo. In addition, the ponds and marshes are home to other water birds also found breeding in other zones to the north, such as Mallard, teal, Northern Shoveler, Graylag Goose, Great Crested and other grebes, Common Coot, Water Rail, Marsh Harrier, Great Reed Warbler, and Eurasian Bittern.

In spring and fall, numerous water birds that nest in the tundra and taiga migrate through ponds of the semi-desert. These migrants, chiefly shorebirds, geese, ducks, gulls, and terns, gather in huge flocks near shores of fresh- and salt-water lakes. Some nonbreeding northern shorebirds that are for the most part juveniles remain on the lakes in semi-desert regions for the entire summer period, and may include Dunlin, Curlew Sandpiper, phalaropes, and Sanderling.

Birds of the Desert Zones. The arid deserts of the southwest Asian portions of the USSR are quite old, biologically speaking, and have evolved some endemic species. Particularly characteristic of sandy regions are Pander's Ground-Jay, Desert Sparrow, and the Northern Raven, a brown-necked subspecies. A large number of typical birds here are restricted to desert environments, such as the Houbara Bustard, Pallas's, Pin-tailed, and Black-bellied Sandgrouse, Cream-colored Courser, Caspian Plover and Sand Plover, Egyptian Nightjar, Blue-cheeked Bee-eater, Striated Scops-Owl, and the local race of the Peregrine Falcon. The passerines also feature many species restricted to this harsh environment, such as the Scrub Warbler, Desert Lark, Desert, Menetrie's and Upcher's Warblers, Trumpeter and Desert Finches, and Saxual Sparrow. Wheatears are particularly numerous here, and are represented by Isabelline, Desert, and Pied Wheatears. The Laughing Turtle-Dove and the Indian Myna are found in the desert, but always in association with human activities.

In the breeding season, bodies of water in the desert zones are home to fewer waterfowl than are marshes to the north. The rather rare Marbled Duck is a typically southern species. However, there is a significant number of herons and ibises, among which are the Great and Little Egrets, Squacco Pond-Heron, Black-crowned Night-Heron, and Eurasian Spoonbill. The Glossy Ibis, in association with the Pygmy Cormorant, form large colonies in reed beds along river floodlands and lake basins. Many widespread and gregarious species such as the Gray and Purple Herons and the Great Cormorant, add to the numbers found in these colonies as well.

Birds of Mountain Zones. Mapping, describing, and understanding the bird life of mountain ranges is a complex task. In the mountains, for every thousand feet in elevation one rises, one is likely to run into vegetation and bird life found at sea-level many hundreds of miles further toward the pole. One often finds many endemic birds (either at the species or subspecies level) in ranges that are surrounded by inhospitable deserts. Many species are limited in their distribution to the mountains, and are not found in similar life-zones further north. One such specialized genus is characteristic of high mountains in the USSR and the Himalayas—the snowcocks: Caucasian, Caspian, Himalayan, Tibetan, and Altai Snowcocks. Space precludes listing all the specialties of each range of mountains. Some mountain non-passerines include the Himalayan Griffon, Caucasian Black Grouse, Ibisbill, Great Knot, Tibetan Sandgrouse, and Snow Pigeon. Passerines are equally well represented: Himalayan, Brown, Black-throated, and Alpine Accentors; Blue Whistling-Thrush, White-capped River Chat, Blue-headed and Guldenstadt's Redstarts, Rufous-tailed Flycatcher, Red-tailed Wheatear, Himalayan Rubythroat, Greater and Lesser Rock Nuthatch, Wallcreeper, Red-breasted and Great Rosefinches, Hodgson's and Brandt's Rosy-Finches, Rock Petronia, and many others. For variety and wealth of species, the southern mountains provide the best birding in the Soviet Union.

Bird Migration in the USSR

The majority of the breeding birds of the USSR winter beyond its borders. The main places for wintering are the countries of Western Europe, shores of the Mediterranean Sea, North Africa, western Asia, India, and southeastern Asia. Some birds even winter in places as far away as central and southern Africa, New Guinea, Australia, and New Zealand. Within the territory of the USSR, many birds winter on the southern shores of the Caspian Sea, in the Transcaucasus, and along the shores of the Black Sea. Corresponding to the location of wintering grounds, the general path of migration routes varies from region to region. Birds from the European part of the USSR primarily fly west and southwest; from western Siberia, most fly south; from eastern Siberia, they fly south and southeast. A number of species from the Chukotski Peninsula even migrate in an easterly direction and winter in Central and South America.

The Five Most Interesting Birding Regions of the USSR

European USSR. This region includes ecological zones that range from tundra in the north to steppe in the south. The variety of birds here is very large, but on the whole the species seen here can readily be seen in countries of Western Europe and in the Mediterranean. As a rule, large species are fairly rare, and the amateur bird watcher is more likely to come across passerine species. If you can get into the right areas and put in enough time, it is possible to observe large species such as the Western Capercaillie, Northern Black Grouse, Hazel Grouse, Common Crane, Common Buzzard, Eurasian Honey-Buzzard, Northern Goshawk, Greater Spotted Eagle, Whooper Swan, Bean Goose, Great Gray Owl, and Ural Owl. Of the passerines, the more interesting birds include the Azure Tit, Blyth's Reed-Warbler, Greenish Leaf-Warbler, Yellow-breasted Bunting, and Booted Warbler. The best time is May to June, when most species are in full song.

Caucasus and Transcaucasus. The beautiful snow-capped peaks of the Caucasus provide the visitor with a greater opportunity to meet birds unfamiliar to him. Among them, it is possible to see Caucasian Black Grouse, Caucasian and Caspian Snowcocks, and Lammergeier; plus such passerines as Wallcreeper, Guldenstadt's Redstart, Great Rose-finch, Persian Robin, Sombre Tit, Rock Nuthatch, Red-billed and Alpine Choughs, Woodchat Shrike, Rock Petronia, and Père David's Snow-Finch. Besides these uncommon and narrow-ranged species, it is also possible to see a significant variety of birds more common to the Mediterranean and West European sectors. The best time for observation is the end of April to July.

Siberia. The territories of Siberia, including both western and eastern regions of this country, encompass portions of all ecological zones except for the semi-desert and desert. Because many tundra and taiga regions of Siberia are either inaccessible or off-limits to visitors, they cannot yet be included into most tourist travel itineraries. The region around Irkutsk on Lake Baikal is open to visitors, and birds such as the Baikal Teal, Solitary and Pin-tailed Snipes, Black-billed Capercaillie, Oriental Cuckoo, Great Gray Owl, Besra Sparrowhawk, and the Asian subspecies of Eurasian Crane can be found. In the delta of the Selenga River, one of the world's rarest shorebirds is found—the Asian Dowitcher. Intensive migrations of shorebirds, ducks, and other birds take place in the Lake Baikal region and along its shores. Of the nesting passerines, those worthy of some special attention are the Olive-backed Pipit; Pine, Meadow, Black-faced, Chestnut-eared, and Yellow-breasted Buntings; Dusky and Radde's Leaf-Warblers, Thick-billed Warbler, Pallas's Leaf-Warbler, Yellow-browed Leaf-Warbler; Siberian Blue Robin, Rufous-tailed Robin, and Scaly Thrush. The best time for observation is the end of May through July, then September.

Soviet Far East. The Soviet Far East is one of the best places for bird observation. However, the large variety of species demands intensive study of this field guide by the bird watcher, as well as the ability to separate out unfamiliar bird calls. In the environs of cities like Khabarovsk, it is possible to see up to thirty species that would be new to a first visitor. They will be primarily passerines, but with luck it is possible to see even the Japanese or White-naped Cranes, the Oriental race of White Stork, and some interesting raptors. Of the passerines, one will definitely see the Azure-winged Magpie and Ashy Minivet; the Gray-backed, Pale, and possibly the Siberian Thrushes; the Chestnut-flanked White-eye and Narcissus Flycatcher; the Azure Tit, Yellow-breasted, Black-faced, and Chestnut-eared Buntings; Japanese Grosbeak, Oriental Greenfinch, Long-tailed Rosefinch, White-cheeked Starling, Purple-backed Starling, Black-naped Oriole, and Large-billed Crow. With optimal circumstances this list can be considerably larger. The best time for such an excursion is May and June.

Central Asia and Kazakhstan. A journey to the famous cities of Central Asia will provide the tourist with fine opportunities for bird watching. Even in the large cities of Alma Ata, Ashkhabad, Tashkent, Samarkand, and others, it is virtually impossible to miss the Laughing Turtle-

Dove, Indian Myna, Desert Finch, Alpine Swift, and the very interesting Bukhara subspecies of the Great Tit that is now regarded by many ornithologists as a separate species. A trip to the mountains or the submountain regions will provide an opportunity to observe Chukar and See-see Partridges, the Eurasian Griffon, Cinereous Vulture, Lammergeier, Golden Eagle, Blue-cheeked Bee-eater, Eurasian Roller, Brown-necked Raven, Blue Whistling-Thrush, Rufous-tailed Rock-Thrush, White-winged Crossbill, Himalayan Rubythroat, Streaked Laughing-Thrush, Severtzov's Tit-Warbler, and Asian Paradise-Flycatcher. It is also not uncommon to see the White-winged Spotted Woodpecker, particularly in places that are wooded or shrubby; also the Central Asian form of Azure Tit and Greater Rock Nuthatch. In plains and in settled areas, birds are numerous, and include the Crested Lark and the Greater and Lesser Short-toed Larks; Pied, Desert, and Isabelline Wheatear; Spanish Sparrow, Red-headed Bunting, and the Central Asian form of Eurasian Goldfinch. With very good luck, it is possible to see the Himalayan Snowcock high in the mountains; and in coniferous forests, the Black-crested Tit, Yellow-browed Leaf-Warbler, and other forest birds. The best time for observing birds is the end of April until the end of June.

THE AUTHORS hope that this book will be helpful to becoming acquainted with birds of the Soviet Union. Since birds are the most wonderful of all the animals, one can only expect that becoming acquainted with them will be pleasant and will bring the reader much happiness.

HOW TO USE THE FIELD GUIDE

Color plates are provided to aid bird identification. If the bird was clearly seen and the illustration supports the identification without a doubt, then it is suggested that the reader turn to the page indicated next to the name of the bird in the caption to the illustration, and read about its habits and range of the species. If some of the illustrations make the identification doubtful, one should read through the entire description. Careful comparison of coloration and habits will aid in making the right diagnosis. If it is breeding season, additional information may be obtained by studying the range maps, although, as mentioned before, this will not be the primary diagnostic source. It is no less important to read closely the section on habits: when brought together with the mental picture, the right answer may emerge.

What if some doubt still remains? Then one should turn to an academic institution that can help make the determination. The best bird collections in the USSR are kept in the Zoological Museum of Moscow State University (No. 6 Herzen Street, Moscow) in the Museum of the Zoological Institute of the Academy of Sciences (No. 1 University Embankment, Leningrad), and in the biology section of the Geography Department at Moscow State University (Department of Geography, Moscow State University, Lenin Hills, Moscow). Any of these institutions can provide an exhaustive and sufficiently competent identification.

In conclusion, we would like to give some advice to the beginning amateur birdwatcher. First, before embarking on an excursion to some distant region such as the Altai or the Crimea, it is useful to make up a list of birds (using the range maps) that may be encountered in that region. This will narrow the number of possibilities and aid identification.

Try to learn the range and ecological requirements of the birds. It would be foolish, for instance, to expect to see Siberian Rubythroats or Blue and White Flycatchers near Moscow, or a Blackbird or Eurasian Crow in the Soviet Far East. One should remember that migration routes are usually (not always) along a meridian, and for this reason migrants can be seen more readily south of their nesting range, and not usually north or east. Warblers, larks, pipits, reed-warblers, and buntings should be identified only within their specific ranges. But identification based solely on geographical isolation is not always reliable.

Second, it is essential to write down all details noted on unfamiliar species for subsequent personal reference and to confirm scientific inquiries. Sightings of banded birds are relatively common, and should definitely be reported to the Banding Center in Moscow. Note the band's letters and numbers, the date and location where the bird was found, the species (if known) and send this information to the Zoological Museum or Geography Department of Moscow State University, or to the Museum of the Zoological Institute of the Academy of Sciences. If the bird is dead, then remove the band and send it with the same information requested above to the same address.

Some Terms

In writing this book, the authors made an effort not to use overly technical terms, but it was not always possible to do so. First, scientific literature uses the symbols ♂ to indicate male and ♀ to indicate female. Monogamous birds are those that form more or less permanent pairs during breeding season; polygamous birds are those that never form pairs, or in which the male may mate with a number of females.

If nestlings emerge from the egg helpless, blind, and cannot leave the nest for some time, their mode of development is called altricial. If the little birds are covered with a thick down, can search for their own food within a few hours, and can leave the nest still barely dry from hatching, their mode of development is called precocial.

The plumage on various parts of the body is named differently. Since all birds are feathered, references to "feathers" are dropped, so that references to "primary wing feathers" becomes simply "primaries," and so on.

Shapes of eggs are described under the section on habits, and are of three main types—ovoid, pear-shaped, and ellipsoid. Each form has three variations, which are shown in Figure 9.

When describing numbers (quantities) of this or that species, the terms "numerous," "common," "uncommon," "rare," and "very rare" are employed. These terms are sufficiently self-explanatory. In some parts of the book, however, the reader will find reference to "rare, in places common." This means that the bird is rare throughout most of its range, but there are some limited regions within that range in which it is common. Sometimes birds of the same species have sharp variations in coloration. Where these variations are individual, they are called phases; where they are geographic, they are called races or subspecies.

BIRDS emerged from ancient reptiles of the Jurassic period, nearly 140 million years ago. They represent a well-isolated group of warm-blooded vertebrates. One of the most characteristic features of birds is their covering of feathers, which protects the body from drastic changes in temperature and which plays a vital role in flight. The ability to fly is the most distinguishing feature (lack of this ability in some present-day birds, such as the ostrich and penguin, is a secondary phenomenon). The body of the bird is designed for this role: its frontal extremities have become wings, the skeleton is lightened, breast muscles are very strong, and special air sacs are located under the skin. In connection with the fact that flight demands great quantities of muscular energy, the level of metabolism is high and the necessity for food is great (the daily food intake equals 12-28 percent of the bird's body weight). Blood temperature is around 42.2° C, and in small birds, it reaches 45.5° C. Of the sense organs, vision and hearing are the most developed. Reproduction is by means of laying eggs that are covered with a hard calcium shell and are normally hatched by the warmth of the nesting bird's body. Birds are found in all parts of the world. Naturally, their appearance varies greatly. Sizes may vary, as well. The largest bird (an ostrich) can reach a weight of 90 kg, and the smallest (a hummingbird) will be barely 2 grams. In feeding habits, birds are as herbivorous as they are carnivorous. There are over 9,000 species of birds in the world, which belong to 40 orders. In the USSR, there are nearly 750 species. It is not possible to give a more exact figure because the classification status of many species is not yet final.

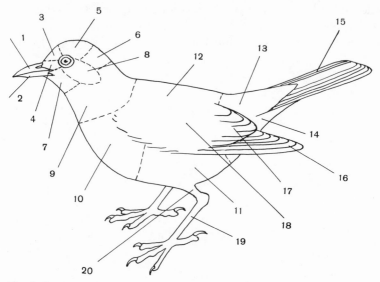

FIG. 1 CHART OF A BIRD

1. upper mandible   2. lower mandible   3. forehead   4. lores   5.crown
6. nape   7. throat   8. ear coverts   9. neck   10. breast   11. belly   12. back
13. rump   14. undertail coverts   15. tail   16. primaries   17. secondaries
18. wing coverts   19. tarsus   20. thigh   *Not illustrated*   cere: fleshy base on
the bill of pigeons and raptors   speculum: rectangular patch on outer portion
of secondaries on ducks

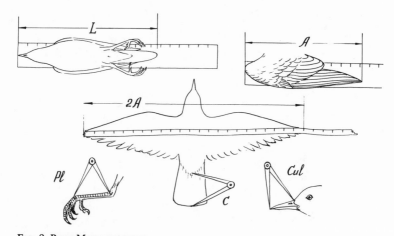

FIG. 2 BIRD MEASUREMENTS

L body length   A wing length   2A wingspan   P1 tarsus length
Cul bill length (culmen)   C tail length

FIG. 3 BIRD CRESTS
1. Bohemian Waxwing   2. Crested Tit   3. Great Crested Grebe   4. Hoopoe
5. Whiskered Auklet   6. Tufted Pochard   7. Northern Lapwing   8. Black-
crowned Night-Heron   9. Wood Lark

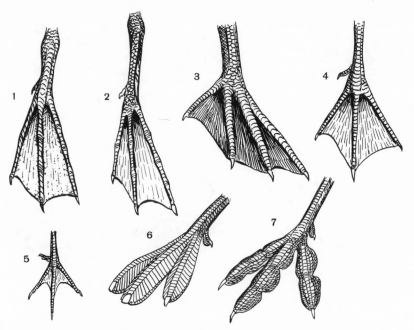

FIG. 4 TYPES OF FEET
1. duck   2. loon   3. cormorant   4. gull   5. tern   6. grebe   7. coot

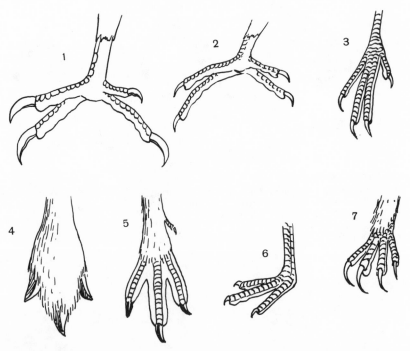

FIG. 5 TYPES OF FEET
1. woodpecker   2. cuckoo   3. kingfisher   4. sandgrouse (*Syrrhaptes*)   5. sand-grouse (*Pterocles*)   6. buttonquail   7. swift

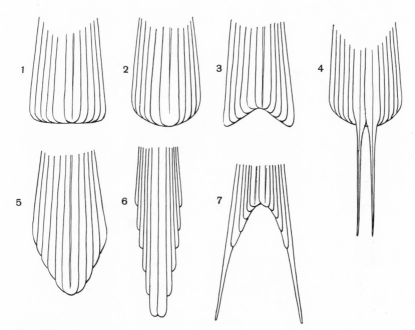

FIG. 6 TAIL TYPES
1. straight   2. rounded   3. slightly forked   4. elongated central tail feathers
5. wedge-shaped   6. graduated   7. forked

FIG. 7 FLOCK FORMATIONS
1. wedge   2. bunched   3. skein   4. line

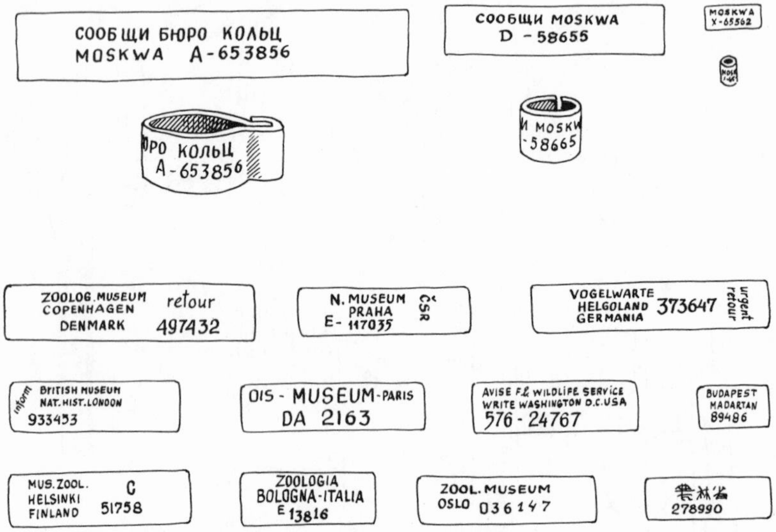

СООБЩИ БЮРО КОЛЬЦ
MOSKWA   A - 653856

СООБЩИ MOSKWA
D - 58655

MOSKWA
X - 65562

ЮРО КОЛЬЦ
A - 653856

И МОСК
- 58665

ZOOLOG. MUSEUM   retour
COPENHAGEN
DENMARK   497432

N. MUSEUM
PRAHA
E- 117035

ČSR

VOGELWARTE
HELGOLAND   373647
GERMANIA

urgent
retour

BFITISH MUSEUM
NAT. HIST. LONDON
933453

OIS - MUSEUM - PARIS
DA 2163

AVISE F.& WILDLIFE SERVICE
WRITE WASHINGTON D.C. USA
576 - 24767

BUDAPEST
MADARTAN
89486

MUS. ZOOL.   C
HELSINKI
FINLAND   51758

ZOOLOGIA
BOLOGNA - ITALIA
E 13816

ZOOL. MUSEUM
OSLO   036147

農林省
278990

FIG. 8 Bird Bands of Various Ornithological Stations

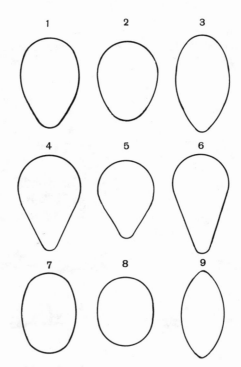

FIG. 9 EGG SHAPES

1. ovoid 2. shortened ovoid 3. elongated ovoid 4. pear-shaped 5. shortened pear-shaped 6. elongated pear-shaped 7. ellipsoid pear-shaped 8. shortened ellipsoid 9. elongated ellipsoid

A FIELD GUIDE TO BIRDS OF RUSSIA AND
ADJACENT TERRITORIES

LOONS: *Gaviiformes*

Large to very large birds with short, narrow wings and short legs set far back. Bill straight or awl-shaped. Three front toes, webbed. Plumage compact and heavy, velvety on the head. Lives at sea and on bodies of fresh water; comes to land only to nest. Locomotion on land is difficult, and is accomplished by pushing itself on its belly with its legs. Monogamous. Eggs are oblong-ovoid or oblong-ellipsoid. Precocial.

Gavia

1. RED-THROATED LOON
Gavia stellata
(Krasnozobaya Gagara)
Plate 1, Map 1
Field marks: 56 cm. Larger than a Mallard. Bill bent slightly upward. Head and sides of the neck gray; white stripes on nape; chestnut spot on the throat; back grayish-brown with small white speckles; belly white. In winter (and juveniles) brown with white belly.
Habits: Inhabits lakes in tundra and taiga; always found in seas and large bodies of fresh water during nonbreeding seasons. Migratory. Common in places. Nests in pairs on open lake shores. Nest: small depression with or without a meager lining of plant material; always built at the very edge of water, most often on islets or small capes. Lays two dark brownish-olive eggs with brown spots from beginning of June. Female sits on the nest very firmly, flushing reluctantly to plunge into the water only when approached too closely. At signs of danger when swimming, submerges with only top of the head and bill showing. Perfect diver; stays immersed for long periods of time. Dives so quickly that it is almost quicker than a rifle shot. Flight heavy, drooping; in flight the neck and hindparts are carried low,

which gives it a sagging look. Paddles along water surface against the wind on takeoff. Cautious. Call: moaning, piercing cries; loud cackle "gag-ga-gagara" before and during flight. Feeds on fish, often flies from lakes to the sea to feed.
Range and distribution: Northern part of European USSR, northern half of Siberia up to the Chukotski and Kamchatka Peninsulas. Winters on the Black Sea and near shores of Western Europe.
Similar species: Differs from Black-throated Loon by lighter back and chestnut spot on the throat.

2. BLACK-THROATED LOON
Gavia arctica
(Chernozobaya Gagara)
Plate 1, Map 1
Field marks: 62 cm. Larger than Red-throated Loon. Bill straight. Head and nape ash-gray; sides of neck and upper breast striped white; back black with bright white bands; belly white; black throat patch.
Habits: Found on lakes in tundra, forest, forest-steppe, and even steppe. During migration, found at sea and on large bodies of fresh water. Migratory. In places common. Unlike Red-throated Loon, nests on variety of lake shores, even reedy lakes in steppe. Nest is always found at water's edge; often on islets or

MAP 1. Black-throated Loon (1), Red-throated Loon (2)

MAP 2. Yellow-billed Loon NOTE: Circled areas indicate heavy concentrations

hummocks emerging from water, sometimes on clumps of grass. In the south, nests from middle of April, when ice melts in tundra lakes. Lays two dark brownish-olive eggs with brown spots (same as Red-throated Loon, but larger). Flight, habits, behavior, and feeding generally same as Red-throated Loon, but call is louder and more diversified.

Range and distribution: Northern half of European USSR; Siberia (except southern re-

gions); northern Kazakhstan. Winters on the Black Sea; near shores of Western Europe, Kamchatka Peninsula, Sakhalin Island, and the Kuril Islands.

Similar species: Differs from Red-throated Loon by a black throat patch and by black back banded white; from Yellow-billed Loon by gray head, black bill, and smaller size.

Note: The eastern race, found on Chukotski Peninsula and in northern Yakutia, is cur-

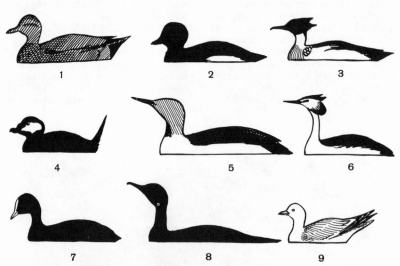

FIG. 10 POSTURE OF BIRDS ON WATER

1. dabbling duck (Gadwall)   2. diving duck (Red-crested Pochard)   3. sawbill (Red-breasted Merganser)   4. stifftail duck (White-headed Duck)   5. loon (Red-throated Loon)   6. grebe (Great Crested Grebe)   7. coot (Common Coot)   8. cormorant (Great Cormorant)   9. gull (Mew Gull)

rently considered to be a separate species. *Gavia pacifica.*

3. YELLOW-BILLED LOON
Gavia adamsi
(Beloklyuvaya Gagara)
Plate 1, Map 2
Field marks: 75 cm. Very large (goose) size. Head and back black; back has frequent large white spots; white stripes on sides of the neck; bill whitish, massive, slightly upturned.
Habits: Inhabits tundra and forest-tundra. Migratory. Fairly common in places, but rare on the whole. Nests on shores of lakes with clear water and stony or sandy bottom. Nest: small depression built on dry land at water's edge. Lays two dark brownish-olive eggs with brown spots from middle to end of June. Eggs resemble those of other loons, but are consid-

erably bigger. Flight, habits, and behavior are similar to those of other loons; call: louder, more harsh.
Range and distribution: Northern regions of Siberia. Winters in offshore regions of the Pacific Ocean; now and then in open waters of the Barents Sea.
Similar species: Differs from other loons by whitish bill and larger size.

[**4.** Vagrants of COMMON LOON (*Gavia immer*) were noted on the Komandorskiye Islands. It resembles the Yellow-billed Loon, but is smaller, with dark straight bill. White back spots are smaller and less frequent. Distribution throughout North America, Greenland, and Iceland. Many ornithologists consider Yellow-billed and Common Loons to be one species, *Gavia immer.*]

GREBES: *Podicipediformes*

Birds of medium and small sizes with short wings and legs set far back. Bill sharp or awl-shaped. All toes lobate-webbed. Plumage dense and compact. Inhabit bodies of fresh water. Monogamous. Eggs are a pointed ellipse or usual ovoid shape. Precocial.

Podiceps

5. GREAT CRESTED GREBE
Podiceps cristatus
(Chomga)
Plate 5, Map 3
Field marks: 48 cm. The largest grebe, but smaller than a Mallard. Magnificent, fluffy, black and orange decorative feathers on the head sweep back to form a collar. Back yellowish-brown; neck and belly white; bill red-

dish. Juveniles without collar; bill yellow-green.
Habits: Found on bodies of water in forest, steppe, and desert. Migratory and common. Nests in pairs, sometimes in colonies. Prefers lakes with open reaches that are overgrown by reed and cane. Nest made of plant stalks, and floats or rests on shoal bottom near shores. Nests from middle of May, laying three or four whitish eggs. Perfect swimmer and diver. Flushes reluctantly. On takeoff, makes a long running start, then flies rapidly with frequent wing beats. Rarely seen in flight. Voice is very

MAP 3. Great Crested Grebe

FIG. 11 A Grebe's Nest

loud and diversified. In spring: guttural cry, "kkua." Call: "kjuik." Feeds on fish, amphibia, insects, mollusks.

Range and distribution: Southern half of European USSR, Kazakhstan, Central Asia, southern regions of West Siberia, southern part of Ussuriski Kray. Winters on the Black and Caspian Seas and on bodies of water in Soviet Central Asia.

Similar species: Differs from Red-necked Grebe by bright collar and reddish bill (in adults); in winter, also by its white neck.

6. RED-NECKED GREBE
Podiceps grisegena
(Seroshchyokaya Poganka)
Plate 5, Map 4

Field marks: 43 cm. Somewhat smaller than Great Crested Grebe. Small crest on the head. Upperparts brownish-gray; head black with gray cheeks; neck rusty red, belly white; bill black, but yellow near mouth. Juveniles duller, with brown neck; adults in winter plumage resemble juveniles.

Habits: Found on bodies of water in forest and steppe. Migratory. Common in places. Nests

in pairs in overgrown lakes, ponds, oxbow lakes. Nesting habits similar to Great Crested Grebe, but eggs are smaller. In typical grebe fashion, it swims and dives perfectly, but flies poorly and reluctantly. Cautious and difficult to see. Call: loud squealing sounds, blending into a kind of neigh. Feeds on small fish, aquatic invertebrates, and water plants.

Range and distribution: European USSR (except northern regions), Kazakhstan, eastern regions of East Siberia. Winters on the Black and Caspian Seas and shores of the Soviet Far East.

Similar species: Differs from Great Crested Grebe by red neck, gray cheeks, black and yellow bill, and lack of collar; from other grebes, by its larger size.

7. HORNED GREBE
Podiceps auritus
(Krasnosheynaya Poganka)
Plate 5, Map 5

Field marks: 33 cm. Small grebe (size of teal). Bill straight. On the head, rusty decorative feathers; black collar. Back is brownish-gray; belly white; neck and stripe on the side rusty. In winter plumage of adults and juveniles, belly, foreside of neck, and cheeks are white; back gray.

Habits: Found on bodies of water in forest, forest-steppe, and steppe. Migratory. Not common. Nests in pairs in small overgrown lakes and back waters; rarely forms colonies. Nest built to float. Lays four or five white eggs in May. As incubation ends, eggs become dirty and brownish-ocher. Habits and behavior like other grebes, but takes wing more readily. Unwary. Call: deep trill and variety of other typically shrill sounds.

Range and distribution: Baltic States, Belo-

MAP 4. Red-necked Grebe (1), Red-throated Dabchik (2)

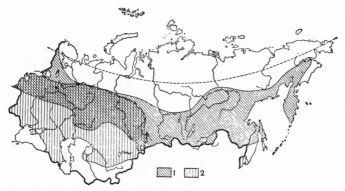

MAP 5. Horned Grebe (1), Black-necked Grebe (2)

russia, central regions of European USSR, southern Siberia, including Sakhalin Island and Kamchatka Peninsula. Winters near bodies of water near southern USSR borders.

Similar species: Differs from Black-necked Grebe by straight, slightly heavier bill; rusty coloration of neck and sides; in winter by pure white cheeks and throat; from Red-throated Dabchik by larger size and decorative feathers.

8. BLACK-NECKED GREBE
Podiceps nigricollis
(Chernosheynaya Poganka)
Plate 5, Map 5

Field marks: 30 cm. Somewhat smaller than Horned Grebe. Bill thin, slightly upturned. Rounded topknot, and rusty decorative feathers behind eyes. Head and neck black; upper parts blackish-brown; belly white. Winter plumage of adults and juveniles is gray with whitish throat and white belly.

Habits: Found on bodies of water in forest, steppe, and desert. Migratory. Common. Nests both separately and in colonies on overgrown lakes, oxbow lakes, reaches, backwaters, and channels. Floating nest made of aquatic plants. Nesting habits and behavior similar to Horned Grebe, which it resembles, but more cautious.

Range and distribution: European USSR except northern regions; Kazakhstan, some areas of Central Asia, southern regions of Soviet Far East. Winters on the Black and Caspian Seas and Lake Issyk-Kul in Kirgizhia.

Similar species: Differs from Horned Grebe by black neck and thin, slightly uptilted bill; in winter by grayish cheeks and forepart of neck; from Red-throated Dabchik by decorative feathers on the head and by the black neck.

Tachybaptus

9. RED-THROATED DABCHIK
Tachybaptus ruficollis
(Malaya Poganka)
Plate 5, Map 4

Field marks: 27 cm. Smallest grebe in USSR. No decorative head feathers. Coloration black-brown; underparts dirty white; cheeks and front of neck rusty red. In winter, upperparts grayish; underparts white.

Habits: Found on bodies of water in forest, steppe, and desert. Migratory; in places non-migratory. Nests in lakes and ponds overgrown with reed and cane; in calm oxbow lakes and backwaters. Floating nests are built far from shore. Lays four to six white eggs at end of May, which quickly become brown-stained during incubation. Very secretive, usually hides

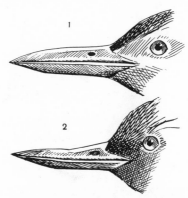

FIG. 12 Bill of 1) Horned Grebe and 2) Black-necked Grebe

in emergent vegetation; usually appears in open water at night and disappears immediately at slightest danger. Otherwise, behavior same as other small grebes. Call: loud, pleasant flute-like trill.

Range and distribution: Southern regions of European USSR, bodies of water in Central Asia and Kazakhstan. Winters on bodies of water in its southern range.

Similar species: Differs from Black-necked and Horned Grebes by smaller size and lack of decorative feathers.

TUBENOSES: *Procellariiformes*

Birds of small to very large sizes, with long, narrow wings. Some birds of this order resemble gulls, terns, or skuas, but differ by structure of the bill, in which nostrils open into tubes (Fig. 13). The three foretoes are webbed. Found in open ocean, appearing on land only during breeding season. Monogamous. Eggs are usual ellipsoid shape. Altricial.

Fulmarus

10. NORTHERN FULMAR
Fulmarus glacialis
(Glupysh)
Plate 21, Map 6

Field marks: 47 cm. Bird of large size; resembles Herring Gull in flight. Monochromatic brownish-gray or white with gray wings and tail. Legs from dark yellowish to olive; bill yellow.

Habits: Inhabits rocky sea coasts and islands; open sea during nonbreeding season. Migratory. Common in places. Nests on high rocky precipices (or at base) in colonies; more rarely in pairs. Often found together with gulls and alcids. Nest thinly lined with dry grass, situated on outcroppings or soil-covered rocky ledges. Lays one large, whitish, brown-speckled egg in early May. Trustful, unwary bird. Active day and night. Stays in flocks. Flight easy, smooth, with infrequent wing beats and long low soarings. Takes flight with some difficulty after a short running start. Swims perfectly; sits high on the water like a gull. Call: deep, gruff cackle. Catches food while swimming by dipping head into water; does not dive. Feeds on fish, sea invertebrates, carrion, and waste.

Range and distribution: Franz Josef Land, northern island of Novaya Zemlya, Sakhalin Island, Komandorskiye Islands, Kurils, and a group of small islands in the basin of the Pacific Ocean. Found in many northern and eastern seas during migration.

Similar species: Differs from gulls by thick-set body, gray wings without black edges, short thick bill.

Oceanodroma

Small birds (size of starling) with long, pointed wings and forked tail.

11. LEACH'S STORM-PETREL
Oceanodroma leucorrhoa
(Severnaya Kachurka)
Plate 23, Map 6

MAP 6. Northern Fulmar (1), Leach's Storm-Petrel (2)

FIG. 13 Bill of 1) Northern Fulmar and 2) Large *Larus* Gull

Field marks: 20 cm. Grayish-brown; rump white with grayish center.
Habits: Inhabits islands and seashores; off-shore during migration. Nomadic. Uncommon. Nests in colonies, often together with Fork-tailed Storm-Petrel, in flat areas with thick soil layer; often far from water. Nests in a hole dug by the bird. Nest entrance is a half-mound, well hidden in grass or bushes. Entrance to the tunnel is slightly inclined, and then runs parallel to the surface, with a length of up to 1.5 meters. Nest is lined with dry grass. Lays one matte white egg in July. Diurnal, but during breeding season prefers night activity. Sleeps and rests on the water. Unwary, generally silent; call is a low twittering. Flight is easy, elegant. Takes wing easily from a flat area; runs well. Gliding flight over surface of water to catch prey with the bill. Feeds on small crustacea, mollusks, various waste.
Range and distribution: Kuril and Komandorskiye Islands. Winters on the Pacific Ocean.
Similar species: Differs from Fork-tailed Storm-Petrel by dark coloration; from Swinhoe's Storm-Petrel by bright white rump.

12. SWINHOE'S STORM-PETREL
Oceanodroma monorhis
(Vilokhvostaya Kachurka)
Plate 23, Map 7
Field marks: 18 cm. Dark brown overall.
Habits: Found at sea and on or near nesting islands. Rare in the USSR. Biology of the bird is unknown. Included in the Red Data Book.
Range and distribution: Islands in Peter the Great Bay near Vladivostok. Winters on the Pacific Ocean.
Similar species: Differs from Leach's Storm-Petrel by dark rump; from Fork-tailed Storm-Petrel, by dark brownish coloration.
Note: Sometimes treated as a race of Leach's Storm-Petrel.

13. FORK-TAILED STORM-PETREL
Oceanodroma furcata
(Sizaya Kachurka)
Plate 23, Map 7
Field marks: 19 cm. Somewhat larger than Swinhoe's Storm-Petrel. Pale gray with dark wings. Juveniles brownish.
Habits: Found on nesting islands during breeding season; open sea during migration and in winter. Nomadic. Common. Nests in colonies on rocky, hilly shores covered with grassy vegetation, sometimes far from water. Builds nest in shallow, long burrows, which are dug by the bird in soft soil or in rock clefts.

MAP 7. Swinhoe's Storm-Petrel (1), Fork-tailed Storm Petrel (2)

Lays one egg with matte white shell, from mid-July on. Stays in flocks. Flight light, rapid, with easy maneuvering and turns, and frequent wing beats; resembles flight of martins. Flies low to the water, catching prey without alighting. Call: twittering and a thin chirp. Feeds on various small swimming crustaceans and on waste (especially from fishing vessels).

Range and distribution: Sakhalin, Komandorskiye, Kuril, and some other islands of the Pacific. Winters on the Pacific through the width of Japan.

Similar species: Differs from Leach's Storm-Petrel and Swinhoe's Storm-Petrel by lighter coloration.

[In summer, the following nomadic albatrosses usually nest on ocean islands: **14.** SHORT-TAILED ALBATROSS (*Diomedea albatrus*), very large, long-winged white bird with dark wing edges and flesh-colored legs. **15.** LAYSAN ALBATROSS (*Diomedea immutabilis*), which resembles Short-tailed Albatross, but smaller, with brown back and wings, flesh-colored legs; **16.** BLACK-FOOTED ALBATROSS (*Diomedea nigripes*), similar in size to Short-tailed Albatross, but all dark with white ring at base of bill and black legs.

Shearwaters that visit the shores of the USSR: **17.** SOOTY SHEARWATER (*Puffinus griseus*), large bird with long bill, long pointed wings, dark brown with pale chin; silvery wing linings. **18.** SHORT-TAILED SHEARWATER (*Puffinus tenuirostris*), greatly resembles Sooty Shearwater but smaller; wing lining light brown. **19.** MANX SHEARWATER (*Puffinus puffinus*), smaller than Sooty Shearwater, upper parts blackish or brownish, underparts white. **20.** BULLER'S SHEARWATER (*Puffinus bulleri*), same size as Sooty Shearwater, upper parts gray with dark "W" pattern, belly white, tail long and wedge-shaped.

[The following vagrants are more rarely seen: **21.** STREAKED SHEARWATER (*Calonectris leucomelas*), upper parts dark brown with light tracery, underparts white, head white with dark streaks, tail long. In recent years discovered nesting on islands near Vladivostok. Included in the Red Data Book. **22.** WHITE-WINGED PETREL (*Pterodroma leucoptea*), of medium size with long, pointed wings; upper parts dark gray, underparts light; forehead and lores white, legs bluish. **23.** EUROPEAN STORM-PETREL (*Hydrobates pelagicus*), similar to the Leach's Storm-Petrel, but tail is not forked.]

PELICANS AND CORMORANTS: *Pelecaniformes*

Birds of large or very large size, with long neck and long, wide wings. All four toes are webbed. Inhabits various bodies of water. Nest in colonies. Monogamous. Eggs oblong-ovoid or oblong-ellipsoid. Altricial.

Pelecanus

Very large birds with massive body, wide wings, and long bill, with large bag of extendable skin under lower mandible. Most species are whitish.

24. DALMATIAN PELICAN
Pelecanus crispus
(Kudryavy Pelikan)
Plate 1, Map 8
Field marks: 171 cm. Plumage white or grayish; wing edges gray-brown. Feathers on nape of neck elongated and curly. Legs and feet black. Nestlings brownish-grey.
Habits: Inhabit bodies of water in steppe and desert. Migratory. Common in places, but total number is small, and continues to decrease. Nests in overgrown reeds in colonies (sometimes together with Eastern White Pelican), on seasides, lakes, deltas, and lower reaches of rivers, where access is difficult. Sometimes single birds are found in open lakes, far from breeding places. Nests are located on remote islets or on floating reed mats, which are built with reed stalks, grass, and branches. Lays two or three, sometimes four or five white eggs from end of April on. Very cautious and will not allow an approach, even to the nest. Take-off for flight is a heavy running start, with a pushing off from the water; but flight is fast, with deep wing flaps, frequent soaring. Flock flies in a file or angle. In spite of the high speed and ease of flight, the pelican appears clumsy due to its wide wings with fingerlike edges. On the ground the bird waddles, moving slowly. Perfect swimmer, but does not dive. Call: muffled roar; outside breeding colonies the bird is silent. Feeds on various species of fish, catching them in upper layers of water or driving them into a shoal. To achieve this, a flock of birds lines up, then drives fish to shore. Cormorants, gulls, and Eastern White Pelicans will usually join this hunt. Included in the Red Data Book.

MAP 8. Dalmation Pelican (1), Eastern White Pelican (2)

Range and distribution: Shores of the Azov Sea, Volga Delta, lower Amu Darya and Syr Darya Rivers, large bodies of water in Kazakhstan. Winters in Iraq, Iran, and northern Hindustan.

Similar species: Differs from Eastern White Pelican by its black legs and long nape feathers.

25. EASTERN WHITE PELICAN
Pelecanus onocrotalus
(Rozovy Pelikan)
Plate 1, Map 8

Field marks: 160 cm. White with pink tint; wing edges black; small crest, pinkish legs. Nestlings dark brown.

Habits: No apparent significant difference from Dalmatian Pelican, with whom it often forms mixed colonies. Eastern White Pelican is even less common. Its breeding season begins slightly later, usually with two eggs in a nest. Minor differences in habits. When in water, the Eastern White Pelican does not keep its neck vertical, as the Dalmatian Pelican does, but more often rests it on its back. Included in the Red Data Book.

Range and distribution: Volga Delta, Aral Sea, large lakes in Kazakhstan, lower Duna River, some bodies of water in the Rostov Oblast. Winters in West Asia, Africa, and India.

Similar species: Differs from the Dalmatian Pelican by its pinkish legs, lack of "mane," and black primaries and secondaries on the underwing.

Phalacrocorax

Large birds of solid build. Tail long. Bill of medium length, hooked at the end; area of bare skin at mouth. Coloration black.

26. GREAT CORMORANT
Phalacrocorax carbo
(Bolshoy Baklan)
Plate 1, Map 9

Field marks: 90 cm. Large cormorant. Plumage black with greenish metallic sheen; throat and cheeks white; white spot on thigh during breeding season; in the race occupying the southern part of its range, the neck and top of head of adults are whitish. Lores and throat pouch yellow. Juveniles are brown with lighter belly.

Habits: Found near seas, large lakes, and rivers. Migratory, sometimes nonmigratory. Common in places. Nests in colonies; sometimes very numerous. Often found together

FIG. 14 Eastern White Pelican in Flight

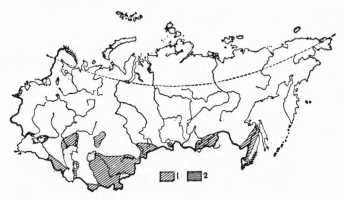

MAP 9. Great Cormorant (1), Temminck's Cormorant (2)

with herons or alcids on rocky seashores, islands, lake shores, and riversides overgrown with reed and arboreal vegetation. Nest built of branches and sticks, situated on nearly inaccessible rock ledges, trees, or on dead reed thickets; less frequently on flat islands. Lays four to six bluish eggs with white blotches from mid-April on. Stays in small flocks outside breeding colonies. Excellent swimmer and diver. Sits deeply in water, slightly uptilting its bill and resting its tail flat on the water surface. Stands vertical when on land and in tree branches. Plumage wets quickly in water, so bird often dries on shore by spreading its wings. Flight heavy but fast, with rapid wing beats; resembles flight of eiders or brants. Flock flies in single file. Takes off from the water heavily by making a running start. Feeds by diving and pursuing prey under water. Call: muffled croaking. Feeds on variety of fish and can be harmful for fish industry where numerous.

Range and distribution: Shores and islands of the Black and Azov Seas, Transcaucasia, shores of the Caspian Sea, and the Volga Delta, lakes of Kazakhstan and Central Asia, Transbaikal, Soviet Far East. Winters on the Black and Caspian Seas and some lakes of Central Asia.

Similar species: Differs from Temminck's Cormorant by the shape of bare skin near bill (see Plate 1); from the others, by larger size; white spot on throat and cheeks; yellow skin near bill.

27. TEMMINCK'S CORMORANT
Phalacrocorax capillatus
(Ussuriysky Baklan)
Plate 1, Map 9
Field marks: 85 cm. Resembles the Great Cormorant, but smaller.

Habits: Inhabits rocky seashores and islands. Migratory, sometimes nomadic. Common in places, but total number is small. Nests in small groups in nearly inaccessible stony precipices and sheer rocks. Lays four bluish eggs with white limelike stains in June. Habits and behavior same as Great Cormorant, but feeds exclusively in the sea. Not found in bodies of fresh water.

Range and distribution: Seashores of the Soviet Far East, Sakhalin Island, southern Kuril Islands. Winters to the south as far as the Ryukyu Islands and southeastern China.

Similar species: Differs from the Great Cormorant by the shape of the bare skin area near the bill (see Plate 1); from the other cormorants, by larger size; white spot on throat and cheeks; yellow bare spot near bill.

28. PELAGIC CORMORANT
Phalacrocorax pelagicus
(Beringov Baklan)
Plate 1, Map 10
Field marks: 70 cm. Medium size. Black with intense metallic green sheen in breeding plumage; neck is streaked white; white spots on thighs; two short crests on head. The area of bare skin near the bill is blackish, the pouch red.

Habits: Inhabits rocky and stony seashores and islands. Migratory; sometimes nomadic or nonmigratory. Common in places. Nests in colonies, often together with alcids. Nest is made of grass and algae, and is situated on rock ledges and in crevices of precipices in nearly inaccessible places. Lays three to five bluish eggs (typical for cormorants) from the middle of May on. Behavior and habits like Great Cormorant. Feeds only on sea fish and crustaceans.

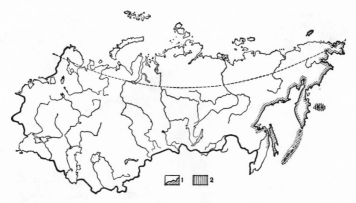

MAP 10. Pelagic Cormorant (1), Red-faced Cormorant (2)

Range and distribution: Shores of Chukotski Peninsula, Bering and Okhotsk Seas, Wrangel Island, Komandorskiye and Kuril Islands, Sakhalin Island. Winters as far south as Taiwan.

Similar species: Differs from Red-faced Cormorant by slender bill and by color and shape of bare skin area near the bill (see Plate 1).

29. RED-FACED CORMORANT
Phalacrocorax urile
(Krasnolitsy Baklan)
Plate 1, Map 10

Field marks: 75 cm. Very similar to Pelagic Cormorant, but has larger area of bare skin near bill, sides of the head red; throat blue.

Habits: Inhabits rocky seashores and islands. Nonmigratory or nomadic. Relatively rare. Nests in colonies on cliffs; nests made of seaweed. Breeding season, number color and

shape of eggs, and feeding habits same as other eastern cormorants.

Range and distribution: Komandorskiye Islands. Winters south to Taiwan.

Similar species: Differs from Temminck's Cormorant by its heavier bill, adults by shape and red color of bare spot near the bill (almost indiscernible from a distance). Juveniles of the two are practically indistinguishable.

30. EUROPEAN SHAG
Phalacrocorax aristotelis
(Khokhlaty Baklan)
Plate 1, Map 11

Field marks: 76 cm. Medium size. Black with green metallic sheen. Area of bare skin at base of bill yellow. Small crest of feathers bent forward on forehead in spring. Juvenile's chin dirty white; belly dark.

Habits: Inhabits rocky seashores and islands.

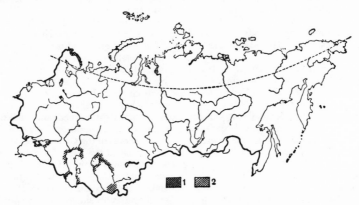

MAP 11. European Shag (1), Pygmy Cormorant (2)

FIG. 15 SHORT-LEGGED WATERBIRDS IN FLIGHT
1. duck (Mallard)   2. cormorant (Great Cormorant)   3. coot (Common Coot)   4. alcid (Razorbill)   5. loon (Red-throated Loon)   6. grebe (Great Crested Grebe)

Nonmigratory or nomadic. Common in places. Nests in colonies (often together with gulls, guillemots, and other cormorants) on steep rocky precipices with ledges, crevices, and niches. Nest massive, built with seaweed, branches, and grass; usually hidden under an overhanging ledge or in a crevice. Nests from early April in the southern part of its range, by mid-May further north. Lays three eggs (typical for cormorants). Behavior, habits, feeding like Great Cormorant, but is not found on bodies of fresh water. Included in the Red Data Book.

Range and distribution: Northern shores of the Kola Peninsula, western shores of the Crimea. Winters on shore regions of open waters in Western Europe and the Azov Sea.

Similar species: Differs from Great Cormorant by smaller size, lack of white throat spot, and by crest (in spring) on the forehead; juveniles, by dark belly.

31. PYGMY CORMORANT
Phalacrocorax pygmaeus
(Maly Baklan)
Plate 1, Map 11

Field marks: 54 cm. Considerably smaller than other cormorants (size of a crow). Greenish-black with small white spots on upper parts; head and neck dark brown. No bare area near bill. Throat of juveniles whitish.

Habits: Inhabits seashores, rivers and lakes of desert areas. Nonmigratory, nomadic, or migratory. Common in places, but generally more rare than other cormorants. Nests in small colonies or pairs, sometimes with other birds, in overgrown reeds or riparian lakes, river deltas, seashores, and islands. Nest is a dome of reed stalks situated in stands or broken heaps of reeds. Sometimes nests in trees. Less sociable than other cormorants; often found singly. Agile climber of reed stalks. Cautious. Habits and behavior like Great Cormorant, but flies faster and lighter. Feeds on small fish.

Range and distribution: Delta of the Duna River, shores of the Caspian Sea, lower reaches and deltas of the Amu Darya and Syr Darya Rivers, shores of the Aral Sea. Winters in the south of the Caspian Sea and in Iran and Iraq.

Similar species: Differs from all cormorants by considerably smaller size; brown head and white-spotted greenish body.

[From time to time other vagrants are noted in the Soviet Union, such as **32.** NORTHERN GANNET (*Sula bassana*, family *Sulidae*): large bird with long conical bill and black legs; adults, white with black-edged wings; juveniles, black-gray with white speckles. In the last century, they were repeatedly observed on the Murman Coast, but specimens were never obtained; also noted in Estonia. Inhabits the Northern Atlantic basin, the south of Africa, Australia, and New Zealand. **33.** The RED-FOOTED BOOBY (*Sula sula*, family *Sulidae*) resembles the Northern Gannet, but legs are red. A specimen was obtained in the Tatar Straits. Inhabits tropical shores of the Atlantic, Pacific, and Indian oceans. **34.** The GREAT FRIGATEBIRD (*Fregata minor*, family *Fregatidae*) is a very large black bird with long pointed wings, long forked tail, and long bill; male has a red, featherless, inflatable throat pouch. Specimen obtained in 1926 near Khabarovsk; later observed near Vladivostok, and in 1962 noted near Komsomolsk on the Amur. Pelagic bird, inhabiting tropical regions of Pacific, Indian, and Atlantic Oceans.]

HERONS, IBISES, STORKS: *Ciconiiformes*

Birds of very large to medium size. Legs, neck, and bill long, and wings broad and rounded. Inhabits shoals, swamps, and flooded stands of reeds. Nests in pairs and in colonies. Monogamous. Eggs ovoid or oblong-ellipsoid. Altricial.

Ardea

Large herons with long legs. Coloration, including the tail, nonwhite. Bill long (more than 10 cm.), straight and sharp. Drooping crest on the head.

35. GRAY HERON
Ardea cinerea
(Seraya Tsaplya)
Plate 6, Map 12
Field marks 91 cm. Gray; crest, wing edges,

FIG. 16 Gray Heron at Its Nest

and stripe on neck black; belly white. Legs yellowish-brown; bill brown.
Habits: Inhabits bodies of water in various landscapes, from taiga to desert. Migratory, in places nonmigratory. Nests in pairs or colonies on river banks, lakes, and reservoirs. Nest is loosely cone-shaped, made of branches and reed stalks, and built on high trees, in flooded osiers, or stands of reed. Nests from April (in the south) and later. Lays four or five light-colored, greenish-blue eggs. Cautious. Flight smooth with slow wing beats, strong and even; takeoff is clumsy, with legs dangling. Head is drawn into shoulders in flight. Usually silent. Call: short, rasping, piercing, unpleasant cry, resembling "krryank," usually uttered in flight. Feeds by wandering through water on shoals, river spits, and sometimes in marshy meadows. Often stays motionless on the bank, with neck drawn in. Feeds on small fish, insects, frogs, and other small animals.
Range and distribution: Southern half of the USSR. Winters in Transcaucasia, Central Asia. Outside the USSR, winters in West Asia, southern Europe, India, and China.
Similar species: Differs from other herons by its gray coloration and large size.

36. PURPLE HERON
Ardea purpurea
(Rizhaya Tsaplya)
Plate 6, Map 12
Field marks: 79 cm. Medium-size bird. Coloration dark; back gray-brown; head, neck, and breast rusty with longitudinal back markings; belly blackish; wings grayish, edged with black; legs and bill yellowish-brown.

MAP 12. Purple Heron (1), Gray Heron (2)

Habits: Found near bodies of water in steppe, desert, and forest-steppe. Migratory. Common in places, but rarer than Gray Heron. Nests in pairs or small colonies near banks of rivers and lakes overgrown with thickets of reed or bushes. Builds loose cone-shaped nests in dry reeds; more rarely in flooded osier thickets. Nests from early May on (in the south). Lays four or five greenish-blue eggs (smaller than Gray Heron's). Active mostly at twilight. Behavior and habits similar to Gray Heron, but rarely perches in trees. Call quieter and less piercing; less cautious. Feeds on small fish, frogs, grass snakes, small rodents, insects.

Range and distribution: Southern regions of European USSR, Kazakhstan, Central Asia, southern regions of Soviet Far East. Winters in Africa, southwestern Asia and China.

Similar species: Differs from other herons by strikingly marked rusty head, breast, and neck.

Egretta

Herons of large and medium size with long legs. Pure white. In spring plumage, long loose feathers (called "little aigrettes" in Russian) on the back.

37. GREAT EGRET
Egretta alba
(Bolshaya Belaya Tsaplya)
Plate 6, Map 13

Field marks: 89 cm. Large. Eye ring yellow; legs black; bill black with yellow base (yellow in winter).

Habits: Inhabits bodies of water in southern treeless landscapes. Migratory. Common in places, but uncommon as a whole. Nests in pairs or colonies on shoals, reedy lakes, and slow rivers or channels with thick riverside

MAP 13. Great Egret (1), Little Egret (2)

FIG. 17 Great Egret Chick

vegetation. Nest is a loose structure built of dead reeds; sometimes situated in low trees. Nests from April on. Lays three to five greenish-blue eggs. Flight and habits same as Gray Heron, but more cautious; rarely perches in trees. Generally silent. Call: gruff, hoarse "crrack." Feeds on small animals, including fish, frog, insects. At the end of the nineteenth and beginning of the twentieth century, the bird was threatened by extermination due to demand for its decorative plumes. It is now protected.

Range and distribution: Southern regions of European USSR, including Volga Delta; Transcaucasus, Central Asia, Kazakhstan, southern Soviet Far East. Winters in southern Central Asia. Outside the USSR, winters in Africa and southern Asia.

Similar species: Differs from Little, Short-billed, and Chinese Egrets by larger size (wing is no less than 36 cm.) and other less obvious differences (see Field marks).

38. LITTLE EGRET
Egretta garzetta
(Malaya Belaya Tsaplya)
Plate 6, Map 13
Field marks: 56 cm. Half the size of Great Egret.

Bill black; lower mandible of adults in winter (and of all juveniles) is yellow (or with yellow base); eye ring black; toes yellow. In spring, two or three long, loose feathers on the nape.

Habits: Found in bodies of water in steppe and desert. Migratory. Common in places. Nests in colonies together with other herons and cormorants on lakes, channels, and estuaries near overgrown banks of reeds, in bushes, on trees. Nests made of dry twigs, situated in trees; occasionally in dry reed. Nest is an inverted cone (typical of herons). Lays five or six greenish-blue eggs from mid-April on. Very sociable, always feeds in small flocks. Unwary. Flight more hurried than other herons. Call: clamorous, croaking "ark-ark-ark." Feeds in shoals or on banks; in field and meadows. Prefers small fish, frogs, insects.

Range and distribution: Southern regions of European USSR, including the Volga Delta and bodies of water of the Caucasus and Transcaucasus; Central Asia. Winters on the Mediterranean, in southwestern Asia, and North Africa.

Similar species: Differs from Great Egret by smaller size, black eye ring, loose feathers on the nape (in spring), and yellow feet.

[In the Soviet Far East, the following vagrants were noted: **39.** CHINESE EGRET (*Egretta eulophotes*), size same as Little Egret, but with yellow bill. Included in the Red Data Book. **40.** SHORT-BILLED EGRET (*Egretta intermedia*), very similar to Great Egret but smaller, and with short bill.]

Bubulcus

41. CATTLE EGRET
Bubulcus ibis
(Yegipetskaya Tsaplya)
Plate 6, Map 14
Field marks: 51 cm. Medium size. Bill and neck short, head large; long, loose feathers on head, neck, and back; overall white with buffy feathers on head, breast, and back; bill yellow with reddish base; legs reddish. Juveniles all white; bill yellow.

Habits: Inhabits swampy lowlands and settled areas. Migratory. Common in places, but not numerous as a whole. Nests in colonies together with other egrets, in clumps of tall trees, near lakes, swamps, river channels, and paddy fields. Builds nest low to the ground, among lianas. Nest is a loose structure, made of thin, dry branches and twigs. Lays five to seven light bluish eggs from end of April to mid-May.

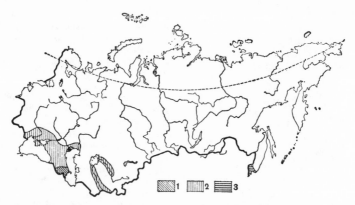

MAP 14. Cattle Egret (1), Squacco Pond-Heron (2), Chinese Pond-
Heron (3)

Feeds in small flocks in meadows and swamps.
Often perches on tree branches. Unwary. Flight
easy but slow, usually low to the ground. Usu-
ally silent. Call: short muffled croaking sound,
"korr-korr-korr." Feeds on insects, sometimes
frogs.
Range and distribution: Transcaucasus, Volga
Delta, Turkmenia (lower reaches of the Atrek
River). Winters in Africa and southwestern
Asia.
Similar species: Differs from Little Egret and
Squacco Pond-Heron by buffy back and breast
and by reddish legs.

Ardeola

Small herons (slightly larger than a crow) with
shorter legs. Long trailing crest, soft, loose
feathers on the back.

42. SQUACCO POND-HERON
Ardeola ralloides
(Zholtaya Tsaplya)
Plate 6, Map 14
Field marks: 46 cm. Head, neck, breast, and
back buffy; wings, belly, and tail white; bill
blue; legs yellow. In winter, upperparts
browner.
Habits: Found in swampy plains, usually by
river valleys and deltas. Migratory. Common
in places. Nesting habits same as other small
herons. In treeless areas, nest may also be situated in stands of dry reed. Lays four or five
elongated greenish-blue eggs in May. When
outside colonies, stays singly or in small groups.
Flight slow with infrequent wing beats, but
easy and graceful. Bird flies low to the ground
in a patternless flock, or fairly high, forming

an angle or oblique line. In flight appears white,
with wide, obtuse wings. Generally unwary and
silent. Call: gruff croaking cry. Feeds on large
insects, frogs.
Range and distribution: Southern USSR, including Volga Delta and the Transcaucasus;
Central Asia. Winters in central Africa.
Similar species: Differs from Cattle Egret by
slightly smaller size, predominance of buffy
in upper parts, and blue bill.

43. CHINESE POND-HERON
Ardeola bacchus
(Belokrylaya Tsaplya)
Not illustrated, Map 14
Field marks: 45 cm. Head and neck red; back
and spots on sides of breast black; rest is white;
bill yellow; legs pale orange. In winter, head,
neck, and back dark brown; remainder of
plumage white with mottling on breast.
Habits: In the USSR, very rare and little-known
habitué of swampy plains. Nesting possible,
but has not been documented.
Range and distribution: Southern regions of
Soviet Far East.
Similar species: Differs from other herons by
its distinctive coloration.

Butorides

44. LITTLE HERON
Butorides striatus
(Zelyonaya Kvakva)
Plate 6, Map 15
Field marks: 45 cm. Small heron with short
legs and long bill. Small crest on head; upper
parts blackish-green; underparts smoky; bill

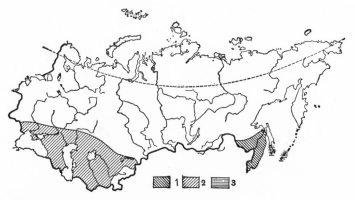

MAP 15. Little Heron (1), Black-crowned Night-Heron (2), Yellow Bittern (3)

black; legs olive. Juveniles less colorful, with mottling on the breast.

Habits: Found along the river banks. Migratory. Common in places. Nests in pairs near river channels, backwaters, and islands overgrown by thick bushes and deciduous trees. Prefers areas heaped with driftwood and fallen trees. Nest is a loose cone situated in trees, usually on branches overhanging water or far from the bank. Lays five (or up to seven or eight) greenish-blue eggs from mid-May. Nesting female sits firmly, allowing a close approach. Flight fast, with frequent wing beats; usually will not rise higher than trees. Flies with neck drawn in. Feeds along river bank channels with rapid current, or fishes while standing in shallows, on snags or underwater tree roots. When threatened, stands stock-still, stretching the neck slightly upward, then flies a short distance and perches again, usually on lower tree branches. Unwary. Rather clamorous call resembles sharp, repeated "tiuu" or "tilk." Feeds almost exclusively on small fish.

Range and distribution: Soviet Far East. Winters in southeastern China and the Philippines.

Similar species: Nothing similar.

Nycticorax

45. BLACK-CROWNED NIGHT HERON
Nycticorax nycticorax
(Kvakva)
Plate 6, Map 15

Field marks: 61 cm. Medium-size heron (slightly larger than a crow), with large head, short legs, and stout bill. Crown and back black; wings gray, underparts white. In spring, a crest

of two to four elongated white feathers is formed on the nape. Bill black; legs yellow but briefly pink during breeding season; eyes red. Juveniles, mottled brown.

Habits: Inhabits swampy lowlands with arboreal vegetation. Migratory. Common. Nests in colonies with other species of herons, cormorants, ibises. Colonies stay in trees, more rarely in reed thickets, not far from water. Nest is a loosely woven cone in the middle part of a tree, but larger and more crudely constructed than that of other herons. Lays three to five light bluish eggs from end of April on. Stays in small flocks outside of breeding colonies. Largely nocturnal; usually perches in trees near water during the day. Flight slow, easy, and smooth; flies up quickly, almost vertically. Feeds while wandering on shoals or staying immobile in water to wait for prey. Unwary, rather clamorous. Call: strong repetitious "kvau . . . kvau." Feeds mostly on fish and frogs, sometimes on large insects.

Range and distribution: Southern regions of European USSR, Central Asia, Kazakhstan. Winters in Africa and southern Asia.

Similar species: Differs from other herons by its black crown and back, and by white underparts.

Ixobrychus

Very small herons (smaller than a crow), with long legs and neck; long bill.

46. LITTLE BITTERN
Ixobrychus minutus
(Volchok)
Plate 6, Map 16

Field marks: 36 cm. Crown and back black;

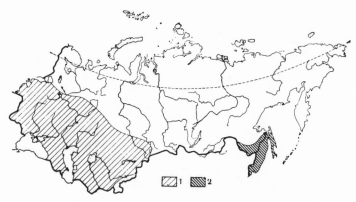

MAP 16. Little Bittern (1), Schrenck's Bittern (2)

neck and breast ocherish; belly whitish, wings black with buffy wing patch; bill greenish; legs green. Back of female brownish. Juveniles mottled brown.

Habits: Found near bodies of water overgrown with reeds and bushes, in a variety of habitats from forest to desert. Migratory. Common but stays hidden singly, and is rarely seen. Nests in pairs near lakes, ponds, reservoirs, and ox-bow lakes overgrown with reed, cane, alder, or osier. Nest situated in broken reeds, bushes, or even in trees, but low to the ground. Nest made of small twigs and reed stalks, and resembles the loosely woven cone of other herons, but smaller. Lays five to nine white eggs with rough matte shell from mid-May on. Crepuscular and nocturnal. If in danger, stays quiet, stretching neck and bill vertically. Flies up easily even from thick brake, and perches soon after. Flight fast, with frequent wing beats, stretching of neck; glides before descending. Agile reed climber. Waits above water for prey. Male call: in spring, muffled, jerky "pumb-pumb"; at other seasons, shrill, quick "ke-ke-ke." Feeds on small fish, frogs, insects.

Range and distribution: Southern half of European USSR, Kazakhstan, Central Asia. Winters in Iran, Iraq, and tropical regions of Africa.

Similar species: Differs from Schrenck's Bittern and Yellow Bittern by black back (not found in same range); from other herons, by small size.

47. SCHRENCK'S BITTERN
Ixobrychus eurythmus
(Amursky Volchok)
Plate 6, Map 16

Field marks: 36 cm. Upperparts chestnut; crown black; underparts ocherish with dark stripe down throat; wings gray, dark-edged. Bill brown and yellow; legs greenish. Females have light mottling on back; juveniles, in addition, have dark mottling on breast.

Habits: Found in open swampy plains in river valleys. Migratory. Not common. Nests in pairs in wet meadows and swamps overgrown with high grass and bushes. Nest situated on the ground, and built with dry stalks fastened together near the base with clay. Lays three to five white eggs at end of May. Feeds in meadows, where there are puddles with open water. Active in twilight, sometimes in daytime. Flight slow, but with rapid wing beats. Does not usually fly high or far. Rarely perches in trees. Usually silent. In spring, call is a repetitive, jerky "gup-gup-gup." Feeds on insects and small fish.

Range and distribution: Soviet Far East along the Amur and Ussuri River, Sakhalin Island. Winters in southern China, in the Philippines, and on Celebes Island.

Similar species: Differs from Little Bittern by chestnut back (species not found together in same range); from Yellow Bittern, by larger size and bare lower shin; from other herons, by smaller size.

48. YELLOW BITTERN
Ixobrychus sinensis
(Kitaysky Volchok)
Plate 6; Map 15

Field marks: 37-38 cm. Smallest bittern, with longest bill. Crown, wing edges, tail, and spots on sides of breast black; back yellow-brown; underparts buffy ocherish and rusty; legs greenish; bill yellow with black ridge.

Habits: Very rare migratory bird. Prefers

swampy plains overgrown with bushes. Biology in USSR unknown.

Range and distribution: Sakhalin Island and Kunashir Island.

Similar species: Differs from the Schrenck's Bittern by lack of dark brown back.

Botaurus

49. EURASIAN BITTERN
Botaurus stellaris
(Vyp)
Plate 6, Map 17

Field marks: 76 cm. Large, short-legged heron with long, massive bill, large head, and thick neck. Rusty brown, dense tracery with dark mottling of stripes and bands; legs and bill greenish-yellow.

Habits: Found near bodies of water in variety of habitat from taiga to desert. Migratory. Common. Nests in pairs in almost inaccessible swampy banks of lakes, flood plains, ponds, and river bays, where dense thickets of reed, cane, and sedge alternate with small pools of water. Large nest is made with stalks and leaves of different plants; situated on the ground, often on hummocks, always in thickets. Lays three to six dull gray eggs from mid-May on. Stays hidden; nocturnal; rarely seen; flushes from reeds on very close approach. Flight easy and quick; flies up clumsily, vertically; alights after flying a short distance. If danger threatens, prefers to stay quiet, stretching neck and bill upward and becoming nearly invisible among dense reedstalks. In spring, call is jerky, muffled, and booming, with deep sounds resembling "prumb-bu-bu." In nonbreeding season, emits gruff cries at night, "kau." Waits for prey near waterline; stays immobile, bent over, with outstretched neck. Feeds on fish, frogs, tadpoles, and water invertebrates.

Range and distribution: Southern half of European USSR and Siberia; Soviet Far East, Sakhalin Island. Winters in south of USSR, in Africa, and southern Asia.

Similar species: Differs from all herons found in USSR by rusty speckled coloration.

[Vagrant **50.** JAPANESE NIGHT HERON (*Gorsachius goisagi*) obtained in Vladivostok area. Small heron with short, slightly curved bill and crest; body chestnut rufous brown with dense tracery of mottled stripes and bands.]

Platalea

51. EURASIAN SPOONBILL
Platalea leucorodia
(Kolpitsa)
Plate 6, Map 18

Field marks: 86 cm. Large bird with long legs and long neck. Bill long and flat, enlarged at end like rounded shovel. Yellowish crest on head; plumage white. Bill black with yellow edge. Legs black. Juveniles without crest; wing tips black; bill reddish.

Habits: Found near large bodies of water in steppe and desert. Migratory. Common in places, but not numerous. Nests in colonies, often together with other birds (herons, cormorants, ibises), on river deltas overgrown with thick reeds, bushes, or trees; or on river islands covered with riparian forest. Nests built in dry reeds, trees, and bushes. Construction is simple and large, made of reed stalks and branches. Lays three or four white eggs with small bright red-brown spots from end of May on. Flight easy, with frequent wing beats and

MAP 17. Eurasian Bittern

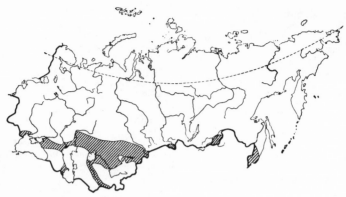

MAP 18. Eurasian Spoonbill

gliding; in flight, bird extends and slightly bends the neck. Unwary; allows closer approach than most herons. Active in twilight, but often feeds during the day. Generally silent; utters grumbling sounds only near nest. Feeds in silty shoals by lowering tip of the bill into water and moving it from side to side ("mowing"). Feeds on water insects, sometimes frogs, fry, mollusks. Included in the Red Data Book.

Range and distribution: Southern regions of European USSR, including the Volga Delta, Transcaucasus, Kazakhstan, Central Asia, Tuva, Transbaikal, Soviet Far East. Winters in East Africa and southern Asia.

Similar species: Differs from herons by distinctive shape of bill and outstretched neck in flight.

Plegadis

52. GLOSSY IBIS
Plegadis falcinellus
(Karavayka)
Plate 6, Map 19

Field marks: 56 cm. Large bird with long legs. Bill long, strongly curved downward. Overall dark chestnut-brown with metallic gloss.

Habits: Found near bodies of water in steppe and desert. Migratory. Common in places, but generally rare. Nests in colonies, often together with herons, spoonbills, and cormorants, in lakes, river deltas, and floodplains overgrown with reed and bushes; or on remote river islets. Small nest situated in dry reeds or in lower parts of trees. Lays three to

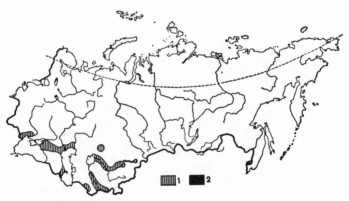

MAP 19. Glossy Ibis (1), Japanese Crested Ibis (2)

five bright blue eggs from early May on. Flight fast, with frequent wing beats alternating with gliding; in flight, flock forms single file. Usually stays in small flocks. Feeds in silty shoals on water insects and their larvae, small crustacea, mollusks, and other invertebrates, sometimes fish and frogs. Usually silent. Call: hoarse, muffled sound.

Range and distribution: Southern regions, including the Duna and Volga Deltas, Transcaucasus, northern Caucasus, deltas of the Amu Darya and Syr Darya; in Turkmenia, the lower course of the Tedzhen and Murgab Rivers. Winters in Africa and southern Asia.

Similar species: Differs from all birds of similar appearance (curlews, ibis, herons) by distinctive coloration.

Nipponia

53. JAPANESE CRESTED IBIS
Nipponia nippon
(Krasnonogy Ibis)
Plate 6, Map 19
Field marks: 60 cm. Large bird, legs shorter than a heron's. Crest on head; bill long and curved downward; overall white with pink or gray tint. Legs brownish-red; bill black-edged red; "face" red.
Habits: Inhabits swampy lowlands with clumps of trees in river valleys and near large lakes. Very rare and apparently near extinction. Has not been observed by any scientists in the USSR for more than a decade. Nests in trees, extremely cautious. Biology nearly unknown. Possibly extinct in the USSR. Included in the Red Data Book.
Range and distribution: Southern regions of Soviet Far East. Winters on the Korean Peninsula.

Similar species: Differs from herons by curved bill and red "face."

[**54.** SACRED IBIS (*Threskiornis aethiopicys*), a native of Africa and Asia Minor, is an occasional vagrant in the Transcaucasus. Bird is white with black head, bill, and tail.]

Ciconia

Very large birds of build typical to this order. Legs and massive bill usually scarlet; coloration, combination of white and black; in flight, neck and legs are stretched.

55. WHITE STORK
Ciconia ciconia
(Bely Aist)
Plate 7, Map 20
Field marks: 102 cm. Coloration white, wings black. Bill and legs are red. In Soviet Far East, bill is black.
Habits: Found in open spaces with clumps of trees and bodies of water from forest to desert, and in settled areas. Migratory. Common in places, but not numerous. Nests in pairs in swampy river valleys and boggy lowlands, both near and far from populated areas. Large, crudely made nest built with boughs and sticks; situated on buildings, in trees, on specially installed poles or posts, sometimes on old haystacks. Same nests are used for many successive years. Lays three to five pure white eggs (the shell is yellow when held up to light) from early April on (later in the north). Easily seen. Flight quiet, with deep wing beats, long and frequent soaring. In contrast, takeoff for flight is heavy, with a running start. Usually silent, but clacks bill loudly when excited, while bending its head back during greeting display

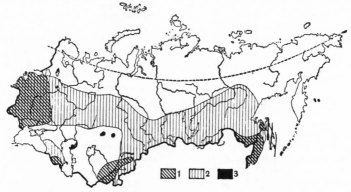

MAP 20. White Stork (1), Black Stork (2), Greater Flamingo (3)

at nest. Feeds in swamps or on banks of reservoirs, on frogs, small rodents, snakes, fish, locusts, and other small animals.

Range and distribution: Baltic States, Belorussia, Ukraine, some western regions of central Russia, Central Asia, Transbaikal. Winters in Africa.

Similar species: Differs from the Black Stork by white coloration; from the Siberian White Crane, by black secondaries.

Note: Races of the Soviet Far East are currently viewed as a separate species, that is, Oriental Stork (*Ciconia boyciana*). Differs by its larger size and black bill. Included in the Red Data Book.

56. BLACK STORK
Ciconia nigra
(Chyorny Aist)
Plate 7, Map 20

Field marks: 90 cm. Black overall; belly white.

Habits: Found in tall forests of plains and mountains; sometimes in open spaces with rocks or clumps of trees. Migratory. Uncommon. Nests in pairs, usually in river valleys or near lakes, where swamps and wet meadows alternate with wooded areas or cliffs. Generally avoids settlements, and prefers the most remote, inaccessible places, but sometimes found feeding near settled areas. Massive, crudely built nest situated in tree or on cliff, usually high up. Same nest used for many years. Lays three to five dirty white eggs (the shell is green when held up to light) from mid-

FIG. 18 White Stork at Its Nest

April on. Very cautious and silent; stays alone; in pairs only at breeding time. Habits, flight, feeding similar to the White Stork. Included in the Red Data Book.

Range and distribution: Central regions of European USSR from Belorussia to the Urals, southern half of Siberia, Soviet Far East. Winters in Africa and southern Asia.

Similar species: Differs from the White Stork by black head, neck, back, and tail.

FLAMINGOS: *Phoenicopteriformes*

Phoenicopterus

57. GREATER FLAMINGO
Phoenicopterus ruber
(Flamingo)
Plate 7, Map 20

Field marks: 127-130 cm. Very large bird with long, thin legs and neck. Bill small, abruptly bent down. Coloration pinkish-white; especially bright on wings; primaries and secondaries black; bill pink with black tip; legs pink. Juveniles gray-white, legs and bill gray.

Habits: Inhabits silty shallow shores of seas and brackish lakes. Migratory. Stays in large flocks, and therefore appears common in places, but total number is small and continues to decrease. Nests in colonies in boggy, silty open shores and on islands surrounded by shallow water. Nest is column-shaped, hollow on the

top, made of hardened clay. Lays one or two oblong-ellipsoid white eggs during the first ten days of May. In July, birds gather on large inaccessible reservoirs for molting; at that time they cannot fly. Feeds in shallow water, dipping the head almost perpendicularly into the water, and filtering water and liquid silt through the bill. Flight resembles that of goose by its speed and frequent wing beats. Takeoff is with difficulty, against the wind and after a long running start; in flight neck and legs are outstretched. Call: long, low cackling. Feeds on algae, small crustacea, mollusks. Included in the Red Data Book.

Range and distribution: Some large lakes in Kazakhstan. Winters on the Caspian Sea, in Iran and Iraq.

Similar species: Differs from all other birds in the USSR by its distinctive appearance and pink coloration.

FIG. 19 LONG-LEGGED WATERBIRDS IN FLIGHT
1. crane (Common Crane) 2. heron (Gray Heron) 3. ibis (Glossy Ibis) 4. stork
(White Stork) 5. flamingo (Greater Flamingo) 6. spoonbill (Eurasian Spoonbill)
7. stork (Black Stork)

MAP 21. Whooper Swan

SWANS, GEESE, DUCKS: *Anseriformes*

Birds of very large to medium size. The bill (with rare exception) is flattened horizontally: its edges have thin plates forming a kind of sieve. Three foretoes are webbed. Plumage compact and elastic, with well-developed down. Inhabits various bodies of water. Excellent swimmer. Polygamous or monogamous. Eggs of usual or oblong-ovoid shape. Precocial.

Cygnus

One of the largest birds in the USSR. Neck very long, thin; wings long and wide; plumage pure white. Juveniles brownish gray, legs black.

58. WHOOPER SWAN
Cygnus cygnus
(Lebed-klikun)
Plate 2, Map 21
Field marks: 147-150 cm. Largest of swans. All white. Extensive yellow area at base of black bill extends out the bill to form an acute angle. Juveniles are gray-brown, and their black bills are pink where the adults' are yellow.
Habits: Inhabits lakes of forest-tundra and taiga. Noted near coast during migration. Migratory. Not numerous. Nests in pairs by remote, large lakes with overgrown banks of sedge and reed. Nest is a heap of moss, grass, or reed, usually built on shallow water or on a hidden island in lake. Lays four to six large white or yellowish eggs from mid-May on. During non-breeding season, stays in small flocks. Feeds by dipping head and neck in water, does not dive. While swimming, neck is usually held upright. Very cautious. Takes off from water after a running start; flight unhurried, but rapid, with deep strong wing beats; neck stretched forward. Call: loud, blaring, extremely beautiful "gang-go, gang-go." Feeds

on water plants and invertebrates. The Whooper Swan is a remarkable beauty of nature; its numbers are decreasing and hunting is forbidden.
Range and distribution: Northern regions of European USSR, western and eastern Siberia except tundra zones. Isolated colonies known on lower Duna and Dnieper Rivers, northern shores of Caspian Sea; in Kazakhstan on the Balkhash and Ala Kul Lakes; Tuva. Winters south by the Mediterranean, Iran, India, southern China. In the USSR, winters on the Black, Caspian, Barents, and Okhotsk Seas.
Similar species: Differs from the Mute Swan by yellow base of the bill and upright posture; from Bewick's Swan, by larger size, more extensive yellow bill, and a more acute angle between the black and yellow parts of the bill.

59. BEWICK'S SWAN
Cygnus bewickii
(Maly Lebed)
Plate 2, Map 22
Field marks: 110-120 cm. All white. Smaller than Whooper Swan. Base of bill yellow; border of yellow and black more nearly at right angles. Juveniles, tip of bill dark but not black.
Habits: Found in low, very swampy tundra; during nonbreeding season prefers seas and large inland bodies of water. Migratory. Not numerous. Nests in grass and low-bush tundra

FIG. 20 SWANS, GEESE, AND SHELDUCKS IN FLIGHT
1. Whooper Swan   2. Mute Swan   3. Snow Goose   4. Canada Goose   5. Brent Goose
(pale-bellied and dark-bellied forms)   6. Barnacle Goose   7. Greater White-fronted
Goose   8. Red-breasted Goose   9. Bean Goose   10. Ruddy Shelduck   11. Red-billed
Shelduck   12. Greylag Goose

near lakes and river channels. Nest is situated on dry prominence or hummock, often near lake or on islet, and is made of moss and sedge, lined with down and feathers. Lays three or four yellowish eggs from early June on. Nest with bird on eggs visible from a distance; at that time female allows close approach, although the Bewick's Swan is extremely cau-

tious during migration. Resembles Whooper Swan on water, but its neck appears shorter. Call similar to Whooper Swan, but clearer, less solemn. Feeds on aquatic plants; often nibbles grass on land. Included in the Red Data Book.
Range and distribution: Band of tundra from Pechora Bay on the Kola Peninsula in the west, to Chukotski Peninsula in the east. Winters in

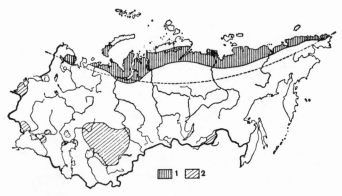

MAP 22. Bewick's Swan (1), Mute Swan (2)

Western Europe and partly in England. In the east, winters on Kamchatka Peninsula, Kuril Islands, Japan, and India.
Similar species: Differs from Whooper Swan by smaller size and shape of spot on base of bill.

60. MUTE SWAN
Cygnus olor
(Lebed-shipun)
Plate 2, Map 22
Field marks: 155-160 cm. All white. Size of Whooper Swan. Bill orange-red with black knob. Juveniles, bill pink with black base and tip.
Habits: Found on large bodies fresh and salt water in variety of habitats. Migratory or nomadic. Not numerous. Nests in lush vegetation of remote lakes, or reed thickets on river deltas, and shallow sea bays. Nest made of reed stalks and lined with bits of down, and situated on fallen reeds. Lays six to eight large dirty bluish eggs from mid-May on. On water, the Mute Swan often takes a typical pose with gracefully bent neck, slightly raised wings, and bill turned downward. When alert, stretches its neck like the Whooper Swan. Very cautious. Call: muffled and hoarse, less clear than Whooper Swan. Feeds in shallows, either on surface of water or by dipping head and neck underwater to feed on the bottom. Feeds on underwater parts of plants, algae, invertebrates. As a rare bird and beauty of nature, the Mute Swan is protected and hunting is forbidden everywhere.
Range and distribution: Baltic States, Lower Duna and Dniester Rivers, Volga Delta, northern Caucasus, southwestern Siberia; in Kazakhstan, along the Turgai, Sarysu, and Syr Darya Rivers. Nests in Transbaikal. Winters on the Black, Caspian, and Mediterranean Seas, in Iran and Central Asia.
Similar species: Differs from other swans by shape of red bill with black knob; juveniles by black base of bill.

[A vagrant **61.** WHISTLING SWAN (*Cygnus columbianus*) was collected on the Anadyr River and on Bering Island (Komandorskiye Islands). On Chukotski Peninsula, a pair of swans with cygnets was sighted; the male was a Whistling Swan and the female a Bewick's Swan. Whistling Swan resembles Bewick's Swan, but is larger, with a black bill and small yellow spot near its base.]

Anser

Size of domestic goose or smaller. Coloration is various tints of gray, brownish gray, and white. Legs and bill pink-orange or yellow. Many ornithologists consider this genus as five separate genera: *Cygnopsis, Philacte, Chen, Eulabeia, Anser*.

62. SWAN GOOSE
Anser cygnoides
(Sukhonos)
Plate 2, Map 23
Field marks: 78 cm. Size of domestic goose. Neck thin and long; coloration brownish-gray; belly and neck whitish in front; dark stripe on nape and crown. Long bill seems disproportionately large for size of the head. Legs orange.
Habits: Inhabits bodies of fresh and brackish water in steppe, forest-steppe, and taiga. Migratory and very rare. Nests in pairs on lakes

MAP 23. Swan Goose (1), Emperor Goose (2)

with swampy banks and reed overgrowth, and near mountain rivers. Builds nest in a dry place in remote, inacessible areas among dense vegetation; seldom in open steppe. Nest is a depression lined with grass and down. Lays four to six large, yellowish eggs from end of April on. Cautious, stays hidden; best seen in flight, when birds gather in small flocks. Call: clear, long cackle. Feeds on land, often far from water's edge. Prefers young sedge and other grasses. Ancestor of some races of domestic geese. Included in the Red Data Book.
Range and distribution: Southern Siberia, Soviet Far East. Winters in Japan, Korean Peninsula, and China.
Similar species: Differs from the Greylag Goose and Bean Goose by large black bill and dark stripe on nape contrasting with the pale throat.

63. EMPEROR GOOSE
Anser canagicus
(Beloshey)
Plate 2, Map 23
Field marks: 76 cm. Smaller than domestic goose with short, thick neck. Coloration bluish-gray with white-edged, dark, scaly pattern; head and nape pure white; bill short and pinkish; legs orange. Juveniles, head and neck dark; bill black.
Habits: Inhabits low seaside tundras, during nonbreeding season found on seashores. Migratory. Very rare. Nests in pairs in boggy, hummock areas of tundra or islands in river estuaries; often among driftwood. Nest is a depression lined with down. Lays four to six white eggs in June. Bird allows close approach while on nest; but very cautious during nonbreeding times. Flight heavy, with frequent wing beats. Flock usually flies low. Generally silent. Call: disyllabic cry "kla-ga, kla-ga." Feeds on sea invertebrates (mollusks, crustacea), sometimes greenery and berries. Included in the Red Data Book.
Range and distribution: Chukotski Peninsula. Winters on Aleutian Islands in North America.
Similar species: Differs from all other geese by its distinct coloration.

64. BAR-HEADED GOOSE
Anser indicus
(Gorny Gus)
Plate 2, Map 24
Field marks: 76 cm. Smaller and more delicately proportioned than domestic goose. Neck long and thin. Coloration ash-gray; head white with two brown bands on nape; neck dark brown with white stripe on sides; wing tips black; bill and legs yellow-orange. Juveniles, similar with dark stripe on neck, nape, and crown.
Habits: Found in fresh and brackish bodies of water in high mountains. Migratory. Uncommon, but common in places. Nests in small colonies on lake banks, spits, or islands, sometimes in swamps. Nests on the ground, like other geese, or on trees and rocks. Nest is a loose structure of thin branches. Lays four to six white eggs in early May. Not cautious near nest. Call: clear, blaring cry. Feeds in shoals or in dry steppe. Prefers new vegetation (sedge, grasses) and various seeds. Number of birds is decreasing. Included in the Red Data Book.
Range and distribution: Central Asia (Tadzhikistan, Kirgizia), Altai, Tuva. Winters in Hindustan, Burma, and southern China.
Similar species: Differs from all other geese by distinctive coloration.

MAP 24. Bar-headed Goose (1), Snow Goose (2)

65. SNOW GOOSE
Anser caerulescens
(Bely Gus)
Plate 2, Map 24

Field marks: 70-78 cm. Smaller than domestic goose. Pure white; wing tips black; often a rust-stained ring around the bill; legs and bill pink. Juveniles, upper parts and head brownish-gray; bill and legs gray.

Habits: Found in hilly, wet tundra; during migration, on seashores. Migratory. Rare as a whole, but common in places. Nests in colonies, which are sometimes enormous (the colony on Wrangel Island numbers thirty to forty thousand pairs in good years, but this is the only place in the USSR where the Snow Goose is still found). Breeding colonies are situated in river valleys and swampy, moss-grass, hummocky tundra, often with thickets of willow. Nests located close to each other, usually on dry hillocks. Nest is a hole generously lined with down. Lays three to six white eggs in early June. Birds trustful and allow close approach to nests and breeding area, but cautious when flying away a short distance, during nonbreeding season, or when far from the colony. Flight easy and strong, with frequent wing beats. When molting, loses ability to fly and gathers in large flocks. Call: clear and diverse cackle. Feeds in tundra, stream valleys, and in wet areas. Prefers young terrestrial plants. Breeding colonies are protected.

Range and distribution: Wrangel Island. Winters in California.

Similar species: Differs from all other geese by white coloration.

66. GREYLAG GOOSE
Anser anser
(Sery Gus)
Plate 2, Map 25

Field marks: 70-82 cm. Size of a domestic goose,

which is derived from this species. Light gray, especially back and rump; black spots on belly (which juveniles lack), undertail white; bill and legs pink.

Habits: Found in fresh-water areas in variety of habitat from taiga to desert. Migratory. Common in places. Nests in pairs in lakes overgrown with reeds, in flood plains and estuaries, marshy grass swamps. Chooses remote, nearly inaccessible areas for nest. Nest made of reed stalks or other plants, and lined with down; situated in dry place (hillock, islet, hummock), on dry, fallen reed, or floating mat of sticks and leaves. Lays four to six white, sometimes yellowish eggs beginning in April (in the south) to June. Hatched goslings and parents stay together until fall, when geese begin to gather in flocks before migration. Very cautious, especially in flocks; except during breeding and hatching, when it allows close approach. When molting, loses ability to fly. Usually feeds in the morning and in the evening in meadows and fields; often far from bodies of water; spends the night and middle of the day on open water. Flight fast, although it appears unhurried. During migration flight pattern is high, forming an angle; when flying to feeding ground, flock forms an irregular line. Call similar to domestic goose. Feeds on various herbs and grasses, pecks at new sprouts, seeds, tubers. The Greylag Goose is the ancestor of a majority of domestic geese.

Range and distribution: In European USSR, nests in colonies of varying sizes in Estonia; also southern Ukraine, Volga Delta, western shores of the Caspian Sea, northwestern oblasts of the Russian Republic. More widely distributed throughout western Siberia, Kazakhstan, southern regions of East Siberia up to the Soviet Far East. Winters in southern Europe and Asia.

Similar species: Differs from the Bean Goose

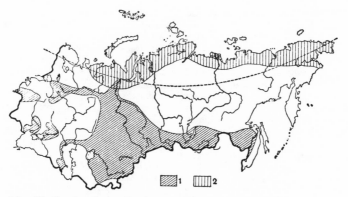

MAP 25. Greylag Goose (1), Greater White-fronted Goose (2)

and Swan Goose by light monochromatic head and pink bill.

67. GREATER WHITE-FRONTED GOOSE
Anser albifrons
(Beloloby Gus)
Plate 2, Map 25

Field marks: 65-70 cm. Smaller than domestic goose. Brownish-gray; black spots on belly; undertail white; white ring around bill up to forehead, but not reaching the crown; pinkish bill and orangish legs. Juveniles lack spots on belly and white forehead.

Habits: Found in wet tundra lowlands and forest-tundra; on seashores and inland bodies of water in various habitats during migration. Migratory. Most common goose in USSR. Nests in areas of low-bush tundra with many lakes and rivers. Builds nest on dry sites; hillocks, high river banks, small hills; often near the nests of Peregrine Falcon or Rough-legged Buzzard. Nest is a depression lined with down. Lays four to six white or slightly ocherish eggs

from mid-April. After eggs hatch, adults molt, at which time they lose the ability to fly. Flight strong, regular, with more rapid wing beats than the Greylag Goose. Flock in flight forms an angle. Call: clear, shrill, jerky cackle. Feeds on land on shoots of grasses, sedges, and so on.

Range and distribution: Tundra and forest-tundra in European and Asian regions of the USSR. Winters in Western Europe, West Asia, Hindustan, China, and Japan.

Similar species: Differs from Lesser White-fronted Goose by larger size, longer bill, small white spot on the forehead (which does not reach the crown), and lack of yellow eye ring (from a distance juveniles difficult to distinguish).

68. LESSER WHITE-FRONTED GOOSE
Anser erythropus
(Piskulka)
Plate 2, Map 26

Field marks: 52-59 cm. Resembles Greater

MAP 26. Lesser White-fronted Goose (1), Red-billed Shelduck (2)

White-fronted Goose, but smaller, bill shorter; white forehead extends onto the crown; narrow yellow eye ring. Juveniles lack white spot on the forehead.

Habits: Found in tundra and forest-tundra; everywhere during migration. Migratory. Bird is less common than the Greater White-fronted Goose. Nests in open tundra and mountain regions, often building nest among rocks or stones. Lays four to seven white or ocherish eggs in June. Call: higher and shriller than Greater White-fronted Goose.

Range and distribution: Tundra and forest-tundra in northern European and Asian regions of the USSR. Winters in central areas of Western Europe; as far as China in the east; as far south as Egypt. In the USSR, wintering grounds are south, on the Caspian Sea.

Similar species: Differs from Greater White-fronted Goose by smaller size, shorter bill, larger white forehead, and yellow eye ring. In flight, appears to have sharper wings. Juveniles difficult to distinguish in the field; usually stay with adults.

69. BEAN GOOSE
Anser fabalis
(Gumennik)
Plate 2, Map 27

Field marks: 65-80 cm. Large goose. Grayish-brown; head and neck darker than back; underparts lighter. Bill long, black with an orange band (bicolored); legs orange.

Habits: Found in lowland tundra, forest-tundra, and taiga; during migration on seashores, lakes, river valleys, in fields and steppe. Migratory. Common in places. Nests in pairs in swampy tundra with abundant lakes (usually in river valleys) or near remote taiga rivers and lakes. Nest situated on dry hillock or slope, often on river islands, among bushes or nearby in the open. Lays three to six ocherish eggs after about the tenth of June. Very cautious, especially when in flocks during migration; but while nesting, stays quiet and allows close approach. When molting (from the middle of July to the middle of August), unable to fly, but runs very fast, helping itself along with wings, and a man is unable to run it down. In flight, flock forms an angle or long oblique line. Call: cackle, but slower, more groaning, and drearier than that of the Greylag Goose. Feeds on land or near bodies of water. Prefers green parts of plants, berries, seeds (particularly seeds of grain crops).

Range and distribution: North in European USSR and West Siberia, East Siberia, Altai, Transbaikal. Winters in Western Europe, Iran, China, Japan.

Similar species: Differs from Greylag Goose by dark color of head and neck and by bicolored bill.

Branta

Smaller than domestic goose. Coloration dark; always with white and black. Bill and legs black.

70. BRENT GOOSE
Branta bernicla
(Chyornaya Kazarka)
Plate 2, Map 28

Field marks: 59 cm. Smallest goose found in USSR, only slightly larger than Mallard. Overall brownish-black head, neck and breast blackish; undertail and neckband white.

Habits: Found in plains and hilly tundra; during migration on flat seashores. Migratory. Uncommon as a whole, but common in places.

MAP 27. Bean Goose

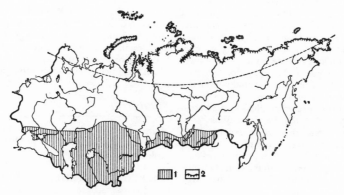

MAP 28. Ruddy Shelduck (1), Brent Goose (2)

Nests in small colonies or pairs in swampy lowlands or dry hummocks, often near nests of Peregrine Falcon or Snowy Owl. Nest situated in a dry place, among hummocks on hills or slopes. Nest is a depression abundantly lined with dark smoky brown down. Lays three to six ocherish eggs from mid-June on. Stays in flocks when molting and in nonbreeding season. Unwary. On the nest, stays quiet, stretching neck to the ground and becoming nearly invisible; if closely approached will flush almost from underfoot. Flight straight, heavy with frequent wing beats. Birds fly single-file or in dense disorderly swarm close to the ground. Call: low, slightly nasal "ong-ong." Feeds on young herbaceous sprouts and algae. Due to decline in numbers, the bird is protected.

Range and distribution: Shores and islands of the Arctic Ocean from Novaya Zemlya to Chukotski Peninsula; shores of the Bering Sea.

Winters in Western Europe, China, and North America.

Similar species: Differs from all other geese and brants by dark, almost black coloration.

71. BARNACLE GOOSE
Branta leucopsis
(Beloschokaya Kazarka)
Plate 2, Map 29

Field marks: 65 cm. Larger than Brent Goose. Crown, neck, and breast black; white forehead, cheeks, and throat; upperparts grayish-brown with banded pattern; belly whitish-gray.

Habits: Found in alpine tundra; during migration on seashores. Migratory. Rare, but numbers have begun to increase. Nests in small colonies; builds nests on slopes and summits of mountain ridges, on cliff ledges. Nest is usually a natural depression, abundantly lined with light gray down. Lays three to six slightly yellowish eggs from mid-June on. Unwary,

MAP 29. Barnacle Goose (1), Red-breasted Goose (2)

especially near the nest. When molting and migrating, stays in flocks, and does not mix with other species of geese. Flight resembles Greater White-fronted Goose. Very clamorous; call loud and audible for a long distance, resembling hoarse barking of a dog. Feeds in dry tundra or silty seacoasts, sometimes in the water. Prefers green leafage of plants, algae, small sea invertebrates (mollusks, small crustacea). Included in the Red Data Book.

Range and distribution: Southern island of Novaya Zemlya, Vaigach Island, Kolguyev Island. Winters on West European shores.

Similar species: Differs from the Canada Goose by shape and size of the white facial markings.

72. RED-BREASTED GOOSE

Branta ruficollis
(Krasnozobaya Kazarka)
Plate 2, Map 29

Field marks: 55 cm. Larger than the Brent Goose; bill short, neck thick. Crown, nape, back, and belly black; sides of neck and breast chestnut-rusty; undertail, stripe on sides, and spot near the bill white.

Habits: Found in dry tundra and forest-tundra; during migration on seacoasts, inland water, or steppe. Migratory. Common in places, although total number is small. Nests in small flocks on steep slopes of river valleys and watersheds; on high banks, always near the nests of raptors. Nest situated in the open and lined with dark down. Lays three to eight olive-greenish eggs from mid-June on. Unwary, especially near breeding area or nest, which the bird leaves when approached. Stays in flocks during nonbreeding season. Agile and clamorous; in flight the flock often changes flight pattern, forming either a line or a disorderly bunch. Flight strong and fast. Call: sharp, short, hoarse cackle. Feeds on various parts of herbaceous plants (sprouts, bulbs, leaves). Due to its declining numbers and narrow range (breeds only in the USSR), the bird is included in the Red Data Book.

Range and distribution: Southern regions of the Taimyr, Gydan, and Yamal Peninsulas. Wintering grounds traditionally located on the Caspian Sea, but in recent years has moved to the Black and Azov Seas and to the lower Duna River.

Similar species: Unique coloration distinguishes the Red-breasted Goose from all other geese and ducks in the USSR.

Note: Many ornithologists consider the Red-breasted Goose a separate genus, *Rufibrenta*.

[Vagrant **73.** CANADA GEESE (*Branta canadensis*) were collected on the Komandorskiye Islands and on the Anadyr River. Single birds were collected on Wrangel Island, in Yakutia, and on the Indigirka River. The goose may have nested in the USSR in the nineteenth century. Back is brownish; underparts brownish gray; head and neck black; white throat and cheeks.]

Tadorna

Large ducks (larger than Mallard) with longish legs. Usually with a pure reddish rust in its coloration.

74. RED-BILLED SHELDUCK

Tadorna tadorna
(Peganka)
Plate 4, Map 26

Field marks: 61-66 cm. Contrasting color: head, neck, and line on belly black; upper breast, sides, belly, and back white; breast rusty red; wings black and white; bill red. Male has swollen red knob on forehead; legs pink. Female is smaller, with thin white ring around base of bill. Juveniles white with brownish-gray upper parts.

Habits: Found in salt lakes of steppe and desert, estuaries; during migration also near fresh water. Migratory. Common. Nests in pairs or small colonies, often far from banks or shores. Nest is a burrow dug in soft ground; deserted burrows of different animals (fox, badger, marmot), or natural caves; rarely builds open nest. Nest lined with white down. Lays seven to ten cream-colored eggs from mid-May on. Several females will often lay eggs in the same nest. Nestlings are cared for by both parents; sometimes several broods gather together. Flight heavy with infrequent wing beats. Call: muffled quack; males whistle. Feeds in water but does not dive. Feeds on water insects, small crustacea, algae.

Range and distribution: Southern regions of European USSR; Kazakhstan, Central Asia, the Minusinsk Basin, Tuva, Transbaikal. Winters in Western Europe, in West Asia, and southern Asia. In the USSR, winters on the Azov Sea, in the Transcaucasus, and Turkmenia.

Similar species: Differs from all other ducks by distinct coloration.

75. RUDDY SHELDUCK

Tadorna ferruginea
(Ogar)
Plate 4, Map 28

Field marks: 62 cm. Rusty-orangeish; head ocherish-white; narrow black band around neck; white patch on wings, black primaries.

Female smaller; head yellowish, no neckband.
Habits: Found in salt-water or fresh-water lakes; rivers of steppe and desert, bodies of water in mountains. When migrating stays on large salt lakes. Migratory. Common. Nests in pairs near open bodies of water with hard-soil banks and sparse vegetation. Nests in deep burrow, which the bird digs; or, more often, uses abandoned or even inhabited burrows of foxes, badgers, or marmots; or nests in deserted structures, broken tombstones, gaps or niches in precipices. Lays eight to twelve cream-colored eggs from early April on. Nest lining is white down with a few rusty feathers. Stays in pairs; when breeding, male stays near the nest. Flight fast but heavy, with strong, infrequent wing beats. Walks on ground easily, often perches on rocks. Call: clear, guttural, and sad "aang-aang." When sitting on nest, female hisses if danger approaches. Feeds on water, seldom dives.
Range and distribution: Southern regions of USSR; Kazakhstan, Central Asia, southern Siberia. Winters in south of Caspian Sea and in Central Asia; some birds fly further south to Iran, Iraq, and Hindustan.
Similar species: Unique coloration of Ruddy Shelduck easily distinguishes it from other ducks.
Note: Many ornithologists classify this bird as a separate genus, *Casarca*.

[A vagrant of **76.** CRESTED SHELDUCK (*Tadorna cristata*) was obtained in 1964 near Vladivostok. Size of Ruddy Shelduck. Male: upper breast black; back and breast dark brownish gray with jetlike tracery; spot and a small green patch on wing; head rusty orange with black trailing crest; bill and legs pink. Female lighter color; upper breast gray; head and neck whitish. Very rare, and apparently either extinct or near extinction. Included in the Red Data Book.]

Anas

Size of domestic duck and smaller. Hind toe lacks paddle like flap. Keeps tail lifted in water.

77. MALLARD
Anas platyrhynchos
(Kryakva)
Plate 3, Map 30
Field marks: 49-57 cm. Size of domestic duck, which is, in turn derived from this species. In male, head is dark green; upper breast chestnut; rump and undertail coverts black; bill yellow; legs orange. Female brown with dark mottling; dark blue speculum; bill orangeish with dark center. In summer, plumage of male resembles female, but bill yellow-green.
Habits: Found in bodies of fresh water in a variety of habitats from forest-tundra to deserts and mountains. Migratory. Common and numerous. Nests near lakes with overgrowth, oxbow lakes, wet grassy swamps and meadows. Nests situated in dense grass, bushes, or under fallen deadwood, usually not far from water. Sometimes uses abandoned nests of herons or crows in trees. Lays seven to twelve white eggs with greenish or olive tint in early April (in the south) and later. Nest is lined with dark down. During hatching, female allows close approach before flushing out from under foot. When eggs hatch, female engages in distraction display to lead the intruder away from the nest. From the end of May, drakes gather in small flocks and fly to molting areas. Some drakes molt near breeding site. Juveniles take wing by August. Migration lasts un-

MAP 30. Mallard (1), Spot-billed Duck (2)

til first frosts. Call resembles quack of the domestic duck. Feeds in water, excellent diver; flight fast and decisive. Feeds on small invertebrates (insects and their larvae, small crustacea, mollusks) and water plants.

Range and distribution: Throughout most of the USSR except near-polar regions and deserts. Winters in North Africa, West Asia, India, and China.

Similar species: Differs from the Spotbill Duck

Fig. 21 Dabbling Ducks and Sawbills in Flight
1. Mallard   2. Northern Pintail   3. Eurasian Wigeon   4. Gadwall (male)   5. Northern Shoveler   6. Garganey   7. Common Merganser   8. Green-winged Teal   9. Red-breasted Merganser (male)   10. Smew

FIG. 22 Mallard Duckling

by entirely yellow bill and lack of white wing spot; from other river ducks, by larger size and blue wing patch.

78. SPOTBILL DUCK
Anas poecilorhyncha
(Chyornaya Kryakva)
Plate 3, Map 30

Field marks: 55 cm. Size of Mallard. Male and female same; brown and black mottling; lighter belly; blue speculum; white tertials; bill black with yellow tip.

Habits: Found in bodies of fresh water with lush vegetation. Migratory. Common in places, but uncommon as a whole. Nests in swampy reedbanks. Builds nest on dry site between hummocks and thickets of sedge. Lays seven to ten eggs (indistinguishable from Mallard eggs) from mid-May on. Nesting and feeding habits same as Mallard. Biology little known.

Range and distribution: Southern regions of East Siberia; Transbaikal, Soviet Far East, Kuril Islands. Winters in Southeast Asia.

Similar species: Differs from female Mallard by black bill with yellow tip (in water, white wing spot is also visible).

79. GREEN-WINGED TEAL
Anas crecca
(Chirok-svistunok)
Plate 3, Map 31

Field marks: 35 cm. Smallest river duck. Head brown with green stripes on side; upper breast ocherish with small black spots; sides gray with fine black vermiculations; speculum green with black. Female dark brown with rusty mottling; underparts whitish; speculum green.

Habits: Found on small inland bodies of water in a variety of habitats from tundra to desert; during migration on seashores as well. Migratory. One of most common ducks. Nests near lakes with overgrowth, oxbow lakes, rivers with slow current, ponds, and swamps, often near large temporary puddles, floods, ditches, and peat quarries. Nest constructed under cover of bushes, fallen deadwood, or in dense grass; sometimes in woods, far from the bank. Lays eight to twelve white, slightly ocherish eggs in May. Female sits tight on nest, allowing close approach, then suddenly flushes out from under foot. Will often do distraction display to lead away from the nest. At onset of nesting, males fly off for molting. Unwary even in nonbreeding season. Usually stays in small flocks.

MAP 31. Green-winged Teal (1), Northern Pintail (2)

Flight noiseless, fast, with frequent wing beats. Birds fly in a dense flock and can rise from water almost vertically. Call of the drake: short, jerky, deep whistle; of female: high shrill quack. In summer, feeds mostly on water invertebrates; in winter, seeds and green parts of water plants.

Range and distribution: Greater part of the USSR except northern tundra and deserts. Winters in south of Western Europe, in Africa, and southern Asia.

Similar species: Differs from Baikal Teal and Garganey by lack of yellow marking or white stripe on head. Female differs from Garganey by having a green speculum and darker coloration; from the Baikal Teal by lack of rounded light spot at base of bill.

80. BAIKAL TEAL
Anas formosa
(Kloktun)
Plate 3, Map 32

Field marks: 47 cm. Slightly large and heavier than the Green-winged Teal. The head has a distinctive green half-moon near the nape and two irregular yellow markings divided by a black stripe under the eye; breast pinkish with small dark spots; sides gray; back brown; speculum green. Female resembles the Green-winged Teal, but has a round light spot near the bill.

Habits: Found in bodies of water in tundra, forest-tundra, and taiga; during migration and on wintering grounds, prefers large lakes and paddy fields. Migratory. Common in places. Nests on taiga river banks; on islands and deltas; mostly in mossy-grassy tundra with many lakes and channels. Nests in dry, hummocky area; in thickets of dry sedge or dwarf birch on small lake islets. Lays six to ten white eggs

(often with yellowish tint) in June. Nesting habits same as other ducks. Stays in large flocks during migration. Flight very fast and low. Call of the drake: muffled frequent "klo-klo-klo"; of female: jerky, wavering quacking.

Range and distribution: East Siberia. Winters in Southeast Asia.

Similar species: The drake differs from the Green-winged Teal by distinctive head markings; the female by a light spot at base of bill (not always distinguishable).

81. FALCATED TEAL
Anas falcata
(Kasatka)
Plate 3, Map 32

Field marks: 49 cm. Smaller than Mallard; long crest; the tertials are particularly long. Head brown and green; neck white; upper breast, belly, and back gray with scaly pattern on upper breast and fine striations on sides and belly; speculum gray-green; bill and legs black. Female dark brownish with rusty underparts; dark scaly ripples on the breast, wing patch gray. In eclipse plumage, drake resembles female.

Habits: Found in various bodies of water in taiga; more rarely in steppe and semi-desert. Migratory. Common in places. Nests in small taiga lakes, rivers, channels, and swamps; occasionally in large lakes. Nest situated in dry place or hummock, and hidden in bushes, deadwood, or in forest, not far from water. Lays seven to ten white eggs tinted pinkish yellow from late May to early June. Female on the nest allows close approach. Birds found in flocks only during migration and on wintering grounds. Flight fast, resembling Mallard's, but lighter. Much less cautious than Mallard. Call of drake: unique, short low sound

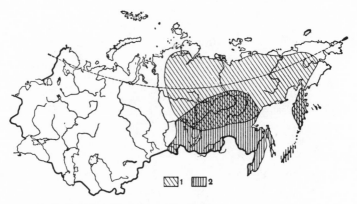

MAP 32. Baikal Teal (1), Falcated Duck (2)

beginning with quiet whistle and ending with a wavering "uit-trr." Call of female: very hoarse, gruff quack. Biology is little known.

Range and distribution: Southern half of East Siberia, Sakhalin Island, Soviet Far East, Kuril Islands. Winters in Southeast Asia.

Similar species: Dark head, light body, scaly ripple on upper breast, green speculum, and black bill distinguish the male. The female resembles Green-winged Teal but is larger.

82. GADWALL

Anas strepera
(Seraya Utka)
Plate 3, Map 33

Field marks: 50 cm. Smaller than Mallard; gray; brownish head with fine black markings; scaly pattern on upper breast and flanks; wings with chestnut-brown over white speculum; undertail coverts black. Female brown with dark mottling on back and breast; in flight, wings similar to male; bill and legs yellowish.

Habits: Found in fresh water; more rarely bodies of salt water in forest-steppe, steppe, and deserts; occasionally in forests. Migratory. Common in places, but does not form large flocks. Nests in small lakes, oxbow lakes, channels, estuaries; or any area with lush water vegetation. Builds nest on dry site, often far from water; in the steppe, under a bush or in the open. Lays seven to eleven white, slightly yellowish or olive eggs from mid-May. Female on nest allows close approach. When molting, males hide in remote areas of lakes. Flight light and fast, rather noisy; the bird flushes from water almost vertically. In flight, the flock communicates often by quacking. Swims with slightly raised hind quarters; rarely dives. Call of male: deep sonorous cry, resembling call of raven; of female: shrill quack. Feeds mostly

on vegetation (terrestrial and aquatic); in shoals, often in steppe.

Range and distribution: Southern half of European USSR and West Siberia, Kazakhstan, Central Asia, south of East Siberia, Transbaikal; isolated populations in the Soviet Far East, Kamchatka Peninsula. Winters in south of Western Europe and Asia.

Similar species: Differs from other ducks by chestnut brown patch with distinct white speculum.

83. EURASIAN WIGEON

Anas penelope
(Sviyaz)
Plate 3, Map 33

Field marks: 46 cm. Smaller than Mallard. Head reddish-brown with golden-yellow forehead; upper breast pinkish-brown; back and sides gray with fine pattern; belly and large area of wing white; speculum green. Female brown with small dark mottling on head; belly white; bill and legs lead-gray.

Habits: Found near bodies of water in forest-tundra and taiga, more rarely in steppe. Migratory. Common in places, but not numerous as a whole. Nests near small quiet rivers and lakes without much vegetation; sometimes in small, brackish steppe lakes. When wintering, concentrates in swampy lowlands. Builds nest in a dry hidden place, in bushes or in dry grass, usually not far from water. Lays seven to eleven pure white eggs from middle or end of May to end of June. Nesting habits similar to other ducks. When molting in June, males gather in areas of forest-steppe with many lakes. Flight fast, easy, and maneuverable. Stays in small flocks; gathers into sizable flocks only when wintering. Rarely dives. Call of drake: shrill, whistling "vhee-hoo"; of female: crack-

MAP 33. Eurasian Wigeon (1), Gadwall (2)

ling quack "rerr. . . ." Feeds on vegetation, more rarely invertebrates.

Range and distribution: Northern regions of European USSR, Siberia, (except northern half of tundra), Kazakhstan, Sakhalin Island, Transcaucasus. Winters in south of Western Europe, North Africa, southern Asia. In the USSR, winters on the Azov Sea and in southern regions of the Caspian Sea.

Similar species: Drake differs from other ducks by brown head with golden forehead; female by white belly and gray bill. In flight, large white spots on wings most characteristic.

84. NORTHERN PINTAIL

Anas acuta
(Shilokhvost)
Plate 3, Map 31

Field marks: 57-70 cm. Slightly smaller than Mallard; neck long and thin; tail long and pointed; head dark brown; neck, breast, and belly white; back and sides gray with fine tracery; wing patch violet-green; undertail black. Female brownish-gray with white trailing edge to wing; speculum rusty, without luster; bill and legs dark gray.

Habits: Found near bodies of water in tundra, forest-tundra, taiga, forest-steppe; in winter, found near estuaries and large lakes. Migratory. Common, numerous in places. Stays in pairs during breeding season; during migration, molting, and on wintering grounds gathers in large flocks. Nest situated in depressions overgrown with bushes on shallow lakes with abundant vegetation, in wet swampy meadows, river valleys, and in tundra. Builds nests in open places: often in dry bed of last year's grasses, in bushes, among hummocks, sometimes completely in the open (in fields or steppe), often far from water. Lays seven to

eleven white eggs of yellowish, bluish, or olive tint, end of April to June. Hatching done by female; males molt on remote reed lakes or deltas of large rivers. Flight fast and light, with the flock forming irregular lines. In flight the birds move head and neck from side to side. Swims with pointed tail uptilted, dives poorly and reluctantly. Call of male: unique cries, "furrr-furrr," and quiet melodious whistle; female: hoarse quack. When flocking, cries of males heard constantly from a great distance. Diet herbivorous and carnivorous, and includes insects and their larvae, small crustacea, and mollusks.

Range and distribution: Nearly all of USSR except southern half of European USSR, Central Asia, northerly tundra regions, and islands of the Arctic Ocean. Winters in Western Europe, on the Nile Delta, and in southern Asia.

Similar species: Male differs from other species by long thin tail; the female, by long neck; rusty, lusterless speculum; gray bill. Pure white belly and breast of drake are most characteristic in flight.

85. MARBLED DUCK

Anas angustirostris
(Mramorny Chirok)
Plate 3, Map 34

Field marks: 46 cm. Small duck, although larger than Green-winged Teal. Male and female have same coloration. Male has small crest; plumage brownish-gray with rounded light spots on the back and dark scaling on upper breast; elongated dark brown eye line spot, which is darker in male. Bill gray, female's is black; legs gray-brown.

Habits: Found in desert. Migratory. Very rare. Nests in shallow lakes with boggy bottom and

MAP 34. Garganey (1), Marbled Duck (2)

reed thickets; in temporary brackish reservoirs. Nests in dry places under cover of dry grass or bushes, nest lined with small quantity of down. Lays seven to twelve white eggs with pale yellow or brownish tint mid-May or later (until end of July). Does not form large flocks even during migration. Not cautious, but stays hidden. Often perches on branches of trees leaning over the water. Flight fast and straight, like other teals. Feeds in shoals and silt banks on plants and small invertebrates. Biology little known. Included in the Red Data Book.

Range and distribution: Western shores of Caspian Sea, Transcaucasus, Central Asia. Winters in Western Europe on the Mediterranean, in southwestern Asia, Hindustan; sometimes found in southern areas of Caspian Sea.

Similar species: Unique coloration permits easy distinction from all other ducks.

86. GARGANEY
Anas querquedula
(Chirok-treskunok)
Plate 3, Map 34

Field marks: 39 cm. Slightly larger than Green-winged Teal. Head brown with white stripe from eye to nape; back, breast, and hindparts brownish with dark vermiculations; belly white; sides and wings gray, speculum greenish-gray, without luster.

Habits: Found in a variety of habitats from forest to desert. Migratory. Common or numerous, especially in mixed forest, forest-steppe and steppe. Nests in small floodplains or meadow lakes with abundant vegetation; in oxbow lakes, channels, ponds, and herbaceous swamps. Builds nest in dry place, under cover of bushes or high grass, among hum-

mocks, usually at water's edge, but sometimes far from it. Lays seven to twelve yellowish, cream, or light olive eggs from mid-May on. Female sits on nest firmly and allows close approach. Unwary even in nonbreeding season. Flight and habits similar to Green-winged Teal. Lands on water easily; almost noiselessly. Call of male: burring, quiet, wooden "kar-r-r"; of female: high, wavering quack. Mostly feeds on water invertebrates, especially mollusks and small crustacea; plants of little importance in diet.

Range and distribution: European USSR except northern borders; Kazakhstan, southern half of Siberia, Soviet Far East, Sakhalin Island. Winters in southern Europe, Africa, and southern Asia.

Similar species: Male differs by white stripe on side of head, easily seen from a distance; female differs from Green-winged, Falcated, and Baikal Teal by blue-gray wing patch and greenish speculum.

87. NORTHERN SHOVELER
Anas clypeata
(Shirokonoska)
Plate 3, Map 35

Field marks: 50 cm. Significantly smaller than Mallard. Bill very wide and long; head and neck dark with green iridescence; breast white; belly and sides brown-rusty; wings with blue patch and green speculum. Female mottled brown; wings similar to male; belly lighter than back. Male's bill is black; female's brown; legs orange.

Habits: Found in a variety of habitats from taiga to desert. Migratory. Common, in places numerous, especially in forest-steppe and steppe. Nests in open shallow lakes with sparse

MAP 35. Northern Shoveler (1), Northern Pochard (2), Red-crested Pochard (3)

vegetation; in forests, near wide river valleys, oxbow lakes, channels, swamps. Usually builds nest near water, but sometimes far away under cover of bush or curtain of high grass, among hummocks, sometimes in the open. Lays seven to eleven eggs from May to June. Female sits on nest very firmly. In June, molting males congregate in remote water bodies and deltas of large rivers. Flight comparatively slow, noisy. In water, holds head low, giving appearance of a very short neck. Does not form large flocks. Unwary, but stays hidden and rather silent. Call of male: muffled, low "kvo-kvo-kvo"; of female: low quack. Feeds almost exclusively on water invertebrates (small crustacea, mollusks).

Range and distribution: Greater part of the USSR except northern regions and deserts. Winters in Western Europe, in Africa as far as the equator, and southern Asia.

Similar species: Differs from all ducks by large bill that widens toward the tip. Characteristic chestnut belly of male is visible in flight.

[Vagrants of **88.** AMERICAN WIGEON (*Anas americana*) were recorded on the Komandorskiye Islands in 1883. Resembling the Eurasian Wigeon, the male's head was gray with green stripe behind the eye; sides and back pinkish. Females appear to be the same in the field. Characteristic feature: pure white axillary ("armpit") feathers, as opposed to dusky axillars in European Wigeon.]

Aix

89. MANDARIN DUCK

Aix galericulata
(Mandarinka)
Plate 3, Map 36

Field marks: 43 cm. Small duck. Coloration: very bright combination of rusty, red-brown, green, black, and white. Crest on the head, "collar," and unique elongated wing feathers reddish; bill red; legs yellow. Female smoky gray with small oval white spots on sides and breast, bill gray.

Habits: Inhabits water bodies of mixed coniferous and broadleaved forests. Migratory. Somewhat rare. Nests on forested islets in river valleys with channels and small forest lakes banked with thickets of willow. Nests in tree hollows, often high (up to 10 m.), choosing the most inaccessible areas, usually at water's edge. Sometimes nests on the ground, under thick bushes or fallen trees. Lays nine to twelve white or slightly yellowish eggs from end of April on. Female sits on nest very firmly,

and does not fly away even if the tree trunk is sharply hit. Stays in small flocks during non-breeding season. Often perches on tree branches, especially when searching for a nesting hollow. Flight fast and maneuverable; flushes from water lightly and noiselessly; seldom dives. Call: melodious whistle; female has a unique quack. Feeds on invertebrates (insects, mollusks), plant seeds, often acorns; less frequently fish and spawn. Included in Red Data Book.

Range and distribution: Soviet Far East, Sakhalin Island, Kuril Islands. Winters in southeastern China, Japan.

Similar species: None in the USSR.

Somateria

Large ducks. Head and bill large; thick-necked; narrow flap on rear toe. Keeps tail low in water.

90. COMMON EIDER

Somateria mollissima
(Obyknovennaya Gaga)
Plate 5, Map 36

Field marks: 59 cm. Very large duck with compact body. Head and back white; breast pinkish; belly black; nape greenish; forehead, crown, and sometimes chin stripe black; bill greenish yellow, legs yellowish. Female overall brown with ocherish tracery; bill and legs gray.

Habits: Found near seashores with islands, stony banks, and bays. Migratory. Common in places. Nests on either heavily forested islands or on stony islands without vegetation, or with moss-

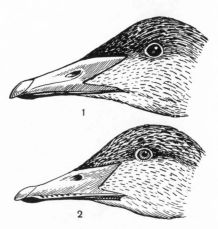

FIG. 23 Bill of Female 1) Common Eider and 2) King Eider

MAP 36. Common Eider (1), Mandarin Duck (2)

tundra vegetation. Often forms colonies. Nest situated in driftwood, clumps of grass under cover of stone, or in the open; on forest islands, under branches of small spruces. Nest abundantly lined with dark down. Lays four to six greenish or light olive eggs from end of May on. Female sits on nest firmly, flushing out from underfoot; sometimes even allows being touched. In mid-June males concentrate on isolated parts of shore. Passes nonbreeding season at sea, staying in flocks. Flight heavy but fast, in a line or dense flock low to the water. Dives often and well. Feeds on mollusks and plants growing in shallow water. Call: resounding "aghuu," heard at a great distance; female: unique hoarse "gag-gag-gag." Eiderdown (from nests) is valued for lining in clothing and camping gear. Hunting prohibited.

Range and distribution: Seashores and islands of the Baltic coast, north European USSR including Novaya Zemlya and Franz Josef Land; in East Siberia: Wrangel Island, shores of the Bering and Okhotsk Seas. Winters on the North, Barents, and Bering Seas. In recent years, a small, nonmigratory population has become established on the Black Sea.

Similar species: Male differs from King Eider by white back and shape of bill; from Spectacled Eider by pink breast, lack of "spectacles" and of black forehead. In the field, female is not distinguishable from King Eider; in the hand, differs by the shape of bill base (Fig. 23) and lack of white speculum; from Spectacled Eider, by lack of light spot around eye ("spectacles").

91. KING EIDER
Somateria spectabilis
(Gaga-grebyonushka)
Plate 5, Map 37

Field marks: 56 cm. Resembles Common Ei-

MAP 37. King Eider

der, but smaller; back black; bluish-gray nape; bill bright orange with large protuberance at base of bill. Female brown, similar to Common Eider, but bill smaller.

Habits: Found in seaside tundra; during non-breeding seasons, found in open sea. Migratory. In places common and numerous. Nests in pairs, often far from sea. Builds nest on dry site under cover of driftwood, clump of grass, or rocks, usually near lake or river, sometimes in the open. Nest lined with thick layer of dark down. Lays four to six greenish or light olive eggs from end of June. Female sits on nest less firmly than Common Eider. Young ducklings stay in lakes. In July and August males gather for molting in remote seaside areas. Flight fast, typical for ducks; small flock flies bunched or in line. Call: loud, repetitive, triple cry "arr-arr-arr"; female: hoarse "gag-gag-gag." Dives well. In summer, feeds on lakes; in other seasons, in deep sea. Feeds from bottom or in silt layer. Prefers fresh-water invertebrates (insects, larvae, small crustacea) or seafood (mollusks). Hunting prohibited.

Range and distribution: Shores and islands of the Arctic Ocean. Winters on northern shores of Western Europe, on the Barents and Kara Seas; waters of the Pacific in northern regions.

Similar species: Male differs from Common and Spectacled Eiders by orange protuberance on forehead and by black lower back; female differs from Common Eider by smaller bill, shape of its base (Fig. 23); from the Spectacled Eider by lack of spot around the eye.

92. SPECTACLED EIDER
Somateria fischeri
(Ochkovaya Gaga)
Plate 5, Map 38

Field marks: 53 cm. Smaller than Common Eider. Breast and belly black, back white, head greenish with prominent yellowish eye ring edged with black. This ring is made of small velvety feathers ("spectacles"); bill and legs yellow. Female brown with light spot around eye.

Habits: Found near seaside tundra on mainland and some islands. Migratory. Common in places. Nests in pairs in marshy tundra with numerous lakes and river channels. Nests along banks of small lakes, often on hummock, completely in the open. Nest lined with dark brown down. Lays five to seven greenish-gray or light olive eggs beginning at the end of June. Female sits on nest firmly. By July males gather in large flocks to fly to molting grounds. Flight fast and light; flock usually flies in close for-

mation; when over water, low and in a line. Feeds on various invertebrates; in lakes: larvae of mosquitos and caddis flies; at sea: mollusks and small crustacea. Hunting is prohibited.

Range and distribution: Coastal tundra of northeastern Siberia from the Lena Delta to Mys Schmidta. Winters on the Bering Sea and further south.

Similar species: Differs from other eiders by characteristic "spectacles" (also visible in females).

93. STELLER'S EIDER
Somateria stelleri
(Sibirskaya Gaga)
Plate 5, Map 38

Field marks: 47 cm. Smaller than Common Eider. Head white with green spots on nape and forehead; small crest; back black; breast and belly rufous rusty; sides white; speculum dark blue; bill and legs black. Female dark brown with dark blue wing patch edged with white.

Habits: Inhabits seaside tundra and islands, in breeding season found in open sea. Migratory. Common in places. Nests in swampy depressions of moss tundra with numerous lakes and in river valleys. Builds nest in dry place, usually near water, under cover of driftwood or in the open. Nest lined with very dark down. Lays six to seven greenish or olive-gray eggs from end of June on. Behavior at nest resembles other eiders. Silent. Usually flies at high altitude or along a river right over the water. Feeds on small invertebrates (larvae of insects, small crustacea, mollusks). Hunting prohibited.

Range and distribution: Tundra near seashores from the Khatanga Bay to Chukotski Peninsula; Novosibirsk Islands. Occasionally nests on shores of Kola Peninsula. Winters on Bering Sea and coast of Kamchatka Peninsula and the Kuril Islands; Murman Coast and Finland.

Similar species: Differs from other eiders by color and smaller size; female, by size and dark blue speculum.

Note: Most ornithologists place Steller's Eider in a separate genus, *Polysticta*.

Netta

94. RED-CRESTED POCHARD
Netta rufina
(Krasnonosy Nyrok)
Plate 4, Map 35

Field marks: 56 cm. Large (Mallard-size) duck.

MAP 38. Steller's Eider (1), Spectacled Eider (2)

Rounded head and upper neck ocherish-rusty; lower neck, breast, and belly black; sides white; back brown; bill red; legs pink. Females brown with light cheeks and belly; dark "cap"; bill black with orange band on upper mandible.

Habits: Inhabits steppe and desert; in winter also found in estuaries. Migratory. Common, in places numerous. Nests in pairs or small colonies on fresh-water lakes with stands of reed and on brackish lakes with deep open stretches. Nest hidden on heaps of drifting reed and floating reed islets, more rarely on banks, peninsulas, or hummocks. Lays six to nine ocherish or grayish-olive eggs from mid-May. Male stays near laying female for a long time. Female flushes quickly and leaves nest quietly if approached. Males gather in large flocks on large lakes to molt. Flight fast and noisy; heavy takeoff from water. Groups of birds fly low over the water, but high above land. Males silent, but in spring produce low whistle; call of female, shrill croak, "keurr-keurr." Feeds by diving or tipping over, like river ducks. Feeds exclusively on leaves, sprouts of water plants, and algae.

Range and distribution: Azov Sea region, northern Caucasus, north and northwestern shores of the Caspian, Central Asia, Kazakhstan, southern regions of West Siberia. Winters on the Mediterranean and in southwestern Asia. In the USSR, southern regions of Caspian Sea, Transcaucasus, Central Asia in places.

Similar species: Differs from other ducks by red bill and light rusty head; female, by light cheeks and reddish band on bill.

Aythya

Ducks of medium size (smaller than domestic duck) and compact build with large head and thick neck. Narrow flap on rear toe. Keeps tail lowered in water.

95. NORTHERN POCHARD
Aythya ferina
(Krasnogolovy Nyrok)
Plate 4, Map 35

Field marks: 45 cm. Considerably smaller than Mallard. Head and neck chestnut; breast, rump, and undertail coverts black; remainder grayish; bill black with bluish-gray band on upper mandible; legs black. No speculum. Female brown with darker head and breast, light (but not white) spot at base of bill and on throat; no speculum.

Habits: Found in a variety of habitats from taiga to steppe. Winters near estuaries. Migratory. Common or numerous, especially in steppe and forest-steppe. Nests in lakes with abundant sedge or reed banks; more rarely in small deep rivers. Builds nests in reed banks or mats of floating reed, in sedge thickets, or on hummocks, usually at water's edge. Lays six to twelve large greenish or olive eggs from

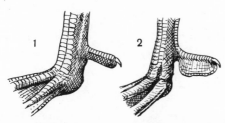

FIG. 24 Rear Toe of 1) Dabbling Duck and 2) Pochard

early May. Nesting female allows close approach, often plunging into the water directly from nest and "leading away from the nest" by imitating a wounded bird. Males gather for molting on large brackish or fresh-water lakes. Flight fast, noisy; takes off from water heavily, usually against the wind. Dives often. Swims like other pochards, sitting deeply in water. Call of male: unique whistle rarely heard and only in spring. Female: shrill croak "karrr." Diet herbivorous (leaves, seeds, roots of water plants) and carnivorous (insect larvae, small crustacea, mollusks).

Range and distribution: European USSR except northern regions and Caucasus; Kazakhstan, southern Siberia. Winters on western shores of Europe, the Mediterranean, Iran, Iraq, Hindustan, Japan. In the USSR, winters on the Black and Azov Seas, southern Caspian Sea, and in the Transcaucasus.

Similar species: Male differs from Red-crested Pochard by dark bill, lack of crest, and chestnut (not reddish) head; female, from other females of pochards by black bill with bluish band, pale gray wing stripe, and light spot at base of bill.

96. FERRUGINOUS POCHARD
Aythya nyroca
(Beloglazy Nyrok)
Plate 3, Map 39

Field marks: 41 cm. Smaller than Red-crested Pochard. Head, neck, breast, and sides rusty brown; back dark brown; belly and undertail white; white wing stripe; bill black; legs gray; eyes white. Female somewhat lighter brown.

Habits: Found near water in forest-steppe, steppe, and desert. Prefers estuaries on wintering grounds. Migratory. Common in places. Nests in pairs or small colonies on deep lakes with reed thickets. Builds nests on floating reed islets or mats, usually at water's edge. Nest abundantly lined with down. Lays six to eleven small brownish-yellow eggs from mid-May. During nonbreeding season stays in small flocks. Flight fast and more maneuverable than other pochards; takes off from water more easily. Silent; unwary. Call of male: low hoarse sound; of female: shrill quack. Feeds mostly on water plants.

Range and distribution: Southern half of European USSR, Central Asia, Kazakhstan, southern regions of West Siberia. Winters on the Mediterranean, Africa, southwestern Asia. In the USSR, in the Transcaucasus, southern areas of the Caspian Sea, and some parts of Central Asia.

Similar species: Differs from other pochards by rusty brown coloration and white undertail; from Baer's Pochard by smaller size and lack of black color on the head (they are not found in the same range together).

97. BAER'S POCHARD
Aythya baeri
(Berov Nyrok)
Plate 4, Map 39

Field marks: 41 cm. Resembles Ferruginous Pochard, but larger; head and neck black with green iridescence; female, black only on crown and nape.

Habits: Rare migratory bird; biology almost unknown. Nests in small overgrown lakes in river valleys and lowlands; builds nests in thickets of sedge near the water. Lays six to ten yellowish eggs in early June. Habits similar to other pochards.

Range and distribution: Southern regions of the Soviet Far East. Winters on the Korean Peninsula, in Japan, and in southeastern Asia.

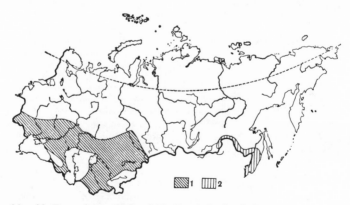

MAP 39. Ferruginous Pochard (1), Baer's Pochard (2)

Similar species: Differs from Ferruginous Pochard by black head (females, by black crown) and larger size. Not found in same range or habitat. Differs from other pochards by white undertail.

98. TUFTED POCHARD
Aythya fuligula
(Khokhlataya Chernet)
Plate 4, Map 40

Field marks: 43 cm. Smaller than Common Pochard. Overall black, with purplish gloss to head; sides and belly white; crest on the head trailing back; bill and legs gray, eyes yellow. Female brown with whitish belly, often with small white feathers near base of bill; crest smaller.

Habits: Found in variety of habitat from tundra, forest-tundra, to semi-desert; in winter found on seashores and bays. Migratory. Common, in places numerous. Stays in flocks during nonbreeding season. Nests in fresh or brackish lakes with thickets of reed or sedge banks; frequently in river valleys. Builds nests on floating mat or islets, on dry reeds hidden among dense vegetation. Nest lined with gray down. Lays seven to twelve large dirty olive eggs from mid-May. Female sits on nest firmly and allows close approach. Flight swift, noisy; usually the small flock flies closely grouped, and takes wing from water heavily, in oblique line. Dives well. Call of male is low indescribable sound; female has shrill hoarse croak, but is usually silent. Diet consists of mollusks, insect larvae, small crustacea, and fish.

Range and distribution: Greater part of USSR except more northerly regions, southern Ukraine, Caucasus, Central Asia, and Soviet Far East. Winters on shores of Europe and North America, Nile Delta, south and southeast Asia. In the USSR, on the Black and Azov Seas, southern Caspian, lakes of the Transcaucasus, and Central Asia.

Similar species: Differs from Greater Scaup by black back and crest; female, by lack of wide white ring at bill base.

99. GREATER SCAUP
Aythya marila
(Morskaya Chernet)
Plate 4, Map 40

Field marks: 44 cm. Larger than Tufted Duck. Head, breast, and rump black; head with greenish gloss; back gray with fine striations; sides and belly white; eyes yellow; bill and legs bluish-gray. Female brown with whitish belly, white ring around base of bill.

Habits: Found in tundra, forest-tundra, and northern taiga; in winter found along seacoast. Migratory. In places common or numerous. Nests in wet lowlands overgrown with sedge near lakes, channels, and rivers. Nest lined with dark down, and situated on dry site among hummocks, in grass, or under cover of bushes. Lays six to ten large eggs in May or later. Stays in small flocks during nonbreeding season, often together with other ducks (Black Scoter, Long-tailed Duck). Flight fast, flushes from water easily; dives well. Carnivorous (mollusks, small crustacea, insect larvae, fish) and herbivorous (leaves, roots, seeds of water plants).

Range and distribution: North European USSR, Siberia, Kamchatka Peninsula, Kuril Islands. Winters on the Baltic Sea, North Sea, and Mediterranean. In the USSR, on the Black and Azov Seas, on the shores of Sakhalin Peninsula, and the Kuril Islands.

Similar species: Differs from Tufted Pochard by lack of crest and gray back; female, by white ring at bill's base.

MAP 40. Tufted Pochard (1), Greater Scaup (2)

Melanitta

Large ducks of solid build with large head, thick neck. Bill set high, swollen at the base. Narrow flap on rear toe. Keep tail low in water, like pochards.

100. WHITE-WINGED SCOTER
Melanitta fusca
(Turpan)
Plate 4, Map 41

Field marks: 54 cm. Size of Mallard. Black with white spot under eye; white speculum; bill bright orange (birds from East Siberia have black protuberance at base of bill); legs red-pink. Female brown with light spots on sides of the head; white speculum; bill brownish-gray.

Habits: Found in tundra, forest-tundra, and taiga. During nonbreeding season, found off seacoasts and on open lakes. Migratory. Uncommon. Nests in pairs in tundra, forest, and mountain lakes with quiet waters and sedge banks. Builds nests in tall grass, among hummocks, under bushes; usually near water's edge but sometimes at considerable distance from the bank. Nest abundantly lined with down. Lays six to ten large creamy white eggs from mid-June. Very wary. Nonbreeding birds spend summer in flocks, feeding and passing the night on water. Seldom appear on land. Takeoff from water heavy and reluctant, flight low but fast; they prefer to escape danger by swimming away, diving frequently. When feeding, dive often and do not appear on surface for long periods of time. Call: gruff, hoarse croak, "kraa-kraa-kra." Feed on mollusks, water insect, larvae, small fish, sometimes leaves and sprouts of plants.

Range and distribution: Estonia, north European USSR, Siberia (except northern tundra), Sakhalin, Kuril Islands; isolated nesters in Georgia and Armenia. Winters on northern and western shores of Europe; shores of China and Japan. In the USSR, winters to southeast of Caspian Sea, and the Komandorskiye and Kuril Islands.

Similar species: Differs from Black Scoter by white speculum and spots on sides of head; from Surf Scoter by speculum and lack of white spots on forehead and nape; females, by white speculum.

Note: Many ornithologists consider the form from East Siberia and North America as a separate species (*Melanitta deglandi*). When so distinguished, the Palearctic form is known as the Velvet Scoter.

101. BLACK SCOTER
Melanitta nigra
(Singa)
Plate 4, Map 41

Field marks: 50 cm. Smaller than White-winged Scoter. Completely black; bill black with orange culmen. Birds from western part of its range (up to the Lena river) have black protuberance at base of bill; legs gray. Female brown with light cheeks and neck, bill brownish-gray.

Habits: Found in tundra, forest-tundra, and taiga. Near large rivers, lakes, and seas during nonbreeding season. Migratory. Common, numerous in places, especially during migration. Nests in open, quiet tundra rivers and lakes with low banks overgrown with sedge; in taiga, on lakes, among mossy bogs, and in swampy river valleys. Usually builds nests at water's edge, well hidden by bushes or dry grass. Nest abundantly lined with down. Lays six to ten pale greenish or brownish eggs from

MAP 41. Black Scoter (1), White-winged Scoter (2)

mid-June. Stays in large flocks during migration and on wintering grounds. Flight fast and maneuverable. Small flock will fly in dense groups close to surface of water, or rather high. In flight, males produce a characteristic ringing sound with their wings, heard especially when the birds fly in a flock. Excellent swimmer and diver, flushes from water re-

FIG. 25 DIVING DUCKS AND SEA DUCKS IN FLIGHT
1. Common Eider 2. Red-crested Pochard 3. Ferruginous Pochard 4. Northern Pochard 5. Common Goldeneye 6. Greater Scaup 7. Tufted Pochard 8. Long-tailed Duck 9. Black Scoter 10. White-winged Scoter

luctantly and heavily. Call of males: melodious cry like "struk-luk"; females: hoarse croak, "re-re-re." Feeds on mollusks, larvae, water plants, sometimes fish, roots of plants.

Range and distribution: Kola Peninsula, north of European USSR, Siberia. Winters on northern and western shores of Europe, shores of the Aleutian Islands, Korea, Japan, China. In the USSR, winters on Latvian and Lithuanian shores, Kamchatka Peninsula, Kuril Islands, occasionally on the Black Sea and Caspian Sea.

Similar species: Both sexes of the White-winged Scoter have a white speculum; the rarer Surf Scoters lack speculum and have white marks on head of both females and males.

[On Komandorskiye Islands and Chukotka Peninsula specimens of vagrant **102.** SURF SCOTER (*Melanitta perspicillata*) were obtained. Resembles White-winged Scoter, but does not have white speculum, male has white nape and forehead.]

Histrionicus

103. HARLEQUIN DUCK
Histrionicus histrionicus
(Kamenushka)
Plate 5, Map 42
Field marks: 44 cm. Smaller than Mallard. Bluish gray with white spots and stripes on head, neck, and wings (looks black at a distance); sides chestnut; bill and legs gray. Females brown with white spots on head.
Habits: Found near mountain rivers and lakes. In nonbreeding season prefers seacoasts. Migratory. Not numerous overall, but gathers in large flocks on wintering grounds. Nests on banks of rivers with swift currents and stony

bottoms in mountains above tree line. Nests from mid-June. Nest is situated under a bush on precipitous cliffs of river shores, and is lined with dark down. Lays up to eight cream-colored eggs. Trustful, allows close approach. Sits high on the water, uplifting tail. Call of male in spring: loud "gi-ek"; in flock they "speak" with low "ek-ek-ek" or hoarse "he-he." Feeds on aquatic insects and their larvae, mollusks, and small crustacea.

Range and distribution: East Siberia including Kamchatka Peninsula, Soviet Far East; Sakhalin, Komandorskiye, and Kuril Islands. Winters on shores of Korea and Japan. In the USSR, on Komandorskiye and Kuril Islands.

Similar species: Male differs from all other ducks by characteristic coloration; female resembles that of Long-tailed Duck in summer plumage, but darker, with no rusty tints on back; characteristic round white spot near ear.

Clangula

104. LONG-TAILED DUCK
Clangula hyemalis
(Moryanka)
Plate 4, Map 42
Field marks: 41-56 cm. Small duck, male with long thin tail. In summer, male's head and breast black, sides and face white; back blackish with rusty tint. In winter, head, neck, sides, and belly white; breast and back black and spot on cheek gray and black. Female in summer, head blackish with whitish face, upper parts brown; sides whitish. Female in winter, head and neck whitish with dark spot under eye; belly and sides white. Depending on the season, representatives of all of these plumages can be seen in the same flock.
Habits: Found in tundra and forest-tundra;

MAP 42. Long-tailed Duck (1), Harlequin Duck (2)

during nonbreeding season near seas, sometimes on lakes. Migratory, in places nonmigratory. Common or numerous. Nests near lakes and rivers in marshy grass tundras. Builds nests on dry places at water's edge, in sedge, under clumps of willows or dwarf birch. Nest lined with dark down. Lays six to eight brown-olive eggs from mid-June. Nesting female allows close approach. Males and nonbreeding females gather in very large flocks in estuaries and lakes. Flight fast, in tight flock low to the water. Very garrulous bird; call: hoarse "a-aue." Noise produced by a flock of Long-tailed Ducks is heard for a long distance. Tail held high while swimming; dives well; flushes reluctantly and heavily. Unwary. Feeds on insect larvae, small crustacea, mollusks, fish.

Range and distribution: North of European USSR and Siberia. Winters on northwest shores of Europe, western shores of North America. In the USSR, winters on waters of the Barents and Baltic Seas, shores of Kamchatka Peninsula, Kuril Islands, northern Sea of Okhotsk, Sea of Japan.

Similar species: Male differs from all ducks except Northern Pintail by long, pointed tail; from Northern Pintail, by coloration; female in summer plumage vaguely resembles female Harlequin Duck, but sides of head whitish with large dark spot under eye.

Bucephala

105. COMMON GOLDENEYE
Bucephala clangula
(Gogol)
Plate 4, Map 43

Field marks: 44 cm. Medium-sized duck with large head on short neck. Male underparts white, back black, head black with green iri-

descence; large white wing patch; rounded white spot near bill. Eyes yellow, bill gray, legs yellow. Female: smaller, gray; head brown, collar white, belly whitish.

Habits: Found in forests; during nonbreeding season on seas and large lakes. Migratory. Common. Nests near taiga rivers and lakes with wooded banks. Builds nests high above ground in tree hollows of aspen, spruce, oak. Nest lined with white down. In nature reserves and game farms, readily occupies man-made nesting boxes. Lays five to twelve greenish-blue eggs, from end of April and later. Flight swift and maneuverable; small flock stays closely grouped or in an irregular line. Characteristic ringing or whistling sound is heard during the flight. Good diver, staying submerged for long periods of time. Flushes from the water easily; when swimming keeps tail lowered. Cautious. Call: hoarse croaking. Feeds almost exclusively on small water animals (mollusks, small crustacea, insect larvae and fish).

Range and distribution: Northern half of European USSR except northerly borders; southern half of Siberia except Transbaikal; Soviet Far East. Winters on northern and western shores of Europe, the Mediterranean, in Iraq, Iran, Pakistan, shores of Korea, Japan, China. In the USSR, on the Black and Caspian Seas, on Komandorskiye and Kuril Islands, Sea of Japan.

Similar species: Differs from Barrow's Goldeneye by rounded (not half-moon) spot at the bill and green iridescence on head (females are practically indistinguishable); from Bufflehead by larger size, lack of white spot on the nape.

[Vagrants of **106.** BARROW'S GOLDENEYE (*Bucephala islandica*) were collected on One-

MAP 43. Common Goldeneye (1), White-headed Duck (2)

zhskoye and Ilmen lakes. Resembles Common Goldeneye but with half-moon spot at base of bill and violet iridescence on head. Females differ only by width of bill tip, which always exceeds 5 mm. Vagrants of **107.** BUFFLEHEAD (*Bucephala albeola*), common to North America, are seen occasionally in the Komandorskiye Islands. It is considerably smaller than Common Goldeneye.

Mergus

Ducks from large to small sizes. Spikelike bill and saw-edged mandibles instead of plates; tip slightly hooked. Most species have crests and keep tail in water like pochards.

108. SMEW
Mergus albellus
(Lutok)
Plate 5, Map 44
Field marks: 43 cm. Small, slightly larger than Garganey. Crest hardly visible; white with black back, a black spot on nape and between bill and eye; legs and bill gray. Female gray with brown head, white cheeks, and light belly.
Habits: Found in forests; during nonbreeding season found near seas and on lakes and rivers in different habitats. Migratory. Uncommon, but common in places. Nests on wooded banks of taiga rivers and lakes, forested ridges, and in swampy river valleys. Builds nests in hollows or trunks of burned trees, sometimes rather high. Nest lined with white down. Lays six to ten white eggs from mid-May and later. Does not form large flocks, usually stays in groups of five to six birds, frequently alone. Flies fast; dives well. Unwary. Call: crackling "krr."

Range and distribution: North European USSR (except tundra); central taiga of East and West Siberia; Chukotski Peninsula; Sakhalin Island. Winters on the Baltic, North, and Mediterranean Seas; shores of Japan, Korea, and China; bodies of water in inland China, India, and Iran. In the USSR, winters in traditional areas of the Caspian, Black, and Azov Sea; lakes of Central Asia.
Similar species: Differs from other mergansers by smaller size (wing up to 20 cm.) and distinctive plumage.

109. RED-BREASTED MERGANSER
Mergus serrator
(Dlinnonosy Krokhal)
Plate 5, Map 45
Field marks: 52-59 cm. Medium size. Ragged crest. In male, head and back black; head with greenish iridescence; neck, belly, and base of wings white; upper breast reddish-brown with black mottling; sides gray with fine striations; bill and legs red. Female grayish; head and neck reddish-brown; belly light; throat and wing patch white; brown coloration blends from neck to lighter upper breast.
Habits: Found near seashores and islands, bodies of water in tundra and taiga, mountain lakes and rivers. Migratory. Common. Nests in wooded or open sea-islands, banks of lakes and rivers. Builds nest in cracks in rocks, hollows under stones, on floating reed mats, dense thickets, in reeds; rarely in the open, and usually not far from water. Nest abundantly lined with dark down. Lays seven to twelve pale olive eggs from mid-May and later (in the north). Female sits on nest so firmly that it is possible to catch it by hand. Does not form large flocks even during migration. Flight fast, with frequent wing beats; paddles to a run-

MAP 44. Common Merganser (1), Smew (2)

MAP 45. Red-breasted Merganser (1), Chinese Merganser (2)

ning start on takeoff from water. Takes flight noisily and heavily. Dives well. Call: hoarse quack, "krekh-krekh." Feeds mostly on fish.

Range and distribution: North European USSR, West and East Siberia, Soviet Far East, Sakhalin Island; isolated nesting found in Crimea, Lake Sevan in Armenia, Lake Balkhash in Kazakhstan, Altai, Tuva. Winters on western and southern shores of Europe, in Iran and eastern Asia. In the USSR, winters on the Black and Caspian Seas, on Lake Sevan, the shores of Kamchatka Peninsula, Komandorskiye and Kuril Islands.

Similar species: Differs from Common Merganser by brown upper breast and gray sides; female, by color blend between neck and belly; from Chinese Merganser, by brown upper

breast and fine striations on sides (females almost indistinguishable).

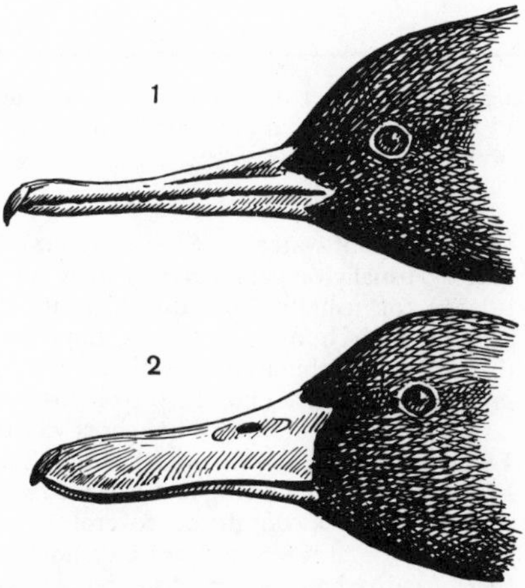

110. CHINESE MERGANSER
Mergus squamatus
(Cheshuychaty Krokhal)
Plate 5, Map 45

Field marks: 57 cm. Male and female resemble Red-breasted Merganser, but male's crest is longer; upper breast pinkish-white; black scaly pattern on sides. On sides of female, the same scaly pattern but fainter.

Habits: Found near rivers in taiga mountain regions. Rare, biology almost unknown. Nest not yet discovered, but ten to twelve nestlings in a brood. Flies little, passes most of the time on water. Flight and call like Red-breasted Merganser. Feeds on fish. Included in the Red Data Book.

Range and distribution: Soviet Far East. Winters in Korea, China, in northern regions of Vietnam and Burma.

Similar species: Differs from Red-breasted Merganser by white upper breast (males) and scaly pattern on sides (both sexes).

111. COMMON MERGANSER
Mergus merganser
(Bolshoy Krokhal)
Plate 5, Map 44

Field marks: 57-80 cm. Size of Mallard. Head and back looks black, underparts and sides pinkish white; crest small, legs and bill red. Female gray; rusty brown head sharply differentiated from gray neck; throat white; underparts light.

Habits: Found in forests and mountains. Migratory. Not common. Nests on banks of rivers with fast current and clear lakes rich in fish but without water plants. Builds nests in

FIG. 26 Bill of 1) Merganser and 2) Dabbling Duck

old tree hollows, sometimes in rock clefts, on driftwood, and under bushes; readily inhabits nesting boxes. Lays eight to twelve cream-white eggs, from mid-May and later; nest lined with white down. Does not form large flocks, stays in groups of eight to ten birds; nestlings often grouped together and watched by one or several females. Flight heavy but fast; takes off from water noisily, with a running start. Dives well. Very cautious, but female sits on nest so firmly that she can sometimes be caught barehanded. Call of male: muffled "ba-bob," female: hoarse "karr-karr." Usually feeds in shoals; in rivers dives facing downstream. Feeds on small fish, rarely on mollusks and insects.

Range and distribution: North European USSR (except tundra); southern half of Siberia; Soviet Far East; Sakhalin Island. Winters on shores of Western Europe and eastern Asia; in the USSR, on the Black and Caspian Seas, shores of Kamchatka Peninsula, Kuril Islands, lakes of Central Asia.

Similar species: Differs from Red-breasted Merganser by larger size, white underparts; female, by sharply defined rusty color on the neck.

Oxyura

112. WHITE-HEADED DUCK
Oxyura leucocephala
(Savka)
Plate 5, Map 43
Field marks: 43 cm. Medium-size duck with short wings and long wedge-shaped tail. Brown with fine dark striations; head white with black crown, nape, and neck; bill bright blue; legs gray. Female differs by dark brown head with white stripe under eye; white neck; bill and legs gray.

Habits: Found in forest-steppe, steppe, and desert. Winters on large lakes and estuaries. Migratory; partly nonmigratory. Uncommon. Nests in fresh-water or deep brackish lakes with thickets of reed and quiet waters. Nests made of stalks and leaves situated in sedge thickets, on floating reed mats at water's edge or directly on water, anchored between reed stalks. Nest sometimes lined with white down. Lays five to seven very large eggs from early June. Shell coarse, grainy, greenish at the beginning of incubation, then dirty yellow by the end. Flies seldom and reluctantly, takes off heavily, with a long running start. Flight fast. While swimming, keeps tail vertical; good diver, submerging without splashing. Silent, furtive. Feeds on seeds and leaves of aquatic plants; also insects and their larvae.

Range and distribution: Lower Volga River, Kazakhstan, Central Asia, southern West Siberia. Winters in North Africa, Iran, India. In the USSR, southeast of Caspian Sea, Turkmenia.

Similar species: Differs from other ducks by long wedge-shaped and sharply uplifted tail with rigid pointed feathers; somewhat resembles Long-tailed Duck in summer plumage from a distance, but completely different in profile.

BIRDS OF PREY: *Falconiiformes*

Birds of medium, large, and very large sizes. Females usually larger than males. Bill and talons hooked, cere well pronounced. Found in a variety of habitats. Monogamous. Eggs usually ovoid or shortened ellipsoid. Altricial.

Pandion

113. OSPREY
Pandion haliaëtus
(Skopa)
Plate 9, Map 46
Field marks: 55 cm. Large bird with long slender wings. Coloration distinctive: upperparts blackish; underparts white with indistinct band on breast; head white with wide black eye stripe. Tarsus bare. Gull-like in flight, with black at bend of wing.

Habits: Found in a variety of habitats except tundra, steppe, and alpine zones. Settles near large bodies of water (lakes, seas, rivers). Migratory, usually very rare. Nest of thick boughs is large and usually situated in high, inaccessible pine, birch, or spruce trees. Lays two or three eggs (combination of white, red-brown and violet-brown) at end of April or early May. Usually silent. Call: a series of short whistles. Feeds almost exclusively on fish (up to 2 or 3 kg.), catches fish by diving feet-first into water, sometimes to a depth of several meters. Searches for prey when soaring or hovering; flies heavily when carrying fish, deeply stroking wings. Due to small number of birds, included in the Red Data Book.

Range and distribution: European USSR ex-

Map 46. Osprey

cept unforested tundra and steppe; Kazakhstan, southern half of Siberia, Soviet Far East. Winters in Africa and southern Asia.

Similar species: Differs easily from all large birds of prey by its shape and coloration (white underparts, dark upperparts, and banded breast.)

Pernis

Large birds (notably larger than a crow) with long tail and slender wings. In flight, the neck seems more stretched than a *Buteo*. Short rigid feathers, resembling scales, on forehead and around eyes. Tarsus, a scaly network of horny plates.

114. EURASIAN HONEY-BUZZARD
Pernis apivorus
(Osoed)
Plate 9, Map 47
Field marks: 55 cm. Color varies greatly; up-

per parts dark brown, underparts vary from all brown to a light whitish with brown spots or mottling. Underwing striped; two dark bands widely separated from broad subterminal band on tail.

Habits: Found in forest and forest-steppe; stays mostly in mature deciduous and mixed forest, also in clearings, meadows. Migratory. Common. Nests in trees, often near a clearing. Nest lined with small green branches and leaves. Lays one or two bright red-brown eggs (often with white) late in the season, end of May to June. Usually flies low, flight light and maneuverable with deep wing beats alternating with short soarings. Call does not resemble the cry of Common Buzzard, sounds like "kii-e!" or quick "kikikiki!" Feeds mostly on larvae of wasps and bumblebees; also insects, rarely on frogs and rodents.

Range and distribution: European USSR except northern regions; southern West Siberia. Winters in Central and South Africa.

Similar species: Differs from Common Buz-

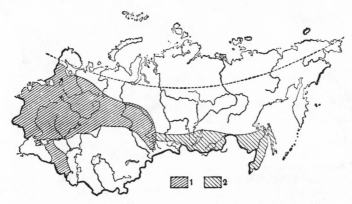

Map 47. Eurasian Honey-Buzzard (1), Crested Honey-Buzzard (2)

zard and Northern Goshawk by its build (long tail, slender wings, neck stretched in flight) and three wide tailbands (also note genus characteristics).

115. CRESTED HONEY-BUZZARD
Pernis ptilorhynchus
(Khokhlaty Osoed)
Plate 9, Map 47
Field marks: 50-56 cm. Resembles Eurasian Honey-Buzzard, but larger. Tail of adults with three wide bands; juveniles have narrower bands. Sometimes a dark horseshoe-shaped spot on throat, often (but not always) well-developed pointed crest. Occasionally brownish color phases are found.

Habits: Inhabits deciduous and mixed forest. Migratory. Rare. Nest made of twigs and lined with new leaves. Lays one or two bright redbrown with white eggs end of May to June.

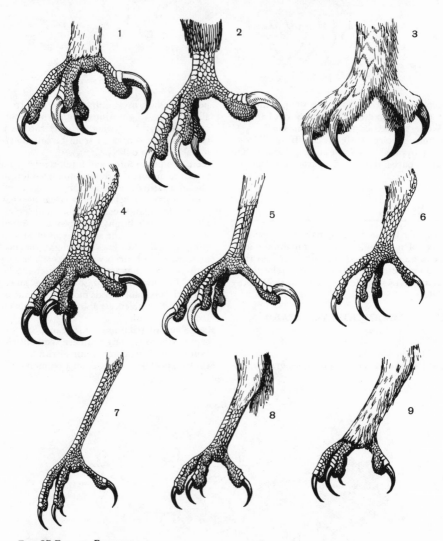

FIG. 27 FEET OF RAPTORS
1. Steppe Eagle 2. White-tailed Sea-Eagle 3. Northern Eagle-Owl 4. Osprey 5. Northern Goshawk 6. Eurasian Honey-Buzzard 7. Marsh Harrier 8. Common Buzzard 9. Rough-legged Buzzard

Flight, habits, and call similar to Eurasian Honey-Buzzard. Feeds on insects, mostly larvae of wasps and bumblebees.

Range and distribution: Southern Siberia, Transbaikal, Soviet Far East, Sakhalin Island. Winters in south of Asia.

Similar species: Differs from Eurasian Honey-Buzzard by larger size, and crest (isolated geographically).

Note: *Pernis ptilorhynchus* is regarded by some as a race of *Pernis apivorus*.

Milvus

Large birds with slender wings and long tail more or less forked.

116. BLACK KITE
Milvus migrans
(Cherny Korshun)
Plate 9, Map 48

Field marks: 57 cm. Dark brown; underparts lighter with rusty tones and dark brown mottling; crown notably lighter than back; forked tail hardly visible. Juveniles have large ocherish tips to body feathers.

Habits: Found in a variety of habitats except northern taiga and tundra. Inhabits forests of various types; often river valleys, areas near lakes or other water bodies; often found near settlements and cities. Migratory. One of the most common and frequently seen raptors. Nests in trees, more rarely in precipice niches. Nest lined with rags, wool, scraps of paper, and other rubbish. Lays two or three white eggs with brown or violet spots end of April to May. Often forms nomadic flocks and nesting colonies. Call: long, tremulous trill, resembling neigh of a foal in the distance. Searches out prey by soaring at a great altitude for a

long time. Feeds on carrion, dead fish, various wastes in dumps and slaughterhouses; more rarely on frogs, lizards, small birds, and rodents.

Range and distribution: European USSR except northern regions and south of the Ukraine; Central Asia, Kazakhstan, southern half of Siberia, Soviet Far East. Winters in Africa and southern Asia.

Similar species: Differs from Red Kite by smaller size, darker color, and shallow forked tail.

117. RED KITE
Milvus milvus
(Krasny Korshun)
Plate 9, Map 48

Field marks: 62 cm. Slightly larger and lighter in color than Black Kite. Upperparts brownish; underparts bright rusty with dark streaks; head light; tail red-brown and deeply forked.

Habits: Found in old deciduous and mixed forest, where it prefers forest edges. Migratory in the USSR. Rare. Nests in trees (oaks, lindens, pines). Lays two or three white eggs with faint rusty brown scribbling in mid-April. Call resembles cry of the Common Buzzard, and sounds like "hiya" or trill, "hi-hi-hiya." Feeds on carrion, small birds, and rodents. Resembles Black Kite in habits. Included in the Red Data Book.

Range and distribution: Southwest European USSR, Transcaucasus. Winters in Mediterranean countries.

Similar species: Differs from Black Kite by rusty color and deeply forked tail.

Haliaëetus

Very large birds. Tarsus half-feathered. Bill massive, very high, pushed in at the sides.

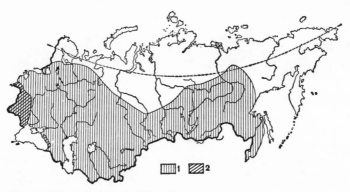

MAP 48. Black Kite (1), Red Kite (2)

118. WHITE-TAILED SEA-EAGLE
Haliaëetus albicilla
(Orlan-belokhvost)
Plate 8, Map 49
Field marks: 77 cm. Large bird with short, slightly wedge-shaped tail. Brown; head and underparts lighter; tail pure white, bill yellow. Juveniles dark brown; underparts with elongated dark spots; tail and bill dark.

Habits: Found in a variety of habitats from tundra to desert, but prefers to be near water; found in river valleys, sea- and lakeshores with

FIG. 28 RAPTORS IN FLIGHT

1. Rough-legged Buzzard   2. Long-legged Buzzard   3. Common Buzzard   4. Eurasian Honey-Buzzard   5. Booted Eagle (light phase)   6. Booted Eagle (dark phase)   7. Peregrine Falcon   8. Northern Harrier (male)   9. Northern Goshawk   10. Black Kite   11. Marsh Harrier (male)

FIG. 29 Black Kite Nestling

trees or rocks. Nonmigratory or nomadic; migratory in the north. Rare as a whole but more common than the other eagles. Massive nest made of thick boughs placed high in trees; more rarely on rocks. The same nests are used for many years in a row. Lays two, rarely three white eggs early March to April. Very cautious, does not allow close approach even near the nest. Rarely soars high in the air; usually catches prey in low flight or from perch on branch or a rock. Flight heavy. Call: barking "kra-kra-kra" or "kiy-kiy-kiy!" Feeds on fish, birds (ducks, gulls, partridge, coot), and mammals (hare, muskrat, suslik—a large, short-tailed ground squirrel); readily feeds on carrion. Included in the Red Data Book.

Range and distribution: Greater part of USSR except unforested tundra and deserts. Winters in southern Europe, Egypt, India, China, Korea, Japan. In the USSR, shores of the Caspian and Black Seas; Central Asia.

Similar species: Differs from other eagles by short, slightly wedge-shaped white tail, massive bill, and bare tarsus (juveniles are more difficult to identify since their tail is dark); from Steller's Sea-Eagle by single color of upper parts (juveniles indistinguishable in the field); from Pallas's Sea-Eagle by unicolor tail and, in juveniles, lack of dark stripe behind eye.

119. PALLAS'S SEA-EAGLE
Haliaëetus leucoryphus
(Orlan-dolgokhvost)
Plate 8, Map 50

Field marks: 74 cm. Resembles White-tailed Sea-Eagle, but lighter, better proportioned, and slightly smaller. Body and wings black-brown, head ocherish; throat light; tail rounded, black with broad white band. Bill horn-color. Females duller. Juveniles: light brown with darker breast and dark tail; dark on sides of head.

Habits: Found in open desertlike habitat, but always near large bodies of water such as river valleys, seashores, and lakes overgrown with reed. Migratory or nomadic. Very rare. Nests early March to April. Nests in trees (willows, cork elms, elaeagnus) or on dry reed. Lays two white eggs. Call: barking "kuok-kuok-kuok." Flight light and swift. Soars well. Often perches motionless on tree or shore ledge, watching prey for long periods of time. Does not harm

MAP 49. White-tailed Sea-Eagle

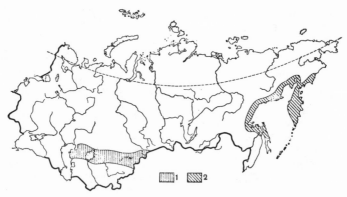

MAP 50. Pallas's Sea-Eagle (1), Steller's Sea-Eagle (2)

hunting or fishing, as it is rare. Included in the Red Data Book.

Range and distribution: Kazakhstan, Central Asia. Winters in India. Occasionally found wintering in USSR in the Amu Darya and Syr Darya Rivers.

Similar species: Adults differentiated from other *Haliaëetus* and *Aquila* by whitish head and broad white band on tail; coloration of body almost black; juveniles differ from White-tailed Sea-Eagle by dark spots behind eyes and unicolor breast and belly.

120. STELLER'S SEA-EAGLE

Haliaëetus pelagicus
(Beloplechy Orlan)
Plate 8, Map 50

Field marks: 85 cm. Slightly larger than Pallas's Sea-Eagle, but more massive. Black-brown with white shoulders; tail white, wedge-shaped. Bill very large and bright yellow. Juveniles brown.

Habits: Found near seashores or wooded river valleys. Winters near ice-free water bodies. Nonmigratory, partly nomadic. Generally uncommon, but locally common. Massive nests made with boughs; situated in trees, more rarely on rocks. Lays two white eggs in April. Very cautious. Flight, habits, hunting technique same as White-tailed Eagle. Call resembles White-tailed Eagle also, but hoarser. Feeds on large fish (salmon), birds (capercaillies, guillemots, ducks), hares, young seals, carrion. Included in the Red Data Book.

Range and distribution: Kamchatka Peninsula, Sakhalin Island, shores of Sea of Okhotsk. Winters on shores of Kamchatka, the Kuril Islands, shores of Primorski Krai. Outside the USSR, in Japan and Korea.

Similar species: Bright yellow bill and white shoulders are diagnostic features when comparing with other raptors; in the field, juveniles are almost indistinguishable from those of White-tailed Sea-Eagles, but slightly more massive.

Accipiter

Birds of large and medium sizes with short blunt wings and long tail. Females notably larger than males. Legs long with large, hooked claws; tarsus bare.

121. NORTHERN GOSHAWK

Accipiter gentilis
(Teterevyatnik)
Plate 10, Map 51

Field marks: 48-58 cm. Large accipiter (larger than a crow). Upperparts dove-gray or brownish-gray; head slightly darker, with white eye stripe; underparts light with dark narrow barring; undertail coverts fluffy white. In the extreme northeast of the USSR, nearly white specimens are occasionally found. Eyes and legs yellow. Juveniles, brownish with elongated spots on breast and belly.

Habits: Found in forest, forest-steppe, and forest-tundra. Prefers coniferous and deciduous forest, where it stays in various areas but avoids dense woods. Nonmigratory and nomadic. Common, but very cautious and not often seen. Nests in trees (pines, spruces, birches, oaks, lindens), often using nests of other birds. Lays three or four white eggs in April. Call: ringing "kyak-kyak-kyak" or "gig-gig-gig." Catches unsuspecting prey by suddenly flying out of ambush. Short wings and long tail permit the bird to change direction readily, and to slow down or accelerate flight sharply while pursuing prey among trees. Feeds on different

MAP 51. Northern Goshawk (1), Eurasian Sparrowhawk (2)

birds (pigeons, woodpeckers, hazel-grouse, black grouses, partridges, and others); also mammals (hares, squirrels).

Range and distribution: Greater part of USSR except true tundra and deserts. Not found in Central Asian mountains. Some of the population is nonmigratory; others migrate south as far as Central Asia.

Similar species: Differs from other accipiters by larger size; from other raptors, by barred underparts and by build (short, rounded wings, long tail).

122. SHIKRA
Accipiter badius
(Tyuvik)
Plate 10, Map 52

Field marks: 36-38 cm. Resembles Northern Goshawk in color and build, but smaller (pigeon-size). Contrasting brownish stripe on whitish throat. Eyes reddish-brown.

Habits: Inhabits riparian and flood-plain forests, groves, and wooded river areas in forest-steppe, steppe, and desert. Stays close to settled areas, and is found in gardens, parks, oases, and even cities. Migratory. Uncommon, but common in places. Builds nest in trees (white willow, cork elm, alder, honey locust), sometimes using magpie nests. Lays three or four (up to seven) bluish-white eggs from mid-May to June. Unwary and noisy near nest. Call: long whistle, "tyuyu-vik, tyuyu-vik." Feeds on lizards, frogs, large insects, more rarely on small birds and animals.

Range and distribution: Southern Ukraine, Central Volga Oblast as far as the Urals, Caucasus, Transcaucasus, Central Asia, Kazakhstan. Winters in Africa and southwestern Asia.

Similar species: Differs from Northern Sparrowhawk by dark stripe on throat, dark eyes, and longer wings; males by gray breast; from Northern Goshawk by smaller size.

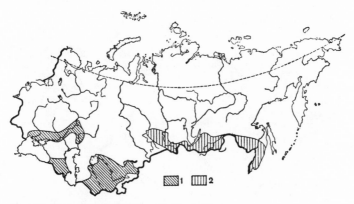

MAP 52. Shikra (1), Besra Sparrowhawk (2)

123. BESRA SPARROWHAWK

Accipiter virgatus
(Maly Perepelyatnik)
Plate 10, Map 52

Field marks: 20-29 cm. Smallest accipiter (smaller than pigeon). Male upperparts gray; underparts pale rust with white and black streaks; tail banded; white throat with dark central stripe. Female, upperparts brown, underparts light gray with elongated brown streaks; broad stripe on light throat; eyes yellow.

Habits: Inhabits coniferous, mixed, and deciduous forests; stays mostly in river valleys. Migratory. Uncommon. Builds nests in trees. Lays four or five white eggs with red-brown spots late in June. Habits and call like Northern Sparrowhawk, which this accipiter resembles. Feeds on small birds (buntings, sparrows, titmice).

Range and distribution: South Siberia, Soviet Far East. Winters in southeastern Asia.

Similar species: Differs from Eurasian Sparrowhawk by smaller size (wing of male does not exceed 17 cm.; of female, 20 cm.); from Shikra by darker upperparts.

124. EURASIAN SPARROWHAWK

Accipiter nisus
(Perepelyatnik)
Plate 10, Map 51

Field marks: 28-38 cm. Looks like a small Northern Goshawk, but barring on male's breast is rusty or rufous-brown; on female's dark brown; eyes yellow. Juveniles resemble females.

Habits: Inhabits forest of various types, but avoids long stretches of forest; usually found at forest edges, in groves, wood-cutting areas, river valleys, in settled areas, and even cities (especially in winter). Nonmigratory and nomadic; migratory in the north. Common in European part of the USSR, uncommon in the east. Builds nests in trees (spruce, pine, birch, larch). Lays three to six white eggs spotted with bright reddish-brown in June. Habits and methods of hunting like Northern Goshawk. Call: loud, very frequent "kik-kik-kik." Feeds almost exclusively on small passerines; females also attack pigeons, jays, young hazel-grouse. Occasionally hunts for small rodents.

Range and distribution: Greater part of USSR except tundra zones, Chukotski Peninsula, and deserts of Central Asia. Winters in Africa and southern Asia. In the USSR, in southern regions.

Similar species: Differs from Northern Goshawk by smaller size; from Shikra by yellow eyes and lack of stripe on the throat. These same diagnostic features, together with its larger size (wings: male no less than 18 cm.; female 22 cm.) distinguish it from Besra Sparrowhawk.

Buteo

Large birds (notably larger than crow) with wide wings and short, slightly rounded tail.

125. COMMON BUZZARD

Buteo buteo
(Kanyuk)
Plate 9, Map 53

Field marks: 53 cm. Coloration varies greatly: upperparts usually dark brown; underparts lighter with elongated mottling. Tail banded, often with wide, dark band at tip. Occasionally some birds very light with whitish underparts and pale mottling. Legs yellow.

MAP 53. Common Buzzard (1), Rough-legged Buzzard (2)

Habits: Found in forest and forest-steppe; in places where wooded areas alternate with open areas (meadows, swamps, wood-cutting areas, forest edges). Migratory. One of the most numerous and often-seen raptors in the central belt of the USSR. Nests made of boughs situated in trees. Lays two to four white eggs spotted with rust in April and May. Unwary near the nest. Noisy; call: mournful, nasal, long "kiiii-kiii." Hunts prey from air. Soars for long periods with motionless wings; sometimes pauses in flight; frequently hovers like the kestrel. Feeds on small rodents, frogs, insects; rarely on birds.

Range and distribution: European USSR except northern borders and Lower Volga region; Kazakhstan, southern half of Siberia, Soviet Far East. Winters in southern Africa and southern Asia.

Similar species: Differs from Eurasian Honey-Buzzard by heavier build and numerous narrow bands on tail (front of tarsus covered with elongated scales); from Long-legged Buzzard by banded tail and lack of contrasting dark spots on the bend of wing; from Rough-legged Buzzard by banded tail and lack of dark belly and striped breast; from Upland Buzzard by smaller size; from Black Kite, by rounded tail; from Northern Goshawk by short tail and longer wings.

126. ROUGH-LEGGED BUZZARD
Buteo lagopus
(Zimnyak)
Plate 9, Map 53

Field marks: 56 cm. Resembles Common Buzzard, but larger and lighter in color. Tail whitish with dark subterminal band; mottling on breast; dark spots on belly and bend of wing;

head and underside of wing light; front of tarsus feathered almost to toes.

Habits: Found in tundra and forest-tundra. Winters in steppe and near settled areas. Migratory, common in places, numerous in some years. Nests mostly in river valleys, building nests (with boughs) on precipices, slopes, in raised places, occasionally in flat places; more rarely in trees. Lays three to six white, rusty-speckled eggs May and June. Behavior and call like Common Buzzard. Feeds on small rodents (lemmings, voles), more rarely on birds.

Range and distribution: North of European USSR and Siberia, Chukotski Peninsula, shores of Sea of Okhotsk, Kamchatka Peninsula. Winters in the Ukraine, central regions of European USSR, Kazakhstan, Caucasus, Transbaikal, Primorski Krai.

Similar species: Differs from Common Buzzard by lighter color, dark spots on breast and bend of wing, dark subterminal tail feathers.

127. UPLAND BUZZARD
Buteo hemilasius
(Mokhnonogy Kurgannik)
Plate 9, Map 54

Field marks: 58 cm. Resembles Common Buzzard, but larger. Coloration varies from dark brown to light brownish-gray with ocherish throat and breast. Several indistinct bands on tail. Tarsus usually feathered in front.

Habits: Found in mountain steppe, forest-steppe, in open hilly areas with rock outcrops, gentle slopes of mountains, and valleys between mountains. Nomadic, nonmigratory in places. Uncommon. Builds bough nests on precipices, stony talus slopes, steppe slopes. Nest lined with wool, rags, dry manure. Lays three or four white eggs with yellowish-brown

MAP 54. Upland Buzzard (1), Long-legged Buzzard (2)

spots in May. Cautious and silent near the nest, in comparison to Common Buzzard. Habits more resemble those of a small eagle. Feeds on various rodents (voles, susliks, gerbils, pikas), occasionally small birds.

Range and distribution: Altai, Tuva, Transbaikal. Winters in southern parts of nesting range in Kazakhstan and southern Soviet Far East.

Similar species: Differs from Common Buzzard by larger size and sometimes by feathered tarsus.

128. LONG-LEGGED BUZZARD

Buteo rufinus
(Kurgannik)
Plate 9, Map 54

Field marks: 58 cm. Resembles Common Buzzard, but larger and usually lighter in color. Upperparts light brown with rusty tint; underparts ocherish or rusty, often mottled; primaries whitish with gray tips, dark spots readily seen at bend of wing; tail lightly banded; but appears to be unbanded from a distance. Dark (entirely brown) specimens are found from time to time.

Habits: Found in desert and semi-desert; prefers slightly hilly plains. Migratory, nomadic in places. Common. Nest made of branches and boughs and situated in trees (saxal, pistachio, and others), on rocks, clay precipices, rubble of buildings. Nest lined with dry wormwood, grains, bark. Lays three to five white eggs with reddish-brown speckles and spots end of March to April. Hunts for prey in flight or perched motionless on poles, mounds, or tombstones in old graveyards. Feeds on rodents (gerbils, voles, susliks), more rarely birds and reptiles.

Range and distribution: Caucasus and Transcaucasus, Central Asia, Kazakhstan. Winters south of nesting range.

Similar species: Differs from other buzzards by lighter base of primaries (with white spots) and light unbarred tail.

Butastur

129. GRAY-FACED BUZZARD

Butastur indicus
(Yastrebny Sarych)
Plate 9, Map 55

Field marks: 46 cm. Large (larger than a crow). Resembles Common Buzzard in build, but smaller and with longer tail. Legs long, tarsus slightly feathered. Upperparts brown; brownish breast with barred underparts; diagnostic

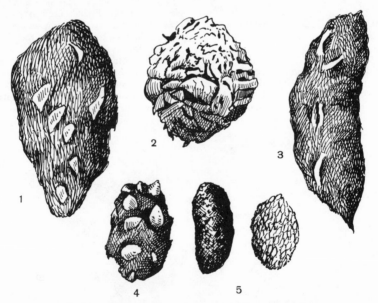

FIG. 30 REGURGITATED PELLETS OF UNDIGESTED MATERIALS
1. Long-legged Buzzard   2. Herring Gull   3. Short-eared Owl   4. Eurasian Crow   5. Blue-cheeked Bee-eater

Map 55. Short-toed Snake Eagle (1), Gray-faced Buzzard (2)

dark stripe on white throat. Juveniles: light underparts with dark streaks.

Habits: Found in deciduous and mixed forests, usually near fields and meadows. Migratory. Rare. Small nest in tree is made of small branches and lined with grass and leaves. Lays three to four white eggs with rusty or red-brown spots in early May. Often perches for a long time on dead limbs of isolated trees. Flies with deep wing beats resembling accipiters. Call: long "ti-viii . . . ti-viii." Feeds on frogs, snakes, lizards, insects, small rodents. Included in the Red Data Book.

Range and distribution: Soviet Far East and the Amur River region. Winters in Southeast Asia and New Guinea.

Similar species: Smaller size, white throat with dark band, and longer legs (tarsus more than 4 cm.) are determinative when compared with Common Buzzard.

Aquila

Large and very large birds with long, wide wings and slightly rounded tail. Bill massive, dark; legs feathered to the toes. In flight, often soars for long periods, spreading primaries wide (like fingers). Identification often difficult.

130. GOLDEN EAGLE
Aquila chrysaetos
(Berkut)
Plate 8, Map 56
Field marks: 82 cm. Large eagle with broad wings and long tail. Black-brown; underparts lighter; pointed golden-yellowish feathers on nape and back of neck. Juveniles: tail white with wide, dark band on outer tail; in old birds base of tail obscurely whitish, but without con-

trasting dark band. Claws very strong, large.
Habits: Found in mountains, forests, and deserts. Settles in areas where cliffs or tall forests alternate with open spaces; in taiga, prefers river valleys; in mountains and deserts is found everywhere. Nonmigratory or nomadic. Rare, more common only in Yakutia and in mountains of Central Asia. Builds massive nests with thick boughs on inaccessible rocks or high trees; in desert, on ruins, or saxal trees. Lays one or two white eggs, usually (not always) mottled a bright reddish-brown in March or April. Very wary. Call: gruff and hoarse "kiek-kiek-kiek." Feeds on different animals (hares, foxes, marmots) and birds; often carrion. In Kazakhstan and Central Asia, used for falconry. Included in the Red Data Book.

Range and distribution: Greater part of USSR except northern regions. Nesting sporadic everywhere. Usually winters within its nesting range.

Similar species: Juveniles (up to three or four years old) differ noticeably from other eagles by two-color tail, old birds only by broad wings, whitish base of tail, often by golden feathers on nape, and by very large claws. From a distance can be confused with Imperial Eagle or Steppe Eagle.

131. IMPERIAL EAGLE
Aquila heliaca
(Mogilnik)
Plate 8, Map 56
Field marks: 75 cm. Large, wide-winged, very dark eagle. Brown; sometimes almost black; crown light yellow; white spots on shoulders. Juveniles: light brown with streaked underparts. Claws smaller and tail shorter than Golden Eagle.
Habits: Found in forest-steppe, steppe, and

FIG. 31 RAPTORS IN FLIGHT
1. Cinereous Vulture   2. Eurasian Griffon   3. Lammergeier   4. Egyptian Vulture   5. Golden
Eagle (juvenile)   6. Golden Eagle (adult)   7. White-tailed Sea-Eagle   8. Pallas's Sea-Eagle
9. Imperial Eagle   10. Osprey   11. Steppe Eagle   12. Short-toed Snake-Eagle

MAP 56. Golden Eagle (1), Imperial Eagle (2)

desert; penetrates far into forests. Stays in plains with isolated trees, in pine forests, and small woods. Migratory. Common in places. Builds nests with thick boughs on trees, usually at the top. Lays one or two pure white or yellowish eggs with rusty spots in April. Call resembles dog's barking, "tyaf-tyaf-tyaf." Feeds on small animals (susliks, marmots, hares), on waterfowl, and on carrion. Included in the Red Data Book.

Range and distribution: South European USSR, Central Asia, Kazakhstan, southern West Siberia; isolated populations in the Baltic states. Winters in Central Asia and Transbaikal.

Similar species: Differs from Steppe Eagle and Golden Eagle by very light "hat"; white spots on shoulders (not always) and lighter primaries in juveniles. Field identification from a distance is difficult without a lot of practice.

132. STEPPE EAGLE
Aquila rapax
(Stepnoy Oryol)
Plate 8, Map 57

Field marks: 75 cm. Large, dark eagle. Brown overall, usually lighter than Imperial Eagle. Sometimes a rusty spot on nape. Juveniles light brown with mottling and spots; primaries darker than body. Claws weak.

Habits: Found in steppe and desert, not usually near arboreal vegetation. More common and more frequently seen than other eagles, although its number has been greatly reduced in the last decades. Builds flat nests with boughs, scraps of skins, and different material on the ground; usually on slope of hill, mound, haystack. Lays two or three white eggs spotted yellowish-brown (sometimes spotless) in April or May. Often perches on telegraph poles,

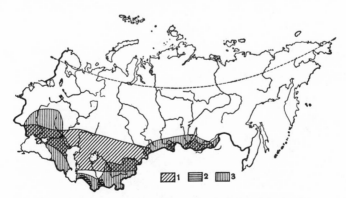

MAP 57. Steppe Eagle (1), Bonelli's Eagle (2), Booted Eagle (3)

tombstones, and other projections. Less cautious than other eagles. Call: hoarse barking. Like other eagles, hunts by watching prey in flight or waiting for it on the ground. Feeds on rodents (susliks, marmots, gerbils), hares, occasionally nestlings and reptiles. Included in the Red Data Book.

Range and distribution: South European USSR, Kazakhstan, Central Asia, Altai, Tuva, Transbaikal. Winters in Africa, India, China.

Similar species: Difficult to distinguish from Imperial and Golden Eagles. Identified unreliably by slightly lighter coloration, lack of light "hat" (which exists on occasion); juveniles distinguished by dark primaries.

133. GREATER SPOTTED EAGLE
Aquila clanga
(Bolshoy Podorlik)
Plate 8, Map 58

Field marks: 70 cm. Large (but smaller than Steppe Eagle), very dark eagle. Plumage of head and body black-brown; sometimes with whitish upper tail coverts. Juvenile's upperparts have light droplike spotting.

Habits: Found in forest and forest-steppe. Found in a variety of habitats: river valleys, pine forests, small steppe forests in wet places (*kolki*), forest swamps, and so on, but always prefers forested areas. Migratory. One of the most common eagles. Builds massive nests exclusively in trees. Lays two white eggs with intense red-brown spots in May. Call: ringing "kiak-kiak" and various trills. Hunts for prey in flight or perching on a bough. Feeds on variety of rodents (including voles), birds, frogs, and even insects.

Range and distribution: Greater part of European USSR except tundra and steppe; northern Kazakhstan, southern Siberia,

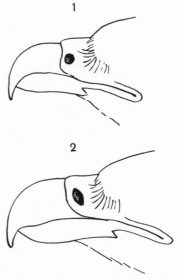

FIG. 32 Nostrils of Juvenile 1) Lesser Spotted Eagle and 2) Steppe Eagle

Transbaikal, Soviet Far East. Winters in southern Europe, southern Asia, and Egypt.

Similar species: Differs from Steppe, Imperial, and Golden eagles by very dark coloration and smaller size. Practically indistinguishable in the field from Lesser Spotted Eagle (a bit larger and darker).

134. LESSER SPOTTED EAGLE
Aquila pomarina
(Maly Podorlik)
Plate 8, Map 58

MAP 58. Lesser Spotted Eagle (1), Greater Spotted Eagle (2)

Field marks: 62 cm. Resembles Spotted Eagle, but smaller and lighter. Gray-brown; head gray. Juveniles: ocherish spots on upper parts becoming stripes on wings, nape ocherish.

Habits: Found in forests and forest-steppes, prefers foliage and mixed tree plantings, river valleys, peripheries of watery meadows. Migratory. Rare, common in places. Builds nest in trees. Lays two whitish or ocherish eggs with rusty mottling and speckling in April or May. Feeds on frogs, lizards, snakes, small rodents, young hares, birds of medium size, insects (grasshoppers, locusts).

Range and distribution: Western USSR, Caucasus, Transcaucasus. Wintering grounds in East Africa and Hindustan.

Similar species: Differs from Greater Spotted Eagle by gray-brown, lighter coloration, smaller size, and lack of white upper tail coverts (diagnostic features unreliable).

Hieraaetus

135. BONELLI'S EAGLE
Hieraaetus fasciatus
(Yastrebny Oryol)
Plate 8, Map 57

Field marks: 69 cm. Large eagle with long tail and contrasting coloration. Upperparts blackish-brown; underparts white or ocherish with narrow, elongated mottling; wide, dark band on outer tail. Juveniles: rusty or rufous-brown, without dark band on tail.

Habits: Found in arid mountains or plains, prefers places overgrown with xerophytic bushes. Nomadic, very rare in the USSR. Builds nests with boughs and sticks on rocks and in niches of precipices. Lays two white eggs with

Fig. 33 Nest of Greater Spotted Eagle

ocherish mottling in April. Feeds mostly on birds, more rarely on rodents, reptiles, insects. Flight swift, with frequent wing beats, seldom soars. Biology little studied.

Range and distribution: Central Asia. Winters within breeding range.

Similar species: Easily identifiable from majority of eagles by contrasting coloration, with white belly; from Booted Eagle by larger size and dark band on tail; from Short-toed Snake-Eagle by dark underwing coverts; from Osprey by lack of dark spots on bend of wing. Juveniles are difficult to differentiate at a distance.

136. BOOTED EAGLE
Hieraaetus pennatus
(Oryol-karlik)
Plate 9, Map 57

Field marks: 52 cm. Small, long-tailed eagle. Two color phases, light and dark. Light phase: upperparts brown, underparts ocherish-whitish with narrow, dark streaks; tail light and unbarred. Dark phase: birds are dark brown with lighter tail.

Habits: Found in forest and forest-steppe; in river valleys, range extends as far as desert zone. Prefers high, old deciduous, sometimes mixed forest stands in plains and mountains. Migratory. Common in places. Builds nests exclusively in trees, often uses nests of other birds (raptors, crows, herons). Lays two white or greenish-white eggs end of April to May. Call: high, thin "yug-yug-yug." Swift and dexterous raptor, frequently catches birds on the wing after frightening them or by flying from ambush. Maneuvers easily between trees. Feeds mostly on birds (from pigeon and magpie to small passerines), more rarely on rodents and frogs.

Range and distribution: Belorussia, central European USSR, Ukraine, Moldavia, Caucasus, Transcaucasus, Central Asia, Kazakhstan, southern Siberia. Winters in Africa and southern Asia.

Similar species: Differs from Short-toed Snake-Eagle, Osprey, Bonelli's Eagle, and some *buteos* by one-color tail; from Long-legged Buzzard by entirely black primaries and secondaries.

Neophron

137. EGYPTIAN VULTURE
Neophron percnopterus
(Stervyatnik)
Plate 8, Map 59

Field marks: 61 cm. Large bird with long, wide

MAP 59. Egyptian Vulture (1), Lammergeier (2)

wings and long, narrow wedge-shaped tail. Bill long and slightly hooked; claws blunt; skin on "face" orange-yellow, featherless; "collar" of pointed feathers on nape and neck. Adults: pure white with black primaries; juveniles: brown with rusty mottling on neck and back.
Habits: Found in low mountains and desert foothills, often near pastures and settlements. Migratory. Common in places. Nests in pairs, often in colonies of Griffon Vultures, in niches and small caves of cliff or forest precipices. Nest lined with scraps of skins, bits of wool, and so on. Lays two ocherish eggs with dense rusty-brown spots end of April to May. Hunts for food while soaring at a high altitude or perching on rocks. Flies with more frequent wing beats than other vultures. Forms flocks in places with abundance of food. Silent and rather cautious. Feeds on carrion and various waste, reptiles (turtles, lizards). Useful because it eliminates carrion. Its small number deserves protection.
Range and distribution: Crimea, Caucasus, Transcaucasus, Central Asia, Kazakhstan. Winters partly in Central Asia, partly migrates to Iran, Turkey, Iraq.
Similar species: Differs from other vultures and Lammergeier by smaller size; adults by white coloration with black primaries. Wedge-like tail, although less pointed than that of Lammergeier, is also a diagnostic feature.

Gypaëtus

138. LAMMERGEIER
Gypaëtus barbatus
(Borodach)
Plate 8, Map 59
Field marks: 108 cm. Very large bird with long,

narrow wings and long, noticeably wedge-shaped tail. In flight resembles a giant falcon, especially from a distance. In contrast to vultures, head and neck are entirely feathered, and the cere is protected by stubble; under the lower mandible there is a unique "beard" of stiffened feathers; legs feathered to the toes; back is dark colored or black; underparts light whitish with an ocherish suffusion. Head whitish with a wide black eyeline.
Habits: Found in high cliff areas. Nonmigratory and rare. Nests in cliffs, preferring inaccessible niches or hollows in overhanging precipices. Lays one or two ocherish eggs, often with brownish spots, from end of February to March. Hunts for food by flying along a planned route at a low height along mountain slopes or circling high in the air. Very wary. Call resembles a whistle. Feeds on carrion (hoofed animals, marmot), also feeds on bones, dried pieces of skin, and dried tendons. Apparently sometimes attacks live prey (young of hoofed animals, birds, turtles). Included in the Red Data Book.
Range and distribution: Mountains of the Caucasus, Central Asia, and Altai.
Similar species: Differs from all other large raptors by its "beard"; long, wedge-shaped tail; long, narrow wings.

Aegypius

139. CINEREOUS VULTURE
Aegypius monachus
(Chyorny Grif)
Plate 8, Map 60
Field marks: 103 cm. Very large bird with wide, long wings; head covered with brownish fluff; neck usually bare, skin bluish. At base of neck,

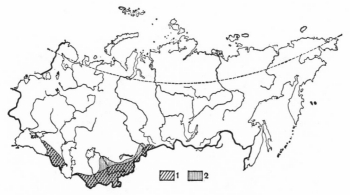

MAP 60. Eurasian Griffon (1), Cinereous Vulture (2)

a ruff of loose, pale brown feathers; nostrils rounded; cere bluish; plumage dark brown; primaries black. Juveniles dark blackish.

Habits: Found in and near mountains. Wanders, and can often be found in plains as well. Nonmigratory or nomadic. Not numerous, but in places with ample food, will collect in large flocks. Nests in upper forest regions or in bare mountains; occasionally found in small colonies. Enormous nests situated either in trees or in mountain slopes and rockslides. Lays one white egg, usually with reddish-brownish spots in March. Searches for food from a great height, where it soars on motionless wings for hours; rarely flies actively. Call: unique hissing. Feeds on carrion, but occasionally attacks live prey (reptiles, birds).

Range and distribution: Crimea, Caucasus, Central Asia, Kazakhstan, Altai.

Similar species: Differs from the Eurasian and Himalayan Griffons by dark plumage and dark fluff on the head.

Gyps

Very large bird with long, wide wings and short, rounded tail. Head and long neck covered with thick, whitish fluff. Distinctive ruff at base of neck. Nostrils are slits.

140. EURASIAN GRIFFON
Gyps fulvus
(Belogolovy Sip)
Plate 8, Map 60

Field marks: 100 cm. Light color overall; upperparts brownish gray; underparts rusty; primaries and tail black. Ruff is a thick, white, fluffy down (juveniles have loose brownish

feathers); rump dove-gray with light spots (not white). Juveniles darker.

Habits: Found in and near mountains; often seen in plains in search of food. Nomadic and fairly common. Nests in colonies. Nests situated in niches of inaccessible cliffs, precipices, and forests, or walls of ravines; more rarely in hollows protected above by cliff ledges. Nests made of twigs and lined with bits of plants. Lays one large white egg, end of February to March. Usually soars, flapping wings only at takeoff. Soars on immobile wings for hours, searching for food at a great height. Usually pulls in neck in flight, giving the Griffon Vulture a unique outline. Feeds exclusively on carrion of domestic and wild animals, sometimes near slaughterhouses.

Range and distribution: Crimea, Caucasus, Central Asia, Kazakhstan. Winters within nesting range.

Similar species: Differs from Himalayan Griffon by dark rump and fluffy ruff (in adult birds); from the Cinereous Vulture by its light ruff and fluff on the head. Juveniles nearly indistinguishable from juveniles of Himalayan Griffon.

141. HIMALAYAN GRIFFON
Gyps himalayensis
(Kumay)
Not illustrated, Map 61

Field marks: 100 cm. Greatly resembles Eurasian Griffon, but significantly lighter: upperparts dove-gray; underparts whitish; rump and underwing white; ruff of loose brownish feathers.

Habits: Found in high mountain regions. Nonmigratory. Very rare. Like the Eurasian Griffon, nests in niches in inaccessible cliff walls and precipices, but does not form colonies.

MAP 61. Northern Harrier (1), Pied Harrier (2), Himalayan
Griffon (3)

Lays one white egg in February. Habits and
flight same as Eurasian Griffon. Feeds exclusively on carrion. Biology little studied. Included in the Red Data Book.
Range and distribution: Mountains of Central
Asia and Kazakhstan.
Similar species: Differs from Eurasian Griffon
by its ruff (of feathers, not fluff), lighter color,
and white rump; from the Cinereous Vulture
by its lighter color and white fluff on the head.
Note: Some researchers consider the Himalayan Griffon to be a subspecies of the Eurasian
Griffon.

[A single vagrant of the **142.** INDIAN WHITE-RUMPED VULTURE (*Gyps bengalensis*). Lower back,
rump, and downy ruff white, remaining
plumage black.]

Circaëtus

143. SHORT-TOED SNAKE-EAGLE
Circaëtus gallicus
(Zmeeyad)
Plate 9, Map 55
Field marks: 65 cm. Large bird with long wings
and large head. Upperparts dark grayish-brownish; underparts nearly white; throat and
upper breast usually darker; tips of primaries
black; three or four indefinite, dark tail stripes.
In juveniles, underparts darker. Eyes yellow
and very large; plumage fluffy, loose; cere
bare.
Habits: Found in a variety of habitats from
forest to desert, preferring boreal vegetation
alternating with open, swampy areas or desert
and steppe regions. Migratory. Rare. Large,
loosely built nests situated in various trees (pine,

oak; in Central Asia, saxal trees, pistachios),
more rarely in cliffs. Lays single large, pure
white egg in April or May. Graceful flight with
extended soaring; often rises in the air, motionless, on an air current. Darker breast readily seen in flight. Usually stays silent. Call:
drawn-out "hee-ee-eeyo" or sad "deey-ee."
Feeds almost exclusively on snakes, lizards,
and frogs. Included in the Red Data Book.
Range and distribution: Southern half of European USSR, Central Asia, Kazakhstan. Winters in Africa, Southeast Asia.
Similar species: Differs from Bonelli's Eagle
by its light underwing; from the Booted Eagle
and the Long-legged Buzzard by its banded
tail; from the Osprey and the Rough-legged
Buzzard by the lack of dark spots at the bend
of the wing.

Circus

Large, graceful birds (larger than crows) with
long wings and tail. Long, thin claws, tarsus
bare. Ring of small, hard feathers surrounds
face, giving the bird the look of an owl.

144. NORTHERN HARRIER
Circus cyaneus
(Polevoy Lun)
Plate 10, Map 61
Field marks: 47 cm. Medium-sized harrier. Male
ash-gray; belly and wide rump stripe pure
white; tip of wing entirely dark. In female,
upperparts dark brownish; underparts light
ocherish with dark streaking; rump white; dark
bands on tail.
Habits: Found in a variety of habitats from
tundra to desert, but prefers fields, meadows,

river valleys, stands of reed, plains, and other open areas. Migratory. Common in places. Nests on the ground, often in swamps or in stands of reed. Flat nest made of grass. Lays four or five white eggs in mid-May. Call: a high "gee-gee-gee" or drawn-out, tremulous "prpee-err." Flight languid, gliding, and low to the ground. Takes prey by surprise. Feeds on small rodents, birds (passerines, sandpipers), lizards, and insects. Deserves protection.

Range and distribution: Greater part of USSR except tundra and true deserts. Winters in Crimea, Transcaucasus, southern Kazakhstan, and Central Asia.

Similar species: Male differs from other harriers by white rump and entirely black wing tip; females and juveniles nearly indistinguishable in the field (white rump somewhat larger, size a bit larger).

145. MONTAGU'S HARRIER
Circus pygargus
(Lugovoy Lun)
Plate 10, Map 62

Field marks: 42 cm. Resembles Northern Harrier, but male a darker dove-gray; rusty streaking on belly; narrow black wing stripe (underwing appears striped in flight); primaries entirely black. Females and juveniles same as Northern Harrier, but smaller; white rump is narrower and mottled.

Habits: Found in steppe and forest-steppe, settled areas, sometimes in forest. Prefers open, wet areas along river valleys, lakes, and swamps, and in thickets. Migratory. Common. Nests on the ground, usually near water, in reed thickets, tall grass. Lays three to six white eggs in early May. Flight and habits same as Northern Harrier. Call: sad "kek-kek-kek." Feeds on small rodents, birds, lizards, and many insects.

Range and distribution: Southern half of European USSR, southern West Siberia, Kazakhstan, Central Asia. Winters in Africa and Hindustan.

Similar species: Male differs from Northern and Pallid Harriers by striped underwing, black stripe on top of wing, and rusty mottling on belly; females and juveniles nearly indistinguishable in the field.

146. PALLID HARRIER
Circus macrourus
(Stepnoy Lun)
Plate 10, Map 62

Field marks: 46 cm. Resembles Northern Harrier but smaller and lighter; breast and belly pure white; dark wing tips; rump light, but not pure white. Appears white from a distance, and somewhat resembles a sea gull. Females and juveniles same as Northern Harrier.

Habits: Found in open areas (steppe, semi-steppe). Found in forest-steppe and near agricultural enterprises. Migratory. Common but number varies from year to year. Nests on the ground or on a hummock, occasionally on heaps of dry reed. Lays four to six white or light blue eggs, usually with dark brownish patches end of April to May. Flight same as other harriers, smooth, languid, unhurried. In spring the mating flight can readily be seen: the male flies high into the air, then, turning over, dives toward the nest with a loud cry. Call: tremulous "pirr," loud "gik-gik-gik," and other sounds. Feeds on small rodents (mice, voles, susliks), more rarely on birds and their eggs, insects, and lizards.

Range and distribution: South and central European USSR, Kazakhstan, Central Asia, southern Siberia to Tuva. Winters in Africa and south of Asia from Iraq to Burma.

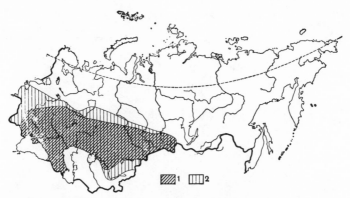

MAP 62. Pallid Harrier (1), Montagu's Harrier (2)

Similar species: Male differs from Northern Harrier by lighter color, lack of pure white rump, and reduced black wing tips; from Montagu's Harrier by the lack of wing bar and rusty mottling on belly. Females and juveniles practically indistinguishable from Montagu's Harrier.

147. PIED HARRIER
Circus melanoleucus
(Pegy Lun)
Plate 10, Map 61

Field marks: 44 cm. Male strikingly patterned: head, neck, upper breast, back, wingstripe, and primaries black; tail dove-gray; remainder of plumage white. Female dark brownish, underparts lighter with rusty clumps of feathers; mottled white rump.

Habits: Found in open areas, with a preference for damp places (river valleys, meadows, swamps, and lake basins). Migratory, in places common. Nests on the ground, in tall grass or bushes. Lays three to six white eggs end of May. Habits and methods of hunting similar to other harriers. Call: loud "kiiy-vee" (resembling call of lapwing). Feeds on small rodents, frogs, passerines and their nestlings.

Range and distribution: Soviet Far East, Transbaikal. Winters further south to Sri Lanka and Borneo.

Similar species: Male readily identifiable from other raptors by its distinct coloration; females and juveniles resemble Northern Harrier, but rump is not pure white and is narrower.

148. MARSH HARRIER
Circus aeruginosus
(Bolotny Lun)
Plate 10, Map 63

Field marks: 52 cm. Largest and darkest of the harriers. Upperparts of male chestnut-brownish with gray tail and wings; wing tips dark. Underparts rusty with mottling; head light ocherish; rump whitish. Female dark brownish with ocherish "cap"; white throat and ocher mottling on the shoulders; no white on rump. Juveniles resemble females.

Habits: Found in open areas, always in damp places. Migratory, in places nonmigratory. Common, sometimes numerous. Nests in swamps, stands of reed on lakes, more rarely in damp meadows. Bulky nest is made of dried reed, twigs, and small branches, and is situated in thickets, on heaps of dried reed, on hummocks, and on old haystacks. Lays four to six white eggs end of April to May. The characteristic mating display consists of flying high into the air, executing complex pirouettes and turns, then diving down. Call: nasal squeak, "pee-you, pee-you," and other sounds. When hunting, smooth, active flight alternates with prolonged glidings. Attack on prey is characteristic: bird rises high into the air with outstretched wings and, lowering its claws, dives straight down. Feeds on rodents (including muskrat), birds (ducks, sandpipers, rails), their nestlings and eggs, insects.

Range and distribution: European USSR except northern regions; Central Asia, Kazakhstan, southern Siberia including Transbaikal and southern Yakutia, Soviet Far East, Sakhalin Island. Winters in the USSR in Transcaucasus and Central Asia.

Similar species: Differs from all other harriers by darker color and lack of white rump.

[A vagrant **149.** BLACK-SHOULDERED KITE (*Elanus caeruleus*) was found near the town of Termez in Uzbekistan. It is a medium-sized raptor with ash-gray upper parts; white underparts; slightly forked tail; black shoulder patch on wing, and black near eye.]

MAP 63. Marsh Harrier

MAP 64. Peregrine Falcon (1), Saker Falcon (2)

Falco

Large and medium-size birds with long, pointed wings. Tail narrow and long. Legs bare. Characteristic tooth on upper mandible (Figure 34). Wing strokes rapid, and flight is decisive.

150. PEREGRINE FALCON
Falco peregrinus
(Sapsan)
Plate 11, Map 64

Field marks: 43 cm. Large falcon (larger than a pigeon), wings pointed; tail slightly wedge-shaped; contrasting coloration. Crown, back, wings, and tail dark; underparts light with narrow, banded pattern on the flanks, belly, and undertail coverts; light spotting on breast; dark moustachial stripe under eye; legs yellow. Juveniles more brown with heavily streaked underparts.

Habits: Found in a variety of habitats from tundra to mountains and desert. Prefers open spaces with small forests or cliffs. Nonmigratory or nomadic; migratory in the north. Rare, but common in the tundra. Nests in cliffs, shoreline precipices, bell towers, sometimes uses nests of other birds (crows, rooks). Lays two to four reddish-brownish eggs in April and May. Actively protects nest; wary away from nest. Call: halting "kyak-kyak-kyak." Feeds on medium-size birds (pigeons, crows, ducks), which it catches in flight; more rarely on small rodents. Included in the Red Data Book.

Range and distribution: Throughout the USSR, except not found on the islands of the Arctic Ocean. Winters in southern USSR.

Similar species: Differs from the Gyrfalcon and the Saker Falcon by the black moustache; from the Lanner Falcon by the dark head; from the Northern Hobby by the lack of rusty color in underparts.

Note: The Central Asian race of the Peregrine Falcon with a rusty head and light gray back is considered by some to be a separate species (*Falco pelegrinoides*), and is listed as such.

151. SAKER FALCON
Falco cherrug
(Baloban)
Plate 11, Map 64

Field marks: 49-54 cm. Large falcon (larger than a crow) with wide wings. Little contrast in coloration; overall ocherish or rusty brown;

FIG. 34 Bill of 1) Peregrine Falcon and 2) Northern Goshawk

underparts lighter, nearly white with drop-shaped streaks. Juveniles are heavily streaked. Moustache slightly visible; legs yellow. Dark brownish races occasionally found in the Altai mountain region and in Central Asia.

Habits: Found in forest-steppe, steppe, and desert. Prefers open spaces with cliffs or tall trees. Migratory or nomadic. Rare, in places common. Nests in trees or cliffs, often using nests of other birds. Lays three to five ocherish or reddish eggs with spots in April to May. Call: loud "kyak-kyak-kyak" or "keek-keek-keek." Feeds on rodents (susliks, hamsters, voles), medium-size and small birds (rooks, magpies, rollers, larks). Catches birds in flight. Used in falconry. Included in the Red Data Book.

Range and distribution: Southern half of USSR from the Ukraine to Transbaikal except the Caucasus. Winters in North Africa and south Asia. In the USSR, in the Transcaucasus, Central Asia, and Transbaikal.

Similar species: Differs from Peregrine Falcon by lack of wide, black moustache and non-contrasting coloration; from the Gyrfalcon by the rusty tones in plumage on legs (tarsus feathered halfway); from the Lanner Falcon by its lighter back.

152. LANNER FALCON
Falco biarmicus
(Sredizemnomorsky Sokol)
Plate 11, no map

Field marks: 43 cm. Large falcon (larger than a pigeon). Upperparts brownish-gray; underparts rusty or whitish with elongated, dark spots and streaks; top of head and crown rusty, occasionally dark; moustache barely visible.

Habits: Found in mountain steppe. Nonmigratory and very rare. Nests in March and April on cliffs, and lays three or four eggs.

Feeds on small and medium-size birds and rodents. Biology little studied. Included in the Red Data Book.

Range and distribution: Armenia, Azerbaijan.

Similar species: Differs from other large falcons by rusty crown in contrast to the very dark back.

153. GYRFALCON
Falco
(Krechet)
Plate 11, Map 65

Field marks: 51-56 cm. Largest falcon (significantly larger than a crow) with slightly blunted wings. Color varies from nearly white to dark brownish-gray upperparts and whitish underparts with mottling. Moustache not noticeable; legs yellow. Juveniles brownish.

Habits: Found on arctic islands and seashores, tundra and forest-tundra, in places in forest. Prefers river plains with steep slopes, seashores near cliffs with rookeries, and mountainous tundra. Nonmigratory or nomadic. Very rare. Does not build nest; uses nest of crow or Rough-legged Buzzard, usually situated in niches or overhanging precipices or cliffs; in forest-tundra occupies nests of crows in trees. Lays two or three, sometimes four or five ocherish eggs with rusty spots in April or early May. Call: hoarse "kyak-kyak-kyak" or drawn-out "keek-keek-keek." Very cautious. Feeds on birds (gulls, guillemots, ptarmigan, sandpipers) that it catches in flight; more rarely feeds on small rodents (lemmings). Included in the Red Data Book.

Range and distribution: Northern USSR from Kola Peninsula to Chukotski Peninsula, Kamchatka (although nest has not yet been found here), Komandorskiye Islands. Winters in central and southern USSR.

Similar species: Differs from Peregrine Falcon

MAP 65. Gyrfalcon (1), Northern Hobby (2)

FIG. 35 Gyrfalcon Nest on a Precipice

by less contrast in coloration and lack of black moustache; from the Saker Falcon by feathered tarsus (feathered two-thirds of the way); and by brownish-gray tones in plumage.

154. NORTHERN HOBBY
Falco subbuteo
(Cheglok)
Plate 11, Map 65
Field marks: 33 cm. Small (pigeon-size), very long wings, and short tail. Contrasting coloration: upperparts dark gray; head blackish; throat white; underparts light with definite elongated streaks; undertail coverts and thighs rusty; moustache wide and obvious. Juveniles duller with an ocher suffusion.
Habits: Found in forest and forest-steppe. Prefers open spaces alternating with clumps of trees, sometimes found in settled areas. Migratory, not numerous, common in places. Nests in trees, using nests of rooks, crows, and other raptors. Lays three, more rarely four or five ocherish eggs with thick reddish-brownish spots in June. Call: loud "klee-klee-klee." Feeds primarily on large insects and birds (swallows, starlings, thrushes), always catching prey in flight.
Range and distribution: Greater USSR except northern tundra regions. Winters in South Africa and Southeast Asia.
Similar species: Differs from Peregrine Falcon by rusty "pants"; from other small falcons by contrasting coloration and wide moustache.

155. MERLIN
Falco columbarius
(Derbnik)
Plate 11, Map 66
Field marks: 28 cm. Small, short-winged falcon. Upperparts and head dove-gray; underparts whitish rusty with elongated streaking. Female upperparts brownish; underparts ocherish with elongated and drop-shaped streaks; head usually same color as back. Tip of tail with broad dark band. Juvenile's upperparts dark brown.
Habits: Found in variety of habitat from tundra to desert. Prefers open spaces mixed with wooded areas. Migratory. Somewhat rare. Nests on the ground, in cliffs, in trees, in nests of other birds, sometimes builds its own nest. Lays three to six ocherish eggs with thick, reddish-brownish mottling May to beginning of June. Call: halting "ke-kek-kek." Hunts in a low, swift

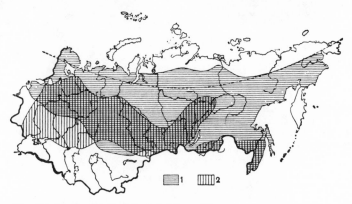

MAP 66. Merlin (1), Red-footed Falcon (2)

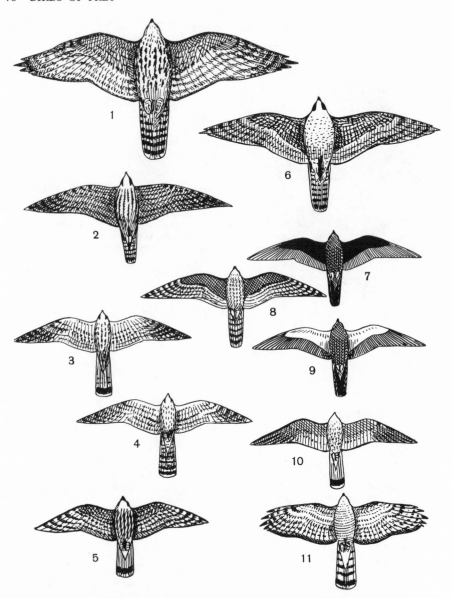

FIG. 36 RAPTORS IN FLIGHT
1. Gyrfalcon   2. Northern Hobby   3. Common Kestrel (male)   4. Common Kestrel
(female)   5. Merlin   6. Peregrine Falcon   7. Red-footed Falcon (male)   8. Red-footed
Falcon (female)   9. Red-footed Falcon (Amur form)   10. Lesser Kestrel   11. Eurasian
Sparrowhawk

flight. Feeds on small birds (pipits, larks, wagtails, etc.) and rodents.

Range and distribution: North European USSR and Siberia except most northerly tundra; Soviet Far East, Sakhalin Island. Winters south as far as North Africa, India, and Southeast China. In the USSR, along southern borders.

Similar species: Differs from female Red-footed Falcon by lack of moustache; females and juveniles of steppe regions in the south, by black claws and smaller size.

156. RED-FOOTED FALCON
Falco vespertinus
(Kobchik)
Plate 11, Map 66

Field marks: 28 cm. Small, pointed-wing falcon. Male slate-black with rusty "pants" and undertail; legs red. In female, upperparts gray with darker bands; underparts ocherish; head rusty; easily seen small moustache. Juveniles, upperparts dark, underparts light ocherish with muddled elongated streaks; head dull rusty. Eastern race is colored differently: male has white underwing; female, gray head, white cheeks and throat.

Habits: Found in forest-steppe and steppe, in settled areas. Prefers open spaces alternating with woods. Migratory. Common. Nests in trees, using nests of rooks, crows, ravens, often forms colonies. Lays three to five rusty red mottled eggs end of May to June. Not cautious. Call: loud "kee-kee-kee." Feeds in flight on insects (locust, grasshopper, bugs), usually flying low to the ground. Also feeds on small rodents.

Range and distribution: Central regions from Ukraine and Kazakhstan to the east as far as north Baikal area. Winters in East and South Africa.

Similar species: Female differs from Merlin by its rusty head and lack of broad subterminal band.

Note: Some ornithologists consider the eastern race (*F. amurensis*), as a separate species. It is found in the Transbaikal and the Soviet Far East.

157. COMMON KESTREL
Falco tinnunculus
(Obyknovennaya Pustelga)
Plate 11, Map 67

Field marks: 34 cm. Small falcon (smaller than a pigeon) with long wings and long tail. In male, upperparts reddish-brownish with round spots; underparts ocherish with elongated streaks; head gray or dove-gray; moustache not prominent; dark subterminal band. Claws black. In female, upperparts rusty rufous with dark barring; head nearly same color as back. Juveniles paler, mottling diffused.

Habits: Found in a variety of habitats from taiga and forest-tundra to mountains and desert. Found in open spaces alternating with wooded areas, sometimes found in settled areas. Migratory. Common. Nests in niches of cliffs, in tree hollows, on the ground, in attics of houses, in trees in old nests of crows and rooks; sometimes forms colonies. Lays four to six (sometimes even eight or nine) ocherish eggs with reddish-brownish speckles end of April to May. Call: loud "kee-kee-kee" or "klee-klee-klee." Often pauses in flight with uplifted wings and lowered tail, hovering in midair. Feeds on mouselike mammals and insects.

Range and distribution: Greater USSR except northern regions. Winters in Crimea, Caucasus, Transcaucasus, southern Kazakhstan, Central Asia.

Similar species: Differs from Lesser Kestrel by

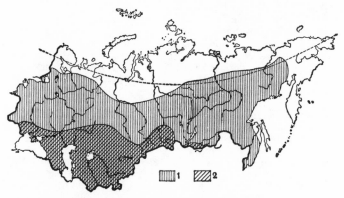

MAP 67. Common Kestrel (1), Lesser Kestrel (2)

its larger size, spotted upperparts (in male) and black claws.

158. LESSER KESTREL
Falco naumanni
(Stepnaya Pustelga)
Plate 11, Map 67
Field marks: 26 cm. Resembles Eurasian Kestrel but smaller and more solid looking. In male, upperparts reddish-brown without spotting; head dark grayish; underparts with small infrequent spots; black subterminal band on tail; claws white; moustache not noticeable.
Habits: Found in variety of habitat from forest-steppe to mountains and desert. Prefers open spaces with outcroppings of cliffs and precipitous slopes. Migratory. Common, in places numerous. Nests in cliffs, rockpiles, in rubble, precipices, or tree hollows; often forms colonies. Lays four to six yellowish-red eggs with dark spots end of May to June. Habits same as Eurasian Kestrel. Feeds on insects (locusts, horseflies, and beetles), more rarely on mouselike mammals.
Range and distribution: South European USSR, Kazakhstan, Central Asia, southern West Siberia, Transbaikal. Winters in Africa, Arabian Peninsula, Iran, and Hindustan.
Similar species: Differs from Eurasian Kestrel by smaller size, white claws, and, in the male, brighter upperparts without black spotting.

[Vagrants of **159.** LAGGAR FALCON (*Falco jugger*) were noted twice in the USSR (in Turkmenia). Resembles Saker Falcon, but smaller and darker, with grayish-brown upperparts and white breast with dark brown flanks, thighs, and belly. In Estonia, an American Kestrel (*Falco sparverius*), was collected; possibly escaped from a zoo.]

GALLINACEOUS BIRDS: *Galliformes*

Birds from very large to small sizes, sturdily built with short, blunt wings. In some species, tail is long; in others, short or hardly noticeable. Feet strong, adaptable to ground locomotion. In grouse and ptarmigan, feathering reaches the claws, but in pheasants, the legs are bare. Females usually smaller and colored differently from males (sexually dimorphic). Usually live on the ground, flying very little, inhabiting variety of habitat from tundra to mountains and desert. Monogamous or polygamous. Eggs of usual or shortened ovoid shape.

Lagopus

Medium-size (crow-size) birds. Tail slightly rounded.

160. WILLOW PTARMIGAN
Lagopus lagopus
(Belaya Kuropatka)
Plate 15, Map 68
Field marks: 38 cm. In winter, white with black tail; in spring, male is white with rusty brown head and neck; in summer, male and female are rusty brownish with barred pattern, wings and belly white; eye wattles red; claws in winter whitish.
Habits: Found in tundra, forest-tundra, taiga, forest-steppe and mountains. Nonmigratory or nomadic. Common. In spring, stays in pairs; in fall and winter, in flocks. Nests in thickets in plains and hilly tundra, near mossy swamps, and in birch groves. Nests on the ground, in a dry place under protection of bushes. Nest situated in a small depression. Lays six to twelve brightly patterned, reddish eggs with brown spots end of May and later. Female allows close approach to nest, then flushes and attempts to distract the intruder from the nest. Male stays in vicinity of nest at breeding time. Call of male: harsh, loud cry resembling laughter, "kerr-er-er-err," and after, a softer "keebeoo-keebeoo." Stays primarily on the ground but occasionally perches in trees. In winter, buries itself in snow to spend the night. Takeoff from ground noisy, flight swift with frequent wing beats and gliding. Feeds on buds, leaves, and shoots of various plants; berries, occasionally insects.
Range and distribution: Northern half of European USSR, north Kazakhstan, Siberia.
Similar species: Differs from Rock Ptarmigan in winter by lack of black eye stripe; in summer, by rusty tones in coloration (females difficult to distinguish from a distance).

161. ROCK PTARMIGAN
Lagopus mutus
(Tundryanaya Kuropatka)
Plate 15, Map 68
Field marks: 34 cm. Resembles Willow Ptarmigan but smaller; bill narrower; in winter, males have black stripe between bill and eye; in summer the plumage is predominantly gray instead of rust-colored. In summer, female is

MAP 68. Willow Ptarmigan (1), Rock Ptarmigan (2)

grayer than Willow Ptarmigan. In winter, claws blackish.

Habits: Found in mountainous tundra. Non-migratory. Not numerous, common in places. Stays in flocks; at breeding times in pairs. Nests near rockpiles with sparse lichens and along sides of hills in dry thicket-filled tundra. Nest is a shallow depression under protection of a rock, hummock, or bush. Nest lined with leaves and grass with a few feathers. Lays six to twelve light ocherish eggs with a thick chocolate speckling from end of June. Eggs lighter in color and more yellow than Willow Ptarmigan's. At the threat of danger, leads intruder away from the nest. Stays on the ground, often perching on high rocks. Flight same as Willow Ptarmigan. Trusting, and allows close approach. Call of male: hoarse cry resembling "krraad-kre-re-reee," entirely dissimilar to the laughter of the Willow Ptarmigan. Feeds on buds and shoots of willows and dwarf birch; berries and leaves; and flowers of grasses.

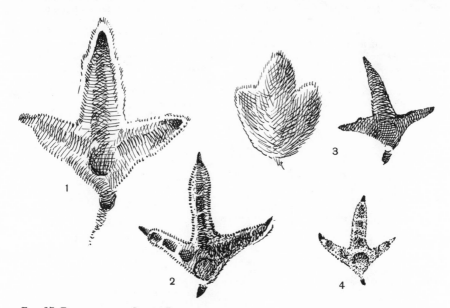

FIG. 37 FOOTPRINTS OF LARGE BIRDS

1. Western Capercaillie   2. Northern Black Grouse   3. Willow Ptarmigan (winter and summer)   4. Northern Hazelhen

Range and distribution: Kola Peninsula, northern Siberia, mountains of East Siberia, Transbaikal, Tuva, Altai.

Similar species: Differs from Willow Ptarmigan in winter by black eye stripe (in male); in summer, by gray tones in plumage. Females nearly indistinguishable both in summer and winter plumage.

Lyrurus

Large (chicken-size) bird. In males, tail is lyre-shaped.

162. NORTHERN BLACK GROUSE

Lyrurus tetrix
(Teterev)
Plate 14, Map 69

Field marks: 42-61 cm. Male shiny black with white undertail coverts and narrow wing bar; lyre-shaped tail tip; red eye wattle. Female brownish-rusty with fine black barring.

Habits: Found in woods and forest-steppe, sometimes in steppe. Nonmigratory, nomadic in places. Common. Does not form pairs (polygamous), nests in thin forest with thick undergrowth, in forest clearings and tree-harvesting areas, avoiding dense, tall forest. Nest is a small depression, usually situated under the protection of fallen branches or thick bushes. Lays five to nine ocherish eggs with red-brown spots from early May. Female sits firmly on nest, allowing close approach. In breeding season, from mid-April, males collect in flocks (leks) in fields, cut-over areas, and mossy swamps in early morning for breeding displays. Mating call is a loud muttering heard from a great distance and reminiscent of the murmuring of pigeons, along

FIG. 38 Northern Black Grouse Chick

with a unique sound resembling "chuffshee." Females visit mating grounds; call: loud "ko-ko-ko." Mating displays have also been observed in fall, beginning at the end of August. In winter, Northern Black Grouse stays in large flocks in birch groves, spending the night under the snow. Very cautious. Flight fast with frequent wing beats and gliding; takeoff very noisy. Feeds on various parts of vegetation, insects, berries; in winter on birch buds and catkins.

Range and distribution: North European USSR except tundra; north Kazakhstan, West Siberia, south of East Siberia, Soviet Far East.

Similar species: Differs from Caucasian Black Grouse by white undertail and wing bar; female by larger size (wing no smaller than 220 cm.). Not found in same range.

MAP 69. Northern Black Grouse (1), Caucasian Black Grouse (2)

163. CAUCASIAN BLACK GROUSE
Lyrurus mlokosiewiczi
(Kavkazky Teterev)
Plate 14, Map 69

Field marks: 50 cm. Resembles Northern Black Grouse, but smaller; dull black; lyre-shaped tail outward and downward curved. Female rusty brownish with black barring.

Habits: Found in alpine and subalpine areas of mountains; winters by moving down the mountain into forested zone. Nonmigratory, sometimes nomadic; rare. Nests in thickets of rhododendron, arborescent juniper, and low-growing birches. Nest situated under bush or rock. Lays five to eight pale ocherish eggs with dark spots end of May. Nesting and hatching behavior same as Northern Black Grouse. Spring mating ritual unusual: males gather singly or in small flocks in early morning and silently hop around, flapping their wings. Stays hidden. In summer, stays singly; in winter, in small flocks, the males separate from the females. Wary, but often becomes disoriented in thick grass and flushes noisily from underfoot. Feeds on leaves, buds, seeds, and flowers of various plants; in winter, on needles and berries of arborescent juniper. Included in the Red Data Book.

Range and distribution: Caucasus and Transcaucasus.

Similar species: Differs from Northern Black Grouse by lack of white undertail and wing bar, and by shape of the tail; females indistinguishable by color, but Caucasian Black Grouse is significantly smaller. The two species are not found in the same range.

Tetrao

Very large, massive bird. Tail long, slightly rounded.

164. WESTERN CAPERCAILLIE
Tetrao urogallus
(Glukhar)
Plate 14, Map 70

Field marks: 67-95 cm. Male grayish black with dark brownish wings and white spots on belly; bill whitish; wing lining white. Female brownish-rusty with black barring.

Habits: Found in old coniferous and mixed (more rarely deciduous) forests in plains and hills. Nonmigratory. Not numerous but common in places. Polygamous, does not form pairs. Nests in forests of various types, but prefers mossy swamp edges and burned areas in inaccessible forested areas with thick undergrowth. Nests under a bush or by a fallen tree. Lays five to nine ocherish eggs with red-brownish spots from early May. Female sits on nest firmly, immobile, and is nearly invisible, melting into the background. Spring mating rituals occur in the same places year after year, usually near mossy swamps with pines, but occasionally in dry pine or fir forest, in mixed and even deciduous forest. The height of the mating season comes at the end of April. The Western Capercaillies arrive at the mating grounds in the evening, and mating calls begin before dawn, while it is still dark. Display call is a unique clicking resembling a distant "kadoo-kadoo," melting into a short trill, then a scraping noise "skzheeshee-skzhee-

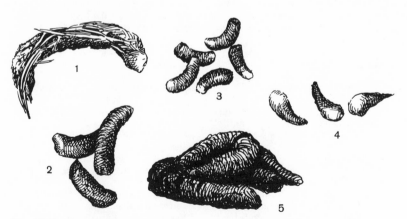

FIG. 39 SCATS OF GAMEBIRDS
1. Western Capercaillie 2. Northern Black Grouse 3. Northern Hazelhen
4. Gray Partridge 5. Mute Swan

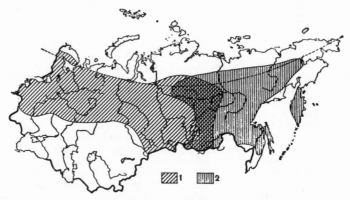

MAP 70. Western Capercaillie (1), Black-billed Capercaillie (2)

shee-skzheeshee." While calling, the bird is apparently oblivious to its surroundings. It gives its display call in trees or on the ground, while fanning its tail, slightly raising its wings, and holding its head high with bill pointing upward. Song is a ferocious "borodoo." Call: a halting and a distant "bak-bak-bak." In summer, stays hidden in dense places; in winter, often forms flocks. Very wary. Flight rapid, with frequent gliding; takeoff from the ground very noisy, positively deafening. Feeds in trees or on the ground; in autumn, on larch and aspen; in winter, on pines. Feeds on various parts of grasses, and berries; in winter, on pine needles.

Range and distribution: Northern half of European USSR except tundra; Siberia to Transbaikal in the east.

Similar species: Differs from Black-billed Capercaillie by white bill and white mottling on tail; female, by rusty upper breast (indistinguishable in the field).

165. BLACK-BILLED CAPERCAILLIE
Tetrao urogalloides
(Kamenny Glukhar)
Plate 14, Map 70

Field marks: 68-97 cm. Resembles Western Capercaillie, but smaller; white spots on back and rump; tail feathers black; bill black. Female darker and browner than female of Northern Black Grouse.

Habits: Found in plains and mountainous taiga; on the Kamchatka Peninsula, prefers birch forests. Nonmigratory. Not numerous, but common in places. Polygamous, and does not form pairs. Usually nests in deciduous taiga, but sometimes in forests of Siberian pine (*Pinus sibiricus*), pine, and deciduous woods. Prefers thin mixed forests in plains and river val-

leys. Nest situated in the open, usually by the trunk of a tree. Lays six or seven ocherish-brownish eggs with small dark spots end of May. Nesting female allows close approach. Spring breeding ritual begins in late April or early May. Stays on the ground, beginning mating call before sunrise. Display call is an odd clicking, becoming a short trill. Contrary to folklore, the ability of the bird to hear is not lost during these displays. Feeds on shoots and buds of larch trees, and various bushes, berries, insects.

Range and distribution: Eastern Siberia to the east from Lake Baikal. Not found in tundra or forest-tundra.

Similar species: Differs from Western Capercaillie by white spots on the back, black bill, and black tail feathers without mottling; female by darker color, particularly on the upper breast. Occasional hybrids between the two species are sometimes found.

Falcipennis

166. SIBERIAN SPRUCE GROUSE
Falcipennis falcipennis
(Dikusha)
Plate 15, Map 71

Field marks: 37 cm. Size of a crow. Outer primaries hard, narrow, and pointed. Brownish-black with white spots on the back and white banded pattern on the breast; white tail stripe. Female brownish with ocherish banded rippling pattern and lighter underparts.

Habits: Found in dense forests of the taiga. Nonmigratory. Rare. Stays in pairs. Nests in silver fir, fir, and deciduous forests, preferring areas near plains, swamp edges, and other areas lush with berry bushes. Lays six to ten

MAP 71. Northern Hazelhen (1), Siberian Spruce Grouse (2)

brownish, finely mottled eggs end of May. Displays by the males on mating grounds in spring consist of fanning the tail, stretching the neck, and hopping while making howling noises. Very trusting, completely fearless of humans, and allows close approach to nest. Feeds on needles of silver fir and on berries. Included in the Red Data Book.

Range and distribution: Southeast Siberia, Far East.

Similar species: Differs from Northern Hazelhen by darker color.

Bonasa

167. NORTHERN HAZELHEN
Tetrastes bonasia
(Ryabchik)
Plate 15, Map 71

Field marks: 66 cm. Larger than a pigeon. Crest on head; brownish-gray with rusty sides and dark barring; black subterminal band on tail broken in center with brown. Male has a black throat; female, white.

Habits: Found in coniferous, mixed, and deciduous forests. Nonmigratory. Common. Stays in pairs (monogamous). Nests in forest with thick undergrowth and thick forest floor near small open fields, along shores of forest streams with alder thickets, and slopes of precipices with thickets of nut trees. Nest is a small depression in the ground, usually under a bush, fallen tree trunk, or stump. Lays seven to ten reddish-yellow eggs speckled brown, beginning of May and later. Female sits on nest so firmly that it is possible to touch her. Mating rituals begin from mid-April. At this time, males from nearby pairs flutter from tree to tree noisily, calling each other to fight. Call: thin,

drawn-out whistle, ending in a trill "teee-teee-tetttereevee." Female: "teee-teeteervee." Flight swift and maneuverable with frequent wing beats and long glides; takeoff noisy, perching in tree quiet. Not wary, and readily attracted with bait. Feeds primarily on the ground; in winter, feeds in trees. Eats buds, seeds, and leaves of various plants; insects, berries, catkins of alder and birch.

Range and distribution: Northern half of European USSR (except tundra); Siberia to the south of the forest-tundra zones; Soviet Far East.

Similar species: Differs from Siberian Spruce Grouse by light gray color.

Coturnix

168. COMMON QUAIL
Coturnix coturnix
(Perepel)
Plate 15, Map 72

Field marks: 17 cm. Smallest bird in the pheasant family (size of a starling). Tail short; ocherish-brownish with dark and light mottling; belly light. In males, throat brownish (white in autumn); in females, whitish; mottled breast.

Habits: Found in meadows and fields in a variety of habitats; steppe. Migratory. Common or numerous. Does not form pairs (polygamous). Nests in open areas with lush vegetation found in grain and other fields, wet and dry meadows near flat depressions in steppe, usually found in farming areas. Nest is a small depression lined with grass. Lays seven to fifteen pear-shaped olive-ocherish eggs with large brownish spots from mid-May. Spends most of its life on the ground; stays hidden in thick

FIG. 40 GALLINACEOUS BIRDS IN FLIGHT
1. Common Pheasant   2. Northern Black Grouse (male)   3. Willow Ptarmigan (summer)   4. Northern Hazelhen

grass; does not perch in trees; seen rarely. Flushes unwillingly nearly out from underfoot, and soon drops into the grass again. Flight straight and swift, with frequent wing beats. Call of male: the well-known "peet-peebeet" from a short distance; also a hoarse "kva, va-kva-va;" female, quiet "ryou-ryou." Feeds on various seeds and insects.

Range and distribution: Southern half of USSR except deserts of Central Asia. Winters in Africa and southern Asia.

Similar species: Differs from other quail and pheasants by small size; from the Yellow-legged Buttonquail by a presence of rear claw, elongated mottling on back.

Note: Some ornithologists consider the eastern races of Common Quail (from Lake Baikal to Soviet Far East) to be a separate species: i.e., Japanese Quail (*Coturnix japonicus*). Differs by smaller size, brighter colors (red-brownish throat) and particularly by its call, which is a soft, muted "choo-peet-trrr."

Ammoperdix

169. SEE-SEE PARTRIDGE
Ammoperdix griseogularis
(Pustynnaya Kuropatka)
Plate 15, Map 72

Field marks: 26 cm. Smaller than a pigeon. Pinkish-gray with a yellowish belly; light eye line capped with a black stripe; brown and

black diagonal lines at the sides; bill orange. Females duller and finely barred.

Habits: Found in desert lowlands. Nonmigratory and not numerous. Stays in pairs or flocks. Nests on dry, rocky mountain slopes with sparse vegetation; in forest areas with occasional cliffs. Nests on the ground, in a niche under a rock. Lays eight to twelve ocherish eggs from mid-May and later. Feeds and stays on the ground, flies up reluctantly and only for a short distance. Usually runs quickly from danger upslope, fluttering up among the rocks. Silent and not wary. Call: light whistle resembling "teetee-teetee" and loud "kvak-kvak-kvak." Feeds on buds and seeds of various vegetation and insects.

Range and distribution: Central Asia.

Similar species: Differs from Chukar Partridge by smaller size; at a distance by absence of black-outlined white throat.

Alectoris

170. CHUKAR PARTRIDGE
Alectoris chukar
(Keklik)
Plate 15, Map 73

Field marks: 37 cm. Size of a crow. Ash-gray with pinkish tones; whitish throat surrounded by a narrow black band that continues in a stripe through the eye and across the fore-

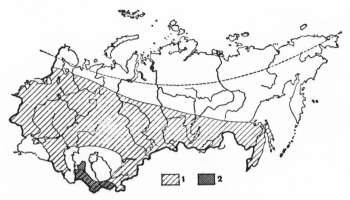

MAP 72. Common Quail (1), See-see Partridge (2)

head; black, brown and white stripes on the sides. Bill, eye ring, and legs red.

Habits: Found on rocky, mountainous slopes higher than the forest belt; desert lowlands near mountains. Nonmigratory. Common and numerous in places. Monogamous, stays in pairs or flocks. Nests in rocky niches on cliff slopes, near rockslides, near clumps of arborescent juniper and pistachio forests. Prefers areas with poor grassy vegetation. Nest situated on the ground, under protection of a bush or rock, sometimes in a niche or crevice near a precipice. Lays seven to eleven ocherish eggs with small indefinite spots from mid-April and later. Feeds on the ground, does not perch in trees, flight swift and maneuverable; take-off noisy, but quieter than that of the gallinaceous forest birds. Runs quickly from danger, usually upslope. Fairly cautious. Raucous voice: loud, frequent singing increasing in speed "kok, kok, kok, kok-kok-kok." Feeds on

green parts of various plants and on insects.

Range and distribution: Mountains of the Crimea, Caucasus, and Transcaucasus; Central Asia, Altai, Tuva.

Similar species: Differs from the See-see Partridge by larger size, black-banded white throat, and strongly patterned stripes at the sides.

Perdix

Size of a pigeon. Tail short. Legs yellow-brownish or grey; bill brownish.

171. GRAY PARTRIDGE
Perdix perdix
(Seraya Kuropatka)
Plate 15, Map 74

Field marks: 29 cm. Upperparts brownish, finely barred with narrow streaking; underparts gray; sides of head, throat, stripes on sides, and outer

MAP 73. Chukar Partridge (1), Black Francolin (2)

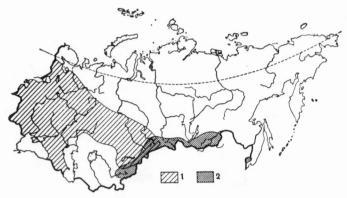

MAP 74. Gray Partridge (1), Daurian Partridge (2)

tail feathers rusty; belly white in males (sometimes in females), with horseshoe-shaped rusty brownish spot, which is characteristic of this species.

Habits: Found in open spaces alternating with overgrown thickets, in a variety of habitats from forest to desert, and settled areas. Nonmigratory. Common or numerous in places. Stays in pairs (monogamous); at wintertime in flocks. Nests at edges of fields overgrown with thickets or tall weeds, in ravines and gullies in steppe, in dry meadows, young forests along side meadows, clumps of birch, and islands of woods in steppe. Nests on the ground hidden in tall grass or under a bush. Lays fourteen to twenty (even up to twenty-four) eggs of a uniform grayish or ocherish-olive color, end of April and later. Incubation and parental duties shared by both parents; bird sits on nest firmly, flushing reluctantly only on close approach. Feeds on the ground in open places. Flight straight and swift; flock takes off from the ground with a characteristic fluttering noise. Call: loud, repetitive "kirr-rek, kirr-rek." Feeds on seeds and shoots of various plants (including cereal grains), insects.

Range and distribution: Southern half of European USSR and West Siberia, northern Kazakhstan.

Similar species: Differs from Daurian Partridge by brownish spot on belly, lack of "beard" (in winter plumage), and lack of ocherish tones in breast.

172. DAURIAN PARTRIDGE
Perdix dauuricae
(Borodataya Kuropatka)
Plate 15, Map 74
Field marks: 28 cm. Resembles Gray Partridge, but side of head, throat, and upper breast

ocherish; spot on belly is black or dark brownish; in fall and winter clumps of stiff, narrow feathers form along the sides of the chin ("beard").

Habits: Habitat, numbers, period of nesting and nesting habits, number and coloration of eggs, habits, call, and feeding same as Gray Partridge. But in comparison, prefers drier and rockier places with thin vegetation, and is often found in the lowlands of mountain regions.

Range and distribution: Central Asia, Kazakhstan, Altai, Tuva, Transbaikal, Soviet Far East.

Similar species: Differs from Gray Partridge by black or dark brownish spot on belly, ocherish upper breast, and "beard" (in fall and winter).

Francolinus

173. BLACK FRANCOLIN
Francolinus francolinus
(Turach)
Plate 15, Map 73
Field marks: 37 cm. Size of a pigeon or slightly larger. Distinctively colored, black with white spotting on nape, spots becoming larger on the flanks; chestnut "collar"; white spot on cheek; bill black; legs reddish. Female with paler upperparts, chestnut nape; breast and belly lighter with heavy black spots.

Habits: Found in plains with thickets. Nonmigratory, rare. Stays in pairs (monogamous). Nests in very thick bushes in overgrowth; often on mats of broken reed along river banks and irrigation canals alternating with fields; in settled areas, along plantings of wheat and cotton. Nest is a shallow depression, nearly unlined; situated under protection of a thick bush or under grasses. Lays six to ten dark olive-brownish eggs with small white dots end of April to May. Female sits on nest; both parents raise chicks. In spring, male displays to the female by turning circles in front of hen, tossing his head and fanning his tail, often hops up and flaps his wings with a unique cry. Stays on the ground, hidden; prefers to run from danger, and will fly up noisily only out of necessity. Bird in flight rises straight up, then flies horizontally and lands soon thereafter. Planes before landing. Feeds on seeds, berries, and shoots of various plants; insects. Included in the Red Data Book.

Range and distribution: Transcaucasus and southwest Turkmenia, Central Asia.

Similar species: Differs from all other gallinaceous birds by distinctive spotted coloration.

Tetraogallus

Large, sturdily built bird.

174. CAUCASIAN SNOWCOCK
Tetraogallus caucasicus
(Kavkazky Ular)
Plate 14, Map 75

Field marks: 56 cm. Grayish with darker streaks on back; black striations on breast, and rufous and whitish heavy streaks on flanks and belly; belly is dark; throat and frontal part of head white; bill black; feet orange-yellow.

Habits: Found in high mountains from alpine meadows and higher. Nonmigratory and scarce. Stays in pairs; in small flocks at nesting time. Nests on steep slopes with rockslides, talus slopes, small rocky meadows. Nest is on

the ground under the protection of a rock or cliff. Lays five to eight grayish-ocher eggs with minute brownish spots; from end of April. The female sits tight on the nest and flushes reluctantly. Very wary during nonbreeding season. Feeds on the ground, runs quickly. The bird generally runs upslope, and flies down or along a slope. Its flight is absolutely straight and consists almost exclusively of gliding. Clamorous voice: either a loud and carrying whistle, or a rough, hoarse clucking resembling "kok-kogok-kok-kok." Flocks of snowcocks often associate with herds of mountain goats. It feeds on various parts of grassy plants. Included in the Red Data Book.

Range and distribution: Caucasus.

Similar species: Differs from the Himalayan Snowcock by its dark breast; from the Caspian Snowcock, by blackish markings on the breast; from the others (which are geographically isolated) by its dark belly.

175. CASPIAN SNOWCOCK
Tetraogallus caspius
(Kaspiysky Ular)
Plate 14, Map 75

Field marks: 56 cm. Resembles Caucasian Snowcock but has black rounded spots on upper breast; belly more brownish.

Habits: Found in alpine and subalpine regions of mountains. Nonmigratory. Scarce. Nests along steep slopes with rockslides, hanging cliffs, in dry meadows in thickets of rhododendron. Period of nesting, breeding habits, habits, call, feeding apparently same as Caucasian Snowcock. Included in the Red Data Book.

Range and distribution: Caucasus, Transcaucasus, Turkmenia (Kopet-Dag Mountains).

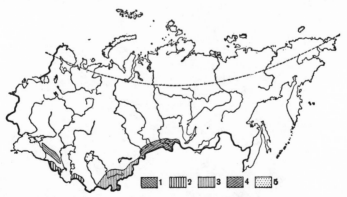

MAP 75. Snowcocks: Caucasian (1), Caspian (2), Himalayan (3), Altai (4), Tibetan (5)

Similar species: Differs from Caucasian Snowcock by rounded spots on upper breast and elongated mottling on belly; from other snowcocks by dark upper breast (also, geographically isolated).

176. HIMALAYAN SNOWCOCK
Tetraogallus himalayensis
(Gimalaysky Ular)
Plate 14, Map 75

Field marks: 59 cm. Resembles Caspian Snowcock, but upper breast whitish with horizontal black spots; head lighter; brown "collar" on neck.

Habits: Found in alpine and subalpine regions of mountains. Nonmigratory or nomadic. Somewhat scarce. Stays in flocks, pairs off in spring. Nests along steep slopes with cliff outcroppings, in thickets of arborescent juniper, and in meadows. Nest situated on ground, under an overhanging rock, under a single pine tree, or in niches of cliffs. Lays seven to eleven brownish-gray or grayish-ocher eggs with small and large brown spots; from end of April. Only the female incubates, sitting tight on the nest and allowing close approach. Extremely wary at other times. Feeds on the ground, moving along the slope with a slow pace, runs rarely and unwillingly. If danger threatens, walks away at an even pace; upon reaching an outcropping or high cliff, flies down. Flight, as with other snowcocks, is unusual. Bird launches itself downward and immediately changes to a gliding flight along the slope, seldom flapping its wings. Call varied: melodic whistle; cry, reminiscent of the call of the Chukar Partridge; clucking; and in flight the bird cries "gul-gul-gul." Feeds on various parts of grassy and shrubby plants, also on bulbs, flowers, insects; in winter, on thin branchlets and seeds.

Range and distribution: Mountains of Central Asia and Kazakhstan.

Similar species: Differs from the Caucasian and Caspian Snowcocks by whitish upper breast with black horizontal spots; from the Tibetan and Altai Snowcocks by dark belly.

177. ALTAI SNOWCOCK
Tetraogallus altaicus
(Altaysky Ular)
Plate 14, Map 75

Field marks: 58 cm. Resembles other snowcocks, but belly white; upper breast gray with black horizontal spots.

Habits: Found in alpine and subalpine regions of mountains. Scarce and nonmigratory. Habits, nesting, peculiarities of behavior, call, feeding apparently same as other snowcocks. On the whole, biology little known. Included in the Red Data Book.

Range and distribution: Altai and Sayan Mountains; Tuva ASSR.

Similar species: Differs from the Caucasian, Caspian, and Himalayan Snowcocks by white belly; from the Tibetan Snowcock by white spots on upper breast and dark mottling on belly.

178. TIBETAN SNOWCOCK
Tetraogallus tibetanus
(Tibetsky Ular)
Plate 14, Map 75

Field marks: 37 cm. Resembles other snowcocks, but belly is white with dark mottling; upper breast gray with white horizontal spots.

Habits: Found in high mountain regions. Nonmigratory and scarce. Nests high in the mountains near rockslides; in winter, moves down to lower elevations and stays in pasture land. Lays five to seven eggs from end of May. Hab-

MAP 76. Common Pheasant

its, call, and feeding same as other snowcocks. Included in the Red Data Book.

Range and distribution: Pamir Mountains (Central Asia).

Similar species: Differs from Caspian, Caucasian, and Himalayan Snowcocks by white belly; from the Altai Snowcock by mottling on belly and white spots on gray upper breast.

Phasianus

179. COMMON PHEASANT
Phasianus colchicus
(Fazan)
Plate 14, Map 76

Field marks: 60-80 cm. Large (larger than a crow). Tail very long and pointed. Red bare area around the eye; feathers along side of crown elongated to form "ears"; coloration subject to geographical variations, but basic form is bright copper-reddish or gold-orange on the back; extensive blackish barring on breast and sides; head blue-green with metallic iridescence; may or may not have white "collar" on the neck. Female buffy brown with dark markings on breast, sides, and back; tail significantly shorter than male's.

Habits: Found in riparian forests, in overgrown thickets and forest along river valleys; also in settled areas. Nonmigratory. In places common or numerous. Monogamous or partly polygamous. Stays alone during nonbreeding season, more rarely in small flocks. Nests in thickets of briars and reedbanks, in small woods with thick undergrowth, in tea plantations, corn fields, and other grain crops. Mainly found nesting in thick riparian forest habitat. Nest situated on the ground under a bush or in grass. Lays eight to twelve brownish or greenish-olive eggs in April. Female alone incubates and sits tight. Pheasants stay hidden, but come out to feed into open areas morning and evening. Prefers to walk away from danger; flushes only out of necessity; runs very rapidly; often perches in trees. On takeoff, rises straight up then changes over to long gliding flight into cover. Crow of cock is reminiscent of the unfinished call of a rooster and is accompanied by wing flapping. Feeds on seeds, plants, insects.

Range and distribution: Northern Caucasus and Transcaucasus, south of Central Asia and Kazakhstan, Soviet Far East.

Similar species: Differs from all other gallinaceous birds by its long tail.

CRANES, BUSTARDS, RAILS, BUTTONQUAIL: *Gruiformes*

CRANES: *Grues*

Very large, well-proportioned birds with long necks and legs. Bill straight and long. Tail short, but appears larger due to elongated and loose tertiaries. Found in variety of habitat from tundra to steppe and semi-desert; but always found in open, often swampy, areas. Monogamous. Eggs elongated ovoid shape. Precocial.

Grus

In adult birds, patches of bare skin on the head covered with sparse hairlike bristles.

180. COMMON CRANE
Grus grus
(Sery Zhuravl)
Plate 7, Map 77

Field marks: 103-120 cm. Large crane with an overall gray coloration, with blackish wing tips. Head and neck black; broad white stripe from cheek down neck; crown is bare and covered with red wartlike skin. Legs black. Head of immatures feathered, and lacks red color.

Habits: Found in a variety of habitats from forest-tundra to desert and mountains; found in open or wooded, swampy places. Migratory. Not numerous, but more common than other cranes. Remains paired throughout year; young stay with parents (in flocks) until following spring. Nest is a flat mound of grass, frequently situated in shallow water or on a reed mat, sometimes in a thicket; nest used several years in a row. Lays two brownish or greenish-olive eggs with red-brownish spots from April to June, depending on location. Very wary; if threatened will usually leave the nest quietly, and not fly until some distance away; will, however, occasionally allow close approach. During breeding season, several birds will gather together and take turns performing characteristic displays, consisting of squatting, hopping, and calling, with half-open

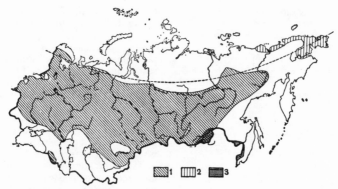

MAP 77. Common Crane (1), Sandhill Crane (2),
White-naped Crane (3)

wings. Flight straight, with even, deep wing
beats, and neck and legs outstretched. During
migration, birds fly in V-shaped formation.
Call: loud, trumpeting, shrill cry, sometimes
a low muted trill. Feeds in dry places, preferring various seeds (including wheat and peas),
berries, young shoots; frequently eats insects,
mollusks, occasionally small vertebrates (frogs,
rodents). Protected everywhere.

Range and distribution: Greater part European USSR except tundra and southern regions; Kazakhstan, West Siberia, southern part
of East Siberia. Winters in Africa, West Asia,
Iran, India, Southeast Asia.

Similar species: Differs from Demoiselle Crane
by presence of red crown and lack of white
ear tufts; from the White-naped Crane by its
black head, throat, and legs.

181. SANDHILL CRANE
Grus canadensis
(Kanadsky Zhuravl)
Plate 7, Map 77

Field marks: 110 cm. Smaller than Common
Crane. Coloration overall gray with brownish
tinge; wing tips blackish; forehead and frontal
part of head bare, covered with brownish-red
skin with black hairlike bristles. Legs black.
Juveniles rusty-brown, head feathered.

Habits: Found in hummocky and hilly thickets
or grassy tundra. Migratory. In places fairly
common. Nests in dry lowlands near lakes and
rivers. Nest situated on a dry spot, often between clumps of thickets. Nest from twigs of
dwarf birch, almost without lining. Lays two
dark brownish or ocher-cream eggs with red-
brown spots in June. Unwary female sits tight
on nest and generally allows closer approach
than other cranes. Feeds on insects, berries,
fruits of plants, and buds. Hunting forbidden.

Range and distribution: Chukotski Peninsula
and tundra to the west as far as the Kolyma
River, Gulf of Anadyr. Winters in North
America.

Similar species: Differs from other cranes by
overall grayish color (not found in ranges of
other cranes).

182. WHITE-NAPED CRANE
Grus vipio
(Daursky Zhuravl)
Plate 7, Map 77

Field marks: 120 cm. Large (larger than the
Common Crane). Light gray; wing tips black;
head and neck white; dove-gray stripe on lower
part of neck; patch of bare red skin around
eye. Legs red. Juveniles rusty; underparts with
ocherish mottling; head feathered.

Habits: Found in swampy plains. Migratory.
Very rare and possibly becoming extinct. Stays
in small flocks during nonbreeding time;
sometimes together with Common Cranes.
Nests in pairs in swampy lowlands in areas of
high grass. Nest is a flat mound of dried grass.
Lays two greenish-olive eggs with reddish-
brown spots (indistinguishable from eggs of
Common Crane) from early May. Nesting period is preceded by courtship displays. Very
wary. Included in the Red Data Book.

Range and distribution: Transbaikal, Soviet Far
East. Winters in Korea and Japan.

Similar species: Differs from the Common
Crane by white head and neck, location of red
head patch, and by its red legs.

183. HOODED CRANE
Grus monachus
(Chyorny Zhuravl)
Plate 7, Map 78

Field marks: 100 cm. Noticeably smaller than

Map 78. Hooded Crane (1), Siberian White Crane (2),
Houbara Bustard (3)

the Common Crane. Coloration dark slate-black; head and neck white; forehead bare with black skin; crown area over eye is similarly bare, but red. Bill greenish; legs black. Juveniles have ocherish head and neck.
Habits: Found in wide, dense, mossy swamps, in taiga regions. Migratory. Very rare. Nests in mossy swamps overgrown with larch and bushes. Nest is small, made of moss and grass. Lays two eggs in May, which are indistinguishable in color from eggs of other cranes, but are considerably smaller than those of Common Crane. Included in the Red Data Book.
Range and distribution: Southern regions of Yakutia, Amur River, Soviet Far East. Winters in Japan.
Similar species: Differs from all other cranes by blackish coloration and white neck and head.

184. SIBERIAN WHITE CRANE
Grus leucogeranus
(Sterkh)
Plate 7, Map 78
Field marks: 137 cm. Large (larger than Common Crane). Plumage pure white; wing tips black; bare red skin on "face"; bill and legs reddish. Juveniles have ocherish mottling.
Habits: Found in tundra and forest-tundra; during migration stays on shores of large lakes. Migratory. Very rare and becoming extinct. Nests in pairs, in damp mossy-grass tundra with a profusion of lakes. Nest is large and flat as a rule, and situated near a lake, often on a hummock or small island in the water. Nest made of dry sedge stalks. Lays two olive or greenish-olive eggs with reddish-brownish spots from early June. Very wary. Call: loud rolling cry. Feeds on roots and shoots of grassy plants, insects, small rodents (lemmings, voles).

Nests only in the USSR. Included in the Red Data Book.
Range and distribution: Two isolated populations; one in the lowlands of the River Ob, the other in Yakutia between the Yana and Alazea Rivers. Winters in India, Iran, and probably in southeast China.
Similar species: Differs from the Japanese Crane by red legs and bill, white neck, and black wing tips; from the White Stork by white tertial plumes.

185. JAPANESE CRANE
Grus japonensis
(Yaponsky Zhuravl)
Plate 7, Map 79
Field marks: 150 cm. Large (the largest crane). Overall white; throat, mid-neck, tertial plumes, and legs black; bill yellowish. "Face" black bare skin; crown red bare skin. Juveniles with ocher mottling.

Fig. 41 Crane's Nest

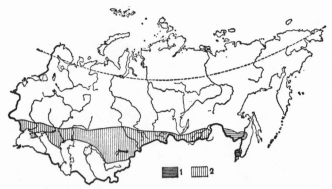

MAP 79. Japanese Crane (1), Demoiselle Crane (2)

Habits: Found in wide, swampy plains with tall grass vegetation. Migratory. Rare and, like the Siberian White Crane, an endangered species. Nests in pairs in reed and grass swamps. Nest is a flattened mound of stalk and grasses. Lays two brownish-olive eggs with red-brownish spots end of April. Call: a trumpeting roll, louder than Common Crane. Feeds on small animals (frogs, fish, aquatic invertebrates) and plants. Included in the Red Data Book.

Range and distribution: Amur River region, Soviet Far East. Winters in Korea and possibly in China.

Similar species: Differs from Siberian White Crane and eastern race of White Stork by its black legs, bill, and neck, and white wing tips.

[An inexplicable vagrant of **186.** BROLGA CRANE (*Grus rubicundus*) was obtained at the end of the last century in Yakutia.]

Anthropoides

187. DEMOISELLE CRANE
Anthropoides virgo
(Krasavka)
Plate 7, Map 79
Field marks: 68-75 cm. Small (smaller than Common Crane). Coloration dove-gray; head, neck, and wing tips black; tufts of long, white feathers ("pigtails") on sides of head; no bare skin on head. Bill yellowish; legs black. Juveniles duller and more brownish.

Habits: Found in steppe and semi-steppe. Migratory. In places still common, but numbers diminishing. Stays paired and in family groups during nonbreeding season; coalesces into flocks. Courtship "dancing" rituals precede breeding period. Nests in dry places with sparse vegetation, preferring stony ground or saline soil areas, usually not far from water. Nest is a small depression without vegetative lining (sometimes lined with small rocks or crusts of saline soil). Nest often situated in a raised area. Lays two, sometimes three, brownish-olive eggs with reddish-brownish spots in early May. Color of eggs matches color of the soil, and the nest is often difficult to see even in an open area. Parents very wary near the nest, and their behavior at this time is the same as that of other cranes. Call: loud rolling sounds. Feeds mostly on seeds, more rarely on insects. Included in the Red Data Book.

Range and distributions: Crimea, south Ukraine, Lower Volga, Kazakhstan, Altai, Tuva, Transbaikal. Wintering grounds in Africa and southern Asia.

Similar species: Differs from all other cranes by tufts of white feathers at the sides of the head and by its smaller size.

BUSTARDS: *Otides*

Large or very large birds with massive build, with long, thick neck and long, strong legs. Plumage hard and compact. Sexual dimorphism occasionally pronounced but lacking in other cases. Found in steppe and desert. Monogamous (Little Bustard, Houbara Bustard) or polygamous (Great Bustard). Eggs are usual or shortened ovoid shape. Precocial.

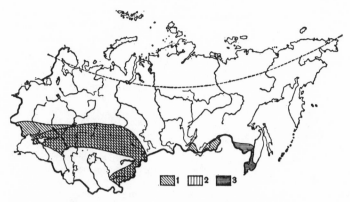

MAP 80. Great Bustard (1), Little Bustard (2), Yellow-legged
Buttonquail (3)

Otis

188. GREAT BUSTARD
Otis tarda
(Drofa)
Plate 7, Map 80
Field marks: 80-103 cm. Very large bird. Head
and neck gray; back rusty with fine black
markings; belly whitish; wings white with dark
tips. In males, tufts of bristlelike feathers
(whiskers) on throat.
Habits: Found in forest-steppe, steppe and
desert. Migratory. Rare, and numbers con-
tinue to decline significantly. Nests in open
spaces, in buffalo grass and other type of
steppe; saline soil areas with sparse vegetation; near river beds, sometimes in grain fields,
but always in places far from civilization. Nest
is a shallow depression without any lining,
completely in the open. Lays two, sometimes
three, olive-greenish eggs with blurry dark spots
from mid-April. Sits tight on nest; if danger
nears, it presses against the ground and is almost invisible. Males do not assist in rearing
young. During nonbreeding time, stays in
"herds." Very wary, but allows close approach
to the nest, then "leads away." Takeoff from
the ground is heavy, with a running start; but
once in the air, flight is swift, strong, with deep
wing beats. Remains silent. Feeds on shoots
and seeds of grasses, insects. Included in the
Red Data Book.
Range and distribution: Steppe of southern
Ukraine, Lower Volga, Kazakhstan, Transbaikal. Winters occasionally on the Crimea, in
the Transcaucasus and Central Asia, but main
wintering grounds further south outside USSR.

Similar species: Differs from Houbara Bustard by larger size and lack of black stripe and
"collar."

189. HOUBARA BUSTARD
Chlamydotis undulata
(Dzhek)
Plate 7, Map 78
Field marks: 63 cm. Large, but much smaller
than the Great Bustard. Sandy rufous with
dark regular mottling on back; belly white,
with black stripe and "collar" of long feathers
at the sides of the neck; crest on head. Black
and white stripes visible on underwing in flight.
Juveniles lack "collar."
Habits: Found in sandy and clay deserts. Migratory. Rare. Nests in pairs in saline soil areas,
sand dunes with sparse vegetation, in takyrs
(dry clay-soil in desert and semi-desert), and
rocky areas; generally in places of sparse vegetation. Nest is a shallow, entirely open
depression without any lining. Lays two or
three greenish-olive eggs with blurred spots,
from mid-April. Only female incubates and
cares for fledglings; sits tight on nest; lays head
down on close approach. During nonbreeding
season, stays singly or in small groups. Very
wary, but does not fly up immediately if danger threatens, preferring to run away rapidly,
crouching and hiding in grass. Takes off with
a running start; flight slow with deep wing
beats; flight always low to the ground. Silent.
Feeds on insects, small lizards, shoots and seeds
of various plants. Included in the Red Data
Book.
Range and distribution: Central Asia, Kazakhstan, Tuva. Winters in West Asia, Iraq, Iran.

Some birds possibly winter in southern Central Asia.

Similar species: Differs from Great Bustard by black stripes on sides of neck and "collar," from Little Bustard by larger size and reduced black on neck.

Tetrax

190. LITTLE BUSTARD
Tetrax tetrax
(Strepet)
Plate 7, Map 80

Field marks: 43 cm. Smallest of the bustards in the USSR (chicken-size). No decorative feathers. Back is grayish-ocherish with dark fine markings; belly white; neck black with two narrow white stripes; wings mostly white with dark tips. Females are brownish mottled, lack black "collar." In winter, coloration of male same as female.

Habits: Found in forest-steppe, steppe, and semi-desert. Migratory. Rare, and has become endangered over the last few years. Nests in areas with short grasses and herbaceous growth, and most often in abandoned fields and in meadows. Nest is a small depression with sparse lining of dry grasses, and is placed in grassy site. Lays three to five shiny olive-greenish eggs with dark, small spots; from early May. Female sits on nest very tightly. Birds flock during nonbreeding season. Wary, and when approached by danger prefers to run away or hide. Flies straight up without a running takeoff; flight swift and straight, low to the ground, often with a characteristic fluttering sound. During the spring breeding period, male displays by fanning his tail, lowering wings, and emitting a frequent, dry, halting "trekk-trek." Feeds on insects, seeds, shoots of various plants. Included in the Red Data Book.

Range and distribution: Reduced to remnant populations in south European USSR, Kazakhstan, and Central Asia. Winters in Transcaucasus and south Central Asia.

Similar species: Differs from Great Bustard and Houbara Bustard by its smaller size and characteristic black collar on the neck (in males).

RAILS, GALLINULES, AND COOTS: *Ralli*

Birds from large to small size with short, blunt wings and short tails. In most species, body somewhat flattened; legs with rare exception are long. Plumage soft and fluffy. In some species, the toes are lobed. Nest found in overgrown thickets near water and in damp meadows. Monogamous. Eggs usual ovoid shape. Precocial.

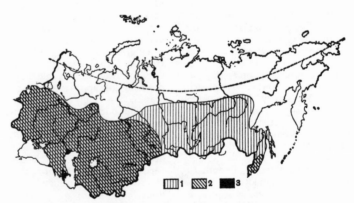

MAP 81. Common Coot (1), Common Gallinule (2), Purple Swamphen (3)

Fulica

191. COMMON COOT
Fulica atra
(Lysukha)
Plate 16, Map 81

Field marks: 38 cm. Larger than a crow. Matte black; grayish belly; frontal shield (forehead) white; toes lobed. Bill conical, short, white; legs gray. Juveniles dark with throat, neck, and underparts grayish-white.

Habits: Found in fresh and salt water in a variety of habitats from taiga to desert. Winters near unfrozen seacoasts, estuaries, and lakes. Migratory, rarely nonmigratory. Common or numerous. Nests on fresh- or salt-water lakes, quiet rivers, and oxbow lakes, shallow areas of seas, and river deltas. Requires thick vegetation such as reed thickets, cattails, rugosa roses, and sedge near water. Flat nest is situated in thick vegetation either directly on water or right next to it. Nest made from stalks and leaves of reeds or sedge. Lays seven to ten (sometimes up to fifteen) grayish-ocherish eggs with minute black speckles from end of April to June. Stays in flocks during nonbreeding season. Not wary. Good swimmer and diver; flies unwillingly; takes off from running start, but flight fairly rapid. Almost never found on dry land. Resembles duck on the water; keeps tail lowered into water, constantly bobbing head slightly. Call: loud "tyok-tyok." Feeds on aquatic plants, more rarely invertebrates and small fish.

Range and distribution: Southern half of USSR from western Ukraine and Moldavia to Soviet Far East. Winters on south Caspian Sea, Central Asia, and south of the USSR borders.

Similar species: Differs from ducks and other rails, gallinules, and coots by distinct white forehead, black coloration, and characteristic silhouette.

Porphyrio

192. PURPLE SWAMPHEN
Porphyrio porphyrio
(Sultanka)
Plate 16, Map 81

Field marks: 48 cm. Somewhat larger than a Common Coot; bill massive, with concave sides; long legs; toes not webbed. Light greenish-blue with metallic iridescence; undertail white; legs, bill, and frontal shield (forehead) orange-red.

Habits: Found in estuaries overgrown with reeds, river deltas, and lakes. Nonmigratory, in places nomadic. Not numerous and even rare. Nests in pairs in thick, nearly inaccessible, watery thickets of reed and cattails. Small but deep nest is situated on a hummock or heaps of broken reed in water. Nest made of stems and leaves of old reed, and well hidden. Lays four to seven cream-ocherish eggs with small brown spots from mid-April. Wary and silent. Stays hidden, and is rarely seen. Moves adroitly through thick reedstalks and is an agile climber. Flies reluctantly and not far. Does not swim in open water. Call: a repeated moan. Feeds on roots and shoots of aquatic plants. Is legally protected. Included in the Red Data Book.

Range and distribution: Transcaucasus, Dagestan, southwest Turkmenia.

Similar species: Differentiated easily from all other birds by coloration and characteristic appearance.

Gallinula

193. COMMON GALLINULE
Gallinula chloropus
(Kamyshnitsa)
Plate 16, Map 81

Field marks: 33 cm. Medium size (smaller than Common Coot); long legs; toes not webbed; dark, matte black on head, neck, and breast; black-brownish on back and wings; undertail and stripes at sides white. Red frontal shield and bill; legs greenish. Juveniles, light brownish, bill gray-yellow.

Habits: Found in a variety of habitats from the forest to desert. Migratory. Common, but due to furtive living habits is rarely seen. Nests in thick stands of reed, cattails, or sedge, on inaccessible lake shores, springs, oxbows, quiet rivers, and reservoirs. Nest made of dry stalks and leaves of reed, and is situated directly over water in reeds or on branches of thickets; sometimes on a hummock or stump. Always hidden in the deepest part of vegetation. Lays six to ten cream or brownish-ocherish eggs with small red-brownish spots from April. Nestlings are black-brownish with red bills. Has two broods. Like other gallinules, the Common Gallinule is an agile walker and climber between reeds; flies well but reluctantly, and lands quickly. Good swimmer and enjoys it, characteristically nodding its head. Call: loud cry "krrook"; when threatened or in flight, a repetitive "kek-kek-kek." Feeds on aquatic invertebrates (insects and their larvae, mollusks).

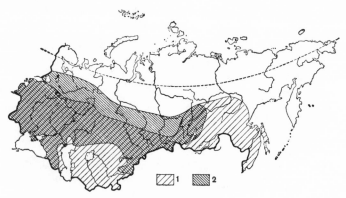

MAP 82. Water Rail (1), Corn Crake (2)

Range and distribution: Southern half of European USSR, Central Asia, Kazakhstan, southern West Siberia, Soviet Far East, Kuril Islands. Winters in the Transcaucasus, southern Central Asia, and south of USSR.
Similar species: Differs from Common Coot by smaller size and red bill and forehead.

Rallus

194. WATER RAIL
Rallus aquaticus
(Pastushok)
Plate 16, Map 82
Field marks: 28 cm. Medium size (but smaller than Common Gallinule). Reddish bill long, slightly curved; neck and breast dark gray; back brown with black spots; black and white barred sides; legs yellow. Juveniles brownish, with indistinctly barred breast.
Habits: Found in a variety of wetland habitats from forest to desert. Migratory, in places nonmigratory. Common. Nests on shores of lakes, oxbows, channels, in damp meadows, all overgrown with thickets of reeds, cattails, and sedge. Prefers the most inaccessible locations. Nest is made of dry stems and leaves, and is situated on a hummock or in reeds, always hidden. Lays seven to ten ocherish and rusty eggs with red-brownish spots in May. Sometimes has two broods. Mostly nocturnal. Agile, quick runner through thick grass; good swimmer and diver; flies reluctantly; appears in open spaces only in search of food. Garrulous; voice: shrill, repetitive "youeet-youeet-youeet" or harsh 'teelk." Feeds on worms, mollusks, and insects.
Range and distribution: Southern half of European USSR, Central Asia, Kazakhstan,

southern West Siberia, southern half of East Siberia, Soviet Far East, Sakhalin Island, Kuril Islands. Winters on shores of Mediterranean, North Africa, Iraq, northern Hindustan, Indochina, Japan. In the USSR: Transcaucasus, southern Kazakhstan, and Central Asia.
Similar species: Differs from Corn Crake and other crakes by longer, curved red bill.

Crex

195. CORN CRAKE
Crex crex
(Korostel)
Plate 16, Map 82
Field marks: 26 cm. Medium size (slightly larger than a thrush). Bill short and yellow; color brownish with black spotting on back, and brown barring on the flanks; wing coverts rusty reddish.
Habits: Found in a variety of habitats from forest to desert. Migratory. Common. Nests in wet meadows in river valleys lush with thick grass; sometimes in thickets near grain and other fields; also in cut forest areas and forest clearings; in boggy lake basins; but avoids very marshy areas. Nest is hidden in tall grass, and can only be found by chance. Lays eight to twelve ocherish eggs with reddish-brown spots and dots from May; occasionally has two broods. Despite coloration and garrulousness, the bird is rarely seen, and only when it flushes. Flies reluctantly, legs dangle in flight. Runs away from danger very rapidly. Primarily nocturnal. Call: scraping cry, "krek-krek-krek-krek," which is heard for a great distance. Feeds on various insects, worms, and seeds.
Range and distribution: European USSR except northern regions, Kazakhstan, southern

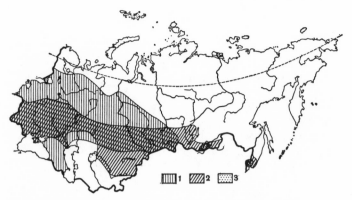

MAP 83. Spotted Crake (1), Baillon's Crake (2), Swinhoe's Yellow Crake (3)

half of west and central Siberia. Winters in Mediterranean countries and Africa.

Similar species: Differs from Water Rail by short bill; from other crakes and rails (except Band-bellied Crake) by rufous wings; from the Band-bellied Crake by lighter color of throat and breast, and spotting on back (but does not occur in same range).

Porzana

Size of a thrush or larger. Bill short, pushed in at the sides.

196. SPOTTED CRAKE
Porzana porzana
(Pogonysh)
Plate 16, Map 83

Field marks: 23 cm. Larger than a thrush. Dark overall; upperparts olive-brownish with large black, and smaller white spots; underparts light bluish-gray with white spots; gray and white barred sides; undertail white; bill yellow with red at base; legs greenish.

Habits: Found in a variety of wetland habitats from forest to desert. Migratory. Common. Nests in thickets of reed or sedge along lake shores; river tributaries and oxbows; flooded areas, grassy swamps, wet meadows, and swampy thickets. Small nest is built from leaves and stems of grasses, and is situated on a hummock or in broken reeds, always well hidden. Lays eight to ten dirty ocherish or greenish-ocherish eggs with reddish or brownish spots; from mid-May to July. Active in the evening, and nocturnal. Stays hidden; flushes rarely and reluctantly; flies a short distance then drops into the grass. Flight is rapid and straight;

takeoff from the ground is nearly soundless. Walks easily through matted plants and leaves of water lilies; rarely swims. Call: harsh, resounding whistle, "youeat-youeat-youeat." Feeds on insects, worms, mollusks, and occasionally seeds.

Range and distribution: European USSR (except northern regions); Kazakhstan, southern half of west Siberia. Winters in southern Europe, North and East Africa, West Asia; in the USSR, in Central Asia.

Similar species: Differs from Little Crake and Baillon's Crake by lack of stripes on undertail and larger size; from the Corn Crake, by darker coloration, reddish base of bill.

FIG. 42 Spotted Crake Chick

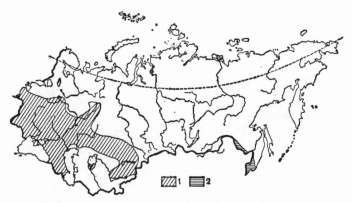

MAP 84. Little Crake (1), Band-bellied Crake (2)

197. LITTLE CRAKE
Porzana parva
(Maly Pogonysh)
Plate 16, Map 84

Field marks: 19 cm. Size of a thrush. Upperparts olive-brownish with dark mottling; neck and underparts slate-gray; undertail barred; yellow bill red at base; legs greenish; in male, chin and throat pale.

Habits: Found in a variety of wetland habitats from forest to desert. Migratory. Common in places. Nests in pairs along thickly vegetated lake shores, river channels, and oxbows, preferring deep bodies of water. Like Spotted Crake, nest is compact and situated on reedstalks over water. The nest lining is always made of a single material, and there is a beaten path to the nest. Lays seven to nine yellowish-gray eggs with rusty puddled spots from mid-May. Usually two broods. Resembles Spotted Crake in habits. Swims readily and dives well; reminiscent of miniature Common Gallinule on water. Agile climber and runner among reeds and aquatic plants. Call resembles a quacking trill, "ka-ka-ka-kakaka." Feeds on small insects and seeds.

Range and distribution: Southern half of European USSR, Kazakhstan, Central Asia, southern West Siberia. Winters in Mediterranean countries, Africa, and West Asia.

Similar species: Differs from Baillon's Crake by red base of bill and lack of definite barring on sides; from the Spotted Crake by smaller size and barred undertail.

198. BAILLON'S CRAKE
Porzana pusilla
(Pogonysh-kroshka)
Plate 16, Map 83

Field marks: 18 cm. Resembles Little Crake, but smaller; strongly barred flanks; bill and legs greenish.

Habits: Found in variety of wetland habitats from forest to desert. Migratory. In places common, but stays hidden and is rarely seen. Nests in same types of places as the Little Crake, but nest is looser, and is more often situated on a hummock or on a heap of broken reed. Lays six to nine eggs resembling those of Little Crake, but darker and smaller, from beginning of May. Habits and manners same as Little Crake, but swims a little more reluctantly. Call: soft characteristic whistle.

Range and distribution: South European USSR except Caucasus and near-Caspian; Kazakhstan, south Siberia to the east as far as Transbaikal, Soviet Far East. Winters in Africa and southern Asia. In the USSR, in Central Asia.

Similar species: Differs from Little Crake by green bill, strongly barred flanks, greenish legs. In the hand, differs by white outer edge of the first primary.

199. SWINHOE'S YELLOW CRAKE
Porzana exquisita
(Belokryly Pogonysh)
Not illustrated, Map 83

Field marks: 20 cm. Smallest of the crakes (significantly smaller than a thrush). Upperparts brownish with black stripes and fine white bars; belly whitish; white spot at bend of wing and speculum.

Habits: Very rare bird, biology completely unknown. Included in the Red Data Book.

Range and distribution: Transbaikal, southern regions of Soviet Far East. Winters in eastern China, Korea, and Japan.

Similar species: Differs from all other small crakes by smaller size and white spot on wings.

200. BAND-BELLIED CRAKE
Porzana paykullii
(Bolshoy Pogonysh)
Plate 16, Map 84

Field marks: 24 cm. Larger than a thrush. Back is uniform olive-brownish, without mottling; sides of head, neck, and breast bright chestnut; strong brownish and white barring on flanks and undertail coverts. Females and juveniles paler.

Habits: Found in meadow lowlands and river valleys near forest zones. Migratory, common in places, but not numerous. Nests on hummocky, not too damp meadows and swamps with thickets; avoids wet places inhabited by Corn Crake; often found near villages and along field edges and fences. Nest is a small depression lined with stalks of grasses, and is situated in a dry place in thick grass. Lays six to nine eggs that resemble eggs of Water Rail but are smaller, from end of May. Primarily nocturnal. Behavior very different from other crakes and more nearly resembles that of the Corn Crake: that is, very fast runner in the thick grass, prefers to fly rather than walk through even shallow puddles. Flushes only when danger is imminent, and then flies only a short distance with legs dangling. Very garrulous; call: short metallic sounds, blending into a fluttering, chirring trill, "urrrrr."

Range and distribution: Near Amur River and southern regions of Soviet Far East. Winters in Indonesia and Moluccas.

Similar species: Differs from other crakes and Corn Crake by bright chestnut-rusty breast.

[Vagrants of **201.** WATERCOCK (*Gallicrex cinereus*) have been noted three times in the USSR: on the Kamchatka Peninsula, on Askold Island, and in the area of the Bay of Ternay. Resembles Common Gallinule, but larger; bare red frontal shield more extensive (to crown); lacks white stripe on side. Its normal range encompasses India and Southeast Asia from the north to Korea. RUDDY-BREASTED CRAKE (*Porzana fusca*) reported frequently in the Amur River regions, on islands near Vladivostok, and south of Soviet Far East. Nesting in the USSR not documented but possible.]

BUTTONQUAIL (HEMIPODES): *Turnices*

Turnix

202. YELLOW-LEGGED BUTTONQUAIL
Turnix tanki
(Tryokhpyorstka)
Plate 15, Map 80

Field marks: 15-17 cm. Small, short-tailed bird, resembling small Common Quail. Wings short and rounded. Lacks hind toe; upperparts brownish with round dark spots on the back; underparts ocherish with rusty suffusion on the breast and dark round spots on the flanks. Female brighter than the male.

Habits: Found in plains and hills overgrown with thickets and grass. Migratory. Rare and very furtive. Nest is a shallow depression lined with dry stalks hidden in dry thicket areas. Lays four pear-shaped gray eggs thickly marked with small brownish dots in June. Male incubates. Reluctant to fly; when in danger, usually hides or runs away rapidly. Flight straight, rapid, but weaker than Common Quail. Call: piercing howl. Feeds on seeds and insects.

Range and distribution: Transbaikal, Amur River region, Soviet Far East. Winters in southern China.

Similar species: Differs from Common Quail by rounded spots on back and sides and by lack of hind toe.

SHOREBIRDS, GULLS, ALCIDS: *Charadriiformes*

Small- and medium-size birds with long legs and thin, usually long bill. Wings, as a rule, are narrow and tail is short. Plumage is dull, usually not very colorful; in many species, coloration changes according to season and age. Found on shores and in swampy areas; more rarely in dry places. Monogamous, with a few exceptions. Eggs are ovoid or shortened pear-shaped. Precocial.

SHOREBIRDS: *Limicolae*

Burhinus

203. STONE THICK-KNEE
Burhinus oedicnemus
(Avdotka)
Plate 17, Map 85
Field marks: 40 cm. Large bustardlike bird with long three-toed legs; short bill, and large yellow eyes; back is sandy gray with dark streaking; underparts whitish with narrow streaks on the breast; bill yellow with black tip. Two definite white wing stripes are visible in flight, whereas only one is visible when the bird is not flying.
Habits: Found in open habitat with sparse vegetation. Migratory. In places common. Nests in sparsely vegetated, sandy, clay or saline soil, desert, and steppe; but, as a rule, in the vicinity of a lake or river. Nest is a scarcely noticeable depression in the ground. Lays two, rarely three, yellowish eggs with dark speckles and dots end of April-May. Stays in pairs during breeding season, otherwise in flocks. Feeds on insects (beetles, locusts), mollusks, sometimes even small turtles. Nocturnal. Hides when approached, then flushes from a running start. Call: loud drawn-out cry, "tar-lee-ee, tar-lee-

ee," which the bird often emits at night in flight.
Range and distribution: South European USSR, Kazakhstan, Central Asia. Winters in Africa and Arabian Peninsula.
Similar species: Characteristic coloration, and particularly the yellow eyes, are diagnostic when comparing with all other shorebirds.

Cursorius

204. CREAM-COLORED COURSER
Cursorius cursor
(Begunok)
Plate 17, Map 85
Field marks: 23 cm. Medium size (size of a thrush). Legs long; bill curved; tail slightly rounded; upperparts uniform yellowish-sandy; underparts somewhat lighter; bold black and white stripes behind eye. Underwing and axillars black; legs yellowish; bill blackish. Juveniles similar but lightly spotted.
Habits: Found in desert, where it prefers flat rocky areas with sparse vegetation. Migratory. Very rare. Probably nests end of May, perhaps later. Nest is a shallow depression in which the female lays two brown-speckled yellowish eggs.

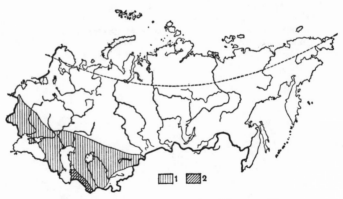

MAP 85. Stone Thick-knee (1), Cream-colored Courser (2)

Stays well hidden; runs well; flies reluctantly, but flight is very rapid and agile. Stands almost vertical when running, extending its neck upward. Call: barking "khek." Feeds on insects (beetles, locusts).

Range and distribution: South Central Asia. Winters on Cape Verde Islands, in the Azores, and East Africa.

Similar species: Characteristic appearance, black underwings, the black and white stripes behind the eye are definitive.

Glareola

Medium-size bird of unique appearance with long narrow wings, long forked tail, and short bill and legs. Throat bordered by a dark stripe. Resembles a large swallow in flight and when perched; does not look like a shorebird.

205. EUROPEAN PRATINCOLE
Glareola pratincola
(Lugovaya Tirkushka)
Plat 18, Map 86

Field marks: 25 cm. Upperparts and breast grayish-brown; throat cream-colored; belly white. Underwing coverts are bright rusty red. Juveniles have white speckling on back.

Habits: Found in open dry habitat, where it prefers places with sparse vegetation. Migratory and common in places. Nests in colonies, usually near water (lakes, rivers). Eggs are laid on the ground in a small depression. Lays three thickly spotted whitish eggs in May or June. Feeds on insects (beetles, locusts), which it catches on the ground as well as in the air. Highly visible and garrulous. Also flies at a great height, frequently for long periods of time. Call: chirring trill "kittee-kirree-kitee-tee."

Range and distribution: Moldavia, southern Ukraine, Crimea, Armenia, northern Caucasus, Kazakhstan, Central Asia. Winters in Africa.

Similar species: Differs from Black-winged Pratincole by its rusty wing lining.

206. BLACK-WINGED PRATINCOLE
Glareola nordmanni
(Stepnaya Tirkushka)
Plate 18, Map 86

Field marks: 25 cm. Closely resembles European Pratincole, but larger; tail more deeply forked; coloration darker. Wing lining black.

Habits: Found in dry open habitat, preferring saline soil with sparse vegetation, sometimes near plowed fields, in steppe or on rocky spits of land. Migratory. Fairly common. Nests in colonies of several hundred pairs situated near water. Nest is a depression in the ground, sparsely lined. Lays three or four eggs end of May to beginning of June. Eggs are olive-greenish or brownish, thickly dotted. Leads away from the nest by pretending it is injured. Call: loud cry, "kirlik-kirlik" or "teerlee." Feeds on insects (beetles, locusts, bees).

Range and distribution: South of European USSR, Kazakhstan. Winters in Africa.

Similar species: Differs from European Pratincole by black wing lining.

207. ORIENTAL PRATINCOLE
Glareola maldivarum
(Vostochnaya Tirkushka)
Plate 18, Map 86

Field marks: 25 cm. Resembles European Prat-

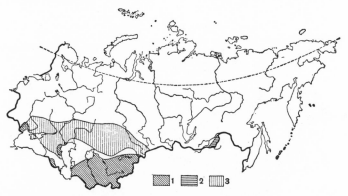

MAP 86. European Pratincole (1), Oriental Pratincole (2), Black-winged Pratincole (3)

incole, but smaller, darker; tail shorter and less forked; secondaries lack white tips.

Habits: Found in grassy steppe. Very rare migrant and occasionally nesting bird. No information regarding its biology.

Range and distribution: Southeast Transbaikal. Winters in southeast regions of Asia, islands of the Indian Ocean to Australia.

Similar species: Differs from European Pratincole by its shorter tail and lack of white tips on secondaries; from the Black-winged Pratincole by its rusty wing lining (although the two species are not found in the same range).

Pluvialis

Fairly large shorebirds, thick-set, with short straight bill.

208. GRAY PLOVER
Pluvialis squatarola
(Tuless)
Plate 18, Map 87

Field marks: 28 cm. Contrasting coloration: underparts, including sides of the head and throat, intense black; black bordered by white stripe on head and neck; back is brightly patterned, with black and white mottling; axillars black; rump white. In winter, underparts are white. Some ornithologists place this species in a separate genus—*Squatarola*.

Habits: Nests in tundra. During migration prefers sandy and rocky seashores, and riversides. Migratory and common in places. Nests in raised areas, in lichen tundra. Nest is a depression lined with lichen. Lays four yellowish or greenish eggs, thickly mottled with black-brownish; end of June. Very wary, and

will not allow close approach even at the height of hatching. One of the most visible birds of the tundra, thanks to its striking plumage and its loud voice (as is the Greater Golden Plover). Call: drawn-out, whining "tuu-lee, tuu-lee" or "tyueerlee." Feeds on various invertebrates.

Range and distribution: Tundra of USSR and Siberia. Winters on southwest shores of Europe, southern Asia, Africa, and Australia.

Similar species: Differs from Greater Golden Plover and Lesser Golden Plovers by its larger size, lack of golden color in its back, black axillars, and white rump.

209. GREATER GOLDEN PLOVER
Pluvialis apricaria
(Zolotistaya Rzhanka)
Plate 18, Map 88

Field marks: 28 cm. Upperparts golden-patterned, underparts, including sides of the head and throat, black and bordered with white; axillars white. Females duller, with white mottling on belly. In winter, black is replaced by a smoky color.

Habits: Found in tundra and forest-tundra, more rarely in forests. Found on seasides during migration. Migratory. Not numerous, in places common. Nests in various types of tundra, from swampy, hummocky areas to raised lichen areas, in forest regions and forest-tundra, in mossy swamps. Nest is a depression lined with lichens, stems, or leaves. Lays four thickly speckled yellowish eggs; from mid-June on. Very wary, and will leave the nest long before approached closely. Flies around or watches from a distance, giving anxious cries. Call: loud whining whistle, "tyouyouyou, tyouyouyou." Feeds on various invertebrates.

Range and distribution: North European USSR and western Siberia within tundra zones. Win-

MAP 87. Gray Plover

ters on the Iberian Peninsula, Nile Delta, and northwestern Africa.

Similar species: Differs from Lesser Golden Plover by its larger size, broader white border to black underparts, and white axillars; from the Gray Plover, by its golden upperparts, white axillars, and dark rump; winter plumage more yellowish-brown than in Gray Plover.

FIG. 43 SHOREBIRDS IN FLIGHT

1. Black-winged Stilt   2. Black-capped Avocet   3. Common Oystercatcher   4. Common Snipe   5. Great Snipe   6. Eurasian Woodcock   7. Eurasian Curlew   8. Black-tailed Godwit   9. Little Ringed Plover   10. Northern Lapwing   11. Greater Golden Plover   12. Gray Plover   13. Common Redshank   14. Greater Greenshank   15. Ruddy Turnstone

MAP 88. Lesser Golden Plover (1), Greater Golden Plover (2)

210. LESSER GOLDEN PLOVER
Pluvialis dominica
(Burokrylaya Rzhanka)
Plate 18, Map 88

Field marks: 24 cm. Closely resembles Greater Golden Plover, but smaller and darker. White border is covered with the wing when the bird is on the ground. Axillars and wing lining smoky gray.

Habits: Found in tundra; on open shores of lakes and rivers during migration; also on fields. Migratory. Rare, but common in places. Nests in dry hummocky or lichen tundra on slopes of small mountains. Nest is a depression lined with lichens. Lays four yellowish eggs with dark, very thick speckles, which blend in with the surroundings perfectly; from mid-June on. Resembles Greater Golden Plover in habits, but call is usually disyllabic, resembling "tyour-lee, tyour-lee," more rarely "tyouee."

Range and distribution: Siberian tundra. Winters in southern Asia and Australia.

Similar species: Differs from Greater Golden Plover by smaller size and darker wing lining and axillars; when on the ground, it is often difficult to observe the white stripe; from the Gray Plover, by its golden upperparts, uniformly dark underparts, and smaller size.

Charadrius

Small- and medium-size shorebirds with short, straight bill and short legs. Head quite large, neck thick. Contrasting coloration.

211. GREATER RINGED PLOVER
Charadrius hiaticula
(Galstuchnik)
Plate 18, Map 89

Field marks: 19 cm. Upperparts brownish-gray; underparts white; black band across upper breast; forehead white, bordered underneath by a black stripe continuing through the eye;

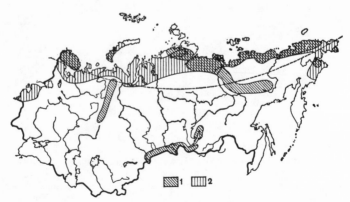

MAP 89. Dotterel (1), Greater Ringed Plover (2)

anterior half of crown blackish; base of bill and legs orange-yellow. In flight, white stripe visible on wing. In winter plumage and in juveniles, the black color is substituted by brownish, and the patterning is less well defined.

Habits: Found in sandy or pebbly regions, usually along seashores, lakes, or rivers. Migratory. Common or numerous. Nests in June, and often has two broods. Nest is a scrape in the sand, sometimes lined with a bolster of cattails. Lays four yellowish eggs with small, dark spots. Vigorous distraction display in which the bird pretends to be hurt; leads intruder away from the nest. Very garrulous and readily noticed, particularly in the area of the nest. When alarmed, its call is a melodic "kyouee"; in breeding season, a repetitive "kveetu-veeu." Feeds on various invertebrates (crayfish, worms, mollusks).

Range and distribution: Baltic States, north European USSR, and Siberia. Winters in south of Caspian Sea. Outside the USSR, in the Mediterranean, Arabian Peninsula, Africa, Madagascar.

Similar species: Differs from Little Ringed Plover by a lack of white stripe over black forecrown, yellow eye rings, orange base of bill, white stripe on wing; from the Kentish Plover, by the complete breast band and orange-yellow legs; from the Long-billed Plover, by the black band between the bill and white forehead (often indistinguishable in the field).

212. LITTLE RINGED PLOVER
Charadrius dubius
(Maly Zuyok)
Plate 18, Map 90
Field marks: 15 cm. Resembles Ringed Plover, but smaller; bill entirely black; yellow eye ring; black stripe on forehead bordered above by white; legs pale pink or yellowish; no white stripe visible in flight.

Habits: Found on sandy or rocky beaches along river shores and lakes, sometimes far from water. Migratory. Common and numerous in places. Nesting habits same as Ringed Plover, but eggs significantly smaller, and are dotted rather than speckled. When alarmed, emits a melodic "peeyou" resembling the call of the Ringed Plover. Feeds on insects and other invertebrates.

Range and distribution: European USSR except northern regions; southern half of West and East Siberia, Soviet Far East. Winters in southern Asia and Africa.

Similar species: Differs from Greater Ringed Plover by all-black bill, white line over black area on forehead, and yellow eye ring, lack of wing stripes (juveniles are difficult to distinguish, except in flight); from the Kentish Plover, by complete breast band; from the Long-billed Plover, by presence of black dividing area between bill and white forehead (often indistinguishable in the field).

213. LONG-BILLED PLOVER
Charadrius placidus
(Ussuriysky Zuyok)
Not illustrated, Map 90
Field marks: 19 cm. Similar to Ringed Plover and Little Ringed Plover, but larger; bill longer, white forehead continues to base of bill; white on outer tail feathers much reduced; black bill (base of lower mandible yellow); yellow eye ring; no wing stripes.

Habits: Found on pebbly beaches and spits on shores of lakes and rivers. Migratory. Rare. Nesting habits same as Little Ringed Plover, but details unknown. When alarmed, emits a short, harsh "peep." Feeds on insects (diptera and their larvae, beetles).

MAP 90. Little Ringed Plover (1), Long-billed Plover (2)

Range and distribution: Soviet Far East. Winters in Hindustan and Indochina.

Similar species: Differs from Greater and Little Ringed Plovers by lack of black between bill and white forehead, darker outer tail feathers, larger size; but often indistinguishable in the field.

214. KENTISH PLOVER
Charadrius alexandrinus
(Morskoy Zuyok)
Plate 18, Map 91

Field marks: 16 cm. Size and shape of Little Ringed Plover. Upperparts pale brownish-gray with rusty nape extending onto crown; belly, forehead, and eye stripe white; forecrown and eye line black; the breast band is divided and reduced to two dark spots on sides of the breast; legs and bill black. Female lacks black on crown, and winter plumage of male is duller.

Habits: Found in open, low-lying shores of salt- and fresh-water bodies. Migratory. In places common and even numerous. Nests on shell and sandy beaches, in saline soil area, alkali and mud flats near lakes. Nest is a shallow scrape, often "decorated" with pebbles and bits of shell. Nesting period is prolonged from the end of April until July. Lays three clay-yellow or pale olive eggs with small dark speckles. Quietly leaves nest on close approach, but quickly returns. Habits similar to those of Little Ringed Plover; runs rapidly, then stops and stands still; flies a short distance. Call: plaintive whistle, "pyoueet." Feeds on mollusks, insects, crayfish, and other invertebrates.

Range and distribution: South European USSR, Central Asia, Kazakhstan, Tuva (in places), Transbaikal, Soviet Far East, Kuril Islands. Winters south of Caspian Sea, Mediterranean, and in southern Asia.

Similar species: Differs from other plovers by incomplete breast band and black legs.

215. MONGOLIAN PLOVER
Charadrius mongolus
(Mongolsky Zuyok)
Plate 18, Map 91

Field marks: 22 cm. Larger than Ringed Plover. Bill short and black; back gray or brownish-gray; broad rusty red breast band and sides, extending onto back and head; throat and belly white; throat (occasionally) bordered by black; forehead white with black border above; black stripe from bill to ear; bill and legs black.

Habits: Found in high-mountain tundra, in barren places; on the Komandorskiye Islands in sand dunes. Migratory. Rare, in places common. Lays two to three brownish-ocher eggs with dark spots in June. Feeds on insects. Biology nearly unknown.

Range and distribution: Chukotski Peninsula, Kamchatka Peninsula, Magadan Oblast, Pamir and Tien-Shan Mountains, some mountains of East Siberia. Winters on eastern shores of Africa, Madagascar, southern Asia and northern Australia.

Similar species: Differs from Sand Plover by shorter bill, smaller size, and less bright coloration (easy to confuse in the field); from the Caspian and Oriental Plovers by black band across the head.

216. SAND PLOVER
Charadrius leschenaultii
(Tolstoklyuvy Zuyok)
Plate 18, Map 92

Field marks: 22 cm. Resembles Mongolian Plover, but larger; bill noticeably longer and thicker; reduced black on head; narrower rusty breast band, and greatly reduced amount of

MAP 91. Kentish Plover (1), Mongolian Plover (2)

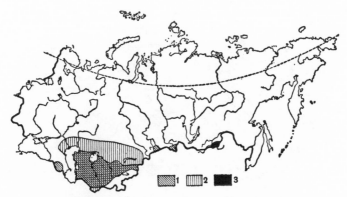

MAP 92. Sand Plover (1), Caspian Plover (2), Oriental Plover (3)

rusty on sides. In female, forehead is white, black entirely replaced by brownish.

Habits: Found in clay deserts, saline soil areas, and rocky plains near mountains. During migration, prefers seashores. Migratory. Rare. Nests in areas with sparse vegetation. Nest is a shallow scrape, thinly lined with twigs of wormwood, surrounded with a bolster of crusts of saline soil or pebbles. Lays three clay-ocherish eggs with large dark spots, often elongated, in April to beginning of May. When disturbed, the bird quietly leaves the nest and does not return for a long period of time. Runs well, often stops and stands stock-still. Usually silent and cautious. Call: muffled trill. Feeds on insects.

Range and distribution: Armenia, Central Asia, Kazakhstan, Altai, Tuva. Winters on eastern shores of Africa, Madagascar, southern Asia, northern Australia.

Similar species: Differs from Mongolian Plover by larger size, longer bill, and narrow breast band; from the Caspian and Oriental Plovers by black pattern on the head.

217. CASPIAN PLOVER
Charadrius asiaticus
(Kaspiysky Zuyok)
Plate 18, Map 92

Field marks: 20 cm. Large, long-legged plover. Top of head and upper parts gray-brownish; forehead, eye stripe, sides of head and throat white; breast rusty and bordered by black below; belly and axillars white; bill black; legs greenish-brown. Females and immatures are pale gray-brown with grayish-yellow breast.

Habits: Found in desert and semi-desert. Migratory. In places common and even numerous. Nests on alkali flats, edges of takyrs (dry

clay-soil areas in desert and semi-desert), along mountain sides, but always in places with sparse vegetation. Nest is a depression, poorly lined with stalks or a few pebbles. Lays three eggs in April or May. Eggs are clay-yellowish with frequent, large black-brownish spots, which match their surroundings closely. Wary and stays silent. Feeds on insects (beetles, locusts).

Range and distribution: Central Asia, Kazakhstan, Lower Volga. Winters in southern and southeastern Africa.

Similar species: Differs from Mongolian Plover and Sand Plover by lack of black on crown and longer legs; from the Oriental Plover, by white axillars and darker head (often indistinguishable in the field).

218. ORIENTAL PLOVER
Charadrius veredus
(Vostochny Zuyok)
Not illustrated, Map 92

Field marks: 22-23 cm. Resembles Caspian Plover, but larger; in old males, head and neck are almost entirely white (in younger males, head more nearly resembles head of Caspian Plover); axillars brownish.

Habits: Found in hummocky, dry steppe; rocky lowlands of mountains; alkali flats. Migratory. Extremely rare. Nesting habits and eggs not recorded. Feeds on insects, primarily beetles.

Range and distribution: Transbaikal. Winters in the Sunda Islands (Malay Archipelago) and in the Philippines; Australia.

Similar species: Differs from Mongolian Plover and Sand Plover by lack of black on the crown; from the Caspian, by brownish axillar patch and (in older males) by white head and neck. Nearly indistinguishable in the field, but ranges are isolated.

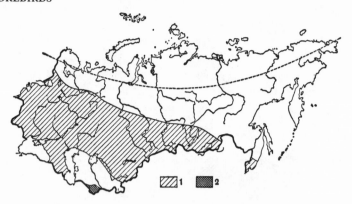

MAP 93. Northern Lapwing (1), Red-wattled Lapwing (2)

219. EURASIAN DOTTEREL
Charadrius (Eudromias) morinellus
(Khrustan)
Plate 18, Map 89

Field marks: 21 cm. Medium-size shorebird, with short bill and legs; in spring, crown in black; eye stripe and throat white; back and breast slate-gray bordered below by white stripe; rusty underparts; black belly; legs yellow; bill black. In winter, plumage is duller; many white feathers on the belly; in juveniles entire underparts are ocherish, upperparts mottled brownish.

Habits: Found in hilly, dry, and rocky tundra; in the mountains, in barren places; during migration, near cultivated lands and alkali flats. Migratory. Common. Nest is a deep depression, lined with leaves and lichens. Usually lays three eggs in June or beginning of July. Eggs are olive-brownish, with large, scattered, irregular black spots. Male incubates, but both sexes engage in distraction display when disturbed. Call: whistling "peet-peet-peet"; when alarmed, it becomes a loud trill. Feeds on insects (beetles, diptera, and their larvae), mollusks and worms.

Range and distribution: Kola Peninsula, southern island of Novaya Zemlya, Urals, mountainous, northern shores of East Siberia from Taimyr to Chukotski Peninsula, some mountains of Central Siberia—Altai, Sayan, Khomar-Daban, Barguzin range; one nesting record for the Caucasus. Winters in North Africa and on the Arabian Peninsula.

Similar species: Distinctive plumage allows easy identification from all other plovers.

Vanellus

220. NORTHERN LAPWING
Vanellus vanellus
(Chibis)
Plate 17, Map 93

MAP 94. Sociable Lapwing (1), White-tailed Lapwing (2), Ruddy Turnstone (3)

Field marks: 32 cm. Large shorebird with short bill and long legs. Wings wide and rounded; long, narrow crest; distinctively marked. Back is a shimmering olive-green; underparts white; top of head and breast band black with metallic suffusion; undertail pale rusty; wide, black subterminal tail band. In winter plumage, head and throat have many white feathers; in juveniles crest is short as well.

Habits: Found in a variety of habitats from taiga to desert, but nests exclusively in damp meadows, grassy swamps, and fields. Migratory. Common or numerous. Often nests in colonies. Nest is a shallow depression lined with grass stalks. Lays four brownish-sandy eggs with thick blackish speckles, merging together on the broader end; from mid-April until June. Feeds on various insects, mollusks, worms. Readily seen. Often flies for long periods of time in display flights, in which the bird rises steeply, drops sharply, and makes deep curves with loud, throbbing wing beats. When guarding nest or brood, aggressively attacks if someone approaches; chases raptors that appear in the vicinity. Call: nasal, plaintive "chyee-vee, chyee-vee."

Range and distribution: European USSR except northern regions, Kazakhstan, Central Asia, south Siberia as far as eastern Transbaikal, southern Soviet Far East. Winters in Transcaucasus and Central Asia. Outside the USSR, western Europe, North Africa; in Asia to the south as far as Pakistan, Burma, southeast China.

Similar species: Easily distinguished from all other plovers by crest; in flight by its distinctive black, rounded wing tips, and black tail band.

Chettusia

Large shorebirds with short bill and long legs.

221. SOCIABLE LAPWING
Chettusia gregaria
(Krechetka)
Plate 17, Map 94

Field marks: 30 cm. Back and breast brownish-gray; crown, eye line, wing tips and band on tail black; forehead, eye stripe, and base of tail white; belly black with rust; bill and legs black. Winter plumage duller; in juveniles, underparts are whitish.

Habits: Found in dry steppe and semi-steppe. Migratory. Numbers are currently decreasing. Nests in steppe areas with sparse vegetation, in saline soil areas, usually near water. Often forms colonies. Nest is a thinly lined depression. Lays four eggs from mid-April

until June. Eggs resemble those of Northern Lapwing, but the spots are reduced in number and size. Easily seen. Actively defends its nest, chasing away raptors and even attacking a person. Not wary away from nest. Flight rapid and strong. Call: scraping "kree-kree." Feeds on various insects (beetles, locusts). Included in the Red Data Book.

Range and distribution: Central and Lower Volga, Kazakhstan, southern West Siberia. Winters in Egypt, the Sudan, Iraq, Pakistan.

Similar species: Differs from White-tailed Lapwing by black "cap," banded tail, white eye stripe, and black legs.

222. WHITE-TAILED LAPWING
Chettusia leucura
(Belokhvostaya Pigalitsa)
Plate 17, Map 94

Field marks: 27 cm. Smaller than Sociable Plover and more long-legged. Crown and upperparts smoky brownish; forehead, cheeks, and throat white; breast ash-gray; belly pinkish-ocher; tail white; wide, white stripe on wings; wing tips black; bill black; legs yellow; eye ring red. In juveniles, upperparts are spotted, and coloration is duller.

Habits: Found near banks of rivers and lakes, in desert zones. Migratory. Rare. Nests in damp, grassy areas, often in colonies. Lays four ocherish clay-colored eggs with dark spots and speckles from end of April to May. Lively, garrulous bird, excellent runner; flight rapid and maneuverable. Call resembles a loud "chetire-chetire." Feeds on insects. Included in the Red Data Book.

Range and distribution: Central Asia, Kazakhstan. Winters in Egypt and India, occasionally in the Transcaucasus and Turkmenia.

Similar species: Differs from Sociable Lapwing by white tail and belly; long, yellow legs; and pale head.

Lobivanellus

223. RED-WATTLED LAPWING
Lobivanellus indicus
(Ukrashenny Chibis)
Plate 17, Map 93

Field marks: 30 cm. Large shorebird; body resembles Northern Lapwing, but legs are longer. Red wattle in front of the eye; small spur at bend of wing. Head, throat, and breast black; belly and sides of neck white; back brownish with a greenish metallic glitter; tail white with black terminal band; base of bill, wattle, and eye-ring red; bill tip black; legs yellow.

Habits: Found in damp, grassy areas along river banks in desert zones. Migratory, common, and biology little known. Habits and flight resemble Northern Lapwing.

Range and distribution: South Turkmenia. Winters in India.

Similar species: Differs from Northern Lapwing by wattle in front of eyes, lack of crest, in flight by significantly lighter (grayish) back.

[An African vagrant, the **224.** SPUR-WINGED LAPWING (*Hoplopterus spinosus*) was noted near Odessa in 1837. In this species, the crown, throat, and breast are black; neck and sides of head, belly, and rump white; upperparts brownish; tail white with black terminal band. Nests in Africa and on the Balkan Peninsula. Vagrants of the **225.** GRAY-HEADED LAPWING (*Microsarcops cinerea*) were found in the areas of Vladivostok and Transbaikal. Head and neck are gray; remaining upperparts brownish; rump white; primaries black, secondaries white; small spur at bend of wing. Nests in Mongolia, southern China, Korea, and Japan.]

Genus Arenaria

226. RUDDY TURNSTONE
Arenaria interpres
(Kamnesharka)
Plate 18, Map 94

Field marks: 23 cm. Small shorebird with stubby bill and short legs. Brightly colored: upper parts rusty with white and black; belly white; upper breast black; head white with dark streaking on crown; intricate black pattern near eye and bill; legs orange. In juveniles, upperparts, head, and breast brownish.

Habits: Found on rocky seashores and islands; pebbled, hilly tundra with sparse vegetation. Migratory. Common or numerous. Nest is a shallow scrape; often hidden under a bush or rock, and always lined with leaves, stems, or lichens. Lays four olive-green eggs with bright brownish mottling in June. Very garrulous near nest; attacks any bird nearby, but when approached by man does not engage in distraction display, but quietly slips away and does not return for a long time, although it runs about and calls in the general area. Feeds on crayfish, mollusks, insect larvae, which it collects by turning over small rocks (thus the name turnstone). Call: clamorous trill, "viti-viti-vi-tititi."

Range and distribution: Shores and islands of the Baltic Sea, Arctic Ocean, and northern seas. Winters on European and Asian shores.

Similar species: Differs from Black Turnstone by rusty back and white throat.

[Vagrants of **227.** BLACK TURNSTONE (*Arenaria melanocephala*) were obtained on Wrangel Island and on the Chukotski Peninsula. Upperparts black, underparts white, legs blackish.]

Calidris

With a few exceptions, small and very small shorebirds with short legs and short, narrow bill. Little contrast in coloration, usually; finely patterned upperparts. Nests in tundra, but in summer, nonbreeding immatures are scattered. Identification difficult.

228. CURLEW SANDPIPER
Calidris ferruginea
(Krasnozobik)
Plate 19, Map 95

Field marks: 19 cm. Bill long, curved; coloration rusty red with blackish patterning on

MAP 95. Dunlin (1), Curlew Sandpiper (2)

back and brownish wings; undertail and rump white; in winter upperparts gray; underparts white with ocherish suffusion on upper breast; rump white.

Habits: Found in dry moss-lichen tundra; late in summer, found in swampy tundra; during migration, on silt shores of water bodies. Migratory. Common in places. Nests in raised areas. Nest is a depression lined with lichens and leaves of willows. Lays four greenish-olive eggs with brownish mottling in June. Female does not engage in distraction display, but runs away furtively. Often found in flocks with other shorebirds. Call: loud "peet-peet" or "r-r-you"; in spring, a variety of trills during breeding flights. Feeds on a variety of invertebrates.

Range and distribution: Tundra of northern Siberian shores from Taimyr Peninsula to the Kolyma Delta in the east. Winters in Africa, Madagascar, southern Asia, and Australia.

Similar species: Differs from Red Knot (in summer) by smaller size and longer, curved bill; from Dunlin (in autumn and summer) by white rump; from other sandpipers by curved bill.

229. DUNLIN
Calidris alpina
(Chernozobik)
Plate 19, Map 95

Field marks: 17-19 cm. Bill like Curlew Sandpiper, but shorter and less decurved. Upperparts rusty with black patterning; upper breast with dark streaks; rump brownish; belly black. In winter, upperparts and upper breast grayish; underparts white; rump dark.

Habits: Found in tundra of various types; during migration, found on silt and sandy shores of seas, rivers, and lakes (same in summer in non-nesting range). Migratory. Common or

numerous. Nests in dry, raised areas with lichen growth, as well as mossy and grass tundra. Nest is a depression lined with willow leaves. Lays four greenish or yellow-olive eggs with red-brownish or olive-brownish mottling in June. Distraction display at nest consists of running away, ruffling its feathers, half-opening its wings, and pulling its neck toward the ground ("runs like a mouse"). Occurs in flocks during nonbreeding season; flies in a tight flock low to the ground or water. Call: loud "trr-trr" or "tree-ree-ree"; during breeding flight, male makes a loud buzzing trill, "tryout-tryou-ryouryouyou." Feeds on various invertebrates (crayfish, mollusks, larvae, insects).

Range and distribution: Baltic States, tundra of European USSR, and Siberia as far as Chukotski Peninsula. Winters on shores of western Europe, North and East Africa, southern Asia.

Similar species: In summer, easily identified by rusty back and black belly; in winter plumage, differs from Curlew Sandpiper by dark rump.

230. LITTLE STINT
Calidris minuta
(Kulik-vorobey)
Plate 19, Map 96

Field marks: 14 cm. Very small (sparrow-size) shorebird with straight, short bill. Upperparts and sides of breast rufous with dark patterning; underparts white; legs black. In winter, upperparts grayer, but individual feathers black with rusty and white edgings; throat and middle of breast white.

Habits: Found in tundra of various types; during migration, found on flat, silty (more rarely sandy) shores of various bodies of water. Migratory. Common, in places numerous. Nests equally in raised areas and in thickets of grassy

MAP 96. Little Stint (1), Rufous-necked Stint (2)

or mossy tundra. Nest is lined with willow leaves and leaves of dwarf birch. Lays four olive-green or yellow eggs with reddish-brownish mottling (always redder than on eggs of Temminck's Stint); end of June to July. Does not usually engage in distraction display, and returns to the nest very quickly. Not wary. Stays in flocks during nonbreeding season, often with other shorebirds. Call: a murmuring "dirr-dirr-eet-ett"; at time of breeding flight, performs a characteristically alternating loud and soft trill. Feeds on insect larvae (mosquitoes), more rarely on other invertebrates.

Range and distribution: Tundra of European USSR and Siberia as far as Chukotski Peninsula in the east. Winters in Africa and southern Asia.

Similar species: Differs from Temminck's Stint by black legs and rusty tones in upperparts (in winter by more colorful back and white throat); from the Rufous-necked Stint, by white throat and rump; from the Long-toed Stint, by black legs and short toes; from other sandpipers, by small size (wings smaller than 10 cm.).

231. RUFOUS-NECKED STINT
Calidris ruficollis
(Pesochnik-krasnosheyka)
Plate 19, Map 96

Field marks: 16 cm. Similar to Little Stint in size and coloration, but throat and upper breast are bright, rusty red.

Habits: Found in dry or sedge-moss tundra. Migratory. In places common, but on the whole rare. Nests in grassy vegetation, on rocky soil, and nest is lined with leaves of willow or dwarf birch. Lays four ocherish eggs with small brick-red speckles melting into each other, early June to July. Either runs away from nest furtively,

or "leads away." At time of breeding flight, emits distinctive prolonged "yek ... yek ... yek ..."; when alarmed, emits a cry similar to "chlek-chlek." Feeds primarily on insects and their larvae.

Range and distribution: Tundra from Taimyr in the east to Chukotski Peninsula and Anadyr. Winters from Malacca to Australia and Tasmania.

Similar species: Differs from Little, Western, Temminck's, and Long-toed Stints by rusty red throat and upper breast (black legs and rusty back are additional features that separate it from the last two sandpipers); from the Spoon-billed Sandpiper, by shape of bill, but nearly indistinguishable in the field at first glance.

232. LONG-TOED STINT
Calidris subminuta
(Dlinnopaly Pesochnik)
Plate 19, Map 97

Field marks: 14 cm. Resembles Little Stint both in coloration and proportions of bill and legs; toes are longer; legs olive-brownish or yellowish.

Habits: Found in grassy, swampy regions and mountain tundra. Migratory. Rare. Nest is a depression on a hummock of sedge. Lays three or four pale grayish-green eggs with small brownish spots in June. Has intensive distraction display. Feeds on a variety of invertebrates.

Range and distribution: Isolated populations nest in Siberia; vicinity of Magadan, Trans-baikal, Verkhoyanski Mountains, Koryak Plateau, Chukotski Peninsula, Komandorskiye and Kuril Islands. Winters in Southeast Asia and Australia.

Similar species: Differs from Temminck's Stint

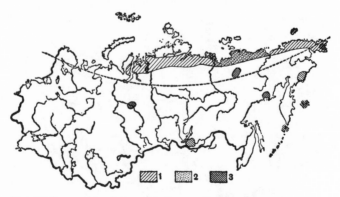

MAP 97. Pectoral Sandpiper (1), Sharp-tailed Sandpiper (2), Long-toed Stint (3)

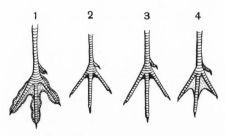

FIG. 44 SHOREBIRD FEET
1. Red-necked Phalarope   2. Little Stint
3. Long-toed Stint   4. Western Sandpiper

by rusty tones in back; from Little Stint and Rufous-necked Stint, by lighter (not black) legs; It differs from all of these three species by its long toes (middle toe is equal to or longer than metatarsus)—obviously not a field character.

233. TEMMINCK'S STINT
Calidris temminckii
(Belokhvosty Pesochnik)
Plate 19, Map 98
Field marks: 14 cm. Same size as Little Stint, but upperparts lack rusty color, and are brownish instead. Outer tail feathers white. Legs greenish-gray or yellowish. In winter plumage, upperparts are a uniform smoky color; throat and upper breast gray.
Habits: Found in low lying tundra of various types; during migration, found on open shores of rivers and lakes, and muddy swamps. Migratory. Numerous. Usually nests near water, between hummocks, in grassy vegetation, or under a bush of willow or dwarf birch. Nest is lined with sedge stems and willow leaves. Lays four eggs in June, like Little Stint, but

with overall brownish (not reddish) tones. If disturbed, quietly walks away from nest, but quickly returns; if sitting on eggs, engages in distraction display. During breeding flight, sings melodic trills, reminiscent of tinkling bells; during nonbreeding season, when birds occur in small flocks, emits characteristic murmuring cry, "dir-dir," which resembles call of Little Stint, but shorter. Feeding habits same as other sandpipers.
Range and distribution: Tundra of European USSR and Siberia from Kola Peninsula and shores of the White Sea to Chukotski Peninsula; occasionally found in forest-tundra. Winters on the Mediterranean, in Africa, and in southern Asia.
Similar species: Differs from other small sandpipers (Little, Rufous-necked, Western, and Long-toed Stints) by brownish (not rusty) tones in back (from the first two, by lighter legs as well); in winter, by gray throat and upper breast, unicolored back, and white outer tail feathers.

234. WESTERN SANDPIPER
Calidris mauri
(Pereponchatopaly Pesochnik)
Plate 19, Map 99
Field marks: 14 cm. Size and coloration resembles Little Stint, but bill significantly longer and slightly drooped at tip; occasionally rusty crown; breast has elongated streaks; three front toes clearly webbed.
Habits: Found in damp, grassy tundra. Migratory. Rare. Nests in swampy areas with sedge and deposits of silt on dry, rocky slopes. Nests under a bush or clumps of grass. Nest lined with sedge stalks and lichens. Lays four cream-colored eggs with reddish-brownish spots and striations in June. Strong distraction display only during latter half of hatching period. Very

MAP 98. Red Knot (1), Temminck's Stint (2), Baird's Sandpiper (3)

lively and garrulous. During breeding flight, male emits soft murmuring trill, "tzree"; when alarmed its cry resembles a police whistle.

Range and distribution: Chukotski Peninsula. Winters in North America, Caribbean islands.

Similar species: Differs from all other small sandpipers by long bill with drooping tip; also from Temminck's Stint by rusty tones in back; from Rufous-necked Stint by lack of rusty color on upper breast and breast. Geographically isolated from all other small sandpipers. Best diagnostic feature is webbed toes.

235. BAIRD'S SANDPIPER
Calidris bairdii
(Berdov Pesochnik)
Plate 19, Map 98

Field marks: 18 cm. Nearly the size of a thrush; upperparts brownish; breast buffy with fine streaking, sharply bordered by white belly. In winter, colors become more gray and streaking less definite.

Habits: Found in rocky tundra, mountain slopes, or rocky areas of moss-grass tundra. Migratory. Rare. Nest is a small depression on bare pebbled ground or in clump of dried grass. Nest lined with willow leaves. Lays four reddish or dove-gray eggs with brownish spots in June. Shows alarm near the nest, but engages in distraction display only during hatching. When alarmed, call resembles "veet-veet-veet." Feeds on various invertebrates.

Range and distribution: Chukotski Peninsula. Winters in South America.

Similar species: Differs from Little Stint and Western Sandpiper and other small sandpipers by larger size, and wing tips that extend beyond the tail; immature, by scaly back.

236. PECTORAL SANDPIPER
Calidris melanotos
(Dutysh)
Plate 19, Map 97

Field marks: 19 cm. Medium-size sandpiper (thrush-size) with long legs, and short, straight bill. Upperparts brown streaked with black, with whitish stripes; brownish breast heavily streaked, sharply defined below; throat and belly white; legs greenish-yellow; female smaller than male.

Habits: Found in plains of tundra of various types. Migratory, common in places. Nests on swampy or dry hummocky areas. Nest is a fairly deep depression, lined with willow leaves, situated under protection of a bush or in grass on a mound. Lays four cream-colored or light greenish eggs with large, reddish-brown spots in June to early July. Call: muffled and very distinct "do-do-do," which the bird emits during breeding time in flight or perched on a mound. When calling, neck of the bird is puffed out. Female engages in distraction display even from freshly laid eggs, and quickly returns to the nest. Feeds on various insects and their larvae (flies, mosquitoes, aquatic insects).

Range and distribution: Tundra from Chukotski Peninsula in the east to Taimyr in the west. Winters in southern South America.

Similar species: Differs from Sharp-tailed Sandpiper by sharp definition between brownish streaked breast and white belly.

237. SHARP-TAILED SANDPIPER
Calidris acuminata
(Ostrokhvosty Pesochnik)
Plate 19, Map 97

Field marks: 19 cm. Resembles Pectoral Sand-

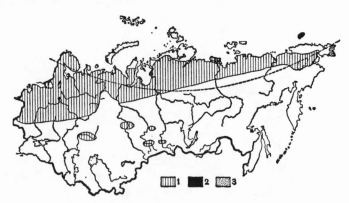

MAP 99. Ruff (1), Buff-breasted Sandpiper (2), Western Sandpiper (3)

piper, but golden colors are more evident in plumage; crown rufous; underparts heavily spotted; characteristic V-shaped mottling on sides; in juvenile and winter, border of lightly streaked buffy breast not sharp.

Habits: Found in tundra plains. Rare and migratory. Nests in damp areas with grassy-mossy vegetation and willow thickets. Nest is a depression lined with willow leaves under clumps of grass. Lays four olive-brownish or greenish eggs with brownish speckles (often blending into a single dark brownish spot on the blunt end of the egg), in June. Female engages in distraction display, but not very energetically; more often flies away, not allowing close approach. Song on breeding grounds: long, muffled trill resembling "trrr." Feeds primarily on mosquito larvae.

Range and distribution: Tundra of northern Yakutia between the rivers Yana in the west and Kolyma in the east. Winters in Australia, New Guinea, Sunda Islands (Malay Archipelago), and in southeastern Asia.

Similar species: Differs from Pectoral Sandpiper, Baird's Sandpiper, and Sanderling in winter or juvenile plumage by blurred border between buffy breast and whitish belly; in summer by V-shaped mottling on the sides, rufous crown, and greenish legs.

238. SANDERLING
Calidris alba
(Peschanka)
Plate 19, Map 100

Field marks: 20 cm. Size of a thrush. Upperparts, head, and breast rusty with frequent black speckling; belly white; legs black; rear toe lacking. In winter, upperparts light gray; underparts white.

Habits: Breeds in hilly, lichen tundra; otherwise stays on sandy or silty shores of seacoasts or other large bodies of water. Migratory. Rarely seen. Nests in dry, rocky areas, with lichens and partridge grass. Nest is a scrape, usually under a willow bush, and is lined with dead leaves. Lays four yellowish-olive eggs with brown spots end of June to July. When endangered, female leaves quickly and runs furtively from the nest for quite a distance. Lively, runs rapidly, but is generally silent. Alarm is a short "veek-veek"; song given during the display flight is a hoarse "trrr-trrr." Feeds on mosquitoes and their larvae, spiders, and other invertebrates; in spring, on plant buds.

Range and distribution: Tundra of Taimyr Peninsula, Severnaya Zemlya, Novosibirsk Islands. Winters in southern Australia and South Africa.

Similar species: Differs from Pectoral, Sharp-tailed, and Baird's Sandpipers by rusty, mottled breast and black legs; in winter, by lighter coloration. In the hand, easily identified by lack of rear toe.

Note: Many ornithologists consider this bird as a separate genus, *Crocethia*.

239. RED KNOT
Calidris canutus
(Islandsky Pesochnik)
Plate 19, Map 98

Field marks: 25 cm. Large sandpiper (larger than a thrush). Upperparts mottled brownish; entire underparts rusty reddish; tail light; legs greenish-brownish; in winter, upperparts gray with white scaling, underparts white.

Habits: Found nesting in mountainous or hilly tundra; otherwise found along seashores. Migratory, common in places. Nests on rocky

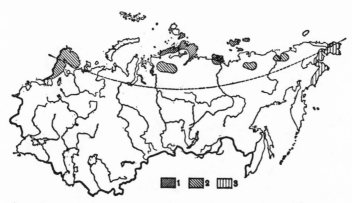

MAP 100. Sanderling (1), Broad-billed Sandpiper (2), Spoon-billed Sandpiper (3)

areas with a heavy cover of lichens. Nest is an open, shallow depression, lined with lichens. Lays four olive-green eggs with brownish splotches at the end of June. Very wary near the nest; sneaks off nest long before danger appears; but energetically engages in distraction display just before or during hatching of nestlings. Call on display flight is a loud whistle resembling "plee-vee, plee-vee," ending with a fast "kuveet-kuveet"; alarm: a short, soft "veek-veek." Feeds on various invertebrates (mosquito larvae, mollusks, crayfish); in spring, on buds and shoots of plants.

Range and distribution: Taimyr tundras, inner regions of Chukotski Peninsula, Wrangel Island. Winters in Australia.

Similar species: Differs from Curlew Sandpiper by larger size and straight bill; in winter, from other sandpipers by larger size and light gray coloration.

240. GREAT KNOT
Calidris tenuirostris
(Bolshoy Pesochnik)
Plate 19, Map 101

Field marks: 20 cm. Largest sandpiper (significantly larger than a thrush). Bill long, almost as long as Greenshank; upperparts mottled brownish with rusty scapulars; underparts white; breast black; large round black spots on flanks; rump light; legs greenish. In winter, upperparts gray with lightly spotted breast. Juveniles duller.

Habits: Found in mountain tundra, but prefers seashores during nonbreeding season. Migratory and rare. Nest in rocky areas with lichens and spots of grassy vegetation. Nest is an open depression in reindeer moss. Lays four grayish-yellow eggs with ovoid red-brownish spots

in mid-June. Male incubates. Call: soft whistling.

Range and distribution: Northeast Siberia. Winters in southern Asia and northern Australia.

Similar species: Differs from Red Knot by larger size; from Greenshank by shorter legs and by its decurved (not upturned) bill, and its call.

241. PURPLE SANDPIPER
Calidris maritima
(Morskoy Pesochnik)
Plate 19, Map 101

Field marks: 19 cm. Size of a thrush, legs short. Entire upperparts and breast grayish-black; scaly mottled back; throat and belly white; heavily mottled sides; base of bill and legs yellow. In winter, more uniformly brownish-gray; juveniles duller.

Habits: Found in mountainous or hilly, dry tundra; during nonbreeding season, stays near seashores. Migratory, in places common. Nests in rocky or pebbly areas, between cliffs and in hummocky tundra. Nest, as with other sandpipers, is lined with leaves and is poorly made. Lays four greenish-olive or brownish eggs with brownish speckles; mid-June. Distraction display consists of running away with ruffled feathers and lowered wings (like Dunlin). Both parents incubate, but young are cared for only by male. In display flight, emits loud trill, resembling "prierrr."

Range and distribution: Kola Peninsula, Novaya Zemlya, Franz Josef Land, northern shores of Taimyr. Winters in southern Europe.

Similar species: Differs from other sandpipers by dark coloration and yellow legs.

Note: Birds nesting on the Chukotski Peninsula and Komandorskiye Islands are currently

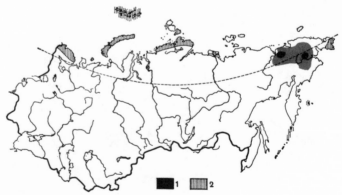

MAP 101. Great Knot (1), Purple Sandpiper (2)

viewed as a separate species, Rock Sandpiper (*Calidris ptilochemis*). They differ by large black spot on the underparts.

[A vagrant of **242.** WHITE-RUMPED SANDPIPER (*Calidris fuscicollis*) was obtained on Franz Josef Land; it was brownish, smaller than a Dunlin, with a pure white rump.]

Tryngites

243. BUFF-BREASTED SANDPIPER
Tryngites subruficollis
(Zholtozobik)
Plate 19, Map 99
Field marks: 16 cm. Small shorebird. Upperparts brownish, with strong scaly pattern; entire underparts buffy. Undersides of wings are whitish, with darker marbled tip and trailing edge. Legs yellowish. In juveniles, legs greenish.
Habits: Found in mossy-lichen, rocky tundra; during migration found on seashores and on swampy shores of tundra lakes. Migratory; very rare.
Range and distribution: Wrangel Island. Winters in South America.
Similar species: Differs from other sandpipers by its erect stance, buffy underparts, whitish underwings, and yellowish legs; in the hand, by marbled pattern on primaries.

Philomachus

244. RUFF
Philomachus pugnax
(Turukhtan)
Plate 19, Map 99
Field marks: 23-25 cm. Large shorebird (smaller than a pigeon) with long legs and short bill. Upperparts brownish, mottled with black and rust; unstreaked breast with yellowish-gray suffusion; belly white; in spring, legs are yellow or orange, in autumn yellowish. Female similar, but noticeably smaller (a little larger than a thrush), and lightly spotted on the sides of the breast. The breeding plumage of the males is exceptional, and consists of a ruff and ear tufts of long, erectile feathers that may be of various colors (usually black, white, and rusty); bare skin around face becomes colorful and "warty." Both sexes have large oval white spots on sides of tail, most readily seen in flight.
Habits: Found in various habitats from tundra to steppe. Migratory. Common. Nests in wet, marshy places with grassy vegetation, along shores of rivers and lakes. Nest is a scrape on a mound, lined with grass and leaves, always well hidden by overhanging grass. Lays four olive or greenish eggs with brownish spots in June. The birds do not pair off; instead, the female is fertilized by a male chosen from a group of males gathered in a display area called a "lek." Here the males engage in courtship displays in which they bow and run about with ruff and ear tufts raised—activities that are intensified by the arrival of the female. Female incubates and raises brood alone; engages in energetic distraction display at nest. Usually silent, but sociable; stays in flocks during nonbreeding season. Feeds on various invertebrates, mostly insects.
Range and distribution: Northern half of European USSR, Northern Siberia as far as Chukotski Peninsula in the east. Winters in Africa and southern Asia.
Similar species: Differs from smaller sandpipers by significantly longer (in spring, orange) legs; from Greenshank, by much shorter straight bill and browner coloration. It is important to note that although breeding-plumaged males are readily identifiable, males and females look alike in winter plumage, and are difficult to distinguish in the field.

Limicola

245. BROAD-BILLED SANDPIPER
Limicola falcinellus
(Gryazovik)
Plate 19, Map 100
Field marks: 16 cm. Small (sparrow-size) shore bird with longish, slightly decurved, and flattened bill. Legs short and blackish; upperparts blackish with brownish mottling; breast ocherish and lightly streaked with black; belly white. White eye stripe becomes double behind eye; two white stripes above each wing. In winter, upperparts are grayer.
Habits: Found in tundra and forest-tundra; during migration, found on silty shores and seashores. Migratory and rare. Nests in sphagnum moss bogs or grassy swamps with hummocks; dry tufts or in sedge clumps. Nest lined with leaves of birch and willow. Lays four brownish eggs thickly covered with small reddish-brownish spots, from mid-June. Secretive and silent. During display flight, emits a Dunlinlike trill. Male sometimes perches in trees for a short period. Call in flight: short "tirr-tirr-terek." Feeds on insects and their larvae, and mollusks.
Range and distribution: Taiga and tundra of

northern European USSR and Siberia. Winters on shores of Mediterranean, in southern Asia, and Australia.

Similar species: Differs from other sandpipers by longer, flattened bill (appears thick); from Jack Snipe, by smaller size (but not always), decurved bill, blackish legs.

Eurynorhynchus

246. SPOON-BILLED SANDPIPER
Eurynorhynchus pygmaeus
(Kulik-lopaten)
Plate 19, Map 100

Field marks: 15 cm. Small (sparrow-size) shorebird with paddlelike flattening on tip of bill. Upperparts rusty, mottled; throat and breast bright rusty; belly white; legs black.

Habits: Found in dry, raised, or swampy lowland tundra; during migration stays on flat seashores. Nests in grassy areas near freshwater puddles, and in dry meadows. Nest is a depression lined with willow leaves. Lays three to four pale brownish eggs with small brown spots from mid-June. Male usually incubates and cares for young; stays hidden and wary near nest; becomes greatly agitated when approached after nestlings emerge. Call during display flight is a buzzing trill, resembling a cicada. Feeds on various invertebrates (insects, small crayfish) that it catches at water edges. Included in the Red Data Book.

Range and distribution: Chukotski Peninsula. Winters in Southeast Asia.

Similar species: Differs from other sandpipers by characteristic shape of bill, but it must be remembered that the "paddle" is not visible in profile, and thus bird can be confused with the Rufous-necked Stint.

Limnodromus

Medium-size shore birds (significantly larger than a thrush), with long legs and very long, straight bill. Head is small and neck is long.

247. LONG-BILLED DOWITCHER
Limnodromus scolopaceus
(Amerikansky Bekasovidny Veretennik)
Plate 20, Map 102

Field marks: 25 cm. Upperparts mottled, blackish-brownish; underparts rusty red; black barring on breast and sides; white wedge up lower back; rump and tail whitish with black barring. In winter, grayish with barred undertail coverts.

Habits: Found in damp lowland tundra and forest-tundra; during migration found on seashores. Migratory and rare. Nests in boggy areas, usually near water. Nest situated on a mound, in moss or dry grass, and lined with willow leaves. Lays four olive-ocher eggs with brownish spots from beginning of June. Sits tight on nest, and flushes at close range; sometimes does distraction display. Nestlings are raised by male, which becomes greatly agitated when approached and flies in circles overhead, crying loudly. Call: murmuring "kreeku-kreeku-kreeku." Feeds on various invertebrates (insects and their larvae, mollusks), by thrusting bill deeply into substrate.

Range and distribution: Tundra from lower Yana River in the west to Chukotski Peninsula and Anadyr lowlands in the east. Winters in South America and southern North America.

Similar species: Differs from Bar-tailed Godwit by smaller size (wing no larger than 15 cm.) and straight bill; from the Asian Dowitcher by its white back (ranges do not overlap).

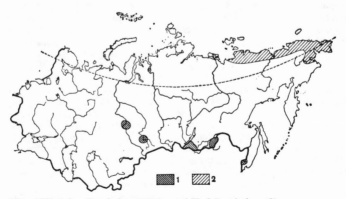

MAP 102. Asian Dowitcher (1), Long-billed Dowitcher (2)

248. ASIAN DOWITCHER
Limnodromus semipalmatus
(Aziatsky Bekasovidny Veretennik)
Plate 20, Map 102

Field marks: 31 cm. Resembles Long-billed Dowitcher, but larger (wing no less than 16 cm.); tail, rump, and lower back whitish with dark barring; underparts without spots or bars.

Habits: Found in swampy regions in various habitats; during migration, on seashores. Migratory. Very rare. Nests in damp, grassy swales in small colonies. Nest situated either on a hummock or on the level ground, well hidden under dried grass. Lays two yellowish-sandy eggs with thick, dark speckles end of May. Not wary near the nest, allows close approach, and does not have a distraction display. Call: soft crying, "kru-ru, kru-ru." Feeds on insect larvae and worms. Included in the Red Data Book.

Range and distribution: Southern shores of Lake Baikal, West Siberia, and Soviet Far East. Winters in India, Indochina, Indonesia.

Similar species: Differs from Bar-tailed Godwit by straight bill and smaller size (wing no larger than 18 cm.); from the Black-tailed Godwit, by lack of wing stripe and black and white tail; from Long-billed Dowitcher, by darker back and larger size (difficult to distinguish, but generally not found in the same range).

Tringa

Medium-size (more rarely large or small), light, and graceful shorebirds, with long bill and legs. Neck is longish and fairly slender. Coloration not bright, usually with a predominance of gray or dark gray.

249. GREEN SANDPIPER
Tringa ochropus
(Chernysh)
Plate 20, Map 103

Field marks: 23 cm. Larger than a starling. Upperparts blackish-brownish; breast and neck gray with mottling; belly and rump white; wing lining dark. Legs are dark greenish. All colors grayer in winter.

Habits: Found in forest habitat; during migration, found everywhere. Migratory. Common. Nests along river shores and streamsides in forest and lake swamps. Sometimes nest is situated on the ground, more often in old nests of thrushes, crows, and jays, usually at a great height (up to 10 m.). Lays four dove-gray eggs with small reddish-brown spots from mid-May to end of June. Wary, but bold and garrulous near nestlings. Often perches in tree branches.

Call: very loud, beautiful, "metallic" song, "tee-t-t-ttv-ttve." Usually flies up from a puddle or streamside in a forest, with a raucous cry and, flashing its bright white rump, disappears. Feeds on various invertebrates (aquatic or terrestrial), but exclusively near water.

Range and distribution: Greater part of the USSR except north and northeast regions of Siberia, Kola Peninsula, Kamchatka Peninsula, Soviet Far East, Caucasus, and deserts of Central Asia. Winters in Central Asia, Transcaucasus, in the Mediterranean, Africa, and southern Asia.

Similar species: Differs from other Tringa by strikingly bright white rump contrasting with a nearly all-black back; similar to but larger than Wood Sandpiper (wing no smaller than 13 cm.), with blackish underwings.

250. WOOD SANDPIPER
Tringa glareola
(Fifi)
Plate 20, Map 104

Field marks: 20 cm. Resembles Green Sandpiper, but smaller (wing no more than 13 cm.). Upperparts noticeably grayer, with whitish spots; legs light, yellowish (in flight, feet visible at end of tail). In winter, grayer, spots on back smaller. Juveniles have rusty spots on back.

Habits: Found in a variety of habitats from tundra to steppe; even in open, swampy places during migration. Migratory. Common. Nests in swampy tundra, in mossy bogs, along forest rivers and lakes, and in grassy meadows. Nest is a depression in moss or grass, lined with sedge stalks or willow leaves, and dwarf-birch leaves; on occasion uses nest of thrush. Lays four greenish eggs with reddish-brown spots from mid-May to end of June. Greatly agitated near the nest, flying around and calling. During nonbreeding season, fairly trusting. Often perches in bushes and trees. Call: disyllabic, characteristic "fee-fee, fee-fee." Feeds primarily on insects and their larvae.

Range and distribution: Northern half of USSR except unforested Siberian tundra. Winters in Africa, southern Asia, and Australia.

Similar species: Differs from Green Sandpiper by lighter and more spotted back, less contrasting rump, light legs, light underwings, and smaller size; from the Common Sandpiper, by spotted back and light rump.

251. GREATER GREENSHANK
Tringa nebularia
(Bolshoy Ulit)
Plate 20, Map 105

Field marks: 30 cm. Nearly the size of a pigeon. Bill slightly upturned; legs greenish, long and,

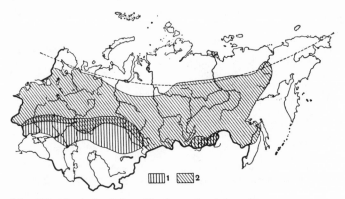

MAP 103. Marsh Sandpiper (1), Green Sandpiper (2)

in flight, extend well beyond tail tip. Upperparts brownish-gray; breast streaked; underparts and rump white; wing lining whitish with brownish barring. In winter similar but lighter colored.

Habits: Found in forest zones; in places, enters forest-tundra. During migration, found on silty beaches of seas, rivers, and lakes. Common and migratory. Nests in forest lakes, streams, and mossy bogs. Nest is a depression lined with bits of moss, usually situated near a hummock or stump. Lays four dove-gray eggs with intense black-brownish spots from mid-May to end of June. Egg-laying is preceded by mating flights, during which time the male emits very loud, beautiful whistles, "tlee-tyouee, tlee-tyoueee." When nest is approached, bird circles with loud cries and perches briefly on tree branches, balancing with its wings. Wary during nonbreeding season. Feeds in the water, often wading nearly up to the belly. Feeds on

insects and their larvae, often eats small fish and fry.

Range and distribution: North European USSR, central and eastern regions of Siberia. Winters on the Mediterranean, in Africa, southern Asia, and Australia.

Similar species: Differs from Common and Spotted Redshanks by greenish legs and upturned bill; from the Gray-tailed Tattler, by white rump; from Spotted Greenshank, by barred wing lining.

252. COMMON REDSHANK
Tringa totanus
(Travnik)
Plate 20, Map 106

Field marks: 28 cm. Large shorebird (but smaller than Greater Greenshank), with short bill and long legs. Upperparts brownish-gray with black mottling; underparts whitish and heavily streaked; rump white; wide, white wing

MAP 104. Wood Sandpiper (1), Gray-tailed Tattler (2)

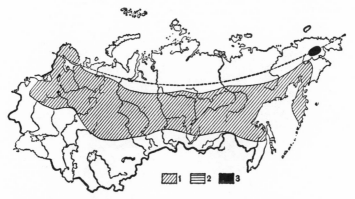

MAP 105. Greater Greenshank (1), Spotted Greenshank (2),
Wandering Tattler (3)

stripe (visible in flight); base of bill and legs
red. In winter, underparts whiter, less mottled
on back.

Habits: Found in variety of habitat from taiga
to mountains and desert, where it prefers grassy
swamps and wet meadows near water. During
migration, stays near silty beaches of seas, rivers, and lakes. Migratory, common, in places
numerous. Often nests in small colonies. Nest
usually situated on hummock or on tuft, well
hidden by overhanging grass. Lays four pale
ocherish eggs with black-brownish spots from
mid-May to mid-June. Nesting habits, same as
other shorebirds; wary during nonbreeding
season. Call: rapid "tyou-lee, tyou-lee," and a
whistle, "te-liyee"; when alarmed, a frequent
"tyout-tyout-tyout." Feeds in shallow water on
a variety of terrestrial and aquatic invertebrates.

Range and distribution: Southern half of Eu-
ropean USSR, southern Siberia, Soviet Far East.
Winters in Africa and southern Asia. In the
USSR, southern part of Caspian Sea.

Similar species: Differs from other shorebirds
by wide white wing stripe and white (wedge-
shaped) rump.

253. SPOTTED REDSHANK
Tringa erythropus
(Shchyógol)
Plate 20, Map 106

Field marks: 30 cm. Smaller than the Greater
Greenshank. Slate-black with white speckles
on back; wing lining white; rump white; long
legs and long straight bill are red. In winter,
grayish with white rump and belly.

Habits: Found in tundra and forest-tundra;
during migration and on wintering grounds
prefers swamps and shores of rivers, lakes,
etc. Migratory. Rare. Nests in grassy or sphagnum moss bogs, more rarely in drier places.
Nest situated on a mound or directly on the
ground (in a dry, raised area, often under a
rock or fallen tree). Nest lined with leaves of
willow or dwarf birch. Lays four greenish eggs
with large dark brownish splotches, from end
of May. Call during display flight: "tyou-vee-
veeyou, tik-tik-tik, tyou-vee-veeyou"; when
alarmed, emits a harsh, disyllabic "tyou-veet."
Very wary, particularly during migration.
Leaves early when nest is approached and does
not return for long period. When young hatch,
loses all fear, and flies about and cries "tek-
tek-tek," and sits on water or in bushes. Usually feeds on shores of shallows, wading in
water up to its belly and feeding on various
insects and their larvae, crayfish, and mollusks.

Range and distribution: Tundra of European
USSR and Siberia except Yamal, Taimyr, and
eastern tip of Chukotski Peninsula. Winters
in Africa and southern Asia; in the USSR, it
winters in southern regions of the Caspian Sea
and occasionally in Central Asia.

Similar species: Differs from all other shorebirds easily by black coloration; in winter, by
red base of mandible.

254. MARSH SANDPIPER
Tringa stagnatilis
(Porucheynik)
Plate 20, Map 103

Field marks: 23 cm. Size of a Green Sandpiper,
but with much longer legs, and more graceful
body. Upperparts brownish-gray with dark
mottling; underparts white with fine streaking
on upper breast and sides; rump and axillars
white; legs greenish.

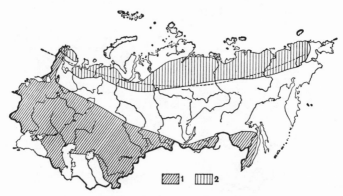

MAP 106. Common Redshank (1), Spotted Redshank (2)

Habits: Found in swampy regions of lakes and in river valleys in steppe and forest-steppe. During migration, found along shores of freshwater bodies. Rare and migratory. Nests in grassy, hummocky swamps and in damp meadows, often in small flocks. Nest situated on a mound or on remains of haystacks, and is lined with dry grass. Lays four cream or yellowish eggs with large, red-brownish spots from early May. During display flight, song resembles "tee-tee-tee." Sits tightly on nest; when disturbed, circles around intruder with loud cries, and attempts to lead him away. Long, often dangling legs are readily seen at this time. Trusting during nonbreeding season. Feeds in damp places and in shallow water on aquatic insects and their larvae.

Range and distribution: South European USSR, Kazakhstan, southern Siberia. Winters in East Africa, southern Asia, Australia. In the USSR, sometimes winters on southern regions of Caspian Sea.

Similar species: Differs from Wood Sandpiper and Green Sandpiper by much longer legs and white wedge-shaped rump; from other Tringa by smaller size (wing no more than 14 cm.), and/or very slender bill.

255. SPOTTED GREENSHANK
Tringa guttifer
(Okhotsky Ulit)
Plate 20, Map 105
Field marks: 30 cm. Resembles Greater Greenshank, but smaller; bill stouter; pure white underwings and axillars.
Habits: Found in swampy lowlands; during migration, stays near seashores. Migratory. Very rare. Nests from beginning of June. Nest, made of moss and lichens, is situated in trees, usually larch. Feeds on aquatic invertebrates and small fish. Included in the Red Data Book.

Range and distribution: Sakhalin Island. Winters in southern Asia as far as Borneo.
Similar species: Difficult to distinguish, but differs from Greater Greenshank by pure white feathers under wings, and yellowish legs.

256. GRAY-TAILED TATTLER
Tringa brevipes
(Sibirsky Pepelny Ulit)
Plate 20, Map 104
Field marks: 25 cm. Bill straight; entire upperparts ash-gray; underparts white; wavy barring on breast and sides (missing in winter).
Habits: Found in mountains and upper regions of forests. During migration, on seashores. Migratory. Rare. Nests on shores and islands in fast rivers with rocky bottoms. Nest situated on the ground between rocks; or uses old nests of thrushes. Lays four light blue eggs with black speckles from early June until July. Sits tightly on nest; when young emerge, is greatly agitated by close approach. Call: disyllabic "tu-ueet." Feeds primarily on insects and their larvae in shallow water and in sand.
Range and distribution: Southern Taimyr, some regions of East Siberia (Yakutia), Koryak Plateau. Winters in Indonesia, in the Philippines, Australia, Polynesia, Tasmania.
Similar species: Differs from Wandering Tattler by white belly, from other Tringa by ash-gray coloration of upperparts and horizonal barring on breast.
Note: Some ornithologists consider the Gray-tailed Tattler and the Wandering Tattler a single species.

257. WANDERING TATTLER
Tringa incana
(Amerikansky Pepelny Ulit)
Not illustrated, Map 105
Field marks: 27 cm. Greatly resembles Gray-

tailed Tattler, but larger, and entire underparts, including belly and undertail, are narrowly barred.

Habits: Found in USSR on several occasions, but nesting has not been determined. Habits are apparently similar to Gray-tailed Tattler.

Range and distribution: Chukotski Peninsula and shores of Sea of Okhotsk probable. Winters in Australia.

Similar species: Differs from Gray-tailed Tattler by entirely barred underparts; from other Tringa, by gray coloration.

Actitis

258. COMMON SANDPIPER
Actitis hypoleucos
(Perevozchik)
Plate 20, Map 107

Field marks: 19 cm. Smallish (size of a thrush); bill and legs fairly short; upperparts brownish with slight iridescence, and narrow, blackish barring. Underparts white with brownish suffusion at sides of upper breast, and narrow streaking on neck and breast; legs gray.

Habits: Found in a variety of habitats from forest-tundra to steppe, but inhabits only shorelines of inland water bodies; found on seashores during migration. Migratory. Common. More frequently seen than other Tringa. Nests in rocky, sandy, and even thickety or forested shores and islands in rivers and lakes. Nest is a shallow depression near the water, lined with dry stems, usually situated under a clump of grass. Lays four light pinkish-gray eggs, speckled red-brownish, from mid-May to end of June. Usually "distracts" from the nest, sometimes circles overhead, crying loudly. Call during breeding flight is "hee-deedee-dee"; when perched: a loud trill 'tee-t-t-t,";

usual call is "tyouee-tyouee." Solitary during nonbreeding season. Often perches on snags of trees or branches emerging from the water, characteristically bobbing its tail. Flies over water with bowed wings, alternating wing beats and gliding. Feeds in shallow water or on water edges on various small invertebrates.

Range and distribution: Most of USSR except tundra and forest-tundra. Winters in Africa and southern Asia.

Similar species: Differs from Green Sandpiper and Wood Sandpiper by lighter upperparts, white wing stripe, and lack of white rump; from stints, by longer legs and uniformly brownish upperparts; from the Terek Sandpiper, by its straight bill; and from all by its bobbing of head and tail.

Xenus

259. TEREK SANDPIPER
Xenus cinereus
(Morodunka)
Plate 20, Map 107

Field marks: 22 cm. Thrush-size shorebird with short legs. Bill noticeably curved upward; upperparts brownish or smoky gray with two irregular black stripes; underparts white with narrow streaking on breast and neck. Legs yellow. In winter, grayer, nearly without mottling.

Habits: Found in a variety of habitats from tundra to forest-steppe, where it lives on freshwater shores. Found on silty seashores as well during migration. Migratory. In places common. Nests alone or in small colonies in remote forest streams and lakes; on large rivers, on open sandy beaches, and on islands. Nest situated in a dry place near the water, under a bush or grasses, sometimes in the open. Nest

MAP 107. Common Sandpiper (1), Terek Sandpiper (2)

lined with grasses, bits of bark, pine needles. Lays four dove-gray eggs, speckled blackish-brownish, from early May to end of June. When approached, female leaves the nest and runs a short distance, loudly calling and twitching its tail; more rarely "distracts." Call during breeding flight: loud, characteristic "kuved-ryouyou." Feeds in shallow water, on silty or sandy shores right at water's edge. Lowers bill into water almost horizontally. Feeds on insects and their larvae, crayfish, and mollusks.

Range and distribution: Forests of European USSR and Siberia. Winters in East Africa, Madagascar, southern Asia, and Australia.

Similar species: Differs from all other small shorebirds by long upcurved bill.

Limosa

260. BLACK-TAILED GODWIT

Limosa limosa
(Bolshoy Veretennik)
Plate 17, Map 108

FIG. 45 Black-tailed Godwit Chick

Field marks: 40 cm. Larger than a pigeon. Upperparts rusty brownish, mottled; head and breast rusty red; belly white with heavy dark barring; tail black with white base; bill slightly upturned. Characteristic white stripe on wing, and long legs extending well beyond the tail, are readily seen in flight. In winter, head and underparts are gray.

Habits: Found in forest-steppe, steppe, and south of forest zones. Common and migratory. Nests in small colonies in grassy and mossy swamps, in damp meadows, and lake lowlands. Nest is situated on a mound or on dry hillock amid sedge. Lays four olive-green eggs with puddled, brownish spots from May to June. During display flight, emits a repetitive

cry that blends into song: "vzotya-vzotya." When nesting area is approached, the godwit flies directly at the intruder with loud cries, circles overhead, often sits on the ground or in trees nearby. In the beginning of summer, feeds in dry places, preferring terrestrial insects; toward autumn, moves closer to shallow shores of water bodies, where it hunts for various invertebrates (crayfish, water insects and their larvae).

Range and distribution: Southern half of European USSR except Lower Volga and the Caucasus; Kazakhstan, Chukotski Peninsula, Soviet Far East. Winters in southwest Europe, Africa, southern Asia, and Australia.

Similar species: Differs from Bar-tailed God-

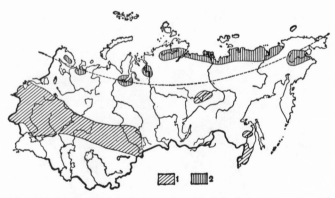

MAP 108. Black-tailed Godwit (1), Bar-tailed Godwit (2)

wit by nearly straight bill, black tail with white base; white wing stripe and long legs also readily seen in flight.

261. BAR-TAILED GODWIT
Limosa lapponica
(Maly Veretennik)
Plate 17, Map 108

Field marks: 37 cm. Smaller than Black-tailed Godwit, bill slightly upturned; breast and belly rusty red; tail white with frequent, dark barring; no wing stripes. In winter, browner than Black-tailed Godwit.

Habits: Found in tundra and forest-tundra; during migration, prefers pine and sandy seasides and swampy lowlands near lakes. Migratory. Not numerous. Nests in mossy, very swampy tundra with lakes, in sedge bogs. Often forms small colonies. Always stays in flocks during nonbreeding season. Nest situated on a hummock or on a dry, raised area, often under a thicket. Lays four olive-greenish or olive eggs with brownish spots from early June. Male and female both incubate. When alarmed, the nesting bird flies out to meet the intruder with loud cries; often perches on a nearby hummock or tree, usually trying to distract from the nest. Sometimes flushes at very close range. If there are nestlings, both parents will circle overhead. Feeds by wading in shallow water and dipping entire bill into water or mud; feeds primarily on insects and their larvae.

Range and distribution: Tundra regions from Kola Peninsula in the west, to Chaun Bay in the east. Winters in East Africa, shores of Persian Gulf, Indonesia, Australia, and New Zealand.

Similar species: Differs from Black-tailed Godwit by lighter, narrowly striped tail, rusty

belly, more slightly upcurved bill; in flight, by lack of white wing stripe and shorter legs.

Numenius

Large- and medium-size curlews with long, deeply curved bills. Brownish gray colors predominate.

262. EURASIAN CURLEW
Numenius arquata
(Bolshoy Kronshnep)
Plate 17, Map 109

Field marks: 57 cm. Larger than a crow. Brownish-gray with black mottling; narrow elongated streaks on head and breast; rump white, sometimes mottled; long downcurved bill.

Habits: Found in forest habitat and steppe. Migratory, and common in places. Nests in mossy and grassy swales in damp lowlands of lakes, in flooded meadows; and further south, in dry steppe. Sometimes forms small colonies. Nest is a shallow depression on the ground or on a mound. Lays four greenish eggs with brownish spots from early May until June. Extremely wary. When spotting danger from a distance, flies up and emits drawn-out, plaintive cry, "kooo-ee" while circling. Will not approach the intruder. When sitting on the nest, prefers to leave it furtively, running hunched over, and will only fly up of necessity. Display song is a loud, varying, whistling trill. Stays in flocks during nonbreeding season. Feeds near water, on silty shores, sometimes in dry places. Dips bill deep into water. Feeds on insects and other invertebrates, sometimes on berries, small fish.

Range and distribution: European USSR and

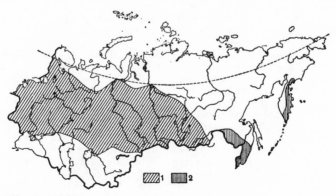

MAP 109. Eurasian Curlew (1), Eastern Curlew (2)

MAP 110. Whimbrel (1), Slender-billed Curlew (2),
Little Curlew (3)

West Siberia except bordering north and Caucasus; Kazakhstan, southern part of East Siberia. Winters in Africa and southern Asia.
Similar species: Differs from Whimbrel by unstriped head and longer bill; from the Eastern Curlew, by light rump and white, nearly unstriped axillars; from the Slender-billed Curlew by lack of rounded spots on lower breast, and larger size.

263. WHIMBREL
Numenius phaeopus
(Sredny Kronshnep)
Plate 17, Map 110
Field marks: 39 cm. Resembles Eurasian Curlew, but smaller; bill shorter, crown black-brownish with light median stripe.
Habits: Found in forest-tundra and taiga, sometimes in steppe. Migratory. Locally rare or common. Nests in mossy bogs, along lake shores in tundra, in swampy, burned areas, in steppe along river valleys and in damp lowlands. Nest is situated in dry place, often on a hummock or under clumps of grass. Nest lined with reindeer moss and leaves of dwarf birch and willow. Lays four elongated greenish or brownish-olive eggs, with brownish spots end of May to June. Runs from nest and hides when approached, then flies up and circles overhead, calling. Often perches in trees. Call of alarm is "kee-küh-rüh-rüh." Display song is similar to that of Eurasian Curlew, but not as pleasant sounding. Call, however, is unique, and unlike whistle of Eurasian Curlew: consists of staccato chirping. Not very wary, particularly during migration. Stays in flocks during nonbreeding season. Feeds on insects and their larvae.
Range and distribution: North European

USSR; Siberia in places. Winters in Africa, southern Asia, and Australia.
Similar species: Differs from other curlews by striped head.

264. EASTERN CURLEW
Numenius madagascariensis
(Dalnevostochny Kronshnep)
Not illustrated, Map 109
Field marks: 57 cm. Greatly resembles Eurasian Curlew, but rump is dark; axillars have dark barring; bill longer.
Habits: Found in broad, mossy swamps, and swampy meadows. Migratory and common in places. Often nests in small colonies. Nest situated on hummock or dry hill. Lays four brownish-olive eggs with brownish spots (darker than those of Eurasian Curlew) end of April to May. Feeds on insects, their larvae, and worms.
Range and distribution: Soviet Far East. Winters in the Philippines, Indonesia, Australia, and Tasmania.
Similar species: Differs from Eurasian Curlew by dark rump and strongly barred axillars.

265. SLENDER-BILLED CURLEW
Numenius tenuirostris
(Tonkoklyuvy Kronshnep)
Plate 17, Map 110
Field marks: 39 cm. Resembles Eurasian Curlew in coloration, but markedly smaller. Large, heart-shaped spots on lower part of breast.
Habits: Found in peat bogs in forest-steppe zones. During migration, in damp meadows along rivers. Migratory. Very rare and, apparently, a dying species. Nests in small colonies. Nest situated on dry, open place, in thickets of sedge or on a mound. Lays four

greenish-olive eggs with brownish spots from mid-may until early June. Nesting habits resemble Eurasian Curlew, but call of alarm is entirely different; it is a unique, trembling whistle, resembling call of the Black Kite. When alarmed, bird also emits loud, halting, "bi-bi-bi." Feeding habits and many other aspects of its biology entirely unknown. Included in the Red Data Book.

Range and distribution: West Siberia. Winters in the Mediterranean and in Iraq.

Similar species: Differs from Eurasian Curlew by smaller size and heart-shaped spotting on breast and sides; from the Whimbrel, by light, unstriped head, and from all other curlews by spots on breast.

266. LITTLE CURLEW
Numenius minutus
(Kronshnep-malyutka)
Plate 17, Map 110

Field marks: 30 cm. Smallest of the curlews (pigeon-size), with short, slightly curved bill. Crown black-brownish with ocherish median stripe; rump dark; indistinct barring on sides.

Habits: Found in stunted forests in subalpine regions of mountains. Prefers swampy meadows near lakes and along river valleys during migration. Migratory. Rare. Nests in varying-sized colonies; old, sedge-covered, burned-over forests; usually on the southern slope of a mountain. Nest is on the ground and lined with dead grass. Lays four greenish eggs, spotted brownish, in the beginning of June. Female sits tight on nest, allowing approach up to two or three meters, then silently flushes off the nest and sits on ground or in dead tree nearby. If eggs are hatched, circles overhead calling loudly. Feeds on beetles and other insects, berries. Included in the Red Data Book.

Range and distribution: Central Yakutia, East Siberia. Winters in Australia.

Similar species: Differs from other curlews by smaller size and short, slightly curved bill.

[A vagrant of the nearly extinct **267.** ESKIMO CURLEW (*Numenius borealis*) of North America was obtained on Chukotski Peninsula at the end of the last century. It resembles the Little Curlew, but is slightly larger. Some ornithologists lump the Little Curlew and the Eskimo Curlew into one species.]

Phalaropus

Small shorebirds (size of thrush or smaller) with short legs and short bill. Toes with lobed webs. Plumage of underparts is very thick and compact. Most often seen swimming on water, characteristically nodding their heads.

268. RED-NECKED PHALAROPE
Phalaropus lobatus
(Kruglonosy Plavunchik)
Plate 18, Map 111

Field marks: 16 cm. Bill long, thin. Upperparts and breast blackish-gray with rusty stripes on back; throat and belly white; sides of neck and throat bright rusty. Male noticeably duller. In winter, upperparts brownish-gray; entire underparts white; black eye line.

Habits: Found in tundra and forest-tundra; during migration, found on bodies of water in a variety of habitats. Migratory. Common and, in places, numerous. Nests in damp, grassy, or hummocky areas near lakes. Nest built by both parents, usually in a thicket of sedge, and lined with dry stalks and leaves of willow. Lays four olive-ocherish eggs with black-

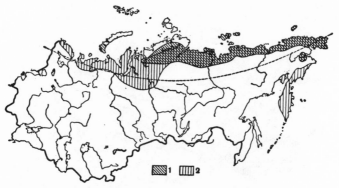

MAP 111. Red Phalarope (1), Red-necked Phalarope (2)

brownish spots from early June. Male incubates alone; after laying, female usually leaves and flies further south. (There have been observations that some females may also incubate the eggs.) Bird flushes from the nest at very close range, dropping down again nearby and quickly returning. During the breeding season, call resembles "kik-kik-kikik-tree-kik"; when alarmed, "chrree-chree." Very trusting, allowing close approach to nest. Feeds on water, primarily on insect larvae, crayfish, and mollusks.

Range and distribution: Northern regions of European USSR and Siberia. Winters in western Africa, southern Asia, and Southeast Asia.

Similar species: Differs from Red Phalarope by coloration; also by smaller size; needlelike, long bill; and dark legs.

269. RED PHALAROPE
Phalaropus fulicarius
(Ploskonosy Plavunchik)
Plate 18, Map 111

Field marks: 20 cm. Slightly larger than Red-necked Phalarope; bill shorter, slightly flattened. Upperparts mottled, rusty black; underparts completely rusty red; cheeks white; cap and throat black; base of bill yellow. Male noticeably duller, with some white on belly and without black cap. In winter plumage, adults and juveniles have smoky gray upperparts; white underparts; black eye line and yellow legs.

Habits: Found in swampy tundra with lakes; during migration found at sea and in larger inland water bodies. Common or numerous. Nesting periods, feeding, and all habits similar to Red-necked Phalarope. Eggs indistinguishable by color but usually slightly larger. Call: rapid "tick-tick-tick," ending in a slightly murmuring "krree-krree."

Range and distribution: Northern Siberia, Novaya Zemlya. Winters on western shores of Africa and on the Persian Gulf.

Similar species: Differs from Red-necked Phalarope in winter plumage by larger size, short, flattened bill, yellow legs, and light gray upperparts.

Himantopus

270. BLACK-WINGED STILT
Himantopus himantopus
(Khodulochnik)
Plate 17, Map 112

Field marks: 38 cm. Large shorebird with straight, thin bill and disproportionately long legs. Color contrasting; top of head, back, and wings black; entire underparts and tail white; legs red. Females have white heads, juveniles have brownish-gray upperparts.

Habits: Found in steppe and desert zones. Migratory. Common. Nests along open shorelines of fresh- and salt-water lakes in grassy swamps, usually in colonies, often with other species. Nest is always situated near water, on hard ground, often on a hummock. It is a depression lined with dry stalks. Bird lays four brownish-olive eggs with black-brownish spots from early May. When disturbed, entire colony flies out to meet the intruder, circling, with legs dangling. Fairly wary during nonbreeding season. Call: harsh monosyllabic cry, "ap-ap-ap." Feeds in shallow water, on silty shores, preferring aquatic insects, mollusks, crayfish.

Range and distribution: South European USSR, Kazakhstan, Central Asia. Winters in Africa and in southern Asia.

Similar species: Differs from Black-capped Avocet by straight bill and red legs.

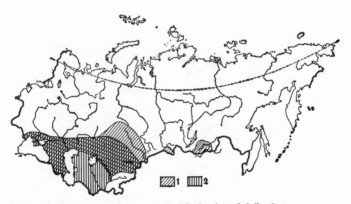

MAP 112. Black-capped Avocet (1), Black-winged Stilt (2)

Recurvirostra

271. BLACK-CAPPED AVOCET
Recurvirostra avosetta
(Shiloklyuvka)
Plate 17, Map 112
Field marks: 43 cm. Large shorebird with long legs and with long, thin, strongly upcurved bill. Coloration contrasting: crown and neck, stripe on wing, and wing tips black; remaining plumage white; legs bluish.
Habits: Found in steppe and desert, sometimes along seashores. Migratory. Common in places. Nests in lowlands nearly devoid of vegetation, in saline soil or sandy lake shores, sometimes on dry or boggy spits of land near seas. Forms colonies, partly with Black-winged Stilts and plovers. Stays in flocks during nonbreeding season. Nest is an open depression, nearly without lining, close to water. Lays four ocherish eggs with small black-brownish spots from early May until mid-June. Behavior same as Black-winged Stilt when nest is approached; a constant screaming and energetic distraction display. Call: very loud 'klee-ee-klee" or "kuik-kuik." Feeds in shallow water, lowering its bill slightly into water and sweeping it from side to side. Good swimmer. Feeds on small crayfish, insect larvae, and mollusks.
Range and distribution: South European USSR, Central Asia, Kazakhstan, south of West Siberia, Tuva, Transbaikal. Winters in USSR in south Caspian Sea. Outside the USSR, in Africa and southern Asia.
Similar species: Differs from Black-winged Stilt by upturned bill and dark legs.

Scolopax

272. EURASIAN WOODCOCK
Scolopax rusticola
(Valdshnep)
Plate 20, Map 113
Field marks: 34 cm. Large (pigeon-size) shorebird with very long bill and short legs. Upper parts rusty red with dark and light mottling; underparts gray with brownish barring. Eyes are large and black.
Habits: Found in plains and hills in forest, more rarely in forest-tundra and forest-steppe. Stays in unfrozen areas of rivers in winter. Migratory and common. Nests in deciduous or mixed forest with thicket, small bogs, damp precipices with thicketed edges. Nest situated under a bush, stump, or fallen tree; often in grass, sometimes on a hummock. Beginning of breeding period varies, depending upon location and an early or late spring. Lays four

ocherish eggs with rusty spots from April to end of June. Female sits tight on nest, flushes reluctantly at close range, and does not engage in a distraction display. Once flushed, prefers to run away. The well-known mating display flight begins during migration, in mid-April, and continues until the end of June. The characteristic mating call is "ook, ook-tsssee, tsssee." Flight occurs in reforested areas, thin woods, along borders of tall forests, and over swampy lowlands. Mating flight begins at sunset, continuing until full darkness; then beginning once more before sunrise. Feeds on worms and larvae of various insects, which it extracts from soft damp ground.
Range and distribution: European USSR (except northern and southern unforested regions); southern Siberia, Soviet Far East, Sakhalin Island. Winters in Transcaucasus and Central Asia. Outside USSR, in southern regions of Western Europe, Mongolia, Japan.
Similar species: Differs from Common Snipe by larger size.

Gallinago

Medium-size shorebird with short legs and very long bill. Brown and ocherish colors predominate in plumage.

273. COMMON SNIPE
Gallinago gallinago
(Bekas)
Plate 20, Map 114
Field marks: 26 cm. Larger than a thrush. Long bill. Upperparts dark brownish with ocherish mottling; breast brownish-ocherish with dark streaks; belly white; crown black with ocherish median stripe; outer tail feathers nearly as wide as central ones, rustier with black bars and narrow white tips.
Habits: Found in a variety of habitats from tundra to steppe, always in damp, swampy regions. Migratory. Common or numerous. Nests in hummocky, grassy, and sphagnum-moss swamps, in flooded meadows, on marshy shores of lakes and rivers, in damp lowlands of steppe, even in swampy forests. Nest situated on a mound or on sedge-covered tuft, usually well hidden by overhanging grass and lined with stems and leaves. Lays four olive-brownish eggs with brownish spots from end of April to June. Female sits tight on nest, and flushes only at close range. Flight is swift, with several zigzags after takeoff, and is accompanied by characteristic quacking notes. In spring, call resembles a plaintive "ta-ke, ta-ke-ta-ke." Display flight is accompanied by fluttering, trembling sounds, reminiscent of

MAP 113. Eurasian Woodcock

bleating; also by sound produced by tail feathers when bird dives from a great height. Feeds in silty places, pulling worms from the soil, also insects and their larvae.

Range and distribution: Greater part of USSR except some regions of northern borders, Central Asia, Caucasus, Soviet Far East, and Sakhalin Island. Winters in Western Europe, Africa, southern Asia. In the USSR, shores of the Black Sea in the Caucasus, in the Transcaucasus, and southern Central Asia.

Similar species: Differs from Great Snipe by clear white belly and by rusty outer tail feathers; from the Pin-tailed Snipe and Swinhoe's Snipe, by wide outer tail feathers.

274. GREAT SNIPE
Gallinago media
(Dupel)
Plate 20, Map 115
Field marks: 28 cm. Greatly resembles Common Snipe, but sides of breast and belly covered with dark barring. Outer tail feathers white, sometimes with black bars.

Habits: Found in forest and forest-steppe zones, more rarely in forest-tundra. Migratory. Common but stays hidden during nesting time and is rarely seen. Nests in damp, hummocky areas, mossy swamps, damp meadows; but, in comparison to Common Snipe, prefers drier areas. Nest usually situated on hummock or raised area, in thick grass, and lined with dry stems of grasses. Lays four ocherish-gray eggs with sparse, large, brownish spots from mid-May to July. Female sits tight on nest, and flushes only at close range. In contrast to the Common Snipe, the Great Snipe takes off silently, with straight flight, unhurried, and low to the ground. The displays of the Great Snipe are a magnificent sight, when males gather after sunset in groups in dry places, run about, lowering their wings and fluffing their feath-

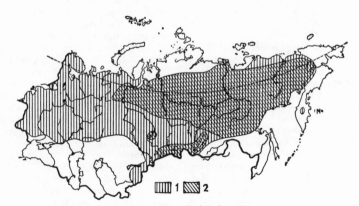

MAP 114. Common Snipe (1), Pin-tailed Snipe (2)

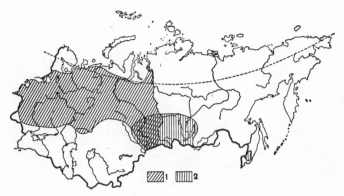

MAP 115. Great Snipe (1), Swinhoe's Snipe (2)

ers, fighting and emitting characteristic twittering sounds. Feeds nocturnally or at dusk, usually on earthworms and larvae of insects.

Range and distribution: European USSR (except northern and southern regions); West Siberia. Winters in subequatorial Africa.

Similar species: Differs from Common Snipe by barred belly and white outer tail feathers; from the Pin-tailed Snipe and Swinhoe's Snipe, by wide outer tail feathers (Figure 47).

275. SWINHOE'S SNIPE
Gallinago megala
(Lesnoy Dupel)
Not illustrated, Map 115

Field marks: 27 cm. Resembles Common Snipe but larger. Outer tail feathers very narrow and noticeably shorter than middle feathers.

Habits: Found in deciduous and thin coniferous forests. Migratory. Common, numerous in places. Nests in more open regions of forest with meadows, patches of thickets, and young growth of aspen or birch. Nest is situated in a dry place with short grass, sometimes on a mound, in the open or under sedge, and is lined with dead grass and leaves. Lays four yellow-cream eggs with intense brownish spots from mid-May to mid-June. Female sits tightly on nest, flushing only at close range and engaging in distraction display. Display flight, which consists of repeated diving from great heights, is accompanied by characteristic sounds that are both vocal (a quacking "chee-ka-chee, chee-ke-chee") and mechanical (by air rushing through the bird's tail feathers. This latter sound resembles a distant jet plane and ends with a loud "ssseeeu." The "chee-ka-chee" call is also given on landing and on the ground. Feeds in wet areas where soil is soft; prefers worms after a rain.

Range and distribution: Southwest Siberia, Transbaikal. Winters in Southeast Asia and Australia.

Similar species: Differs from Great Snipe and Common Snipe by narrow outer tail feathers; from the Pin-tailed Snipe, by wider (nearly 3 mm.) outer tail feathers (Figure 47).

276. PIN-TAILED SNIPE
Gallinago stenura
(Aziatsky Bekas)
Plate 20, Map 114

Field marks: 27 cm. Greatly resembles Common Snipe, and virtually impossible to iden-

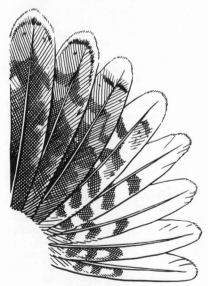

FIG. 46 Tail Feathers of Great Snipe

FIG. 47 TAIL FEATHERS OF SNIPE
1. Pin-tail Snipe   2. Swinhoe's Snipe   3. Solitary Snipe

tify in the field but, in the hand, the outer tail feathers are narrower than in Swinhoe's Snipe and noticeably shorter than the middle feathers.

Habits: Found in forests and alpine regions of mountains, plains of larch taiga, forest-tundra. Migratory. Common in places. Nests in damp meadows and in swamps (both grassy and mossy), in wet areas of mountain tundra, flooded forest-fire areas, and river valleys. Nests on hummock or dry, raised area, and nest is lined with dry leaves, larch needles, and grasses. Lays four olive or yellowish or greenish eggs with large brownish spots from early June. Female sits tightly on nest and engages in distraction display. Display flight is similar to Swinhoe's Snipe, but buzzing sound caused by the tail feathers when diving is higher and its call differs ("chvin-chvin-chvin"). Feeds on various invertebrates.

Range and distribution: Northern half of West Siberia, East Siberia except northern borders, Transbaikal. Winters in southern Asia.

Similar species: Differs from Great Snipe, Common Snipe, and Swinhoe's Snipe by narrower outer tail feathers (only 1 mm. wide; Figure 47).

277. SOLITARY SNIPE
Gàllinago solitaria
(Gorny Dupel)
Plate 20, Map 116

Field marks: 28 cm. Resembles Common Snipe, but bill shorter; upperparts blackish-brown with fine rusty barring; breast earth-brown with white streakings. Tail has wide outer tail feathers like Swinhoe's Snipe.

Habits: Found in alpine regions of mountains. Nomadic and rare. Nests in damp river valleys

and by streams, near springs, on mountain slopes covered with sedge, in small islands of dwarf birch, and in boggy areas. Lays four cream-yellowish eggs with large, brownish spots, which are indistinguishable from the eggs of Swinhoe's Snipe, beginning of June. Display flight same as Swinhoe's Snipe, but does not call on the ground. As a rule stays singly, which accounts for its name. In winter, found near unfrozen springs. Active at dusk, and nocturnal. Feeds on beetles and their larvae, mollusks, and other invertebrates.

Range and distribution: Pamirs, Tien-Shan, Altai, Sayan Mountains; some ranges of East Siberia, Soviet Far East. Winters in areas sheltered from wind and cold within nesting range.

Similar species: Differs from all other snipes by brownish breast with white streaks and fine rusty barring on back.

[**278.** LATHAM'S SNIPE (*Gallinago hardwickii*) is found as a nesting bird of Sakhalin Island and Kunashir Island in the Kuriles. It resembles Swinhoe's Snipe, but is larger (wing no less than 14 cm.). Included in the Red Data Book.]

Lymnocryptes

279. JACK SNIPE
Lymnocryptes minimus
(Garshnep)
Plate 20, Map 116

Field marks: 19 cm. Small shorebird (smaller than a thrush) with a shortish, straight bill and short legs. Back is blackish-brownish with a metallic iridescence and long, ocherish stripes; breast is dove-gray with dark streaks; belly white. Light eye stripe and narrow whitish

MAP 116. Jack Snipe (1), Solitary Snipe (2)

stripes on each side of black crown; legs yellowish-brownish.

Habits: Found in forest and forest-tundra, but nests only in grassy or sphagnum bogs. Prefers silty shores of inland bodies of water and swamps during migration. Migratory. Rare but common in places during migration. Nests in marshy areas near streams overgrown with horsetails (*Equisetum*) and sedge. Nest often situated on a hummock in a completely inaccessible place. Lays four dove-gray or olive-brownish eggs with rusty mottling from early June. Female sits tight on nest and flushes out from very close range. Display vocalizations resemble sounds of a distantly clopping horse, "tok-tok-tok, tok-tok" (with an emphasis on the last syllable); on takeoff, often emits a smacking cry, "chee-veek." Flight unhurried. Stays hidden, moves very little, rarely seen. When alarmed, flies a short distance and settles once again in the grass. Feeds at dusk and at night in silty places, on worms, insect larvae, and mollusks.

Range and distribution: North European USSR and Siberia. Winters in Africa and southern Asia. In the USSR, in the Transcaucasus and Central Asia.

Similar species: Differs from other snipe by small size (wing no larger than 11 cm.), by black median head-stripe; from Broad-billed Sandpiper, by straight bill.

Ibidorhyncha

280. IBISBILL
Ibidorhyncha struthersi
(Serpoklyuv)
Plate 17, Map 117

Field marks: 43 cm. Large shorebird with short legs and long, often strongly downcurved bill. Crown, throat, and band across lower breast

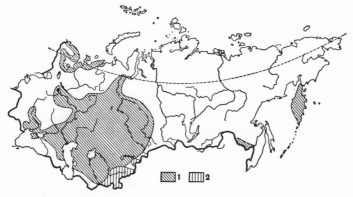

MAP 117. Common Oystercatcher (1), Ibisbill (2)

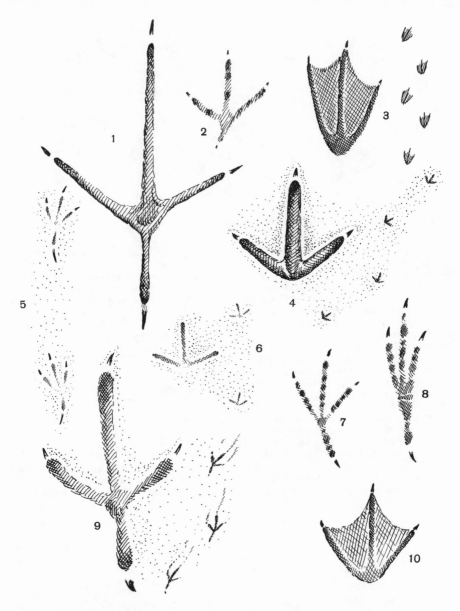

FIG. 48 BIRD FOOTPRINTS
1. Little Egret   2. Common Quail   3. Garganey   4. Common Oystercatcher   5. White Wagtail   6. Little Ringed Plover   7. European Turtle-Dove   8. Eurasian Jay   9. Eurasian Crow   10. Little Gull

black; back and upper breast gray; underparts white; bill and eyes red; legs pale pink. Juveniles duller, legs gray.
Habits: Found in high mountain regions. Nonmigratory or nomadic. Very rare. Nests in pairs on pebbly beaches and islands in mountain rivers. Nest is a shallow depression, lined with flat pebbles. Lays three or four greenish-gray eggs with yellowish-brownish spots from early to mid-May. When alarmed, female quietly leaves nest and walks away; occasionally hides; after eggs hatch, both parents circle over the intruder and emit loud cries. Wary during nesting time. Call: melodic, flutelike cry, "tee-lee, tee-lee." Feeds by wading into water nearly up to its belly and dipping its head and neck in the water. Feeds on insects and their larvae, small fish. Included in the Red Data Book.
Range and distribution: Central Asia, Kazakhstan. Winters within its breeding range.
Similar species: Curved bill and characteristic coloration permit quick identification.

Haematopus

281. COMMON OYSTERCATCHER
Haematopus ostralegus
(Kulik-soroka)
Plate 17, Map 117
Field marks: 43 cm. Large, thickset shorebird with long, straight, bright red bill and pinkish legs. Coloration contrasting: upperparts and breast black; underparts white.
Habits: Found on seashores and shores of large rivers in a variety of habitats. Migratory. Common. Nests on rocky or sandy spits of land and islands. Stays in pairs, more rarely in small colonies. Nest is an open depression, lined with shells, pebbles, or a variety of rubbish. Lays three, occasionally four, pale ocherish eggs with dark brownish spots from mid-May until mid-June. When endangered, female leaves the nest early and flies out screaming to meet the intruder squarely. Sometimes will even attack a person. Wary when away from eggs and nestlings, and is the first to sound an alarm on the beaches. Call is loud, resembling a fast, repetitive "kee-pit, kee-pit." Feeds primarily on mollusks, also insects and their larvae, crayfish, and other invertebrates, catching them by turning over pebbles, as does the Ruddy Turnstone.
Range and distribution: European USSR, Kazakhstan, Central Asia, West Siberia, Amur River region, Kamchatka Peninsula. Winters in Africa and southern Asia.
Similar species: Characteristic coloration permits easy distinction from all other shore birds.

[Vagrants of **282.** PAINTED-SNIPE (*Rostratula benghalensis*) have been found in Primorski Krai; this shorebird is larger than a thrush, with a long, reddish bill, decurved at tip; mottled brownish upperparts with conspicuous buffy V; gray-brownish streaked breast, bordered by black, and contrasting with white underparts; buffy crown stripe and ring around the eye. In the more brightly colored female, the back is darker, the eye ring is white, and the neck and upper breast chestnut-brown. It is a member of the family *Rostratulidae*.]

JAEGERS, GULLS, TERNS: *Lari*

Birds of large and medium sizes with long wings. Short tail, but sometimes individual feathers are significantly longer. Foretoes are webbed; plumage is fluffy but compact. Biologically tied to various bodies of water. Monogamous. Eggs are usual ovoid shape. Semi-altricial.

Stercorarius

Medium-size bird with long, narrow wings and elongated middle tail feathers. Tip of bill is hooked. There are two color phases: dark and light.

283. PARASITIC JAEGER
Stercorarius parasiticus
(Korotkokhvosty Pomornik)
Plate 21, Map 118
Field marks: 46 cm. Size of a pigeon, but wings much longer. Middle pair of tail feathers are long and pointed, and extend well beyond the other tail feathers. Dark-phase birds are uniformly brownish-gray; light-phase birds have a black "cap," grayish-brown upperparts, and whitish underparts. However, plumage is variable. Juveniles are heavily barred with central tail feathers barely longer than the other tail feathers.
Habits: Found in tundra; on seashores of open seas during nonbreeding season. Migratory. Common. Nests both in swampy lowland areas with lakes, and in dry, lichen tundra mountainsides. Nest is a shallow depression thinly lined with moss, lichens, or sedge, and is situated on a mound or a dry, raised place. Lays two brownish or greenish-olive eggs with dark

MAP 118. Long-tailed Jaeger (1), Parasitic Jaeger (2)

spots in June. Actively attacks an intruder near the nest by dive-bombing and by pretending to be hurt and falling on its side, dragging its wing. Call: characteristic meowing cry; near the nest, a thin squeak. Flight is light and even, with frequent gliding. Feeds on fish, which it usually obtains from gulls by harassing them until they regurgitate their recently swallowed food. During breeding season, primarily feeds on lemmings, nestlings, and eggs of various birds, insects, and berries.

Range and distribution: Tundra of European and Asian USSR, shores of Bering and Okhotsk seas, Kamchatka Peninsula. Winters south as far as Australia and New Zealand.

Similar species: Differs from Long-tailed Jaeger by shorter middle tail feathers.

284. LONG-TAILED JAEGER
Stercorarius longicaudus
(Dlinnokhvosty Pomornik)
Plate 21, Map 118

Field marks: 53 cm. Resembles the Parasitic Jaeger in its light (more contrasting) coloration, but is smaller and more compact; middle tail feathers are significantly longer.

Habits: Found in tundra; along seashores or on the open seas during migration. Migratory. Common, in places numerous. Nests in dry regions of tundra; swampy lowlands are avoided. Nest always situated in a dry place and lined with lichens. Attacks intruder near the nest and engages in distraction display similar to that of the Parasitic Jaeger. Lays two eggs in June. By coloration eggs are indistinguishable from those of the Parasitic Jaeger, but are usually smaller. Food and feeding habits similar to Parasitic Jaeger.

Range and distribution: Tundra of European and Asian USSR, shores of Bering and Okhotsk

seas, Kamchatka Peninsula. Winters on oceans to the south as far as Australia and New Zealand.

Similar species: Differs from Parasitic Jaeger by its very long middle tail feathers (more than twice the length of the tail). Juveniles are nearly indistinguishable in the field, but Long-tail is smaller, grayer, with less white in wing.

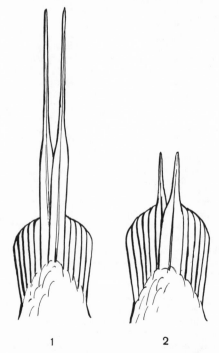

FIG. 49 Tail of Adult 1) Long-tailed Jaeger and 2) Parasitic Jaeger

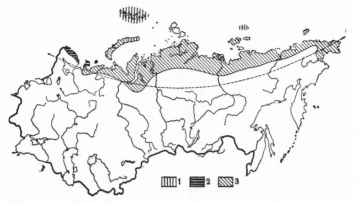

MAP 119. Ivory Gull (1), Great Black-backed Gull (2), Pomarine Jaeger (3)

285. POMARINE JAEGER
Stercorarius pomarinus
(Sredny Pomornik)
Plate 21, Map 119

Field marks: 51 cm. In coloration resembles Parasitic Jaeger, but is significantly larger (almost as large as a Herring Gull). Middle tail feathers are long, rounded (not pointed), and twisted 180°. Juveniles are large and heavy-billed with only a suggestion of longer tail feathers.

Habits: Found in tundra; near seashores or on open seas during nonbreeding season, and often in flocks. Migratory. Not numerous. Nests in dry, lichen tundra and in swampy lowland regions near lakes and rivers. Nest is situated on a dry prominence or a mound, and lined with lichens and moss. Lays two eggs like Parasitic Jaeger, but larger; in June. Differs from other jaegers near the nest by its wary attitude; will not attack an intruder. Flight is straight, with even wing beats; in flight, widened central tail feathers give the appearance of long, extended legs. Call is more harsh and hoarse than in other jaegers, and is rarely heard. Like other jaegers, takes food away from gulls, but also feeds on lemmings, nestlings, and eggs of other birds in the tundra.

Range and distribution: Tundra along shores of Arctic Ocean, polar islands. Winters on the Atlantic and Pacific Oceans.

Similar species: Adults separated from other jaegers easily by the long central tail feathers that are rounded and completely twisted.

[Rarely visiting vagrants of the **286.** GREAT SKUA (*Catharacta skua*) have been found in the European section of the Arctic; it is larger than the Pomarine Jaeger; has a monochromatic dark brownish color with large white patches at the base of the primaries; and lacks the elongated feathers in the tail.]

Pagophila

287. IVORY GULL
Pagophila eburnea
(Belaya Chayka)
Plate 22, Map 119

Field marks: 44 cm. Medium size (like a crow). Coloration pure white; legs black; bill yellow-tipped. Juveniles white with sparse brownish spots on body, end of tail, and tips of flight feathers.

Habits: Inhabits cliffs, sometimes open sea-

FIG. 50 Gull Chick

shores of polar islands; stays on open seas near ice floes during nonbreeding season. Migratory. Rare. Nests in small colonies on overhanging rock ledges. Nest made of dry grass, moss, and feathers. Lays two ocherish-white eggs with dark brownish spots; from early July. Flight is rapid and light; rarely lands on water. Call: harsh, loud "kree-kree." Feeds on carrion left by hunters and bears, and on excrement of seals and walruses. Included in the Red Data Book.

Range and distribution: Franz Josef Land, Severnaya Zemlya. Winters on Arctic Ocean.

Similar species: Differs from all gulls by its pure white coloration.

Rissa

Medium size (like a crow); with only three foretoes. Gonys on lower mandible not prominent.

288. BLACK-LEGGED KITTIWAKE
Rissa tridactyla
(Moevka)
Plate 22, Map 120

Field marks: 40 cm. Wings dark gray with black tips; remainder of plumage white; legs black; bill yellow. Juveniles have black band on upper neck; black tip to tail; small, black spot behind the eye; black, diagonal stripe on wing visible in flight.

Habits: Found in cliffs of seashores; stays in flocks near seashores, often well out to sea during nonbreeding season. Migratory. Numerous. Nests in huge colonies (rookeries) on precipitous, inaccessible coastal cliffs. Nests are on ledges, closely spaced, and are made of grass and feathers. Lays two to three ocherish

eggs with dark spots from mid-May to June. Young leave the nest only after they are fully feathered. Black-legged Kittiwakes are very garrulous in their colonies; call: a loud "kitti-vey, kitti-vey," a plaintive "eea-eea-eea," and other sounds. Flight is light with frequent wing beats. Feeds on small fish (capelin and pollock), more rarely on crayfish and mollusks, catching food in eddies of water, either on the wing or while swimming. Eggs are considered edible.

Range and distribution: Shores of the Barents Sea, Novaya Zemlya, Novosibirskiye Islands, Severnaya Zemlya, Wrangel Island, shores of Chukotski Peninsula, Bering Sea, Sea of Okhotsk, Kamchatka Peninsula, Komandorskiye Islands. Winters on waters of the Atlantic and Pacific.

Similar species: Differs from all gulls by its medium size, black-tipped wings, yellowish bill, and black legs; juveniles by distinctive markings.

289. RED-LEGGED KITTIWAKE
Rissa brevirostris
(Krasnonogaya Govorushka)
Plate 22, Map 120

Field marks: 39 cm. Resembles Black-legged Kittiwake, but underwing is gray, not white; legs yellow or red. Juveniles lack black terminal band on tail and diagonal stripe on wing.

Habits: Place and method of nesting, feeding, and habits same as Black-legged Kittiwake. Apparently lays only a single egg. More wary than Black-legged Kittiwake.

Range and distribution: Komandorskiye Islands. Winters on the northern Pacific.

Similar species: Differs from Black-legged

MAP 120. Red-legged Kittiwake (1), Lesser Black-backed Gull (2), Black-legged Kittiwake (3)

Kittiwake by red legs; juveniles by lack of black band on tail.

Rhodostethia

290. ROSS'S GULL
Rhodostethia rosea
(Rozovaya Chayka)
Plate 22, Map 121
Field marks: 32 cm. Small gull with characteristic wedge-shaped tail. Coloration is very beautiful: back is uniformly ash-gray with white trailing edge on wing; narrow, black band around the neck ("necklace"); remainder of plumage is white with a bright pink tone. Dark underwings. Bill is black; legs and eye ring bright red. In winter it is similar, but without black neck band. In juveniles, upperparts are brownish with dark diagonal pattern similar to Black-legged Kittiwake immature; underparts white; tail with black subterminal band.
Habits: Found in tundra and forest-tundra; stays in open seas near ice floes during nonbreeding season. Migratory. Rare, in places common. Nests in small colonies of various sizes, in swampy lowlands near lakes. Nest made of dry grass and situated on hummocks in water. Lays three brownish or greenish-olive eggs with brownish spots in June. If nest is approached, dives at the intruder, crying loudly and flying toward the nest. Flight is light, slightly dipping. Variety of calls. In summer, feeds primarily on insects; in winter, on small fish and aquatic invertebrates. Included in the Red Data Book.
Range and distribution: Tundra of North Yakutia from Khroma River in the west to Kolyma River and Chaun Bay in the east. Winters on Arctic and Pacific Oceans.
Similar species: Differs from all other gulls by

wedge-shaped tail and characteristic coloration.

Xema

291. SABINE'S GULL
Xema sabini
(Vilokhvostaya Chayka)
Plate 22, Map 121
Field marks: 33 cm. Small gull with forked tail; back and wings gray; head with slate-gray hood; outermost primaries entirely black; remaining plumage white. Legs blackish; bill black with yellow tip; eyes bright red. In winter, head is white. Juveniles have brownish upperparts, and black subterminal band near tip of forked tail.
Habits: Found in tundra; during nonbreeding season, stays on open seas. Migratory. Rare, in places common. Nests in swampy, moss-sedge tundra with many lakes; forms small, mixed colonies. Nest is made of grass and is situated directly on damp ground or in moss, frequently near water's edge. Lays three greenish or brownish-olive eggs in mid-June. Very aggressive near the nest, attacks an intruder, silently distracts when chicks are hatched. Call: a chirring "krrrrree." Flight is light with many dives. Feeds in flight from the surface of the water, sometimes swims in water or searches on land. In summer, feeds on insects and their larvae; in winter, on aquatic invertebrates.
Range and distribution: Taimyr, Wrangel Island, northern Yakutia, Chaun Bay, lower Anadyr River. Winters on the Arctic Ocean.
Similar species: Differs from all other gulls by forked tail. In flight, by characteristic triangle formed by black primaries and white secondaries.

MAP 121. Sabine's Gull (1), Ross's Gull (2)

Larus

Sizes from small to large; wings are wide, tail slightly rounded. Juveniles (up to two years) of many species are nearly indistinguishable from each other in the field.

292. GREAT BLACK-BACKED GULL
Larus marinus
(Morskaya Chayka)
Plate 21, Map 119
Field marks: 68 cm. Largest of the gulls in the USSR. Back and wings slate-black; remaining plumage white. Legs pinkish; bill yellow with red spot on gonys of lower mandible. Juveniles are gray-brownish; head and breast lighter, mottled; wide, dark subterminal band on tail.
Habits: Found on seashores and cliff islands. Migratory. Common in places. Nests in small colonies, often together with Herring Gull; occasionally in pairs, on cliff ledges, on single crags, or on grass-covered plateaus. Nest made of dry grass and feathers. Lays two or three large, grayish-ocherish eggs with brownish-olive and black spots; from mid-May on. Very wary and does not allow close approach to nest. Chicks are gray with black spots, and leave the nest shortly after hatching, but stay nearby. Call: laughing, halting, bass "kha-ga-ga," loud "yeeah-yeeah-yeeah," or a throaty "kai." Feeds on beaches close to the water and on open seas; prefers fish (cod, herring, and capelin) and leavings of commercial fishing; also eggs and nestlings of other seabirds, lemmings, carrion, aquatic invertebrates, berries, and will often steal food from other gulls.
Range and distribution: Shores and islands of the Barents Sea, Kanin Peninsula. Winters on shores of Western Europe.
Similar species: Differs from Lesser Black-backed Gull by larger size and pinkish legs; from the Slaty-backed Gull by pure black wings.

293. SLATY-BACKED GULL
Larus schistisagus
(Tikhookeanskaya Chayka)
Plate 21, No map
Field marks: 60 cm. Resembles Great Black-backed Gull, but smaller, with lighter mantle. Bill is short and massive. Juveniles are gray-brownish with lighter underparts.
Habits: Found on shores and islands of the Sea of Okhotsk. Prefers sandy beaches and precipitous cliff benches. Nonmigratory and nomadic. In places numerous. Nests in colonies on separate crags or on the top of cliff ledges. Nest is made of dry grass and feathers, and is situated among thick vegetation, and as a rule, near the edge of the precipice. Lays two or three ocherish or greenish-olive eggs with black spots from early May. Call similar to Great Black-backed Gull. Feeds on aquatic invertebrates (crabs, sea urchins), fish, nestlings, eggs, carrion, and offal. Often flies well inland, where it catches voles and insects.
Range and distribution: Sea of Okhotsk, Kamchatka Peninsula; Sakhalin, Shantarskiye, and Kuril Islands.
Similar species: Differs from Great Black-backed Gull and the Lesser Black-backed Gull by its lighter mantle; also ranges widely separated.

294. BLACK-TAILED GULL
Larus crassirostris
(Chernokhvostaya Chayka)
Plate 21, Map 122
Field marks: 44 cm. Medium size (like a crow). Wings dark gray with black tips; tail has wide, black subterminal band; remaining plumage white. Legs greenish-yellow; bill is massive, yellow with black subterminal ring and red tip. Juveniles are brownish.
Habits: Found on seashores with sandy beaches and rocky precipices. Nonmigratory and nomadic. In places numerous. Nests in colonies on islands and single cliffs. Nest made of dry grass and situated on ledges and gentle slopes amid vegetation. Lays two or three greenish-ocherish eggs with dark spots from early May until June. Call is a bass "kaoo-kaoo." Feeds on small fish (smelt, greenlings); in winter, on waste from commercial fisheries.
Range and distribution: Sakhalin, Kuril Islands, coastal Soviet Far East. Winters further south on the Pacific Ocean.
Similar species: Differs from other gulls by black tail band.

295. LESSER BLACK-BACKED GULL
Larus fuscus
(Klusha)
Plate 21, Map 120
Field marks: 53 cm. Resembles Great Black-backed Gull, but smaller; legs yellow or orange. Juveniles are brownish mottled.
Habits: Found on shores and islands of small lakes; also on major rivers during nonbreeding season. Not numerous, migratory. Nests in small colonies in pairs, on grassy shores with cliffs, or on separate crags; in lakes, prefers to nest on islands. Nest is made of dry stalks, lichens, and feathers. Lays two or three greenish-ocher or light blue eggs with black spots; from end of May to June. Call and habits same as other large gulls. Feeds on small fish, aquatic invertebrates, nestlings and eggs of other birds,

MAP 122. Herring Gull (1), Black-tailed Gull (2)

wastes of aquatic animals. Often forages in commercial fishing areas. On land, feeds on berries and hunts for small rodents.

Range and distribution: Kola Peninsula, southwestern regions of European USSR. Winters on Mediterranean, Persian Gulf, and eastern Atlantic. In the USSR, on the Azov and Black seas.

Similar species: Differs from Great Black-backed Gull by smaller size and yellow legs; from the Slaty-backed Gull, by its darker wings and less massive bill (also ranges widely separated). Juveniles nearly indistinguishable from juveniles of Herring Gull and Great Black-backed Gull.

296. HERRING GULL
Larus argentatus
(Serebristaya Chayka)
Plate 21, Map 122

Field marks: 56 cm. Large gull (much larger than a crow). Mantle is gray in varying shades (from slate-gray to light gray) with black tips; remaining plumage is white. Bill yellow with red spot on gonys of lower mandible. Legs pink or yellow. Juveniles are mottled brownish-gray with lighter underparts.

Habits: Found in a variety of habitats from tundra to desert. Prefers valleys of large rivers during migration. In the north, migratory; in the south, nomadic or nonmigratory. Common and numerous in places. Nests in colonies or separate pairs on cliff shores of seas and on islands, often together with other gulls and alcids; on sandy or silty spits of land, and on small islands in steppe lakes; in tundra, on heaps of reeds or hummocks; in swampy lowlands near lakes and on river islands. Nest made of dry grass and feathers and is situated in inaccessible cliffs, on gentle, grassy slopes,

or on flat, lichen-covered areas. Start of nesting depends on region, and begins mid-April until the end of June. Lays two or three brownish-green or ocherish-olive eggs with dark spots. Fairly aggressive near the nest, but on the whole very wary. Call is a laughing "ha-ga-ga" (in flight); loud "eeah-eeah-eeah" that is emitted on the ground while the bird leans its head back and opens its bill wide; or, occasionally, a throaty "kyaoo," emitted in flight when alarmed. Feeds on a variety of prey: fish, aquatic invertebrates, commercial fishing waste, and hunting offal; on dry land, hunts for susliks, voles, lizards, insects; on seas, follows fishing vessels; also feeds on nestlings and eggs of other birds; carrion, berries.

Range and distribution: Greater part of USSR except central regions of European USSR, the mountain ranges of Siberia, and deserts of Central Asia; shores of Okhotsk and Kamchatka.

Similar species: Differs from the Glaucous Gull and Glaucous-winged Gull by black wing tips; from the Mew Gull by larger size. Experience is required to identify juvenile Herring Gulls from juveniles of the Great Black-backed Gull and other gulls in the field.

297. MEW GULL
Larus canus
(Sizaya Chayka)
Plate 22, Map 123

Field marks: 40 cm. Resembles Herring Gull in coloration, but much smaller (slightly larger than a crow). Bill and legs greenish-yellow. In winter, head is mottled. Juveniles are brownish with light underparts and dark band on tail tip.

Habits: Found in a variety of habitats from tundra to steppe and semi-desert; found on

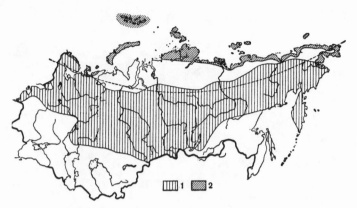

MAP 123. Mew Gull (1), Glaucous Gull (2)

river valleys during migration. Migratory. Common, in places numerous. Nests in small colonies or in pairs, often together with other gulls and terns on small islands in seas; more often on lakes of various types (fresh or salt water). Nest made of grass or bits of reed, and situated close to water's edge, usually on little islands, on heaps of reed, or on hummocks. Lays three greenish or brownish-olive eggs from early May until mid-June. Call: alarmed, piercing "keeaa-keeaa" or "chak-chak." Feeds on small fish (sand eel, capelin, stickleback), aquatic invertebrates (crayfish, mollusks), insects; feeds on garbage near settlements and leavings from commerical fishing.

Range and distribution: Northern half of European USSR, Kazakhstan, south and central Siberia, Kamchatka Peninsula. Winters on the Black and Caspian seas; in Southeast Asia.

Similar species: Differs from Herring Gull by smaller size, unmarked yellow bill, and by its voice; from the Black-legged Kittiwake, by its yellow legs; from the Slender-billed Gull, Black-headed Gull, and Mediterranean Gull (in fall), by larger size, yellow legs, and gray mantle with white-spotted black wing tips. Juveniles differ from other juveniles of gulls by medium size and broad tailband.

298. GLAUCOUS GULL
Larus hyperboreus
(Burgomistr)
Plate 21, Map 123

Field marks: 66 cm. One of the largest gulls. Mantle light gray with white tips; legs pink; bill yellow with red spot on lower mandible. Juveniles are uniformly light-colored; dark bill had flesh-colored base.

Habits: Found on cliffs of seashores and on islands, in tundra; stays on seashores during nonbreeding season. Migratory. Not numer-

ous. Nests in pairs, more rarely in small flocks together with Herring and Great Black-backed Gulls on precipitous ledges, usually near rookeries; in tundra, on lake islands. Nest made of dry aquatic plants and grass. Lays two or three brownish-olive eggs with dark spots from mid-May to June. Very wary. Call similar to Herring Gull, but harsher. Feeds on fish and aquatic invertebrates; in rookeries, feeds on nestlings and eggs of guillemots and Black-legged Kittiwake; in tundra, hunts for lemmings; also feeds on wastes of fishing industry. Flight and habits same as other large gulls.

Range and distribution: Shores and islands of Arctic Ocean. In winter, south to France and Japan.

Similar species: Differs from Glaucous-winged Gull and other large gulls by white primaries; juveniles differ from Iceland Gull by larger size and bicolored bill; from others by larger size and pale coloration.

299. GLAUCOUS-WINGED GULL
Larus glaucescens
(Serokrylaya Chayka)
Not illustrated, No map

Field marks: 62 cm. Resembles Glaucous Gull, but smaller, with darker mantle and white-tipped gray primaries. Juveniles are smoky brown.

Habits: Found on cliffs near seashores of the Kamchatka Peninsula and the Komandorskiye Islands. Nomadic. In places numerous. Nests in pairs or colonies in inaccessible cliffs or on peaks of rocky ledges of precipices near rookeries. Nest made of dry aquatic plants, grass, and feathers. Lays three greenish-olive eggs with dark spots from mid-May. Habits, flight, and call same as other large gulls. Feeds on remains of commercial walrus hunting, on eggs and nestlings of other birds, fish, aquatic invertebrates (sea urchins, crabs, mollusks), and carrion.

Range and distribution: Komandorskiye Islands, Kamchatka. Winters south to Japan.

Similar species: Differs from Glaucous Gull by darker coloration and smaller size (difficult to distinguish in the field); from the Herring Gull, by white wing tips.

300. GREAT BLACK-HEADED GULL
Larus ichthyaëtus
(Chernogolovy Khokhotun)
Plate 21, Map 124

Field marks: 63 cm. Large (larger than Herring Gull). Back and wing coverts gray; primaries and most secondaries white; wing tips with black subterminal band; head black; remaining plumage white. Legs yellowish; bill red-yellow with black band. In winter, head is white with brownish-black streaks and spots. Juveniles are grayish-brown with outermost primaries black and underparts white; wide black band on tail.

Habits: Found on shores and islands of seas, and large saline lakes. Migratory and partly nomadic. In places common, but on the whole not numerous. Nests in large colonies, often together with other birds. Stays in small flocks and singly during nonbreeding season. Colonies are situated on islands that are either flat with cliffs, sandy, or with shells. Nest made of dry aquatic plants, feathers, and small roots. Lays three creamy or ocherish-white eggs with black spots from mid-April. In contrast to other gulls, the chick's down is not gray, but a silvery white with grayish spots. Very wary, and even near the nest avoids close contact with intruders. Call: harsh, low "ai"; bird generally remains silent. Feeds on fish, consuming sick

fish or waste of commercial fishing; often eats rodents (susliks, voles), more rarely nestlings, lizards, and insects. Included in the Red Data Book.

Range and distribution: Crimea, south Caspian Sea, Kazakhstan, south of West Siberia. Winters on the Black, Caspian, and Mediterranean Seas.

Similar species: Differs from all large gulls by its black head; juveniles larger than Herring Gull, with white underparts and head, and broad band at tip of white tail.

301. BLACK-HEADED GULL
Larus ridibundus
(Ozernaya Chayka)
Plate 22, Map 124

Field marks: 37 cm. Medium-size gull (size of a crow). Head is coffee-brown; mantle gray; outermost primaries white with black tips and black undersides; remaining plumage is white. Bill and legs red. In winter, head is white with brownish spot behind the eye. Juveniles have brownish upperparts and white underparts; tips of primaries black; dark terminal band on tail.

Habits: Found in a variety of habitats from forest to desert; also in river valleys during migration. Migratory, and one of the most common gulls. Nests near lakes, marshes, lagoons (limans), and in old river beds; prefers places where there is lush vegetation near water. Forms large colonies, often together with other gulls and terns. Nest is made of grass and is situated on a floating mat, in broken reeds, or on a hummock; sometimes on dry, grassy, or sandy islets. Lays three greenish-brownish or light olive-bluish eggs with dark brownish spots from mid-April to May. Circles overhead with alarmed cries when intruder approaches nest-

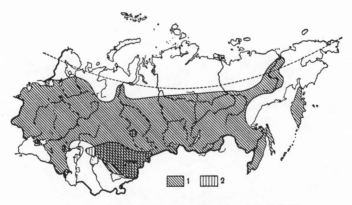

MAP 124. Black-headed Gull (1), Great Black-headed Gull (2)

ing colony; circles aggressively. Call is a harsh, chirring "kyarr." Feeds from the surface of the water by flying low, or swimming; often searches for food on land. Feeds on aquatic and terrestrial insects and their larvae, small fish (usually dead or sick), often on rodents (voles).

Range and distribution: European USSR except northern regions, Kazakhstan, southern half of Siberia, Soviet Far East. Winters on shores of Western Europe, Black and Caspian Seas.

Similar species: Differs from Mediterranean Gull by black tips to primaries (juveniles by white, not blackish primaries); from the Slender-billed Gull (in fall and winter), by shorter bill; from the Brown-headed Gull, by its smaller size and lighter wing tips (also these gulls are generally not found in the same range).

302. BROWN-HEADED GULL
Larus brunnicephalus
(Burogolovaya Chayka)
Not illustrated, No map

Field marks: 45 cm. Resembles Black-headed Gull, but larger; head is browner, with a black "collar" bordering this brownish area; has black wing tips (not just tips of primaries).

Habits: Found in the high mountains of the Pamirs; stays on seashore and inland bodies of water in plains during nonbreeding periods. Migratory. In places common, but rare on the whole. Nests in colonies along shores of mountain lakes. Nest made of grass, or entirely unlined. Lays three ocherish eggs with brownish spots, from early July. Feeds on small fish, aquatic invertebrates. Included in the Red Data Book.

Range and distribution: High mountain lakes of the Pamirs. Winters in India.

Similar species: Differs from Black-headed Gull

by more well-defined black wing tip; also not usually found in the same range.

303. RELICT GULL
Larus relictus
(Reliktovaya Chayka)
Plate 22, Map 303

Field marks: 39-40 cm. Resembles Black-headed and Brown-headed Gulls, but slightly larger than both. Brown on nape and neck graduates to black; less black on primaries; white half-moon patch over and behind the eye; bill dark red. After first autumn molting, juveniles have white head with brownish, drop-shaped mottling; dark band on tail. The downy chicks are whitish without mottling (similar to those of Great Black-headed Gull).

Habits: Found in fresh- or salt-water lakes in steppe or semi-desert. Migratory. Very rare on the whole. Nests in colonies of around twenty pairs; nesting colonies situated on flat, open, lake islands. Nest made of dry grasses and feathers, and situated on the ground, usually in association with Caspian Terns. Nests are very close to each other, about one-half meter apart. Lays three whitish eggs with brownish or blackish speckles mid-May. Feeds on variety of food, especially insects, aquatic invertebrates, and small fish. Included in the Red Data Book.

Range and distribution: Nests on Lake Barun-Toray in the Transbaikal, and on Lake Alakol in southeastern Kazakhstan; possibly also in Mongolia. Winters in China.

Similar species: Differs from the Black-headed, Brown-headed, and Mediterranean Gulls by characteristic coloration of head: coffee-brown on front of crown, blending to pure black on the nape and lower throat. The white half-moon patch near the eye is another distinguishing feature.

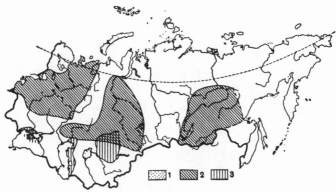

MAP 125. Mediterranean Gull (1), Little Gull (2), Slender-billed Gull (3)

304. MEDITERRANEAN GULL
Larus melanocephalus
(Chernogolovaya Chayka)
Plate 22, Map 125

Field marks: 38 cm. Resembles Black-headed Gull, but head is a shiny black; wing tips are white. Bill is larger than in Black-headed Gull; it is red with a thin black ring. In winter, head is white. Juveniles resemble juveniles of Black-headed Gulls, but the black on the wing tips is more extensive.

Habits: Found on seashores, and in vicinity of seashores during nonbreeding season. Migratory and nomadic. Numerous in places. Nests in large colonies on sea islands or in swampy lowlands near sea. Nests situated close to each other, and made from dry grass stalks and feathers. Lays two or three light ocherish eggs with small black spots from mid-May. Feeds on small fish, aquatic invertebrates, and insects (for which it forages in the steppe). Call is more harsh and rough than that of the Black-headed Gull.

Range and distribution: Shores and islands of Black and Azov Seas, range expanding into the Baltic states. Winters on the Mediterranean and Black Seas.

Similar species: Differs from Black-headed Gull and from the Slender-billed Gull in autumn by its white wing tips.

305. LITTLE GULL
Larus minutus
(Malaya Chayka)
Plate 22, Map 125

Field marks: 30 cm. Somewhat resembles Black-headed Gull in coloration, but much smaller; head is black, wing tips white, and underwings are blackish-gray. In winter, head is whitish with dusky cap and a spot behind the eye. Juveniles have gray-brownish upperparts; white underparts; wings have strong black stripes that form a inverted W pattern; narrow, black stripe on tail tip.

Habits: Found in forest, forest-steppe, and steppe. Prefers river valleys, and seashores during nonbreeding season. Migratory. Common (or even numerous) in places. Nests in colonies, often together with terns and other gulls. Prefers lakes with overgrowth, old river beds, swampy lowlands. Nest is made of bits of dried stalks, reeds, and cattails, and is situated on hummocks, heaps of reeds, or simply on the ground. Lays three brownish or greenish-olive eggs with brownish spots from end of May until July. Very aggressive near the nest, but generally peaceful and trusting. Flight is light, uneven, almost fluttering. Call: quiet, melodic "kek-kek-kek." Obtains food in flight from the water surface or the ground; some-

times catches insects in mid-air. Feeds primarily on insects and their larvae, crayfish; and on wintering grounds, on small fish.

Range and distribution: Northern half of European USSR, Kazakhstan, West Siberia, Transbaikal, southern Yakutia. Winters on shores of Western Europe, Black and Caspian Seas.

Similar species: Differs from most gulls by its much smaller size (wing no larger than 24 cm.); from other small gulls and terns by its uniformly gray mantle and blackish underwings.

306. SLENDER-BILLED GULL
Larus genei
(Morskoy Golubok)
Plate 22, Map 125

Field marks: 43 cm. Medium-size gull. Wings gray with outermost primaries white, and all primaries edged with black; head, tail, and underparts are white with pinkish tone on belly and breast; legs and long, thin bill are red. Juveniles similar to adults with mottled grayish upperparts, and narrow, black stripe on tail tip.

Habits: Found on seashores and islands; on salt- and, rarely, fresh-water lakes in steppe and desert zones. Migratory. In places numerous but rare on the whole. Nests in colonies, sometimes together with other gulls and terns, but always as a discrete unit. Colonies are situated in sandy or silty islands, more rarely on marshy shores. Nest is a small depression, thinly lined with vegetation, and nests are often built close to each other. Lays three white or cream-colored eggs with black-brownish spots; from mid-May. Very wary even near the nest, and never attempts to attack an intruder, as is the case with most other gulls. Flight is light and even. A peaceful, tolerant bird, staying in flocks even during nonbreeding season. Call is a characteristic nasal "kerr-kerr." Feeds on small fish, aquatic invertebrates, and insects that it catches by flying far inland to the steppe.

Range and distribution: Shores and islands of Black and Azov Seas, Central Asia, Kazakhstan. Winters from Canary Islands to the Persian Gulf. In the USSR, occasionally on the Caspian Sea.

Similar species: Differs from all gulls except Black-headed and Little by its dark underwings. Both adults and young differ from Little Gull by much larger size; from the Black-headed Gull, by its darker wing lining and, in summer, lack of a dark head. Juveniles similar, but larger with a longer bill.

[Vagrants of **307.** ICELAND GULL (*Larus glau-*

coides) were twice obtained on Novaya Zemlya; it greatly resembles the Glaucous Gull, but is smaller and has a more slender bill. In the Kurils, on Sakhalin Peninsula, and in Vladivostok, vagrants of **308.** SAUNDER'S GULL (*Larus saundersi*) were obtained; resembles the Black-headed Gull but smaller and with a black bill.]

Chlidonias

Small size. Tail slightly forked; very long, narrow wings; short legs; coloration of adult birds is dark.

309. BLACK TERN
Chlidonias niger
(Chyornaya Krachka)
Plate 23, Map 126

Field marks: 25 cm. Slate-black; darker on head and throat; wing lining is pale gray; undertail white; legs reddish-brownish; bill black. In winter, forehead and entire underparts are white; dark spots on sides of upper breast. Juveniles resemble winter plumage of adults.

Habits: Found in a variety of habitats from forest to desert. Migratory. Common or numerous. Nests in colonies, often with other species of terns or gulls, on shores and islands overgrown with cattails, reeds, or sedge in lakes, springs, and quiet rivers; more rarely in swamps. Nest situated on a floating mat, on floating aquatic plants, or on heaps of reeds. Nest made of stalks of grass or leaves of reeds. Lays three ocherish or dark brownish eggs with dark spots; from end of May to June. Blissfully unwary; ignores intruder near the nest even on close approach. Call: soft "kek-kek-kek." Flight is uneven, fluttering, often pausing in mid-air, or hovering. Walks awkwardly. Feeds by flying low and catching prey close to or on the water surface in flight; dives into the water rarely and more weakly than Common Terns. Feeds on aquatic invertebrates and occasionally small fish. Also feeds on insects, for which it forages far from water.

Range and distribution: Southern half of European USSR, Kazakhstan, Central Asia, south of West Siberia. Winters in Africa.

Similar species: Differs from White-winged Tern by its black tail, light wing lining and dark top of wing; from the Whiskered Tern, by its entirely black head, and in winter plumage, by its characteristic dark spots on the sides of the breast.

310. WHITE-WINGED TERN
Chlidonias leucopterus
(Belokrylaya Krachka)
Plate 23, Map 126

Field marks: 23 cm. Resembles Black Tern, but wing lining is black; top of wing and tail are white; bill and legs bright red. Adults in winter plumage and juveniles resemble Black Tern, but usually do not have dark spots on sides of breast, and have whitish rump and tail.

Habits: Found in bodies of fresh water with lush vegetation close to the shore. Migratory. Common and numerous in places. Nests in colonies, often together with other birds. Prefers deeper bodies of water than Black Tern. Nest usually situated on heaps of reeds or on hummocks. Construction of nest, number of eggs and their coloration are same as Black Tern. These two birds greatly resemble each other in habits, flight, feeding peculiarities, and by food preferences.

Range and distribution: Southern half of European USSR, Kazakhstan, southern West

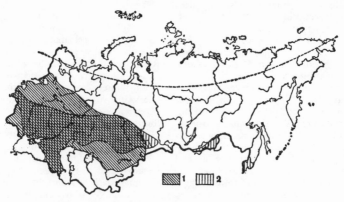

MAP 126. Black Tern (1), White-winged Tern (2)

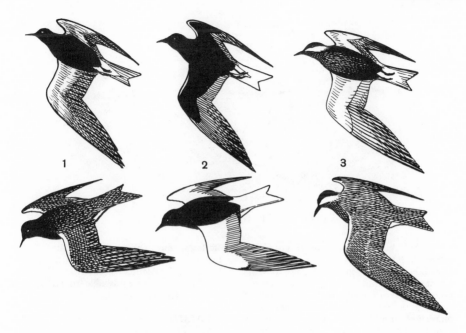

FIG. 51 MARSH TERNS IN FLIGHT (SUMMER)
1. Black Tern   2. White-winged Tern   3. Whiskered Tern

Siberia, Transbaikal, Soviet Far East. Winters in Africa, southern Asia, and Australia.
Similar species: Differs from Black Tern by white wings and tail, red legs; from the Whiskered Tern by its entirely black head. Juveniles differ from Whiskered Tern by lack of dark spots on sides of the breast and by black crown.

311. WHISKERED TERN
Chlidonias hybrida
(Beloschokaya Krachka)
Plate 23, Map 127
Field marks: 33 cm. Coloration dark slate-black; lighter on wings and tail; black "cap" on head; chin, cheeks, undertail and wing lining are white. Tail forked. Bill and legs are red. In winter, upperparts pale gray; eye line dark; forehead white, crown white narrowly streaked with black.
Habits: Found near fresh water in a variety of habitats. Migratory, not as numerous as Black Tern or White-winged Tern. Nests in pairs in colonies, in thickets near lakes, quiet rivers, or bogs. Nest situated on floating plants or on hummocks. Lays three greenish or light blue eggs with black spots (usually easily identifiable from eggs of Black Tern); end of June.

Habits, feeding methods, and food are same as Black Tern.
Range and distribution: Baltic states, southern half European USSR, Transcaucasus, Kazakhstan, Central Asia, south of West Siberia, Soviet Far East. Winters in Africa.
Similar species: Differs from Black Tern and White-winged Tern by lighter coloration, white cheeks and chin, red bill; in winter, by whiter, streaked crown.

Sterna

Small to medium sizes; tail is deeply forked; coloration light.

312. COMMON TERN
Sterna hirundo
(Rechnaya Krachka)
Plate 23, Map 128
Field marks: 35 cm. Medium size; wings very long and narrow. Outer tail feathers greatly elongated; upperparts gray; underparts white with grayish sides; black "cap" on the head; legs red or red-brownish; bill red with black tip, sometimes entirely black (in eastern races). In winter, forehead is white; upperparts lighter;

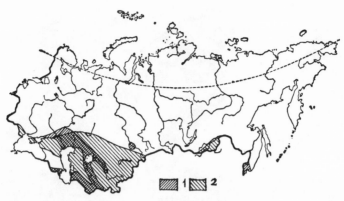

MAP 127. Whiskered Tern (1), Gull-billed Tern (2)

bill blackish. When bird is sitting, tips of folded wings reach tip of tail.

Habits: Found in a variety of habitats from forest to desert. Migratory. Common and numerous. Nests on sandy and pebbly spits of land and on islands in seas, rivers, and lakes, on reed-covered flats (on lower reaches of rivers), in boggy meadows. Nests in colonies; sometimes singly. Nest situated on flat, sandy beaches or on heaps of reeds. Lays three ocherish eggs with black spots from mid-May until June. Very aggressive near the nest, attacks intruders, chases away raptors. Flight is light and direct, usually hovers before diving for fish near the water surface (seldom becomes completely submerged); rarely sits on water. Call: harsh, unpleasant "kirrryaya" or quiet "kee-kee-kee." Feeds on aquatic invertebrates, small fish, flying insects.

Range and distribution: Greater part of the USSR except northern regions. Winters in Africa.

Similar species: Differs from the Arctic Tern by its lighter underparts and black color on bill; from the Aleutian Tern, by its black forehead. Almost indistinguishable from these terns in its winter plumage.

313. ARCTIC TERN
Sterna paradisaea
(Polarnaya Krachka)
Plate 23, Map 129

Field marks: 35 cm. Greatly resembles Common Tern, but underparts grayer; bill entirely red. When bird sits, end of tail extends noticeably beyond folded wing tip. In winter, forehead is white, bill blackish.

Habits: Found on northern seashores, islands, tundra, forest-tundra during nonbreeding season. Migratory. Common or numerous. Nests in pairs or colonies, on rocky or grassy shores not far from water, often in reed-covered flats, on sandy spits of land and small islands; also in lakes of swampy tundra.

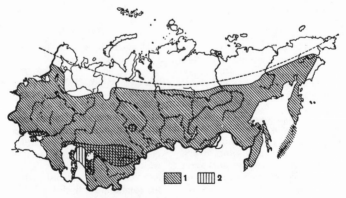

MAP 128. Common Tern (1), Caspian Tern (2)

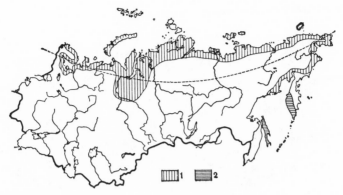

MAP 129. Arctic Tern (1), Aleutian Tern (2)

Nest made of sea grass, bits of wood, sea shells, and is poorly lined. Lays two, more rarely three, ocherish, brownish or greenish-olive eggs with dark spots from early June until July. Very aggressive in colonies, often dive-bombing and sometimes pecking an intruder while giving loud alarm cries. Considerably more cautious when nesting in pairs. Call: a piercing, chirring "kirrrya-kirri-kirri." Flight and feeding habits same as Common Tern. Feeds on small fish (stickleback, capelin) and aquatic invertebrates (amphipods); often follows fishing vessels.

Range and distribution: Tundra from Kola Peninsula in the west to Chukotski Peninsula and shores of the Bering and Okhotsk Seas in the east. Winters on subequatorial seas.

Similar species: Differs from Common Tern by its darker coloration and red bill; from the Aleutian Tern, by black forehead and red legs. In winter, the two species are nearly indistinguishable.

314. ALEUTIAN TERN
Sterna aleutica
(Aleutskaya Krachka)
Plate 23, Map 129

Field marks: 35-37 cm. Resembles Common Tern but smaller; generally darker and smokier overall; forehead, throat, rump, and tail are white; lores, legs, and bill black. In winter, same but with white streaking on head.

Habits: Found on interior bodies of water on islands; along seashores during nonbreeding season. Nonmigratory or nomadic. Rare on the whole. Nests in mixed colonies and in pairs on sandy or pebbly shores of rivers and lakes covered with sparse vegetation; on islands and on spits of land. Nest is a shallow depression lined with plant material, situated near the

water. Lays two dark, olive-brown eggs with black spots in June. Feeds on small fish, which it catches at sea or in overgrown lakes. Included in the Red Data Book.

Range and distribution: Kamchatka Peninsula, Sakhalin Island.

Similar species: Differs from Common and Arctic Terns by its darker coloration overall, white forehead, and black legs. In winter, nearly indistinguishable in the field.

315. LITTLE TERN
Sterna albifrons
(Malaya Krachka)
Plate 23, Map 130

Field marks: 24 cm. Small tern with light gray upperparts, white forehead, black cap, and white underparts; wing tips are dark; legs yellow; bill yellow with black tip. In juveniles, cap is grayish; upperparts mottled; bill brownish with yellow base.

Habits: Found in a variety of habitats from forest to desert. Migratory. Not numerous, but common in places. Nests in small colonies or in pairs, in colonies of other terns; prefers sandy, pebbly, and shell-strewn islands, spits of land on seashores, rivers, more rarely lakes. Nest is a depression without any lining. Lays three ocherish eggs with small, black spots from early June. Appearance, habits, and methods of feeding resemble the Common Tern; but flight is lighter and more graceful. Feeds primarily on small fish, usually on various fry, more rarely on aquatic invertebrates.

Range and distribution: Southern half of European USSR, Kazakhstan, Central Asia, southern regions of West Siberia. Winters on shores of Africa and southern Asia.

Similar species: Differs from other terns by smaller size and yellow bill.

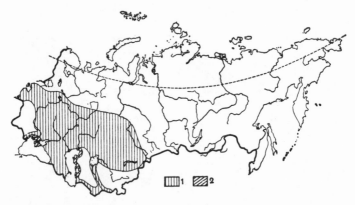

MAP 130. Little Tern (1), Sandwich Tern (2)

316. SANDWICH TERN
Sterna sandvicensis
(Pestronosaya Krachka)
Plate 23, Map 130
Field marks: 43 cm. Large, crested tern with long, narrow bill. Cap black; upperparts gray; underparts and tail white; bill black with yellow tip; legs black. In winter, forehead and forecrown are white, remainder of crown dark-streaked. Juveniles have brownish mottled upper parts and a dark cap.
Habits: Found on seashores and islands. Migratory. Not numerous on the whole. Nests on sandy and shell-strewn flat beaches in colonies. Nest is a shallow depression, sometimes thinly lined with grass. Lays two whitish or cream-colored eggs with small, black spots from early June. Flight, habits, and call similar to Common Tern. Feeds primarily on small fish, more rarely on insects.
Range and distribution: Shores and islands of Black and Azov Seas, eastern shores of the Caspian. Winters on the Mediterranean and shores of Africa.
Similar species: Differs from other terns by its long, black, yellow-tipped bill.

317. GULL-BILLED TERN
Sterna nilotica
(Chaykonosaya Krachka)
Plate 23, Map 127
Field marks: 39 cm. Large tern. The whitest of the terns; upperparts are light bluish-gray; underparts white; black cap; legs and shortish, thick bill are black. In winter, head is white with lightly marked nape and black eye line, back is lighter-colored than in summer. In juveniles, upperparts are mottled brownish with whitish crown and ocherish nape.
Habits: Found on islands and shores of seas,

in fresh- or salt-water lakes, large rivers. Migratory. Not numerous on the whole. Nests in colonies, on sandy or shell-strewn islands, more rarely on spits of land and on shores of saline soil with lichen vegetation. Lays three ocherish eggs with infrequent brownish spots; from mid-April. Aggressive near the colony and dives at intruder with loud cries. Call: soft, pleasant "ke-vek, ke-vek." When alarmed, emits a harsh, chirring cry. Usually feeds in dry steppe, far from water, where it eats insects (particularly locusts) and lizards; catches fish only occasionally.
Range and distribution: South European USSR, Transcaucasus, Central Asia, Kazakhstan, Transbaikal. Winters in Africa and southern Asia.
Similar species: Resembles Sandwich Tern in size, but differs by its short, black bill and less forked tail; also by its different call.

318. CASPIAN TERN
Sterna caspia
(Chegrava)
Plate 23, Map 128
Field marks: 51 cm. Largest of the terns (larger than a crow). Upperparts dark gray; underparts white; black cap has a metallic glitter, and is obviously crested; massive red bill; legs black. In winter, top of head is white with dark streaks; sides of head black.
Habits: Found on shores and islands of seas, inland bodies of water in steppe and desert regions. Migratory. Common in places but rare on the whole. Nests in large colonies; more rarely singly along sandy and shell-strewn beaches with sparse vegetation; more often on islands in seas, lakes, and large rivers. Nest is a shallow depression, sometimes lined with fish bones and situated close to each other. Lays

two or three ocherish eggs with blackish spots at end of May. Very garrulous and aggressive near colonies; when an intruder approaches, circles overhead with loud cries, and dive-bombs. Wary away from the nest. Call: harsh, twittering cawing, nearly unpleasant. Like other terns, catches its prey by diving into water, but usually not deeply. Feeds on small fish, more rarely on aquatic invertebrates.

Range and distribution: Estonia, Crimea, Azov Sea, Caspian Sea, Central Asia, Kazakhstan, southern Siberia, Transbaikal, Soviet Far East. Winters on shores of Africa and southern Asia.

Similar species: Differs from other terns by its larger size; from gulls, by its forked tail and large, red bill.

ALCIDS: *Alcae*

Medium- to small-sized birds with heavy bodies, short, pointed wings and short tails. Toes are webbed. Plumage very compact; velvety on head and neck. Spends the greater part of its life on water, and only goes on land during the breeding period. Flight is fast with rapid wing beats, usually close to the water. On land, walks clumsily and unwillingly; many species cannot take off from the ground. Good swimmer and diver. Stays in flocks, and, as a rule, nests in colonies. Monogamous. Eggs are pear-shaped, elongated pear-shaped, or usual ovoid shape. Semi-altricial mode of development.

Cepphus

Medium-size birds (like a pigeon). Bill is pointed, not flattened.

319. BLACK GUILLEMOT
Cepphus grylle
(Chistik)
Plate 24, Map 131
Field marks: 33 cm. Coloration black; large white patch on wing; bill black; legs red. In winter, underparts and wing patch are white; upperparts mottled gray; remainder of wing black.
Habits: Found on cliffs and pebbled shores of seas and on islands. In winter, stays on open seas. Migratory or nonmigratory. Common. Nests in mixed colonies; stays in flocks during nonbreeding season. Builds nests in clefts and hollows under rocks, lining them with small pebbles. Lays two white or ocherish eggs with small, dark spots in June. On land, stays nearly horizontal. Call: thin, quiet whistle. Feeds on small fish and aquatic invertebrates.

Range and distribution: Shores and islands of White and Barents Seas, islands of the Arctic Ocean, Chukotski Peninsula, Komandorskiye and Kuril Islands. Winters on open seas.

Similar species: Differs from the Spectacled Guillemot by its all-black head and large white spot on wing; from murrelets (in winter), by its larger size, lighter head, and red legs.

320. SPECTACLED GUILLEMOT
Cepphus carbo
(Ochkovy Chistik)
Plate 24, Map 131
Field marks: 40 cm. Resembles Black Guillemot, but is larger; wings entirely black; white

MAP 131. Black Guillemot (1), Spectacled Guillemot (2)

spot circles the eye. In winter, underparts white; upperparts uniformly blackish.

Habits: Found on cliffs and islands of seasides. Nonmigratory and not numerous. Nests in pairs or in small groups in hollows under rocks and in deep cliff crevices. Lays one or two white eggs with blackish spots in June. Feeding, habits, and call similar to Black Guillemot.

Range and distribution: Shores of Okhotsk Sea, Kamchatka Peninsula, Sakhalin Island and Soviet Far East. Winters on open seas.

Similar species: Differs from Black Guillemot by lack of white wing patch and presence of white eye ring; in winter, by bicolored appearance.

Alca

321. RAZORBILL
Alca torda
(Gagarka)
Plate 24, Map 132

Field marks: 42 cm. Large (larger than a crow). Bill laterally flattened, and black with a vertical white stripe; a similar white stripe extends from the base of the bill to the eye; legs black. Head and upperparts black, underparts white. In winter, chin and throat are white.

Habits: Found on islands and cliffs near seashores; in winter, stays on unfrozen regions of ocean. Migratory or nomadic. Common. Nests singly or in small groups together with other alcids, but slightly distant from them. Nests in niches or crevices of overhanging cliffs high over the water. Nest is a depression thinly lined with pebbles or bits or seaweed. Lays one ocher-cream egg with black-brownish spots end of May. In flight, head is pulled back into the shoulders; characteristically cocks its tail in

water; sits vertically on land, balancing against the tail, usually on fairly high cliffs. Generally silent. Call: scraping cry, very rarely heard. Feeds on small fish (capelin, sand eel, young cod).

Range and distribution: Shores of Barents and White Seas. Winters on northern and western shores of Europe.

Similar species: Differs from murres by its massive black bill with distinct white, vertical stripe.

Plautus

322. DOVEKIE
Plautus alle
(Lyurik)
Plate 24, Map 132

Field marks: 20 cm. Small (thrush-size). Upperparts, throat, and breast brownish-black; underparts white; white wingstripe; bill short, conical, black; legs gray. In winter, cheeks and entire underparts are white.

Habits: Found on rocky seashores and islands; stays on open seas near ice floes in winter. Nomadic and numerous. Nests in enormous colonies on coastal rockslides and cliffs, as well as far inland. Nest is not lined, and is situated in hollows under rocks. Lays a single bluish-white egg in mid-June. Habits and flight same as other alcids. Very garrulous; call: chirring, harsh cry. Feeds primarily on aquatic invertebrates (crustaceans); more rarely on small fish.

Range and distribution: Franz Josef Land, northern island of Novaya Zemlya, Severnaya Zemlya. Winters in waters of the Barents Sea.

Similar species: Differs from murres by smaller size; from Black Guillemot by its white belly.

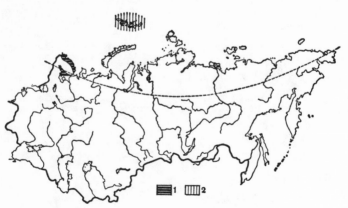

MAP 132. Razorbill (1), Dovekie (2)

MAP 133. Thick-billed Murre (1), Thin-billed Murre (2)

Uria

Large bird. Bill fairly long, needle-shaped, black.

323. THIN-BILLED MURRE
Uria aalge
(Tonkoklyuvaya Kayra)
Plate 24, Map 133

Field marks: 43 cm. Head, neck, back, and wings are black; underparts white; sparse, diagonal streaking on sides; legs black. In some races, a white ring circles the eye, connecting to a stripe that reaches to the ear ("spectacled murre"). In winter, cheeks and entire underparts are white.

Habits: Found on cliff shores of seas and on islands; winters on unfrozen seas. Nomadic. Numerous. Nests in huge colonies, often together with Black-legged Kittiwakes, on inaccessible, overhanging rock ledges. Eggs are laid directly on ledges and prominences of cliffs without any lining, usually close together. Lays a single egg, end of May to June. Eggs have an elongated pear shape that prevents them from rolling off the ledge; color varies from greenish-blue to white with various shapes of black, brownish, or brown spots and curlicues. Young leave the nest before they know how to fly by jumping from cliffs into the water, often from a great height. Habits and flight similar to other guillemots. In flight, neck is drawn out; when turning in flight, the toes, which are spread wide, act as a steering mechanism. On water, stays in tight flocks; tail is not cocked. Call: distant, hoarse, roaring cawing. Feeds on small fish (capelin, sand eel, and cod) and crustaceans.

Range and distribution: Shores of Barents Sea, Novaya Zemlya, shores of Kamchatka Penin-

sula, Kuril Islands, Sakhalin Island. Winters on open water near its breeding range.

Similar species: Differs from the Thick-billed Murre by the diagonal streaking on the sides, and entirely black bill; in winter, by the white cheek that is nearly bisected by a narrow line behind eye.

324. THICK-BILLED MURRE
Uria lomvia
(Tolstoklyuvaya Kayra)
Plate 24, Map 133

FIG. 52 Murre Chick

MAP 134. Marbled Murrelet (1), Kittlitz's Murrelet (2)

Field marks: 45 cm. Greatly resembles Thin-billed Murre, but bill is shorter and thicker; thin, light streak at the corner of the mouth near the lower mandible. Border between black upperparts and white underparts is very sharp. There is no "spectacled" variety. In winter, underparts entirely white; upperparts black.

Habits: Mode of nesting and location, habits, feeding similar to Thin-billed Murre, with whom it often resides.

Range and distribution: Shores of Barents Sea, Novaya Zemlya, Franz Josef Land, Severnaya Zemlya, Novosibirskiye Islands, Wrangel Island, Chukotski Peninsula, shores of Kamchatka, Kuril Islands, Sakhalin Island. Winters on open water near its breeding range.

Similar species: Differs from Thin-billed Murre by thin, light line on the bill, and strongly contrasting border between dark back and light belly caused by lack of diagonal streaking.

Brachyramphus

Medium-size bird with small, conical, black bill and dull, mottled coloration.

325. MARBLED MURRELET
Brachyramphus marmoratus
(Dlinnoklyuvy Pyzhik)
Plate 24, Map 134

Field marks: 33 cm. Smaller than a pigeon. Upperparts dark brown with darker barring; underparts lighter with brownish speckles. Legs pinkish. In winter, underparts pure white; upperparts grayish-black; dark cap extends below the eye.

Habits: Found along seashores. Nonmigratory and nomadic. Rare. Nests far from ocean; the single known nest was found situated on a branch of a larch tree at the height of seven meters, and was made from lichens. Lays a single light bluish-green egg with dark spots in June.

Range and distribution: Kamchatka, Kuril Islands, Sakhalin Island, shores of Okhotsk Sea. Winters on open seas near its breeding range.

Similar species: Differs from Kittlitz's Murrelet by its bicolored appearance, entirely dark tail, and long (longer than 1 cm.) bill; in winter, by the black cap extending below the eye, and strongly contrasting white scapulars.

326. KITTLITZ'S MURRELET
Brachyramphus brevirostris
(Korotkoklyuvy Pyzhik)
Plate 24, Map 134

Field marks: 32 cm. Same size as Marbled Murrelet. Upperparts brownish-gray, thickly mottled and barred with white; underparts lighter, but similarly marked, especially thick on the upper breast; outer tail feathers white; legs gray. In winter, underparts are white, dark cap much reduced by white that extends well above the eye and forms a nearly unbroken collar.

Habits: Found near seashores. Very rare. Nests inland, far from water; feeds along seashores; in winter, also found at sea. Nest is a shallow depression situated on open ground. Lays one greenish egg with black spots in June. Feeds on aquatic invertebrates and, apparently, small fish.

Range and distribution: Shores of Chukotski Peninsula. Winters on coastal Kamchatka Peninsula, Kuril Islands.

Similar species: Differs from Marbled Murrelet by more nearly uniform coloration and by short bill; in winter, by reduced dark cap

PLATE 1

50 CM

1. Pelagic Cormorant *28*   2. Great Cormorant *26*   3. Red-faced Cormorant *29*
4. Temminck's Cormorant *27*   5. Great Cormorant *26*   6. Pelagic Cormorant *28*
7. European Shag *30*   8. Pygmy Cormorant *31*   9. Yellow-billed Loon *3*   10. Black-throated Loon *2*   11. Red-throated Loon *1*   12. Northern Gannet *32*   13. Eastern White Pelican *25*   14. Dalmatian Pelican *24*

PLATE 2

1. Whooper Swan *58*   2. Bewick's Swan *59*   3. Mute Swan *60*   4. Snow Goose *65*
5. Swan Goose *62*   6. Greylag Goose *66*   7. Bean Goose *69*   8. Lesser White-fronted
Goose *68*   9. Bar-headed Goose *64*   10. Barnacle Goose *71*   11. Brent Goose *70*
12. Greater White-fronted Goose *67*   13. Emperor Goose *63*   14. Red-breasted Goose *72*
15. Canada Goose *73*

PLATE 3

50 CM

1. Mallard 77   2. Northern Pintail 84   3. Spot-billed Duck 78   4. Eurasian Wigeon 83
5. Garganey 86   6. Gadwall 82   7. Baikal Teal 80   8. Green-winged Teal 79
9. Northern Shoveler 87   10. Ferruginous Pochard 96   11. Marbled Duck 85
12. Falcated Duck 81   13. Mandarin Duck 89

PLATE 4

1. White-winged Scoter *100* la. eastern form   2. Black Scoter *101*   3. Surf Scoter *102*
4. Tufted Pochard *98*   5. Barrow's Goldeneye *106*   6. Common Goldeneye *105*
7. Bufflehead *107*   8. Northern Pochard *95*   9. Baer's Pochard *97*   10. Greater Scaup *99*
11. Red-crested Pochard *94*   12. Long-tailed Duck *104*   12a. winter   13. Ruddy
Shelduck *75*   14. Red-billed Shelduck *74*   15. Crested Shelduck *76*

PLATE 5

1. Common Eider *90* 2. Spectacled Eider *92* 3. King Eider *91* 4. Steller's Eider *93*
5. Harlequin Duck *103* 6. Red-breasted Merganser *109* 7. Chinese Merganser *110*
8. Common Merganser *111* 9. Smew *108* 10. White-headed Duck *112* 11. Black-
necked Grebe *8* 12. Red-throated Dabchick *9* 13. Horned Grebe *7* 14. Red-necked
Grebe *6* 15. Great Crested Grebe *5* 15a. Winter plumage

PLATE 6

50 CM

1. Eurasian Spoonbill *51*   2. Japanese Crested Ibis *53*   3. Glossy Ibis *52*   4. Gray Heron *35*   5. Purple Heron *36*   6. Great Egret *37*   7. Cattle Egret *41*   8. Little Egret *38* 9. Squacco Pond-Heron *42*   10. Little Heron *44*   11. Black-crowned Night-Heron *45* 12. Eurasian Bittern *49*   13. Little Bittern *46*   14. Schrenck's Bittern *47*   15. Yellow Bittern *48*

PLATE 7

1. Common Crane *180*   2. Sandhill Crane *181*   3. White-naped Crane *182*   4. Hooded
Crane *183*   5. Siberian White Crane *184*   6. Demoiselle Crane *187*   7. Japanese Crane
185   8. Greater Flamingo *57*   9. White Stork *55*   10. Black Stork *56*   11. Great Bustard
188   12. Houbara Bustard *189*   13. Little Bustard *190*

PLATE 8

1. Golden Eagle *130*   2. Pallas's Sea-Eagle *119*   3. Steller's Sea-Eagle *120*   4. Eurasian Griffon *140*   5. Cinereous Vulture *139*   6. Lammergeier *138*   7. White-tailed Sea-Eagle *118*   8. Egyptian Vulture *137*   9. Imperial Eagle *131*   10. Steppe Eagle *132*   11. Greater Spotted Eagle *133*   12. Lesser Spotted Eagle *134*   13. Bonelli's Eagle *135*

PLATE 9

50 CM

1. Booted Eagle *136*   2. Common Buzzard *125*   3. Long-legged Buzzard *128*   4. Upland
Buzzard *127*   5. Rough-legged Buzzard *126*   6. Gray-faced Buzzard *129*   7. Eurasian
Honey-Buzzard *114*   8. Black-shouldered Kite *149*   9. Short-toed Snake-Eagle *143*
10. Black Kite *116*   11. Red Kite *117*   12. Crested Honey-Buzzard *115*   13. Osprey *113*

PLATE 10

1. Eurasian Sparrowhawk *124*   2. Northern Goshawk *121*   2a. East Siberian form
3. Shikra *122*   4. Besra Sparrowhawk *123*   5. Montagu's Harrier *145*   6. Pallid Harrier
146   7. Northern Harrier *144*   8. Pied Harrier *147*   9. Marsh Harrier *148*

PLATE 11

1. Peregrine Falcon *150* 1a. rusty-headed form 2. Saker Falcon *151* 2a. Altai form
3. Lanner Falcon *152* 4. Gyrfalcon *153* 5. Merlin *155* 6. Northern Hobby *154*
7. Common Kestrel *157* 8. Lesser Kestrel *158* 9. Red-footed Falcon *156* 9a. eastern form

PLATE 12

1. Snowy Owl *359*   2. Northern Eagle-Owl *360*   3. Great Gray Owl *375*   4. Ural Owl *374*
5. Tawny Owl *373*   6. Blakiston's Fish-Owl *361*

PLATE 13

1. Long-eared Owl *366*   2. Short-eared Owl *367*   3. Northern Hawk-Owl *372*   4. Barn Owl *376*   5. Brown Hawk-Owl *368*   6. Striated Scops-Owl *364*   7. Eurasian Scops-Owl *362*   8. Eurasian Pygmy-Owl *371*   9. Eastern Scops-Owl *365*   10. Collared Scops-Owl *363*   11. Little Owl *370*   12. Boreal Owl *369*

PLATE 14

1. Northern Black Grouse *162*   2. Western Capercaillie *164*   3. Caucasian Black Grouse
163   4. Black-billed Capercaillie *165*   5. Himalayan Snowcock *176*   6. Altai Snowcock *177*
7. Tibetan Snowcock *178*   8. Caucasian Snowcock *174*   9. Caspian Snowcock *175*
10. Common Pheasant (Soviet Far Eastern form) *179*   10a. Caucasus form

PLATE 15

1. Willow Ptarmigan (summer, winter) *160* 2. Rock Ptarmigan (summer, winter) *161*
3. Siberian Spruce Grouse *166* 4. Northern Hazelhen *167* 5. Common Quail *168*
5a. Soviet Far East form 6. Daurian Partridge *172* 7. See-see Partridge *169* 8. Chukar
Partridge *170* 9. Gray Partridge *171* 10. Black Francolin *173* 11. Yellow-legged
Buttonquail *202*

PLATE 16

1. Water Rail *194*   2. Little Crake *197*   3. Spotted Crake *196*   4. Corn Crake *195*
5. Band-bellied Crake *200*   6. Baillon's Crake *198*   7. Common Gallinule *193*   8. Purple
Swamphen *192*   9. Watercock (male) *201*   10. Common Coot *191*

PLATE 17

1. Stone Thick-knee *203*   2. Cream-colored Courser *204*   3. Black-capped Avocet *271*
4. Black-winged Stilt *270*   5. Sociable Lapwing *221*   6. White-tailed Lapwing *222*
7. Northern Lapwing *220*   8. Red-wattled Lapwing *223*   9. Little Curlew *26*   10. Slender-
billed Curlew *265*   11. Eurasian Curlew *262*   12. Whimbrel *263*   13. Ibisbill *280*
14. Black-tailed Godwit *260*   15. Bar-tailed Godwit *261*   16. Common Oystercatcher *281*

PLATE 18

1. Gray Plover *208*   2. Greater Golden Plover *209*   3. Lesser Golden Plover *210*   4. Little Ringed Plover *212*   5. Eurasian Dotterel *219*   6. Kentish Plover *214*   7. Greater Ringed Plover *211*   8. Caspian Plover *217*   9. Mongolian Plover *215*   10. Sand Plover *216*
11. Black-winged Pratincole *206*   12. European Pratincole *205*   13. Oriental Pratincole *207*   14. Ruddy Turnstone *226*   15. Black Turnstone *227*   16. Red Phalarope *269*   17. Red-necked Phalarope *268*

PLATE 19

1. Curlew Sandpiper *228*   2. Dunlin *229*   3. Buff-breasted Sandpiper *243*   4. Little Stint *230*   5. Pectoral Sandpiper *236*   6. Baird's Sandpiper *235*   7. Western Sandpiper *234*   8. Long-toed Stint *232*   9. Temminck's Stint *233*   10. Sanderling *238* 11. Red Knot *239*   12. Great Knot *240*   13. Rufous-necked Stint *231*   14. Spoon-billed Sandpiper *246*   15. Broad-billed Sandpiper *245*   16. Purple Sandpiper *241* 17. Sharp-tailed Sandpiper *237*   18. Ruff *244*

PLATE 20

20 CM

1. Spotted Redshank *253*   2. Common Redshank *252*   3. Marsh Sandpiper *254*   4. Green
Sandpiper *249*   5. Greater Greenshank *251*   6. Spotted Greenshank *255*   7. Gray-tailed
Tattler *256*   8. Wood Sandpiper *250*   9. Common Sandpiper *258*   10. Terek
Sandpiper *259*   11. Common Snipe *273*   12. Pin-tailed Snipe *276*   13. Jack Snipe *279*
14. Great Snipe *274*   15. Eurasian Woodcock *272*   16. Long-billed Dowitcher *247*
17. Asian Dowitcher *248*   18. Solitary Snipe *277*

PLATE 21

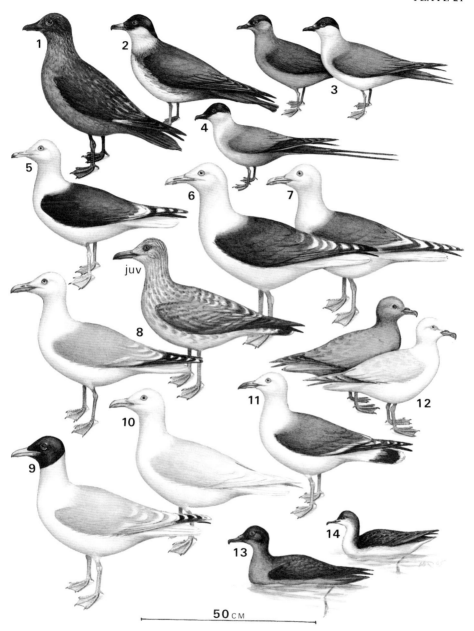

1. Great Skua *286*   2. Pomarine Jaeger *285*   3. Parasitic Jaeger *283*   4. Long-tailed
Jaeger *284*   5. Lesser Black-backed Gull *295*   6. Great Black-backed Gull *292*   7. Slaty-
backed Gull *293*   8. Herring Gull *296*   9. Great Black-headed Gull *300*   10. Glaucous
Gull *298*   11. Black-tailed Gull *294*   12. Northern Fulmar *10*   13. Sooty Shearwater *17*
14. Manx Shearwater *19*

PLATE 22

1. Sabine's Gull *291*   2. Ross's Gull *290*   3. Black-legged Kittiwake *288*   4. Red-legged Kittiwake *289*   5. Ivory Gull *287*   6. Mew Gull *297*   7. Mediterranean Gull *304*   8. Black-headed Gull *301*   9. Little Gull *305*   10. Slender-billed Gull *306*   11. Relict Gull *303*

PLATE 23

1. Black Tern *309* 2. White-winged Black Tern *310* 3. Whiskered Tern *311* 4. Gull-billed Tern *317* 5. Sandwich Tern *316* 6. Little Tern *315* 7. Caspian Tern *318*
8. Arctic Tern *313* 9. Common Tern *312* 10. Aleutian Tern *314* 11. Swinhoe's Storm-Petrel *12* 12. Leach's Storm-Petrel *11* 13. Fork-tailed Storm-Petrel *13*

PLATE 24

25 CM

1. Razorbill *321*   2. Dovekie *322*   3. Thin-billed Murre *323*   4. Thick-billed Murre *324*
5. Marbled Murrelet *325*   6. Black Guillemot *319*   7. Spectacled Guillemot *320*
8. Kittlitz's Murrelet *326*   9. Ancient Murrelet *327*   10. Parakeet Auklet *332*   11. Crested
Auklet *329*   12. Whiskered Auklet *330*   13. Least Auklet *331*   14. Rhinoceros Auklet *333*
15. Tufted Puffin *336*   16. Atlantic Puffin *334*   17. Horned Puffin *335*

PLATE 25

1. Rock Pigeon *341* 2. Hill Pigeon *342* 3. Snow Pigeon *343* 4. Eastern Stock Pigeon *344*
5. Western Stock Pigeon *345* 6. Wood Pigeon *346* 7. European Turtle-Dove *347*
8. Oriental Turtle-Dove *348* 9. Collared Turtle-Dove *349* 10. Laughing Turtle-Dove *350* 11. Japanese Green-Pigeon *352* 12. Tibetan Sandgrouse *340* 13. Pallas's Sandgrouse *339* 14. Pin-tailed Sandgrouse *338* 15. Black-bellied Sandgrouse *337*

PLATE 26

30 CM

1. Eurasian Cuckoo *353*   2. Indian Cuckoo *356*   3. Lesser Cuckoo *355*   4. Hodgson's Hawk-Cuckoo *357*   5. Eurasian Roller *386*   6. Hoopoe *395*   7. Broad-billed Roller *387* 8. European Bee-eater *393*   9. Blue-cheeked Bee-eater *394*   10. Eurasian Kingfisher *388* 11. Pied Kingfisher *391*   12. Black-capped Kingfisher *390*   13. European Nightjar *377* 14. Gray Nightjar *379*   15. Egyptian Nightjar *378*

PLATE 27

1. Gray-headed Green Woodpecker *398*   2. Eurasian Green Woodpecker *397*   3. Black
Woodpecker *396*   4. Scaly-bellied Green Woodpecker *399*   5. Great Spotted Woodpecker
401   6. Syrian Woodpecker *403*   7. Northern Three-toed Woodpecker *400*
8. Lesser Spotted Woodpecker *406*   9. Middle Spotted Woodpecker *405*   10. White-
backed Woodpecker *404*   11. Gray-headed Pygmy Woodpecker *408*   12. Japanese Pygmy
Woodpecker *407*   13. Eurasian Wryneck *409*

PLATE 28

1. Alpine Swift *382*   2. White-throated Needletail *385*   3. Northern Swift *381*   4. Pacific Swift *383*   5. House Swift *384*   6. Crag Martin *431*   7. Northern House Martin *428* 8. Barn Swallow *425*   9. Red-rumped Swallow *426*   10. Wire-tailed Swallow *427* 11. Sand Martin   *429*

PLATE 29

1. Snow Bunting (summer and winter) *650*   2. Northern Skylark *410*   3. Gray
Lark *415*   4. Lesser Short-toed Lark *414*   5. Wood Lark *412*   6. Crested Lark *413*
7. Greater Short-toed Lark *416*   8. Desert Lark *423*   9. White-winged Lark *419*
10. Mongolian Lark *420*   11. Calandra Lark *421*   12. Bimaculated Lark *422*   13. Hume's
Short-toed Lark *417*   14. Black Lark *418*   15. Horned Lark *424*

PLATE 30

1. White Wagtail *447* 1a. European form 1b. Central Asian form 1c. Kamchatka form
2. Gray Wagtail *446* 3. Yellow-backed Wagtail *444* 4. Yellow Wagtail *443* 4a. black-headed form 5. Citrine Wagtail *445* 6. Forest Wagtail *442* 7. Meadow Pipit *439*
8. Petchora Pipit *438* 9. Tawny Pipit *435* 10. Tree Pipit *436* 11. Water Pipit *441*
12. Olive-backed Pipit *437* 13. Red-throated Pipit *440* 14. Richard's Pipit *434*

PLATE 31

20CM

1. Great Gray Shrike *452*   2. Chinese Gray Shrike *453*   3. Lesser Gray Shrike *454*
4. Long-tailed Shrike *456*   5. Tiger Shrike *458*   6. Bull-headed Shrike *455*   7. Bay-
backed Shrike *460*   8. Brown Shrike *459*   Top: Central Asian form   Middle: Siberian
form   Bottom: European form   9. Woodchat shrike *457*   10. Ashy Minivet *449*
11. Hypocolius *464*   12. Bohemian Waxwing *462*   13. Japanese Waxwing *464*

PLATE 32

1. Fieldfare *470* 2. Mistle Thrush *471* 3. Song Thrush *472* 4. Red-winged Thrush *473* 5. Scaly Thrush *468* 6. Gray Thrush *481* 7. Gray-backed Thrush *476* 8. Pale Thrush *477* 9. Dark-throated Thrush *475* form Left: Black-throated Right: Red-throated form 10. Siberian Thrush *469* 11. Gray-cheeked Thrush *480* 12. Naumann's Thrush *474* (three color variations)

PLATE 33

1. Ring Thrush *478*   2. Streaked Laughing-Thrush *519*   3. Eurasian Blackbird *479*
4. Blue Whistling-Thrush *483*   5. White-backed Rock-Thrush *484*   6. White-throated
Rock-Thrush *486*   7. Blue Rock-Thrush *485*   7a. Soviet Far Eastern form   8. Himalayan
Accentor *622*   9. Brown Accentor *619*   10. Siberian Accentor *618*   11. Black-throated
Accentor *617*   12. Japanese Accentor *616*   13. Alpine Accentor *621*   14. Dunnock *615*

PLATE 34

1. Northern Wheatear *487*   2. Desert Wheatear *488*   3. Pied Wheatear *489*   3a. Caucasus form *489*   4. Finsch's Wheatear *490*   5. Red-Tailed Wheatear *492*   6. Variable Wheatear *493*   7. Isabelline Wheatear *491*   8. Whinchat *494*   9. Stonechat *495*   10. Pied Bushchat *496*

PLATE 35

1. Siberian Blue Robin *512*   2. Orange-flanked Bush-Robin *498*   3. European
Robin *514*   4. White-capped River Chat *499*   5. Guldenstadt's Redstart *504*   6. Japanese
Robin *515*   7. Eurasian Redstart *500*   8. Black Redstart *501*   9. Eversmann's Redstart *502*
10. Daurian Redstart *503*   11. Blue-headed Redstart *505*

PLATE 36

15 CM

1. Barred Warbler *570*   2. Garden Warbler *569*   3. Lesser Whitethroat *573*
4. Blackcap *571*   5. Desert Warbler *574*   6. Greater Whitethroat *572*   7. Orphean
Warbler *568*   8. Ménétries's Warbler *575*   9. Streaked Scrub Warbler *577*
10. Nightingale *507*   11. Thrush-Nightingale *508*   12. Rufous-tailed Robin *511*
13. Siberian Rubythroat *509*   14. Bluethroat *513*   15. Himalayan Rubythroat *510*
16. Rufous Scrub-Robin *518*   17. Persian Robin *516*

PLATE 37

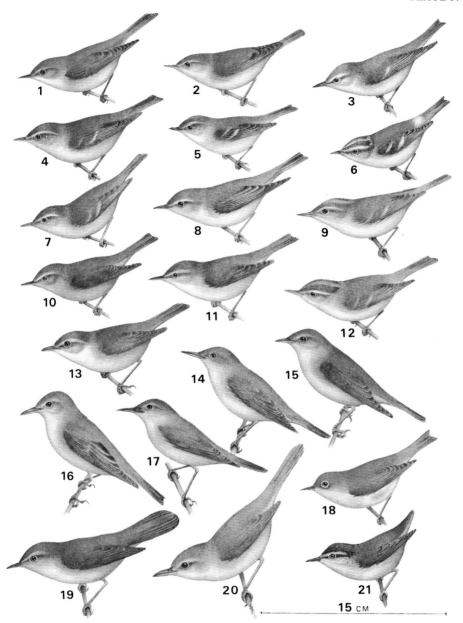

1. Chiffchaff *525*   2. Willow Warbler *524*   3. Greenish Warbler *528*   4. Arctic
Warbler *527*   5. Yellow-browed Warbler *532*   6. Pallas's Warbler *533*   7. Pale-legged
Leaf-Warbler *529*   8. Wood Warbler *526*   9. Eastern Crowned Warbler *531*
10. Olivaceous Leaf-Warbler *535*   11. Dusky Leaf-Warbler *536*   12. Western Crowned
Warbler *530*   13. Radde's Warbler *539*   14. Upcher's Warbler *563*   15. Booted
Warbler *565*   16. Icterine Warbler *563*   17. Olivaceous Warbler *566*   18. Chestnut-
flanked White-eye *614*   19. Cetti's Bush-Warbler *542*   20. Japanese Bush-Warbler *541*
21. Stub-tailed Bush-Warbler *540*

PLATE 38

1. Spotted Bush-Warbler *543*   2. European Grasshopper-Warbler *552*   3. Lanceolated
Warbler *553*   4. Gray's Grasshopper-Warbler *547*   5. Savi's Warbler *549*
6. Middendorff's Grasshopper-Warbler *551*   7. River Warbler *548*   8. Pallas's
Grasshopper-Warbler *550*   9. Moustached Warbler *546*   10. Thick-billed Reed-
Warbler *554*   11. Great Reed-Warbler *555*   12. Paddyfield Warbler *559*   13. Marsh
Warbler *557*   14. European Reed-Warbler *556*   15. Blyth's Reed-Warbler *558*   16. Black-
browed Reed-Warbler *560*   17. Sedge Warbler *561*   18. Aquatic Warbler *562*

PLATE 39

1. Spotted Flycatcher *581*   2. Dark-sided Flycatcher *582*   3. Gray-streaked Flycatcher *583*
4. Asian Paradise-Flycatcher *592*   5. Japanese Paradise-Flycatcher *593*   6. Rufous-tailed
Flycatcher *585*   7. Asian Brown Flycatcher *584*   8. Pied Flycatcher *586*   9. Collared
Flycatcher *587*   10. Red-throated Flycatcher *588*   11. Narcissus Flycatcher *590*
12. Mugimaki Flycatcher *589*   13. Blue-and-white Flycatcher *591*

PLATE 40

1. Great Tit *594*   1a. Central Asian form   2. Blue Tit *596*   3. Azure Tit *595*   3a. Central Asian form   4. Coal Tit *598*   5. Black Crested Tit *599*   6. Varied Tit *597*   7. Sombre Tit *604*   8. Willow Tit *602*   9. Crested Tit *600*   10. Siberian Tit *603*   11. Marsh Tit *601* 12. Little Forktail *517*   13. Eurasian Dipper *465*   14. Brown Dipper *466*   15. Northern Wren *467*

PLATE 41

1. Wallcreeper *610*   2. Northern Treecreeper *611*   3. Short-toed Treecreeper *612*
4. Himalayan Treecreeper *613*   5. Eurasian Nuthatch Caucasus form *606*   5a. European
form   6. Kruper's Nuthatch *607*   7. Greater Rock Nuthatch *608*   8. Lesser Rock
Nuthatch *609*   9. Bearded Reedling *520*   10. Eurasian Penduline-Tit *605*   Top: Caspian
form   Middle: European form   Bottom: black-headed form   11. Severtzov's Tit-
Warbler *580*   12. Long-tailed Tit *523*   12a. Southern European form   13. Vinous-
throated Parrotbill *521*   14. Firecrest *579*   15. Goldcrest *578*

PLATE 42

15 CM

1. Cirl Bunting *647*   2. Yellowhammer *624*   3. Corn Bunting *623*   4. Yellow-throated Bunting *630*   5. Yellow-breasted Bunting *629*   6. Cretzschmar's Bunting *648*   7. Ortolan Bunting *634*   8. Gray-necked Bunting *635*   9. Red-headed Bunting *627*   10. Black-headed Bunting *626*   11. Yellow-browed Bunting *631*   12. Chestnut Bunting *628* 13. Japanese Gray Bunting *646*   14. Black-faced Bunting *632*

PLATE 43

1. Rustic Bunting *640*   2. Meadow Bunting *637*   3. Rock Bunting *636*   3a. Siberian
form   4. White-capped Bunting *633*   5. Pallas's Reed Bunting *645*   6. Pine Bunting
625   7. Little Bunting *641*   8. Japanese Reed Bunting *643*   9. Jankowski's Bunting *638*
10. Northern Reed Bunting *644*   11. Tristram's Bunting *642*   12. Lapland
Longspur *649*   13. Chestnut-eared Bunting *639*   14. Northern Junco *651*

PLATE 44

1. Chaffinch *687*   2. Brambling *688*   3. Oriental Greenfinch *664*   4. Eurasian
Goldfinch *665* 4a. South Asian form   5. European Greenfinch *663*   6. Eurasian Siskin *666*
7. Twite *668*   8. Linnet *667*   9. European Serin *672*   10. Common Redpoll *669*
11. Red-fronted Serin *671*   12. Hoary Redpoll *670*

PLATE 45

1. Long-tailed Rosefinch *673* 2. Northern Bullfinch *677*   2a. gray form 2b. Ussuri form   3. White-winged Crossbill *684*   4. Scarlet Rosefinch *681*   5. Red Crossbill *685* 6. Great Rosefinch *678*   7. Pallas's Rosefinch *680*   8. Red-mantled Rosefinch *679*   9. Red-breasted Rosefinch *682*   10. Pine Rosefinch *683*   11. Parrot Crossbill *686*

PLATE 46

1. Black-billed Desert-Finch *676* 2. Hodgson's Rosy-Finch *689* 3. Brandt's Rosy-Finch *690* 4. Trumpeter Finch *674* 5. Crimson-winged Finch *675* 6. Arctic Rosy-Finch *691* 6a. Komandorskiye form 7. Desert Sparrow *702* 8. White-winged Snow-Finch *692* 9. Rock Petronia *695* 10. Theresa's Snow-Finch *694* 11. Pale Petronia *696* 12. Père David's Snow-Finch *693* 13. Saxual Sparrow *699* 14. Cinnamon Sparrow *701* 15. House Sparrow *697* 16. Spanish Sparrow *698* 17. Tree Sparrow *700*

PLATE 47

1. Pander's Ground-Jay *723* 2. Henderson's Ground-Jay *724* 3. Spangled Drongo *714*
4. Black Drongo *713* 5. Northern Starling (fall and spring) *703* 6. White-cheeked
Starling *705* 7. Red-cheeked Starling *708* 8. Daurian Starling *707* 9. Yellow-billed
Grosbeak *662* 10. Rose-colored Starling *704* 11. Indian Myna *706* 12. Japanese
Grosbeak *661* 13. White-winged Grosbeak *660* 14. Hawfinch *659* 15. European Golden
Oriole *711* 16. Black-naped Oriole *712*

PLATE 48

1. Northern Raven *715*   1a. desert form   2. Eurasian Crow *716*   2a. black form 2b. gray form   3. Large-billed Crow *717*   4. Eurasian Rook *718*   5. Jackdaw *719*   .5a. Daurian form   6. Black-billed Magpie *725*   7. Eurasian Jay *727* with examples of various races.
8. Siberian Jay *728*   9. Azure-winged Magpie *726*   10. Red-billed Chough *720*
11. Alpine Chough *721*   12. Spotted Nutcracker *722*

MAP 135. Ancient Murrelet (1), Crested Auklet (2)

and white "face" that extends well above the eye.

Synthliboramphus

327. ANCIENT MURRELET
Synthliboramphus antiquus
(Starik)
Plate 24, Map 135
Field marks: 27 cm. Small (smaller than a pigeon). Bill short and conical, whitish; head and throat are black; back is slate-black; breast and belly white; narrow white eyebrow extends onto the nape. In winter, the white eyebrow is lacking; throat is white, chin gray.
Habits: Found on islands and seashore cliffs. Nomadic, rare, common in places. Nests in colonies, in crevices and hollows between rocks, sometimes far inland. Eggs are laid directly on the ground. Lays two ocherish eggs speckled brownish in June. Stays in small flocks on the water. Call: melodic, thin whistle. Feeds on aquatic invertebrates, small fish.
Range and distribution: Shores of Kamchatka Peninsula, Sakhalin Island, Kuril Islands, shores of Soviet Far East. Winters south to Taiwan.
Similar species: Differs from other small alcids of the Soviet Far East by its tufts of white feathers over the eye and small, conical bill; from other murrelets (in winter) by lack of white scapulars, gray chin, and shorter bill.

[Vagrants of the **328.** JAPANESE MURRELET (*Synthliboramphus wumizusume*) have occasionally been found along shores of Sakhalin Peninsula and the Kuril Islands. It resembles the Ancient Murrelet, but has broad white stripes on each side of a crest of long, narrow, black feathers. Crest is lacking in winter.]

Aethia

Medium and small sizes. Bill very short with high ridge. In summer, head is decorated with elongated feathers.

329. CRESTED AUKLET
Aethia cristatella
(Bolshaya Konyuga)
Plate 24, Map 135
Field marks: 27 cm. Size of a pigeon. Crest of forward-curving long, black feathers on forehead; white, threadlike feathers behind the eye; uniformly brownish-gray, slightly darker on the back; bill red with decorative platelets on upper mandible; legs gray. In winter, crest is shorter (entirely lacking in juveniles), bill yellowish.
Habits: Found near cliffs and on rocky seashores and islands; in winter, stays on unfrozen regions of the sea; often far from land. Nonmigratory and nomadic. Numerous in places. Nests in cliff crevices and in rock slides, also in open spaces between rocks; often forms large colonies. Lays a single large, white egg directly on the ground in June or July. Feeds primarily at dusk and at night, staying in flocks. Very garrulous and not cautious. Feeds on crustaceans that it catches by diving to a great depth.
Range and distribution: Shores of Chukotski Peninsula, Komandorskiye and Kuril Islands, Sakhalin Island. Winters on open seas near nesting range.
Similar species: Differs from Whiskered Auklet by larger size (wing larger than 12 cm.) and

Map 136. Parakeet Auklet (1), Whiskered Auklet (2), Least Auklet (3)

dark belly; from the Parakeet Auklet, by the crest on the forehead and dark belly.

330. WHISKERED AUKLET
Aethia pygmaea
(Malaya Konyuga)
Plate 24, Map 136

Field marks: 22 cm. Resembles Crested Auklet but smaller; belly light; tufts of white, thread-like feathers before (above and below) as well as behind eye. Crest is smaller in winter, lacking in juveniles.

Habits: Found on precipitous cliff seashores. Nomadic and nonmigratory. Common, in places numerous. Nests in crevices of inaccessible, overhanging ledges, under rocks. Forms colonies, often together with Storm-Petrels and Crested Auklets. Lays single white egg directly on the ground in June. Feeds both day and night. Stays in flocks on water, very garrulous. Call: piercing cry. Feeds on small crustaceans.

Range and distribution: Komandorskiye and Kuril Islands. Winters on open regions of seas near its breeding range.

Similar species: Differs from Crested Auklet by smaller size (wing less than 12 cm.), lighter belly, and three sets of longer white feathers on head; from the Parakeet Auklet, by crest on head and small size.

331. LEAST AUKLET
Aethia pusilla
(Konyuga-kroshka)
Plate 24, Map 136

Field marks: 21 cm. Smaller than a thrush. Bill short, swollen; small knob at base of upper mandible; upperparts and head blackish; throat and belly pure white; dark band across breast; short, threadlike white feathers behind the eye;

bill red; legs gray. In winter, bill is brownish and lacks knob.

Habits: Found along rock-strewn seashores, and cliffs with rock slides of large boulders; in winter, found on unfrozen seas. Nomadic. Not numerous. Nesting habits similar to other auklets. Lays a single egg in June. In winter, stays in huge flocks. Walks over land easily, often climbing on rocks. Very lively, garrulous, and unwary. Flies over colonies for long periods of time. Call: thin, gentle whistle. Feeds on small crustaceans, which it finds in the upper layers of water.

Range and distribution: Shores of Chukotski Peninsula. Winters on shores of Sakhalin, Komandorskiye, and Kuril Islands.

Similar species: Differs from other auklets by significantly smaller size, lack of crest on forehead, and dark breast-band.

Cyclorrhynchus

332. PARAKEET AUKLET
Cyclorrhynchus psittacula
(Belobryushka)
Plate 24, Map 136

Field marks: 27 cm. Size of a pigeon. Bill short, heavy, and upturned. Long, white stripe of threadlike feathers goes from the eye to the nape; lacks crest on forehead; upperparts black with diffuse barring on flanks; underparts white except for chin and throat, which are blackish; bill red; legs light bluish-gray.

Habits: Found on seashore cliffs; in winter, stays in unfrozen parts of seas. Nomadic and common. Nests in small colonies on cliffs, using crevices and hollows under rocks. Lays a single white egg directly on the ground in mid-July. Feeds at sea; stays in flocks and in pairs;

moves about on dry land quickly and easily; usually silent. Feeds on crustaceans.

Range and distribution: Shores of Chukotski Peninsula, Kamchatka Peninsula, Sea of Okhotsk, Komandorskiye Islands, Kuril Islands. Winters on coasts of Japan.

Similar species: Differs from Crested and Whiskered Auklets by lack of crest on forehead and by white breast and belly.

Cerorhinca

333. RHINOCEROS AUKLET
Cerorhinca monocerata
(Tupik-nosorog)
Plate 24, Map 137
Field marks: 32 cm. Larger than a pigeon. Short orange bill has a horn near the base of the upper mandible. Two stripes of white plumelike feathers on sides of head; upperparts black; breast brownish; belly white; legs yellow. In winter, similarly marked, but lacks horn on bill and tufts of feathers on sides of head.

Habits: Found on small islands covered with grassy vegetation; stays on unfrozen patches of seas during nonnesting season. Nomadic. Common in places. Nests in colonies on gentle slopes with a thick layer of soil, in which it digs a deep burrow (up to 2 or 3 meters). Lays a single white egg with violet spots in May. Nest is lined with dry grass. Primarily nocturnal. Like other auklets, feeds on water in small flocks or singly, far from shore. Usually silent except on breeding grounds. Food is small fish and crustaceans.

Range and distribution: Kuril Islands, Shantarskiye Islands, Moneron and Sakhalin Islands. Winters south to Japan.

Similar species: In summer, differs from all auklets by horn on its bill; in winter, differs

from Parakeet Auklet and other auklets by larger size and longer yellowish bill.

Fratercula

Size of a pigeon. Bill large, short, set very high, greatly compressed, brightly colored with vertical furrows; folds of orange skin located at the corners of the mouth.

334. ATLANTIC PUFFIN
Fratercula arctica
(Tupik)
Plate 24, Map 137
Field marks: 32 cm. Upperparts and neck black; breast and belly white; cheeks light bluish-gray; small horny excrescence over the eye; bill light bluish-gray near the base with outer half orange-red; legs orange. In winter, bill decreases in size; is much smaller in juveniles.

Habits: Found on flat or cliff islands with well-developed peat bogs or thick layers of soil; in winter, found on open seas. Nomadic and common. Nests on grassy slopes or on tops of plateaus in colonies. Nest is a deep burrow, which the bird digs in the ground and occupies for many successive years. The burrow is sloping or horizontal, with the nesting chamber located at the end. It is lined with grass and feathers. Entrance to the nest is wide, and an old colony resembles a badger village. Lays a single white egg with indefinite gray spots in June. Feeds at sea, usually not far from the nesting colony, singly or in flocks. Stands straight, often associating with Razorbills on cliffs situated over colonies of guillemots and Black-legged Kittiwakes. Fairly cautious. Call: grumbling "arrr," rarely heard. Feeds on small fish, rarely on crustaceans.

Range and distribution: Shores of Barents Sea,

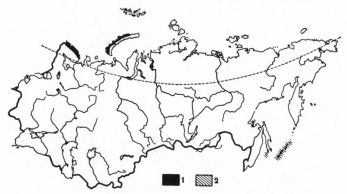

MAP 137. Atlantic Puffin (1), Rhinoceros Auklet (2)

MAP 138. Horned Puffin (1), Tufted Puffin (2)

Novaya Zemlya. Winters on open waters near breeding range or shores of Western Europe.
Similar species: Differs from Horned Puffin by grayish cheeks (also not found in the same range); from the Tufted Puffin, by white belly and lack of tufts of long, yellow feathers on sides of head.

335. HORNED PUFFIN
Fratercula corniculata
(Ipatka)
Plate 24, Map 138

Field marks: 32 cm. Greatly resembles Atlantic Puffin, but larger, with white cheeks; basal half of bill yellow, tip red; small, erectile dark horn over the eye. In winter, bill is smaller, base dark with red tip; horn over eye lacking.
Habits: Found on seashore cliffs and on islands; in winter, stays near seashores. Nonmigratory and nomadic. Common. Nests on precipitous cliffs in small colonies. Nest is situated in cliff crevice and is lined with dry grass. Lays a single white egg, sometimes with indefinite gray-violet speckles in June. Active diurnally, feeds and swims like the Atlantic Puffin, but often sits on land, bracing itself on its tarsus. Silent except on breeding grounds. Call: a muted "orr-orr." Feeds on small fish, more rarely on crustaceans and mollusks.
Range and distribution: Shores of Chukotski Peninsula, Kamchatka Peninsula, Komandorskiye, Kuril, Shantarskiye, and Sakhalin Islands. Winters on open seas near nesting range.
Similar species: Differs from Atlantic Puffin by white cheeks; also not found in the same range; from the Tufted Puffin, by white belly and lack of feathery tufts on sides of the head.

Lunda

336. TUFTED PUFFIN
Lunda cirrhata
(Toporik)
Plate 24, Map 138

Field marks: 33 cm. Large (crow-size). Bill very massive, high-arched, and laterally flattened, with three or four vertical furrows and a small scutum over the nostrils. Upperparts black, underparts black-brownish; cheeks white; tufts of long, soft, yellow feathers behind the eye; bill red with greenish base; legs red; bare red eye ring. In winter, cheeks are brownish, ear tufts are gone, bill is smaller, red-tipped, and brownish near the base.
Habits: Found on headlands and sea islands with an adequately thick layer of soil or peat; in winter, stays in open seas. Nonmigratory and nomadic. Common, in places numerous. Nests on grassy slopes of plateaus, often in large colonies. Nest situated in deep burrows, and lined with dry grass and feathers. Lays a single egg, sometimes with indefinite violet-gray speckles in mid-June. Active diurnally, feeds in flocks on the ocean; flies to nesting area high over the water; sits almost vertically on dry land, well up on its feet; walks well. Call: muffled growling, rarely heard. Feeds primarily on small fish; occasionally on crustaceans and seas urchins.
Range and distribution: Shores of Chukotski Peninsula, Kamchatka, Komandorskiye, and Kuril Islands, Sakhalin, continental shores of Sea of Okhotsk. Winters on open seas near nesting range.
Similar species: Differs from Horned Puffin

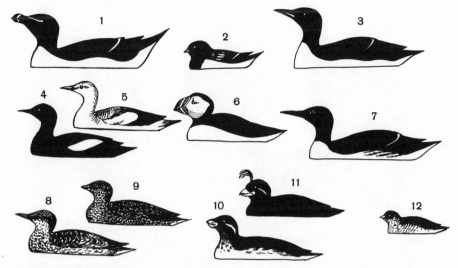

FIG. 53 ALCIDS IN WATER
1. Razorbill 2. Dovekie 3. Thick-billed Murre 4. Black Guillemot (summer) 5. Black Guillemot (winter) 6. Atlantic Puffin 7. Thin-billed Murre 8. Marbled Murrelet 9. Kittlitz's Murrelet 10. Parakeet Auklet 11. Crested Auklet 12. Least Auklet

and Atlantic Puffin by dark underparts and tufts of feathers on the sides of the head. Juveniles differ by their yellowish bill, and grayish, not white, underparts.

SANDGROUSE, PIGEONS, DOVES: *Columbiformes*

SANDGROUSE: *Pterocletes*

Medium (pigeon-size) birds, stocky, with long, pointed wings and tail and short legs. Feathers are short and hard. Sexual dimorphism is pronounced. Found in desert and semi-desert. Monogamous. Eggs are usual-ellipsoid shape. Precocial.

Pterocles

Four unfeathered toes on the leg.

337. BLACK-BELLIED SANDGROUSE
Pterocles orientalis
(Chernobryukhy Ryabok)
Plate 25, Map 139
Field marks: 35 cm. Tail short and pointed. Upperparts yellowish-brownish with dark pattern. Chestnut chin, small, black throat patch, gray upper breast; yellowish lower breast; narrow, black stripe separating the upper and the lower breast; black belly and sides. In fe-

male, chin and throat are yellowish, and belly is black.
Habits: Found in clay deserts. Migratory; in places nonmigratory. Common in only a few places. Nests in pairs in plains or hilly regions with sparse vegetation, wormwood, and crushed stones; in saline soil areas and edges of takyrs (dry clay-soil areas in Central Asia). Nest is a depression on the ground. Eggs are often laid on the ground, without any lining and only a few pebbles that keep the eggs from rolling. Lays three shiny clay-yellow eggs with soft brownish spots from early May. Both parents incubate and engage in distraction display. Stays in flocks when feeding and drink-

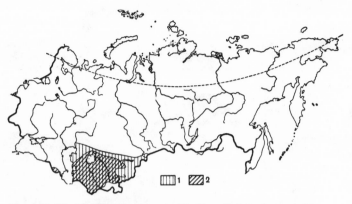

MAP 139. Black-bellied Sandgrouse (1), Pin-tailed Sandgrouse (2)

ing. Feeds on the ground, runs easily, with small steps, keeping its body horizontal. Good flier; flight is very fast, with frequent wing beats, and takeoff is noisy. Will fly up to fifty or sixty kilometers daily to get to a drinking area. Call, which is usually heard in flight, resembles a murmuring "tchurr-tchurr." Feeds on seeds, more rarely on shoots of plants and insects.

Range and distribution: Central Asia and Kazakhstan. Winters in southwestern Asia. In the USSR, occasionally winters in the Transcaucasus and in southern Central Asia.

Similar species: Differs from Pin-tailed Sandgrouse and Pallas's Sandgrouse by its shorter tail, and black flight feathers.

338. PIN-TAILED SANDGROUSE
Pterocles alchata
(Belobryukhy Ryabok)
Plate 25, Map 139

Field marks: 35 cm. Tail is long and pointed. Back greenish with yellow spots; belly pure white; chin and throat black; upper breast greenish-yellow; breast rusty and bordered by two black stripes. Legs white and feathered. In female, chin and upper throat whitish, with two gray-black stripes bordering the clear yellowish breast.

Habits: Found in sandy desert and semi-desert. Migratory, nonmigratory in the south. Common in places. Nests in hilly, semi-stable or developing sand dunes, alternating with clay or saline soil areas. Stays in large flocks but is a semi-colonial nester, not forming any real colonies. Nest is a shallow depression, usually situated on the slope of a sand dune, sometimes entirely in the open, sometimes in the shade of a clump of grass. Lays three yellowish-ocherish eggs with thick, bright brown spots

from early May. Flight, habits, and mannerisms similar to Black-bellied Sandgrouse; call, however, is entirely different and resembles a nasal, halting "gang-gang." Feeds on various seeds.

Range and distribution: Central Asia and Kazakhstan. Winters in Africa and southwestern Asia.

Similar species: Differs from Black-bellied Sandgrouse and Pallas's Sandgrouse by pure white belly; from the Tibetan Sandgrouse, by lack of horizontal barring on the breast and by black throat in the male.

Syrrhaptes

Has three toes joined together so that they have a single sole; feathered on top.

339. PALLAS'S SANDGROUSE
Syrrhaptes paradoxus
(Sadzha)
Plate 25, Map 140

Field marks: 37 cm. Tail very long, almost threadlike; outermost primaries are similarly attenuated. Upperparts sandy ocherish with heavy black barring; forehead and throat rusty; breast gray-yellow with narrow belt of short black and white bars; belly black; white feathered legs. In female, sides of grayish-yellow upper breast are covered with small black spots; lacks band; chin is bordered below by a narrow, black stripe. In juveniles, tail is not elongated.

Habits: Found in desert and semi-desert. Nonmigratory and nomadic. Sometimes accomplishes tremendous flights far from its nesting area (as far as southern Europe and Scandinavia; in the USSR, as far as Arkhangelsk).

Fig. 54 Pallas's Sandgrouse (left) and Black-bellied Sandgrouse (right) in Flight

Common. Nests in areas of firm turf; in clayey, forested saline soil, or pebbly desert and semi-desert, equally in plains and hills. Always stays in flocks, and often forms colonies during nonbreeding period. Nest is a shallow depression, either in the open or under a wormwood bush. Lays three yellowish-ocherish eggs with soft pale brownish spots from mid-April. Egg is not shiny, unlike other sandgrouse eggs. Habits and mannerisms similar to other sandgrouse, but flight is even more rapid and graceful; bird itself generally appears more graceful. Call: melodic, resonant "ten-ten" or a murmuring "tryou-ryou." Not wary, particularly on drinking grounds. Feeds on seeds of various plants, more rarely on shoots and buds.

Range and distribution: Kazakhstan, Central Asia, Altai, Tuva.

Similar species: In flight, differs from Black-

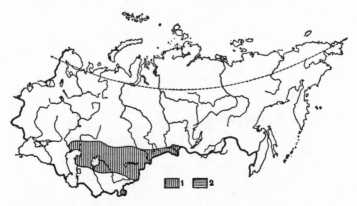

Map 140. Pallas's Sandgrouse (1), Tibetan Sandgrouse (2)

bellied Sandgrouse by elongated tail and wings; from the Pin-tailed and Tibetan Sandgrouse, by its black belly.

340. TIBETAN SANDGROUSE
Syrrhaptes tibetanus
(Tibetskaya Sadzha)
Plate 25, Map 140
Field marks: 40 cm. Resembles Pallas's Sandgrouse, but is larger; primaries not elongated. Crown and upper breast are gray with fine, wavy, black bars; sides of head are yellowish; back is sandy with black mottling; belly white; wing tips black.
Habits: Found in high mountains. Nonmigra-

tory or nomadic, rare. Nests in rocky, high mountain desert, along river valleys strewn with pebbles. Solitary nester; stays in flocks during nonbreeding season. Lays three eggs in May. Call resembles a halting "ka-ga, ka-ga" or a quacking "yak-yak-kaga." Not wary. Biology not well studied. Included in the Red Data Book.
Range and distribution: Central Asia (Tadzhikistan).
Similar species: Differs from Pallas's Sandgrouse and the Black-bellied Sandgrouse by white belly; from the Pin-tailed Sandgrouse, by its gray breast with fine, black barring, and a lighter throat. Also not found in the range of any other sandgrouse.

PIGEONS AND DOVES: *Columbae*

Birds of medium size with proportional bodies. Compact plumage. Fleshy cere. Found in forest and mountain habitat; a number of the species are found near settled areas. Monogamous. Eggs are of usual ellipsoid, more rarely shortened ellipsoid shape. Altricial.

Columba

Tail is straight or slightly rounded, with dark band at the tip; dove-gray color predominates. Legs are red or pink.

341. ROCK PIGEON
Columba livia
(Sizy Golub)
Plate 25, Map 141
Field marks: 34 cm. Coloration is a dark bluish-gray; wings light gray with two broad dark stripes; dark terminal band on tail; whitish rump. In semi-tame Rock Pigeons, plumage is often variable.

Habits: Found in settled areas, mountain habitats, steppe, and desert. Nonmigratory, nomadic in places. Common or numerous. Nests in colonies along cliffs or clay precipices, in caves, deserted buildings and wells, in towns and other settled areas—in attics and eaves of roofs, in towers, bell towers, etc. Nests are situated either in the open on a ledge or cornice, or in burrows, clefts, and niches. Nest is flat, loosely made of twigs and feathers. Lays two white, shiny eggs from February or March on. Multibrooded; may nest three to four times. Occurs in flocks. Flight is very fast and strong, with frequent, deep wing beats; agile flier; takeoff often accompanied by loud flapping of wings. Call: gurgling coo; also emits a faint

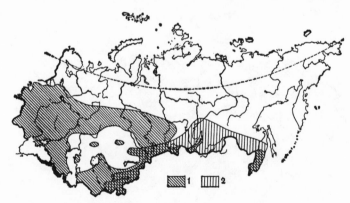

MAP 141. Rock Pigeon (1), Hill Pigeon (2)

"voi" near the nest, resembling a drawn-out "oo-oo-oo" (with emphasis in the beginning). Feeds on the ground. Prefers seeds of a variety of plants (including cereal crops).

Range and distribution: European USSR except northern regions; Kazakhstan, Central Asia, Altai, southern West Siberia, Transbaikal, south of Soviet Far East.

Similar species: Resembles Stock Pigeon and Hill Pigeon; differs from the first by its white rump and heavy black wing stripes; and from the second, by its darker tail. Differs from Eastern Stock Dove by its lighter color, particularly noticeable in the wing lining.

342. HILL PIGEON
Columba rupestris
(Skalisty Golub)
Plate 25, Map 141

Field marks: 34 cm. Resembles Rock Pigeon, but smaller; tail white with dark terminal band. Bill black.

Habits: Found in mountains, rocky ledge outcroppings in open country, and in settled areas. Nonmigratory. In places common and even numerous. Solitary or semi-colonial nesters. Nest situated in a niche or crevice in rocky ledges; in attics of buildings, or in outlying deserted houses in steppe. Lays two white eggs starting in early April. Multibrooded. Always stays in flocks. Flight, habits, and feeding habits same as Rock Pigeon. Call: a gurgling sound somewhat like that of the Rock Pigeon, but shorter, more halting, and much higher in tone. More often, the Hill Pigeon gives a characteristically thin and sharp moan. Feeds on various seeds.

Range and distribution: Mountains of Central Asia, Altai, southern regions of Central and East Siberia, southern Soviet Far East.

FIG. 55 PIGEONS IN FLIGHT
1. Rock Pigeon   2. Hill Pigeon   3. Western Stock Pigeon

Similar species: Differs from the Rock Pigeon and the Eastern Stock Dove by white tail and black terminal band.

343. SNOW PIGEON
Columba leuconota
(Belogrudy Golub)
Plate 25, Map 142

Field marks: 34 cm. Size same as Rock Pigeon. Head is slate-gray; neck and breast white, sometimes with an ocherish suffusion; back and wings brownish-gray; tail dove-gray with broad white band in center; legs are red.

Habits: Found in high mountain cliffs. Nomadic. Very rare. Biology of the Snow Pigeon in the USSR in entirely unknown. Included in the Red Data Book.

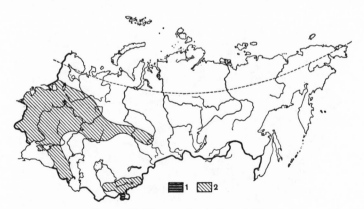

MAP 142. Snow Pigeon (1), Western Stock Pigeon (2)

Range and distribution: Confirmed only in the Altai range. Has been observed in the Pamirs and in mountains of southern Kazakhstan.
Similar species: Differs from all other pigeons by its white breast.

344. EASTERN STOCK PIGEON
Columba eversmanni
(Bury Golub)
Plate 25, Map 143
Field marks: 30 cm. Resembles Rock Pigeon, but smaller and darker, particularly the wing lining; back and wings are brownish; bill yellowish, cere white.
Habits: Found in desert and in settled habitats. Migratory. Common in places. Nests in clay and forested precipices along river banks; in old groves; in deserted buildings, ruins, and wells; in old burrows of other animals, old tree hollows, holes in buildings, etc. Nest is unlined. Lays two white eggs (smaller than Rock Pigeon's) at end of April. Stays in small flocks. Flight like Rock Pigeon, but somewhat lighter and weaker. Often perches in trees, choosing the thickest part of the crown. Feeds exclusively on the ground, usually in the morning and before evening. Call: monotonous, muffled "oo, oo-oo, oo." Feeds on seeds of various plants.
Range and distribution: Plains and valleys of Central Asia from Konet-Dag and the Aral Sea to western Tadjhikistan. Winters in southern Iran, Afghanistan, and northern Hindustan.
Similar species: Differs from all other pigeons by its brownish tones in the back and wings; in flight, resembles the Rock Pigeon, but tail is shorter; lower back and upper rump whitish, wing lining dark. Differs from Western Stock Pigeon by white patch on lower back.

345. WESTERN STOCK PIGEON
Columba oenas
(Klintukh)
Plate 25, Map 142
Field marks: 34 cm. Resembles Rock Pigeon, but has gray rump and reduced wing stripes and dark underwings; bill is yellowish.
Habits: Found in deciduous and mixed forests. Migratory. Not numerous. Nests in pairs along edges of old, primarily oak forests, and in groves; avoids thick, forested areas. Nest situated in a tree hollow, often high above the ground, and is not lined by the bird, who uses whatever material is available in the hollow already. Lays two white eggs from end of April on; multi-brooded. Stays in flocks during nonbreeding season. Flight like other pigeons, but a characteristic whistling sound of the wings is heard during takeoff. Very wary and hard to see in the forest. Call: a loud, hoarse "hoo-hooo," which is repeated several times in a row. Feeds on the forest floor; during the latter half of the summer, in open fields. Feeds on various seeds.
Range and distribution: Forests of European USSR, Caucasus, Transcaucasus, southern West Siberia, northern Kazakhstan. Isolated populations in south of Central Asia and in Kazakhstan. Winters in southern Europe and southwestern Asia.
Similar species: Differs from the Rock, Eastern Stock, and Hill Pigeons by its dark rump. The underwings are dark, in contrast to the Rock Pigeon, whose wing lining is white.

346. WOOD PIGEON
Columba palumbus
(Vyakhir)
Plate 25, Map 143
Field marks: 41 cm. Much larger than Rock

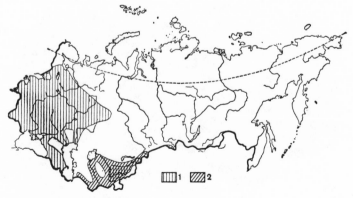

MAP 143. Wood Pigeon (1), Eastern Stock Pigeon (2)

Pigeon. Coloration dove-gray; breast pink-gray; white patches on neck and wings; dark, wide terminal band on tail; bill yellow with reddish base and white cere; legs raspberry-red.

Habits: Found in mixed, deciduous, or coniferous forests, more rarely in forest-steppe. Migratory. Not numerous. Nests in pairs, usually in dense and rarely visited sections of the forests. Thin, loosely constructed nest made of twigs and situated in a tree, sometimes high near the trunk or on a branch. Lays two white, large eggs from end of April on (later in the north); multibrooded. Flocks during nonbreeding season. Flight like other pigeons, but appears slower and unhurried. Very wary, even near the nest. Often perches in the open on tall trees; on low trees, stays hidden. Call: a very loud, hooting, rythmical "hoo, oo-rooo-ra, hoo, oo-rooo-ra, hooo-ra." Feeds on seeds and grain from fields.

Range and distribution: European USSR, southwestern Siberia, mountains of southern Kazakhstan and Central Asia. Winters in southern Europe, Iran, Hindustan.

Similar species: Differs from other pigeons by white patches on neck and wings; larger size.

Streptopelia

Smaller and more graceful than pigeons. Long tail rounded with a white band at the end; sandy and rose-gray colors predominate in the plumage. Legs are red.

347. EUROPEAN TURTLE-DOVE
Streptopelia turtur
(Obyknovennaya Gorlitsa)
Plate 25, Map 144
Field marks: 27 cm. Medium size. Back is

ocherish-brown with a scaly pattern; underparts gray-pink; patch of diagonal black and white stripes on the neck; fan-shaped tail black with a narrow, white terminal band. Juveniles lack spots on the neck.

Habits: Found in deciduous and mixed, more rarely coniferous forests, forest-steppe, in steppe and desert zones, settled areas, and river valleys. Migratory and common. Nests in pairs along forest edges and in clearings, in woods along a river, in lumbering areas, parks, gardens, in areas bordered by fields, and even in thickets. Nest is flat, loosely built, and is situated in trees or bushes, often fairly low. Lays two white eggs in May; doublebrooded. Often seen in flocks in summer and autumn. Flight resembles that of the pigeon, but is lighter, and the bird is thinner and more graceful. Fairly trusting, sits in the open in trees. Call: loud, pleasant purring, resembling "turr-turr, turr-turr," Feeds on the ground in open places and in forests along roads; prefers various seeds.

Range and distribution: European USSR, southwestern Siberia, lower region of mountains in southern Kazakhstan and Central Asia. Winters in Africa, northwestern Hindustan, and Arabian Peninsula.

Similar species: Differs from the Collared and the Laughing Turtle-Doves by scaly pattern on the back, black-and-white patch on the neck; from the Oriental Turtle-Dove, by its smaller size, lighter coloration, and grayish upper breast (often indistinguishable in the field).

348. ORIENTAL TURTLE-DOVE
Streptopelia orientalis
(Bolshaya Gorlitsa)
Plate 25, Map 145
Field marks: 33 cm. Resembles European Tur-

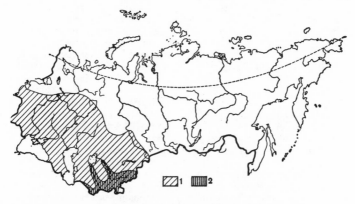

MAP 144. European Turtle-Dove (1), Laughing Turtle-Dove (2)

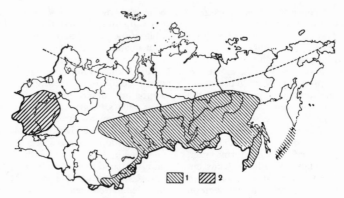

MAP 145. Oriental Turtle-Dove (1), Collared Turtle-Dove (2)

tle-Dove, but is larger and more thickset; coloration darker and browner.

Habits: Found in various types of forests and boreal plantings in open habitat. Migratory and common. Usually nests in woodland, with thick undergrowth or young trees; in riparian woodlands. Nest is larger than that of other doves, built with twigs and small branchlets, and is situated in a tree, usually on lower branches. Lays two white or slightly yellowish eggs in May. Stays in small flocks during nonbreeding season. Flight strong and swift. Resembles European Turtle-Dove in appearance, but call is entirely different: bass, resonant, and harsh "hoo-boo, hoo-boo, hoo-boo," reminiscent of the gurgling of a Wood Pigeon. Generally unwary, but in some areas will not allow close approach. Feeds on various seeds.

Range and distribution: Siberia from southern Urals to Sakhalin and southern Kuril Islands, mountains of southern Kazakhstan and Central Asia. Winters in southern Asia.

Similar species: Differs from European Turtle-Dove by its larger size and darker color, but ranges do not overlap.

349. COLLARED TURTLE-DOVE
Streptopelia decaocto
(Kolchataya Gorlitsa)
Plate 25, Map 145

Field marks: 28 cm. Size of European Turtle-Dove. Head, neck, and breast are gray-pink; back is uniform brownish-gray; white-edged black half-moon on nape; tail is long, with terminal half white.

Habits: Found in settled areas. Nonmigratory; some partly migratory. Not numerous, common in places. Nests in cities, villages, and in gardens; on eaves and balconies of houses or in trees. Nest is made of twigs and dry stalks.

Lays two pure white eggs in March. Flight and habits similar to other doves, but is trusting and does not avoid human neighbors. Feeds close to houses. Call: muted, repetitive "hoo-hoo-hoo." Male usually gives display coo while perched in a tree or on a roof.

Range and distribution: City parks of west European USSR. Range actively expanding north and east. Currently noted in Moscow, Bryansk, Kursk, Baltic States. Also nests in southeastern Turkmenia.

Similar species: Differs from all other doves by characteristic black half-moon on the nape, and wide, white tail band; differs from European and Oriental Turtle-Doves by even-colored back; from the Laughing Dove, by its larger size.

350. LAUGHING TURTLE-DOVE
Streptopelia senegalensis
(Malaya Gorlitsa)
Plate 25, Map 144

Field marks: 26 cm. Noticeably smaller than other doves. Back is uniformly brownish-sandy; head and underparts are gray-pink; blackish spots on sides of neck.

Habits: Found in settled areas. Nonmigratory. Common, numerous in places. Nests in pairs or in small colonies in large and small towns, villages, kichlaks (villages of Central Asia), and auls (mountain villages in Caucasus); in central squares, and in suburbs with gardens and parks. Not found in unsettled areas. Nest is loosely constructed and situated on a cornice, under eaves, in house attics, and other buildings; in parks and gardens in trees, sometimes low to the ground, sometimes very high. Lays two white, almost round eggs from February on; multiple-brooded (as many as four broods). Resembles other doves in habits, but is significantly more trusting, feeding directly on streets under the feet of passers-by. Call: loud, halting "ku-ku-kuu." Feeds on various seeds, often depends on being fed.

Range and distribution: Cities and towns of southern Kazakhstan and Central Asia.

Similar species: Differs from other doves by its small size and black spots on the side of the neck.

[Vagrants of **351.** RED TURTLE-DOVE (*Streptopelia tranquebarica*) have been found in the USSR; it resembles the Laughing Dove, but tail is shorter, coloration more pink or reddish, with a black half-moon on the nape. Vagrants of the **352.** JAPANESE GREEN-PIGEON (*Treron sieboldi*), which nests in Japan, were found in 1962 on Kunashir Island in the Kurils; it is smaller than the Rock Pigeon, back and tail are olive-green, breast is yellow-green, wing coverts reddish. How they got there has not been determined.]

CUCKOOS: *Cuculiformes*

Medium-size bird with long, rounded, or fan-shaped tail and long, pointed wings. Does not build its own nest, but adds its eggs to the nest of small insect-eating birds. Altricial.

Cuculus

Upperparts gray, underparts white with dark barring.

353. EURASIAN CUCKOO
Cuculus canorus
(Obyknovennaya Kukushka)
Plate 26, Map 146

Field marks: 33 cm. Smaller than a pigeon. Upperparts, head, throat, and upper breast gray; underparts white with narrow, blackish barring; white terminal tips to tail feathers. Underwings whitish; marginal coverts at wrist of wing are white with black barring. Females have two color phases: gray and, more rarely, rusty.

Habits: Found in forest and thickets in variety of habitat. Migratory. Common. Solitary; rarely in pairs. Lays eggs in nests of other birds (thrushes, warblers, wagtails, flycatchers). Eggs often resemble those in parasitized nests, but are usually larger. In flight, resembles a Eurasian Sparrowhawk. When calling, male cocks its tail up and lowers its wings. Call of male: the well-known "cuck-coo"; call of female is a loud trill, "klee-klee-klee." Feeds on various insects and their larvae, also on fuzzy caterpillars.

Range and distribution: Found throughout USSR except northerly border regions. Winters in Africa and southern Asia.

Similar species: Differs from Indian Cuckoo by its call and lack of black subterminal band on tail; from the Oriental Cuckoo, by its voice, lighter barring, and barred marginal coverts.

354. ORIENTAL CUCKOO
Cuculus saturatus
(Glukhaya Kukushka)
Not illustrated, Map 146

Field marks: 32 cm. Resembles Common

MAP 146. Eurasian Cuckoo (1), Oriental Cuckoo (2)

Cuckoo, but darker, more heavily barred below. Underwings yellowish; white marginal coverts at wrist of wing. Two color phases, gray and rusty; females usually rusty.

Habits: Found in tall trees of coniferous and mixed, damp forests; more rarely in deciduous forest and in thickets. Migratory and common. White eggs with dark spots are usually laid only in nests of warblers. Solitary, sometimes in pairs; usually hidden in thickest part of tree. Very wary. Call: muted, but resonant "do-do-do." Habits, flight, and feeding habits similar to Common Cuckoo.

Range and distribution: Taiga zones of USSR from Pechora River to eastern boundaries. Winters in Indonesia, Australia, New Guinea, Solomon Islands.

Similar species: Differs from Common Cuckoo by its darker coloration, white marginal coverts on wrist of wing, and its call; from the Indian Cuckoo, by lack of black stripe on tail tip.

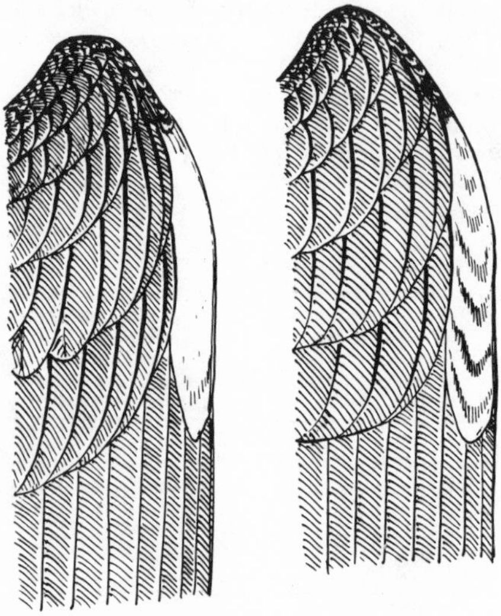

355. LESSER CUCKOO
Cuculus poliocephalus
(Malaya Kukushka)
Plate 26, Map 147

Field marks: 22 cm. Slightly larger than a thrush. Head, throat, upper breast, and entire back are gray; wings and tail are blackish-brown; tail feathers with white tips; breast and belly buffy white with wide, black bars.

Habits: Found in thin, deciduous forest with thickets. Migratory. Not numerous. Stays hidden in crowns of trees. Very wary. Call: fairly loud sounds, resembling "vot-tut-to, te-tyouhe."

Range and distribution: Southern Primorski Krai in the Soviet Far East. Winters in southeastern Asia.

1   2

FIG. 56 Wing of 1) Oriental Cuckoo and 2) Eurasian Cuckoo

Similar species: Nearly indistinguishable from Common and Oriental Cuckoos, but smaller and with different call.

356. INDIAN CUCKOO
Cuculus micropterus
(Indiyskaya Kukushka)
Plate 26, Map 147

Field marks: 33 cm. Greatly resembles Com-

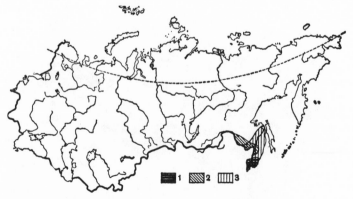

MAP 147. Lesser Cuckoo (1), Indian Cuckoo (2), Hodgson's Hawk-Cuckoo (3)

mon Cuckoo, but head is gray and back has a brownish suffusion; wide, black band on tail tip.

Habits: Found in damp, mature forests. Migratory and rare. Stays hidden in crowns of trees.

Range and distribution: Southern Soviet Far East (from upper reaches of Zeya River to Komsomolsk on the Amur River). Winters in southeastern Asia.

Similar species: Differs from the Oriental and Common Cuckoos by black band on tail tip.

357. HODGSON'S HAWK-CUCKOO
Cuculus fugax
(Shirokokrylaya Kukushka)
Plate 26, Map 147

Field marks: 33-35 cm. Smaller than a pigeon. Upperparts dark brownish-gray; throat whitish; tail dark gray with wide, black bands and narrow rusty tip; in males, breast and upper belly are pinkish-rusty; in females, underparts are whitish with narrow, brownish streaks on breast and belly.

Habits: Found in Siberian pine (*Pinus sibericus*), silver fir, and mixed taiga. Migratory. Rare, but common in places. Stays hidden in crowns of large trees, and usually detected only by its call. Call: a repetitive cry beginning weakly, then getting stronger, "zheeyou-eechee, zheeyou-eechee" or "cheel-chee, cheel-chee." Bird usually calls in flight, at dusk.

Range and distribution: Southern Soviet Far East. Winters in southeastern Asia.

Similar species: Differs from other cuckoos by its banded tail and shape (short broad wings and long tail).

[In Moldavia and Turkmenia, vagrants of **358.** GREAT SPOTTED CUCKOO (*Clamator glandarius*) were noted; it is a large cuckoo with white (or buffy) underparts, brownish upperparts, conspicuous crest, and a long tail with large white spots.]

OWLS: *Strigiformes*

Birds from very large to small sizes. Wings wide, rounded; tail short; plumage fluffy and soft. Legs usually feathered to the claws. Bill short, upper mandible hooked sharply. Claws sharp and hooked. Plumage on head forms a flattened facial disc; eyes large. Many owls have tufts of feathers ("ears") over their ears. When quiet, sits very straight and upright. Found in a variety of habitats from tundra to desert. Nocturnal, with a few exceptions. Monogamous. Eggs are a rounded-ellipsoid shape. Altricial.

Nyctea

359. SNOWY OWL
Nyctea scandiaca
(Belaya Sova)
Plate 12, Map 148

Field marks: 57 cm. Very large owl. Coloration snow-white; in female, with dark barring on belly, sides, and back; juveniles are more heavily barred. Eyes bright yellow; no "ears."

Habits: Found in tundra and arctic prairies. During nonbreeding season, found in forest-tundra, in steppe, in forest (prefers open woods). Nomadic. Rare on the whole, but common in places. Nests on hillocks, slopes, and shores of small rivers. Nest is a thinly lined hollow. Lays four to seven eggs from end of May to June. Call: loud "kee-kee-kee" and "kra-aoo." Feeds on rodents (lemmings, voles), often catches birds (even birds as large as ducks and geese). Hunts for prey while perched on a rise or flying low in an unhurried flight.

Range and distribution: Tundra from Kanin Peninsula to Chukotski Peninsula and islands of the Arctic Ocean. Winters south of breeding range within USSR.

Similar species: Differs from other owls by its white coloration.

Bubo

360. NORTHERN EAGLE OWL
Bubo bubo
(Filin)
Plate 12, Map 149

Field marks: 67 cm. Very large owl with well-developed "ears." Coloration variable; upperparts from dark rufous with black mottling to an ocherish with infrequent spots; breast is rusty or ocherish with blackish streaks over fine, dark barring on sides and belly; legs feathered to the claws; eyes orange-yellow.

Habits: Found in a variety of habitats from taiga to desert and mountains; inhabits all unpopulated, remote areas, and avoids contact with people. Nonmigratory or nomadic. Generally rare. Nests in cliffs, in inaccessible parts of the forest, in ravines, in rock slides, under

MAP 148. Snow Owl (1), Blakiston's Fish-Owl (2)

precipices. Nest is on the ground, in hollows of rocky ledges, in hollow trees; occasionally uses nest of a raptor. Lays two or three white eggs in April. Searches for prey in flight or while perched in tree. Flight is slow, silent, usually low to the ground. Call: a loud, distant "oo-hoo."

Range and distribution: Entire USSR except tundra, basin of the Anadyr River, and Kamchatka Peninsula.

Similar species: Differs from Blakiston's Fish-Owl by feathered toes, orange eyes, and more contrasting coloration; from all other owls, by its very large size and noticeable "ears."

Ketupa

361. BLAKISTON'S FISH-OWL
Ketupa blakistoni
(Ribny Filin)
Plate 12, Map 148

FIG. 57 Snowy Owl Nestling

Field marks: 72 cm. Appearance resembles Eagle Owl, but coloration more uniform; brownish overall; finely barred underparts with thin dark streaks; tarsus feathered, but toes are bare or covered with sparse, bristly feathers.

Habits: Found in mixed taiga, where it stays exclusively in river plains and river islands overgrown with thickets and other vegetation. Nonmigratory. Very rare. Feeds on fish and crabs; catches food by walking into water and wading through the shallows. Included in the Red Data Book.

Range and distribution: Soviet Far East, Sakhalin, and southern Kuril Islands.

Similar species: Differs from Northern Eagle-Owl by its unfeathered toes and noncontrasting coloration.

Otus

Small owls (wing smaller than 20 cm.) with readily noticeable "ears." Toes are bare or partially feathered. Dark, narrow, elongated streaking on underparts.

362. EURASIAN SCOPS-OWL
Otus scops
(Splyushka)
Plate 13, Map 150

Field marks: 19 cm. Two color phases and intermediates ranging from rusty gray to rufous; underparts lighter, finely barred, with heavier, dark streaks. Tarsus feathered, toes unfeathered.

Habits: Found in a variety of habitats with boreal vegetation; found in deciduous and mixed mature forests, stands of pine, groves, gardens, and mountain forests. Migratory. Common. Nests in tree hollows and in old magpie

MAP 149. Northern Eagle-Owl (1), Long-eared Owl (2)

nests, more rarely in crevices, burrows, precipices, and other hidden areas. Lays four to six white eggs at the end of May. Nocturnal. In daytime, perches close to the trunk of a tree. Call: sad, melodic whistle, resembling "splyou-you." Feeds on insects, occasionally catches small rodents and small birds.

Range and distribution: Southern half of USSR from Belorussia to western Transbaikal. Winters in Equatorial Africa and southwestern Asia.

Similar species: Differs from Striated Scops-Owl by its more contrasting coloration and bare toes; from the Collared Scops-Owl, by lack of "collar"; from the Eastern Scops-Owl, by its entirely feathered tarsus.

363. COLLARED SCOPS-OWL
Otus bakkamoena
(Osheynikovaya Sovka)
Plate 13, Map 151
Field marks: 25 cm. Back is yellowish-brown

with small, dark crosslike markings, and buffy nuchal collar; underparts ocherish with light barring and thin streaks; tarsus feathered for two-thirds of length.

Habits: Found in deciduous forests. Nonmigratory. Rare. Feeds on insects, small birds, and small rodents. Very little information about its biology in USSR is available.

Range and distribution: Southern Soviet Far East, Sakhalin, and southern Kuril Islands. Winters in southeastern Asia.

Similar species: Differs from other owls by having tarsus feathered two-thirds of its length, and buffy "collar" on the nape.

364. STRIATED SCOPS-OWL
Otus brucei
(Bulanaya Sovka)
Plate 13, Map 151
Field marks: 20 cm. Pale coloration, two color phases: pale gray and yellowish, with well-de-

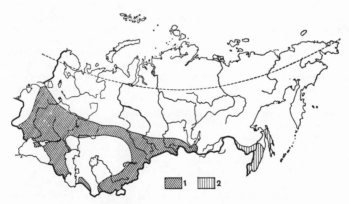

MAP 150. Eurasian Scops-Owl (1), Eastern Scops-Owl (2)

MAP 151. Short-eared Owl (1), Striated Scops-Owl (2), Collared Scops-Owl (3)

fined blackish streaking. Tarsus and toes feathered.

Habits: Found in boreal plantings near settled areas (gardens, parks) and clearings of woods along river valleys. Migratory and common in places. Nests in tree hollows, very often using old nests of magpies. Lays four to six white eggs in April. Nocturnal; unafraid in daytime and allows a very close approach. Call: muffled, drawn-out "kooo" followed by "kuh-kuh-kuh," which the bird repeats for long periods of time. Catches prey from the ground or in branches while in flight. Like other owls, feeds on insects, more rarely on small rodents and small birds.

Range and distribution: Southern Kazakhstan and Central Asia. Winters in Hindustan and on the Arabian Peninsula.

Similar species: Differs from other owls by pale plumage and feathered toes.

365. EASTERN SCOPS-OWL
Otus sunia
(Ussuriyskaya Sovka)
Plate 13, Map 150

Field marks: 19 cm. Upperparts uniformly rufous or gray-brownish, without well-defined mottling. Underparts are lighter with small, frequent barring and infrequent elongated streaks; lower part of tarsus is not feathered.

Habits: Found in deciduous forests along river valleys and in plains, more rarely on edges of coniferous taiga. Migratory. Common in places. Nests in hollows of old trees, lays eggs end of May to June. Nocturnal. Call: disyllabic, melodic "ke-vyouyou" or loud "klok-klok-klok." Feeds on insects, but also preys on small rodents.

Range and distribution: Soviet Far East and Sakhalin Island. Winters in southeastern Asia.

Similar species: Differs from other owls in its range by its unfeathered lower tarsus.

Asio

Medium-size owls (wing 27-33 cm.) with well defined "ears." Legs and toes thickly feathered. Upper mandible is dark. Eyes are yellow or orange.

366. LONG-EARED OWL
Asio otus
(Ushastaya Sova)
Plate 13, Map 149

Field marks: 34 cm. Upperparts brownish with dark, marbled pattern; underparts rusty yellow with extensive streaking and less prominent barring: "ears" long (up to 5 cm.).

Habits: Found in various types of forests (including montane); prefers coniferous areas, and avoids settled areas (gardens and parks). Nonmigratory and nomadic; in places migratory. Common. Nests in old nests of other birds (crows, raptors), more rarely in tree hollows. Lays four to six white eggs end of April. Nocturnal; roosts in trees close to the trunk. Call: muted "hoo-hoo-oo" or plaintive "oo-oo-oo" and other sounds. In spring, sometimes claps wings very loudly in flight. In autumn, often gathers in roosts of fifteen to twenty individuals. Feeds on small rodents, more rarely on birds.

Range and distribution: Entire forest zone of USSR except northern regions. Migratory populations winter in southern USSR, southern Asia, and North Africa.

Similar species: Differs from the Short-eared Owl by its long "ears" and barred feathers on the belly and sides; from the Strix owls by smaller size, orange-yellow eyes, and black bill.

367. SHORT-EARED OWL
Asio flammeus
(Bolotnaya Sova)
Plate 13, Map 151

Field marks: 37 cm. Resembles Long-eared Owl, but coloration buffier; back ocher-brownish; underparts lighter and streaked, but without barring on belly and sides; "ears" are short but noticeable (up to 1-2 cm.). Dark spots at the bend of the underwing are conspicuous in flight.

Habits: Found in a variety of habitats from tundra to desert and mountains. Always inhabits open areas (flooded meadows, swamps, lake shores, sometimes sown fields or dry steppe). Nonmigratory, nomadic, or migratory. Common. Nests on the ground, building its nest of dry grass. Lays four to six eggs end of April to May. In years when there is ample food, lays up to eight or ten white eggs. Feeds almost exclusively on small rodents. Hunts at dusk, often continuing into the day. Rarely perches in trees; roosts on the ground. Flight is unhurried, slightly rocking, and low to the ground. In spring, the breeding flight can be observed, when the bird emits a characteristic mating call, "boo-boo-boo-boo," alternating with deep wing-beats.

Range and distribution: Entire USSR except extreme north and Chukotski Peninsula. Migratory populations winter in the Transcaucasus and Central Asia.

Similar species: Differs from the Long-eared Owl by its short "ears" and lack of barring at the belly and sides; from the Strix owls, by smaller size and black bill.

Ninox

368. BROWN HAWK-OWL
Ninox scutulata
(Iglonogaya Sova)
Plate 13, Map 152

Field marks: 27 cm. Medium-size owl (wing up to 23 cm.) with long wings and tail. Facial disc is less pronounced than in other owls; no "ears"; tarsus is feathered almost to the toes; toes covered with characteristic sparse, hard bristles. Plumage is compact. Back is uniformly chocolate-brownish; belly light-colored with heavy streaks; eyes yellow.

Habits: Found in deciduous forests mixed with Siberian pine and silver fir, in plains, and lower regions of mountains; also found near river thickets. Migratory bird. Rare. Call: disyllabic "kukh-kukh, kukh-kukh." Feeds primarily on insects.

Range and distribution: Southern Soviet Far East.

Similar species: Differs from other owls by lack of obvious facial discs, uniformly brown back, and broadly streaked underparts.

Aegolius

369. BOREAL OWL
Aegolius funereus
(Mokhnonogy Sych)
Plate 13, Map 152

Field marks: 25 cm. Small owl (wing up to 19 cm.). Legs thickly feathered to the claws; no "ears"; prominent facial disc; back is grayish-brown with white spots; numerous small, white spots on the head; belly is whitish with soft, brownish streaks; eyes and bill are yellow.

Habits: Found in coniferous and mixed for-

MAP 152. Boreal Owl (1), Brown Hawk-Owl (2)

ests; stays in remote areas as well as forest meadows and cleared areas. Nonmigratory or nomadic. Common, but stays hidden and is rarely seen. Nests early in April and lays three to six white eggs in a tree hollow. Like the Little Owl and Northern Pygmy-Owl, sits so tight on the nest that it can be picked up. Feeds on small rodents, shrews, and small birds; in winter, caches food in holes in tree. Flight is swift, slightly wavy; hunts from perch or in flight. Call: rapid and high-pitched "koo-koo-koo."

Range and distribution: Entire taiga zone of USSR; evergreen forests of Caucasus; Central Asia.

Similar species: Differs from other owls by lack of nuchal collar or feathering of claws; from the Little Owl, by the white spots, not streaks, on the head, grayish-brown back, and rounder facial disc; from the Northern Pygmy-Owl, by its larger size (wings always larger than 10 cm.) and shorter tail.

Athene

370. LITTLE OWL
Athene noctua
(Domovoy Sych)
Plate 13, Map 153

Field marks: 23 cm. Resembles Boreal Owl, but facial disc flatter. Back is light brownish to rufous-sandy color, and is lightly spotted. Whitish streaks on the head.

Habits: Found in a variety of habitats from forest-steppe to mountains and deserts; always inhabits open terrain; often seen in settled areas. Nonmigratory. Common. Nests in burrows, caves, precipices, gullies or cliffs; holes in deserted buildings, in attics, and rubble or heaps of rocks; occasionally the bird digs fairly

FIG. 58 Flight Silhouettes of Typical 1) Nightjar and 2) Owl

deep burrows in clay precipices. Lays four to eight white eggs from April to beginning of May. Feeds on small rodents (gerbils, jerboas, voles), on birds (sparrows, larks), lizards, and insects. Feeds at dusk as well as during the day. Often perches on telegraph poles and other such lookouts, thus is seen more frequently than other owls. Hunts by waiting for prey to pass or pursuing from a low flight. Flight is swift, bounding. Call: harsh "ku-veet, ku-veet" and other sounds.

Range and distribution: Central and southern USSR from the Baltic States through Lake Zaisan as far as eastern Transbaikal.

Similar species: Differs from Otus owls by feathered toes and lack of "ears"; from the Boreal Owl, by light streaks on the head, incomplete facial disc, and browner coloration;

MAP 153. Little Owl (1), Eurasian Pygmy-Owl (2)

from the Eurasian Pygmy-Owl, by larger size (wings always much larger than 10 cm.).

Glaucidium

371. EURASIAN PYGMY-OWL
Glaucidium passerinum
(Sych-vorobey)
Plate 13, Map 153
Field marks: 16 cm. Resembles Boreal Owl, but much smaller (wing no larger than 10 cm.), facial disc poorly developed. Upperparts brownish with white spots; more finely speckled on the head; breast is light with dark spots and streaks. Tail with five narrow, white bands.
Habits: Found in mature coniferous and mixed forests. Nonmigratory, nomadic in places. Rare; inconspicuous. Nests at the end of April to May, usually in tree hollows, sometimes in nesting boxes, and sits tight on nest. Lays four to six white eggs. Mostly nocturnal, but sometimes hunts during the day. Call: monotonous, repetitive "dyou, oob-oob" and many other sounds. Feeds on small rodents, shrews, small birds, and caches food in tree hollows in winter.
Range and distribution: Entire taiga zone of USSR.
Similar species: Differs from Otus owls by lack of "ears"; from the Boreal and Little Owls, by smaller size.

Surnia

372. NORTHERN HAWK OWL
Surnia ulula
(Yastrebinaya Sova)
Plate 13, Map 154
Field marks: 37 cm. Medium-size owl with no "ears" and long, rounded tail. Upperparts grayish-brown with white spots; numerous small white spots on forehead and crown; facial disc is white, bordered with black; belly is white and heavily barred with brownish; eyes and bill are yellow.
Habits: Found in mature forests, primarily coniferous, in forest-tundra; stays in river valleys; in forest-steppe, prefers cut-over areas. Nonmigratory or nomadic. Rare, but common in places. Often nests in hollows of trees with broken tops; occasionally uses tree hollow or old nests of other birds. Lays three to five white, slightly elongated eggs from early April; during peaks of prey cycles lays up to nine or ten eggs. Flight is swift with alternating wing-flapping and gliding; reminiscent of a hawk. Unwary and readily seen; often perches on tops of trees or on telegraph poles. Call: hawk-like "kee-kee-kee" and characteristic "ool-ool-ool." Often hunts diurnally; usually in morning and evening. Hunts for prey either from an ambush, or circling around fields and forest clearings. Feeds on small rodents (voles, lemmings), sometimes on birds.
Range and distribution: Entire taiga zone of USSR and central Tien Shan mountain range.
Similar species: Differs from all owls by its distinctive shape and barring on breast and belly.

Strix

Large, big-headed owl with fluffy, loose plumage. Bill is light, usually yellow; "ears" are lacking; toes are feathered to the claws; facial disc is well developed.

373. TAWNY OWL
Strix aluco
(Seraya Neyasyt)
Plate 12, Map 154
Field marks: 38 cm. Large, slightly larger than a crow; with short tail. Two color phases: gray or rusty brown; upperparts of the gray type are grayish-brown with dark mottling, belly is light with elongated dark mottling; the rusty types are similarly marked, but rusty red is substituted for the gray tones. The Caucasus race is darker. Eyes are black.
Habits: Found in deciduous, mixed, and coniferous forests, old groves and parks. Nonmigratory or nomadic. Common. Nests in hollows of various trees, sometimes inhabits old nests of raptors and crows, or occupies attics of deserted buildings. Lays three to five white eggs from early April. Strictly nocturnal. Call of the male: "hoo-hoo-hoooo," of the female: "kyouyouyouveeh." Feeds on small rodents and other small mammals; more rarely on various birds, frogs, and insects.
Range and distribution: European USSR and mountains of southern Kazakhstan and Central Asia.
Similar species: Differs from Long-eared and Short-eared Owls by lack of "ears," yellow bill, and black eyes; from the Ural Owl, by its smaller size, short tail (shorter than 22 cm.) and its nearly unmarked central tail feathers; from the Great Gray Owl, by its black eyes, lack of concentric circles on the facial disc, and by its smaller size.

374. URAL OWL
Strix uralensis
(Dlinnokhvostaya Neyasyt)
Plate 12, Map 155
Field marks: 56 cm. Large (significantly larger

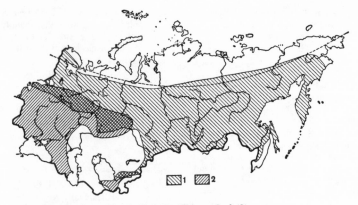

MAP 154. Northern Hawk Owl (1), Tawny Owl (2)

than a crow), with long, barred tail. Light buffy brown color thickly streaked with dark brown. Unmarked facial disc; eyes are black.

Habits: Found in mature coniferous or mixed forests. Nonmigratory or nomadic. Rare. Nests in tree hollows, in old nests of raptors, or simply on the ground. Lays two to four white eggs in April. Call: barking, high-pitched "hey-hey-hey" or "kaoo-vekk." Feeds primarily on rodents, but attacks birds as well. Usually watches for prey while perched in a tree.

Range and distribution: Forest zones of northern and central USSR from Belorussia to southern Kuril Islands.

Similar species: Differs from Long-eared and Short-eared Owls by larger size, lack of "ears," and by black eyes; from the Tawny Owl by long, sharply barred tail (longer than 22 cm.) and larger size; from the Great Gray Owl, by its lighter color, black eyes, and unmarked facial disc.

375. GREAT GRAY OWL
Strix nebulosa
(Borodataya Neyasyt)
Plate 12, Map 155

Field marks: 70 cm. Very large, with long tail and rounded head; plumage dark, smoky gray, and thickly mottled; dark concentric circles on the facial disc; eyes and bill yellow.

Habits: Found in remote sections of mature forests, primarily coniferous. Nonmigratory or nomadic. Rare, but common in regions of East Siberia. Nests early from mid-April to the beginning of May, and occupies old nests of large raptors, where it lays three to five white eggs. Call: loud and muffled "hoo-hoo-hoo." Often hunts diurnally. Feeds primarily on various rodents (voles, lemmings, squirrels), occasionally on birds (grouse).

Range and distribution: Taiga zone of the USSR.

Similar species: Differs from Ural Owl by dark

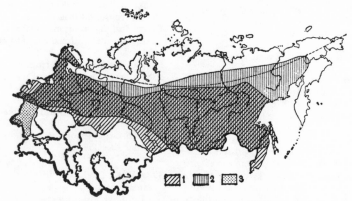

MAP 155. Ural Owl (1), Great Gray Owl (2), Barn Owl (3)

concentric circles on facial disc and by yellow eyes; from the Northern Eagle-Owl, by lack of "ears" and by grayer coloration.

Tyto

376. BARN OWL
Tyto alba
(Sipukha)
Plate 13, Map 155
Field marks: 34 cm. Medium-sized owl with fairly long legs and heart-shaped facial disc. Claw of middle toe is saw-toothed. "Ears" lacking; coloration light, back is golden-brown with soft, grayish pattern of narrow barring, and fine dark and light spots; belly is white or ocherish, sometimes sparsely speckled; facial disc outlined with dark edge; eyes are black.
Habits: Found in settled areas. Nonmigratory and rare. Nests in church bell-towers, in old deserted buildings, and in rubble; more rarely in tree hollows near forest edges. Lays four to seven white, slightly elongated eggs from end of April to beginning of May. Strictly nocturnal. Call: hissing. Feeds on small rodents and insects, sometimes attacks birds.
Range and distribution: West of European USSR.
Similar species: Differs from other owls by its heart-shaped facial disc, slightly hooked bill, and long legs.

NIGHTJARS: *Caprimulgiformes*

Medium-size birds, active at dusk and nocturnally, with long tail and wings. Plumage is soft and fluffy. Legs are short and weak; eyes are large; bill short, mouth opening is very large and edged with bristle- and hair-like feathers in the corners. Found in a variety of habitats, in plains and hills. Eggs are ovoid-ellipsoid shape. Monogamous. Altricial.

Caprimulgus

377. EUROPEAN NIGHTJAR
Caprimulgus europaeus
(Obiknovenny Kozodoy)
Plate 26, Map 156
Field marks: 26-28 cm. Size of a small pigeon. General coloration dark; upperparts gray-brownish and variously mottled with grayish and blackish barring, spots, and streaks; underparts barred. Narrow white bar across throat (both sexes); males have small white wing patch and white tips to the outer tail feathers.
Habits: Found in forest, forest-steppe, in thickets and semi-desert, unforested slopes of mountains, groves. Migratory. Common. Occurs singly or in pairs; in small flocks during migration. Nests in a depression without any lining. Lays two gray eggs with indefinite dark spots from May to July. In daytime, sits immobile on a tree branch or on the ground. At dusk, flies quietly in open spaces (lumbered areas, fields, meadows) or over water. Flight

MAP 156. European Nightjar (1), Egyptian Nightjar (2), Gray Nightjar (3)

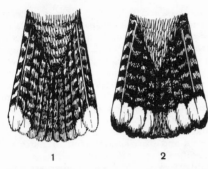

1   2

FIG. 59 Tail of 1) European Nightjar and 2) Gray Nightjar

uneven, with frequent, sharp turns. Call: harsh "kuvik" or a dry, very drawn-out trill, reminiscent of a motor's hum. Feeds on insects (moths, mosquitoes) that it catches in flight.

Range and distribution: European USSR (except the north), Kazakhstan, Central Asia, Altai, southern Siberia as far as southeast Transbaikal. Winters in Africa.

Similar species: Differs from Egyptian Nightjar by its dark coloration; from the Gray Nightjar by the white corners on its tail tip.

378. EGYPTIAN NIGHTJAR
Caprimulgus aegyptius
(Bulany Kozodoy)
Plate 26, Map 156

Field marks: 25 cm. Resembles European Nightjar, but coloration gray-sandy; mottling is gold with brownish. Throat white, but white spots on tail reduced or absent.

Habits: Found in plains in desert and semi-desert, where soil is soft. Migratory. Common. Nest is an unlined depression. Lays two gray-ocherish eggs with indefinite rusty brownish spots from May to June. Flight, habits, methods of hunting and feeding similar to European Nightjar. Call: rapid, repetitive, metallic "kre-kre-kre."

Range and distribution: Plains of southern Kazakhstan and Central Asia. Winters in Africa.

Similar species: Differs from other nightjars by light golden upperparts and even paler underparts.

379. GRAY NIGHTJAR
Caprimulgus indicus
(Bolshoy Kozodoy)
Plate 26, Map 156

Field marks: 27-28 cm. Greatly resembles European Nightjar, but larger and darker, with subterminal white patch on outer tail feathers.

Habits: Found in plains and mountain forests, stays primarily in cut-over areas. Migratory. Common in places. Nest, as with other nightjars, is an unlined depression. Lays two grayish-white eggs with marbled gray patterning in June. Flight and habits similar to European Nightjar. Call: loud, increasingly rapid sounds, "vak-vak-vak."

Range and distribution: Southern Soviet Far East and southeast Transbaikal. Winters in southern Asia.

Similar species: Differs from European Nightjar by subterminal white patch on tail.

[Vagrants of **380.** PLAIN NIGHTJAR (*Caprimulgus inornatus*) have been obtained near Tbilisi.]

SWIFTS: *Apodiformes*

Small birds (no larger than a thrush), stocky, with very long, pointed wings; short, slightly flattened bill; wide mouth; short legs; hard, compact plumage. Appearance similar to swallows; spends most of the day in the air; helpless on the ground; cannot take off from a flat surface. Found in a variety of habitats. Monogamous. Eggs are elongated-ovoid shape. Altricial.

Apus

Small- to medium-sized swifts with forked tails; undertail dark; all four toes of the foot are pointed forward.

381. NORTHERN SWIFT
Apus apus
(Chyorny Strizh)
Plate 28, Map 157

Field marks: 16 cm. Medium-size swift. Throat whitish, remaining plumage is brownish-black.

Habits: Found in a variety of habitats from forest to desert, but prefers open spaces, cities, and other settled areas. Migratory. Common or numerous. Nests in colonies, in tree hollows, in cliff crevices, in burrows in precipices, under roofs, and in crevices of buildings. Lays two or three white eggs in June. Call: harsh, squealing "vzz-vzz." Flight is swift, strong, with frequent wing beats. Feeds on winged insects (flies, mosquitoes), which it catches in flight.

Range and distribution: European USSR (ex-

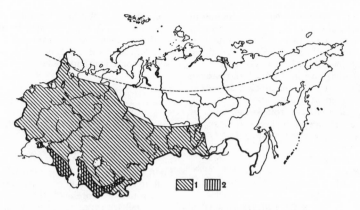

MAP 157. Northern Swift (1), Alpine Swift (2)

cept northern regions), Kazakhstan, southern Siberia as far as Transbaikal, and Central Asia. Winters in tropical and southern Africa.

Similar species: Differs from other swifts by monochromatic brownish-black coloration, with dark rump; from swallows, by crescent-shaped wings.

382. ALPINE SWIFT
Apus melba
(Belobryukhy Strizh)
Plate 28, Map 157

Field marks: 21 cm. Large swift. Upperparts, wings, tail, undertail, and wide band across upper breast are gray-brownish; throat, breast, and belly white.

Habits: Found in dry open habitat, primarily in mountains, where it stays near cliffs; at lower elevations, it is found along seashore cliffs; also found in suburbs, towns, and villages. Migratory. Common, in places numerous. Nests in colonies. Builds nest in cliff crevices or under roofs of buildings. Lays two or three white eggs from May to June. Habits similar to Northern Swift, but flight is even more rapid. Call: harsh "skree-skree."

Range and distribution: Crimea, Caucasus, Central Asia, and southern Kazakhstan. Winters in Africa and India.

Similar species: Differs from other swifts by white underparts with dark band on upper breast.

383. PACIFIC SWIFT
Apus pacificus
(Belopoyasnichny Strizh)
Plate 28, Map 158

Field marks: 16 cm. Size same as Northern Swift. Overall coloration black-brownish; throat and rump white; light, scaly pattern on belly. Tail deeply forked.

Habits: Found in mountains and in settled areas.

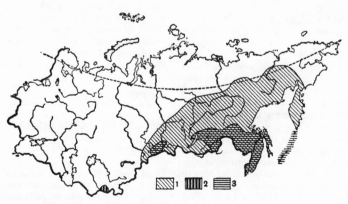

MAP 158. Pacific Swift (1), House Swift (2), White-throated Needletail (3)

Migratory and common. Nests in colonies in cliff crevices and under roof eaves, usually close to water. Lays two or three white eggs in June. Flight and habits similar to Northern Swift. Call: harsh, disyllabic "spee-err."

Range and distribution: Central and eastern Siberia (from Altai to Kamchatka); Soviet Far East. Winters in Australia.

Similar species: Differs from House Swift by larger size and deeply forked tail; from the Northern Swift by white rump.

384. HOUSE SWIFT
Apus affinis
(Maly Strizh)
Plate 28, Map 158

Field marks: 13 cm. Small swift (much smaller than Northern Swift). Top of head and neck, wings, and tail brownish; back, breast, and belly black; throat and rump white. Short tail only slightly forked.

Habits: Found in mountain habitat, where it stays in flocks near precipices and in crevices, preferring shady, damp places. Often found with other swifts. Nests in colonies in clefts of cliffs or occupies old nests of Northern House Martins. Lays two or three white eggs from May to June. Flight similar to Northern Swift, but lighter and less rapid. Call: soft "vzz-vzz," resembling call of Northern Swift, but weaker.

Range and distribution: Mountains of southern Central Asia. Winters in Africa and India.

Similar species: Differs from other swifts by smaller size; from the Pacific Swift, also by its slightly forked tail and blackish unmarked belly.

Hirundapus

385. WHITE-THROATED NEEDLETAIL
Hirundapus caudacutus
(Iglokhvosty Strizh)
Plate 28, Map 158

Field marks: 19 cm. Large swift with shortish tail, in which the quill of each feather resembles a needle. Forehead, throat, flanks, and undertail are white; wings black with metallic glitter. Back is light brownish; upper breast, breast, and belly black-brownish; three toes forward, one back.

Habits: Found in forests and groves with old oak trees. Migratory, common in places. Stays in flocks in the air, flight incredibly swift. Nests in tree hollows high over the ground. Lays three to six white eggs in June. Call is a soft cry.

Range and distribution: Southern East Siberia and Soviet Far East. Winters in Australia.

Similar species: Differs from other swifts by white undertail.

ROLLERS: *Coraciiformes*

Birds of medium and small sizes with compact, hard plumage. Plumage of most species is bright and colorful. Found in a variety of habitats from forest to desert and mountains. Monogamous. Eggs are shortened ellipsoid shape. Altricial.

Coracias

386. EURASIAN ROLLER
Coracias garrulus
(Sizovoronka)
Plate 26, Map 159

Field marks: 32-33 cm. Size of a pigeon. Overall coloration light greenish-blue with reddish-brown back; light blue patches on wings and tail; long heavy bill. Juveniles are paler.

Habits: Found in a variety of habitats from desert to forest; often seen in settled areas. Migratory and common. Nests in tree hollows near forest edges and in groves, in burrows of clay precipices, sometimes in house cracks. Lays four to six shiny white eggs from May to June. Occurs singly or in pairs; in groups during autumn migration. Often seen perched motionless on overhead wires, on a dead branch, or haystack. Feeds on large insects and small vertebrates (lizards, rodents). Call: harsh, chattering "rak-rak."

Range and distribution: European USSR (central and southern regions), Central Asia, Kazakhstan, southern West Siberia. Winters in subequatorial Africa.

Similar species: No similar species in the USSR.

Eurystomus

387. BROAD-BILLED ROLLER
Eurystomus orientalis
(Shyrokorot)
Plate 26, Map 159

Field marks: 30 cm. Larger than a thrush. Bill short, wide at the base, and red. Head and wings brownish-black; remaining plumage darker greenish-blue, greener on the back.

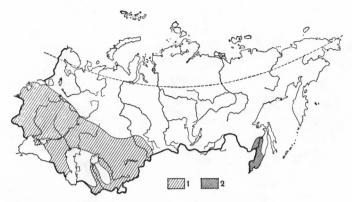

MAP 159. Eurasian Roller (1), Broad-billed Roller (2)

Round light blue patch at base of primaries, most conspicuous in flight.

Habits: Found near fields, areas of cut trees, and along river valleys. Migratory and common in places. Nests in hollows of large trees. Lays four to six white eggs in June. Occurs singly, in pairs, and flocks in crowns of trees, often flying out from dead branches. Flight is swift. Call: harsh "cher-cher." Feeds on variety of insects, which it usually catches in flight, but sometimes in trees.

Range and distribution: Southern Soviet Far East. Winters in Japan and southern Asia.

Similar species: No similar species in the USSR.

Alcedo

Small, occasionally medium-size birds with straight, pointed bill and short, weak legs with toes half-grown together. Coloration is bright and colorful.

388. EURASIAN KINGFISHER
Alcedo atthis
(Obyknovenny Zimorodok)
Plate 26, Map 160

Field marks: 16-18 cm. Larger than a sparrow. Upperparts light bluish-green; rump glittering azure-blue; white throat and patch on side of neck; underparts and cheeks rusty red; bill brownish.

Habits: Found on narrow rivers and streams, lake shores, and other bodies of water with clear water, and in a variety of habitats. Migratory. Not numerous. Nests in clay or sandy precipices on shores. Nest is a burrow that the bird digs out. Lays five to eight rounded, shiny white eggs from May to July. Occurs singly or in pairs. Usually seen perched close to the

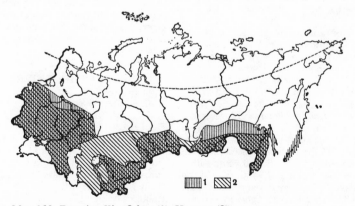

MAP 160. Eurasian Kingfisher (1), Hoopoe (2)

FIG. 60 BIRDS IN FLIGHT
1. Barn Swallow   2. Northern House Martin   3. Northern Swift   4. Little Tern
5. European Bee-eater   6. European Pratincole

water, looking down. Flies directly over water, in swift flight with frequent wing beats. Call: harsh "peek-peek-peek." Feeds on small fish and aquatic invertebrates.
Range and distribution: European USSR (north to 60° N latitude), Kazakhstan, Central Asia, southern Siberia, and Soviet Far East.
Similar species: No similar species in the USSR.

[In Lenkoran (a town on the Caspian Sea in Azerbaijan) vagrants of **389.** WHITE-THROATED KINGFISHER (*Halcyon smyrnensis*) were obtained; blue upperparts, white throat, reddish-brown head and belly, red bill. On islands of Peter the Great Bay and in the Sudzuhinsky nature reserve vagrants of **390.** BLACK-CAPPED KINGFISHER (*Halcyon pileata*) were observed; black cap, white throat, buffy underparts, deep blue upperparts, and red bill. In the Crimea, vagrants of **391.** PIED KINGFISHER (*Ceryle rudis*) were observed; it was black and white with a broadly banded black and white tail. In the Kuril Islands (Kunashir), vagrants of **392.** CRESTED KINGFISHER (*Ceryle lugubris*) were ob-

served; heavy crest, white underparts, and heavy black-and-white barring above.]

Merops

Small (thrush-size) birds with thin, slightly downcurved bill; long, pointed wings; and long tail in which the middle feather is narrow and protrudes out much farther than the others. Legs are short and weak, foretoes are partly grown together.

393. EUROPEAN BEE-EATER
Merops apiaster
(Zolotistaya Shchurka)
Plate 26, Map 161
Field marks: 26-30 cm. Eye line and narrow breast band are black; throat yellow; head and back golden-brown in adults and greenish in juveniles; forehead is whitish with light blue tinge; wings brownish and blue; tail greenish; belly is light blue.
Habits: Found in open steppe regions with

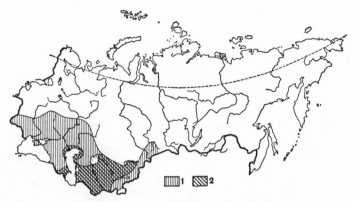

MAP 161. European Bee-eater (1), Blue-cheeked Bee-eater (2)

precipices and gullies, river valleys, and at the foot of mountains. Migratory. Common and numerous. Nests in colonies in burrows that it digs into overhanging precipices. Lays five to eight shiny white eggs in May and June. Flight is swift and light with alternating gliding and frequent wing beats. Stays in flocks, often perches on overhead wires, dead branches, and in bushes. Call: loud, but gentle "kryou-kryou." Feeds on large insects, which it catches in flight.

Range and distribution: Southern USSR from Transcarpathia to the Altai. Winters in Africa, Arabian Peninsula and western Hindustan.

Similar species: Differs from Blue-cheeked Bee-eater by its light blue underparts and yellow throat.

394. BLUE-CHEEKED BEE-EATER
Merops superciliosus
(Zelyonaya Shchurka)
Plate 26, Map 161

Field marks: 33-34 cm. Resembles European Bee-eater, but overall coloration is green. Black eye line; forehead and eye stripe light blue; throat rusty yellow becoming rusty on the upper breast.

Habits: Found in steppe, semi-desert, and desert, on precipices, in gullies, and in river valleys. Migratory. In places numerous. Time of nesting, habits, flight, and feeding habits similar to European Bee-eater. Call: harsh "kree-kree."

Range and distribution: Caucasus, Central Asia, and Kazakhstan. Winters in Africa and southern Asia.

Similar species: Differs from European Bee-eater by overall greenish coloration.

Upupa

395. HOOPOE
Upupa epops
(Udod)
Plate 26, Map 160

Field marks: 28-32 cm. A little larger than a pigeon. Bill thin, long, slightly downcurved. Large fan-shaped crest on the head; wings wide and rounded, boldly marked with black-and-white stripes; tail black with single broad white band; lower belly and undertail coverts whitish; remaining plumage brownish-pink, brighter on the breast and on the crest.

Habits: Found in thinly wooded open spaces, in groves and thickets, gardens and parks. Migratory and common. Nests in a tree hollow, on a heap of rocks, in niches of cliffs and precipices, in burrows. Lays three to nine grayish eggs from April to June. Found singly, in pairs, and small groups on the ground or in trees and bushes, often near settled areas. Flight is fairly slow and undulating. Feeds on the ground on insects and other small invertebrates. Call: muted "up-up-up" and a harsh hissing.

Range and distribution: European USSR (south of the Baltic States and Leningrad Oblast), Kazakhstan, Central Asia, southern Siberia, and the Soviet Far East. Winters in Africa and southern Asia.

Similar species: No similar species in the USSR.

WOODPECKERS: *Piciformes*

Medium-sized to small birds with straight, chiseled bills (except the Wryneck), short, powerful, zygodactyl feet (usually two toes front, two rear). Wings are broad, tail is stiff and pointed at the tip (except Wryneck). Found in forested regions. During breeding period, in spring, males "drum" by rapping dry trees with their beaks, emitting a characteristic dry drumming sound. Monogamous. Eggs ovoid or shortened ovoid shape. Altricial.

Dryocopus

396. BLACK WOODPECKER
Dryocopus martius
(Zhelna)
Plate 27, Map 162
Field marks: 45 cm. Large, size of a crow. Matte black; eyes white. Male has a raspberry-red crown; the female has a red nape.
Habits: Found in mature coniferous and mixed, sometimes deciduous forests. Nonmigratory. Not numerous. Nests in a hole in a tree, hollowed out by the bird; nest usually situated high above the ground, and entrance to the nest is at a right angle to trunk. Lays three to five white eggs in April or May. The spring "drumming" is very loud, low in tone. Found singly or in pairs; climbs tree trunks and stumps by hopping up the trunk. Wary. Call: loud "kree-kree-kree" or plaintive, nasal "klyoue." Feeds on insect larvae and ants.
Range and distribution: Forest zones of USSR, mountain forests of the Caucasus.
Similar species: Differs from other woodpeckers by larger size and black coloration.

Picus

Medium-size woodpecker with predominance of green on the back.

397. EURASIAN GREEN WOODPECKER
Picus viridis
(Zelyony Dyatel)
Plate 27, Map 163
Field marks: 32-37 cm. Back is bright green; rump is golden-yellow; underparts greenish-white; wings and tail brownish with light barring; forehead and "moustache" are black (with red speckles in the male); crown and nape are red. Bill is gray-black.
Habits: Found in deciduous and mixed forests, groves, and parks, preferring thin plantings. Nonmigratory. Common. Nests in tree hollows; entrance to the nest is round. Lays three to six white eggs, April to June. Occurs singly or in pairs, on the ground and on tree trunks; often seen tearing ant hills apart. Call: loud,

laughing cry, "kley-kley-kley." Ants are its primary food source.
Range and distribution: Southern half of European USSR.
Similar species: Differs from Scaly-bellied Green Woodpecker by its blackish bill and lack of scaly pattern on the belly; from the Gray-headed Green Woodpecker, by more extensive red on head.

398. GRAY-HEADED GREEN WOODPECKER
Picus canus
(Sedoy Dyatel)
Plate 27, Map 163
Field marks: 30 cm. Resembles Eurasian Green Woodpecker, but smaller; head and nape are gray, males have a red forehead; underparts grayish.
Habits: Found in thin, deciduous, mixed, and partly coniferous forests. Nonmigratory and nomadic bird. Not numerous. Stays on trunks of thickly branched trees, on the ground on ant hills. Nesting, habits, and feeding same as Eurasian Green Woodpecker. Call: loud, nasal cry, "klai-klai-klai-klai."
Range and distribution: Central European USSR, southern Siberia, and Soviet Far East.
Similar species: Differs from Eurasian Green Woodpecker by smaller size and gray head.

399. SCALY-BELLIED GREEN WOODPECKER
Picus squamatus
(Cheshuychaty Dyatel)
Plate 27, Map 163
Field marks: 30 cm. Resembles Eurasian Green Woodpecker, but underparts have dark, scaly pattern; bill is yellow.
Habits: Found in tugay (riparian woods: various poplars, thorny shrubs, and reeds) having scattered large trees with dead branches. Nonmigratory. Very rare, apparently becoming extinct. Builds nest in tree hollow, lays four to six white eggs from March to May. Occurs singly and in pairs on the ground and in trees; feeds primarily on ants. Call: harsh "tee-tee-you" or "klyou-klyou." Included in the Red Data Book.
Range and distribution: Groves on the flood-

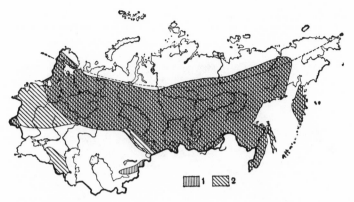

MAP 162. Northern Three-toed Woodpecker (1), Black Wood-pecker (2)

plain of the Murgab River (southern Turk-menia).
Similar species: Differs from other green woodpeckers by scaly pattern on breast and belly.

Picoides

400. NORTHERN THREE-TOED WOODPECKER
Picoides tridactylus
(Tryokhpaly Dyatel)
Plate 27, Map 162
Field marks: 22 cm. Medium size (larger than a thrush). Black and white striped head and neck; wings, tail black with white barring; underparts and back white. In male, crown is golden-yellow; in female, whitish with fine blackish streaks. Three toes on the foot.
Habits: Found in remote coniferous forests, in plains and hills. Nonmigratory. Fairly common. Nest is situated in a tree hollow; entrance to the nest is round; lays three to six white eggs in May or June. More secretive than other woodpeckers; found singly and in pairs. Usually silent; call: harsh, monosyllabic cry. Feeds on insects and their larvae (primarily woodborers).
Range and distribution: Taiga of USSR.
Similar species: Differs from other woodpeckers by yellow or white crown and three toes on the foot.

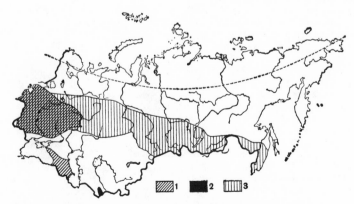

MAP 163. Eurasian Green Woodpecker (1), Scaly-bellied Green Woodpecker (2), Gray-headed Green Woodpecker (3)

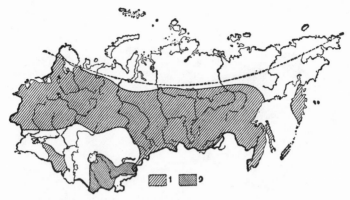

MAP 164. Great Spotted Woodpecker (1), White-winged Spotted Woodpecker (2)

Dendrocopos

Medium-size and small woodpeckers of a bright black-and-white coloration. Bill is dark.

401. GREAT SPOTTED WOODPECKER
Dendrocopos major
(Pyostry Dyatel)
Plate 27, Map 164
Field marks: 23 cm. Medium size (larger than a thrush). Back, crown, neck, wings, tail, and stripe from bill to the nape are black; cheeks, forehead, throat, breast, belly, barring on wings and tail, wide shoulder stripe is white; undertail is red. The nape of the male and the entire top of head in juveniles are red.
Habits: Found in variety of forests, in plains and in hills. In winter, also found in groves and old parks. Nonmigratory and nomadic. Fairly common, and is seen more often than others. Nest situated in a hole in a tree (usually aspen), which the bird hollows out, and is occasionally very high. Entrance is round. Lays four to six white eggs in April or May. "Drumming" during breeding time is much weaker than that of the Black Woodpecker. Flight is swift, characteristically undulating. Occurs singly and in pairs in trees, on trunks or in branches, sometimes on the ground. Call: harsh "keek-keek." Feeds on insects; in winter, on seeds of coniferous trees. Caches pine cones in a stump or a dead tree trunk.
Range and distribution: Forests of European USSR, central and southern Siberia, Soviet Far East.
Similar species: Differs from White-winged Spotted Woodpecker by predominance of black

in the wings; from the Syrian Woodpecker by black pattern on the head.

402. WHITE-WINGED SPOTTED WOODPECKER
Dendrocopos leucopterus
(Belokryly Dyatel)
Not illustrated, Map 164
Field marks: 22-23 cm. Greatly resembles Great Spotted Woodpecker, but white is such a predominant color in the wings that they appear entirely white.
Habits: Found in tugay (riparian woods consisting of various poplars, thorny shrubs, and reeds), saxal thickets in deserts, groves in mountains and plains, and in gardens and parks. Nonmigratory and nomadic. Common. Habits and call similar to Great Spotted Woodpecker, but nests earlier, in March.
Range and distribution: Forests in mountains

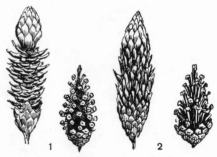

FIG. 61 Fir and Pine Cones: Seed Removal by 1) Woodpecker and 2) Crossbill

and plains of southern Kazakhstan and Central Asia.

Similar species: Difficult to distinguish from Great Spotted Woodpecker except by predominance of white coloration, particularly on the wings.

403. SYRIAN WOODPECKER
Dendrocopos syriacus
(Siriysky Dyatel)
Plate 27, Map 165

Field marks: 23 cm. Greatly resembles Great Spotted Woodpecker, except black stripe from corner of the bill does not reach the nape, so that the white cheeks connect with the white of the neck.

Habits: Found in deciduous, mixed, more rarely coniferous forests, in riparian forests, gardens, and groves in plains and hills. Nonmigratory. Not numerous. Habits and call similar to Great Spotted Woodpecker. Feeds on insects; in winter and fall, also on seeds.

Range and distribution: Southwestern USSR and Transcaucasus.

Similar species: Differs from Great Spotted Woodpecker by unbroken white pattern on head.

404. WHITE-BACKED WOODPECKER
Dendrocopos leucotos
(Belospinny Dyatel)
Plate 27, Map 165

Field marks: 26-30 cm. Resembles Great Spotted Woodpecker, but lower back and rump are white; has broader stripes on wings, and outer tail feathers have more extensive white; sides pinkish. In male, entire crown is red; female, black.

Habits: Found in thin forests of various types.

Nonmigratory and nomadic. Common in places. Nesting, habits, flight, feeding, and call similar to Great Spotted Woodpecker.

Range and distribution: Mixed and deciduous forests in central European USSR, southern Siberia, and Soviet Far East.

Similar species: Differs from Great Spotted, Middle Spotted, and Gray-headed Pygmy Woodpeckers by white lower back and rump.

405. MIDDLE SPOTTED WOODPECKER
Dendrocopos medius
(Sredny Pyostry Dyatel)
Plate 27, Map 166

Field marks: 21 cm. Resembles Great Spotted Woodpecker, but smaller; wide white band on shoulders and wings; belly and sides yellow-ocherish; undertail and crown red.

Habits: Found in deciduous, sometimes mixed forests in plains and hills. Nonmigratory and nomadic. Not numerous. Nesting and habits similar to Great Spotted Woodpecker. Occurs singly and in pairs, usually on branches, sometimes on the ground. Call: frequent "kik-kik-kik."

Range and distribution: Central and southern regions of European USSR.

Similar species: Differs from Great Spotted Woodpecker by smaller size and red crown.

406. LESSER SPOTTED WOODPECKER
Dendrocopos minor
(Maly Pyostry Dyatel)
Plate 27, Map 166

Field marks: 14 cm. Small (sparrow-size) woodpecker. Heavily barred black and white upperparts; underparts white with black streaks. Male has red crown; female, black.

Habits: Found in deciduous and mixed forests,

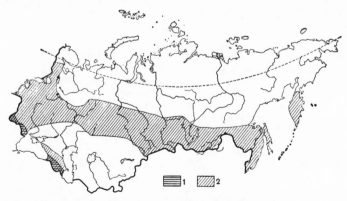

MAP 165. Syrian Woodpecker (1), White-backed Woodpecker (2)

MAP 166. Middle Spotted Woodpecker (1), Lesser Spotted Woodpecker (2)

parks, gardens. Nonmigratory and nomadic. Common. Nests in a tree hollow that the woodpecker often digs out of rotten trees low to the ground. Lays five to eight white eggs in May or June. Stays singly and in pairs, in trees, climbing along branches and rarely on trunks. In winter, is nomadic together with tits. Call: loud "kee-kee-kee-kee-kee" blending together, resembling cry of a small hawk. Feeds on various insects.

Range and distribution: All regions of USSR except Kazakhstan and Central Asia.

Similar species: Differs from other woodpeckers by its small size and lack of red undertail coverts; from Pygmy Woodpeckers by white belly that lacks streaking and (in males) by red crown.

407. JAPANESE PYGMY WOODPECKER
Dendrocopos kizuki
(Maly Ostrokryly Dyatel)
Plate 27, Map 167

Field marks: 13 cm. Size of Lesser Spotted Woodpecker. Head brownish-gray; black and white barring on the back; underparts whitish with brownish streaks on flanks. Male has a small patch of red feathers behind the eye.

Habits: Found in various types of woods, in plains and hills. Nonmigratory. Common in places but rare on the whole. Habits similar to Lesser Spotted Woodpecker, but nests later, in June. Found on smaller branches of trees, in bushes, and even on large grassy plants.

Range and distribution: Soviet Far East, Japan.

Similar species: Differs from Lesser Spotted Woodpecker by brownish-gray head and brown streaked flanks; from the Gray-headed Pygmy

Woodpecker by smaller size, whitish nape, and black-and-white barred back.

408. GRAY-HEADED PYGMY WOODPECKER
Dendrocopos nanus
(Bolshoy Ostrokryly Dyatel)
Plate 27, Map 167

Field marks: 15 cm. Resembles Japanese Pygmy Woodpecker but is slightly larger; upper back is black; crown blackish. Male has a few red feathers located on the sides behind the head.

Habits: Found in plains and mountain forests, primarily in deciduous forests. Nonmigratory. Uncommon, but apparently common in places.

Range and distribution: Southern Central Asia.

Similar species: Differs from Lesser Spotted Woodpecker by dark underparts; from the Japanese Pygmy Woodpecker by black upper back and larger size.

Jynx

409. EURASIAN WRYNECK
Jynx torquilla
(Vertisheyka)
Plate 27, Map 167

Field marks: 16 cm. Size of a sparrow. Upperparts brownish-gray with light and dark mottling; wings and tail rusty with blackish and gray bars and mottling; underparts ocherish-gray with narrow, dark barring. Small straight bill, weak. Barred tail soft, rounded at the tip.

Habits: Found in thin forests in a variety of habitats, preferring forest edges, fields and

MAP 167. Eurasian Wryneck (1), Japanese Pygmy Woodpecker (2),
Gray-headed Pygmy Woodpecker (3)

planted groves. Migratory and common. Nests in natural hollows in trunks of trees and in stumps. Lays seven to twelve white, slightly elongated eggs in May and June. Stays on thick branches of trees, often walks on the ground. When alarmed, stretches its neck and turns its head like a snake. Call: loud "kyaee-kyaee-kyaee"; when startled in the tree cavity, it hisses. Differs from other woodpeckers in that it does not drill into the bark of a tree in search of food; instead it feeds exclusively on ants and their pupa.

Range and distribution: Forest zone from Kola Peninsula to Sea of Okhotsk (as far north as 63°-66° latitude). Does not nest in Kazakhstan or Central Asia. Winters in Africa and southern Asia.

Similar species: No similar species in the USSR.

LARKS, SWALLOWS, WARBLERS, BUNTINGS, STARLINGS, CROWS, THRUSHES, ETC.: *Passeriformes*

Birds of very small to medium and large sizes. Bill can be of various shapes; usually straight. Four toes—three facing forward, one back. Most species are songbirds. Inhabit a variety of landscapes, but usually associated with woodsy or shrubby growth. Eggs are typically ovoid shaped, but sometimes rounder. Monogamous. Altricial.

Alauda

Small birds (no larger than a starling) with a compact body, relatively short tail, and wide wings. Back of tarsus rounded and scaled. Feeds on insects and grass seeds. Long, nearly straight claw on hind toe.

410. NORTHERN SKYLARK
Alauda arvensis
(Polevoy Zhavoronok)
Plate 29, Map 168

Field marks: 17-20 cm. Somewhat larger than a sparrow. Coloration of upperparts ocher and interspersed grayish-brown, with finely streaked head and nape, and broader blackish streaks on the back; underparts ocher-white with fine brownish streaks on the breast. A noticeable wide crest. White outer tail feathers.

Habits: Found in open country, where it inhabits farmland, grassland, plains, alpine meadows. Commonly migrates. Stays in pairs or flocks. Nests in a hole or depression in the ground. Lays four or five grayish or reddish eggs with dark spots, April to June. Call: a soft "chri-ik" or "chrr-ik." Song: a variety of loud trills.

Range and distribution: Greater part of the USSR except deserts of Central Asia and northernmost areas. Winters in southern regions of European USSR, Transcaucasus, and Central Asia.

Similar species: In the field, almost indistin-

MAP 168. Northern Skylark (1), Oriental Skylark (2)

guishable from the Oriental Skylark, but is larger, with a longer tail.

411. ORIENTAL SKYLARK
Alauda gulgula
(Maly Polevoy Zhavoronok)
Not illustrated, Map 168
Field marks: 16 cm. Similar to Northern Skylark, but smaller.
Habits: Found in open, grassy country in plains and hills. Generally migrates. Stays in pairs and in flocks on the ground. Often perches in bushes. Nests on ground. Lays three to five grayish spotted eggs, April to June. Call and song similar to Northern Skylark.
Range and distribution: Southern Transcaucasus and Central Asia. Winters in India.
Similar species: Differs from Northern Skylark by shorter tail and smaller size (nearly indistinguishable in the field). The Oriental

Skylark is found only south of the Aral Sea, and is absent throughout most of the Northern Skylark's range.

Lullula

412. WOOD LARK
Lullula arborea
(Yula)
Plate 29, Map 169
Field marks: 14-16 cm. Small (sparrow-size) lark. Upperparts buffy brown with streaked crown and nape, and heavier black streaks on back; throat and belly white; eye stripe and breast buffy white; narrow brownish streakings on breast. Small but visible crest. Tail short.
Habits: An uncommon lark that inhabits forest edges and scrub-covered hilly steppes. Migra-

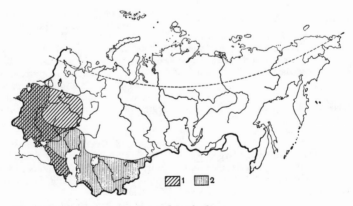

MAP 169. Wood Lark (1), Crested Lark (2)

tory. Stays on the ground, sometimes perches in trees and bushes. Found in pairs and flocks. Nests on ground. Lays four or five white eggs spotted brown or red, April to June. Sings high in the air. Alarm and call are a short trill. Song: loud clear whistle, "yuli-yuli-yuli-yul-yul-yul-yuloo-yuloo."

Range and distribution: Central, western, and southern regions of European USSR; Caucasus. Winters in south of Europe, southern Africa, and Southeast Asia.

Similar species: Differs from other skylarks by light eye stripe, small size, short tail, and habitat.

Galerida

413. CRESTED LARK
Galerida cristata
(Khohlaty Zhavoronok)
Plate 29, Map 169

Field marks: 19-20 cm. Large (but smaller than a starling). Upperparts brownish-gray with dark streaks—smaller on the head, heavier on the back. Underparts whitish with brown streaks on buffy breast. Long, pointed crest.

Habits: Inhabits open settled areas, dry plains, and semi-deserts. Nonmigratory. Stays on the ground in flocks. Lays three to six whitish eggs with dark spots, April to June. Call: a melodic "eeree-eeree-tree-treee" and a quiet "jnoi." Song: a variety of quiet trills.

Range and distribution: Western and southern regions of European USSR, Caucasus, Central Asia, and Kazakhstan.

Similar species: Differs from other larks by its long, pointed crest.

Calandrella

Small (sparrow-size) larks. Inhabits dry expanses of steppe in flat areas and hills. Bill rather narrow and conical, legs comparatively long.

414. LESSER SHORT-TOED LARK
Calandrella leucophaea
(Solonchakovy Zhavoronok)
Plate 29, Map 170

Field marks: 14-17 cm. Upperparts light ashy brown; wings and tail brownish; underparts, eye stripe, wing bars, and outer tail feathers whitish; narrow brownish streakings on the breast.

Habits: Found in dry saline soil areas and in steppe with sparse vegetation. Common. Migratory. Stays on the ground in pairs and flocks. Nest is built on the ground and is tightly woven from stems and blades of grass. Lays four or five whitish eggs with brownish spots, May to July. Call: a soft chirp. Song: a series of short, disyllabic twitterings. Usually sings in flight.

Range and distribution: South of European USSR, Transcaucasus, Kazakhstan, Central Asia, Transbaikal. Winters in northeastern Africa, Iraq, India, and China.

Similar species: Differs from other small larks by its light ashy-brown coloration; and from Short-toed Lark by its streaked breast and lack of dark patches on neck.

415. GRAY LARK
Calandrella pispoletta
(Sery Zhavoronok)
Plate 29, Map 170

Field marks: 14 cm. Upperparts brownish with dark streakings; underparts, outer tail feath-

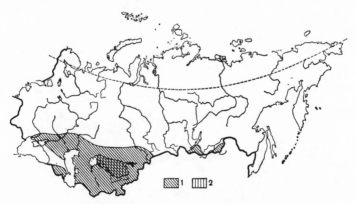

MAP 170. Gray Lark (1), Lesser Short-toed Lark (2)

ers, and eye stripe ocher-white; breast has brownish streaks that coalesce at the sides into patches; wings and tail brownish.

Habits: Found in dry steppe, pastures, stream beds, and fields with sparse vegetation. Usually migrates. Stays on the ground in pairs and in flocks. Nest, made of grasses, is on the ground. Lays four or five whitish or greenish eggs with brownish spots from May to July. Sings in flight. Song: a string of short twitters and warbles.

Range and distribution: From southern Ukraine to southeast Transbaikal. Winters in northeastern Africa, Iran, India, and China.

Similar species: Differs from the Lesser Short-toed Lark by the dark coloration of the upperparts. Practically indistinguishable in the field from the Short-toed Lark and Hume's Short-toed Lark. Streaking on the breast visible at short range.

Note: *Calandrella leucophaea* and *Calandrella pispoletta* are currently considered as races of *Calandrella rufescens* in the West.

416. GREATER SHORT-TOED LARK
Calandrella cinerea
(Maly Zhavoronok)
Plate 29, Map 171

Field marks: 14-17 cm. Similar to Lesser Short-toed Lark, except the breast is unstreaked, and there are brownish patches on the sides of the upper breast.

Habits: Inhabits open steppe with sparse vegetation. Usually migrates. Stays on the ground in pairs and in flocks. Nests on the ground in a depression under cover of a clump of grass. Lays four or five whitish or pinkish-brown eggs with small brown and gray spots from April to July. Usually sings in flight, ascending upward in bobbing flight. Song: a variety of short twitters, "veeti-veeti-veet-ti, tiriy-tee-tee-tee."

Range and distribution: South of European USSR, Caucasus, Kazakhstan, Central Asia, Transbaikal. Winters in southern Europe and Asia.

Similar species: Differs from the Lesser Short-toed Lark by the presence of brownish patches on sides of breast and by the lack of streakings on the breast.

417. HUME'S SHORT-TOED LARK
Calandrella acutirostris
(Tonkoklyuvy Zhavoronok)
Plate 29, Map 171

Field marks: 14 cm. Coloration similar to Greater Short-toed Lark, but the back is darker and the underparts whiter.

Habits: Found in dry mountain steppe and semideserts with sparse vegetation. Usually migrates. Stays on the ground in pairs and in flocks. Nests on the ground. Usually lays three grayish eggs with brownish speckles from May to July. Sings in flight. Song: a variety of twitters.

Range and distribution: Central Asia and Kazakhstan. Winters in India.

Similar species: Differs from the Lesser Short-toed Lark by its darker upperparts. Almost indistinguishable in the field from the Greater Short-toed Lark, except by its darker upperparts and whiter underparts.

Melanocorypha

Large (starling-size) larks of solid build with massive, fairly long bill.

418. BLACK LARK
Melanocorypha yeltoniensis
(Chyorny Zhavoronok)
Plate 29, Map 172

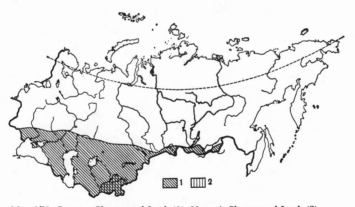

MAP 171. Greater Short-toed Lark (1), Hume's Short-toed Lark (2)

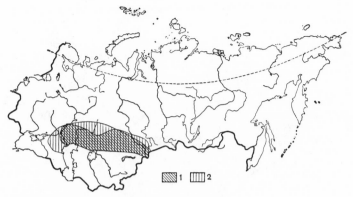

MAP 172. Black Lark (1), White-winged Lark (2)

Field marks: 18-22 cm. Male in summer dull black. Fall and winter: upperparts ash-gray with black spots showing through. Female and juvenile upperparts brownish-gray with dark mottling; underparts white with a brown-streaked ocher suffusion on the breast; underwing coverts black.

Habits: Inhabits dry areas of high salinity, and feather-grass steppes. Usually nomadic. Stays in pairs during nesting season and in flocks the remainder of the year. Moreover, males and females stay in separate flocks. Nest located in a depression on the ground. Lays four or five eggs that are light ocher with brownish speckles, April to June. Sings sitting on the ground or while flying. Song is a variety of trills and imitations of other bird songs. Feeds on the ground.

Range and distribution: Lower Volga and Kazakhstan. In winter, nomadic through south of European USSR, Kazakhstan, and Central Asia.

Similar species: Male differs from other larks by all-black coloration. Females and juveniles differ from the Calandra Lark by the absence of black spots on the sides of the throat.

419. WHITE-WINGED LARK
Melanocorypha leucoptera
(Belokryly Zhavoronok)
Plate 29, Map 172
Field marks: 17-20 cm. Top of head, auriculars, shoulders, and upper tail coverts rusty. Back is brownish-gray, with blackish-brown streaks; tail and wings are blackish. Underparts are white, as is the large white wing patch (most conspicuous in flight) and outer tail feathers.

Habits: Found in areas of high salinity, feather-grass steppe, and saline soil areas. Usually a nomadic and migratory bird. Solitary nester;

flocks at other times. Nests on the ground. Lays four to six light green or yellowish brown-spotted eggs from May to July. Sings from the ground; occasionally flies into the air. Call: a quiet, prolonged cry. Song: a simple trill that sometimes imitates other bird voices.

Range and distribution: Central Caucasus, Lower Volga, Kazakhstan. In winter, nomadic southwest of its nesting habitat.

Similar species: Differs from the Mongolian Lark by the absence of black patches on the sides of the throat and from other larks by the white secondaries.

420. MONGOLIAN LARK
Melanocorypha mongolica
(Mongolsky Zhavoronok)
Plate 29, Map 173
Field marks: 20-22 cm. Resembles White-winged Lark, but noticeably larger, with large black patches at the sides of the throat.

Habits: Inhabits steppe, preferring damp areas with lush grass. Usually migrates. Solitary nester; the rest of the time in flocks. Nests on the ground. Lays three or four grayish eggs with brown spots in May or June. Sings in flight. Song: a selection of trills.

Range and distribution: Tuva, Transbaikal. Winters in southern Mongolia and further south.

Similar species: Differs from White-winged Lark by black patches on sides of throat; from the Calandra Lark by its rufous cap and shoulders, white wing patch.

421. CALANDRA LARK
Melanocorypha calandra
(Stepnoy Zhavoronok)
Plate 29, Map 173
Field marks: 19-22 cm. Upperparts brownish-

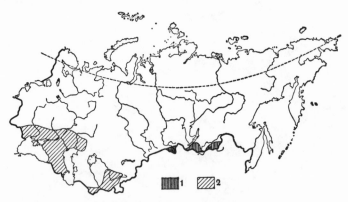

MAP 173. Mongolian Lark (1), Calandra Lark (2)

gray with brownish streaking. Wings and tail brownish. Outer tail feathers, trailing edge of the wing, and underparts white. Large black patches at the sides of the throat. Breast buffy with small brownish streaks. Underwings blackish.

Habits: Inhabits grassy steppes and sown grass fields. Common. Nonmigratory and nomadic. Stays on the ground. Solitary during nesting; otherwise in flocks. Nests on the ground. Lays four or five dirty white or greenish eggs spotted brown from April to July. Sings on the ground or in a bush; often sings in flight. Song: a variety of loud, sonorous trills and whistles, which often includes imitations of other bird calls.

Range and distribution: South of European USSR, Caucasus, lower Volga, western Kazakhstan, and Central Asia.

Similar species: Differs from the Mongolian Lark by the absence of rufous tones and lack of white wing patch. In the field, difficult to distinguish from the Bimaculated Lark, but differs by its white stripe on the trailing edge of the wing, by its white outer tail feathers and heavier patches on the breast.

422. BIMACULATED LARK

Melanocorypha bimaculata
(Dvupyatnisty Zhavoronok)
Plate 29, Map 174

Field marks: 18-19 cm. Resembles Calandra Lark but smaller; does not have white stripes at trailing edge of wing, and streaking on the breast is reduced or absent. Instead of white outer tail feathers, the tail is white-tipped.

Habits: Found in argillaceous and sandy steppe with sparse vegetation; also rocky steppe areas. Solitary during nesting season; flocks the rest of the year. Common, in some areas numer-

ous. Sings on the ground and during high ascent. Song: a variety of loud, sonorous trills and whistles with imitations of other birds.

Range and distribution: Transcaucasus, Central Asia, and southern Kazakhstan. Winters in northeast Africa and northwest India.

Similar species: Closely resembles Calandra Lark, differing by white-tipped tail, lack of white on wing, and reduced or absent streaks on the breast.

Ammomanes

423. DESERT LARK

Ammomanes deserti
(Pustinny Zhavoronok)
Plate 29, Map 174

Field marks: 15-18 cm. Somewhat smaller than a starling. Uniformly clay-gray with rosy overtones; underparts lighter; faint streakings on the breast.

Habits: Inhabits sandy foothills and argillaceous desert plains with sparse vegetation. Generally nonmigratory; nomadic. Occurs in flocks and in pairs. Nest, made of small stones, is situated on the ground. Lays four or five grayish-white eggs with brown spots from April to June. Call: melodic whistles and chirps.

Range and distribution: Southern regions of Central Asia.

Similar species: Differs from other larks by its uniformly pinkish coloring.

Eremophila

424. HORNED LARK

Eremophila alpestris
(Rogaty Zhavoronok)
Plate 29, Map 175

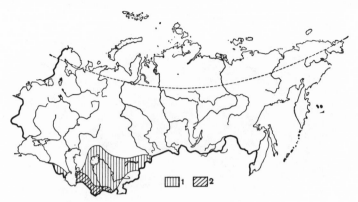

MAP 174. Bimaculated Lark (1), Desert Lark (2)

Field marks: 16-20 cm. Somewhat smaller than a starling. Long narrow feathers or "horns" on each side of the head. Fairly long tail in comparison to other larks. Upperparts pinkish-gray with dark streaks on the back. Forecrown "horns," lores, malar area, band on upper breast, bill, legs, and tail are black. Underparts, forehead, and outer tail stripes are white (cheeks, forehead, and throat occasionally yellow).

Habits: Found in dry mountains and steppe; alpine and subalpine meadows and rocky mountains; tundra. Northern populations migratory, southern mostly nomadic. Solitary nesters, but stay in flocks in winter, when often seen in cattle-yards and by the roads. Nests on the ground. Lays three to five greenish or brownish eggs with brown spots. Call: quiet whistle, "fyee-fee-teetee." Song: high-pitched tinkling, often given in the air.

Range and distribution: Near-polar area of the USSR, Caucasus, in places in Kazakhstan and Central Asia, Altai mountain regions, Transcaucasus. Winters in southern USSR.

Similar species: No similar species in the USSR.

Hirundo

Small (sparrow-size) birds with long pointed wings; short, weak legs; short, flattened bill; wide mouth, and forked tail with the outermost feathers long and narrow. No sexual dimorphism in coloration. Feeds on insects, which are usually caught in flight.

425. BARN SWALLOW
Hirundo rustica
(Derevenskaya Lastockha)
Plate 28, Map 176

Field marks: 18-21 cm. Upperparts and a wide stripe across the breast are a shining blue-black. Forehead and throat rusty brown; spots

MAP 175. Horned Lark

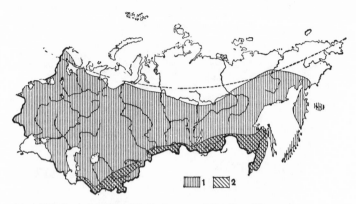

MAP 176. Barn Swallow (1), Red-rumped Swallow (2)

on tail white; breast and belly whitish or rusty. Forked tail narrow and long.

Habits: Found in settled areas; often seen in villages and towns. Migratory. Common, sometimes numerous. Stays in flocks both in the air and while perched on wires or dead tree branches. Nest is a cup fashioned from bits of clay and located under eaves of buildings, on the wall of a well, under a bridge, etc. Lays four to six white eggs speckled with brownish-red in May or June. Call: loud "tvee-veet." Song: twittering "teel-veedee, teelee-veelee-trrr."

Range and distribution: Greater part of USSR except northern regions. Winters in Africa and southern Asia.

Similar species: Differs from other swallows by its rusty brown throat, blackish breast band.

426. RED-RUMPED SWALLOW
Hirundo daurica
(Ryzhepoyasnichnaya Lastochka)
Plate 28, Map 176

Field marks: 18-20 cm. Top of head, back, wings, and tail blue-black; nape and upper tail coverts rusty red; underparts ocherish with narrow brownish streaks. Has long, forked tail.

Habits: Found in steep river valleys, hills, villages, and towns. Nests in cliffs, precipices, or walls and under eaves of houses. Migratory. Common. Flocks during flight or while perched on wires, cliff ledges, or dead tree branches, etc. The clay nest is fastened to a wall and is in the shape of a bottle with one or several entrances. Lays five or six white eggs in May or June. Call: quiet chirping. Song: chirping and sounds reminiscent of a cat's meowing.

Range and distribution: Central Asia, Altai, Tuva, Transbaikal, Amur River region, Soviet Far East. Winters in southern Asia.

Similar species: Differs from other swallows by rusty rump and narrow streakings on underparts.

427. WIRE-TAILED SWALLOW
Hirundo smithii
(Nitekhvostaya Lastochka)
Plate 28, Map 177

Field marks: 22-26 cm. Top of head rusty; back, wings, and tail blue-black; underparts pure white. Outer tail feathers very long and narrow, even threadlike.

Habits: Found in steep river valleys and inhabited areas. Migratory. Uncommon. Stays in pairs and flocks. Nests on cliff walls, in caves, under bridges, more rarely on walls of buildings—but usually in the vicinity of water. Nest is in the form of a cup or bowl. Lays three or four white eggs speckled reddish-brown from June to July. Call: quiet chirping.

Range and distribution: Central Asia. Winters in southern Asia.

Similar species: Differs from other swallows by its rusty cap, white underparts, and long, wirelike outer tail feathers.

Delichon

428. NORTHERN HOUSE MARTIN
Delichon urbica
(Gorodskaya Lastochka)
Plate 28, Map 177

Field marks: 13-15 cm. Top of head, back, wings, and tail blue-black; rump and entire underparts white. Sharply forked tail.

Habits: Lives in hilly and inhabited areas. Nests on walls of cliffs and on buildings. Migratory. Common, sometimes numerous. Stays in flocks

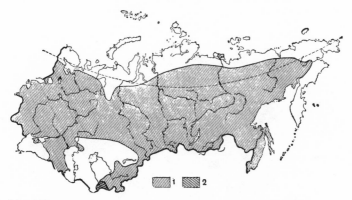

MAP 177. Northern House Martin (1), Wire-tailed Swallow (2)

in flight or perched on wires; sits on ground more often than other swallows. Colonial nester. Globular clay nest has a side entrance. Lays four to six white eggs in May or June. Call: a ringing "teerch-teerch."

Range and distribution: Larger part of the USSR except northern regions, deserts of Central Asia and Kazakhstan, and Kamchatka Peninsula. Winters in Africa and southern Asia.

Similar species: Differs from other swallows by its white rump.

Riparia

429. SAND MARTIN
Riparia riparia
(Beregovushka)
Plate 28, Map 178

Field marks: 12-14 cm. Top of head, neck, back, wings, tail, and band across breast are grayish-brown. Throat, breast, and belly white. Tail is slightly forked.

Habits: Inhabits river valleys, where it nests in clay or sand banks. Migratory. Common, sometimes numerous. Stays in flocks; nests in colonies. Builds nest in burrows along river banks. Lays four to six white eggs from May to July. Call: a dry "chirr-chirr."

Range and distribution: Larger part of USSR except northern border areas. Winters in south of Africa and Asia.

Similar species: Differs from Plain Martin by distinct brownish band across the breast.

430. PLAIN MARTIN
Riparia paludicola
(Malaya Lastochka)
Not illustrated, Map 178

Field marks: 13 cm. Resembles Sand Martin, but somewhat smaller and paler; lacks breast band; tail only slightly forked.

MAP 178. Sand Martin (1), Crag Martin (2), Plain Martin (3)

MAP 179. Richard's Pipit (1), Tawny Pipit (2)

Habits: Found in river valleys with steep banks of clay or sand. Migratory. Fairly rare. Stays in flocks; nests in colonies together with Sand Martins. Nest is a burrow along steep embankments. Lays two to four white eggs in May or June. Call: quiet twittering.
Range and distribution: Central Asia. Winters in southern Asia.
Similar species: Differs from the Sand Martin by its lack of a breast band.

Ptyonoprogne

431. CRAG MARTIN
Ptyonoprogne rupestris
(Skalistaya Lastochka)
Plate 28, Map 178
Field marks: 14-15 cm. Overall coloring brownish-gray; lighter underparts; white spots on the narrowly forked tail.

Habits: Found in unforested mountain ravines. Usually migrates. Stays in flocks. Flight slower than other swallows. Nests on walls of cliffs, where it builds an open nest of clay. Lays three or four brown-speckled white eggs from May to July. Call: quiet chirping.
Range and distribution: Caucasus, mountains of Central Asia and Altai. Winters on Arabian Peninsula and in East Africa.
Similar species: Differs from other swallows by its brownish underparts and white spots on tail.

[The **432.** CLIFF SWALLOW (*Petrochelidon albifrons*) with blackish upperparts, buffy forehead, and whitish belly; rufous throat and upper tail coverts; and the **433.** TREE SWALLOW (*Iridoprocne bicolor*) with bluish-green upperparts and white underparts, were both collected on Wrangel Island, but are rare vagrants.]

MAP 180. Tree Pipit (1), Olive-backed Pipit (2)

Anthus

Small, rather long-legged, sparrow-size bird. Thin, awl-shaped or straight bill. Tail does not exceed the length of the body; when on the ground, the bird constantly wags it. Feeds on insects.

434. RICHARD'S PIPIT
Anthus richardi
(Stepnoy Konyok)
Plate 30, Map 179

Field marks: 18 cm. Largest of the pipits. Upperparts rusty brown with dark streaking; underparts and outer tail feathers white; throat and breast suffused with ocher, with the breast sparsely brownish-streaked; eye stripe whitish.

Habits: Found in open steppe and expanses of meadow. Common. Found singly, in pairs and, when migrating, in flocks on the ground. Nest is built in a depression and is usually hidden by a clump of grass. Lays four to six grayish-white eggs with fine olive-chocolate speckling in May and June. Sings while flying in a high circular flight pattern. Call: a loud "rreep" and short "peet." Song: a monotonous "tree-ee-aya-eeya, tree-eeya-eeya-eeya-eeya."

Range and distribution: Southern Siberia, Transbaikal, Soviet Far East. Winters in southern Asia.

Similar species: Differs from other pipits by its larger size.

435. TAWNY PIPIT
Anthus campestris
(Polevoy Konyok)
Plate 30, Map 179

Field marks: 16 cm. Very similar to Richard's Pipit, but somewhat smaller and grayer, with underparts ocher-whitish with rufous overtones on breast and sides; white outer tail feathers. Immature has streaked breast.

Habits: Found in dry open country and hills; sometimes found in forest meadows and forest edges. Common. Occurs singly and in pairs; in flocks while migrating. Nests in depression on the ground. Lays four to six whitish, greenish, or reddish eggs with dark spots from May to July. Sings on the ground and from the topmost branches of bushes. Call: short "tvee" or "tsiriyoi." Song: a short trill.

Range and distribution: Western and southern part of European USSR, Caucasus, Central Asia, Kazakhstan, southern Siberia. Winters in Africa and southwestern Asia.

Similar species: Differs from Richard's Pipit by its grayer upperparts and smaller size.

Note: Populations that nest in Tuva and Trans-baikal are currently considered by many to be Godlewski's Pipit (*Anthus godlewskii*).

436. TREE PIPIT
Anthus trivialis
(Lesnoy Konyok)
Plate 30, Map 180

Field marks: 15 cm. Small pipit. Upperparts olive-gray with rufous streakings on head and back; belly and outer tail feathers white; sides and breast streaked with blackish-brown. Rear claw relatively short and curved.

Habits: Found along the edges of forests and rarely in plains. Often numerous. Stays on the ground and in trees, singly or in pairs; flocks during migration. Nests in depression on the ground. Lays four to six grayish, greenish, or rusty eggs with small dark spots from May to July. Sings perched on the top of a tree or bush; flies into the air while singing, then, after turning, once again perches in a tree or on the ground. Call: short "tseet-tseet." Song: a loud "seep-seep-seep-sia-sia-sia."

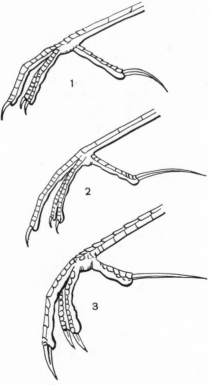

Fig. 62 Feet of 1) Tree Pipit, 2) Meadow Pipit, and 3) Northern Skylark

Range and distribution: European USSR, Caucasus, southern part of West Siberia, mountains of Central Asia. Winters in south of Europe, Africa, and southwestern Asia.

Similar species: In the field, practically indistinguishable from the Meadow, Olive-backed, or Petchora Pipit. In the hand, can be seen to differ from Meadow and Petchora Pipit by the short curved claw of the hind toe. Differs from Olive-backed Pipit by its brownish (not greenish) upperparts.

437. OLIVE-BACKED PIPIT
Anthus hodgsoni
(Pyatnisty Konyok)
Plate 30, Map 180

Field marks: 14 cm. Resembles Tree Pipit, but upperpart of body is greenish-olive.

Habits: Inhabits woods in plains and hills, often along river banks, in bogs, and in mountainous tundra. Common. Feeds and nests on the ground. Lays four or five eggs, light violet or grayish with dark spots in June and July. Song and call: similar to Tree Pipit, but more ringing.

Range and distribution: Siberia except northern parts, Transbaikal, Soviet Far East. Winters in southern Asia.

Similar species: In the field, practically indistinguishable from the Tree Pipit, Meadow Pipit, and Petchora Pipit. Can be distinguished in the hand from Meadow Pipit and Petchora Pipit by the short rear claw, and from Tree Pipit by its olive-green upperparts.

438. PETCHORA PIPIT
Anthus gustavi
(Sibirsky Konyok)
Plate 30, Map 181

Field marks: 16 cm. Resembles Tree Pipit, but has black-brownish upperparts with two whitish streaks down back. Claw of rear toe is long, slightly curved.

Habits: Inhabits brushy tundra and remote taiga swamps. Uncommon. Usually found on the ground, singly and in pairs, but also perches in trees and shrubs. Nests on the ground. Lays four to six greenish eggs with dark spots in June or July. Sings while ascending.

Range and distribution: Northern Siberia (except tundras), Soviet Far East. Winters in the Philippines and Indonesia.

Similar species: In the hand differs from Tree Pipit and Olive-backed Pipit by its long, slightly curved rear claw. Differs from Meadow Pipit by its coloration, which is rather dark with prominent whitish streaks on the back.

439. MEADOW PIPIT
Anthus pratensis
(Lugovoy Konyok)
Plate 30, Map 181

Field marks: 14 cm. Very similar to Tree Pipit, but rear claw is longer and less curved.

Habits: Found in damp meadows, grassy bogs, mossy and rocky tundra. Common. Stays in pairs; flocks during migration. Feeds on the ground. Nests on the ground. Lays four to six grayish, yellowish, or greenish eggs with brownish spots from April to July. Sings in flight. Call: short "peet." Song: monotonous "eet-eet-eeteeteetee."

Range and distribution: North and west of European USSR. Winters in southern Europe, southern Africa, Iran, Iraq. In the USSR, winters in the Transcaucasus and Central Asia.

Similar species: Differs from Tree Pipit and Olive-backed Pipit by longer rear claw; from Petchora Pipit by its relatively light olive-gray upper body.

MAP 181. Petchora Pipit (1), Meadow Pipit (2)

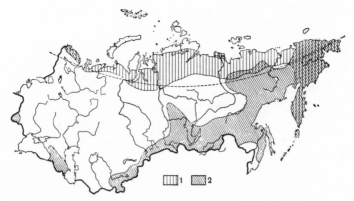

Map 182. Red-throated Pipit (1), Water Pipit (2)

440. RED-THROATED PIPIT
Anthus cervinus
(Krasnozoby Konyok)
Plate 30, Map 182
Field marks: 14 cm. One of the small pipits. Color of upperparts same as Tree Pipit. Male has rusty reddish eye stripe, sides of head, throat, and breast. Females and juveniles resemble Tree and Meadow Pipit, but have a reddish tone on throat and breast. Adult females may be more strongly marked.
Habits: Inhabits hummocky, damp tundra. Common, numerous in places. Solitary nester, but flocks during migration. Occasionally found in steppe and meadows of the central and southern belt of the USSR during migration. Builds nest in a depression in the ground, usually under a clump of grass or a bush. Lays five or six eggs, light blue or olive-gray with dark spots in June or July. Sings on the ground and in flight. Call: quiet "psaoriss." Song: several loud trills.
Range and distribution: North of European and Asian sections of USSR. Winters in Africa and southwestern Asia.
Similar species: Differs from other pipits by reddish underparts.

441. WATER PIPIT
Anthus spinoletta
(Gorny Konyok)
Plate 30, Map 182
Field marks: 16 cm. Top of head and upper tail coverts gray, back brownish-gray, wings and tail brownish, belly and outer tail feathers white, throat and breast light ocher-pinkish.
Habits: Inhabits subalpine and alpine meadows and mountain tundra. Common. Found in pairs during breeding season; in flocks during migration and winter. Feeds on the ground.

Nests on the ground under the protection of a rock or shrub. Lays four to six eggs, grayish or greenish with black spots from April to July. Sings in air and on the ground. Call: a soft "tsit-tsit." Song: loud and similar to song of the Tree Pipit.
Range and distribution: Carpathian Mountains, Caucasus, mountains of Central Asia and Siberia. Winters in south of Western Europe, southern Africa, and southern Asia. In the USSR, winters in Transcaucasus and southern Central Asia.
Similar species: Differs from other pipits by nearly total lack of streakings and the light pinkish lower body.

Dendronanthus

442. FOREST WAGTAIL
Dendronanthus indicus
(Drevesnaya Tryasoguzka)
Plate 30, Map 183
Field marks: 15 cm. Smaller than a sparrow. Length of tail equals length of body. Upper body olive-brownish; eye stripe, outer tail feathers, underparts and stripes on upper wing white; tail, wings, and two breast stripes brownish-black.
Habits: Inhabits thin, mixed, and deciduous woods, gardens, and parks. Migratory. Common. Stays singly, in pairs, and occasionally in flocks in trees. Constantly wags tail. Nest is little basket in a tree, woven of grass, thin roots, cobwebs, horsehair, and lichens. Lays five blue-gray eggs speckled brownish-rust. Voice: a rather loud "pyeu-pyeu."
Range and distribution: Amur River region of the Soviet Far East. Winters in southeastern Asia.

MAP 183. Yellow Wagtail (1), Forest Wagtail (2)

Similar species: Differs from White Wagtail by its arboreal preference, shorter tail, and broad white wing bars.

Motacilla

Small (sparrow-size) birds with a long tail that often significantly exceeds the length of the body.

443. YELLOW WAGTAIL
Motacilla flava
(Zholtaya Tryasoguzka)
Plate 30, Map 183
Field marks: 16 cm. Tail fairly long, but does not exceed the length of the body. In the male, the crown is gray or black, back olive-green, wings and tail brownish-black, outer tail feathers white, entire underparts yellow. Upperparts of female duller and underparts whitish-yellowish. Upperparts of juveniles brownish; underparts ocherish; sides of throat and band across the breast black-brownish.
Habits: Found in meadows, grassy swamps, often in brakes on plains and in hills. Common; numerous in some areas. Feeds on the ground. Often perches in shrubs and on tall grasses. On approach to the nest, it circles the intruder's head with cries of alarm or flies from bush to bush. Nest is on the ground under a hummock or clump of grass. Lays five or six grayish-white eggs with dark gray speckles in May and June.
Range and distribution: Greater part of the USSR except some regions of the far north and Sakhalin Island.
Similar species: Differs from Gray Wagtail by shorter tail and smaller size, from the Citrine Wagtail by the darker crown. Juveniles prac-

tically indistinguishable from juvenile Citrine Wagtails in the field. Differs from Yellow-backed Wagtail by its gray or black head.

444. YELLOW-BACKED WAGTAIL
Motacilla lutea
(Zheltospinnaya Tryasoguzka)
Plate 30, Map 184
Field marks: 16 cm. Tail fairly long, but does not exceed length of body. Back is greenish-yellow in male; wings and tail brownish; outer tail feathers white; head and entire underparts yellow. Female and juveniles less colorful, with brownish suffusion on back, head, and breast.
Habits: Found in damp, grassy meadows. Stays in pairs and flocks. Not numerous; common in some areas. Habits same as Yellow Wagtail. Nests on ground by hummock or clump of grass. Usually lays five light blue-grayish eggs with brownish and dark gray spots in June.
Range and distribution: Lower Volga, Kazakhstan, south of East Siberia, Sakhalin Island. Winters in East Africa, India, and southeastern Asia.
Similar species: Differs from Yellow Wagtail by its yellow or green head; from the Citrine Wagtail by its green back.

445. CITRINE WAGTAIL
Motacilla citreola
(Zheltogolovaya Tryasoguzka)
Plate 30, Map 184
Field marks: 16 cm. Tail fairly long, but does not exceed length of body. Male has gray, blackish-gray, or occasionally black back; wings and tail black with white outer tail feathers; head and underparts yellow. Females less colorful, with top of head greenish-gray. Juve-

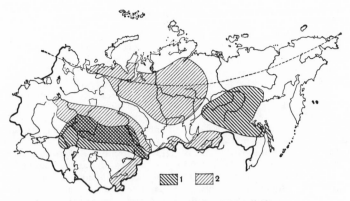

MAP 184. Yellow-backed Wagtail (1), Citrine Wagtail (2)

niles have same coloring as juvenile Yellow Wagtails.

Habits: Found in damp meadows and grassy swamps in hills and plains. Stays on the ground in pairs and flocks, often perching on grass stems and in bushes. Builds nest on ground by hummock or clump of grass. Lays four or five ocher or light blue eggs with brownish spots, April to July. Male often flies up and sings while fluttering in place. Call: a loud "tsuili." Song: several short loud chirps.

Range and distribution: Central, northeast, and southeast parts of European USSR, Kazakhstan, Central Asia, West Siberia, western regions of East Siberia, Transbaikal. Winters in southern Asia.

Similar species: Differs from Yellow Wagtail by its yellow or greenish head. Juveniles indistinguishable in field from juvenile Yellow Wagtails. Differs from Yellow-backed Wagtail by its gray or black back.

446. GRAY WAGTAIL
Motacilla cinerea
(Gornaya Tryasoguzka)
Plate 30, Map 185

Field marks: 18 cm. Tail long, exceeding length of body. Upperparts blue-gray; tail and wings brownish-black; outer tail feathers white; chin and throat black; belly whitish; remainder of underparts and upper tail coverts yellow. Throat of male is whitish in winter.

Habits: Found along banks of mountain reservoirs. Common. Stays singly and in pairs on rocks along the shore and on the ground. Occasionally perches in trees. Nests in rocky crevices, beside a rock, or on tree roots overhanging water. Lays four to six yellowish-gray eggs with dark spots from March to June. Call: loud "tsit-tsit."

Range and distributions: Caucasus, mountains of Central Asia, southern half of Siberia, Kamchatka Peninsula, Sakhalin Island, Soviet

MAP 185. Gray Wagtail (1), White Wagtail (2)

Far East. Winters in Africa, southern Asia, and New Guinea.

Similar species: Differs from Yellow Wagtail by its long tail, yellow upper tail coverts, and in the male a black throat.

447. WHITE WAGTAIL
Motacilla alba
(Belaya Tryasoguzka)
Plate 30, Map 185

Field marks: 18 cm. In adults, top of head, throat, upper breast, tail, and wings are black; back is gray or black; forehead white, as is wide band through the eye to the ear (and occasionally sides of the head); outer tail feathers, some wing feather edgings, and entire underparts white. Juveniles are gray without black markings.

Habits: Found in wetlands, shores of reservoirs, ponds, and lakes, and inhabited areas. Common, numerous in places. Stays singly and in pairs; in flocks during migration. Usually seen on the ground and on rocks, but sometimes perches in bushes and trees. Nests in hollows of dead trees, under eaves, in niches and cracks in cliffs and precipices, etc. Lays five or six eggs with gray spots, April to July. Call: a loud "tsiti-tsuri" and a short "cherlich." Song: repetition of these sounds.

Range and distribution: Greater part of USSR except some near-polar regions. Winters in Africa, southern Asia to Sri Lanka, and the Philippines.

Similar species: Differs from Forest Wagtail by its long tail, black throat and cap.

[In Sakhalin and in the Vladivostock regions, a vagrant of **448.** the JAPANESE WAGTAIL (*Motacilla grandis*) was obtained. It resembles the White Wagtail, but has a mostly black head and breast.]

Pericrocotus

449. ASHY MINIVET
Pericrocotus divaricatus
(Sery Lichinkoed)
Plate 31, Map 186

Field marks: 18 cm. Size of a sparrow. Long tail, bill slightly hooked. Upperparts gray; wings, tail black (and male has black crown and nape); underparts, forehead, and outer tail feathers white.

Habits: Found in deciduous and mixed woods and groves. Migratory. Common. Stays singly, in pairs, and in flocks in crowns of trees; often perches on dead branches. Nest in tree is in cup form, made of grass stems, cedar needles, and lichens. Lays four to five bluish-gray eggs with dark spots in May or June. Call: loud melodic trill.

Range and distribution: Amur River region and Soviet Far East. Winters in Taiwan, Philippines, and Indonesia.

Similar species: No similar species in USSR.

[A specimen of **450.** BROWN-EARED BULBUL (*Microscelis amaurotis*) was obtained in southern Sakhalin and in the Vladivostok region. It was brown with a yellow rump. **451.** The WHITE-CHEEKED BULBUL (*Pycnonotus leucogenys*), which is dark brown with white cheeks and yellow undertail coverts, was found near the Surhandaria and Pyandje Rivers.]

Lanius

Small, more rarely medium-size bird with soft, fluffy feathers. Strong, hooked bill with upper mandible notched. Tail usually acuminate, sometimes wedge-shaped. Wings fairly short

MAP 186. Great Gray Shrike (1), Ashy Minivet (2)

and rounded. Strong legs and toes with sharp curved claws. Feeds on a variety of animals: small vertebrates, insects, and other invertebrates. Characteristically impales food on thorns and sharp twigs. Usually quietly perched; when alarmed, often twitches tail from side to side. Perches on dead tree branches, bushes, or telephone wires. Taking flight, the bird drops and flies low to the ground, rising sharply to perch once again on a topmost branch. Song: an imitation of other bird calls.

452. GREAT GRAY SHRIKE

Lanius excubitor
(Sery Sorokoput)
Plate 31, Map 186

Field marks: 25-27 cm. A large shrike (somewhat larger than a starling). In adults, the top of the head, back, and rump are light ashy gray; a wide blackish stripe runs from the bill through the eye to the ear; wings and tail are black; outer tail feathers, wing patches and entire underparts white. Juveniles are brownish, with brownish vermiculations on underparts.

Habits: Found in bushes in open areas, forest edges, and forest-tundra. Partly nonmigratory and nomadic. Common. Stays singly or in pairs. Nests in tree or bush. Lays five or six whitish-greenish eggs with brownish spots from April to June. Call: a harsh "check-check."

Range and distribution: Greater part of USSR except near-polar tundra; south of European USSR, Caucasus, Kazakhstan, Kamchatka Peninsula. Winters in central and southern USSR.

Similar species: Differs from Chinese Gray Shrike by its smaller size and shorter tail. From the Lesser Gray Shrike, by its larger size and whitish forehead.

FIG. 63 Bill of 1) Shrike and 2) Thrush

453. CHINESE GRAY SHRIKE

Lanius sphenocercus
(Klinokhvosty Sorokoput)
Plate 31, Map 187

Field marks: 28 cm. Large shrike (larger than a starling). Coloring similar to Great Gray Shrike, but with large white bands on shoulders and wings. Tail long and strongly wedge-shaped, and graduated.

Habits: Found in wide river valleys, meadows, and slopes of hills with single trees and clumps of bushes. Migratory. Common. Stays singly and in pairs. Nests in trees. Lays five or six white eggs with rusty brownish spots in April to May. Call: harsh "check-cherr."

Range and distribution: Southern Soviet Far East. Winters in Korea and eastern China.

Similar species: Differs from Great Gray Shrike

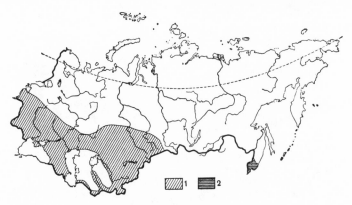

MAP 187. Lesser Gray Shrike (1), Chinese Gray Shrike (2)

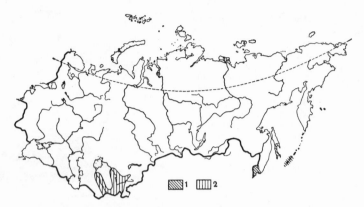

MAP 188. Bull-headed Shrike (1), Long-tailed Shrike (2)

by its longer, more strongly graduated tail and larger size.

454. LESSER GRAY SHRIKE
Lanius minor
(Chernoloby Sorokoput)
Plate 31, Map 187
Field marks: 20-23 cm. Large shrike (size of a starling). Top of head and body gray; forehead and band through the eye to the ear black; wings and tail black; wing patch, outer tail feathers, and entire underparts white; pink blush on breast and sides.
Habits: Found in open steppe areas with clumps of bushes and trees. Stays singly and in pairs. Migratory. Common. Nests in bushes or trees. Nest is often woven entirely of wormwood twigs. Lays five or six pale green eggs with brownish or violet-brownish spots in May and June. Call: harsh "chok-chok" or "chzhuck-chok."
Range and distribution: South European USSR, Caucasus, Kazakhstan, Central Asia. Winters in subequatorial Africa.
Similar species: Differs from Great Gray Shrike by its more extensive black mask and smaller size.

455. BULL-HEADED SHRIKE
Lanius bucephalus
(Yaponsky Sorokoput)
Plate 31, Map 188
Field marks: 20 cm. In male, top of head and nape rusty; back and rump gray; black mask; wings and tail brownish-black; base of primaries, eyebrow, throat, and belly white; sides rusty red. The females and juveniles are brownish, and their underparts are marked by a faint scaly pattern. Juveniles are scaly-backed as well.

Habits: Found in thickets of meadows, river valleys, gardens, and parks. Migratory. Uncommon. Stays singly and in pairs. Nests in bushes. Lays four to six greenish eggs with gray spots in April and May. Call: loud "chi-chi-tyo-tyo."
Range and distribution: Southern Soviet Far East and Sakhalin Island. Winters in eastern China and Japan.
Similar species: Differs from Brown Shrike by its rusty sides and white wing patch.

456. LONG-TAILED SHRIKE
Lanius schach
(Dlinnokhvosty Sorokoput)
Plate 31, Map 188
Field marks: 22-24 cm. Medium-sized shrike. Long graduated tail. Top of head gray; back and rump rufous; forehead, wide stripe from bill through the eye to the ear, wings, and tail are black; underparts white with an intense rusty suffusion on the sides and undertail coverts.
Habits: Found in clumps of bushes and trees

FIG. 64 Beetle Impaled on Thorn by Shrike

MAP 189. Woodchat Shrike (1), Tiger Shrike (2)

in steppe and semi-deserts; also gardens and parks. Migratory. Common. Nests on trees or bushes. Lays four to six greenish eggs with brownish spots from May to July. Call: a harsh chatter.

Range and distribution: Central Asia. Winters in southern Asia.

Similar species: Differs from Bay-backed Shrike by its longer tail and absence of white outer tail feathers; also by the absence of white patches on the wings.

457. WOODCHAT SHRIKE
Lanius senator
(Krasnogolovy Sorokoput)
Plate 31, Map 189

Field marks: 19 cm. Small shrike. Upperparts black except for reddish-brown crown and nape; black mask; forehead, underparts, wide shoulder patches and outer tail feathers white.

Habits: Found in groves, thickets, and gardens

in steppe areas. Migratory. Common. Stays singly and in pairs. Nests in bushes or trees. Lays four or five pale green eggs with dark spots in May or June. Call: rough "kresk-kresk" or "skerr-skerr."

Range and distribution: Transcaucasus. Winters in Africa and on the Arabian Peninsula.

Similar species: Differs from other shrikes by its black back and reddish-brown head.

458. TIGER SHRIKE
Lanius tigrinus
(Tigrovy Sorokoput)
Plate 31, Map 189

Field marks: 19 cm. In male, crown and nape gray; forehead and mask black; back, wings, and tail brownish-rusty with narrow dark transverse bars; underparts white. Female duller with dark barring on breast and sides. Juveniles' upperparts are rusty brown; underparts dirty white with overall barring.

MAP 190. Brown Shrike (1), Bay-backed Shrike (2)

Habits: Found in thickets, forest edges, gardens, and parks. Migratory. Uncommon. Stays singly and in pairs. Nests in trees and bushes. Lays three to six light orange eggs with dark spots in May or June. Call: a rough chatter.
Range and distribution: Southern Soviet Far East. Winters in Southeast Asia and on the Sunda Islands (Malay Archipelago).
Similar species: Differs from other shrikes by its barred back.

459. BROWN SHRIKE
Lanius cristatus
(Zhulan)
Plate 31, Map 190
Field marks: 18-20 cm. Smaller than a starling. In the males of the European and western Siberian races, the top of the head and neck are gray; the back chestnut; tail, wings, and mask black; basal half of outer tail feathers and underparts are white; breast and sides rosy. In males of Central Asian and Soviet Far Eastern races, top of head, back, wings, and tail are clay-brown of various shades; mask brownish. Upperparts of females ocher-brown; underparts whitish with dark scaly pattern.
Habits: Lives in thickets in open areas, along river valleys, forest edges, in gardens and parks. Migratory. Common. Stays singly and in pairs. Nests in bushes or trees, more rarely on the ground. Lays four to seven pinkish or whitish eggs with brownish spots in May or June. Call: a harsh "check-check" and a loud "jaya-jaya."
Range and distribution: Greater part of USSR except northern regions. Winters in Africa, Arabian Peninsula and southern Asia.
Similar species: Differs from Bull-headed Shrike by range and lack of white spot on wings.
Note: The taxonomy of the Brown Shrike (*Lan-*

ius cristatus), Red-backed Shrike (*Lanius collurio*), and Central Asian Shrike (*Lanius isabellinus-phoenicuroides*) is still insufficiently clear. Although we regard this group as one species, they are so distinctive that we have shown them individually on Plate 31.

460. BAY-BACKED SHRIKE
Lanius vittatus
(Indiysky Zhulan)
Plate 31, Map 190
Field marks: 18 cm. Gray head and rump, reddish back, graduated tail black with white outer feathers. Small white patch on black wing. Underparts whitish with rusty flanks.
Habits: Found in pistachio bushes on dry hills. Migratory. Uncommon. Stays singly and in pairs. Nests in bushes or in trees. Usually lays four whitish eggs with purple and rusty brown spots in May. Call: rough "chirr-chirr."
Range and distribution: Southern Turkmenia (Central Asia). Winters in India.
Similar species: Differs from Long-tailed Shrike, which lacks white wing patches and white outer tail feathers. Tail shorter.

[The **461.** MASKED SHRIKE *Lanius nubicus* is a vagrant (or rare visitor) to several parts of Central Asia.]

Bombycilla

462. BOHEMIAN WAXWING
Bombycilla garrulus
(Sviristel)
Plate 31, Map 191
Field marks: 18-23 cm. Size of a starling. Conspicuous crest. Thick, fluffy feathering. Pinkish-gray overall; wings black with narrow yel-

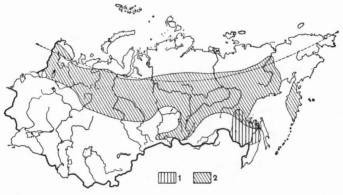

MAP 191. Japanese Waxwing (1), Bohemian Waxwing (2)

low and white marking; secondaries with waxy red tips; tail, throat, and eyeline black; undertail coverts rufous; tip of tail yellow.
Habits: Found nesting in pine and birch woods. When wandering, found in any type of woods, gardens, and parks. Nomadic. Common. In pairs during the breeding season, otherwise in flocks. Nests in trees. Lays three to seven gray-blue eggs with small black spots in May or June. Call: soft "sveereeree-sveereeree." Feeds on insects, which are often caught in flight, and berries.
Range and distribution: Northern European USSR and central regions of Siberia and Kamchatka Peninsula. Nomadic wanderer in winter south of its breeding range.
Similar species: Differs from Japanese Waxwing by yellow band at tail tip.

463. JAPANESE WAXWING
Bombycilla japonica
(Amursky Sviristel)
Plate 31, Map 191
Field marks: 17-19 cm. Resembles Bohemian Waxwing, but tail is red-tipped; wings lack yellow stripe. Undertail coverts in male are reddish, in females, brown.
Habits: Nests in deciduous and cedar taiga with thickets of Bog Whortleberry (*Vaccinium uliginosum*). In fall and winter, found in various types of woods, parks, and gardens. Nomadic. Uncommon. Stays in flocks in trees. Nesting habits not studied. Call: a silvery trill. Feeds on berries and insects.
Range and distribution: Southeastern Siberia. Winters in Japan, Taiwan, sometimes along the coast.
Similar species: Differs from Bohemian Waxwing by red-tipped tail.

464. HYPOCOLIUS
Hypocolius ampelinus
(Sviristelivy Sorokoput)
Not illustrated, Map 303
Field marks: 23 cm. Smaller than a starling, tail fairly long. Upperparts brownish-gray; underparts pinkish-gray; tail tipped with black terminal band. In adults, wing tips white. In male, wide black band extends from bill through eye to back of head.
Habits: Stays in small groups, in riparian forests. Very rare migratory bird that is not seen each year. Nests in fork of branches in bushes. Nest is massive, built of thin twigs and grasses, and is lined with bast fibers and plant fluff. Lays three to five white eggs speckled brownish-gray. Feeds on insects and berries. Voice: melodic trill. Included in the Red Data Book.
Range and distribution: Southern Turkmenia

(Tedzhen River). Winters in southwestern Asia.
Similar species: Differs from Waxwings by its lack of crest, white wing tips, long, black-tipped tail, and wide, black mask.

Cinclus

Small (starling-size) birds, chunky with a short tail; long, strong legs, short rounded wings. Thickly feathered. Bill is straight; nostrils protected by skinlike covering. Nest is a massive ball of moss and roots with a side entrance, usually located behind a waterfall, bank depression, or similar streamside location. Feeds on small invertebrates, which it catches by diving into water and running along the bottom.

465. EURASIAN DIPPER
Cinclus cinclus
(Olyapka)
Plate 40, Map 192
Field marks: 17-20 cm. Top and sides of head and neck brownish; back, tail, and rump brownish-gray; throat and breast white. In the European race the belly is rufous or brownish, in Asian races white. Juveniles are grayish-brown; underparts dirty white with grayish speckling.
Habits: Lives along banks of clear, fast-flowing streams with rocky bottoms in mountains; more rarely in valleys with permanent streams. Nonmigratory. Common. Found singly and in pairs on rocks in water and on the shore. Builds nest near water. Lays four to six white eggs in May or June. Call: a rough "dzeet-dzeet." Song: a variety of ringing trills.
Range and distribution: Karelia, Kola Peninsula, Carpathians, Caucasus, Urals, mountains of Central Asia and southwestern Siberia. Winters south of its nesting range.
Similar species: Differs from Brown Dipper by white throat and breast.

466. BROWN DIPPER
Cinclus pallasii
(Buraya Olyapka)
Plate 40, Map 192
Field marks: 21-23 cm. Resembles Eurasian Dipper but somewhat larger, and uniformly rusty or blackish-brown. Upperparts of juveniles gray-brownish; underparts whitish with brownish scales.
Habits: Found on shores of clear, fast-flowing, rocky mountain streams. Usually nonmigratory, but some may engage in short migrations. Common. Found alone and in pairs on rocks in water or on shore. Flies low over the water. Usually builds nest under cover of wa-

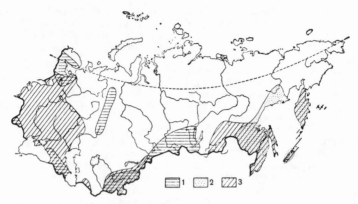

MAP 192. Eurasian Dipper (1), Brown Dipper (2), Northern Wren (3)

terfall, on a cliff wall or rock. Lays four to six white eggs from April to June. Call similar to Eurasian Dipper.

Range and distribution: Mountains of Central Asia and southeastern Siberia, Soviet Far East, Kamchatka Peninsula, Sakhalin Island. Winters in eastern China and Korea.

Similar species: Differs from Eurasian Dipper by its uniformly brownish coloring.

Troglodytes

467. NORTHERN WREN
Troglodytes troglodytes
(Krapivnik)
Plate 41, Map 192

Field marks: 9-12 cm. Very small, energetic bird with short, cocked tail. Slender, straight bill; short, rounded wings. Upperparts, wings, and tail chestnut-brown with dark barring; underparts grayish or brownish with dark barring.

Habits: Lives in thickets in a variety of habitats: in valleys and mountains. Prefers damp ravines or forest with heaps of fallen branches or trees. Nomadic and migratory. Common. Found alone or in pairs low to the ground. Very lively. Nest ball-shaped with side entrance, usually found in holes of moss-covered tree trunks, under roots, or in heaps of fallen branches. Lays four to seven white eggs with brownish-red speckles in May or June. Call: a harsh "chirr-chirr." Song: loud, ringing trills. Feeds on small invertebrates.

Range and distribution: Western part of European USSR, Caucasus, mountains of Central Asia, southeastern Siberia, Soviet Far East,

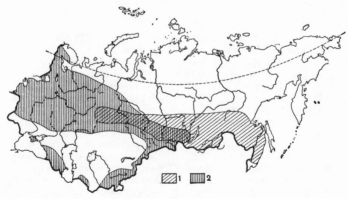

MAP 193. Scaly Thrush (1), Mistle Thrush (2)

Kamchatka Peninsula and Sakhalin Island. Winters south of its nesting range.

Similar species: Can be confused with the Stubtailed Bush Warbler where their ranges overlap in the Far East and Sakhalin; the warbler has white underparts, however, and a light buffy eye stripe, which the wren lacks.

Turdus

Birds the size of a starling or larger (rarely smaller), well proportioned, with upright stance. Feeds on small invertebrates, fruits, and berries. Usually feeds on the ground, foraging in the forest floor. Nest is cup-shaped; interior often smeared with clay or mud.

468. SCALY THRUSH
Turdus dauma
(Pyostry Drozd)
Plate 32, Map 193

Field marks: 31 cm. Largest of the thrushes. Tail fairly short. Upperparts golden-olive with wide black crescents. Underparts whitish with brownish-black crescent-shaped marks; tip of tail feathers whitish.

Habits: Found in various types of woods; particularly in taiga, along stream banks. Migratory. Fairly common. Stays well hidden on the ground, but flies up noisily and perches in tree. Flight rapid. Nest is on ground or in tree, and is made of ferns, twigs, moss, and soil. Lays four or five brick-ocher eggs with rusty spots in May or June. Call: faint "horr-horr." Song: quiet chirping and loud, sad whistle.

Range and distribution: Southern Siberia and Soviet Far East. Winters in southeastern Asia.

Similar species: Differs from other thrushes by its large size, golden upperparts, and scaly appearance; the black and white underwings are best seen in flight.

469. SIBERIAN THRUSH
Turdus sibiricus
(Sibirsky Drozd)
Plate 32, Map 194

Field marks: 20 cm. Medium-size thrush. Adult male is black and blue-gray with a wide white eye stripe and white belly. Female and juvenile upperparts are olive-brownish; underparts white with extensive brownish barring on breast and sides.

Habits: Found in various types of woods; prefers river valleys in plains and in mountains. Migratory. Uncommon. Stays hidden in trees and bushes; feeds on the ground. Nests in tree or large bush. Lays four or five pale blue eggs

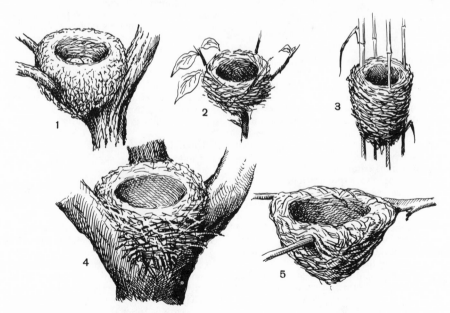

FIG. 65 PASSERINE NESTS
1. Chaffinch   2. Typical Warbler   3. Reed-Warbler   4. Song Thrush   5. European Golden Oriole

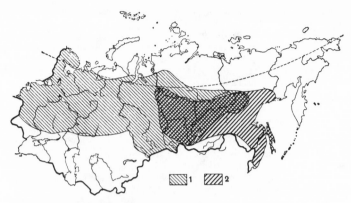

MAP 194. Fieldfare (1), Siberian Thrush (2)

with brownish spots in May or June. Male usually sings on top of tree. Call: loud "chirr." Song: disyllabic flutelike whistle and quiet chirping.

Range and distribution: Southern and southeastern Siberia, Soviet Far East. Winters in southern Asia from Hindustan to Borneo.

Similar species: No similar species in the USSR.

470. FIELDFARE
Turdus pilaris
(Ryabinnik)
Plate 32, Map 194

Field marks: 25-28 cm. Large thrush. Top of head, neck, and rump light blue-gray; back chestnut brown, wings and tail blackish-brown; underparts white with blackish spotting on breast and sides. Ocher suffusion on the breast.

Habits: Variety of forest types. Migratory and nomadic bird. Common. Stays in flocks; nests in colonies. Feeds in trees and on the ground. Noisy, conspicuous bird. Nest cup-shaped and made of dry grasses, twigs and mud; located in trees. Lays four to seven greenish eggs with brownish spots from May to July. Call: loud chuckle. Song: a variety of harsh noisy sounds. In spring and summer feeds on invertebrates; in fall and winter mostly on fruit and berries.

Range and distribution: European USSR, West Siberia except southern regions, East Siberia to Lake Baikal and Lena River basin. Winters in the Crimea, Caucasus, Tadzhikistan, southern Africa, southwestern Asia.

Similar species: Differs from other thrushes by its blue-gray crown and rump.

471. MISTLE THRUSH
Turdus viscivorus
(Deryaba)
Plate 32, Map 193

Field marks: 25-29 cm. Large thrush. Upperparts, wings, and tail olive-gray; underparts white with black spots; underwings white.

Habits: Found in a variety of forests in flatlands and hills. Migratory and nomadic. Common. Found in pairs during breeding season, in flocks the rest of the time. Wary. Nests in trees, usually high above the ground. Lays four or five pinkish eggs with brownish and gray spots from April to July. Call: noisy "trrrr." Song: a variety of flutelike whistles.

Range and distribution: European part of USSR except north; Crimea, Caucasus, mountains of Central Asia, southern Siberia to the east as far as Lake Baikal. Winters in Africa, southwestern Asia, Asia Minor.

Similar species: Differs from Song Thrush by its larger size, white spots on tail, and white underwing, seen in flight. The Fieldfare also lacks the wing stripe, spotted underparts, and monochromatic gray upperparts.

472. SONG THRUSH
Turdus philomelos
(Pevchy Drozd)
Plate 32, Map 195

Field marks: 23-24 cm. Small thrush. Upperparts olive-gray, underparts whitish with black spots. Breast and underwing buffy.

Habits: Found in a variety of woods in flatlands and hills. Migratory. Common. Found in pairs during breeding season; the rest of the time in flocks. Nests in trees, in spruces as a rule. Inside of nest lined with a gluelike material from rotten wood mixed with the bird's saliva. Usually lays five light blue eggs with black spots from April to June. Male sings in trees while perched. Call: harsh "tyek-tyek" or "tseeu." Song: ringing "spiridon-spiridon-chaipeet-chaipeet-veetu-veetu."

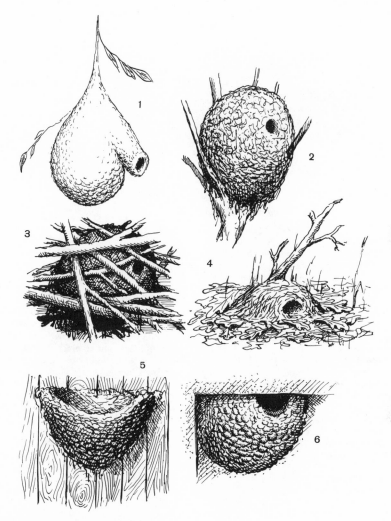

FIG. 66 PASSERINE NESTS
1. Eurasian Penduline-Tit 2. Long-tailed Tit 3. Northern Wren 4. Leaf-warbler 5. Barn Swallow 6. Northern House-Martin

Range and distribution: European USSR, Caucasus, Siberia bordered by Lake Baikal on the east (except the north). Winters in the Crimea and Transcaucasus. Outside the USSR, in southern Europe, southern Africa, Iran.
Similar species: Differs from Mistle Thrush by its smaller size and buffy underwing coverts (best seen in flight). From the Red-winged Thrush by its buffy, not reddish, underwings.

473. RED-WINGED THRUSH
Turdus musicus
(Belobrovik)
Plate 32, Map 195
Field marks: 21 cm. Resembles Song Thrush, except for creamy white eye stripe; sides and underwings rusty red.
Habits: Found in variety of woods and thickets along river valleys. Migratory. Common. Stays

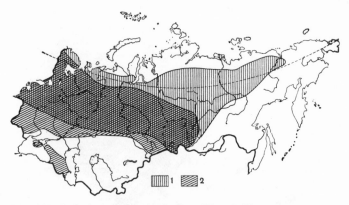

Map 195. Red-winged Thrush (1), Song Thrush (2)

in pairs during nesting season; in flocks in trees, bushes, and on the ground the remainder of the time. When singing, perches in the tops of trees. Builds nest in trees, stumps, bushes, or on the ground. Lays five or six light bluish-green eggs with reddish-brown spots in May or June. Call: raucous "tse-tek-tek." Song: a variety of clacking sounds and loud whistles, "ee-tew-tew-tew."

Range and distribution: Northern half of European USSR, western Siberia, central region of East Siberia to the Kolyma River in the east. Winters in the Crimea, Transcaucasus, Turkmenia. Outside the USSR, winters in southern Europe, North Africa, southeastern Asia.

Similar species: Differs from Song Thrush by its light eye stripe; rusty sides; and reddish, not buffy, underwing.

474. NAUMANN'S THRUSH
Turdus naumanni
(Drozd Naumanna)
Plate 32, Map 196

Field marks: 23 cm. Medium-sized thrush. There are two races that are strikingly dissimilar: the northern race (*T. n. eunomus*) is dark, with the top of the head, back, rump, tail, and sides of head mottled blackish; the underparts are white with a broken black band across breast and black mottled sides; wings are rusty brown. In the southern race (*T. n. naumanni*) there is no black at all. Eye stripe, chin, throat, and belly are whitish. Upperparts are brownish-gray; upper breast, sides, tail and undertail coverts rusty red.

Habits: Found in various types of woods and thickets. Migratory and common. Stays in pairs

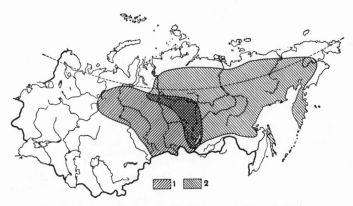

Map 196. Dark-throated Thrush (1), Naumann's Thrush (2)

during nesting period; otherwise, found in flocks. Feeds on the ground. Builds nest on horizontal tree branch, on a stump, on the ground, sometimes in a hedge, more rarely on a cliff. Interior of nest lined with clay. Lays four to six light bluish-green eggs with brownish spots in May or June. Male perches in tree, immobile, while singing. Call: harsh "chak-chak," "tsepit-chak-chak," or "kvevetch." Song: a variety of beautiful whistles.

Range and distribution: Siberia (except northern borders and Transbaikal). Winters in eastern Asia.

Similar species: Nominate race (*T. n. naumanni*) differs from the red-throated race of the Dark-throated Thrush by having light eye line and more extensive rusty coloration on the breast and flanks.

Note: Many ornithologists are currently inclined to consider the northern (dark) and southern (light) races as separate species.

475. DARK-THROATED THRUSH
Turdus ruficollis
(Temnozoby Drozd)
Plate 32, Map 196

Field marks: 23-25 cm. Medium-sized thrush. Two dissimilar races. In *T. r. atrogularis*, the male has top of head, back, wings, and middle tail feathers olive-gray; remainder of tail brownish; sides of head, chin, throat, and upper breast black; lower breast and belly white. The male *T. r. ruficollis* has olive-gray upperparts, but with a reddish breast, rufous eye stripe and tail. Both races have rusty underwings. Females and juveniles are less distinctive, with grayish upperparts, off-white underparts with broken breast band.

Habits: Inhabits various types of woods and thickets in plains and hills. Migratory. Common. Found in pairs during nesting; otherwise in flocks in trees and bushes. Nest in trees low to the ground. Lays four to seven pale blue eggs with brownish spots in May and June. Call: harsh "chak-chak." Song: a selection of loud noises.

Range and distribution: Northeastern European USSR, West Siberia east to Lake Baikal. Winters in the Altai region, in the south of West Siberia, Transcaucasus, Central Asia. Outside the USSR, to Iraq and Burma.

Similar species: Red-throated race differs from Naumann's Thrush (*T. n. naumanni*) by less extensive red breast, white sides and belly, and rufous eyebrow.

476. GRAY-BACKED THRUSH
Turdus hortulorum
(Sizy Drozd)
Plate 32, Map 197

Field marks: 25 cm. Medium-sized thrush. Head, back, wings, and tail dark gray; throat whitish; sides rusty; belly white.

Habits: Found in flood-plain thickets, thin oak woods, and pine-hornbeam forests. Migratory. Common. Feeds on the ground. Nest is situated in bush or tree, and is made from soil and dry grass. Usually lays five light green eggs with rusty spots in May or June. Sings from the tops of trees. Call: harsh "chak-chak." Song: several loud whistles.

Range and distribution: Southeastern Siberia, Soviet Far East. Winters in southeastern China.

Similar species: Differs from Pale Thrush by gray head and upperparts.

MAP 197. Pale Thrush (1), Gray-backed Thrush (2)

477. PALE THRUSH
Turdus pallidus
(Bledny Drozd)
Plate 32, Map 197

Field marks: 22 cm. Resembles Gray-backed Thrush, but back is olive-brown; sides and breast paler, sometimes almost gray.

Habits: Found in pine and deciduous forest and thickets. Migratory. Common. Found in pairs during nesting season; otherwise in flocks in trees, bushes, and on the ground. Nest is made of grass and soil and is built in tree or bush. Lays four to six greenish eggs with reddish-brown spots in May and June. Call: loud "tsee" and a dry cracking noise. Song: loud monotonous whistle, "tuvee-tulee, tulee-tuvee."

Range and distribution: Southern half of eastern Siberia, Soviet Far East, Sakhalin Island, Kamchatka Peninsula. Winters in Japan and eastern China.

Similar species: Differs from Gray-backed Thrush by its rufous back and pale coloring of the sides.

Note: The Eyebrowed Thrush (*T. p. obscurus*) and Red-bellied Thrush (*T. p. chrysolaus*) are usually considered to be species separate from *Turdus pallidus*.

478. RING THRUSH
Turdus torquatus
(Belozoby Drozd)
Plate 33, Map 198

Field marks: 24 cm. Medium-sized thrush. Male blackish, lightly scaled with white; large white crescent on breast. Wing feathers have whitish edges, so that wings appear pale when bird is in flight. Female brownish-gray with buffy crescent on breast. Juveniles gray-brownish with lighter wings; spotted breast.

Habits: Inhabits mountain thickets and upper regions of forest belt. Migratory. Common. Stays in pairs. When migrating, stays in flocks on cliffs, rocks, in bushes, and on the ground. Builds nest on ground near a rock, in a tree or bush. Lays four or five light bluish-green eggs with rusty spots in May and June. Call: harsh "trek-chek-chek" or "tseee." Song: a variety of beautiful whistles.

Range and distribution: Carpathian Mountains, Caucasus, Turkmenia. Winters in mountains bordering Mediterranean Sea and in northwestern Africa.

Similar species: Distinguished easily from the Eurasian Blackbird even at a distance by its light-colored wings and white breast.

479. EURASIAN BLACKBIRD
Turdus merula
(Chyorny Drozd)
Plate 33, Map 198

Field marks: 25-27 cm. Medium-sized thrush. Male entirely black. Bill and eyelids orange. Females and juveniles brownish-gray with a dark beak.

Habits: Found in various types of woods, primarily deciduous and mixed; overgrown thickets; gardens and parks. Migratory but permanent resident in the south. Common. Stays singly and in pairs; more rarely in small flocks on the ground, in bushes and trees. When hopping, often flicks its tail. Nests on the ground, in a bush, or on horizontal tree branches low over the ground. Lays four to seven light bluish-green eggs with rusty-brown spots from April to July. When singing, male usually perches at the top of a tree. Call: harsh "chak-chak" or "terre-chok-chok." Song: a variety of sad, flutelike whistles.

Range and distribution: West and central Eu-

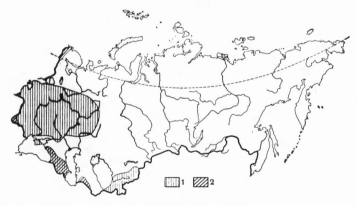

MAP 198. Eurasian Blackbird (1), Ring Thrush (2)

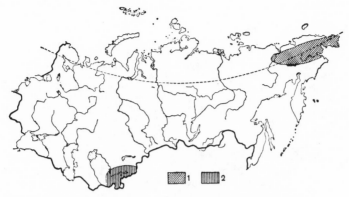

MAP 199. Gray-cheeked Thrush (1), Blue Whistling-Thrush (2)

ropean USSR, Caucasus, mountains of Central Asia. Winters in Central Asia and Transcaucasus.

Similar species: Differs from Ring Thrush by its blackish wings and lack of white on the breast.

Catharus

480. GRAY-CHEEKED THRUSH
Catharus minimus
(Maly Drozd)
Plate 32, Map 199

Field marks: 19 cm. Small thrush (significantly smaller than a starling). Upperparts olive-gray; underparts white with blackish spots on the throat and breast.

Habits: Found in forest tundra and in the upper boundaries of taiga in mountain regions. Nests in bushes or low in a tree. Lays 5-6 greenish-light-blue eggs with red or yellow-brownish spots; in June. Male sings while perched in top of tree. Call: harsh "drzhee" and loud "tsokh." Song: rolling buzzy notes dropping down the scale.

Range and distribution: Chukotski Peninsula, west to the Kolyma River. Migrates through North America to South American wintering grounds.

Similar species: Differs from other Palearctic thrushes by its small size.

[On Sakhalin and Moneron Islands, vagrants of **481.** GRAY THRUSH (*Turdus cardis*) have been seen. Males are slate-gray or black, with a black-spotted white belly and a yellow bill and eye ring. The upperparts of the female are olive-brownish, and the throat, breast, and sides are rusty red with blackish streaks and spots. In Kharkov Oblast, a **482.** SWAINSON'S THRUSH (*Catharus ustulatus*) from North America was obtained. It closely resembles the Gray-cheeked Thrush, but has a buffy eye ring.]

Myophonus

483. BLUE WHISTLING-THRUSH
Myophonus caeruleus
(Sinaya Ptitsa)
Plate 33, Map 199

Field marks: 33 cm. Size of a jackdaw. Tail long; wings short and rounded. Black-blue with silver-violet suffusion on back, head, and breast; wings and tail dark blue. From a distance, appears to be black.

Habits: Found in mountains. Inhabits mountain crevices near streams and waterfalls. Nonmigratory, occasionally nomadic. Common. Stays singly and in pairs on cliffs and rocks; more rarely in bushes and trees. When perched, raises and lowers tail, also moves it side to side. Nest is made of moss, grasses, roots, and soil, and is situated in cliff over water. Lays four or five pale green or pinkish eggs with faint dark speckles in May and June. Call: harsh "dzhee." Song: a variety of loud, beautiful whistles.

Range and distribution: Mountains of Central Asia.

Similar species: Differs from other thrushes by its large size and bluish color.

Monticola

Bright colors; fairly short-tailed, and the size of a starling.

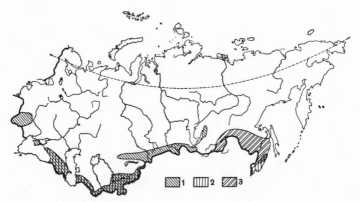

MAP 200. White-backed Rock-Thrush (1), Blue Rock-Thrush (2),
White-throated Rock-Thrush (3)

484. WHITE-BACKED ROCK-THRUSH
Monticola saxatilis
(Pyostry Kamenny Drozd)
Plate 33, Map 200
Field marks: 18-19 cm. In male, head and neck
blue-gray; back and wings brownish-black;
lower back and rump white; breast, belly, and
tail rusty red. Females and juveniles rusty gray
with brownish mottling.
Habits: Found in hilly steppe. Inhabits dry,
rocky mountain slopes with sparse vegetation.
Migratory. Common. Stays singly and in pairs
on rocks and cliffs. Often bobs and flicks its
tail. Builds nest between rocks or in crevices
of cliff walls. Lays four to six greenish-blue
eggs in May and June. Call: harsh "chek-chek"
and a whistle, "feweet." Song: a variety of trills,
whistles, and imitations of other bird calls. Male
occasionally flies into air while singing.
Range and distribution: Carpathians, Crimea,
Caucasus, mountains of Central Asia, Altai,
Sayan, Transbaikal. Winters in Africa and
southern Asia.
Similar species: Female differs from female
Blue Rock-Thrush by its reddish tail.

485. BLUE ROCK-THRUSH
Monticola solitarius
(Siny Kamenny Drozd)
Plate 33, Map 200
Field marks: 19-22 cm. Male uniformly gray-
blue; wings and tail brownish-black. Females
and juveniles brownish-gray with light barring
and a bluish suffusion on the back; males of
the far eastern race have reddish-brown bel-
lies.
Habits: Found in dry hilly steppe and in cliffs

near the shores of the Sea of Japan. Migratory. Common. Found singly and in pairs on
cliffs, rocks, and on the ground. Nests between rocks or in crevices of a cliff. Lays four
to six light blue-greenish eggs, sometimes with
brownish-red speckles in May and June. Male
sometimes flies up while singing. Call: harsh
"chek-chek." Song: loud, melodic, with beautiful whistles and imitations of other bird calls.
Range and distribution: Caucasus, mountains
of Central Asia, Soviet Far East. Winters in
Africa and southern Asia.
Similar species: Female differs from female of
the White-backed Rock-Thrush by its uniform
dark-brownish coloring and lack of reddish
tail.

486. WHITE-THROATED ROCK-THRUSH
Monticola gularis
(Lesnoy Kamenny Drozd)
Plate 33, Map 200
Field marks: 15 cm. In male, top of head is
light blue; back, sides of head, wings, and tail
are brownish-black; rump and underparts rusty
brown; throat and patch on wings white. In
females and juveniles, wings and tail are
brownish-gray; there is dark scaly mottling on
the back; top of head is gray; throat white;
underparts whitish with dark brownish barring.
Habits: Found in mixed and pine forests on
mountainsides. Migratory. Uncommon. Occurs singly and in pairs. Nest is built on the
ground, in a fallen tree or a stump. Lays five
to seven white eggs with rusty brown speckles
in May and June. Song is a variety of beautiful
whistles.
Range and distribution: Amur River region,

MAP 201. Northern Wheatear (1), Desert Wheatear (2)

Soviet Far East. Winters in southeastern China. **Similar species:** No similar species in the USSR.

Oenanthe

Size of a sparrow. Long-legged. When perched, often bobs and moves tail up and down. Most species are migratory. Feeds on insects and other small invertebrates.

487. NORTHERN WHEATEAR
Oenanthe oenanthe
(Obyknovennaya Kamenka)
Plate 34, Map 201
Field marks: 14 cm. In spring and summer, male has ash-gray back and top of head; black eye line and cheeks; black wings and tail; base of outer tail feathers, rump, and entire underparts white. Females and juveniles, and males in autumn, have ocher-brownish upperparts with rusty throat and breast, and white rump and belly.
Habits: Found in open, usually dry, areas in plains and hills. Occurs singly and in pairs. Nests in a rodent burrow, cliff crevice, between rocks or stacks of wood. Lays four to seven pale blue eggs in May and June. Call: loud "chek-chek." Song: a selection of different sounds and imitations of other bird songs. Male sings during ascent and continues while hovering.
Range and distribution: All territories of the USSR except northern borders, Kamchatka Peninsula, and Soviet Far East. Winters in southwestern Asia and equatorial Africa.
Similar species: Male differs from other wheatears by its gray back. Females and juveniles differ from other female wheatears by small

but detectable differences, except for the Isabelline Wheatear, which it closely resembles.

488. DESERT WHEATEAR
Oenanthe deserti
(Pustynnaya Kamenka)
Plate 34, Map 201
Field marks: 14 cm. In male, top of head and back are ocher-grayish; throat, sides of head, and sides of neck, wings, and tail black; underparts whitish; rump and upper tail coverts are white. Females and juveniles are pale brown above and whitish below; wings and tail are a dark brownish.
Habits: Found in deserts, rocky and sandy areas in plains and hills. Common. Occurs alone or in pairs on the ground and on rocks. Nests in a burrow, or between roots of saxal tree and rocks. Lays four to six light blue eggs from April to June. Call: harsh "chek, chek." Song consists of imitations of other birds.
Range and distribution: Transcaucasus, Central Asia, southern Kazakhstan, Altai, Tuva. Winters in Africa and in southern Iran.
Similar species: Males differ from other wheatears by the all-black tail. Females and juveniles greatly resemble females of other wheatears, differing by their lighter overall coloring and all-dark tail.

489. BLACK-EARED WHEATEAR
Oenanthe hispanica
(Pleshanka)
Plate 34, Map 202
Field marks: 14-15 cm. Males have two color phases. In the pale form, the lores, cheeks, wings, middle and tip of tail are black, whereas the other has a black throat in addition to the above. In both forms, the remainder of the

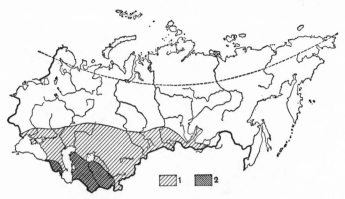

MAP 202. Black-eared Wheatear (1), Finsch's Wheatear (2)

plumage is sandy buff with lighter underparts and a white rump. Females and juveniles have the back and top of the head brownish-gray, white rump, and the same tail pattern as the male; underparts ocherish.

Habits: Found in dry, rocky steppe in plains and hills. Common. Found singly and in pairs. Nests in cliff crevices or between rocks. Lays four to six pale blue eggs with reddish-brown speckles in May and June. Call: loud "chek-chek." Song: a variety of calls and songs imitating other birds.

Range and distribution: South of European USSR, Caucasus, Central Asia, Kazakhstan, southern Siberia. Winters on Arabian Peninsula and in Africa.

Similar species: In the field, male similar to Finsch's Wheatear but lacking white in wing. Asian races characterized by a black back. In Caucasus races, the black on the sides of the throat is not connected to the wings. Females and juveniles often resemble females of other wheatears, but differ by a blackish tail.

Note: Many ornithologists consider the Caucasus race, Black-eared Wheatear (*Oenanthe hispanica*), and the European-Asian race, Pied Wheatear (*Oenanthe pleschanka*), to be individual species.

490. FINSCH'S WHEATEAR
Oenanthe lugens
(Chernosheynaya Kamenka)
Plate 34, Map 202

Field marks: 16-17 cm. Male has black throat, upper breast, sides of the head and neck, wings, central tail feathers, and end of tail. Upperparts pale gray and underparts whitish. In females and juveniles, upperparts are grayish-brown; wings brownish; throat and upper breast blackish-gray; belly, rump, and upper tail coverts white.

Habits: Found in clay sands, rocky steppe, dry rocky gorges in low mountains. Winters to some extent within breeding grounds. Uncommon. Nests in a burrow. Lays four to six light blue eggs in May and June. Call: harsh "chek-chek." Song: imitations of other birds' songs and calls.

Range and distribution: Caucasus and Central Asia. Winters in Transcaucasus and Turkmenia, and in East Africa.

Similar species: Male differs from males of Variable Wheatear by its pale back; from the Caucasian races by the black stripe from the neck to the wing. Females and juveniles differ from other female wheatears by the blackish-gray throat and upper breast.

491. ISABELLINE WHEATEAR
Oenanthe isabellina
(Kamenka-plyasunya)
Plate 34, Map 203

Field marks: 16-18 cm. Brownish-gray with ocher tones; wings brownish; rump and upper tail coverts white; tail black with base of outer tail feathers white.

Habits: Found in dry, open areas in plains and hills. Common. Occurs singly and in pairs. Nests in burrow, in crevice of a cliff, or between rocks. Lays four to six light blue eggs from March to June. Call: loud "chek-chek." Song: imitations of a variety of other bird songs and calls.

Range and distribution: South of European USSR, Caucasus, Central Asia, Kazakhstan, southern Siberia. Winters in northeastern Africa and India.

Similar species: Resembles females of the

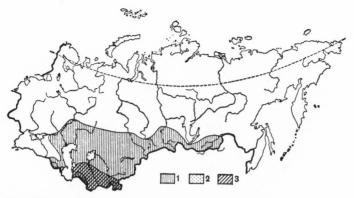

MAP 203. Isabelline Wheatear (1), Red-tailed Wheatear (2),
Variable Wheatear (3)

Northern Wheatear and other wheatears, but duller.

492. RED-TAILED WHEATEAR
Oenanthe xanthoprymna
(Zlatoguzaya Kamenka)
Plate 34, Map 203

Field marks: 16-18 cm. Brownish overall; throat and upper breast whitish; wings brownish; rump and base of tail rusty, remainder of tail black. Male and female have same general coloration.

Habits: Found on bare, rocky mountain slopes. Somewhat rare. Occurs singly and in pairs. Nests in crevices of cliffs or between rocks. Lays four or five white eggs with occasional brownish-red speckles from March to June. Call: loud "chek-chek." Song: imitations of calls and sounds of other birds.

Range and distribution: Transcaucasus, Turkmenia, Tadzhikistan. Winters in Egypt and southwestern Asia.

Similar species: Differs from other wheatears by its rusty rump and basal half of tail.

493. VARIABLE WHEATEAR
Oenanthe picata
(Chyornaya Kamenka)
Plate 34, Map 203

Field marks: 15 cm. In male, undertail coverts, rump, and basal two-thirds of outer tail feathers are white (sometimes breast, belly, and top of head are white); remainder is black. Females and juveniles are brownish.

Habits: Found in rocky hillocks in desert areas as well as in low mountains with sparse vegetation. Common. Migratory; settled in southern ranges. Occurs singly and in pairs. Nests

in cliff crevices, piles of rocks, and burrows. Lays four to seven pale blue eggs with reddish-brownish speckles from March to June. Call: loud "chek-chek." Song: imitates various sounds of other birds.

Range and distribution: Mountains of Central Asia. Winters in India and Iran.

Similar species: Differs from males of other wheatears by its black head; from the Pied Bushchat by its larger size and white in tail. Females differ from female of other wheatears by the dark brownish coloring.

Saxicola

Very small (smaller than a sparrow), long-legged, and relatively short-tailed. Head seems large. Feeds on insects, finding them on the ground or catching them in midair. Usually seen perched upright in high grass, prominent bush branches, telephone wires, and the like. Alarmed, it gives a loud call, "tooee-chek-chek," and bobs its tail. All species are migratory.

494. WHINCHAT
Saxicola rubetra
(Lugovoy Chekan)
Plate 34, Map 204

Field marks: 12-15 cm. Upperparts brownish, streaked with dark brown; dark brownish ear patch; wings and tail brownish; wide stripes on the shoulder, eyebrow, and belly are white; throat and breast ocher-rusty. Female duller than male. Juveniles ocher-brownish with lighter mottling.

Habits: Found in meadows in clumps of bushes. Common. Occurs singly and in pairs. Nests

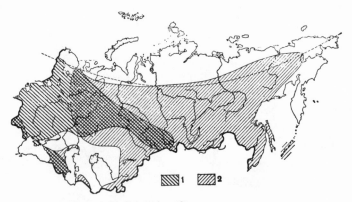

MAP 204. Whinchat (1), Stonechat (2)

on the ground. Lays five or six greenish-blue eggs with rusty spots in May or June. Song: short twittering trill.

Range and distribution: European USSR, Caucasus, central regions of West Siberia. Winters in Africa.

Similar species: Differs from Stonechat by its light eye stripe and throat.

495. STONECHAT
Saxicola torquata
(Chernogolovy Chekan)
Plate 34, Map 204

Field marks: 12-13 cm. In the male, head, throat, back, wings, and tail are black; breast rusty red; belly, wide stripe across the shoulder, rump, and sometimes upper tail coverts are white. In the female, the black is replaced by brownish-gray. Juveniles are brownish with lighter mottling.

Habits: Found in dry steppe, damp meadows, in plains, and in hills. Common. Occurs singly and in pairs. Nests on the ground. Lays five to eight greenish-blue eggs with rusty-red spots in May or June. Song: twittering trill.

Range and distribution: Eastern half of European USSR, Carpathians, Caucasus, mountains of Central Asia and Kazakhstan, Siberia except extreme north, and Kamchatka Peninsula. Winters in northeastern Africa and southern Asia.

Similar species: Differs from Whinchat by its black or brownish head.

496. PIED BUSHCHAT
Saxicola caprata
(Chyorny Chekan)
Plate 34, Map 205

Field marks: 12 cm. The male is all black with a white wing patch; lower belly and rump are white. Females and juveniles are brownish with rusty rump. Underparts are lighter.

MAP 205. Pied Bushchat

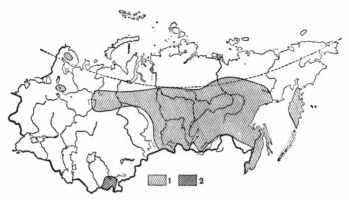

MAP 206. Orange-flanked Bush-Robin (1), White-capped
River Chat (2)

Habits: Found in damp meadows and inhabited areas, usually near water. Not numerous but common in places. Found singly and in pairs. Nests on the ground. Lays three to five greenish to light blue eggs with reddish-brown spots from April to June. Song: loud trill.
Range and distribution: Central Asia. Winters in Iran, Afghanistan, Pakistan.
Similar species: Differs from the other stonechats by dark coloration.

[**497.** HODGSON'S BUSHCHAT (*Saxicola insignis*) was found in Zaysan, and nests in southeast Altai regions, according to recent information. It resembles the stonechat but is larger; the throat is white. Included in the Red Data Book.]

Tarsiger

498. ORANGE-FLANKED BUSH-ROBIN
Tarsiger cyanurus
(Sinekhvostka)
Plate 35, Map 206
Field marks: 13-15 cm. Size of sparrow. In the adult male, the upperparts are dark blue with azure-blue eye stripe, wing coverts, and rump; wings are brownish-blue; throat and belly are white; breast grayish; sides of body rusty. Females and juveniles have brownish-gray upper parts of bluish rump and tail; underparts like male, but duller.
Habits: Found in tall forest taiga in plains and hills. Migratory. Common. Found both in trees and on the ground alone, in pairs, or in flocks. Very lively. On the ground, it makes high bouncy hops while bobbing its tail. Male sings while perched in tree, often at the very top.

Nests in a stump, on fallen trees, or on the ground. Lays five to seven white eggs with light brown crown at the rounded end in May or June. Call: a loud "fyeet-trr." Song consists of single whistles. Feeds on insects.
Range and distribution: Southern half of Siberia, Kamchatka Peninsula, Soviet Far East; isolated nester on Kola Peninsula and in north European USSR. Winters in southeastern Asia.
Similar species: No similar species in the USSR.

Chaimarrornis

499. WHITE-CAPPED RIVER CHAT
Chaimarrornis leucocephala
(Beloshapochnaya Gorikhvostka)
Plate 35, Map 206
Field marks: 17 cm. Somewhat larger than a sparrow. Tail long and rounded, wings short, long-legged. Top of head is sparkling white; forehead, cheeks, throat, breast, wings, and end of tail black; rump, tail, and belly reddish-brown. In juveniles, the white cap has a gray, scaly design and the belly is rustier.
Habits: Inhabits mountains. Found near rushing rivers and streams with precipitous banks. Nonmigratory. Uncommon. Stays singly and in pairs on rocks jutting out of water and along the banks. Fans its tail when perched, and moves it up and down and from side to side. Nests in cliff crevices or between rocks. Lays three or four light bluish-green eggs with rusty brown spots in June or July. Call: long, prolonged whistle, "teeeet." Feeds on small water creatures, invertebrates, and insects.
Range and distribution: Mountains of Central Asia.
Similar species: Differs from Guldenstadt's

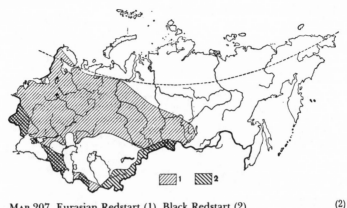

MAP 207. Eurasian Redstart (1), Black Redstart (2)   (2)

Redstart by the lack of white on the wings, and by its white, not gray, cap.

Phoenicurus

Very small and (more rarely) small, long-legged, well-proportioned birds. All species are sexually dimorphic. When perched, tail often bobs and trembles. Feeds on insects and other small invertebrates.

500. EURASIAN REDSTART
Phoenicurus phoenicurus
(Obyknovennaya Gorikhvostka)
Plate 35, Map 207
Field marks: 14-16 cm. Smaller than a sparrow. In male, top of the head, neck, and back are ash-gray; forehead white; sides of the head and throat are black; wings brownish; underparts and tail bright rust. In female, tail is rusty; belly ocher-whitish; the rest is brownish-gray. Juveniles are brownish with lighter mottling and rusty tail.
Habits: Found in thin woods, parks, and gardens. Migratory. Common. Stays in lower part of trees, in bushes, and on the ground. Nests in tree hollows, cracks in houses, nesting boxes. Lays six or seven light blue eggs from May to July. While singing, the male will occasionally fly to the top of the tree. Call: loud "fyeet-tee-teek." Song: resonant trill.
Range and distribution: European USSR (north as far as Murman, lower Pechora River), Siberia to the east as far as Lake Baikal, north as far as Salekhard on the Ob River and Turukhansk on the Yenisei River; Stony Tunguska River, and upper reaches of the Lower Tunguska River; mountains of southern Ka-

zakhstan, Central Asia, and Altai. Winters in Africa and Arabian Peninsula.
Similar species: Male differs from male Black Redstart by its white forehead; from the male Daurian Redstart by its lack of a white wing patch. Female closely resembles female of Black Redstart, but is somewhat lighter. They are practically indistinguishable in the field, but found in different environments.

501. BLACK REDSTART
Phoenicurus ochruros
(Gorikhvostka-chernushka)
Plate 35, Map 207
Field marks: 14-16 cm. In male, top of head and back are ash-gray; sides of head, throat, and breast are black; belly and tail rusty; sometimes belly is gray. Female is brownish-gray with rusty tail. Juveniles are dark brownish-gray with lighter mottling and a rusty tail.
Habits: Found near cliffs and rock slides in mountain areas and near stone buildings in cultivated areas. Migratory. Common. Stays singly and in pairs on rocks and cliffs. Nests in cliff crevices, between rocks, and under roof eaves. Lays four to six white or pale blue eggs from April to July. Call: loud "fyeet-teek-teek." Song: short trills and chattering noises.
Range and distribution: West European USSR; in recent years range has expanded east as far as Moscow; mountains of the Caucasus, Central Asia; south Kazakhstan; southern Sayan and Tannu-Ola mountains. Winters in southern Europe, northern Africa, Arabian Peninsula, Iran, and India.
Similar species: Differs from Eurasian Redstart male by its black throat and breast and grayish (not white) forehead. Females and juveniles are very similar, but somewhat darker

than females of Eurasian Redstart. Each tends to remain in its own environment.

502. EVERSMANN'S REDSTART
Phoenicurus erythronotus
(Krasnospinnaya Gorikhvostka)
Plate 35, Map 208

Field marks: 15 cm. In male, top of head and nape are gray; forehead is grayish; eye line and cheek patch that extends to wing are black; wings brownish with white patch; belly whitish; back, throat, breast, and tail rusty red.

Habits: Found in mountain forest with nearby bushy overgrowth. Migratory; in places, tends to stay and winter. Common. Occurs alone, in pairs, and small groups in trees, bushes, on rocks, and on the ground. Nests on the ground under roots or between rocks. Lays three to five light green eggs with brownish-gray speckles in June and July. Call: loud, whistling "few-eet" and soft "trr."

Range and distribution: Mountains of Central Asia, southern Kazakhstan, and southern Siberia. Winters in southern Central Asia, Iraq, Iran, Afghanistan, and India.

Similar species: Male differs from other Redstarts by its large size and rusty back. Female and juveniles greatly resemble those of other redstarts, especially the Eurasian Redstart, but are larger.

503. DAURIAN REDSTART
Phoenicurus auroreus
(Sibirskaya Gorikhvostka)
Plate 35, Map 208

Field marks: 14 cm. In male, forehead, sides of head, throat, lower back, and wings are black; crown, nape, and upper back are gray; large wing patch is white; rump, breast, belly, and tail are rusty (tail has black central tail feathers). Female is brownish-gray with lighter underparts, rusty tail, and white wingpatch. Juveniles are dark brownish with lighter mottling and rusty tail.

Habits: Found in woods, riverside thickets, gardens, and parks. Migratory. Common. Stays in trees, bushes, or on the ground, singly or in pairs. Nests in tree hollows, cliff crevices, piles of rocks, and construction sites. Lays five or six pinkish or light blue eggs with red speckles, April to June. Call: loud "fyeet-teek-teek." Song: fairly loud trill.

Range and distribution: Southern Siberia from Krasnoyarsk to Sakhalin in the east. Winters in Japan and Southeast Asia.

Similar species: Differs from Eurasian Redstart by white wing patch.

504. GULDENSTADT'S REDSTART
Phoenicurus erythrogaster
(Krasnobryukhaya Gorikhvostka)
Plate 35, Map 209

Field marks: 17 cm. Noticeably larger than other Redstarts. In male, top of head and large wing patch are white; back, wings, sides of head, throat, and upper breast black; tail, breast, belly, and rump rusty reddish. Female and juveniles brownish-gray with lighter mottling; lighter underparts; rusty red tail. Juvenile males have white wing patch.

Habits: In spring, summer, and fall, found in upper treeline areas of mountains near permanent snows. In winter, moves down to thickets along mountain river valleys. Nonmigratory and nomadic. Common. Stays singly, in pairs, or in groups of varying sizes. Often seen perched on large rock or top of bush. Nests in cliff crevices or between rocks.

MAP 208. Daurian Redstart (1), Eversmann's Redstart (2)

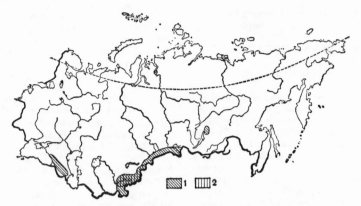

MAP 209. Guldenstadt's Redstart (1), Blue-headed Redstart (2)

Lays three to five white eggs with reddish speckles in June and July. Call: loud "tyeet-teek-teek." Song: a variety of quiet chirping sounds interspersed with imitations of other bird calls.

Range and distribution: Mountains of the central Caucasus, Central Asia, south Kazakhstan, Altai, Sayan, mountains of the Transbaikal.

Similar species: Differs from White-capped River Chat by its white wingpatch.

505. BLUE-HEADED REDSTART
Phoenicurus caeruleocephalus
(Sedogolovaya Gorikhvostka)
Plate 35, Map 209

Field marks: 14 cm. Smaller than a sparrow. In male, crown and nape are light bluish-gray; back, wings, tail, throat, and breast are black; broad shoulder stripe and belly are white. Fe-

males and juveniles are brownish-gray with rusty rump.

Habits: Found in mountain forests of pine and arborescent juniper with an undergrowth of thicket. Migratory. Uncommon. Occurs singly and in pairs; during migration, in flocks of various sizes in trees, bushes, or rocks and on the ground. When perched, moves tail from side to side. Nests on the ground under tree roots or under rocks. Lays three to five light bluish-white eggs in May and June. Call: loud "teek-teek."

Range and distribution: Pine forest of Tien-Shan Mountains; arborescent juniper forests of the Pamir-Altai ranges. Winters in the Himalayan and Hindu Kush valleys.

Similar species: Differs from other redstarts by its black or brownish tail.

[In the Turkestan mountain ridges the **506.**

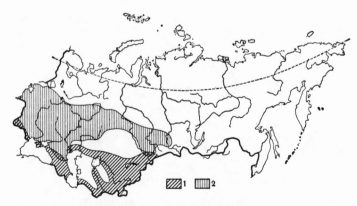

MAP 210. Nightingale (1), Thrush Nightingale (2)

PLUMBEOUS WATER REDSTART (*Rhyacornis fuliginosus*) has been found. It is all gray with a rusty red tail.]

Luscinia

Well-proportioned and long-legged. Size of a sparrow or a bit larger. Tail is straight, slightly rounded at the tip. When perched, constantly raises and lowers its tail. Some species are sexually dimorphic. When singing, usually sits immobile, with head lifted and throat puffed out. Feeds on various small invertebrates.

507. NIGHTINGALE
Luscinia megarhynchos
(Yuzhny Solovey)
Plate 36, Map 210

Field marks: 16-18 cm. Tail fairly long. Upper parts, wings, and tail light rufous-brownish; underparts dirty white.

Habits: Found in thin deciduous and mixed woods, thickets, gardens, and planted shrubbery. Common, in places numerous. Occurs singly or in pairs, well hidden on the ground, in bushes, or on lower tree branches; but easily located by its song. Nests on the ground or in lower part of bushes. Lays four to six brownish-olive eggs in May and June. Call: low "feeyoueet-trr." Song is loud, resonant, and varied.

Range and distribution: Southwestern European USSR, Crimea, Caucasus, Central Asia, southern Kazakhstan. Winters in central Africa.

Similar species: Differs from Thrush-Nightingale by its lighter color, long tail, and unspotted breast.

508. THRUSH-NIGHTINGALE
Luscinia luscinia
(Obyknovenny Solovey)
Plate 36, Map 210

Field marks: 16-18 cm. Greatly resembles Nightingale, but somewhat smaller; tail is slightly shorter, upperparts are dark brownish-gray, and breast is finely speckled.

Habits: Found in thickets, deciduous woods, gardens, and glades near water or in damp places. Migratory. Common, in places numerous. Nests on the ground. Lays four or five olive or brownish-olive eggs in May and June. Call: low "fyoueet-trr." Song: a variety of loud sounds.

Range and distribution: European USSR and Siberia east as far as the upper reaches of the Yenisei River; northern borders from the Karelian Isthmus to 60°-61° in Siberia; south to the Central Caucasus, Volgagrad, 49° latitude to the Ural River, the Kokchetavsky Highlands, and upper reaches of the Irtysh River. Winters in East Africa.

509. SIBERIAN RUBYTHROAT
Luscinia calliope
(Solovey-krasnosheyka)
Plate 36, Map 211

Field marks: 14 cm. In male, upperparts, wings, and tail are brownish-olive; eye line black; eye stripe and malar stripes are white; brilliant red throat outlined in black; breast, flanks, and sides of neck gray-brown, belly lighter. In females throat is white and coloration is duller. Juveniles are brownish-gray with light spots.

Habits: Found in forests with tangled thickets, woodcutting areas, and river floodlands. Migratory. Common. Found singly and in pairs on the ground, in bushes, and in lower part

MAP 211. Siberian Rubythroat (1), Himalayan Rubythroat (2)

of trees. Nest, nearly globular with side entrance, is on the ground. Lays four to six light blue eggs, sometimes with brownish spots, in May and June. Call: loud whistle, "feeyoueet-feeyoueet." Song: a variety of loud whistles and clicks.

Range and distribution: From western slopes of the Urals, east through all Siberia except northern regions as far as the Koryak District, Kamchatka, Kuril Islands, and the Soviet Far East. Winters in southern Asia.

Similar species: Differs from Himalayan Rubythroat by the lack of black on the breast in the male and by the olive, not gray, upperparts of the female.

510. HIMALAYAN RUBYTHROAT
Luscinia pectoralis
(Chernogrudaya Krasnosheyka)
Plate 36, Map 211

Field marks: 14 cm. In male, throat is brilliant red; forehead, lores, cheeks, eye stripe, breast, and tail are black; superciliary, belly, and basal half of outer tail feathers white; upperparts light blue-gray with a brownish suffusion. Females and juveniles lack black or red; throat is white and upperparts and breast are brownish-gray.

Habits: Lives in thickets in mountain forests and meadows. Migratory. Uncommon. Occurs singly and in pairs on rocks, in bushes, and on the ground. Male sings with head and tail uplifted. Nests on the ground. Lays three to five greenish light-blue eggs with brownish speckles in May and June. Call: low whistles and noises. Song: a variety of loud trills.

Range and distribution: Mountains of Tien-Shan and Pamir-Alai. Winters in India.

Similar species: Differs from Siberian Ruby-

throat by the black breast in males and light blue-gray upperparts of females.

511. RUFOUS-TAILED ROBIN
Luscinia sibilans
(Solovey-svistun)
Plate 36, Map 212

Field marks: 14 cm. Upperparts brownish-rufous; underparts whitish with scaly brownish pattern on breast and sides.

Habits: Found in damp forests, in thickets and fallen trees. Migratory. Common. Stays singly and in pairs near the forest floor or on the ground. Wary and stays hidden. Usually nests on a stump. Lays five or six light blue eggs in June and July. Call: quiet whistle ending in glass-clinking sounds. Song: loud tremulous whistle, resembling the neigh of a colt from a distance.

Range and distribution: Taiga of southern Siberia and Soviet Far East. Winters in Southeast Asia.

Similar species: Differs from other Luscinias by the scaly pattern on the breast and sides.

512. SIBERIAN BLUE ROBIN
Luscinia cyane
(Siny Solovey)
Plate 35, Map 212

Field marks: 13 cm. In male, upperparts are dark blue; forehead, lores, and broad "moustache" that extends to the wing are black; underparts white. In female, olive-brownish upperparts have a blue cast; rump and tail are bluish; buffy breast is mottled. Juveniles similar, but without bluish cast.

Habits: Found in taiga near fallen trees and branches. Common and migratory. Stays on the ground hidden in thickets, or near the

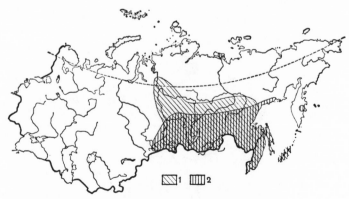

MAP 212. Rufous-tailed Robin (1), Siberian Blue Robin (2)

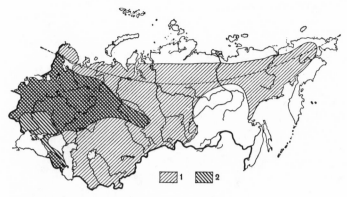

MAP 213. Bluethroat (1), European Robin (2)

forest floor, singly or in pairs. Nests on the ground. Lays four to six light blue eggs in May and June. Call: harsh "chok-chok." Song: a variety of melodic whistles.
Range and distribution: Southern Siberia and Soviet Far East. Winters in Southeast Asia.
Similar species: Differs from other Luscinias by its blue upperparts.

513. BLUETHROAT
Luscinia svecica
(Varakushka)
Plate 36, Map 213
Field marks: 14 cm. Upperparts of male are olive-gray; wings brownish; tail is black with basal half of outer tail feathers rusty; throat and breast are bright blue edged below with black, white, and rust; in the center of the upper breast there is either a white or rusty spot (or none) depending on the subspecies; belly is white. In female, throat is whitish and the breast is dusky with blackish streaks. Juveniles are dark brownish with light spots; rusty at base of tail.
Habits: Found in overgrown thickets, commonly near reservoirs of water. Migratory. Common, in places numerous. Stays on the ground or in bushes. Nests on the ground. Lays four to seven gray-green eggs with small brownish spots in May and June. The male raises his head and tail high while singing. Call: loud "chak-chak." Song: loud trills and imitations of other birds.
Range and distribution: Entire USSR except extreme northern Siberia, central and upper Lena River, Soviet Far East, Chukotski Peninsula and Kamchatka Peninsula. Winters in northern Africa and southern Asia.
Similar species: Differs from other Luscinias

by the rusty patches at base of tail; the male by his blue throat and breast.

Erithacus

514. EUROPEAN ROBIN
Erithacus rubecula
(Zaryanka)
Plate 35, Map 213
Field marks: 13-15 cm. Small (sparrow-size), long-legged bird. Upperparts, tail, and wings are olive-brown; forehead, cheeks, throat, and breast are orange-rust; belly white. Juveniles are brownish with light spots.
Habits: Found in woods, gardens, and parks. Migratory. Common, numerous in places. Occurs singly and in pairs on the ground, in bushes and trees. Nests in a hollow in the ground or in a rotting stump; occasionally in a hollow tree. Lays five or six pinkish eggs with red-brownish speckles, May or June. Male sings while perched upright with slightly lowered wings. Call: harsh "teek-teek-teek." Song: loud ringing trill.
Range and distribution: European USSR and West Siberia north to 63°-64° N latitude. Winters in southern Europe and northern Africa.
Similar species: Differs from the Japanese Robin by its olive-brown back.

515. JAPANESE ROBIN
Erithacus akahige
(Yaponskaya Zaryanka)
Plate 35, Map 214
Field marks: 14-16 cm. Resembles the European Robin, but upperparts are reddish-brown; throat, sides of head, and upper breast rusty-orange; belly and undertail yellowish-white.

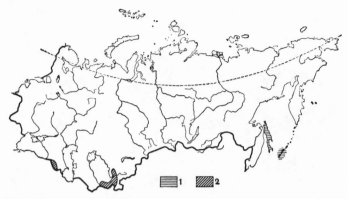

MAP 214. Japanese Robin (1), Persian Robin (2)

Habits: Found in a variety of woods. Migratory. Uncommon. Occurs in darker areas of the forest; often seen hopping on forest paths, flicking its tail. Nests on the ground. Usually lays five light greenish-blue eggs, May or June. Male raises head and tail and lowers wings when singing. Call: short chatter. Song: loud, short trill.

Range and distribution: Southern Sakhalin and southern Kuril Islands. Winters in Japan and southeastern China.

Similar species: Differs from European Robin by its reddish-brown upperparts.

Irania

516. PERSIAN ROBIN
Irania gutturalis
(Solovey-belosheyka)
Plate 36, Map 214

Field marks: 17 cm. Larger than a sparrow, long-legged. Upperparts of male are ash-gray; lores, cheeks, sides of neck, wings, and tail black; eyebrow, throat, and belly are white; breast and flanks orange. The female is grayish-brown, with only the flanks orange. Juveniles are brownish with light spots.

Habits: Found in dry, rocky mountain slopes in areas of scrub. Migratory. Common, in places rare. Occurs singly and in pairs on the ground, in bushes, and on rocks. Bobs and fans tail while perched. Nests in bush, or log; more rarely in a tree or on the ground. Lays four to six light greenish-blue eggs with rusty-brown spots in May or June. Male sometimes flies into the air while singing. Call: quiet whistle ending in a faint chatter. Song: a variety of loud trills.

Range and distribution: Transcaucasus and

mountains of Central Asia. Winters in southwestern Arabian Peninsula and Ethiopia.

Similar species: No similar species in the USSR.

Enicurus

517. LITTLE FORKTAIL
Enicurus scouleri
(Belonozhka)
Plate 40, Map 215

Field marks: 12 cm. Small, distinctive bird, smaller than a sparrow. Forehead, upper tail coverts, rump, breast, belly, wing patch, and outer tail feathers are white; remainder is black. Short, slightly forked tail. Legs are whitish.

Habits: Found on banks of shallow, turbulent mountain streams with waterfalls and steep drops. Occurs singly or in pairs on rocks in the water or on banks. Nonmigratory. Uncommon. While perched, constantly bobs and fans tail. If startled, flies low over the water. Nests on rocks and in cliff crevices near water; entrance is often hidden by waterfall. Lays three to four white eggs with reddish speckles in June. Song: loud "ts-youeee."

Range and distribution: Pamir-Alai and southwestern Tien-Shan Mountains.

Similar species: No similar species in USSR.

Erythropygia

518. RUFOUS SCRUB-ROBIN
Erythropygia galactotes
(Tugayny Solovey)
Plate 36, Map 215

Field marks: 15 cm. Small bird (larger than a sparrow), stoutly built, long-legged, and with a long wedge-shaped tail. Upperparts are

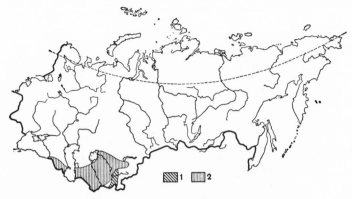

MAP 215. Little Forktail (1), Rufous Scrub-Robin (2)

grayish-brown; underparts and eyebrow are ocher-whitish; tail rusty brown with black and white corners.
Habits: Found in thickets in plains and steppe, gardens and vineyards. Migratory. Common. Found singly and in pairs on the ground and in bushes. On the ground, raises and lowers tail; fans it when in flight. Often perches immobile in the top of a bush. Nests in bushes; more rarely on the ground. Lays three to five pale green or light blue eggs with brownish speckles in May or June. Call: harsh "tsee-tsi." Song: variety of loud whistles and trills.
Range and distribution: Transcaucasus and plains of Central Asia and south Kazakhstan. Winters in southwestern Asia and Africa.
Similar species: Differs from nightingales by its black-and-white-tipped rusty tail.

Garrulax

519. STREAKED LAUGHING-THRUSH
Garrulax lineatus
(Polosataya Timeliya)
Plate 33, Map 216
Field marks: 20 cm. Smaller than a starling. Thickly feathered and fluffy; wings short and rounded; broad tail long and graduated. Olive-gray with narrow, light ocherish stripes; rump ash-gray; wings olive rust; tail tip has narrow grayish-white and wide black bands.
Habits: Found in overgrown mountain thickets. Nonmigratory as well as nomadic. Common. Found paired during nesting season; the remainder of the year occurs in small flocks on the ground and in bushes. Agile climber, but heavy in flight; quiet; when hopping on the ground, often holds its tail high. Nests in bushes. Lays three to five light bluish-green

eggs in May or June. Call: drawn-out whistle, "tyou-tee-tee-vee" and a soft "dzhee-dzhee." Feeds on insects and other small invertebrates, berries, and seeds.
Range and distribution: Mountains of southern Tadzhikistan and Uzbekistan.
Similar species: No similar species in USSR.

Panurus

520. BEARDED REEDLING
Panurus biarmicus
(Usataya Sinitsa)
Plate 41, Map 216
Field marks: 16-18 cm. Pointed tail, long and graduated. In male, head and neck are gray; back and tail rusty brown; wings rusty with black-and-white markings; underparts whitish with a pinkish suffusion; undertail coverts and moustachial stripe black. Females and juveniles are rusty, with similarly marked wings, but lack black moustache and undertail coverts.
Habits: Found in stands of reeds and cattails in marshes, and along lake and river shores. Nonmigratory as well as nomadic. Common, in places numerous. Occurs in pairs and flocks; readily climbs stalks of reeds and cattails. Often nests in colonies. Nest, in form of a deep cup, is found at base of bushes, in piles of fallen reeds or cattails over water. Lays five to seven white eggs with dark speckles in April and May. Song: loud "chveen-chveen."
Range and distribution: Reedstands in Lithuania (Lake Tuvintas) and in south European USSR, Kazakhstan, southwestern Siberia, Central Asia, Tuva, southern Transbaikal.
Similar species: No similar species in USSR.

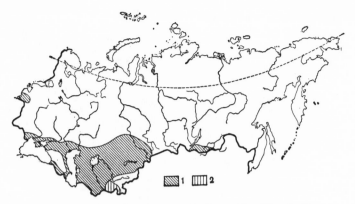

MAP 216. Bearded Reedling (1), Streaked Laughing-Thrush (2)

Suthora

521. VINOUS-THROATED PARROTBILL
Suthora webbiana
(Sutora)
Plate 41, Map 217
Field marks: 12 cm. Small fluffy bird with long, graduated, squared-off tail and thick, bulbous bill. Uniformly brownish-ocher, but lighter on belly.
Habits: Found in thickets along river banks and forest edges. Nonmigratory and nomadic. Uncommon. Stays in pairs and flocks. Climbs in thickest part of bushes or grasses. Nest is a deep cup or ball, and is located in bushes or on the ground. Lays five or six light blue eggs in May. Voice is not recorded.
Range and distribution: Southern Soviet Far East.
Similar species: No similar species in USSR.

Paradoxornis

522. REED PARROTBILL
Paradoxornis heudei
(Trostnikovaya Sutora)
Not illustrated, Map 303
Field marks: 18 cm. Small, sparrow-size bird with long, graduated tail and short, swollen bill. Coloration rusty brownish; underparts whitish; wide, brownish-black eye line extending to the nape.
Habits: Secretive; occurs in pairs and flocks in thick reed beds. Nonmigratory. Rare. Nest is a deep cup made from leaves of reeds and sedge, and is situated between two or three stalks low to the water. Lays three or four light blue eggs. Call: short trills and nasal whistles. Included in the Red Data Book.
Range and distribution: Lake Khanka (on boundary between China and Primorski Krai, north of Vladivostok).
Similar species: No similar species in the USSR.

Aegithalos

523. LONG-TAILED TIT
Aegithalos caudatus
(Dlinnokhvostaya Sinitsa)
Plate 41, Map 217
Field marks: 14-17 cm. Fluffy bird with a very long, graduated tail. Back, wings, and tail black; shoulder stripe pinkish; head, underparts, and outer tail feathers white; on belly and flanks, a dirty pink tone. Juveniles and adults of southern races have a dark stripe over the eyes.
Habits: Found in mixed and deciduous woods. Nonmigratory and nomadic bird. Common. Found in pairs during nesting season, the rest of the year in flocks—flying from tree to tree and into bushes, constantly calling to each other. Agile climber along thin branches, often hanging from them. Nest is globular with side entrance, and is found in crotch of tree or bush. Lays nine to twelve white eggs with violet-pink markings from April to June. Call: loud "cherr-cherr."
Range and distribution: From western boundaries to Kamchatka Peninsula. North as far as 59°-61° N latitude.
Similar species: No similar species found in USSR.

MAP 217. Long-tailed Tit (1), Vinous-throated Parrotbill (2)

Phylloscopus

Very small lively birds, significantly smaller than a sparrow. Tail straight; bill thin and oval-shaped. All species migratory. All warblers resemble each other and are practically indistinguishable in the field. However, all are clearly distinguishable by their song. Feed on a variety of insects and other small invertebrates.

524. WILLOW WARBLER
Phylloscopus trochilus
(Penochka-vesnichka)
Plate 37, Map 218
Field marks: 11 cm. Top of head, back, rump, wings, and tail brownish-gray or greenish-gray; underparts yellowish-white; indefinite whitish-yellowish brow over the eye. Legs light brownish.

Habits: Found in variety of forest types, thickets, and stands of reed from tundra to desert; in plains and hills. Common, in places numerous. Occurs singly, in pairs, and flocks in bushes and trees. Very lively. Often flies to top of tree or bush when singing. Nest is a loosely woven "house" (shalashik) on the ground. Lays four to eight white eggs with small brownish-red spots in May or June. Call: short whistle, "fyoueet." Song: a variety of clear whistles melting into a trill.

Range and distribution: From western boundaries of the USSR across Siberia to the Anadyr River Basin. Not found in southern European USSR, Kazakhstan, southern Siberia, or the entire Soviet Far East. Winters in Africa.

Similar species: Differs from Chiffchaff by its light-colored legs.

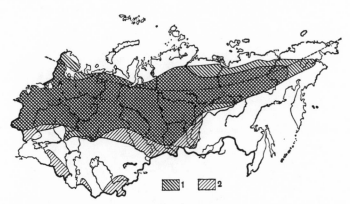

MAP 218. Willow Warbler (1), Chiffchaff (2)

525. CHIFFCHAFF
Phylloscopus collybitus
(Penochka-tenkovka)
Plate 37, Map 218

Field marks: 11 cm. Smaller than a sparrow. Coloration same as Willow Warbler, but upperparts often brownish; legs black.

Habits: Found in various types of woods and overgrown thickets in plains and hills. Common. Stays singly or in pairs in leafy parts of trees and bushes. Very lively. Nest, in the form of a loosely woven "house" (shalashik), is situated on the ground or in a bush low to the ground. Lays five to seven white eggs with small red-brownish spots in May and June. Call: short whistle, "fyoueet." Song: loud repeated "tyen-tyin-tyan-tyoun ... tr ... tr ... ten-tin."

Range and distribution: Found in forested regions from the western boundaries of the USSR east to the upper reaches of the Kolyma River, excluding eastern Siberia, Soviet Far East, Kazakhstan (south from upper reaches of Irtysh River and middle reaches of the Ural River). Winters in Africa, West Asia, and India.

Similar species: Indistinguishable from Willow Warbler in the field except for its song. In the hand, it is readily distinguished by its black legs.

526. WOOD WARBLER
Phylloscopus sibilatrix
(Penochka-treshchotka)
Plate 37, Map 219

Field marks: 13 cm. Large warbler. Top of head, back, and rump are yellow-green; tail and wings blackish-brownish with greenish margins; eyebrow, throat, upper breast, and flanks yellow; lower breast and belly white.

Habits: Found in various types of woods. Common. Stays singly and in pairs. Fast and lively.

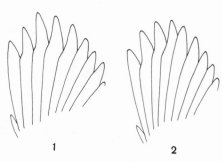

FIG. 67 Wings of 1) Chiffchaff and 2) Arctic Warbler

When singing, male often flits from branch to branch. Nest is a loosely woven "house" (shalashik) on the ground. Lays five to seven white eggs with small violet-gray spots from May to July. Call: sad whistle, "tyouyou-tyouyouoo." Song: loud "seep-seep-seepseepseepseerrr."

Range and distribution: European USSR and western Siberia. Winters in Africa.

Similar species: Differs from other warblers by its larger size, bright yellow face and throat, and yellow-green back.

527. ARCTIC WARBLER
Phylloscopus borealis
(Penochka-talovka)
Plate 37, Map 219

Field marks: 12 cm. Upperparts greenish-brownish; there are two whitish wing bars (one obvious, one indefinite); eyebrow yellowish-white; underparts whitish with a yellowish cast on the breast; legs pale.

Habits: Found in coniferous and mixed forests and thickets. Common. Found singly or in pairs in crowns and trees or in the thickest parts of

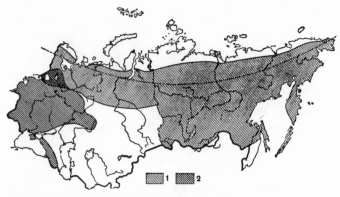

MAP 219. Arctic Warbler (1), Wood Warbler (2)

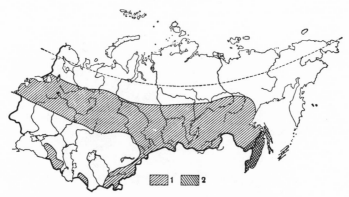

MAP 220. Greenish Warbler (1), Pale-legged Leaf-Warbler (2)

bushes. Very lively. Nest is a loosely woven domed cap (shalashik), and is situated on the ground; more rarely on a stump or on the trunk of a fallen tree. Lays three to six white eggs (sometimes with red speckles) in June or July. Call: soft "tzet-tzet," "tseet-tseet," or "drr-drr." Song: loud sounds, "tzee-tzee-tzee."

Range and distribution: North of European USSR and West Siberia, East Siberia, northern Soviet Far East, Kamchatka Peninsula, Sakhalin and Kuril Islands. Winters in Southeast Asia.

Similar species: Differs from other warblers in the field by its voice. Initially, almost indistinguishable from the Greenish Warbler in the field, but somewhat larger. The first primary is longer than the primary coverts, and the second primary is shorter than or equals the sixth. There are two light wing bars.

528. GREENISH WARBLER
Phylloscopus trochiloides
(Zelyonaya Penochka)
Plate 37, Map 220

Field marks: 11 cm. Coloring similar to Arctic Warbler but greener; one light wing bar.

Habits: Found in a variety of woods and overgrown thickets. Common. Found singly and in pairs, sometimes in flocks. Lively, active bird that hops about in the crown of a tree or bush. Nest in the form of a loosely woven domed cup (shalashik) on the ground or in a bush low to the ground. Lays five or six white eggs in June or July. Call: quiet whistle, "pee" or "psueel." Song: fairly loud, consisting of whistles and trills resembling "tee-pseetu-pseetu-psee-tee-tee-tee-psee."

Range and distribution: From the Baltic States to the Kolyma Plateau and Sikhote-Alin range.

Mountain forests of the Caucasus and Central Asia. Winters in India and Indochina.

Similar species: As with all Phylloscopus, nearly indistinguishable from others at a distance. Differs from Arctic warbler by its slightly smaller size and single wing bar; also by the shorter length of the first primary, and longer second primary that equals the fourth.

529. PALE-LEGGED LEAF-WARBLER
Phylloscopus tenellipes
(Blednonogaya Penochka)
Plate 37, Map 220

Field marks: 11 cm. Wings, tail, and upperparts brownish with rusty rump; one or two faint wing bars; eyebrow yellowish-white; underparts whitish, with buffy sides and undertail coverts. Legs grayish-yellow.

Habits: Found in deciduous woods and thickets along river banks. Uncommon but numerous in places. Found alone and in pairs. Nesting habits unknown in USSR. Call: harsh "che-che-che." Song is short, and reminiscent of a cricket chirping.

Range and distribution: Southern Soviet Far East. Winters in Indochina.

Similar species: Differs from other warblers in the field by its song and rusty rump. In the hand, it differs by its light legs.

530. WESTERN CROWNED WARBLER
Phylloscopus occipitalis
(Zelenokrylaya Penochka)
Plate 37, Map 221

Field marks: 12 cm. Upperparts dull green; tail and wings brownish with greenish edges to feathers; eyebrow greenish-yellow; crown dark with median yellowish-white stripe; two light wing stripes. Underparts grayish-white with a greenish suffusion at the sides.

MAP 221. Western Crowned Warbler (1), Eastern Crowned Warbler (2)

Habits: Found in mountains, deciduous forests, and groves. Uncommon. Found singly or in pairs. Lively, like all warblers, constantly moving about in tree branches or shrubs. Nest is a loosely woven domed cup (shalashik) situated on the ground near tree roots, on bushes, or in ground hollows. Lays four or five white eggs in June or July. Call: loud "cheep-cheep" or "cheep-veee." Song: loud repeated syllables, "cha-chee-cha-chee. . . ."

Range and distribution: Mountains of Central Asia and south Kazakhstan. Winters in India.

Similar species: Differs from other warblers by its striped head. Not found in same range as Eastern Crowned Warbler.

531. EASTERN CROWNED WARBLER
Phylloscopus coronatus
(Svetlogolovaya Penochka)
Plate 37, Map 221
Field marks: 12 cm. Upperparts gray-green-ish; underparts whitish; undertail coverts yellow; eye stripe yellowish-white; median crown stripe light greenish; single light wing bar.

Habits: Found in coniferous and mixed taiga, where it inhabits thinned-out areas. Common. Found singly and in pairs in tree crowns. Nests in lower tree branches or mountainsides. Lays five to seven white eggs in May or June. Call: short whistle. Song: short, loud "pichu-pichu-vin" or "tseet-eet . . . tsu-eet . . . tsaya."

Range and distribution: Soviet Far East (south of the Amur River). Winters in Indochina and Indonesia.

Similar species: Differs from other warblers by its striped head. Range does not overlap with Western Crowned Warbler.

532. YELLOW-BROWED WARBLER
Phylloscopus inornatus
(Penochka-zarnitchka)
Plate 37, Map 222

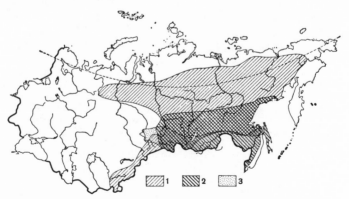

MAP 222. Yellow-browed Warbler (1), Pallas's Warbler (2), Radde's Warbler (3)

Field marks: 10 cm. Very small warbler. Upperparts, wings, and tail brownish-green; light stripes over the eye and faint stripe on crown; two light-yellowish wing stripes; underparts whitish.

Habits: Found in various types of woods in plains and hills. Common. Stays singly or in pairs. Very lively. Nest in the form of a loosely woven domed cup (shalashik) is situated on the ground. Lays five to seven white eggs with red speckles in June. Call: quiet "veet." Song: short, ringing "veet-veet-tzheee."

Range and distribution: Northern forests from Perm to shores of Sea of Okhotsk, mountains of southern Kazakhstan and Central Asia. Winters in southern Asia.

Similar species: Differs from Pallas's Warbler by its greenish rump and inconspicuous crown stripe; from others by its small size.

533. PALLAS'S WARBLER
Phylloscopus proregulus
(Korolkovaya Penochka)
Plate 37, Map 222

Field marks: 9 cm. Very small warbler. Upperparts olive-green; head brownish; wings and tail brownish with feather edges greenish; two prominent yellowish wing bars; eyebrow, stripe in center of head, and rump are yellow; underparts whitish with a yellow suffusion at the belly and sides.

Habits: Found in coniferous and mixed taiga in plains and hills. Common, in places numerous. Found singly and in pairs. Nest is loosely woven domed cup (shalashik) in a tree. Lays five or six white eggs with small grayish and red-brownish spots in June or July. Call: loud "tveet." Song: loud, varied melodic trills.

Range and distribution: Central and southern Siberia and Soviet Far East. Winters in Southeast Asia.

Similar species: Differs from Yellow-browed Warbler by its bright yellow rump and head stripes.

534. PLAIN LEAF-WARBLER
Phylloscopus neglectus
(Iranskaya Penochka)
Not illustrated, Map 223

Field marks: 10-11 cm. Small. Upperparts, wings, and tail grayish-brown; underparts whitish with brownish flanks; eyebrow yellowish-whitish.

Habits: Found in mountain forests and thickets. Stays in thick groves of arborescent juniper, pistachio trees, and similar foliage. Locally common. Stays singly, in pairs, and small flocks. Nesting habits not studied in USSR. It is reported that in Iran the nest is a loosely woven domed cup (shalashik) situated in a bush low to the ground. Eggs are white. Call: harsh chirping "gurrr."

Range and distribution: Mountains in south of Central Asia. Winters in south of Iran and India.

Similar species: Differs from Olivaceous Leaf Warbler and the Chiffchaff by its whitish eyebrow and light underparts. Differs from the Willow Warbler by its shorter tail, but nearly indistinguishable in the field.

535. OLIVACEOUS LEAF-WARBLER
Phylloscopus griseolus
(Indiyskaya Penochka)
Plate 37, Map 223

Field marks: 11 cm. Small. Upperparts, wings, tail, throat, breast, and sides grayish-brownish; belly yellowish; eyebrow bright yellow.

Habits: Found in rocky mountain slopes with sparse vegetation. Found singly, in pairs, or small flocks usually on rocks. Uncommon. Nest is a loosely woven domed cup (shalashik) on

MAP 223. Dusky Leaf-Warbler (1), Olivaceous Leaf-Warbler (2), Plain Leaf-Warbler (3)

the ground or low to the ground in a thick bush. Lays four or five white eggs with rusty red speckles in May or June. Call: short, chirping "trr-trr" or "chilyee." Song: short trill.

Range and distribution: Mountains of south Kazakhstan, Central Asia, Altai, and Tarbagatai. Winters in India.

Similar species: Differs from other warblers by its bright yellow eyebrow on its dark head.

536. DUSKY LEAF-WARBLER
Phylloscopus fuscatus
(Buraya Penochka)
Plate 37, Map 223

Field marks: 11 cm. Upperparts rusty brown; underparts brownish-whitish; eyebrow buffy white.

Habits: Found in forest and thicket zones of mountains. Common. Occurs singly or in pairs in bushes and trees. Nest is a loosely woven domed cup (shalashik) situated on the ground, or close to the ground in a bush or tree. Lays four to six white eggs in May or June. Call: harsh "chek-chek." Song: loud whistles ending in trills.

Range and distribution: Siberia from Tomsk, Novosibirsk, and Central Altai to Lower Anadyr River, Kamchatka Peninsula, Sakhalin Island, and Sikhote-Alin. Winters in southern China, Indochina, and India.

Similar species: Differs from other warblers by its dark rusty brown coloring; from Radde's Warbler by its darker coloring.

[In the southern part of the Crimea, **537.** BONELLI'S WARBLER (*Phylloscopus bonelli*) has been recorded. It resembles the Plain Leaf-Warbler. **538.** BROOK'S LEAF-WARBLER (*Phylloscopus subviridis*), which resembles Yellow-browed Warbler, was obtained in the Turkmen and Fergana mountain ranges and near the city of Orenburg.]

Herbivocula

539. RADDE'S WARBLER
Herbivocula schwarzi
(Tolstoklyuvaya Penochka)
Plate 37, Map 222

Field marks: 13 cm. Large. Upperparts olive-brownish; rump yellowish-olive; underparts whitish; sides and undertail coverts olive-brown; long eyebrow light buffy.

Habits: Found in thin mixed and deciduous forests. Common, in places numerous. Usually stays near the forest floor, at the base of a bush or in grass. Wary. When singing, the male perches upright in the uppermost crown of a tree, with its throat puffed and its bill

pointed upward, and it quivers its wings. Nest is a slightly flattened dome situated low to the ground or in grass. Lays four to six white eggs with small rusty spots, June or July. Call: quiet whistle, "tveet-tveet," and harsh "tsok-tsok."

Range and distribution: Southern Siberia and Soviet Far East. North as far as 51°-55° N latitude. Winters in Indochina.

Similar species: Differs from Dusky Leaf-Warbler by its lighter coloring and yellowish-olive rump.

Cettia

Very small, similar to reed-warblers.

540. STUB-TAILED BUSH-WARBLER
Cettia squameiceps
(Korotkokhvostka)
Plate 37, Map 224

Field marks: 10 cm. Short tail. Rufous-brown upperparts; dark, scaly crown: buffy yellow eyebrow; blackish-brown eye stripe; white underparts with buffy undertail coverts.

Habits: Found in taiga of the southern Ussuri region, where it inhabits mixed and occasionally deciduous woods. Migratory. Common, and numerous in places. Found in remote corners of the forest, where it hops about on fallen trees and branches. Tail is always cocked upward. Nests on the ground under a bush or pile of fallen branches. Lays five to seven pinkish-white eggs with small lilac or purple-pink spots in May or June. Call: chirping and peculiar "chmok-chmok." Song: sound reminiscent of a cicada chirping.

Range and distribution: Southern Soviet Far East, southern Sakhalin Island and Kunashir Island. Winters in southeastern Asia.

Similar species: Differs from Northern Wren by its conspicuous whitish eyebrow and white underparts.

541. JAPANESE BUSH-WARBLER
Cettia diphone
(Korotkokrylaya Shyrokokhvostka)
Plate 37, Map 224

Field marks: 14 cm. Large warbler. Tail wide, tip rounded. Upperparts brownish; underparts buffy; indefinite buffy eyebrow.

Habits: Found in overgrown thickets and grasses in a variety of topography in hills and valleys. Migratory. Common. Stays hidden in thickets, revealing itself by its call or song. Domed nest is situated near the ground, on clumps of grasses or bushes. Lays four or five dark pink or rusty red eggs in June. Male sings while perched immobile in the thick crown of a tree or bush. Call: harsh "tyok-tyok." Song is short

MAP 224. Japanese Bush-Warbler (1), Stub-tailed Bush-Warbler (2), Cetti's Bush-Warbler (3)

and loud, with beautiful whistles, "koo-goo-oo-oo-oo-ook . . . tu-lee-tulee . . . koo-goo-oo-oo-ook . . . tulee-tulee."

Range and distribution: Southern Soviet Far East (Primorski Krai), southern Sakhalin, and southern Kuril Islands. Winters in southeastern Asia.

Similar species: Differs from reed-warblers by its rounded tail and lighter upperparts.

542. CETTI'S BUSH-WARBLER
Cettia cetti
(Solovinaya Shirokokhvostka)
Plate 37, Map 224

Field marks: 14 cm. Tail wide and rounded. Upperparts rusty or pale brownish; underparts dirty white; sides gray-brownish; eyebrow whitish.

Habits: Found in overgrown thickets and thick grasses along rivers. Migratory. Common. Stays hidden in grasses or thickets. Cup-shaped nest situated in bush or grasses near the ground. Lays three to five (usually four) shiny brick-red eggs from April to June. Call: loud "tsveet-tsveet," "chveets," or "teech-eech-chee." Song: short, loud "tseet-tseeveet-tseevoy-tseevoy-tseevoyt."

Range and distribution: Caucasus, Lower Volga, Kazakhstan as far as Lake Zaisan, Central Asia. Winters in the Mediterranean, southwestern Asia, and in northwestern Hindustan.

Similar species: Differs from reed-warblers by voice and wide, rounded tail.

Bradypterus

Very small, dun-colored birds with a characteristically graduated tail.

543. SPOTTED BUSH-WARBLER
Bradypterus thoracicus
(Malaya Pestrogrudka)
Plate 38, Map 225

Field marks: 11 cm. Back reddish-brown; wings and tail dark brownish; crown brownish-gray; underparts whitish; breast and upper breast has brownish spots; undertail rufous-brown with whitish spots.

Habits: Found in taiga with luxuriant undergrowth and thickets, in forest meadows, mountain plains with thick grass and bushes. Migratory. Rare, but in places common. Stays low and hidden. Nest, in form of loosely woven domed cup, is situated in a heap of brush or in branches of a fallen tree. Lays four to six pinkish white eggs with some brownish spots in June or July. Sings from the densest part of thickets. Song: harsh "trzee-trzee."

Range and distribution: Southern Siberia from northeast Altai as far the southern Soviet Far East. Winters in southern Asia.

Similar species: Differs from Chinese Bush Warbler by its darker back.

544. CHINESE BUSH WARBLER
Bradypterus taczanowskia
(Sibirskaya Pestrogrudka)
Not illustrated, Map 225

Field marks: 11 cm. Greatly resembles Spotted Bush Warbler. Upperparts brownish with faint stripes; underparts whitish, with upper breast, sides of breast, and belly buffy, and brownish spots on the breast; faint pale yellow eyebrow.

Habits: Found in woods along river valleys in areas of thickets, in meadows, and dry mountain plains with lush grass and few bushes. Migratory. Rare. Stays hidden in thick grass. Nest is situated in thick clumps of grass. Usually lays five light pink eggs with violet-gray

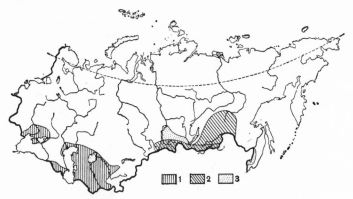

MAP 225. Moustached Warbler (1), Spotted Bush-Warbler (2), Chinese Bush-Warbler (3)

spots in June or July. Sings in the evening, at night, and at dawn. Song: scraping "tze-tze-tze. . . ."

Range and distribution: Southern Siberia and the Soviet Far East from eastern Sayan to south of Khabarovsk Krai. Winters in southern China and in Indochina.

Similar species: Differs from Spotted Bush-Warbler by its lighter back and darker sides.

[A juvenile **545.** LARGE-BILLED BUSH-WARBLER (*Bradypterus major*) was obtained in the eastern Pamirs. It had grayish-olive upperparts and white underparts, with an ocher suffusion on the upper breast and lower flanks.]

Acrocephalus

(See 554-562 for remainder of Genus)

546. MOUSTACHED WARBLER
Acrocephalus melanopogon
(Tonkoklyuvaya Kamyshovka)
Plate 38, Map 225

Field marks: 12 cm. Very small, with a slightly graduated tail. Upperparts rusty brown with wide blackish streaks on back; rump slightly paler; head olive-gray with dark brownish streaks, and a prominent white stripe over the eye; underparts whitish with brownish suffusion on the sides of the breast.

Habits: Found in riverside stands of cattails, in sedge, and thickets in plains and hills. Migratory. Common. Stays hidden in lower part of growth. Nest in the form of a cup is situated in stands of cattails, in sedge, in clumps of fallen reeds, and in bushes. Lays four to six greenish eggs with brownish speckles in May or June. Call: soft "churr." Song: a variety of loud whistles and chirring.

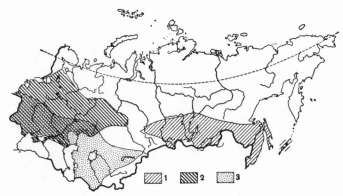

MAP 226. Gray's Grasshopper-Warbler (1), River Warbler (2), Savi's Warbler (3)

Range and distribution: Southern USSR from the Duna Delta to the Ila River delta and the Lower Vakhsh River. Winters in southern Central Asia, southern Iran, Pakistan, and northern Africa.

Similar species: Greatly resembles Sedge Warbler, but crown is darker and back rustier. Nearly indistinguishable in the field, except by call.

Locustella

Very small birds (with rare exceptions). Tail graduated, wings wide and short. Bill long and straight. Flies reluctantly, low to the ground.

547. GRAY'S GRASSHOPPER-WARBLER
Locustella fasciolata
(Taezhny Sverchok)
Plate 38, Map 226

Field marks: 18 cm. Largest of the grasshopper-warblers (somewhat larger than a sparrow). Upperparts dark olive-brown; tail and rump have a rusty tone; throat and belly whitish; breast and sides olive-brownish.

Habits: Found in grassy thickets of river valleys, in meadows, along mountain slopes, in thin forests, gardens, and parks. Migratory. Common. Stays hidden in thick grass. Nests on the ground. Usually lays four dirty white eggs with small lilac-gray spots in June. Begins its song on the ground, then hops to the top of a bush, branch by branch. Song: short, loud "pootee-rootee," "rootee-tootee."

Range and distribution: Southern Siberia and Soviet Far East from Novosibirsk and the Shors Highlands to the Lower Amur, south of Sakhalin Island, southern Kuril Islands. Winters in Indonesia, the Philippines, and New Guinea.

Similar species: Differs from others of its genus by its song and larger size.

548. RIVER WARBLER
Locustella fluviatilis
(Rechnoy Sverchok)
Plate 38, Map 226

Field marks: 12 cm. Upperparts dark olive-brownish; underparts whitish; throat lighter; throat and breast with faint dark streaks; undertail coverts are ocher-brownish with light tips.

Habits: Inhabits damp meadows, river valleys, swamps, woods, gardens, and parks with thickets of grass and shrubs. Migratory. Common. Stays well hidden in thick vegetation. Nests on the ground. Lays five to seven white eggs speckled gray and red-brownish in June. Readily identified by its song. Song: lengthy, monotonous chirring, "zer-zer-zer-zer. . . ."

Range and distribution: European USSR except the Caucasus, southern West Siberia. Winters in southern and southeastern Africa.

Similar species: Differs from other Locustella warblers found in the same area by its streaked breast and by its song.

549. SAVI'S WARBLER
Locustella luscinioides
(Soloviny Sverchok)
Plate 38, Map 226

Field marks: 14 cm. Upperparts rusty brownish; underparts whitish-buffy with brownish sides.

Habits: Found in osier thickets and dense growth in damp, swampy areas. Common. Stays hidden in thickest part of grass or bushes, making its presence known by its song. Nests on ground or low to the ground in clumps of grass. Lays four or five white eggs with small brownish spots in May and June. Call: harsh "chk-chk." Song: sound resembles "zirrrrr . . . ," increasing in intensity.

Range and distribution: Southern half of USSR east to Barnaul and Lake Zaisan. Winters in northeastern and tropical Africa.

Similar species: Differs from reed-warblers by its habits and manner of staying very hidden. From other Locustella warblers by its uniformly rusty upperparts.

550. PALLAS'S GRASSHOPPER-WARBLER
Locustella certhiola
(Pevchy Sverchok)
Plate 38, Map 227

Field marks: 13 cm. Upperparts brownish; rump rusty; nape grayish; heavily streaked with dark brown on head, back, and shoulders; tail rusty with dark tip; underparts whitish; undertail coverts buffy; eyebrow buffy gray.

Habits: Lives in grassy meadows with bushes and rank growth in both dry and damp areas. Common. Stays hidden in thickets. Nests on the ground in thick grass. Lays four to six plain pink eggs or pink eggs spotted red-brownish in June and July. Male often flies into the air out over an open area, or perches on top of stems when singing. Call: harsh chirring. Song: a variety of loud whistles, trills, and chirring.

Range and distribution: Siberia and Soviet Far East. Winters in southern Asia.

Similar species: Differs from Lanceolated Warbler by its darker upperparts and lack of streaking on the breast. From the European Grasshopper-Warbler by the dark subterminal band on the tail.

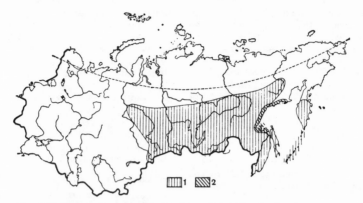

MAP 227. Pallas's Grasshopper-Warbler (1), Middendorff's Grass-hopper-Warbler (2)

551. MIDDENDORFF'S GRASSHOPPER-WARBLER
Locustella ochotensis
(Okhotsky Sverchok)
Plate 38, Map 227
Field marks: 13 cm. Upperparts rusty brown with a darker, rusty rump and indistinct dark streaks on the head and back; underparts whittish with white throat, brownish breast and sides; dark bars on tail underfeathers, tail tip whitish; faint whitish stripe over eye.
Habits: Found in thick grass and bushes in plains and hills. Common. Stays hidden. Nests on the ground or in grass close to the ground. Lays five or six pink eggs with blackish stripes in June and July. Easily identified by its voice. Song: harsh, gnashing "veeche-veeche-veech."
Range and distribution: Shores of Sea of Okhotsk from Magadan to the Lower Amur, Sakhalin Island, Kamchatka Peninsula, Kuril Islands. Winters in the Philippines and Indonesia.
Similar species: Differs from Lanceolated Warbler by indefinite streaking on the back and light eye stripe.

552. EUROPEAN GRASSHOPPER-WARBLER
Locustella naevia
(Obyknovenny Sverchok)
Plate 38, Map 228
Field marks: 12 cm. Smaller than a sparrow. Upperparts olive-brownish with black-brownish broken streaks; eye stripe indistinct; underparts light brownish with whitish throat and belly.
Habits: Found in both dry and moist areas covered with rank vegetation and clumps of bushes, as well as thick, damp, young woods.

Migratory. Common. Very secretive and hard to see. Nests on the ground. Lays four to seven white or pinkish eggs with small pink spots in June and July. Identified most readily by its song. The male sometimes sings from the top of stalks. Song: lengthy, reminiscent of a grasshopper's chirring, "zee-zee-zeezeezee-zeezee."
Range and distribution: From the Baltic States and Moldavia to Tuva, except Central Asia, and western and southern Kazakhstan. Winters in Spain, northwestern Africa, Iran, and India.
Similar species: Differs from other grasshopper-warblers by its song. From the Lanceolated Warbler, by the lack of streaks on the sides of the throat and breast.

553. LANCEOLATED WARBLER
Locustella lanceolata
(Pyatnisty Sverchok)
Plate 38, Map 228
Field marks: 12 cm. Upperparts brownish-olive and heavily streaked; eye stripe indistinct or nonexistent; underparts whitish with sharp brownish streaks on sides of throat and breast.
Habits: Found in grassy clumps along shores of bodies of water, in both damp and overgrown meadows. Common, but rare in European part of USSR. Stays hidden in thick grass, but is identifiable by its song. Nest situated on the ground. Lays five white eggs with reddish-brown and gray spots in June. Male visible during song, when it climbs onto top of stalk. Call: loud "chirr-chirr." Song: lengthy, reminiscent of a grasshopper's chirring, but with harsh jingling and whistling sounds.
Range and distribution: North European USSR, Siberia, Soviet Far East, Sakhalin Is-

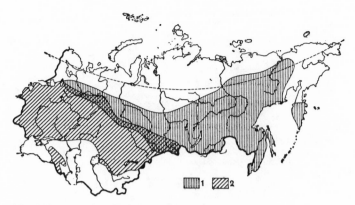

MAP 228. Lanceolated Warbler (1), European Grasshopper-Warbler (2)

land, Kuril Islands. Winters in Southeast Asia.
Similar species: Differs from European and Pallas's Grasshopper-Warblers by its darker upperparts and streaked breast; from Middendorf's Grasshopper-Warbler by the heavy streaking on the back and indistinct eye stripe. Also distinguished from all by its song.

Acrocephalus

Small to very small birds; usually with a short graduated tail. Bill straight. Flight hesitant. Wings short and rounded. Migratory. Feeds on insects. Most reed-warblers closely resemble each other and are difficult to identify in the field.

554. THICK-BILLED REED-WARBLER
Acrocephalus aëdon
(Tolstoklyuvaya Kamyshovka)
Plate 38, Map 229
Field marks: 18 cm. Smaller than a starling. Tail long, graduated. Upperparts rusty brownish, underparts dirty white. Lacks eyebrow.
Habits: Found in overgrown bushes at forest edges, plains, river valleys, and gardens. Common, in places rare. Migratory. Stays hidden in bushes but often flies out onto tops of bushes or trees. Nests in a bush. Lays four to six pinkish or yellowish eggs with brownish lines and curls in June and July. Call: harsh "chok-chok" or "chok-chok-cherre-chok-chok." Song: loud, ringing, with beautiful whistles.
Range and distribution: Southern Siberia and Soviet Far East. Winters in Southeast Asia.
Similar species: Differs from Great Reed-Warbler by its long graduated tail and lack of eyebrow.

555. GREAT REED-WARBLER
Acrocephalus arundinaceus
(Drozdovidnaya Kamyshovka)
Plate 38, Map 229
Field marks: 19 cm. Large (starling-size) reed-warbler. Upperparts dark brownish; underparts dirty white. Conspicuous light eyebrow.
Habits: Found in overgrown reeds and osier thickets, along shores of water bodies. Common, in places numerous, but hidden in overgrowth. Nests in reeds or bushes. Lays three to six greenish-white eggs with brownish speckles from May to July. Call: harsh "chok-chok." Song: variety of raucous, unmusical clacking sounds, "dlin-dlin-kar-r-ra-betch-betch-vak-vak."
Range and distribution: Southern USSR from western borders to south of Soviet Far East. Winters in India, West Asia, tropical Africa, and Indochina.
Similar species: Differs from Thick-billed Reed-Warbler by its short, ungraduated tail and prominent eyebrow.

556. EUROPEAN REED-WARBLER
Acrocephalus scirpaceus
(Trostnikovaya Kamyshovka)
Plate 38, Map 230
Field marks: 12 cm. Medium-size reed-warbler. Upperparts light brownish; underparts whitish with rusty tone.
Habits: Found in osier thickets, cattails, and reeds along the shores of reservoirs. Uncommon. Favors reed or osier stalks for perching. Lays three to six greenish or bluish-white eggs with brownish or gray spots from May to June. Call: harsh "cherr-cherr." Song: a variety of beautiful sounds, imitating calls and noises of other birds.

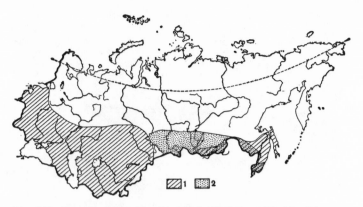

MAP 229. Great Reed-Warbler (1), Thick-billed Reed-Warbler (2)

Range and distribution: Southern half of USSR from the Baltic States to Lake Zaisan and the lower Vakhsh River. Winters in tropical Africa.

Similar species: Practically indistinguishable in the field from the Marsh or Blyth's Reed-Warbler. In the hand, differs from Marsh Warbler by having a deeper emargination of the inner web of the ninth primary, and having the ninth primary equal the seventh; by the claw on the rear toe, which is equal to the toe in length. Differs from Blyth's Reed-Warbler by having the ninth primary equal to the sixth primary.

557. MARSH WARBLER
Acrocephalus palustris
(Bolotnaya Kamyshovka)
Plate 38, Map 230
Field marks: 12 cm. Greatly resembles Euro-

pean Reed Warbler, but emargination on the inner web of the ninth primary is not as deep, and the ninth primary is longer than the seventh.

Habits: Found in thickets in a variety of open landscapes in plains and hills, avoiding swampy meadows. Common. Stays in undergrowth and is an agile stalk climber. Nests in a bush or between stalks of grasses. Lays four to seven white or greenish-white eggs with small gray or brownish spots from May to July. In song, male usually flies to top of bush or grass clump. Call: harsh "chek-chek-cher." Song: musical and variable, consisting of imitations of other birds, noises, and whistles.

Range and distribution: European USSR and Kazakhstan. North as far as Estonia, also Leningrad, Kostroma, and Perm Oblasts. Winters in eastern and southern Africa.

Similar species: In the field, almost indistin-

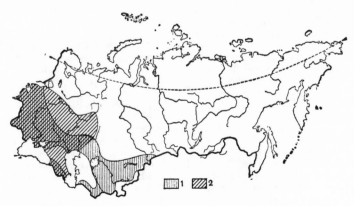

MAP 230. European Reed-Warbler (1), Marsh Warbler (2)

guishable from Blyth's Reed-Warbler and European Reed-Warbler. In the hand, differs from the European by the reduced emargination on the inner vane on the ninth primary; and the claw of the rear toe which is shorter than the toe. From Blyth's, by the second primary which is shorter than the fifth.

558. BLYTH'S REED-WARBLER
Acrocephalus dumetorum
(Sadovaya Kamyshovka)
Plate 38, Map 231

Field marks: 12 cm. Resembles the Marsh Warbler. Upperparts grayish-brown; underparts whitish with brownish suffusion; light, indistinct eye stripe; ninth primary equal to the sixth primary.

Habits: Found in thickets in forests and open areas; in plains and hills, gardens and parks. Common, but in places rare. Stays in dense cover, hopping with agility between stalks or among branches. Nests in bushes or grasses. Lays four to six pinkish or white eggs with brownish spots in May and June. Call: harsh "chek-chek," which is also included in the song. Song varies: consists of bird imitations and its own chirrs and whistles. Often sings nocturnally.

Range and distribution: From the Baltic States to central Vilyui River (western Yakutsk ASSR), upper reaches of the Lower Tunguska and Lena Rivers. Not found in southern half of European USSR or in southwestern Kazakhstan. Winters in India, Sri Lanka, and Burma.

Similar species: Nearly indistinguishable from European Reed-Warbler or Marsh Warbler in the field except for its grayer upperparts, indistinct white eye stripe, and ninth primary, which is equal to the sixth primary.

559. PADDYFIELD WARBLER
Acrocephalus agricola
(Indiyskaya Kamyshovka)
Plate 38, Map 232

Field marks: 12 cm. Upperparts rusty brownish; top of head rather dark; eye stripe whitish; underparts white with a buffy suffusion.

Habits: Found in reeds, osier and birch groves in marshy areas, along reservoir banks, in gardens, and along small open canals. Common; in places numerous. Stays in thickets near water. Nests in reeds. Lays four or five light olive or greenish eggs with small brownish spots in May and June. Call: harsh "chek-chek." Song varies, with beautiful whistles and imitations of other birds.

Range and distribution: Shores of the Black and Azov Seas, western Siberia, Kazakhstan, Central Asia, steppes of Minusinsk and Abakansk, Tuva. Winters in India and Indochina.

Similar species: Difficult to distinguish from the European Reed Warbler, Marsh Warbler, and Blyth's Warbler except possibly by its more conspicuous whitish eye stripe.

560. BLACK-BROWED REED-WARBLER
Acrocephalus bistrigiceps
(Pestrogolovaya Kamyshovka)
Plate 38, Map 232

Field marks: 12 cm. Upperparts rusty olive-brown; underparts whitish with buffy sides; white eyebrow bordered above and below by black.

Habits: Found in grassy or osier thickets near bodies of water, marshes, damp areas; more rarely in dry meadows and clearings. Common; in places numerous. Lively, agile. Nests in grassy stubble and lays four to six olive eggs with brownish spots in June or July. Male usually sings from top of stubble or bushes. Call:

MAP 231. Blyth's Reed Warbler (1)

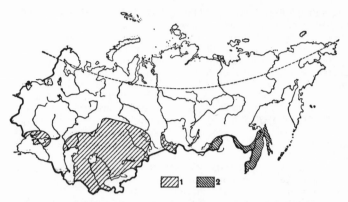

MAP 232. Paddyfield Warbler (1), Black-browed Reed-Warbler (2)

harsh "chirrr." Song: a variety of chirrings.

Range and distribution: Southern Siberia and Soviet Far East from southeastern Transbaikal to the lower Amur River, southern Sakhalin Island, and the southern Kuril Islands. Winters in Southeast Asia.

Similar species: Differs from other warblers by the distinctive black-and-white eyebrow.

561. SEDGE WARBLER
Acrocephalus schoenobaenus
(Kamyshovka-barsuchok)
Plate 38, Map 233

Field marks: 12 cm. Upperparts brownish with streaked back and unstreaked rump; wide, whitish eyebrow; underparts whitish with ocher suffusion on the flanks.

Habits: Found in reeds, sedge, and osier thickets along shores of bodies of water. Common. Stays in thickets. Nests in grass or bushes. Lays four to six yellowish eggs with brownish or

reddish speckles in May and June. Call: soft "chrr-chrr-chrr" or "feweet-klee-klee." Song: a variety of chirrings.

Range and distribution: Entire European USSR, West Siberia to the east as far as the Yenisei River, northern part of Kazakhstan as far as Lake Zaisan in the south. Winters in tropical and southern Africa.

Similar species: Differs from Aquatic Warbler by lack of crown stripe.

562. AQUATIC WARBLER
Acrocephalus paludicola
(Vertlavaya Kamyshovka)
Plate 38, Map 233

Field marks: 12 cm. Resembles Sedge Warbler, except for striped head, buffy eyebrow, and streaked rump.

Habits: Found in marshes, overgrown sedge meadows, and osier thickets. Rare. Nests in grassy thicket near a bush. Lays five or six

MAP 233. Sedge Warbler (1), Aquatic Warbler (2)

olive-spotted greenish-yellow eggs in May and June. Male occasionally flies into the air while singing. Call: soft "tak-tak" or "trr-tr." Song: a variety of chirrings.

Range and distribution: European USSR from the Baltic States to the Black and Azov Seas, in the east as far as central Ob River in West Siberia, to the south as far as Bashkiria. Winters in Africa.

Similar species: Differs from Sedge Warbler by its boldly striped blackish and buffy head.

Hippolais

Small birds with a long, wide bill. Somewhat resemble the Phylloscopus warblers, but differ from them by their larger size and wide bill. Feed on insects.

563. ICTERINE WARBLER
Hippolais icterina
(Zelyonaya Peresmeshka)
Plate 37, Map 234
Field marks: 13 cm. Greenish-gray upperparts; light yellow underparts; thin, black eye stripe, yellow eyebrow; bluish legs.
Habits: Found in a variety of woods, gardens, and parks. Common. Stays in the thickest and leafiest part of trees and bushes. Nests in trees. Lays four to six pinkish eggs spotted brown and blackish in June and July. Call: loud "vet-vet" or "tse-tse-dedevin" or "chrek-chrek." Song: imitations of other birds as well as its own nasal sounds.
Range and distribution: European USSR (except northeast, extreme south, Karelia, and the Kola Peninsula), extending into southwestern Siberia. Winters in Africa.
Similar species: Differs from other Hippolais

warblers in USSR by its greenish upperparts and yellowish underparts.

564. UPCHER'S WARBLER
Hippolais languida
(Pustynnaya Peresmeshka)
Plate 37, Map 234
Field marks: 13 cm. Larger than other Hippolais warblers in USSR. Upperparts, sides of head, and neck pale grayish-brown; underparts whitish with a brownish-buff tone on the sides; indefinite light eye stripe.
Habits: Found in remote bushy thickets in montane plains and mountainsides. Common. Found singly or in pairs in bushes; very lively. Nests in trees or bushes. Lays three to five gray- or blackish-spotted pinkish eggs from May to July. Call: soft chirring. Song: imitations of other bird songs.
Range and distribution: Southern Transcaucasus, Central Asia, and southern Kazakhstan. Winters in East Africa.
Similar species: Differs from the Booted Warbler by its larger size and voice.

565. BOOTED WARBLER
Hippolais caligata
(Bormotushka)
Plate 37, Map 235
Field marks: 11 cm. Smaller than a sparrow. Upperparts brownish-gray; underparts whitish-buff.
Habits: Found in thickets at forest edges, in burnt-over or cut-over forest areas, in birch and oak groves, wild rose bushes; sometimes in reeds, gardens, and parks. Common, but in places rare. Stays hidden in thick bushes and on the ground. Nests on the ground and in bushes. Lays four to six pinkish eggs spotted red-brownish or black in May or June.

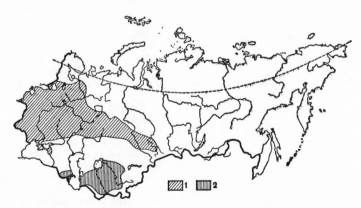

MAP 234. Icterine Warbler (1), Upcher's Warbler (2)

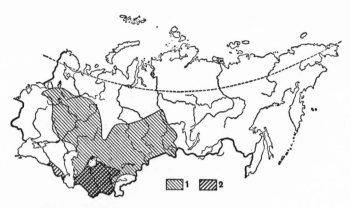

MAP 235. Booted Warbler (1), Olivaceous Warbler (2)

Call: harsh "chrek-chrek." Song: a variety of chirrings.

Range and distribution: Central and southwestern European USSR, Bashkiria, Kazakhstan, West Siberia in the east as far as the Yenisei River and Tuva, north to 57°-61° N latitude; Central Asia except the Pamirs. Winters in Somalia, southern Arabia, India.

Similar species: Differs from other Hippolais Warblers by its small size.

566. OLIVACEOUS WARBLER

Hippolais pallida
(Blednaya Peresmeshka)
Plate 37, Map 235

Field marks: 13 cm. Upperparts pale gray-brownish with a light olive tone; underparts whitish with an ocher suffusion that darkens at the sides.

Habits: Found in thickets near reservoirs, gardens, and parks. Common. Stays hidden in bushes or trees. Male sometimes flies up while singing. Nests in bushes. Lays four or five whitish-pinkish eggs with gray and reddish or black spots in May and June. Call: harsh "chek-chek." Song: a variety of monotonous chirring sounds.

Range and distribution: Transcaucasus, shores of the Black Sea in the Caucasus, Central Asia, southern Kazakhstan. Winters in North and East Africa.

Similar species: Differs from the very similar Upcher's Warbler by song; from the Garden Warbler by its flattened, not rounded, head.

[The **567.** OLIVE-TREE WARBLER (*Hippolais olivetorum*), which is the largest Hippolais in the region has been reported in the Crimea and Transcaspian regions.]

Sylvia

Small and very small. Tail straight. Greater contrast in coloration than leaf- or reed-warblers. Feeds on insects and occasionally berries in autumn.

568. ORPHEAN WARBLER

Sylvia hortensis
(Pevchaya Slavka)
Plate 36, Map 236

Field marks: 15 cm. Size of a sparrow. Nape, back, rump, wings, and tail are brownish-gray; top and sides of head black; underparts whitish; outer tail feathers white; eye white.

Habits: Found in bushy thickets in a variety of habitats. Not numerous. Stays in trees and bushes; fast and lively. Nests in bushes, and lays four to six greenish-white eggs with gray, greenish, and brown spots in June and July. Call: harsh "chek-chek." Song: a variety of sonorous whistles.

Range and distribution: Transcaucasus, mountains of Turkmenia, Pamir-Alai, and western Tien-Shan.

Similar species: Differs from Blackcap by its white eye, whitish underparts, white outer tail feathers, and black cheeks and crown.

569. GARDEN WARBLER

Sylvia borin
(Sadovaya Slavka)
Plate 36, Map 236

Field marks: 14 cm. Olive-gray overall; somewhat lighter underparts.

Habits: Found in groves and thickets in marshy meadows. Common. Stays in tree crowns and the thickest part of bushes. Nests in bushes. Lays four to six gray eggs spotted brownish

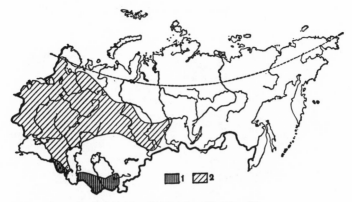

MAP 236. Orphean Warbler (1), Garden Warbler (2)

from May to July. Call: harsh "chek-chek." Song: a variety of burbling trills.

Range and distribution: European USSR (except Kola Peninsula and northeast), central and southern regions of western Siberia. Winters in tropical and southern Africa.

Similar species: Differs from other Sylvia by its uniform grayish coloration that lacks distinctive marks; from Olivaceous Warbler by rounded head and lack of eyebrow.

570. BARRED WARBLER
Sylvia nisoria
(Yastrebinaya Slavka)
Plate 36, Map 237

Field marks: 15 cm. In the male, the head, back, and rump are ash-gray; underparts whitish with a dark, crescentic barring. In females and juveniles, the gray is replaced by brownish-gray, and barring is restricted to the flanks. Eyes of adults are yellow.

Habits: Found in thin woods and thickets. Not numerous but locally common. Stays in tree crowns or in the thickest part of bushes; very lively. Nests in a bush or tree. Lays five or six whitish eggs with gray spots in June or July. Call: harsh "chek-chek." Song: a variety of loud whistles.

Range and distribution: European USSR (except northern regions), West Siberia, Central Asia (except central and western areas). Winters in eastern Africa.

Similar species: Differs from other Sylvia by the barring on its underparts.

571. BLACKCAP
Sylvia atricapilla
(Slavka-chernogolovka)
Plate 36, Map 237

Field marks: 14 cm. Upperparts brownish-gray, underparts lighter. Male has a black cap; fe-

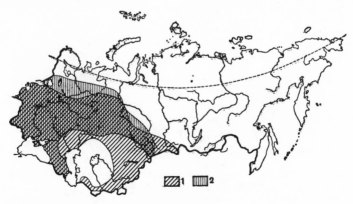

MAP 237. Barred Warbler (1), Blackcap (2)

males and juveniles are similar, but with rusty brown cap.

Habits: Found in mixed and deciduous woods, gardens, and parks. Common. Stays in the leafiest part of bushes or trees; very lively. Nests in bushes; rarely in lowest tree branches. Lays four to six dirty white eggs spotted brownish from May to July. Call: harsh "chek-chek." Song: a variety of sonorous flutelike whistles.

Range and distribution: European USSR and southwestern Siberia. Winters in Africa.

Similar species: Differs from Orphean Warbler by its gray cheeks and underparts, lack of white outer tail feathers, and lack of white eyes.

572. GREATER WHITETHROAT
Sylvia communis
(Seraya Slavka)
Plate 36, Map 238

Field marks: 14 cm. Head gray; throat white. Back, wings, and tail brownish-rufous; shoulders rusty; underparts pinkish-white.

Habits: Found in thickets in open areas and forest edges. Common. Stays in thickest part of bushes; agile hopper from branch to branch. Nests in bush. Lays four to six white or greenish eggs with brownish spots in June. Male often flies into the air while in song. Call: loud "chek-chek." Song: a variety of chirping, something like "terlee-viturlee-chet-chit-tee-teerlee."

Range and distribution: European USSR, southern Siberia (east as far as southwest Transbaikal), Central Asia, and southern Kazakhstan. Winters in southwestern Asia and Africa.

Similar species: Differs from Lesser White-

throat by its rusty shoulders and lack of dark cheeks.

573. LESSER WHITETHROAT
Sylvia curruca
(Slavka-melnichek)
Plate 36, Map 238

Field marks: 13 cm. Resembles Greater Whitethroat, but smaller; upperparts grayer with no rufous on the wing; lores and cheeks dark; throat white.

Habits: Found in a variety of woods and thickets. Common, in places rare. Stays in tree crowns or in the thickest part of bushes; very lively. Nests in tree or bush. Lays four to six grayish-white eggs with dark spots in May or June. Call: soft "chek-check." Song: a variety of chirping interspersed with loud "klyo-klyo-klyo-klyo."

Range and distribution: European USSR and Siberia as far as the Lena River and Transbaikal; Central Asia and Kazakhstan. Winters in southern Iran, India, and equatorial Africa.

Similar species: Differs from Greater Whitethroat by its dark cheeks and grayer upperparts.

574. DESERT WARBLER
Sylvia nana
(Pustynnaya Slavka)
Plate 36, Map 239

Field marks: 12 cm. Smallest of the warblers in the USSR. Upperparts light yellowish-gray; underparts whitish with buffy flanks; tail brownish with white outer feathers.

Habits: Desert inhabitant. Found in thickets of scrub and saxal trees. Common. Stays in bushes; very lively. Nests in bushes, and lays four or

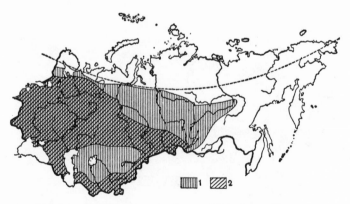

MAP 238. Lesser Whitethroat (1), Greater Whitethroat (2)

MAP 239. Desert Warbler

five white eggs speckled brownish or gray from April to June. Call: soft chirring. Song: ringing "teere-teetyou-tyou-tyou-tyouyou."
Range and distribution: Deserts of Kazakhstan and Central Asia. Winters in southern West Asia and in northeast Africa.
Similar species: Differs from Streaked Scrub Warbler by its unstreaked upperparts, and by its more typical warbler behavior.

575. MÉNÉTRIES'S WARBLER
Sylvia mystacea
(Belousaya Slavka)
Plate 36, Map 240
Field marks: 12 cm. Resembles Lesser Whitethroat, but plumage more contrasting; head, wings, and tail blackish; back dark brownish-gray; outer tail feathers white; throat and breast pink; malar stripe white; belly whitish. Red

eye, yellow eye ring. Females and juveniles: upperparts are grayish-brownish; underparts ocherish-white.
Habits: Found in thickets along river valleys in steppe, and on dry mountainsides; has a predilection for tamarisk. Common. Stays in bushes; very lively. Male flies up while singing. Nests in bush. Lays four or five white eggs with pinkish cast and dark speckles in May and June. Call: loud "cherrr." Song: short chirping trill.
Range and distribution: Deserts and semi-deserts of Central Asia and Kazakhstan. Winters in western regions of the Arabian Peninsula and in Somalia.
Similar species: Differs from other warblers by its white "whiskers."

[The **576.** SARDINIAN WARBLER (*Sylvia melano-cephala*) has been recorded in Bessarabia.]

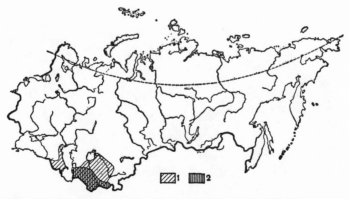

MAP 240. Ménétries's Warbler (1), Streaked Scrub Warbler (2)

Scotocerca

577. STREAKED SCRUB WARBLER
Scotocerca inquieta
(Skototserka)
Plate 36, Map 240
Field marks: 12 cm. Very small and lively. Color a light pinkish-gray; belly whitish; long, graduated, dark brownish tail with whitish tip; long brownish streaks on the head, back, and breast.
Habits: Found in thickets in dry desert and semi-desert. Non-migratory and nomadic. Common. Found singly, in pairs and groups. Hops about in bushes or on the ground with tail cocked. Nests in bush. Lays five to eight pinkish-white eggs speckled brownish-red from March to June. Call: prolonged whistle, changing to chirring.
Range and distribution: Deserts of Central Asia and southern Kazakhstan.
Similar species: Differs from Desert Warbler by its long tail and streaked head and back.

Regulus

578. GOLDCREST
Regulus regulus
(Zheltogolovy Korolyok)
Plate 41, Map 241
Field marks: 9-11 cm. Small fluffy bird (the smallest bird in the USSR) with a short tail. Upperparts olive-green; underparts whitish; two whitish wings bars; top of male's head is orange with lemon-yellow edges, of female's, lemon-yellow, crowns of both have black bordering stripes that do not connect at the forehead.
Habits: Found in coniferous and mixed forest;

in old pine trees during nesting. Nonmigratory and nomadic. Common. At nesting, stays in pairs; in flocks the remainder of the time. Nest is a domed cup, and is located high on the tip of a pine branch. Lays eight to ten pale red eggs speckled brownish-red in May and June. Call: quiet "tsee-tsee-tsee." Song: quiet, ringing "tsee-flee-heen, tsee-flee-heen."
Range and distribution: European USSR, southern West Siberia, Tien-Shan Mountains, southern Soviet Far East, Sakhalin Island, southern Kuril Islands.
Similar species: Differs from Firecrest by its lack of black eye stripe and by joining of black crown stripes at forehead.

579. FIRECREST
Regulus ignicapillus
(Krasnogolovy Korolyok)
Plate 41, Map 241
Field marks: 9 cm. Resembles Goldcrest, but with black eye stripe; forehead and eyebrow pure white; cheeks light bluish-gray; crown orange-yellow (male) or yellow (female) bordered by black stripe that meets at the forehead.
Habits: Found in mixed and coniferous woods and thickets of Labrador-tea. Nonmigratory and nomadic. Not numerous. At nesting, stays in pairs, the rest of the time, in flocks. Nest is a cup situated on the tip of a branch. Lays seven to twelve pink eggs with small brownish-red spots in May or June. Call: similar to Goldcrest's. Song: slowly rising thin whistle, "fee-fee-feefeefee-fyou."
Range and distribution: Carpathians, western Caucasus, the Crimea.
Similar species: Differs from Goldcrest by its white eye stripe, gray cheeks, and black band across the forehead.

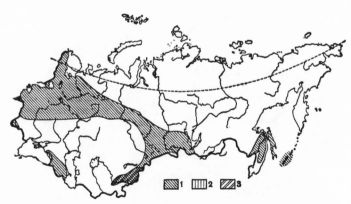

MAP 241. Goldcrest (1), Firecrest (2), Severtzov's Tit-Warbler (3)

Leptopoecile

580. SEVERTZOV'S TIT-WARBLER
Leptopoecile sophiae
(Raspisnaya Sinichka)
Plate 41, Map 241
Field marks: 9-10 cm. One of the smallest birds in the USSR. Tail long, with rounded tip. Softly feathered and fluffy. Crown rusty, back and upper neck gray; wings and tail blackish-brownish; outer tail feathers and eye stripe lighter; throat, breast, sides, and rump violet-blue; belly whitish-rusty. Females and juveniles are duller, with brownish-gray underparts.
Habits: Found in forests of arborescent juniper and thickets in upper mountain regions. Nonmigratory and nomadic. Common. Paired during nesting; otherwise in flocks. Agile climber in thick bushes. Nest is a cup situated in a bush. Lays four to six white eggs speckled red-brownish in April and May. Voice: quiet, charming "tsee-tsee."
Range and distribution: Mountains of Central Asia and southern Kazakhstan.
Similar species: No similar species in the USSR.

Muscicapa

Small birds with a wide, flat bill. Tail short, straight; often forked. Found in a variety of woodlands. Characteristically perches immobile; occasionally flicks its wings while perched on a prominent branch; also flies up to catch an insect and returns to the same place. Migratory.

581. SPOTTED FLYCATCHER
Muscicapa striata
(Seraya Mukholovka)
Plate 39, Map 242
Field marks: 14 cm. Upperparts, tail, and wings brownish-gray; darker brownish streaks on the head and fainter streaks on back; underparts white; breast has a brownish suffusion and indistinct brownish streaking; white streaks on the forehead; tenth primary is longer than primary coverts.
Habits: Found in planted woods in a variety of habitats. Common. Stays singly and in pairs. Nests behind loose bark, in tree crotches, in shallow tree hollows, in nesting boxes, etc. Lays four to six greenish eggs with rusty spots in May and June. Call: loud "tseet-teet."
Range and distribution: European USSR, southern Siberia as far as the Transbaikal, mountains of Central Asia and southern Kazakhstan. Winters in Africa.
Similar species: At first glance, similar to the Dark-sided Flycatcher, Gray-streaked Flycatcher, and the Asian Brown Flycatcher. In the hand, differs from the Dark-sided Flycatcher by its streaked, whitish forehead; from the Gray-streaked Flycatcher by lack of streaking on the belly; from the Asian Brown Flycatcher by streaked breast.

582. DARK-SIDED FLYCATCHER
Muscicapa sibirica
(Mukholovka-kasatka)
Plate 39, Map 242
Field marks: 12 cm. Resembles Spotted Flycatcher, but upperparts, including forehead, are darker. Underparts darker with white stripe from throat to belly; tenth primary shorter than primary coverts.
Habits: Found in mixed taiga with a predom-

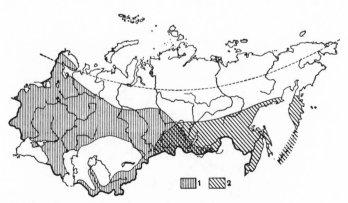

MAP 242. Spotted Flycatcher (1), Dark-sided Flycatcher (2)

inance of coniferous forest in plains and hills. Common. Found singly and in pairs. Nest is made of bits of lichen and lined with larch needles, and is situated in tree crotch or in thick branches. Lays four or five greenish eggs with small rusty-brown spots in May and June. Call is a soft chirring.

Range and distribution: Southern Siberia from the Altai to the shores of the Okhotsk Sea, Soviet Far East, Kamchatka Peninsula, Sakhalin and Kuril Islands. Winters in southeastern Asia.

Similar species: In the field, practically indistinguishable from the Spotted, Gray-streaked, or Asian Brown Flycatcher. Differs from the Spotted Flycatcher by lack of whitish streaks on the forehead (and in the hand, by the tenth primary, which is shorter than the primary wing coverts); from the Gray-streaked Flycatcher by its darker underparts; from the Asian Brown Flycatcher by its longer wings and darker underparts.

583. GRAY-STREAKED FLYCATCHER
Muscicapa griseisticta
(Pestrogolovaya Mukholovka)
Plate 39, Map 243

Field marks: 12 cm. Greatly resembles Spotted Flycatcher, but streaking on breast and belly more distinct; forehead white (not white-streaked).

Habits: Found in variety of woods. Not numerous. Found singly and in pairs. Nesting habits not studied in USSR. Call: fairly loud "speet-teet-teet."

Range and distribution: Southeastern Siberia, Soviet Far East, southern Kamchatka Peninsula, Sakhalin Island, Kuril Islands. Winters in Southeast Asia and Indonesia.

Similar species: Greatly resembles Dark-sided Flycatcher, Spotted Flycatcher, and Asian Brown Flycatcher. Differs from the Spotted and Dark-sided by the distinct streaking on the belly; from the Asian Brown, by its streaked breast.

584. ASIAN BROWN FLYCATCHER
Muscicapa latirostris
(Shirokoklyuvaya Mukholovka)
Plate 39, Map 243

Field marks: 12 cm. Greatly resembles Spotted Flycatcher, but has a light ring around the eye; underparts are white with a grayish-brown suffusion on the breast and flanks.

Habits: Found in a variety of forests, but prefers deciduous woods. Occurs singly and in pairs. Common. Nest is a compact cup of moss and lichens, and is situated in tree crowns or crotches. Lays four or five olive-gray eggs in May and June. Call: loud "seeet-seet."

Range and distribution: Southern Siberia, Soviet Far East, southern Sakhalin Island, and southern Kuril Islands. Winters in southern Asia and in the Philippines.

Similar species: Greatly resembles Dark-sided, Spotted, and Gray-streaked Flycatchers; differs by lack of streaking on breast.

585. RUFOUS-TAILED FLYCATCHER
Muscicapa ruficauda
(Ryzhekhvostaya Mukholovka)
Plate 39, Map 243

Field marks: 13 cm. Brownish-gray overall; belly whitish; rump and tail rusty brown.

Habits: Found in mostly deciduous forests with old trees in mountain areas. Somewhat rare, although common in places. Occurs singly and in pairs. Nests in tree branches. Lays three or four olive-green eggs in May and June. Call: quiet whistle. Song: loud "nee-tee-tee-teee."

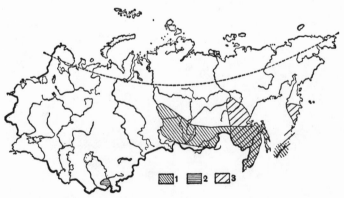

MAP 243. Asian Brown Flycatcher (1), Rufous-tailed Flycatcher (2), Gray-streaked Flycatcher (3)

MAP 244. Pied Flycatcher (1), Collared Flycatcher (2)

Range and distribution: Deciduous forests of the Pamir-Alai Mountains. Winters in India.
Similar species: Differs from other flycatchers by its rusty tail. In the field, differs from female Redstarts by its flycatcher behavior. In the hand, by its wide, flat bill.

586. PIED FLYCATCHER
Muscicapa hypoleuca
(Mukholovka-pestrushka)
Plate 39, Map 244

Field marks: 13-14 cm. In male, top of the head and neck, back, wings, and tail are black; narrow white band on forehead; wide wing patch; outer tail feathers and entire underparts are white. In females and juveniles the black is replaced by gray-brownish.
Habits: Found in a variety of woods, gardens, and parks. Common, in places numerous. Found singly and in pairs. Often lowers wings and raises fanned tail while perched on dead branch. Nests in tree hollow or nesting boxes. Lays five to seven light blue eggs in May and June. Call: loud "peek-peee." Song: a variety of loud trills resembling "peechee-peechee-kooleeleechi."
Range and distribution: European USSR (except southern regions) and souther West Siberia (as far as the upper reaches of the Yenisei River). Winters in north equatorial Africa.
Similar species: Resembles Collared Flycatcher, but the two are seldom seen together, since ranges do not overlap. Differs by lack of white collar. Females practically indistinguishable.

587. COLLARED FLYCATCHER
Muscicapa albicollis
(Mukholovka-belosheyka)
Plate 39, Map 244
Field marks: 13-14 cm. Greatly resembles Pied

Flycatcher, but white of underparts extends around the neck, occasionally coming full circle.
Habits: Prefers tall deciduous trees in plains and hills. Not numerous. Found singly and in pairs. Behavior and call similar to Pied Flycatcher. Nests in tree hollow. Lays four to seven light blue eggs in May and June.
Range and distribution: Central and western regions of European USSR, Caucasus, western Central Asia. Winters in tropical Africa.
Similar species: Male differs from Pied Flycatcher by its white collar. Females practically indistinguishable.

588. RED-THROATED FLYCATCHER
Muscicapa parva
(Malaya Mukholovka)
Plate 39, Map 245
Field marks: 11-12 cm. Smallest flycatcher in the USSR. In male, top and sides of head and neck are ash-gray; back and rump brownish-gray; wings and tail brownish; throat and upper breast rusty; breast, belly, and basal half of outer tail feathers white. Females and juveniles are similar but without rusty throat, and the ash-gray is replaced by brownish-gray.
Habits: Found in mature forests in plains and hills. Not numerous, but common in places. Nests in tree hollow or cavity. Lays five or six pinkish-yellow or greenish eggs with rusty-pink spots in May and June. Call: dry chirring "trr" or whistle, "hu-lee, hu-lee." Song: a loud trill.
Range and distribution: Forest zones from western borders to Kamchatka Peninsula and the lower Amur River; mountains of the Caucasus. Winters in southern Asia.
Similar species: Male differs from Mugimaki Flycatcher by its gray upperparts; females by the lack of any rust on the throat.

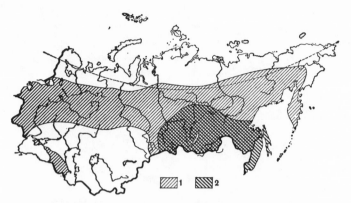

MAP 245. Red-throated Flycatcher (1), Mugimaki Flycatcher (2)

589. MUGIMAKI FLYCATCHER

Muscicapa mugimaki
(Taezhnaya Mukholovka)
Plate 39, Map 245

Field marks: 11 cm. In male, top and sides of head, back, wings, and tail are black; shoulder patch white; stripe behind the eye and belly are white; throat, breast, and flanks are rusty red. In females and juveniles, the black is replaced by brownish-gray, and the rusty-red by a yellowish-rust.

Habits: Found in plains with tall trees and damp, mountainous taiga. Common. Stays singly and in pairs in lower crown of trees. Nest is made of moss and lichens, lined with dry grass, animal hair, moss, and the like, and is situated on branches close to the trunk. Lays four to eight olive-green eggs with red-brown spots in May and June. Call: dry, scraping chirring. Song: loud trill.

Range and distribution: Taiga of southern Siberia (from Tomsk and Krasnoyarsk), Soviet Far East, southern Sakhalin Island. Winters in Malaysia and Indonesia.

Similar species: Differs from the Red-throated Flycatcher by the less extensive (sometimes absent) white on basal half of outer tail feathers. The male differs by its black upperparts; the female by its rusty breast.

590. NARCISSUS FLYCATCHER

Muscicapa narcissina
(Zheltospinnaya Mukholovka)
Plate 39, Map 246

Field marks: 11 cm. In male, head, nape, back, wings, and tail are black; belly, eyebrow, and wing bar are white; throat, breast, flanks, and rump are yellow. Females and juveniles are brownish-gray with an olive-greenish rump, dirty white underparts, and a whitish throat

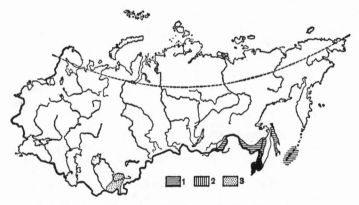

MAP 246. Narcissus Flycatcher (1), Blue-and-white Flycatcher (2), Asian Paradise-Flycatcher (3)

spotted with grayish-brown. Flycatchers of the Kuril Islands and Sakhalin Peninsula have a yellow eyebrow.

Habits: Found in forests, wooded areas, and thickets near river deltas. Common. Found singly and in pairs in lower tree branches and in bushes. Nests in a tree hollow. Lays four to seven white eggs with brick-red speckles in May and June. Call: short whistle. Song: quiet trill resembling "pee-pee-peetyou-eeto-foyee."

Range and distribution: Southern Soviet Far East, Sakhalin Island, southern Kuril Islands. Winters in Indochina, Indonesia, Philippines.

Similar species: No similar species in the USSR.

591. BLUE-AND-WHITE FLYCATCHER
Muscicapa cyanomelana
(Sinaya Mukholovka)
Plate 39, Map 246

Field marks: 15 cm. In male, top of head, back, and tail are bright blue; wings have brownish tips; sides of head, throat, and breast are black; belly white; sides blackish-gray. The females and juveniles are brownish-gray with a rusty rump; they have buffy white underparts with a brownish breast.

Habits: Found in forests with a thick undergrowth; more often along banks and cliffs of rivers. Common. Occurs singly and in pairs. Nest is made from moss and is situated on rock pinnacles, in stump cavities, or shallow tree hollows. Lays four or five white-pinkish eggs in June and July. Song: a variety of loud, beautiful trills.

Range and distribution: Southern areas of Soviet Far East and southern Kuril Islands. Winters in Indochina, Philippines, and Borneo.

Similar species: No similar species in the USSR.

Terpsiphone

592. ASIAN PARADISE-FLYCATCHER
Terpsiphone paradisi
(Rayskaya Mukholovka)
Plate 39, Map 246

Field marks: 20-30 cm. Large flycatcher (larger than a sparrow) with long tail and prominent pointed crest. In the male, back, tail (and in Far East races, the wings) are a bright reddish-rust; head and crest are black with a blue-green gloss; underparts white; breast is gray in Far Eastern races; wings are white with black feather shafts; tail very long. In females and juveniles, tail is shorter and underparts gray. Bill, legs, and bare ring around the eyes are light blue.

Habits: Found in deciduous woods, old gardens, and groves. Not numerous, but common in places. Found singly, in pairs, or in groups of three to five in the thickest part of the tree and bushes. Very lively, and does not remain long in one place. Nest, small and compact, is woven of bast fibers. Lays two to five white-pinkish eggs with small reddish-brown spots in May and June. Call: harsh "chet-trkh-chettr" or "dzh-zee, dzh-zee." Song: lovely low whistle, "ee-tym-lyou-lyou-goo."

Range and distribution: Deciduous mountain forests in Central Asia and southwestern Tien-Shan Mountains, southern Soviet Far East. Winters in India and Southeast Asia.

Similar species: No similar species in the USSR.

[In the southern Ussuri River region, vagrants of **593.** JAPANESE PARADISE FLYCATCHER (*Terpsiphone atrocaudata*) were noted. The bird has a black head, throat, breast, and tail; a whitish belly and a rusty metallic glitter on its back. Prominent blue bill and eye ring.]

Parus

Small birds with short, straight bill and longish, strong legs. Thickly and softly feathered; wings comparatively short. In fall and winter stays in flocks that are often made up of several species. Feeds on insects. May also feed on berries in fall and winter.

594. GREAT TIT
Parus major
(Bolshaya Sinitsa)
Plate 40, Map 247

Field marks: 13-17 cm. Largest of the USSR tits. Head, throat, breast, and belly stripe black; wings and tail light bluish; back is greenish or light blue-gray; breast and belly yellow or white; cheeks and nape are white.

Habits: Found in deciduous and mixed woods in plains, hills, gardens, and parks. Nonmigratory and nomadic. Common. At nesting, stays in pairs. The remainder of the time in flocks, often with other species of tit. Very spry and lively. Like other tits, it prepares its food by banging it while clutching it in its claws. Nests in a stump. Lays nine to thirteen white eggs with small red-brownish spots from March to June. Call: a loud "peen-peen-cherzhzh." Song: loud whistles resembling "tsee-tsee-tsee-pee, in-cha-in-cha."

Range and distribution: European USSR, southern Siberia, Soviet Far East, Kazakhstan, Central Asia.

Similar species: Differs from other tits by its large size.

MAP 247. Great Tit (1), Varied Tit (2)

595. AZURE TIT
Parus cyanus
(Belaya Lazorevka)
Plate 40, Map 248

Field marks: 12-14 cm. Back is light blue-gray; wings, tail, and eye stripe are light blue; tail has white tip and white outer tail feathers; extensive patches of white on wings; head is white or grayish; underparts are white (may be yellow locally) with short black stripe.

Habits: Found in deciduous and mixed forest, riverbank thickets, and thickets near lakes and ponds in plains and hills. Found in pairs at nesting time; in flocks the rest of the time. An agile climber in bushes or along thin tree branches, often hanging upside down. Nonmigratory and nomadic. Not numerous. Nests in a stump, more rarely in a cliff crevice. Lays three to eleven white eggs with red-brown speckles in May and June. Call: loud "tsee-tsee-tsee-trrzh." Song: a short trill.

Range and distribution: Central belt of Eu-ropean USSR (from Belorussia east), southern Siberia, Soviet Far East. Pamir-Alai and Tien-Shan Mountains.

Similar species: Differs from other tits by its white or gray head.

596. BLUE TIT
Parus caeruleus
(Lazorevka)
Plate 40, Map 248

Field marks: 11-13 cm. Blue cap, wings, and tail; greenish back; cheeks and forehead white; throat, belly stripe, and stripe around cheeks black; breast and belly yellow.

Habits: Found in deciduous woods, gardens, and parks. Nonmigratory and nomadic. Common. Stays in pairs during nesting period; in flocks the remainder of the time, often with other species. Agile climber on thin branches of trees and bushes. Nests in stumps. Lays five to ten white eggs with small red-brown spots

MAP 248. Azure Tit (1), Blue Tit (2)

MAP 249. Coal Tit (1), Crested Tit (2), Rufous-naped Tit (3)

in April and May. Call: loud "tsee-tsee-tsirrzz."
Song: short trill.
Range and distribution: Deciduous and mixed
woods of central and southern belt of European USSR.
Similar species: Differs from other tits by its
blue cap.

597. VARIED TIT

Parus varius
(Yaponskaya Sinitsa)
Plate 40, Map 247
Field marks: 12 cm. Back, wings, and tail are
light blue-gray; head and throat black; forehead, cheeks, rear crown, and nape are yellowish-white; upper back, belly, and sides are
brownish-rusty.
Habits: Found in coniferous (prefers yew-tree)
forests. Nonmigratory and nomadic. Common. Found in pairs during nesting; in flocks
the rest of the time. Nests in stump, and lays
seven or eight white eggs with small red-brown
spots in April or May. Voice: harsh "tsee-tsee"
or 'tsi-tsi-shh."
Range and distribution: Southern Kuril Islands.
Similar species: Differs from other tits by its
rusty brown belly.

598. COAL TIT

Parus ater
(Moskovka)
Plate 40, Map 249
Field marks: 11-12 cm. Back is light blue or
olive-gray; wings and tail brownish-gray; head,
throat, and upper breast black; cheeks, spot
on nape, breast, and two narrow wing bars are
white; underparts whitish with buffy sides.
Habits: Inhabits coniferous and mixed woods
in plains and hills. Nonmigratory and nomadic. Common. Found in pairs during nest-

ing season; in flocks the rest of the time, often
with other species. Lively and bold; often climbs
in tree crowns. Nests in stumps or holes in the
ground. Lays six to eleven white eggs with
small reddish spots from April to June. Call:
loud "tsee-pee, tsee-pee" or "tee-tee-tyouee."
Range and distribution: Entire USSR, mountain forests of the Crimea, Caucasus and Tien-
Shan Mountains.
Similar species: Differs from Rufous-naped Tit
by its light belly.

599. RUFOUS-NAPED TIT

Parus rufonuchalis
(Ryzhesheynaya Sinitsa)
Plate 40, Map 249
Field marks: 12 cm. Slightly crested; back,
breast, and belly are light blue-gray; wings
and tail brownish-gray; head, throat, and upper breast black; cheeks and nape spot are
white; undertail and neck spot rusty red.
Habits: Found in mountain forests of spruce
and arborescent juniper. Nonmigratory and
nomadic. Common. Pairs during nesting; the
remainder of the year found in flocks, which
are often joined by other species of tits. Nests
in stump. Lays eggs in May and June. Eggs of
birds that nest in the USSR not available for
description. Call: loud "tsee-fyouee." Song:
loud trill.
Range and distribution: Mountain forests of
Pamir-Alai and Tien-Shan.
Similar species: Differs from Coal Tit by its
gray belly.

600. CRESTED TIT

Parus cristatus
(Khokhlataya Sinitsa)
Plate 40, Map 249
Field marks: 11-12 cm. Large pointed crest on
the head. Back, wings, and tail gray-brownish;

throat, crescentic stripe behind the eye and speckling on crest are black; head, crest, and entire underparts are white with a brownish suffusion on the flanks.

Habits: Coniferous forests. Found in pairs at nesting time; in flocks with other species the rest of the year. Found in middle and lower sections of trees and on the ground. Non-migratory and nomadic. Common. Nests in a stump. Lays five to ten white eggs with small red-brown spots from April to June. Call: loud "tsee-tsee-trrch."

Range and distribution: European USSR except southern half.

Similar species: Differs from other tits by its prominent crest.

601. MARSH TIT
Parus palustris
(Chernogolovaya Gaichka)
Plate 40, Map 250

Field marks: 11-13 cm. Back, wings, and tail are brownish-gray; top of head and chin are black; cheeks and underparts dirty white.

Habits: Prefers deciduous, more rarely mixed forests, thickets of river floodlands, groves, and parks. Nonmigratory and nomadic. Common. In pairs at nesting time; in flocks with other tits the remainder of the year. Agile and lively; often hangs from the end of a branch. Nests in a stump. Lays six to ten white eggs with small reddish-brown spots from April to June. Voice: loud "tsee-tsee-chzhee-chzhee" or a sorrowful whistle, "pyouyouee-pyouyouee-pyouee." Voice of Caucasus race: a loud trill.

Range and distribution: European USSR (from the Baltic States and Moldavia to Bashkiria), southern Siberia (from Altai), Soviet Far East,

Sakhalin Island, southern Kuril Islands. Isolated populations in the Caucasus.

Similar species: In the field, practically indistinguishable from the Willow Tit. In the hand, differs by its smaller, blue-tinged glossy cap and thicker bill.

602. WILLOW TIT
parus montanus
(Boorogolovaya Gaichka)
Plate 40, Map 250

Field marks: 11-14 cm. Greatly resembles Marsh Tit, but cap and bib are slightly larger, with a brownish tone.

Habits: Found in coniferous and mixed forests. Nonmigratory and nomadic. Common. Behavior same as Marsh Tit, but has a preference for coniferous plantings. Nests in stump. Lays seven or eight white eggs with small red-brown spots from April to June. Call: loud "tsiye-tsiiye" or "dzee-dzee."

Range and distribution: Entire forest zone of the USSR from western borders to Anadyr River, Kamchatka Peninsula, Sakhalin Island.

Similar species: Nearly indistinguishable from Marsh Tit in the field. In the hand, it differs by having the dull (not glossy) black cap reach the back; also by its slightly thinner bill.

603. SIBERIAN TIT
Parus cinctus
(Serogolovaya Gaichka)
Plate 40, Map 251

Field marks: 12-14 cm. Back, wings, and tail grayish-brownish; cap brownish; chin blackish-brown; cheeks and underparts dirty white with a rusty suffusion on the flanks.

Habits: Found in coniferous, more rarely deciduous forests. Nonmigratory and nomadic. Not numerous. Stays in pairs and flocks to-

MAP 250. Marsh Tit (1), Willow Tit (2)

gether with other species of tits. Nests in a stump. Lays six to nine white eggs with small reddish-brown spots in May or June. Voice: loud "tsin-tsin."

Range and distribution: Northern forest zones from the Kola Peninsula to Anadyr River and shores of the Okhotsk Sea.

Similar species: Differs from other species by its brownish cap.

604. SOMBRE TIT
Parus lugubris
(Sredizemnomorskaya Gaichka)
Plate 40, Map 251

Field marks: 14 cm. Resembles Marsh Tit, but larger. Black cap, throat, and upper breast; cheeks and outer tail feathers white; breast and belly dirty white. Noticeably heavy bill.

Habits: Inhabits mountainous deciduous forests. Stays in pairs and flocks in tree crowns. Nonmigratory. Rare. Nests in a stump. Lays six to ten white eggs with reddish speckles from April to July. Voice: loud "tsee-tsee" or "tsee-tsee-tsee."

Range and distribution: Southwestern Transcaucasus.

Similar species: Differs from other tits by its white outer tail feathers, pure white cheeks, and larger black bib.

Remiz

605. EURASIAN PENDULINE-TIT
Remiz pendulinus
(Remez)
Plate 41, Map 251

Field marks: 9-12 cm. Small (significantly smaller than a sparrow). Back and shoulders rusty brown; broad black mask; wings and tail blackish with light edgings; head pale gray, brown, or black; underparts whitish with a buffy suffusion.

Habits: Found in deciduous forest near floodland, thickets near bodies of water, and stands of reed and cattail. Migratory. Common. Goes to mountain elevations of 2,000 meters. Stays in pairs during nesting; the rest of the time, in flocks. Climbs about on thin branches of bushes and trees and reed stems. Nest is made of plant fluff in the shape of a mitten, and is suspended on thin branches. Sometimes it is woven in the shape of a bag from leaves and fluff from reeds, and is situated between reed stems. Lays five to ten white eggs in May or June. Voice: thin whistle, "tsee-tsee."

Range and distribution: Southern half of USSR from the Baltic States to the Amur River area. Winters in the Transcaucasus, Central Asia, northern India, and China.

Similar species: No similar species in the USSR.

Sitta

Small (sparrow-size) birds with a pointed, straight bill and strong short legs with sharply curved claws. Feathering is thick and fluffy. Tail short and straight. Thick-set body. Agile cliff or tree-trunk climber, often moving down head first. Feeds on insects.

606. EURASIAN NUTHATCH
Sitta europaea
(Obyknovenny Popolzen)
Plate 41, Map 252

Field marks: 14-17 cm. Upperparts uniformly light blue-gray; wings and tail brownish-black;

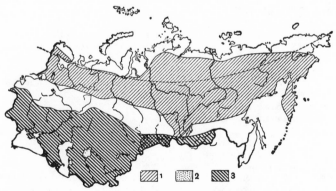

MAP 251. Siberian Tit (1), Sombre Tit (2), Eurasian Penduline-Tit (3)

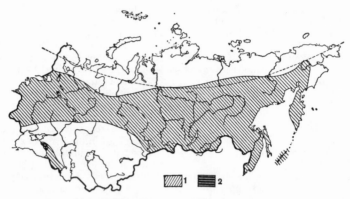

MAP 252. Eurasian Nuthatch (1), Kruper's Nuthatch (2)

eye stripe black; "corners" on tail white; throat white; breast and belly white or rusty; flanks rusty brown.

Habits: Found in wooded habitat where it lives in large trees of deciduous, mixed, or coniferous forests; sometimes found in gardens and parks. Nonmigratory and nomadic. Common. Found singly and in pairs; climbs on tree trunks; often joins flocks of tits. Very lively and noisy. Nests in stump; entrance to nest smeared with clay. Lays six to eight white eggs with red-brownish speckles from April to June. Call: loud "tyochtyoch-tyoch" or "tseet-tseet." Song: loud whistle.

Range and distribution: Forest zone throughout USSR except Central Asia and Kazakhstan.

Similar species: Differs from Kruper's Nuthatch by its larger size, and by the lack of a black cap and rufous patch on the upper breast. From the Rock Nuthatches by its rusty flanks.

607. KRUPER'S NUTHATCH
Sitta krüperi
(Chernogolovy Popolzen)
Plate 41, Map 252

Field marks: 12 cm. Smallest of the USSR nuthatches. Upperparts bluish-gray; wings brownish; tail and crown black; white tips on the outer tail feathers; underparts whitish-gray; large rusty spot on upper breast.

Habits: Found in mountain forests where it mostly lives in old plantings of silver fir (*Abies alba, Abies pectinata*). Nonmigratory. Not numerous. In habits, resembles Eurasian Nuthatch, but usually stays on branches, not trunk. Nests in stump, and nest entrance is not smeared with clay. Lays five or six white eggs with reddish spots in May. Call: harsh "pshsh-pshsh." Song: loud, sad, interrupted whistle.

Range and distribution: Mountain forests of northwestern Caucasus.

Similar species: Differs from Eurasian Nuthatch by its black cap, rusty spot on upper breast, and smaller size.

608. GREATER ROCK NUTHATCH
Sitta tephronota
(Bolshoy Skalisty Popolzen)
Plate 41, Map 253

Field marks: 15-17 cm. Resembles Eurasian Nuthatch; belly and sides light ocher-rusty. Lacks rusty flanks and white on tail.

Habits: Found in mountain cliffs. Nonmigratory. Common. Stays singly and in pairs on rocks and cliffs. Agile climber. Nest in cliff crevice is walled up with clay, and has a tunnel-shaped entrance. Lays six to eight white eggs with small red-brown spots from March to May. Call: loud whistle, "ploi-tyouee-tyouee" or "seet-seet." Song: a variety of loud whistles.

Range and distribution: Mountains of Armenia, Central Asia, and southern Kazakhstan.

Similar species: Differs from Eurasian Nuthatch by its larger size and uniform whitish-buff underparts. In the field, almost indistinguishable from the Lesser Rock Nuthatch. In the hand, differs by its larger size and longer, heavier bill.

609. LESSER ROCK NUTHATCH
Sitta neumayer
(Maly Skalisty Popolzen)
Plate 41, Map 253

Field marks: 14 cm. Resembles Greater Rock Nuthatch but smaller; bill is thinner.

Habits: Similar to Greater Rock Nuthatch. Lays up to thirteen eggs.

Range and distribution: Transcaucasus.

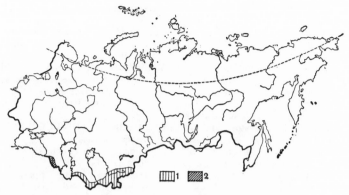

MAP 253. Greater Rock Nuthatch (1), Lesser Rock Nuthatch (2)

Similar species: In the field, nearly indistinguishable from Greater Rock Nuthatch. In the hand, differs by smaller size and thinner bill.

Tichodroma

610. WALLCREEPER
Tichodroma muraria
(Stenolaz)
Plate 41, Map 254

Field marks: 16-17 cm. Thin and long decurved bill. Top of head, back, and belly ash-gray; wings, tail, breast, and throat are black; broad, rounded wings with raspberry-red shoulders and wing patches; large white spots on outer primaries and outer tail feathers. Fall and winter throat is whitish.

Habits: Found in high cliffs of upper mountain regions. In winter, it moves down into the valleys, where it is found on steep slopes and shoreline precipices. Nonmigratory and nomadic. Not numerous. Climbs about on cliff walls and on rocks, constantly fluttering its wings. Flight reminiscent of a butterfly. Nests in cliff crevice. Lays three or four white eggs with small red-brownish spots in May and June. Call: low whistle, "tseeoo."

Range and distribution: Mountains of Carpathia, Caucasus, Central Asia, southern Kazakhstan, southeastern Altai.

Similar species: No similar species in the USSR.

Certhia

Very small birds with a thin, long, downcurved bill. Feathering is thick and fluffy. Legs have short tarsus and long toes with sharp claws. The tarsus is scutellated. Broad wings. Good tree-trunk climbers. Feeds on insects that it finds under bark.

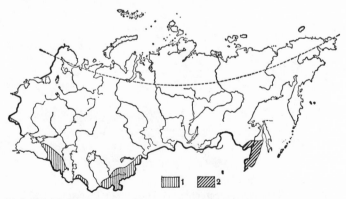

MAP 254. Wallcreeper (1), Chestnut-flanked White-eye (2)

611. NORTHERN TREECREEPER
Certhia familiaris
(Obyknovennaya Pishchukha)
Plate 41, Map 255

Field marks: 12-15 cm. Upperparts rufous-brown with whitish streaks and unstreaked rusty rump; wings with light irregular markings; underparts white. Claw of rear toe is no shorter than 9 mm.

Habits: Found in coniferous and mixed forest in plains and hills. Nonmigratory and nomadic. Common. Found singly and in pairs; climbs on tree trunks. Nests in stump or behind loose bark. Lays five to eight white eggs with small red-brown spots from April to June. Call: quiet "tsee-tsee." Song: loud trill.

Range and distribution: European USSR, southern Siberia, and Soviet Far East.

Similar species: Nearly indistinguishable from Short-toed Treecreeper in the field, but is whiter below and lacks brownish flanks. In the hand, differs by the longer claw on its hind toe.

612. SHORT-TOED TREECREEPER
Certhia brachydactyla
(Korotkopalaya Pishchukha)
Plate 41, Map 255

Field marks: 12-16 cm. Greatly resembles Northern Treecreeper, but eye stripe less distinct; underparts whitish with a brownish suffusion on the belly and flanks. Claw of the rear toe is no longer than 7.5 mm.

Habits: Found in deciduous and mixed woods, parks, and gardens. Nonmigratory and nomadic. Common. Found singly and in pairs on tree trunks. Nests in stump or behind loose bark. Lays six to eight white eggs with red-brownish speckles in April and May. Call: loud

"tveet-tveet." Song: short trill, "krootee-ver-ree."

Range and distribution: Transcarpathia, Black Sea coast of the Caucasus, and the Talysh Mountains.

Similar species: Practically indistinguishable from Northern Treecreeper in the field, but differs by its brownish sides in the hand. Also, claw of hind toe is no longer than 7.5 mm.

613. HIMALAYAN TREECREEPER
Certhia himalayana
(Gimalayskaya Pishchukha)
Plate 41, Map 255

Field marks: 13-16 cm. Upperparts brownish-gray with light and dark streaking; wings brownish; tail brownish and narrowly barred; underparts and eye stripe whitish; long, curved bill.

Habits: Found in mountain forests primarily of arborescent juniper. Nonmigratory, nomadic. Not numerous. Climbs tree trunks like other tree creepers. Found singly and in pairs. Lays four to six white eggs with small reddish-brown spots in May and June. Call: thin "tsee." Song: loud, whistling trill.

Range and distribution: Pamir-Alai and southwestern Tien-Shan Mountains.

Similar species: Differs from other tree creepers by its barred tail and longish bill. Also, range differs from other species.

Zosterops

614. CHESTNUT-FLANKED WHITE-EYE
Zosterops erythropleura
(Beloglazka)
Plate 37, Map 254

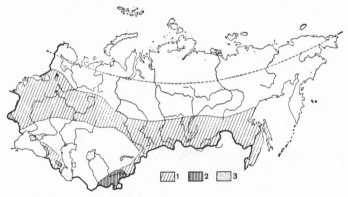

MAP 255. Northern Treecreeper (1), Himalayan Treecreeper (2), Short-toed Treecreeper (3)

Field marks: 12 cm. Very small bird. Upper parts, wings, and tail greenish; throat and upper breast yellow; belly and eye ring white; chestnut flanks vary in size (sometimes missing).

Habits: Found in groves and thickets along river banks. Migratory. Not numerous. Occurs singly, in pairs, and in flocks in trees and bushes. Nests in trees. Lays five or six eggs in June, but nesting habits little studied in USSR. Call: loud "tseeplee." Feeds on insects.

Range and distribution: Southern Soviet Far East. Winters in southeastern China.

Similar species: Differs from warblers by white eye ring.

Prunella

Small (sparrow-size or slightly larger) birds. Tail straight and notched. Upper mandible slightly flattened; bill is wide and straight at the mouth. Feathering is thick and fluffy. No sexual dimorphism in coloration. Feeds on small invertebrates. In winter, some species also feed on seeds.

615. DUNNOCK
Prunella modularis
(Lesnaya Zavirushka)
Plate 33, Map 256

Field marks: 14-16 cm. Upperparts dark brownish with dark streaking on back; head and breast dark gray; belly whitish.

Habits: Found in a variety of woods with thick undergrowth. Migratory in the north and nomadic in the south. Common. Stays hidden on the ground and in lower parts of trees and bushes, singly and in pairs. Nest, in tree or bush, is situated low to the ground. Lays four to six light greenish blue eggs in May and June. Male often perches at top of tree while singing. Call: soft trill, "trrree." Song: several loud trills.

Range and distribution: Northern forest zone of European USSR, Crimea, Caucasus. Winters in southern Europe, Iran, Iraq.

Similar species: Differs from Japanese Accentor by lighter coloration. Also found in entirely different ranges.

616. JAPANESE ACCENTOR
Prunella rubida
(Yaponskaya Zavirushka)
Plate 33, Map 256

Field marks: 14-16 cm. Resembles Dunnock, but darker and more rufous; underparts brownish-gray.

Habits: Found in overgrown thickets and pine (*Pinus sibiricus*) forest floor. Probably nomadic. Somewhat rare. Stays hidden on the ground or in lower trees and thickets. Nests in bush. Lays three or four greenish light blue eggs in June. Song and call same as Dunnock.

Range and distribution: Southern Kuril Islands. Winters in Japan.

Similar species: Differs from Dunnock by darker coloring; also the two species are not found in the same range.

Note: Some zoologists consider the Japanese Accentor to be a race of the Dunnock.

617. BLACK-THROATED ACCENTOR
Prunella atrogularis
(Chernogorlaya Zavirushka)
Plate 33, Map 256

Field marks: 15-16 cm. Upperparts, wings, and tail brownish-gray; brownish streaking on the

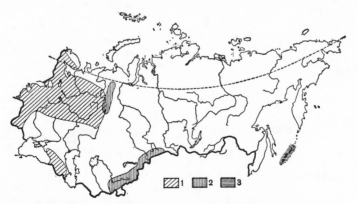

MAP 256. Dunnock (1), Black-throated Accentor (2), Japanese Accentor (3)

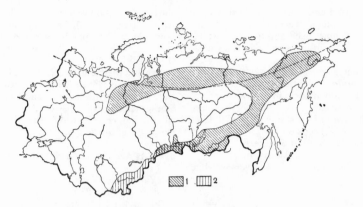

Map 257. Siberian Accentor (1), Brown Accentor (2)

back; throat, cheeks, and top of head brown-ish-black; eye stripe buffy; underparts buffy; belly whitish.

Habits: Found in coniferous and mixed forest with bushes and thickets of mountain shrubbery. Migratory in the north and nomadic in the south. Common. Stays hidden on the ground or in lower part of bushes singly, in pairs, or small flocks. Nests in bush or tree. Lays four or five light blue eggs in June or July. Call: soft trill. Song: several loud trills.

Range and distribution: Northern Urals, lower Yenisei River, mountain forests of the Altai, Tien-Shan, and northern ranges of the Pamir-Alai. Winters on Central Asian plains.

Similar species: Differs from Brown Accentor and Siberian Accentor by black throat.

618. SIBERIAN ACCENTOR
Prunella montanella
(Sibirskaya Zavirushka)
Plate 33, Map 257

Field marks: 15-16 cm. Upper neck and back dark brownish with brownish streaking; rump gray; wings and tail brownish, top and sides of head black; eye stripe and underparts ocherish.

Habits: Found in overgrown thickets in taiga, usually along river valleys. Migratory. Not numerous. Stays hidden in thickest part of bushes. Nests in tree low to the ground. Lays four to six light blue eggs in June and July. Male sings while perched in treetop. Call: quiet trill, "tirrl." Song: loud trills.

Range and distribution: Forest zones of northern Siberia from the Urals to Anadyr: mountain forests of East Siberia: Altai, Sayan, Sikhote-Alin. Winters in eastern China and Korea.

Similar species: Differs from Black-throated

Accentor by its light throat; from the Brown Accentor by its bright coloration.

619. BROWN ACCENTOR
Prunella fulvescens
(Blednaya Zavirushka)
Plate 33, Map 257

Field marks: 15-19 cm. Upper neck, back, and rump brownish-gray; brownish streaks on the back; wings and tail brownish; top and sides of head brownish-black; throat and eye stripe whitish; underparts buffy whitish.

Habits: Inhabits mountains. Found in regions of overgrown mountain thickets on dry, rocky slopes. Nomadic. Common. Found paired at nesting time; the rest of the time, in flocks on the ground, on rocks, and in bushes. Nests on the ground. Lays four or five light blue eggs from May to July. Call: soft trill. Song: a variety of loud trills.

Range and distribution: Mountains of Central Asia, southern Kazakhstan, Tarbagatai, Altai, western Sayan, Tannu-Ola, Khamar-Daban, and Barguzin ranges. Winters at lower elevations.

Similar species: Differs from Black-throated Accentor by its light throat; from the Siberian Accentor by its light color. Nearly indistinguishable from Radde's Accentor, but the two species are not found in the same ranges.

620. RADDE'S ACCENTOR
Prunella ocularis
(Pestrogrudaya Zavirushka)
Not illustrated, Map 258

Field marks: 15-16 cm. Greatly resembles Brown Accentor, but cheeks and spots on back are black.

Habits: Found in overgrown bushes on dry,

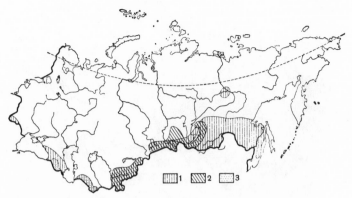

MAP 258. Alpine Accentor (1), Himalayan Accentor (2), Radde's Accentor (3)

rocky mountain slopes. Nomadic. Not numerous. Habits and voice similar to Brown Accentor. Nesting habits unknown.

Range and distribution: Mountains of Armenia and Nakhichevan ASSR.

Similar species: Nearly indistinguishable from Brown Accentor, but their ranges do not overlap.

621. ALPINE ACCENTOR
Prunella collaris
(Alpiyskaya Zavirushka)
Plate 33, Map 258

Field marks: 18-19 cm. Larger than other accentors. Brownish-gray overall; wings brownish-black with whitish wing bars; blackish tail with white tips; throat whitish with black spotting; flanks broadly spotted with rusty red or rusty brown. In juveniles, throat and sides are brownish-gray.

Habits: Found in mountains in alpine meadows, cliffs, glacial moraines, and rockslides. Nonmigratory and nomadic. Not numerous. Found singly, in pairs, and in flocks on the ground and on rocks. Nest situated in a cliff crevice or under a rock. Lays four or five light blue eggs in June and July. Call: soft "cheerk-cheerk." Song: a variety of loud trills.

Range and distribution: Caucasus, Central Asia, southern Kazakhstan, central Altai, and mountains of southern East Siberia.

Similar species: Differs from Himalayan Accentor by its larger size and rusty sides.

622. HIMALAYAN ACCENTOR
Prunella himalyana
(Gimalayskaya Zavirushka)
Plate 33, Map 258

Field marks: 16 cm. Similar to Alpine Accentor. Upperparts brownish-gray with brownish streaks; tail and wings black-brownish; tail white-tipped; throat white with only a few small darkish spots near chin; underparts whitish with large areas of rusty brown mottling that nearly come together at the breast.

Habits: Mountain inhabitant; found in alpine meadows, cliffs, rockslides, and glacial moraines. Not numerous, in places common. Stays singly, in pairs, and flocks on the ground and on rocks. Nests on the ground. Lays four to six light blue eggs in June and July. Voice: melodic trill.

Range and distribution: Pamir-Alai, Tien-Shan, Tarbagatai, Altai, Sayan, Khamar-Daban, and Barguzin ranges. Wintering grounds unknown.

Similar species: Differs from Alpine Accentor by smaller size, dark-streaked (not rusty) sides, and a bright white throat.

Emberiza

Small birds. Bill is small and conical; sometimes blunt and swollen. The bill shape is distinctive; edges of the upper and lower mandible turn inward.

623. CORN BUNTING
Emberiza calandra
(Prosyanka)
Plate 42, Map 259

Field marks: 17-19 cm. Large bunting (larger than a sparrow). Upperparts, wings, and tail grayish-brownish with dark streaks. Throat, breast, and belly dirty white with brownish streaks.

Habits: Found in dry open spaces with clumps

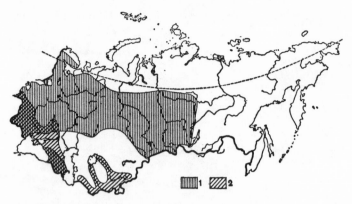

MAP 259. Yellowhammer (1), Corn Bunting (2)

of bushes or dry grass in plains and hills. Non-migratory and nomadic. Common. Found singly, in pairs, and in flocks. Feeds on the ground. Often perches on tops of bushes, small trees, and tall grass stalks. Nests on the ground. Usually lays five grayish-white eggs with a pinkish tint and brownish spots from April to July.

Range and distribution: Southern regions of European USSR, Central Asia, and southern Kazakhstan. Winters in the Transcaucasus, Central Asia, Arabia, and North Africa.

Similar species: Larger and more softly colored than other buntings.

624. YELLOWHAMMER
Emberiza citrinella
(Obyknovennaya Ovsyanka)
Plate 42, Map 259

Field marks: 16-18 cm. The male's head, throat, breast, and belly are yellow with sparse dark-brownish mottling; back and flanks are streaked with chestnut, and the rump is rusty; wings and tail brownish; outer tail feathers white. Females and juveniles are duller, with more extensive streaking on breast and belly.

Habits: Found in forest-steppe and thin forests, where it lives in thickets, forest clearings, glades, cut forest, and inhabited areas. Stays near settlements along with sparrows in winter. Common and nomadic. Feeds on the ground. Found paired during breeding season, otherwise occurs in flocks. Nests on the ground. Lays four or five white eggs with pinkish tone and fine dark veins and curlicues. Male sings while perched on top of tree or bush. Call: loud "tsik-tsik." Song: ringing "zeen-zeen-zeen-zeeee-tseek."

Range and distribution: European USSR, western and central Siberia. Winters in the Transcaucasus and Central Asia. Part of the population is nonmigratory.

Similar species: Differs from other buntings

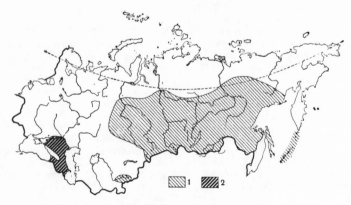

MAP 260. Pine Bunting (1), Black-headed Bunting (2)

by its yellow and brownish mottling on the head and underparts.

625. PINE BUNTING
Emberiza leucocephala
(Beloshapochnaya Ovsyanka)
Plate 43, Map 260

Field marks: 16-18 cm. In male, the gray-brown back is streaked; the rump, throat, breast, and sides of head are chestnut-brown, and the flanks are broadly streaked with chestnut; tail and wings brownish; upper breast, top of head, belly, and outer tail feathers white. Females and juveniles are duller and more streaked.

Habits: Found in thin woods, forest clearings, and glades, where it prefers overgrown bushes. Common and migratory. In spring, found in pairs; the rest of the time in flocks. Nests on the ground. Lays four or five grayish-white eggs with rusty brown spots from May to July. Feeds on the ground. Male sings while perched on top of tree or bush. Call: soft "tsik-tsik." Song: loud "tin-tin-teee."

Range and distribution: Siberia, Soviet Far East, Sakhalin and Kuril Islands. Isolated populations in the Tien-Shan Mountains. Winters in southern Central Asia. Part of population is nonmigratory.

Similar species: Differs from Meadow Bunting by its white crown and chestnut throat.

626. BLACK-HEADED BUNTING
Emberiza melanocephala
(Chernogolovaya Ovsyanka)
Plate 42, Map 260

Field marks: 16 cm. In male, top and sides of head black; wings and tail blackish-brown; back and rump rusty brown; entire underparts bright yellow. In females and juveniles, upper parts yellowish-gray; underparts dirty yellow-ish-white. Females have yellow undertail coverts.

Habits: Found in open steppe, around clumps of bushes. Migratory. Common. Feeds on the ground. Paired during breeding season; in flocks the rest of the time. Male sings while perched on tall grass stalks, top of bush, or on electric wires. Nests in bush or on the ground. Lays four or five light blue-white eggs with small brownish spots from May to July. Call: soft "tsik-tsik." Song: loud "tee-tee-tee-teeooreeooree."

Range and distribution: South European USSR from the Azov Sea and Volgograd to the Transcaucasus. Winters in India.

Similar species: Male differs from other buntings by its black head. Females resemble females of Red-headed Bunting, but not found in the same range.

627. RED-HEADED BUNTING
Emberiza bruniceps
(Zholchnaya Ovsyanka)
Plate 42, Map 261

Field marks: 16-17 cm. In male, head, throat, and breast are rusty brown; back and rump brownish-green; tail and wings brownish; underparts bright yellow. In females and juveniles, upperparts are yellowish-gray; underparts are dirty yellowish-white.

Habits: Found in dry, open steppe, in plains and hills, where it prefers thickets. Migratory. Common. Found in pairs during breeding season; in flocks the rest of the year. Nests in bush or amid grass stalks. Lays four or five greenish-white eggs with brownish spots in May and June. Feeds on the ground. Male sings while perched on top of a bush or on telephone wires. Call: soft "tsik-tsik." Song: loud "choot-choot-choot-treeooreeooree."

Map 261. Red-headed Bunting (1), Chestnut Bunting (2)

Range and distribution: Central Asia and Kazakhstan. Winters in India.

Similar species: Male resembles male of Chestnut Bunting, but differs by its greenish back and bright yellow underparts. The two species are not found in the same range. Female greatly resembles female of Black-headed Bunting, but they are not found together in the same range.

628. CHESTNUT BUNTING
Emberiza rutila
(Ryzhaya Ovsyanka)
Plate 42, Map 261
Field marks: 14 cm. Small bunting, resembling Red-headed Bunting. In male, head, throat, breast, and upperparts are chestnut-rufous; tail and wings brownish; breast and belly yellow. In females and juveniles, top of head, wings, tail, and back are rufous-brownish; throat, breast, and belly are yellowish-white; brownish streaking on the head, breast, and sides.
Habits: Found in taiga, where it prefers thickets of Labrador-tea, Great Bilberry, and osier. Migratory. Not numerous. Stays in pairs and in small flocks. Usually nests on the ground. Lays four or five white eggs with light blue-gray tone and small dark spots in June. Feeds on the ground. Male sings while perched in tree or bush. Call: soft "tik-tik." Song: loud "töi-töi-tööi-öö-öi-öi-see-see-see."
Range and distribution: Southeastern Siberia and Soviet Far East except southern Primorski regions. Winters in southern Asia.
Similar species: Male differs from male of Red-headed Bunting by its rufous back and pale yellow underparts. Females and juveniles greatly resemble those of the Yellow-breasted Bunting, but differ by rusty overtones.

629. YELLOW-BREASTED BUNTING
Emberiza aureola
(Dubrovnik)
Plate 42, Map 262
Field marks: 14 cm. In male, top of head, breast-band, back, and rump are chestnut-brown; forehead, sides of head, and throat black; wings and tail brownish; large white patch over narrow wing bar; underparts yellow. In females and juveniles, the upperparts are brownish-gray with dark streaking; sides of head are brownish; underparts yellowish.
Habits: Found in meadows, hills with sparse birches, osier thickets by river floodlands, and in peat bogs. Migratory. Common. Occurs in pairs and flocks. Feeds on the ground. Nests on the ground. Lays four or five greenish-gray

or olive-light blue eggs with brownish spots in June and July. Male sings while perched in tall grasses or bushes. Call: soft "tik-tik." Song: loud "filyou-filyou-filee-filee-filee-tyou-tyou."
Range and distribution: Northern and central belt of European USSR, Siberia, Soviet Far East. Winters in southern Asia.
Similar species: Females and juveniles differ from females of Chestnut Bunting by the brownish sides of the head and grayish upperparts.

630. YELLOW-THROATED BUNTING
Emberiza elegans
(Zheltogorlaya Ovsyanka)
Plate 42, Map 262
Field marks: 15 cm. Small but noticeable crest. In male, top of head, eye stripe, and large crescent on upper breast are black; wings and tail brownish; back brown with dark streaks; rump gray; underparts and outer tail feathers white; eyebrows and throat yellow. Coloration is duller in females and juveniles, with black being replaced by brownish.
Habits: Found in deciduous woods, where it prefers young plantings; more rarely in high-grass meadows. Migratory. Common. Stays in pairs and flocks. Nests on the ground. Lays four or five dirty white eggs with brownish speckles in May and June. Voice: soft "tik-tik." Song: loud, beautiful trill.
Range and distribution: Southern Soviet Far East. Winters in Japan and southeastern China.
Similar species: Differs from Yellow-browed Bunting by its yellow throat and black or brownish crescent on breast.

631. YELLOW-BROWED BUNTING
Emberiza chrysophrys
(Zheltobrovaya Ovsyanka)
Plate 42, Map 263
Field marks: 14-16 cm. Back is brownish with dark brownish streaks; rump is rufous-brownish; wings and tail brownish; median stripe of the head, outer tail feathers, and entire underparts are white, with brownish streaks on breast and flanks; yellow eye stripe.
Habits: Inhabits taiga, where it prefers thickets. Migratory. Rare bird that stays hidden. Found in pairs and flocks. Feeds on the ground. Nests in trees. Its nest, found in June, contains four grayish-white eggs with gray and brownish speckles. Call: gentle whistle.
Range and distribution: Central regions of East Siberia. Winters in southeastern China.
Similar species: Differs from Yellow-throated Bunting by its white throat and lack of black or brownish patch on breast.

Map 262. Yellow-breasted Bunting (1), Yellow-throated Bunting (2)

632. BLACK-FACED BUNTING
Emberiza spodocephala
(Sedogolovaya Ovsyanka)
Plate 42, Map 264

Field marks: 14-15 cm. Small bunting. In male, head, neck, and upper breast are dark gray; back is brownish with dark streaks; wings and tail brownish; breast and belly pale yellow with streaked flanks; outer tail feathers white. Upperparts of females and juveniles are brownish-gray with dark streakings; underparts yellowish with brownish streaks.

Habits: Found in thickets in river valleys, at forest edges, more rarely in fir groves. Migratory. Common. Found paired during nesting period; the remainder of the time in flocks. Nests on the ground or low in a bush. Lays four or five pale blue eggs with brownish spots from May to July. Coloration of eggs varies greatly. Feeds on the ground. Male sings while perched on top of a bush. Call: soft "tik-tik." Song: fairly loud "tee-tee-teee."

Range and distribution: South Central Siberia, Soviet Far East, Sakhalin Island, southern Kuril Islands. Winters in Southeast Asia.

Similar species: Differs from Japanese Gray Bunting by its yellow underparts.

633. WHITE-CAPPED BUNTING
Emberiza stewarti
(Ovsyanka Styuarta)
Plate 43, Map 264

Field marks: 15 cm. In male, top of head and cheeks are gray; throat and eye stripe black; back, rump, and breast band are chestnut-brown; tail, wings, and streaks on breast and sides brownish; breast, belly, and outer tail feathers white. Upperparts of females and juveniles are grayish-brown; underparts are ocher-whitish with brownish streaking.

Map 263. Yellow-browed Bunting (1), Tristram's Bunting (2)

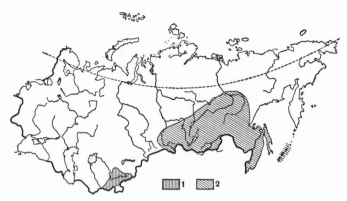

MAP 264. White-capped Bunting (1), Black-faced Bunting (2)

Habits: Found on dry, precipitous mountain slopes with sparse bushes and trees. Migratory. Common. Found in pairs and flocks. Feeds on the ground. Call: soft "tsik-tsik." Song: a ringing trill. Nest is situated on the ground under the protection of a rock or bush. Usually lays four grayish-white eggs with small gray and brown spots from May to July.

Range and distribution: Mountains of Central Asia and southern Kazakhstan. Winters in northern India.

Similar species: Males differ from other buntings by the contrasting gray and black on the head. Females and juveniles resemble females of Ortolan Buntings, but are smaller.

634. ORTOLAN BUNTING
Emberiza hortulana
(Sadovaya Ovsyanka)
Plate 42, Map 265

Field marks: 16 cm. In male, head and breast are light gray; throat and eye ring yellowish; wings and tail brownish; outer tail feathers white; remainder of plumage is ocher-brownish with dark brownish streaks on the back. Bill is reddish. In females and juveniles, top of head, cheeks, and back are brownish; throat, upper breast, breast, and belly are ocher-whitish, streaked with brownish on the back and upper breast.

Habits: Found in open landscapes, thickets by river floodlands, in hilly steppe, along slopes of steppe gullies and in inhabited areas. Migratory. Common. Found in pairs and flocks. Feeds on the ground. Nest situated on the ground and is overhung by a bush or by grass. Lays four to six dirty white eggs with small brownish spots from May to July. Male sings while perched on bush or tree branch. Call: soft "tsik-tsik." Song: loud "tym-tyou-tyourr."

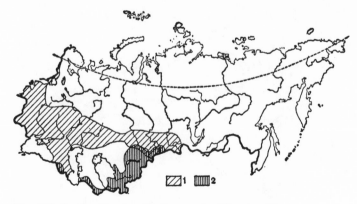

MAP 265. Ortolan Bunting (1), Gray-necked Bunting (2)

Range and distribution: Central and southern belt of European USSR, northern Kazakhstan, southern Siberia to Irkutsk.

Similar species: Females and juveniles differ from females of White-capped Bunting by its greater size; from the Gray-necked Bunting by its streaked breast.

635. GRAY-NECKED BUNTING
Emberiza buchanani
(Skalistaya Ovsyanka)
Plate 42, Map 265

Field marks: 16-17 cm. Cheeks, top of head, and nape gray; back is brownish-gray with thin, dark streaks; wings and tail brownish; malar stripe, outer tail feathers, and belly white; throat, breast, and flanks pale reddish-brown; bill reddish.

Habits: Found on dry, rocky mountain slopes and rockslides with sparse vegetation. Migratory. Common. Found in pairs and flocks. Feeds on the ground. Nests on the ground, protected by a bush or overhanging grass. Usually lays five light blue-green eggs with small brownish and gray spots in May and June. Male sings while perched on rock or in bush. Call: soft 'tsik-tsik." Song: fairly loud trill.

Range and distribution: Mountains of Transcaucasus, Central Asia, Kazakhstan, and southern Altai. Winters in India.

Similar species: Differs from female Ortolan Bunting by lack of brownish streaking on the breast and by its reddish underparts.

636. ROCK BUNTING
Emberiza cia
(Gornaya Ovsyanka)
Plate 43, Map 266

Field marks: 16-17 cm. In male, back and belly rufous-brown; head, throat, and upper breast gray; wings and tail brownish; outer tail feathers white; black stripes through, over, and below the eye. Females and juveniles duller. In Siberian races, black stripes on the head are replaced by rusty brown.

Habits: Found in dry, open hilly spaces with sparse vegetation. Nonmigratory and nomadic. Common. Stays in flocks and in pairs. Feeds on the ground. Nests on the ground below an overhanging rock or bush. Lays four or five grayish-white eggs with small brownish spots from May to July. Call: soft "tsik-tsik." Song: short chirps.

Range and distribution: Mountains of southern USSR from the Crimea to Tuva.

Similar species: Differs from the other mountain-dwelling buntings by its gray head with black or brown stripes.

637. MEADOW BUNTING
Emberiza cioides
(Krasnoukhaya Ovsyanka)
Plate 43, Map 266

Field marks: 16-18 cm. In male, forehead, crown, eye line, cheek patch, and "whisker" as well as a broad band across breast and streaks on flanks are chestnut-rusty; back, rump, and shoulders brown; throat, eyebrow, neck, outer tail feathers and belly are whitish; wings, tail, and streaks on back are brownish. Females and juveniles duller.

Habits: Found in cut-over forests, thickets, plantings near roadsides and gardens; both in plains and hills. Nomadic. Common. Feeds on the ground. Stays in pairs and flocks. Nests on the ground under protection of a bush or grasses; more rarely in the lower part of a bush. Lays four or five dirty white eggs with

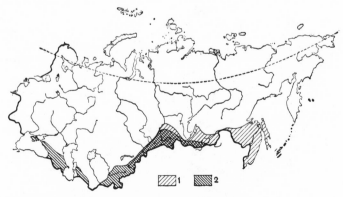

MAP 266. Meadow Bunting (1), Rock Bunting (2)

small brownish spots from May to July. Call: soft "tsik-tsik." Song: loud trill.

Range and distribution: Regions of southern Asian USSR from Tien-Shan to the Sea of Japan.

Similar species: Differs from Pine Bunting by its rusty cap.

638. JANKOWSKI'S BUNTING
Emberiza jankowskii
(Ovsyanka Yankovskovo)
Plate 43, Map 267

Field marks: 16-17 cm. Top of head, back, and rump are rusty brownish; streaks on back, wings, tail, and eye line brownish; "whisker" mark is black; eye stripe, throat, breast, belly, and outer tail feathers are white; brown spot in center of belly.

Habits: Found in open spaces, where it stays among low hills with overgrown bushes and grass. Nonmigratory, with a very limited range. Very rare. Feeds and nests on the ground. Apparently nests in May. Call: soft "tsik-tsik." Song: short trill. Included in the Red Data Book.

Range and distribution: Southern Primorski regions of the Soviet Far East.

Similar species: Differs from other buntings in the USSR by its brown belly spot.

639. CHESTNUT-EARED BUNTING
Emberiza fucata
(Osheynikovaya Ovsyanka)
Plate 43, Map 267

Field marks: 16 cm. Head and neck gray; cheeks chestnut; back brown with black streaks; throat, breast, and belly whitish; rusty band across breast below a band of short, black streaks; wings and tail brownish; outer tail feathers white.

Habits: Found in open landscapes with thickets, river valleys, fields, wet meadows, cleared portions of forest. Migratory. Generally rare, but common in places and even numerous. Found in pairs and flocks. Feeds on the ground. Nest situated under the protection of grasses. Usually lays five dirty white eggs with small brownish spots in May and June. Call: soft "tsik." Song: short distinguishing trill.

Range and distribution: Southern Transbaikal and southern Soviet Far East. Winters in southern Asia.

Similar species: Differs from other buntings by the double breast bands.

640. RUSTIC BUNTING
Emberiza rustica
(Ovsyanka Remez)
Plate 43, Map 268

Field marks: 14-15 cm. In male, head is black; back, rump, and wide breast band are rusty brown; wings, tail, and streaks on back are dark brownish; eye stripe (behind eye), throat, belly, and outer tail feathers white. Females and juveniles are duller and brownish with darker streakings.

Habits: Found in forest belt, where it lives at coniferous forest edges; in thickets of Labrador-tea in mossy swamps; in birch groves along riverbanks and swamps. Migratory. Common. Found in pairs and flocks. Stays hidden. Feeds on the ground. Nests on the ground. Lays four or five gray eggs with small dark spots from May to July. Sings while perched in tree or bush. Call: soft "tik-tik." Song: loud, beautiful trill.

Range and distribution: Taiga zone from the Kola Peninsula to the Kamchatka Peninsula. Winters in Japan and eastern China.

Similar species: Differs from Tristram's Bun-

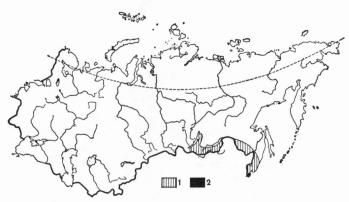

MAP 267. Chestnut-eared Bunting (1), Jankowski's Bunting (2)

ting by its white throat and chestnut breast band.

641. LITTLE BUNTING
Emberiza pusilla
(Ovsyanka Kroshka)
Plate 43, Map 268

Field marks: 13-14 cm. Small bunting. Rusty crown and cheek patch outlined in black; upperparts grayish-brown; throat and outer tail feathers white; underparts whitish; back, breast, and flanks are streaked with blackish-brown.

Habits: Found in thickets of tundra, forest-tundra, and northern taiga. Migratory. Common. Feeds on the ground. Stays in pairs and flocks. Nests on the ground, and lays four to six whitish eggs with small brownish spots in June and July. Call: soft "tseek-tseek." Song: loud "tee-tee-tee-teerch."

Range and distribution: Winters in mountains and nearby in southern Siberia and Central Asia. Forest-tundra and northern borders of taiga throughout the USSR.

Similar species: Differs from other buntings by its small size and by rusty crown and cheeks.

642. TRISTRAM'S BUNTING
Emberiza tristrami
(Taezhnaya Ovsyanka)
Plate 43, Map 263

Field marks: 14 cm. Head and throat black; crown stripe, eyebrow, and malar stripe white; upper parts rusty-brown with black streaks on the back; whitish, unstreaked underparts with rusty brown flanks and breastband. Juveniles duller.

Habits: Found in plains and hills of taiga with a predominance of silver fir. Migratory. Somewhat rare. Stays in pairs and flocks. Nests in bushes. Usually lays four pinkish eggs with

small dark spots in June and July. Call: quiet "tsik."

Range and distribution: Coniferous forest of southern Soviet Far East. Winters in southeastern China.

Similar species: Differs from Rustic Bunting by its black throat.

643. JAPANESE REED BUNTING
Emberiza yessoënsis
(Ryzhesheynaya Ovsyanka)
Plate 43, Map 269

Field marks: 14 cm. In male, head and throat black; back is brown with black streaks; nape and rump chestnut-rust; wings and tail brownish; underparts and outer tail feathers whitish. Females and juveniles duller, and black is replaced by brownish.

Habits: Found in swampy areas with tall grass and bushes. Migratory. Not numerous. Found singly and in flocks in bushes or grass. Nests in bush or in bed of grass low to the ground. Lays five brownish eggs with small dark spots in June and July. Male flies to top of bush or stalks while singing. Call: stretched-out "tsik." Song: quiet disyllabic trill.

Range and distribution: Southern Soviet Far East. Winters in eastern China.

Similar species: Differs from Pallas's Reed Bunting and Northern Reed Bunting by rusty nape and lack of white stripes on its black head.

644. NORTHERN REED BUNTING
Emberiza schoeniclus
(Kamyshovaya Ovsyanka)
Plate 43, Map 270

Field marks: 15-19 cm. In male, head and throat black; back rusty gray with black streaks; rusty shoulders on wings; wings and tail are brown-

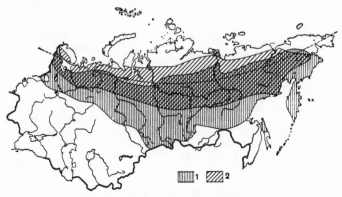

MAP 268. Rustic Bunting (1), Little Bunting (2)

MAP 269. Pallas's Reed Bunting (1), Japanese Reed Bunting (2)

ish; breast, belly, outer tail feathers, and malar stripe white. Females and juveniles lack black on the head, which is streaked; similar mottling on the breast. In southern steppe regions, there is a larger race of the Northern Reed Bunting with a thick, puffed bill.

Habits: Found in reeds and thickets along banks of various bodies of water. Migratory. Common. Stays in pairs and flocks. Nests on the ground, more rarely in a bush or grasses. Lays four to six grayish-pink eggs with a dark pattern from May to July. Call: soft "tseek-tseek." Song: loud "shree-shree-teeree-teeree."

Range and distribution: Found in European USSR, Kazakhstan, Central Asia, Siberia to the east as far as Podkamennaya, Tunguska River and eastern Transbaikal, southern Soviet Far East, Kamchatka Peninsula, Kuril Islands, and southern Sakhalin Island. Winters in southern USSR.

Similar species: Differs from Pallas's Reed Bunting by larger size; from the Japanese Reed Bunting by the lack of a rusty nape.

645. PALLAS'S REED BUNTING
Emberiza pallasi
(Polarnaya Ovsyanka)
Plate 43, Map 269

Field marks: 13-15 cm. Resembles Northern Reed Bunting, but noticeably smaller.

Habits: Found in overgrown thickets in tundra, along riverbanks, and in mountain tundra. Migratory. Fairly common. Found singly, in pairs and flocks, in bushes and on the ground. Nests on the ground or at base of bush. Lays four or five pink eggs with dark spots in June and July. Call: quiet "tsee-see." Song: soft trill.

Range and distribution: Central and East Siberia. Winters in southern Primorski region

in the USSR; also in Korea, China, and Mongolia.

Similar species: Differs from Northern Reed Bunting by smaller size; from the Japanese Reed Bunting by the lack of rusty nape.

646. JAPANESE GRAY BUNTING
Emberiza variabilis
(Yaponskaya Ovsyanka)
Plate 42, Map 270

Field marks: 14 cm. Male is dark gray overall; lighter on belly; dark streaks on brownish back. The females and juveniles are lighter and more brownish, with a rusty suffusion on the back; throat, breast, and belly are whitish with dark streaks.

Habits: Found in coniferous and mixed forest and thickets of dwarf bamboo, primarily in hilly or mountainous areas. Migratory. Not numerous. Found in pairs or flocks, remaining hidden in the thickest part of bushes. Nests in bush low to the ground. Lays five white eggs with small reddish-gray spots in June. Call: soft "tsik." Song: short "youee-tseeye-tseeye."

Range and distribution: Southeast Kamchatka Peninsula, Kuril Islands and southern Sakhalin Island. Winters in Japan.

Similar species: Differs from Black-faced Bunting by lack of yellow underparts.

[In the Caucasus, the Crimea, and the Ukraine, vagrant **647.** CIRL BUNTING (*Emberiza cirlus*) was noted. In male, top of head and breast band greenish-gray; back rusty brown; "face" and throat black with eyebrow and cheeks yellow. Underparts yellow. Female is duller; throat, breast, and belly yellowish with brownish streaks. In the Caucasus and the Crimea, vagrant **648.** CRETZSCHMAR'S BUNTING (*Em-*

MAP 270. Northern Reed Bunting (1), Japanese Gray Bunting (2)

beriza caesia) was noted. It resembles the Ortolan Bunting, but differs by its rufous, not
yellow, throat.]

Calcarius

649. LAPLAND LONGSPUR
Calcarius lapponicus
(Laplansky Podorozhnik)
Plate 43, Map 271

Field marks: 15-17 cm. Small (sparrow-size)
bird. In male, forehead, crown, sides of head,
throat, and upper breast black; nape rusty;
back and rump brownish-gray; black streaks
on back and sides; wings and tail brownish;
stripe from back of eye, sides of neck, and
belly white. Rear claw long and nearly straight.
Females and juveniles are brownish and heavily streaked; throat is white; band of brownish
streaks across upper breast.

Habits: Found in tundra with hummocks;
sometimes in osier thickets and dwarf birches.
Migratory and nomadic. Common, in places
numerous. Occurs in pairs and flocks on the
ground. Nests in depression under a tussock.
Lays four to six brownish eggs with black-
brownish spots in June and July. Call: short,
plaintive whistle. Song: several loud trills, often
sung in flight.

Range and distribution: Tundra throughout
the USSR. Winters in southern Europe, Kazakhstan, and Central Asia.

Similar species: Male differs from males of
Northern Reed Bunting and Japanese Reed
Bunting by its light eye stripe. Female practically indistinguishable in the field; but in the
hand, easily differentiated by its markedly long
rear claw (longer than the toe).

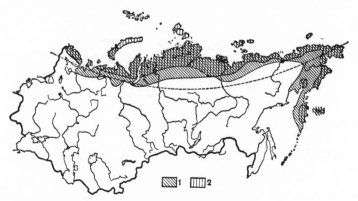

MAP 271. Lapland Longspur (1), Snow Bunting (2)

MAP 272. White-winged Grosbeak (1), Hawfinch (2)

Plectrophenax

650. SNOW BUNTING
Plectrophenax nivalis
(Poonochka)
Plate 29, Map 271

Field marks: 16-18 cm. Small bird (smaller than a starling). Mostly white. In spring, back, wing tips, and central tail feathers of male are black. In autumn, upperparts are rusty brown and the back is streaked; the underparts are whitish with a buffy suffusion of breast. Females and juveniles are similar but duller.

Habits: Found in rocky tundra, seasides, precipices, and cliffs along riverbanks. Winters in open areas, usually inhabited landscapes (roads, barns, forest edges). Migratory and wintering bird. Common, often numerous. Found in pairs during nesting and in flocks at other times on the ground and on rocks. Nests in hidden places (among rocks, cliff crevices, in piles of logs, etc.). Lays four to seven greenish-white eggs with blackish spots in June and July. Call: loud trill. Song: short, loud trill.

Range and distribution: Shores of the Arctic Ocean.

Similar species: No similar species in the USSR.

[On Chukotski Peninsula and Wrangel Island the following American vagrants were collected: **651.** NORTHERN JUNCO (*Junco hyemalis*); **652.** BROWN TOWHEE (*Pipilo fuscus*); **653.** GOLDEN-CROWNED SPARROW (*Zonotrichia atricapilla*); **654.** SAVANNAH SPARROW (*Passerculus sandwichensis*); **655.** WINTER SPARROW (*Spizella arborea*); **656.** FOX SPARROW (*Zonotrichia iliaca*).

Vagrants of **657.** YELLOW-RUMPED WARBLER (*Dendroica coronata*) and **658.** NORTHERN

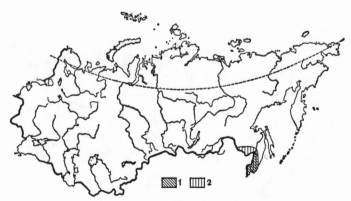

MAP 273. Japanese Grosbeak (1), Yellow-billed Grosbeak (2)

WATERTHRUSH (*Seirus noveboracensis*) were noted on Chukotski Peninsula. Both belong to the family *Parulidae*: wood warblers.

659. HAWFINCH
Coccothraustes coccothraustes
(Obyknovenny Dubonos)
Plate 47, Map 272
Field marks: 18 cm. Size of starling; bill is thick and massive; tail short. In male, head is dark brownish; throat, ring around base of bill, wings, and tail are black; back chestnut; wide, whitish shoulder stripe; underparts pinkish-gray; belly, tip of tail, and wing patches white. Female duller. In juveniles, head and underparts have short dark barring.
Habits: Found in deciduous and mixed forests, plantings with a predominance of maples, ash, and other species with large seeds. Nomadic. Not numerous, stays hidden. Stays in pairs and flocks in crowns of trees; sometimes on the ground under them. Nests in April and May in trees at a height of two to six meters. Lays three to seven greenish eggs with dark spots and curlicues. Call: soft "tsik-tsik." Song: a variety of harsh, chattering sounds. Feeds on seeds of maple, ash, and linden; also berries.
Range and distribution: European USSR, southern Siberia, Soviet Far East, Kamchatka Peninsula, Sakhalin and Kuril Islands. Isolated populations in mountains of Central Asia.
Similar species: Differs from Yellow-billed Grosbeak and Japanese Grosbeak by its brown head.

Mycerobas

660. WHITE-WINGED GROSBEAK
Mycerobas carnipes
(Archyovy Dubonos)
Plate 47, Map 272
Field marks: 18 cm. Size of a starling. Bill thick, black, and massive. Tail fairly long. In male, head, breast, back, wings, and tail are matte black; belly and rump green-yellow; wing spot white. In females and juveniles, black is replaced by gray.
Habits: Found in upper region of mountain forest belt. Prefers arborescent juniper. Non-migratory. Common everywhere. Stays in pairs and flocks in trees and bushes of arborescent juniper. Nests in bushes and trees low to the ground. Lays three to five white eggs with purple-brownish spots in May and June. Call: hoarse croaking sounds. Song: repetition of

these sounds as well as harsh whistles. Feeds on juniper berries.
Range and distribution: Mountains of Central Asia and southern Kazakhstan.
Similar species: No similar species in the USSR.

Eophona

661. JAPANESE GROSBEAK
Eophona personata
(Bolshoy Chernogolovy Dubonos)
Plate 47, Map 273
Field marks: 18 cm. Size of a starling. Bill thick, massive, bright yellow; tail fairly long. Male (and female) ash-gray; top of head, ring around base of bill, wings, and tail black; belly and wing spot white. Juveniles lack black on head.
Habits: Found in deciduous taiga. Stays hidden in pairs and flocks in tree crowns. Migratory. Common in places. Nests in trees at the height of two to six meters. Lays three or four light blue eggs with dark spots in June. Call: soft "täk-täk." Song: variety of loud flutelike whistles. Feeds on pine nuts, seeds of berries, and insects.
Range and distribution: Arrives at taiga in March and leaves in October. Southern Soviet Far East. Winters in southeastern China.
Similar species: Differs from Hawfinch by its black crown; from the Yellow-billed Grosbeak by its larger size and black wing tips.

662. YELLOW-BILLED GROSBEAK
Eophona migratoria
(Maly Chernogolovy Dubonos)
Plate 47, Map 273
Field marks: 15 cm. Resembles Japanese Grosbeak, but noticeably smaller; wings and head (in males) are black; wing tips white.
Habits: Inhabits deciduous taiga. Found in forests on hillsides, river valleys, gardens, and parks. Migratory. Common. Stays in leafy part of trees and thickets singly, in pairs, and in flocks. Nests in trees at a height of 1.5 to 3 meters. Lays three to five pale blue eggs with blackish spots in June. Call: loud "tek-tek." Song: a variety of whistles. Feeds on seeds and insects.
Range and distribution: Migrates in May, then in August-September. Southern Soviet Far East. Winters in southeastern China.
Similar species: Differs from Hawfinch by its black head and yellow bill; from the Japanese Grosbeak by its smaller size and white wing-tips.

Chloris

Small (sparrow-size) birds with thick, conical bill and generally uniform coloration.

663. EUROPEAN GREENFINCH
Chloris chloris
(Zelenushka)
Plate 44, Map 274
Field marks: 14-16 cm. Male is greenish-yellow; brighter on the belly; top of head gray. Female upperparts gray-green; underparts dirty white. Both sexes have yellow patches in wings and base of tail; female duller. Juveniles same as females but with brownish streaks on breast.
Habits: Found in mixed and deciduous forest and inhabited areas. Lives in cleared forests, gardens, and parks. Nomadic, migratory in the north. Common. Stays in pairs at breeding season; in flocks the remainder of the year. Prefers thickets and plantings of hemp and sunflowers. Nests in trees and bushes, usually no higher than three meters. Lays four to six light blue-gray eggs with blackish-violet or dark-red spots in April and May. Call: babbling trill. Song: a variety of these trills, ending in a harsh "vzhzhzh." Feeds on seeds and insects.
Range and distribution: Forest and forest-steppe zones of European USSR; mountain forests of Central Asia and southern Kazakhstan.
Similar species: Female differs from female House Sparrow by its greenish tones; from Eurasian Goldfinch and Eurasian Siskin by its larger size.

664. ORIENTAL GREENFINCH
Chloris sinica
(Kitayskaya Zelenushka)
Plate 44, Map 274
Field marks: 14 cm. Male greenish with chestnut-brown nape and back; crown and rump gray; wing stripes, tail, and belly yellow; wings and tail black. Females and juveniles duller.
Habits: Found in coniferous and deciduous forests. Lives in cleared forests, gardens, and parks. Nonmigratory. Common. Found in pairs during breeding season; in flocks the remainder of the year. Nests high in trees. Lays three to five light blue eggs with brown spots in May and June. Call: distinctive babbling trill. Feeds on seeds and insects.
Range and distribution: Eastern Transbaikal, Soviet Far East, Kamchatka Peninsula, Sakhalin Island, Kuril Islands. Winters as far as Taiwan (Formosa) and the Ryukyu Islands.
Similar species: No similar species in the USSR.

Carduelis

665. EURASIAN GOLDFINCH
Carduelis carduelis
(Shchegól)
Plate 44, Map 275
Field marks: 12-14 cm. Size of a sparrow. Bill long, sharp, conical. Plumage of adult is distinctive. Red "face," white cheeks; wings and tail black; yellow band on wings. Juveniles lack red "mask" and are finely streaked on back and breast. In European and Siberian (black-headed) races, the crown is black; back brown. In Central Asian and southern Siberian (gray-headed) races, top of the head, back, and breast are uniformly brownish-gray.
Habits: Found in mixed deciduous forest. Found in light-filled, cleared forest areas, gardens, and parks. Feeds on thistle, burdock, and plantings of hemp. Nomadic. Common. At breeding season stays in pairs; in flocks the remainder of the year. Nests in trees at a height of four to six meters in April and May. Lays four or five light blue or greenish eggs with small violet-brownish or violet-purplish spots in May and June. Call: loud "peet-peelee-peet." Song: a variety of loud trills. Feeds on seeds and insects.
Range and distribution: European USSR, southern West Siberia, mountains of Central Asia and Kazakhstan.
Similar species: No similar species in the USSR.

Spinus

666. EURASIAN SISKIN
Spinus spinus
(Chizh)
Plate 44, Map 275
Field marks: 12-13 cm. Small bird. Bill sharply pointed. Male greenish-yellow; crown, chin, wings, and tail black; yellow stripes on wings and base of tail; belly whitish. Upperparts of females and juveniles greenish-gray; underparts whitish with dark streaks.
Habits: Found in coniferous and deciduous forest. Feeds in groves of birch and alder. Nonmigratory and nomadic. Common. Stays in flocks except at breeding time, when it pairs. Often hangs upside down when feeding on cones of alder. Nests high in branches of coniferous trees from April to June. Lays five or six blue or greenish eggs with small rusty spots in May and June. Call: loud "tee-ee-lee, teee." Song has great variety, but basic sounds

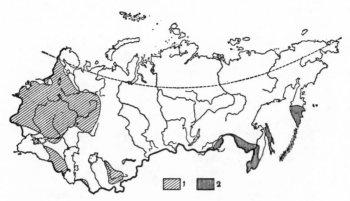

MAP 274. European Greenfinch (1), Oriental Greenfinch (2)

are "tseevee-teevee-tseevee-teevee-keee." Feeds on seeds and insects.

Range and distribution: European USSR, West Siberia, Transbaikal, Soviet Far East, Sakhalin Island.

Similar species: Differs from European Serin by its pointed bill, yellow patches at base of tail, and black cap of male.

Acanthis

Very small bird with sharp, short bill and fairly long tail. Plumage of males includes red or pink.

667. LINNET
Acanthis cannabina
(Konoplyanka)
Plate 44, Map 276

Field marks: 13 cm. Upperparts dark chestnut-brown; underparts whitish. Male has grayish head with raspberry-red forehead and crown; blood-red breast. Females and juveniles are brownish with darker streaks.

Habits: Found in forest steppe and inhabited areas. Prefers forest edges, roadside plantings, and thickets in mountain steppe. Nonmigratory and nomadic. Common. Pairs off in spring; stays in flocks in bushes and on the ground the remaining time. Nests in bushes from April to June. Lays four to six greenish light blue eggs speckled reddish-brown from May to July. Call: chirping "tk-tk-tk." Song: a variety of whistles and trills. Feeds on insects and seeds.

Range and distribution: European USSR and southern West Siberia, mountains of Central Asia, and southern Kazakhstan.

Similar species: Differs from Twite and Common Redpoll by its chestnut-brown back.

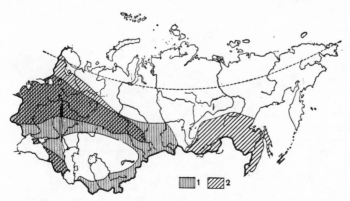

MAP 275. Eurasian Goldfinch (1), Eurasian Siskin (2)

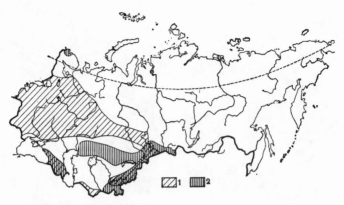

MAP 276. Linnet (1), Twite (2)

668. TWITE
Acanthis flavirostris
(Gornaya Chechetka)
Plate 44, Map 276

Field marks: 13 cm. Upperparts brownish-gray with broad brownish streaks. Underparts and outer tail feathers whitish; upper breast and throat buffy with blurred streaking. Appears white in flight. Male has bright pink rump.

Habits: Found in rocky steppe, subalpine and alpine meadows. Found in open steppe with sparse vegetation. Nonmigratory and nomadic. Very common in nesting range. Stays in pairs at breeding time; in flocks the remainder of the year. Nests in bushes in April. Lays four to six light bluish-green eggs speckled reddish-brown in May and June. Call: loud "peee-tee-tee." Song: a variety of chirps. Feeds on seeds and insects.

Range and distribution: Mountains of the Caucasus, Central Asia, Kazakhstan, south-east Altai, Tannu-Ola, Kola Peninsula, steppes of central Kazakhstan.

Similar species: Differs from Linnet by brownish-gray streaked back; from Common Redpoll by lack of raspberry cap.

669. COMMON REDPOLL
Acanthis flammea
(Obyknovennaya Chechetka)
Plate 44, Map 277

Field marks: 12 cm. Upperparts grayish-brownish with dark streaking; underparts white with dark streaks on the flanks; raspberry cap; throat black. In male, breast suffused with bright raspberry. Females and juveniles have streaked breast; bill yellowish with dark tip.

Habits: Found in tundra, forest-tundra and taiga. Prefers tundra scrub, stunted forests, and open taiga. Migratory and nomadic. Common. When wintering, nomadic through groves of birch and alder and in inhabited

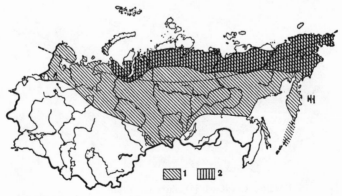

MAP 277. Common Redpoll (1), Hoary Redpoll (2)

areas. Stays in flocks in bushes, trees, and on the ground. Nests in bushes and trees low to the ground. Lays four to six light blue eggs speckled brownish in May and June. Call: loud "che-chet" or "pee-you-ee." Song: a variety of twitters. Feeds on seeds and insects.

Range and distribution: Throughout northern USSR.

Similar species: Differs from Linnet by brownish-gray back and black throat; from the Twite, by its raspberry cap; from the Hoary Redpoll, by its darker back and lightly streaked rump.

670. HOARY REDPOLL

Acanthis hornemanni
(Tundryanaya Chechetka)
Plate 44, Map 277

Field marks: 12 cm. Resembles Common Redpoll but color lighter; rump white; in males, breast is a soft rose. Appears white in flight.

Habits: Inhabits tundra, stunted forests, and northern regions of taiga. Found in rockslides, tundra scrub, and cut-over taiga. Nonmigratory and nomadic. Common within nesting range but rare elsewhere. Stays in flocks. In May, nests in bushes, cliff crevices, and between rocks. Lays four to six light bluish eggs with brownish speckles in June. Call same as Common Redpoll. Feeds on seeds and insects.

Range and distribution: Tundra and forest-tundra zones throughout the USSR. Found with Common Redpoll on wintering grounds.

Similar species: Differs from Common Redpoll by its light ash upperparts; white rump; males by pale pink breast.

Serinus

Very small birds with short, thick bill.

671. RED-FRONTED SERIN

Serinus pusillus
(Korolevsky Vyurok)
Plate 44, Map 278

Field marks: 11 cm. Adults sport a flame-red cap on the head; throat, upper breast, and head are black; rump orange; belly white; remaining plumage is yellow-orange with blackish streaks. Juveniles lack red cap, and head is brownish-rusty.

Habits: Found in upper and middle regions of mountains. Prefers subalpine meadows and tops of forests. Nonmigratory and nomadic. Common. Stays on rocks, on the ground, and in bushes in flocks and pairs. Nests in cliff crevices or in trees and bushes close to the ground in April and May. Lays three to five pale blue eggs with small brown spots end of May to July. Call: loud trill. Song: a variety of loud trills. Feeds on seeds and insects.

Range and distribution: Mountains of the Caucasus, Central Asia, and southern Kazakhstan.

Similar species: No similar species in the USSR.

672. EUROPEAN SERIN

Serinus canaria
(Kanareechny Vyurok)
Plate 44, Map 278

Field marks: 11 cm. Male is yellow-green; brighter on breast and head; belly white; wings, tail, and streaking on back and sides are brownish. Females and juveniles similar but duller, with streaked breast.

Habits: Found in cultivated areas and lower regions of mountains. Prefers gardens, parks, and groves. Nonmigratory in southern part of its range; migratory in northern part. Common in nesting area. Stays in flocks and pairs in trees, bushes, and on the ground. Nests in

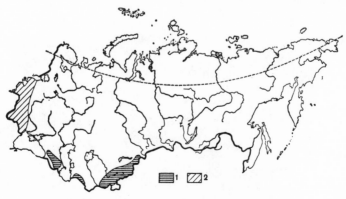

MAP 278. Red-fronted Serin (1), European Serin (2)

tree crowns (prefers coniferous) and in bushes in April. Lays four or five light blue eggs with small brownish spots from May to July. Call: short trill. Song: variety of trills resembling cicada noises. Feeds on seeds and insects.

Range and distribution: Western regions of European USSR.

Similar species: Differs from European Siskin by shorter bill and lack of black cap.

Uragus

673. LONG-TAILED ROSEFINCH
Uragus sibiricus
(Dlinnokhvosty Snegir)
Plate 45, Map 279

Field marks: 17-18 cm. Smaller than a sparrow. Bill short and swollen; tail long. In male, back is gray or reddish-brownish with blackish streaks; tail and wings black-brownish; belly, outer tail feathers, and wing bars white; silvery feathers on head and throat; remaining plumage is raspberry-pink. Females and juveniles gray with brownish streaks on back and breast.

Habits: Found in forest floodlands. Prefers thickets in river floodlands and along lower mountain slopes. Nonmigratory and nomadic. Fairly common. Stays in pairs and flocks; agile bush climber. Fluttering flight. Nests in May in trees and bushes. Lays four or five blue-green eggs with small dark spots. Call: loud "pee-you-een." Song: a variety of trills. Feeds on seeds.

Range and distribution: Southern Siberia and Soviet Far East.

Similar species: Differs from Pallas's Rosefinch by long tail and smaller size.

Rhodopechys

674. TRUMPETER FINCH
Rhodopechys githagineus
(Pustynny Snegir)
Plate 46, Map 279

Field marks: 12 cm. Smaller than a sparrow. Clay-gray overall; wing feather edges and suffusion on breast pink; belly white. Bill short, thick, conical, reddish color. Female similar, but only tinged with pink. Bill pale-colored.

Habits: Found in desert and semi-desert. Prefers gravelly desert regions of steppe and mountain slopes with sparse grassy vegetation and small bushes. Nonmigratory and nomadic. Not numerous. Stays in flocks on the ground. Nests in cliff crevices, precipices, and between rocks. Usually lays five light blue eggs with small blackish spots in April and May. Call: clear "ke-ke-ke."

Range and distribution: Mountains of the Transcaucasus, Central Asia, southern Kazakhstan, Altai.

Similar species: Differs from Desert Finch by smaller size, grayer plumage, lack of contrast in plumage, and lighter-color bill.

675. CRIMSON-WINGED FINCH
Rhodopechys sanguinea
(Krasnokryly Chechevichnik)
Plate 46, Map 280

Field marks: 15 cm. Larger than a sparrow. Bill thick, conical, yellow with dark tip. Male upperparts and sides of breast dark brownish with dark streaks; wings, tail, and cap brownish-black with large pink patch at base of tail and fore-edge of wing; cheeks and lores pink; belly and tips of tail feathers white. Females and juveniles duller, without a black cap.

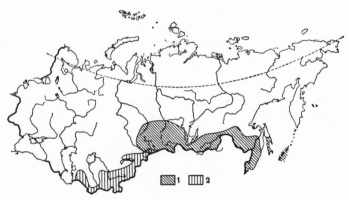

MAP 279. Long-tailed Rosefinch (1), Trumpeter Finch (2)

MAP 280. Northern Bullfinch (1), Black-billed Desert-Finch (2), Crimson-winged Finch (3)

Habits: Usually found on gravelly mountain slopes with sparse vegetation. Nonmigratory and nomadic. Fairly rare, but common and even numerous in places. Stays in flocks on the ground and on rocks; more rarely in bushes and trees. Nests on the ground between rocks. Lays four or five pale blue eggs with small brown spots in June and July. Call: harsh chirping and loud, beautiful whistle. Song: a variety of chirps and whistles. Feeds on seeds.
Range and distribution: Mountains of the Transcaucasus, Central Asia, and southern Kazakhstan.
Similar species: No similar species in the USSR.

Rhodospiza

676. BLACK-BILLED DESERT FINCH
Rhodospiza obsoleta
(Bulany Vyurok)
Plate 46, Map 280
Field marks: 14 cm. Size of a sparrow. Male is a soft dove-gray; has wide, pink wing patch; tail and wings have broad white edges to the feathers; lores black; bill massive, black. Females and juveniles duller.
Habits: Found in dry mountainous regions and in argillaceous plains of steppe, semi-desert, and desert. Found in forest plantings near shores of bodies of water, saxal trees, gardens, and parks. Nomadic. Common. Found paired during breeding season; in flocks the remainder of the year. Nests in bushes and trees. Lays five or six light blue eggs with small dark spots in April and May. Call: quiet whistle, "feenk-feenk." Song: a variety of beautiful trills. Feeds on seeds.

Range and distribution: Plains of Central Asia and southern Kazakhstan.
Similar species: Differs from Trumpeter Finch by its contrasting black-white-pink wings and black bill.

Pyrrhula

677. NORTHERN BULLFINCH
Pyrrhula pyrrhula
(Snegir)
Plate 45, Map 280
Field marks: 14-17 cm. Size of a sparrow. In male, cap, wings, and tail black; back is light blue-gray; rump, undertail, and single wing bar white; underparts red. Females similar, but red is replaced by brownish-gray. Juveniles are like females, but without cap. In males of eastern Siberian races, underparts are gray; in Kamchatka races, pinkish-gray.
Habits: Found in mixed and coniferous forest. At nesting time, prefers mature forests with an undergrowth of thickets; in fall and winter is a nomadic wanderer; prefers gardens, parks, plantings of sunflowers and hemp. Common; stays hidden in summer; in fall and winter easily spotted. Found in pairs at breeding time; in flocks the remainder of the year, both in trees and bushes. Nests in trees high up, in March. Lays four to six light blue eggs with reddish-brown speckles in May and June. Call: a melodic whistle, "few-few." Song: a variety of scraping sounds. Feeds on seeds and insects.
Range and distribution: Throughout the USSR.
Similar species: No similar species in the USSR.

Carpodacus

Birds varying in size from sparrow to starling, with massive conical bills and fairly long tails. Coloration of adult male always includes red or pink. Females, and young males for three years, are grayish-brown with dark streaking.

678. GREAT ROSEFINCH
Carpodacus rubicilla
(Bolshaya Chechevitsa)
Plate 45, Map 281
Field marks: 20-21 cm. Large (starling-size) finch. Bill thick, light-colored; in male, back is grayish-red; tail and wings brownish; rest of plumage raspberry-red with white spots. Females and juveniles gray with dark brownish streaks.
Habits: Found in alpine meadows. Prefers treeless mountain regions no lower than 2,000 meters. Winters by flying down to overgrown thickets of mountain river valleys. Nonmigratory, altitudinal nomadic. Fairly common. In spring, stays in pairs; in flocks the rest of the time. Nests in cliff crevices or between rocks in May and June. One nest (which was found in July) contained five light blue eggs with dark speckles. Call: soft whistle, "fyou-in, fyou-in." Song: a variety of loud rolling whistles. Feeds on seeds; possibly insects.
Range and distribution: Caucasus, Central Asia, southern Kazakhstan, Altai.
Similar species: Differs from Red-breasted Rosefinch by thick, massive bill and raspberry, not red, color in males. Females and juveniles differ from females of Red-mantled Rosefinch by larger size.

679. RED-MANTLED ROSEFINCH
Carpodacus rhodochlamys
(Rozovaya Chechevitsa)
Plate 45, Map 281
Field marks: 15-20 cm. Male lilac-pink; back and crown brownish; wings and tail dark brown; silver-pink eye stripe. Females and juveniles gray with dark brownish streaks.
Habits: Found in upper regions of forest belt in mountains. Prefers overgrown arborescent juniper and deciduous thickets in subalpine meadows. Nonmigratory and nomadic. Fairly common, but stays hidden. Stays in bushes and trees in pairs and flocks. Nests in bushes. Lays four to six light blue eggs with small brown spots from May to July. Call: harsh "chzh-zhay." Song: several drawn-out whistles resembling "cheeyou-cheefew." Feeds on seeds.
Range and distribution: In winter, found in all forest regions of mountains. Mountains of Central Asia, southern Kazakhstan, Altai.

Similar species: Male differs from other finches by its lilac tones. Females and juveniles differ from Great Rosefinch by smaller size.

680. PALLAS'S ROSEFINCH
Carpodacus roseus
(Sibirskaya Chechevitsa)
Plate 45, Map 282
Field marks: 16 cm. Smallest of the rosefinches (sparrow size). Male is raspberry-pink; back brownish with dark streaks; wings and tail black-brownish; belly and wing bars white; head and throat spotted silvery-white. Females and juveniles reddish-gray with elongated brownish streaks.
Habits: Found in taiga forests. At nesting time, prefers mountain taiga and its upper limits. Nomadic through river floodlands, aspen and birch groves, seen in gardens and parks. Nomadic. Not numerous. In spring, stays hidden and in pairs; stays in flocks on the ground, in bushes, and in trees the remainder of the time. Nesting habits unknown. Call: quiet whistle. Song: repetition of same whistles. Feeds on seeds and partly on insects.
Range and distribution: Mountains of central and southern Siberia.
Similar species: Differs from Long-tailed Rosefinch by its short tail and significantly larger size.

681. SCARLET ROSEFINCH
Carpodacus erythrinus
(Obyknovennaya Chechevitsa)
Plate 45, Map 282
Field marks: 14-15 cm. In adult males, back, tail, and wings brownish-red; head, upper breast, and breast bright red; belly whitish-pink. Females and juveniles greenish-gray; lighter on breast and belly.
Habits: Found in thickets near river floodlands, forest edges, and in mountains. Migratory. Common. Arrives April-May, migrates again August-September. Found in pairs; while migrating, in flocks on the ground, in bushes, and in trees. Nests in bushes or trees close to the ground. Lays three to six light bluish-green eggs with brownish speckles from May to July. Call: soft "chooee-ee." Song: loud whistle, "cheero-veecheeoo." Feeds on seeds and insects.
Range and distribution: Throughout USSR except tundra and desert zones. Winters in southern Asia.
Similar species: Male differs from other rosefinches by brighter red coloration; from the Red-breasted Rosefinch, by its much smaller size. Females and juveniles differ from European Greenfinch by lack of yellow in wing or tail.

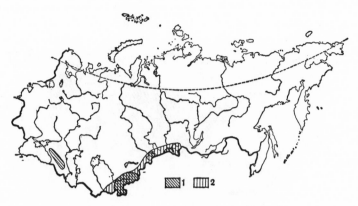

MAP 281. Great Rosefinch (1), Red-mantled Rosefinch (2)

682. RED-BREASTED ROSEFINCH
Carpodacus puniceus
(Krasny Vyurok)
Plate 45, Map 283

Field marks: 20 cm. Large finch (size of a starling). Bill thin and long. Crown and back brownish-gray with darker elongated streaks; tail and wings brownish; belly whitish with dark mottling at sides. In male, forehead, sides of head, throat, and breast bright red with indefinite white speckles; rump pink. In females, throat whitish; brownish streaking; breast and rump lemon- or orange-yellow. In juveniles, breast and rump brownish with brownish streaking.

Habits: Found in upper regions of mountains near glaciers. Prefers cliffs, rockslides, and moraines with alpine meadows no lower than 2,800 meters. Stays in flocks on the ground and on rocks. Nonmigratory. Not numerous. Call: harsh, rude "dzhee-oo, dzhee-oo." Song: a variety of loud whistles. Nesting habits unknown. Feeds on seeds and partly on insects.

Range and distribution: Mountains of Central Asia and southern Kazakhstan.

Similar species: Differs from Great Rosefinch by its longer thinner bill and red, not raspberry, coloration; from the Scarlet Grosbeak by significantly larger size of male.

Pinicola

683. PINE ROSEFINCH
Pinicola enucleator
(Shchur)
Plate 45, Map 283

Field marks: 19-24 cm. Size of a starling. Bill short and thick. Tail long. In males, head, back, rump, and breast raspberry-pink; belly gray; wings and tail blackish-brownish; two white wing bars. Females and juveniles similar, but raspberry color is replaced by yellow-orange.

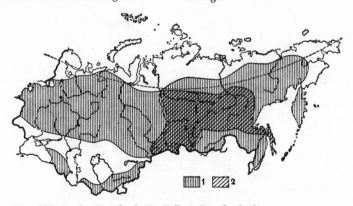

MAP 282. Scarlet Rosefinch (1), Pallas's Rosefinch (2)

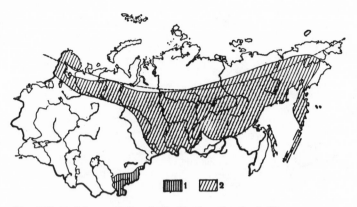

MAP 283. Red-breasted Rosefinch (1), Pine Rosefinch (2)

Habits: Found in northern taiga forest and Siberian mountains. Prefers deciduous woods with some alder and birch, and mountain regions with Siberian pine (*Pinus sibiricus*). In summer, is nomadic and stays hidden. Fairly common. In spring, stays in pairs; in flocks in trees the remainder of the year. Nests in branches of coniferous trees and in undergrowth. Lays three to five light blue eggs darkly speckled in June and July. Call: melodic whistle, "pyou-you, lee." Song: a variety of melodic whistles. Feeds on conifer seeds and berries.
Range and distribution: Taiga throughout USSR.
Similar species: Differs from other finches by coloration, larger size, and longer tail.

Loxia

Birds of sparrow size or somewhat larger; thick-set with short tail and long bill, in which the upper and lower mandible cross each other. Red or raspberry tones predominate plumage of male. Females and juveniles are greenish-gray. In juveniles, head and underparts have brownish streaks. Nomadic. Common. Stays in flocks in coniferous trees, often hanging from pine cones on which it feeds. Constantly calls in flight, but silent when perched. Call: loud "kle-kle." Song: a variety of chirps with loud whistles. Differs from Pine Rosefinch by crossed bill, smaller size, and shorter tail. Feeds on seeds of conifers.

684. WHITE-WINGED CROSSBILL
Loxia leucoptera
(Belokryly Klyost)
Plate 45, Map 284
Field marks: 14-16 cm. Smallest crossbill in the USSR. Wings and tail black-brownish; two wide,

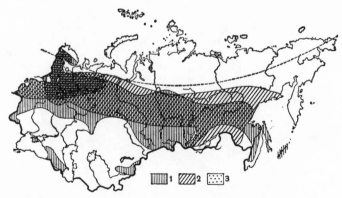

MAP 284. Red Crossbill (1), White-winged Crossbill (2), Parrot Crossbill (3)

white wing bars. Male is raspberry-pink color. Female similar, but greenish with yellowish rump. Juveniles like female, but streaked.

Habits: Found mainly in deciduous taiga; also in fir groves and stands of Siberian pine. Nests in trees. Lays four or five light-blue eggs with black-brownish speckles from April to June.

Range and distribution: From north European USSR to Sea of Okhotsk.

Similar species: Differs from other crossbills by white wing bars.

685. RED CROSSBILL
Loxia curvirostra
(Klyost-yelovik)
Plate 45, Map 284

Field marks: 16-17 cm. Wings and tail black-brownish. Male brick-red; size of bill varies between subspecies. Females similar but greenish. Juveniles streaked.

Habits: Found in fir and mixed forest; more rarely in pine and deciduous forest in plains and mountains. Nests in coniferous trees (usually fir). Lays three or four pale greenish-blue eggs with brownish spots from March to May.

Range and distribution: Northwest European USSR.

Similar species: In the field difficult to distinguish from Parrot Crossbill, but differs by thinner bill and smaller size.

686. PARROT CROSSBILL
Loxia pytyopsittacus
(Klyost-sosnovik)
Plate 45, Map 284

Field marks: 17-20 cm. Largest crossbill (larger than sparrow). Thick bill, swollen at base. Plumage same as Red Crossbill.

Habits: Primarily found in dry, tall coniferous forest, but also seen in fir-pine forests and in groves of pines near swamps. Nests in fir and pine in May. Lays three or four pale greenish-blue eggs with brownish spots (same as Red Crossbill).

Range and distribution: Coniferous forest throughout forest zones and mountains of the USSR.

Similar species: Differs from Red Crossbill by more massive bill and larger size. Difficult to distinguish the two species in the field.

Fringilla

687. CHAFFINCH
Fringilla coelebs
(Zyablik)
Plate 44, Map 285

Field marks: 15-16 cm. Size of sparrow. Bill thin and conical. Wings and tail black-brownish; outer tail feathers and wing bars white. In spring and summer, male has gray-blue crown; chestnut back; black forehead; reddish-brown underparts. In fall, crown is brownish. Females and juveniles similar but brownish-gray with lighter underparts.

Habits: Found in a variety of forests, gardens, and parks. Migratory in northern and central regions and nomadic in southern. Migrates in April; then September-October. Common, numerous in places. In spring stays in pairs; the remainder of the time in flocks in trees and bushes. Nests in trees. Always weaves bits of lichen into outer wall of nest. Lays four to seven light bluish-green eggs speckled pink-violet in May and June. Call: loud "peenk-

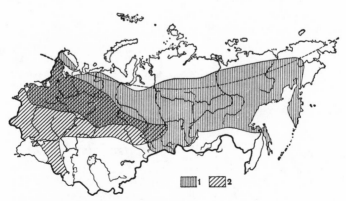

MAP 285. Brambling (1), Chaffinch (2)

peenk." Song: loud trill with a harsh ending, "fyeet-fyeet-lya-lya-vee-cheeyou-keek." Feeds on seeds and insects.

Range and distribution: Entire forest zone through European USSR, southern Siberia as far as the Angara River. Winters in the Crimea, Caucasus, and Central Asia.

Similar species: No similar species in the USSR.

688. BRAMBLING
Fringilla montifringilla
(Vyurok)
Plate 44, Map 285

Field marks: 15-16 cm. Build similar to Chaffinch. In male, head, back, wings, and tail black in spring (brownish in autumn); throat, rump, upper wing bar and belly white; breast and lower wing bar orangish. Females and juveniles duller; black is replaced by grayish-brownish; orange by dirty ocherish.

Habits: Found in a variety of forests, usually with predominance of birch. Migratory in the north, wintering in the south. Spring migration March-April; fall migration in October. Common. Stays in pairs at breeding time; in flocks the remainder of the year. Nests in trees. Always weaves bits of birchbark into outer nest wall. Lays five to seven greenish eggs with reddish-violet speckles in May and June. Call: harsh "chzhe"; in flight, short sounds, "tk-tk-tk." Song: harsh, loud "chzhzhzh." Feeds on seeds and insects.

Range and distribution: From Baltic States and Kola Peninsula to Anadyr, Kamchatka Peninsula, and shores of Sea of Okhotsk. Winters in southern USSR, southwestern Asia, China, and Japan.

Similar species: No similar species in USSR.

Leucosticte

Small (sparrow-size or slightly larger) birds; long tail deeply forked; fairly thick conical bill.

689. HODGSON'S ROSY-FINCH
Leucosticte nemoricola
(Gimalaysky Vyurok)
Plate 46, Map 286

Field marks: 15 cm. Brownish-gray overall; wide brownish streaks on back; indefinite light wing bars. In juveniles, head is rusty.

Habits: Found in alpine and subalpine meadows. Prefers cliffs and rockslides in upper mountain zones. Nomadic. Common. Stays in flocks on the ground and on rocks, perches in trees and bushes. Nests under rocks, often in burrows. Lays four or five eggs in July. Call: loud "chyee-chyee." Song: a variety of twitters. Feeds on seeds and partly on insects.

Range and distribution: Mountains of Central Asia, southern Kazakhstan, and southern Siberia.

Similar species: Differs from female House Sparrow by range, darker coloring, and by deeply forked tail.

690. BRANDT'S ROSY-FINCH
Leucosticte brandti
(Zhemchuzhny Vyurok)
Plate 46, Map 286

Field marks: 16-19 cm. Gray overall; darker with brownish tone on back; forehead black in spring; rump and bend of wing pinkish.

Habits: Found in upper, treeless zones of mountains. Prefers cliffs, rockslides, and crests of mountain ranges over 2,000 meters. Nonmigratory and nomadic. Common. Stays in flocks on the ground and on rocks. Nests in colonies in June-July. Nest undiscovered in USSR. Call: loud, melodic chirping. Song: soft trill.

Range and distribution: Mountains of the Altai, southern Kazakhstan, and Central Asia.

Similar species: Differs from snow-finches by lack of white in plumage.

691. ARCTIC ROSY-FINCH
Leucosticte arctoa
(Sibirsky Vyurok)
Plate 46, Map 287

Field marks: 16 cm. Size same as previous finches (sparrow-size), but on the Komandorskiye Islands there is a larger (nearly starling-size) race. Dark-brownish overall; wings, rump, and belly with areas of raspberry-pink; crown gray or buffy gray. In the Altai and Sayan mountain regions, local races have gray-white on wings and tail.

Habits: Found in rocky areas of tundra in plains and hills. Stays in flocks on the ground and on rocks. Nests in cliff crevices and between rocks. Lays three or four white eggs in June and July. Call: soft chirping. Song: a variety of twitters. Feeds on seeds and insects.

Range and distribution: Mountains of southern and East Siberia, Kamchatka Peninsula, Kuril Islands, Komandorskiye Islands. Winters to southern Transbaikal and southern Soviet Far East.

Similar species: Differs from Brandt's Rosy-Finch by darker brownish color.

Montifringilla

692. WHITE-WINGED SNOW-FINCH
Montifringilla nivalis
(Snezhny Vyurok)
Plate 46, Map 287

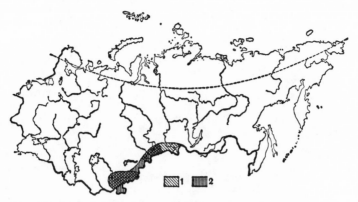

MAP 286. Hodgson's Rosy-Finch (1), Brandt's Rosy-Finch (2)

Field marks: 18-19 cm. Larger than a sparrow. Tail straight, wings long and pointed. In adult, back is dark brown; head gray; wings white with black tips; tip of tail and central tail feathers black; chin and throat black; underparts white. Juveniles similar, but lack throat spot, and upperparts are a dull brownish-gray.

Habits: Found in high mountain steppe and subalpine and alpine meadows, where it prefers cliffs, rockslides, and buildings. Usually in flocks. Feeds on the ground. Usually nonmigratory. Nests in colonies in cliff crevices or animal burrows. Lays four or five white eggs from May to July. Call: loud chirping. Song: harsh, nasal sounds.

Range and distribution: Mountains of the Caucasus, Central Asia, southern Kazakhstan, Altai.

Similar species: Differs from Brandt's Rosy-Finch by white in its plumage; from Père David's Snow-Finch by its brownish back.

Pyrgilauda

693. PÈRE DAVID'S SNOW-FINCH
Pyrgilauda davidiana
(Mongolsky Zemlyanoy Vorobey)
Plate 46, Map 288

Field marks: 13 cm. Smaller than a sparrow. Back and crown ocher-grayish; wings and tail brownish; forehead, lores, throat, and upper breast black; sides of head, belly, breast white with an ocher suffusion; spots on tail are white.

Habits: Found in steppe near cliffs and argillaceous plains in mountains; rocky areas of mountain steppe; and semi-desert with sparse vegetation. Nonmigratory and nomadic. Rare. Stays in flocks on the ground. Nests in a burrow. Lays five or six white eggs from May to July. Call: quiet twittering.

Range and distribution: Southeastern Altai, southeastern Transbaikal.

MAP 287. White-winged Snow-Finch (1), Arctic Rosy-Finch (2)

MAP 288. Rock Petronia (1), Père David's Snow-Finch (2) Pale Petronia (3)

Similar species: Differs from White-winged Snow-Finch by buffy back and black forehead.

[Vagrant of **694.** THERESA'S SNOW-FINCH (*Pyrgilauda theresae*) was obtained in southeast Turkmenia. It looked like a female House Sparrow, but with light outer tail feathers.]

Petronia

Small bird, similar to sparrow in size and structure.

695. ROCK PETRONIA
Petronia petronia
(Kammeny Vorobey)
Plate 46, Map 288
Field marks: 14 cm. Brownish-gray overall; back with heavy brownish streaks; flanks indistinctly streaked; crown with two dark stripes; light eyebrow; dark eye stripe and cheeks; lemon-yellow spot on breast; white spots near tail tip.
Habits: Found in mountain steppe near cliffs, rockslides, precipices, and sparse vegetation. Nomadic. Common. Stays in flocks on the ground and on rocks. Usually nests in colonies between rocks, cliff crevices, or buildings. Lays four to seven greenish-brownish eggs with brownish spots from May to July. Call: loud "gi-you-eeb."
Range and distribution: Southern USSR from the Volga-Ural steppes and the Caucasus to southeastern Transbaikal.
Similar species: Differs from female House Sparrow by striped crown, white spots on tail, and yellow spot on breast; from the Pale Petronia by the streaked back, crown stripes, and yellow spot on breast.

696. PALE PETRONIA
Petronia brachydactyla
(Korotkopaly Vorobey)
Plate 46, Map 288
Field marks: 14 cm. Uniformly brownish-gray. White spots near tip of tail.
Habits: Found in dry, desert mountain regions with sparse vegetation. Migratory. Fairly common. Stays in flocks on the ground and on rocks. Nests in cliff crevices, precipices and holes in buildings. Lays four or five white eggs speckled brownish from May to July. Call: drawn-out twittering.
Range and distribution: Southern Transcaucasus and southern Turkmenia. Winters in Arabia and northeastern Africa.
Similar species: Differs from Rock Petronia by lack of streaked back; from female House Sparrow by white spots on tail.

Passer

Small birds with sturdy build, short tail and wings. Feed on seeds and insects.

697. HOUSE SPARROW
Passer domesticus
(Domovoy Vorobey)
Plate 46, Map 289
Field marks: 14 cm. In male, crown is gray; throat and upper breast black; upperparts chestnut-brown; underparts whitish; cheeks and single wing bar white. Females and juveniles brownish-gray overall; lighter underparts; back with black streaks.
Habits: Found in settled areas, where it lives in towns and villages; in central Asia, found near ravines and precipices. Nonmigratory, but migratory in central Asia. Numerous. Stays

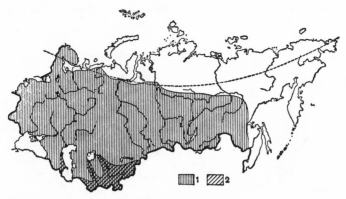

MAP 289. House Sparrow (1), Spanish Sparrow (2)

in flocks; often nests in colonies. Nests under roofs and in house cracks, artificial nesting boxes, in burrows along slopes of gullies, and in precipice walls. Lays five or six white or light grayish-blue eggs with brownish spots from April to July. Call: loud "dzheev-dzheev."

Range and distribution: Throughout European USSR, Siberia as far as Yakutsk and Khabarovsk (except the northern regions), Central Asia, Kazakhstan. Central Asian populations winter in India.

Similar species: Male differs from Hodgson's Rosy-Finch by lighter coloring and tail, which lacks notch. Female from female of European Greenfinch by lack of green in plumage; from the Rock and Pale Petronia by lack of white spots in tail; nearly indistinguishable from female Spanish Sparrow. Male differs from male Spanish Sparrow by lack of black on back and less extensive black on the breast.

698. SPANISH SPARROW
Passer hispaniolensis
(Chernogrudy Vorobey)
Plate 46, Map 289

Field marks: 14 cm. Resembles House Sparrow, but in males entire breast and stripes on flanks are black; crown of head brown; cheeks white.

Habits: Found in settled areas, preferring young tree plantings in towns and villages. Migratory and nomadic. Numerous. Stays in flocks and nests in colonies. Large, enclosed nest situated in tree. Lays four to eight light bluish-white eggs with gray spots from May to July. Call: harsh "dzheev-dzheev."

Range and distribution: Caucasus, Central Asia, southern Kazakhstan. Winters in southwestern Asia.

Similar species: Male differs from male House Sparrow by more black on breast and flanks;

brown cap and white cheeks. Females nearly indistinguishable from female House Sparrow.

699. SAXAUL SPARROW
Passer ammodendri
(Saksaulny Vorobey)
Plate 46, Map 290

Field marks: 14 cm. In male, back and rump yellowish-gray; crown, throat, and streaks on back are black; wide rusty ocher eyebrow; wings and tail brownish; breast, belly and sides of head whitish. Females and juveniles similar but paler, with gray replacing black.

Habits: Found in desert, where it prefers saxal thickets and scrub along river valleys. Migratory. Not numerous. Stays in flocks; nests in tree hollows, more rarely in buildings. Lays

FIG. 68 Sparrow Nestling

FIG. 69 Nests of Spanish
Sparrow

four to six white eggs with small gray-rust spots
from May to July. Call: melodic chirping and
short whistle.

Range and distribution: Deserts of Central Asia
and Kazakhstan. Winters south of its nesting
range, and does not migrate to distant lands.

Similar species: Differs from other sparrows
by rusty eyebrow.

700. TREE SPARROW
Passer montanus
(Polevoy Vorobey)
Plate 46, Map 291

Field marks: 14-15 cm. Smaller than a House
Sparrow. Back dark brown with dark brown
streaks; wings and tail brownish; crown chestnut-brown; sides of head white; throat and
cheek spot black; underparts whitish.

Habits: Found in settled areas, where it prefers
young tree plantings during breeding season;
barnyards and crop sowings the rest of the
year. Nonmigratory. Common. Stays in flocks.
Nests in pairs and in small colonies. Nests in
tree hollows, under roof eaves, burrows in
precipices, artificial nesting boxes, and near
rim of nest of large raptors. Lays four to eight
white or grayish eggs speckled dark from April
to July. Call: harsh "chirr-chirr."

Range and distribution: Throughout the USSR
except the north, northeastern Siberia, and
Kamchatka Peninsula.

Similar species: Differs from Cinnamon Sparrow by black cheek spot; from House Sparrow, by brown head and characteristic cheek
spot.

701. CINNAMON SPARROW
Passer rutilans
(Rizhy Vorobey)
Plate 46, Map 290

Field marks: 14 cm. Resembles Tree Sparrow.
In male, throat and eye stripe are black; crown,
back, and rump brownish-rusty with blackish
streaks; sides of head white; breast and belly
grayish-white; wings and tail brownish. Females and juveniles lack black and rusty colors;
back is brownish; eye stripe light.

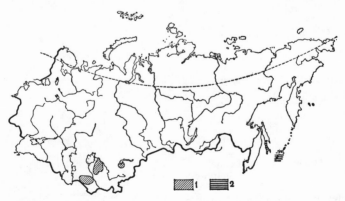

MAP 290. Saxual Sparrow (1), Cinnamon Sparrow (2)

MAP 291. Tree Sparrow (1), Desert Sparrow (2)

Habits: Found in damp, deciduous, riparian forest. Migratory and nomadic. Rare. Stays in pairs and flocks. Nests in tree hollows. Lays five or six whitish eggs with brownish spots in May and June.

Range and distribution: Southern Sakhalin Island and southern Kuril Islands. Winters in Japan.

Similar species: Differs from Tree Sparrow by lack of black cheek spot.

702. DESERT SPARROW
Passer simplex
(Pustynny Vorobey)
Plate 46, Map 291

Field marks: 13 cm. Smaller than a House Sparrow. Upperparts light gray; lores and throat black; tail and wings brownish with lighter edgings; wing bar, cheeks, breast, and belly white with ocher tone. Females and juveniles similar, with black replaced by brownish.

Habits: Found in deserts with saxal grasses or thickets. Nonmigratory. Rare. Stays in pairs or small flocks on the ground and in bushes. Large, globular nest with cylindrical entrance is situated in a tree. Lays five or six white eggs with dark spots in April or May. Call: short trill. Included in the Red Data Book of the USSR.

Range and distribution: Eastern regions of the Kara Kum Desert.

Similar species: Differs from other sparrows by light gray color.

Sturnus

Small birds with sturdy body; bill long and pointed; long, strong legs; some part of plum-age with metallic iridescence. Feeds on insects, berries, and fruit.

703. NORTHERN STARLING
Sturnus vulgaris
(Obyknovenny Skvorets)
Plate 47, Map 292

Field marks: 20-24 cm. Adult is blackish with a shining, metallic iridescence; wings and tail brownish. In autumn, entire body is covered with thick, white speckles. Juveniles brown with lighter throat.

Habits: Found in inhabited areas and cut forest; nearly always in the vicinity of a settlement. Migratory. Common and numerous. Feeds mostly on the ground, sometimes in trees. Stays in flocks. Usually nests in artificial boxes and buildings; outside settled areas, in tree hollows and burrows. Lays five to seven light blue eggs from April to July. Call: harsh and scraping. Song: mostly mimics other birds.

Range and distribution: European USSR (as far north as the Arctic Circle), central and southern Siberia to Lake Baikal, Central Asia, and Kazakhstan. Winters in southern USSR, West Asia, and northern Africa.

Similar species: Differs from Blackbird by shorter tail and iridescent sheen; in autumn by speckled appearance. Juveniles differ from juveniles of Rose-colored Starlings by darker color.

704. ROSE-COLORED STARLING
Sturnus roseus
(Rozovy Skvorets)
Plate 47, Map 292

Field marks: 21-24 cm. Adult crested; head, neck, wings, and tail black with metallic iridescence; remainder pink. Juveniles light grayish-brownish with lighter underparts.

Habits: Found in dry open spaces with preci-

MAP 292. Northern Starling (1), Rose-colored Starling (2)

pices, cliffs, heaps of rock; often seen in settled areas as well. Migratory. Common and numerous. Stays in large flocks, more rarely in pairs or singly. In flight, flock is a tight knot or ribbonlike. Nests in colonies in crevices of cliffs, precipices; in heaps of adobe and pressed dung, in stacks of firewood and between rocks. Lays four to six light blue eggs in May and June. Call and song: harsh, scraping, hoarse sounds. Usually feeds on the ground, sometimes in trees and bushes.

Range and distribution: Southern USSR from the Ukraine to the Altai. Winters in southwestern Asia.

Similar species: Juveniles differ from juveniles of Northern Starling by lighter coloration.

Spodiopsar

705. WHITE-CHEEKED STARLING
Spodiopsar cineraceus
(Sery Skvorets)
Plate 47, Map 293

Field marks: 22-23 cm. Gray overall; crown and sides of head white with dark streaks; belly white; neck and nape black; bill bright yellow, brownish at tip. Female duller; juveniles rusty brownish.

Habits: Found in deciduous forest and groves, often in settled areas. Migratory. Common. Stays in flocks; nests in colonies in tree hollows. Lays four to eight light blue eggs in May and June. Call: harsh cracking noises.

Range and distribution: Southeast USSR from southeastern Transbaikal to southern Sakhalin and southern Kuril Islands. Winters in southeastern China, North Vietnam, and in the Philippines.

Similar species: No similar species in the USSR.

Acridotheres

706. INDIAN MYNA
Acridotheres tristis
(Mayna)
Plate 47, Map 293

Field marks: 25-27 cm. Larger than a starling. Head, neck, wings, and tail black; belly, wing patch and tip of tail white; remainder is brownish-pinkish; bill, legs, and bare spot under the eye yellow.

Habits: Found in settled areas. Nonmigratory. Common. Gregarious, nests in colonies. Nest situated under roofs and in cracks of buildings; in burrows and niches of precipices. Lays three to six light blue eggs from March to July. Call: hoarse, scraping cries and whistles.

Range and distribution: Central Asia and southern Kazakhstan.

Similar species: No similar species in USSR.

Sturnia

707. DAURIAN STARLING
Sturnia sturnia
(Maly Skvorets)
Plate 47, Map 294

Field marks: 18-19 cm. Smaller than a starling. Male is light gray; back, tail, wings, and spot on nape are black with a metallic violet iridescence; wide white wing bar. Females and juveniles are duller, and females lack black spot on nape.

Habits: Found in groves and forest edges. Migratory. Common. Gregarious, often nests in colonies in tree hollows. Lays five or six light blue eggs in May and June. Call: loud cracking

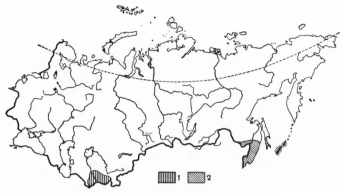

MAP 293. Indian Myna (1), White-cheeked Starling (2)

noises. Song: a variety of trills, whistles, and mimics of other bird calls.

Range and distribution: Southeast USSR from southeastern Transbaikal to the lower Amur River and southern Primorski region. Winters in southern China, Indochina, and Indonesia.

Similar species: Male differs from Red-cheeked Starling by lack of rusty spots on cheeks. In the field, female nearly indistinguishable from female Red-cheeked Starling, but is lighter.

708. RED-CHEEKED STARLING
Sturnia philippensis
(Yaponsky Skvorets)
Plate 47, Map 294

Field marks: 18-19 cm. Resembles Daurian Starling, but male has bright rusty brown spots on cheeks; spots sometimes connected to form a band that reaches the throat.

Habits: Found in groves in deciduous forests among fields. Migratory. Not numerous. Stays in pairs and flocks. Nests in tree hollows. Lays five or six light blue eggs in May and June. Call same as Daurian Starling.

Range and distribution: Shores and islands of Peter the Great Bay, southern Sakhalin Island, southern Kuril Islands. Winters in the Philippines and in the Greater Sunda Isles.

Similar species: Male differs from Daurian Starling by rusty spots on cheeks; female, by its lighter color.

[Vagrants of **709.** BRAHMINY MYNA (*Sturnus pagodarum*) were found in the Kugitangtai Mountains: brownish-gray upperparts, rusty underparts, black crest, and whitish rump. Vagrants of **710.** RUSTY BLACKBIRD (*Euphagus carolinensis*) were obtained on the southwest shores of the Chukotski Peninsula; color blackish with light bluish-green iridescence.]

MAP 294. Red-cheeked Starling (1), Daurian Starling (2)

Oriolus

Birds of medium size (larger than a starling) and sturdy build. Males brightly colored with a predominance of yellow. Feed on insects and furry caterpillars.

711. EUROPEAN GOLDEN ORIOLE
Oriolus oriolus
(Ivolga)
Plate 47, Map 295
Field marks: 24-27 cm. In male, wings, tail, and lores black; outer corners of tail, spot on wings, and remaining plumage bright yellow. In females and juveniles, upperparts yellowish-green; underparts yellowish-white with narrow, brownish streaks.
Habits: Found in thin deciduous and mixed forests, gardens, and parks. Migratory. Common. Found singly, in pairs, and more rarely in small flocks. Stays hidden in leafy part of trees. Nest is a basketlike pouch with a "bolster" along the inner rim, hung from from tip of tree branch. Lays three or four white eggs speckled black in May and June. Easily identifiable by call, which is a harsh "vzhyaya-aa," and beautiful flutelike whistle, "flew-teeyou-leyou."
Range and distribution: Deciduous and coniferous forests from Karelia east to the Yenisei River and south to the borders of the USSR, except deserts of Central Asia and Kazakhstan. Winters in Africa, India, Madagascar, and Sri Lanka.
Similar species: Differs from Black-naped Oriole by lack of black stripe on nape.

712. BLACK-NAPED ORIOLE
Oriolus chinensis
(Chernogolovaya Ivolga)
Plate 47, Map 295
Field marks: 24-28 cm. Resembles European Golden Oriole, but black eye line wider, and extends around the head completely. Juveniles have olive-green upperparts; underparts whitish with dark streaks.
Habits: Found in deciduous woods. Migratory. Common. Found singly, in pairs, and flocks in tree crowns. Nests in fork of tree at tip of branch. Lays three or four pinkish-white eggs with small rusty brown spots in May and June. Easily identified by call, which is a drawn-out whistle, "tyou-you-you." Song: loud flutelike whistle, "gree-goree."
Range and distribution: Southern Soviet Far East. Winters in Sri Lanka, southern India, and southeastern China.
Similar species: Differs from European Golden Oriole by continuous black band across nape.

[Vagrants of **713.** BLACK DRONGO (*Dicrurus macrocercus*) and **714.** SPANGLED DRONGO (*Chibia hottentota*) were obtained in southern coastal areas. The birds are the size of a starling or slightly larger, plumage black with bright metallic iridescence.]

Corvus

Large bird with powerful, straight, and fairly thick bill. Black or gray with black and metallic sheen. Wings long, tail short. Open nest (without roof) situated in trees or cliff ledges.

715. NORTHERN RAVEN
Corvus corax
(Voron)
Plate 48, Map 296
Field marks: 62-64 cm. Large bird (much larger than a crow). Black with metallic bluish luster; tail wedge-shaped. In desert races, head, neck, back, and upper breast have chocolate-brown-

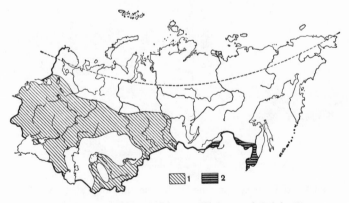

MAP 295. European Golden Oriole (1), Black-naped Oriole (2)

MAP 296. Northern Raven (1), Large-billed Crow (2)

ish tint. Some ornithologists consider it a separate species, i.e., BROWN-NECKED RAVEN (*Corvus ruficollis*).

Habits: Found in forests, river valleys, seashores, mountains, and desert. Nonmigratory. Not numerous. Occurs singly, in pairs, or small flocks. Nests in trees, cliff ledges, or precipices. Lays three to seven light greenish-blue eggs with brownish spots from February to May. Call: loud "krook-krook" and cawing. Feeds mostly on rodents, insects, carrion.

Range and distribution: Throughout the USSR except northern Asian borders.

Similar species: Differs from other crows by larger size and wedge-shaped tail.

716. EURASIAN CROW

Corvus corone
(Vorona)
Plate 48, Map 297

Field marks: 47-48 cm. Divided into two races, black and gray. The black race is uniformly black with bluish metallic glint. The gray (hooded) race has black wings, head, and tail and the rest of the plumage is gray. Some ornithologists consider them separate species, i.e., *C. corone* and *C. cornix*.

Habits: Found in all habitats, especially settled areas; in places lives only in inhabited areas. Nonmigratory or nomadic or migratory. Common. In breeding season, stays in pairs; in flocks the rest of the year. Usually feeds on the ground. Nest situated in trees, more rarely on rock ledges or heaps of cattails. Lays four or five light greenish-blue eggs speckled brownish from March to June. Call: hoarse "karr-karr."

Range and distribution: Throughout the USSR except northern borders. Gray race found in European USSR, West Siberia, and Kazakh-

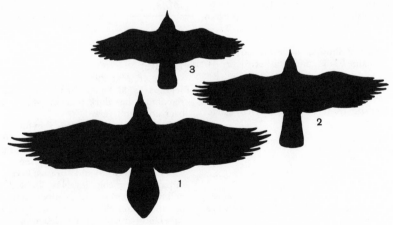

FIG. 70 CORVIDS IN FLIGHT
1. Northern Raven   2. Eurasian Rook   3. Jackdaw

MAP 297. Eurasian Crow: Gray race (*C. corone*) (1), black race (*C. cornix*) (2)

stan. Black race found in Central Asia, southern Kazakhstan, central and eastern Siberia, and Soviet Far East.

Similar species: Eurasian Crow nearly indistinguishable from juvenile Rook in the field. In the hand, differs by thicker bill and heavier body.

717. LARGE-BILLED CROW

Corvus macrorhynchos
(Bolsheklyuvaya Vorona)
Plate 48, Map 296

Field marks: 50 cm. Large crow with long, thick bill. Black with greenish glitter on head; tip of tail wedge-shaped.

Habits: Found in thin forests of plains and hills. In winter, stays in flocks near towns and villages. Nonmigratory. Common. Usually feeds on the ground. Nests in trees. Lays five or six light greenish-blue eggs speckled brownish in April and May. Call: loud "kroo-kroo" or "kaoo-kaoo."

Range and distribution: Southern Soviet Far East, Sakhalin Island, and southern Kuril Islands.

Similar species: Differs from other crows by long, massive bill; from the Eurasian Crow, by smaller size; from Northern Raven by range.

718. EURASIAN ROOK

Corvus frugilegus
(Grach)
Plate 48, Map 298

Field marks: 46 cm. Black with dark bluish, metallic iridescence. Adults have grayish-white skin around bill.

Habits: Found in settled areas and thin forests.

Stays in flocks, nests in colonies. Numerous and migratory. Common. Usually feeds on the ground. Nests in trees; often several in the same tree. Lays five or six light greenish-blue eggs speckled brownish from April to June. Call: hoarse "kraaa."

Range and distribution: European USSR (except northern regions and the Transcaucasus), Kazakhstan, southern Siberia, to the east as far as the central Primorski region. Winters in southern USSR.

Similar species: Adult Eurasian Rooks differ from other crows by bare white skin near bill. Juveniles indistinguishable from Eurasian Crow. Since adult and juvenile Eurasian Rooks always stay together in large flocks, the identification of juveniles is not usually a problem.

Coloeus

719. JACKDAW

Coloeus monedula
(Galka)
Plate 48, Map 298

Field marks: 33-36 cm. Crown and neck gray; remainder has dark blue metallic sheen on back and shoulders.

Habits: Found in settled areas, thin forests, open spaces with cliffs and precipices. Nonmigratory, nomadic, and migratory. Common; in place numerous. Gregarious, often together with Eurasian Crows and Eurasian Rooks. Nests in pairs and in colonies. Nest situated in tree hollows, under roofs, in pipes, burrows in precipices and cliff crevices. Lays four to six light bluish-green eggs speckled brownish from April to June. Call: loud "caw-caw."

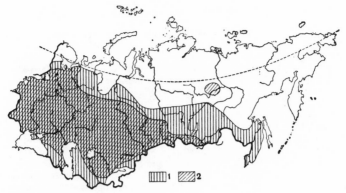

MAP 298. Jackdaw (1), Eurasian Rook (2)

Range and distribution: European USSR (except most central regions), southern Asian regions (except the Pamirs). Part of the population is nonmigratory; part migrates to the south.

Similar species: Differs from other crows by its smaller size.

Note: In Tuva, the Transbaikal, and in the Soviet Far East, there are two races of jackdaw: one is significantly darker, particularly the head; the other has head, wings, and tail black, with the rest of the plumage nearly white. Some ornithologists consider the eastern jackdaws as a separate species, DAURIAN JACKDAW (*Coloeus dauricus*).

Pyrrhocorax

720. RED-BILLED CHOUGH
Pyrrhocorax pyrrhocorax
(Klusheetsa)
Plate 48, Map 299

Field marks: 45 cm. Black with dark bluish sheen. Long, slightly downcurved bill; legs are coral-red. Wings long and tail short.

Habits: Found in open mountain areas; prefers meadow steppe and plowed fields. Nonmigratory. Common. Stays in flocks. Nests in crevice or niche of cliff. Lays three to nine grayish-green eggs speckled brownish from April to July. Call: loud "klyaa-klyaa." Feeds on the ground.

Range and distribution: Mountains of the Caucasus, Central Asia, southern Kazakhstan, and southern Siberia.

Similar species: Differs from Alpine Chough by red bill and shorter tail.

721. ALPINE CHOUGH
Pyrrhocorax graculus
(Alpiyskaya Galka)
Plate 48, Map 299

Field marks: 42 cm. Black; short yellow bill; legs red. Wings and tail long.

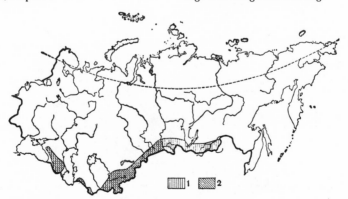

MAP 299. Red-billed Chough (1), Alpine Chough (2)

Habits: Found in open areas in upper mountain regions, where it prefers cliffs, rockslides, and meadows. Stays in flocks, nests in colonies. Usually feeds on ground or in bushes. Non-migratory; in winter, flies down to river valleys, where it feeds on berry bushes. Common. Nests in cracks and niches of cliffs. Nests not yet found in USSR. Call: gentle "keeree-keeree" and loud "kreeya."

Range and distribution: Mountains of the Caucasus, Central Asia, southern Kazakhstan, and the Altai.

Similar species: Differs from Red-billed Chough by shorter yellow bill.

Nucifraga

722. SPOTTED NUTCRACKER
Nucifraga caryocatactes
(Kedrovka)
Plate 48, Map 300

Field marks: 34-38 cm. Crown, wings, and tail black; rest of plumage chestnut-brownish and thickly spotted on back, neck, breast, and belly with white; undertail coverts and tip of tail white; bill long and blackish.

Habits: Found in coniferous taiga. Nomadic. Common. Occurs singly, in pairs, and in flocks. When nesting, stays hidden and silent; the rest of the time is noisy and easily seen. Flight heavy; wings wide. Nests in trees, on cliff ledges, or precipices. Lays four or five greenish eggs with dark spots in April and May. Call: hoarse, drawn-out "rezh-rezh" or "kray-kray."

Range and distribution: All taiga zones throughout the USSR, also coniferous forests of the Tien-Shan Mountains.

Similar species: No similar species in USSR.

Podoces

Unique birds; larger than a starling.

723. PANDER'S GROUND-JAY
Podoces panderi
(Saksaulnaya Soyka)
Plate 47, Map 300

Field marks: 25 cm. Crown and back light gray; lores, wings, tail, and large upper breast patch black; throat, undertail, and wing patches white; breast and belly pinkish-yellowish; bill and legs long.

Habits: Found in desert scrub singly and in pairs. Nonmigratory. Not numerous. Stays on the ground; runs fast, with head raised. Roofed nest situated in a bush. Lays four or five light bluish-greenish eggs spotted brownish from March to June. Call: loud "tse-tse-tse."

Range and distribution: Sandy deserts of Kazakhstan and Central Asia.

Similar species: Differs from Henderson's Ground-Jay by gray crown and black breast spot.

724. HENDERSON'S GROUND-JAY
Podoces hendersoni
(Mongolskaya Saksaulnaya Soyka)
Plate 47, Map 301

Field marks: 28 cm. Crown, wings, and tail black; elongated white stripe on wing; remainder of plumage gray-rusty; underparts lighter; bill and legs long.

Habits: Found in rocky and desert plains with thickets. Nonmigratory. Rare. Stays singly and in pairs. Good, fast ground runner. Often digs at base of bush. Nesting habits little known.

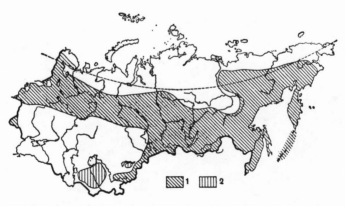

MAP 300. Spotted Nutcracker (1) Pander's Ground-Jay (2)

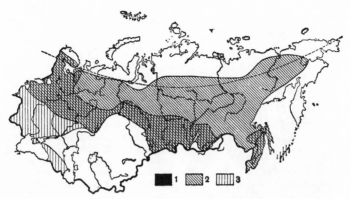

MAP 301. Henderson's Ground-Jay (1), Siberian Jay (2), Eurasian Jay (3)

One open nest was found situated on the ground under a bush. No record in USSR of eggs. Call: harsh whistle.

Range and distribution: Zaisan Basin.

Similar species: Differs from Pander's Ground-Jay by black crown and lack of black spot on upper breast.

Pica

725. BLACK-BILLED MAGPIE
Pica pica
(Soroka)
Plate 48, Map 302

Field marks: 45-48 cm. Medium-size bird (like Jackdaw) with long, graduated tail. Head, neck, upper breast, back, rump, tail, and wings black with iridescent gloss; breast, belly, large shoulder, and wing patches white.

Habits: Found in wooded and thicket areas in a variety of habitats. Avoids deep forest. Stays singly, in pairs, and in flocks. Flight heavy with frequent beats of its short wings. Raises tail when walking on the ground. Roofed nest situated in bushes or trees. Lays five to eight light bluish-greenish eggs with brownish spots from April to July. Call: loud, harsh chattering.

Range and distribution: European USSR, West Siberia, southern regions of central Siberia as far as southeastern Transbaikal, southern Soviet Far East, basin of the Anadyr River, Koryak National Okrug, Kamchatka Peninsula, Kazakhstan, and Central Asia.

Similar species: No similar species in USSR.

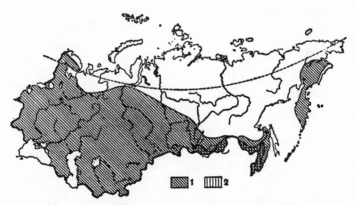

MAP 302. Black-billed Magpie (1), Azure-winged Magpie (2)

FIG. 71 Nest of Black-billed Magpie

Cyanopica

726. AZURE-WINGED MAGPIE
Cyanopica cyana
(Golubaya Soroka)
Plate 48, Map 302
Field marks: 35 cm. Long, graduated tail; head black; back and rump brownish-gray; tip of tail and throat white; breast and belly whitish with brownish suffusion; wings and tail light blue.
Habits: Found in deciduous forest and thickets in river valleys. Nonmigratory and nomadic. Common. Found in pairs and flocks in trees and bushes; more rarely on the ground. Open nest situated in tree. Lays three to seven light grayish-bluish eggs speckled dark in May and June. Call: loud "feeell-cheen-cheen."
Range and distribution: Southwest and southeastern Transbaikal, southern Soviet Far East.
Similar species: No similar species in the USSR.

Garrulus

727. EURASIAN JAY
Garrulus glandarius
(Soyka)
Plate 48, Map 301
Field marks: 35-37 cm. Jackdaw-size bird with fluffy, loose plumage; crest conspicuous when excited; short wings and long tail. Wings, tail (and in Caucasian and Crimean races top of head) black; rump white; bright blue wing coverts narrowly barred with black; remaining plumage brownish-gray. In Siberian races, head is rusty; in European, whitish with brownish streaks.
Habits: Found in deciduous and mixed forest, more rarely in coniferous forests. Nomadic. Common. Stays hidden in breeding season, but raucous and readily seen at other times. Stays in pairs and flocks in trees, bushes, and on the ground. Flight quiet and heavy. Nests on outer branches of tree. Lays five to seven greenish eggs spotted brownish-gray from April to June. Call: harsh "chzhe-chzhzhe." Song: a variety of loud sounds and imitations of other birds.
Range and distribution: European USSR, Siberia, and Soviet Far East.
Similar species: Differs from Siberian Jay by white rump and black tail.

Cractes

728. SIBERIAN JAY
Cractes infaustus
(Kuksha)
Plate 48, Map 301
Field marks: 28-30 cm. Reminiscent of Eurasian Jay, but smaller. Grayish-brownish overall; crown and wings dark brownish; rump and wing patches rusty; tail rusty with dark median stripe.
Habits: Found in coniferous taiga. Silent and hidden during breeding season; noisy and easily seen the remainder of the year. Occurs in pairs and flocks in trees and on the ground. Flight is quiet and heavy, with tail fanned. Nonmigratory and nomadic. Common. Nests in trees. Lays three to five greenish-gray eggs with dark mottling in March and April. Call: loud "kzhe-kzhe" and pleasant, low whistle, "kook-kook." Song: a variety of whistles and faint sounds.
Range and distribution: All taiga zones from the Kola Peninsula and the Baltic States to Anadyr and shores of the Sea of Okhotsk.
Similar species: Differs from Eurasian Jay by dark coloration and rusty rump.

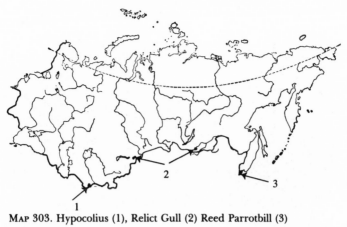

MAP 303. Hypocolius (1), Relict Gull (2) Reed Parrotbill (3)

BIBLIOGRAPHY

Dementiev, G. P., Gladkov, N. A., eds. *Birds of the USSR*. Vols. 1-6. Moscow, 1951-1954. In Russian.

Dolgushin, I. A., and others. *Birds of Kazakhstan*. Vols. 1-5. Alma Ata, 1960-1974. In Russian.

Fauna of the USSR. *Birds*. Vol. 1, editions 3, 4, 5. Vol. 2, editions 1 and 3. Leningrad, 1937-1962. In Russian.

Gladkov, N. A.; Dementiev, G. P.; Ptushenko, E. S.; Sudilovskaya, A. M. *Guide to Birds of the USSR*. Moscow, 1964. In Russian.

Ivanov, A. I. *Catalog, Birds of the USSR*. Leningrad, 1976. In Russian.

Ivanov, A. I.; Kozlova, E. V.; Portenko, L. A.; Tugarinov, A. Ya. *Birds of the USSR*. Vols. 1-4. Leningrad, 1951-1960. In Russian.

Ivanov, A. I., Shtegman, B. K. *Brief Guide to Birds of the USSR*. 2nd edition. Leningrad, 1978. In Russian.

Stepanyan, L. S. *Structure and Distribution of Bird Fauna in the USSR*. Vols. 1-2. Moscow, 1975-1978. In Russian.

Vaurie, C. *The Birds of the Palearctic Fauna*, Vols. 1-2, London, 1959 and 1965.

INDEX OF ENGLISH NAMES

THIS is an index of suffixes and unprefixed proper names, with reference to species number. Included are the names in use in this book as well as alternate names mentioned only in the cross-reference list. For example, *Apus melba* is known as Alpine Swift in English. Its species number will be included under Swift 381-385. As a convenience to users of this book, both parts of a compound name are indexed to the consecutive species numbers. Number 723, the Pander's Ground-Jay will be found listed under G (Ground-Jay) as well as J (for Jay). You may wish to turn directly to the text page on which that species is described, or refer to the cross-reference index to look up its alternate vernaculars, scientific name(s), or where to find the color plate, map, or additional figure.

Accentor 615-622
Albatross 14-16
Auk 301-322
Auklet 322, 329-333
Avocet 271

Bee-eater 393-394
Bittern 41, 46-49
Blackbird 479, 710
Blackcap 571
Bluetail 498
Bluethroat 513
Booby 33
Brambling 688
Brant 70
Bufflehead 107
Bulbul 450-451
Bullfinch 674, 677
Bunting 623-650
Bushchat 494-497, 518
Bush-Robin 498, 518
Bush-Warbler 540-545
Bustard 188-190
Buttonquail 202
Buzzard 114-115, 125-129
Buzzard-Eagle 129

Capercaillie 164-165
Chaffinch 687
Chat 494-497, 499, 518
Chickadee 603
Chough 720-721
Chukar 170
Coot 191-192
Cormorant 26-31
Corncrake 195
Courser 204
Crake 195-200
Crane 180-187
Creeper 610-613
Crossbill 684-686
Crow 716-717
Cuckoo 353-358
Curlew 203, 262-267

Dabchick 9
Desert-Finch 674-676
Dikkop 203
Dipper 465-466
Diver 1-4
Dollarbird 387
Dotterel 215-216, 218-219
Dove 341-351
Dovekie 322
Dowitcher 247-248
Drongo 713-714
Duck 74-89, 96, 98, 103-104, 112
Dunlin 229
Dunnock 615

Eagle 118-120, 130-136, 143
Eagle-Owl 360
Egret 37-41
Eider 90-93

Falcon 150-159
Fieldfare 470
Finch 674-676, 692-694
Firecrest 579
Fish-Owl 361
Flamingo 57
Flycatcher 581-593
Forktail 517
Francolin 173
Frigatebird 34
Fulmar 10

Gadwall 82
Gallinule 192-193
Gannet 32
Garganey 86
Godwit 260-261
Goldcrest 578
Goldeneye 105-106
Goldfinch 44
Goosander 111
Goose 62-73
Goshawk 121-122
Grasshopper-Warbler 546-553

Grebe 5-9
Greenfinch 663-664
Green-Pigeon 352
Greenshank 251, 254-255
Griffon 137-142
Grosbeak 660-662, 681, 683
Ground-Jay 723-724
Grouse 160, 162-163, 166
Guillemot 319-320, 323-324
Gull 287-308
Gyrfalcon 153

Harrier 144-148
Hawfinch 659-662
Hawk 126, 144
Hawk-Cuckoo 357
Hawk-Owl 368, 372
Hazelhen 167
Hen 167
Heron 35-37, 41-45, 50
Hobby 154
Honey-Buzzard 114-115
Honey-Kite 114-115
Hoopoe 395
Horned-Owl 360
Houbara 189
Hypocolius 464

Ibis 52-54
Ibisbill 280
Irania 516

Jackdaw 719
Jack Snipe 279
Jaeger 283-285
Jay 723-724, 727-728
Junco 651

Kestrel 156-158
Kingfisher 388-392
Kite 116-117, 149
Kittiwake 288-289
Knot 239-240

Lammergeier 138
Lapwing 220-225
Lark 410-424
Laughing-thrush 519
Leaf-Warbler 524-539
Linnet 667
Little-Bittern 46-48
Longspur 649
Loon 1-4

Magpie 725-726
Mallard 77
Marsh-Tern 309-311
Martin 428-432
Merganser 109-111

Merlin 155
Minivet 449
Moorhen 193
Murre 323-324
Murrelet 305-328
Myna 706, 709

Needletail 385
Night-Heron 45, 50
Nightingale 507-508, 511
Nightjar 377-380
Nutcracker 722
Nuthatch 606-609

Oldsquaw 711-712
Osprey 113
Ouzel 478
Owl 359-376
Oystercatcher 281

Painted-snipe 282
Paradise-Flycatcher 592-593
Parrotbill 521-522
Partridge 169-173
Parula 657
Pastor 704
Pelican 24-25
Penduline-Tit 605
Peregrine 150
Petrel 11, 22-23
Petronia 695-696
Phalarope 268-269
Pheasant 179
Pigeon 341-346, 352
Pintail 84
Pipit 434-441
Plover 208-225
Pochard 94-98
Pond-Heron 42-43
Pratincole 205-207
Ptarmigan 160-161
Puffin 334-336
Pygmy-Owl 371

Quail 168

Rail 194, 199
Raven 715
Razorbill 321
Redpoll 669-670
Redshank 252-253
Redstart 499-506
Redwing 473
Reedhen 192
Reedling 520
Reed-Warbler 555-560
Robin 498, 511-518
Rock-Thrush 484-486
Roller 386-387

Rook 718
Rosefinch 673, 678-683
Rosy-Finch 689-691
Rubythroat 509, 510
Ruff 244

Sanderling 238
Sandgrouse 337-340
Sandpiper 228-259
Scaup 99
Scops-Owl 362-365
Scoter 100-102
Scrub-Robin 518
Sea-Eagle 118-120
Serin 671-672
Shag 30
Shearwater 17-21
Shelduck 74-76
Shikra 122
Shoveler 87
Shrike 452-461
Siskin 666
Skua 283-286
Skylark 410-411
Smew 108
Snake-Eagle 143
Snipe 273-279, 282
Snowcock 174-178
Snow-Finch 692, 694
Sparrow 615, 653-656, 695-702
Sparrowhawk 123-124
Spoonbill 51
Sprosser 508
Starling 703-709
Stilt 270
Stint 230-234
Stonechat 495-497
Stonecurlew 203
Stork 55-56
Storm-Petrel 11-13, 23
Swallow 425-433

Swamphen 192
Swan 58-61
Swift 381-385

Tattler 256-257
Teal 79-81, 85-86
Tern 309-318
Thick-knee 203
Thrush 468-486, 519
Thrush-Nightingale 508
Tit 520, 523, 594-605
Tit-Warbler 580
Towhee 652
Treecreeper 611-613
Turnstone 226-227
Turtle-Dove 347-351
Twite 668

Vulture 137-142

Wagtail 442-448
Wallcreeper 610
Warbler 518, 524-580, 657
Watercock 201
Waterthrush 658
Waxwing 462-463
Wheatear 487-493
Whimbrel 263, 266
Whinchat 494
Whistling-Thrush 483
White-eye 614
Whitethroat 572-573
Wigeon 83, 88
Willow-Warbler 524, 534, 538-539
Woodcock 272
Woodlark 412
Woodpecker 396-408
Wren 467
Wryneck 409

Yellowhammer 624

CROSS-REFERENCE LIST

Peter Alden, Massachusetts Audubon Society

THIS list of birds found in the USSR is consecutively numbered from 1 to 728 following the exact order of their appearance in the text. The sequence of orders and families is modern. Some rare and accidental species are briefly mentioned after the full accounts of the commoner species of a family. These will be somewhat out of proper taxonomic sequence.

Assignment of a species number will facilitate the reader's use of color plates, figures, maps, and this list of names.

The scientific name in use in this work appears first. In some cases additional names are inserted afterwards. These other names will be in use in various other books and technical papers. Some have been used for forms now considered to be subspecies. Others reflect continuing discussion on which genus the form should be included in (often requiring a change in gender). Still others are suppressed names appearing only in older works.

The English names (or vernaculars) selected for use in this work appear first. This name is often followed by two or more alternate names. These other names have been rejected for a variety of reasons such as inaccuracy, lack of prefixes, implication of wrong family relationship, or validity for only one subspecies. Ornithologists of wide experience and bird students who travel have long had to be aware of a variety of English and scientific names. Presenting most of these other names adjacent to each other should greatly increase the value of this work to individuals.

Additional columns after the names of the birds give the reader the color plate number (1-48) and map number.

GAVIIFORMES		Plate	Range Map
LOONS (DIVERS) GAVIIDAE			
1 Gavia stellata	Red-throated Loon Red-throated Diver	1	1
2 G. arctica incl. G. (a.) pacifica	Black-throated Loon Black-throated Diver Arctic Loon Green-throated Loon	1	1
3 G. adamsi	Yellow-billed Loon White-billed Diver	1	2
4 G. immer	Common Loon Great Northern Diver	—	—

		Plate	Range Map

PODICEPEDIFORMES

GREBES: PODICIPEDIDAE

5 Podiceps cristatus	Great Crested Grebe Crested Grebe	5	3
6 P. grisegena	Red-necked Grebe	5	4
7 P. auritus	Horned Grebe Slavonian Grebe	5	5
8 P. nigricollis	Black-necked Grebe Eared Grebe	5	5
9 P. ruficollis Tachybaptus ruficollis	Red-throated Dabchick Little Grebe	5	4

PROCELLARIIFORMES

ALBATROSSES: DIOMEDEIDAE
SHEARWATERS: PROCELLARIIDAE
STORM-PETRELS: HYDROBATIDAE

10 Fulmarus glacialis	Northern Fulmar Fulmar	21	6
11 Oceanodroma leucorrhoa	Leach's Storm-Petrel Leach's Petrel	23	6
12 O. monorhis	Swinhoe's Storm-Petrel	23	7
13 O. furcata	Fork-tailed Storm-Petrel Pale Storm-Petrel	23	7
14 Diomedea albatrus	Short-tailed Albatross	—	—
15 D. immutabilis	Laysan Albatross	—	—
16 D. nigripes	Black-footed Albatross	—	—
17 Puffinus griseus	Sooty Shearwater	—	—
18 P. tenuirostris	Short-tailed Shearwater	—	—
19 P. puffinus	Manx Shearwater	—	—
20 P. bulleri	Buller's Shearwater New Zealand Shearwater Gray-backed Shearwater	—	—
21 Calonectris leucomelas Puffinus leucomelas Procellaria leucomelas	Streaked Shearwater White-faced Shearwater	—	—
22 Pterodroma leucoptera	White-winged Petrel Gould's Petrel	—	—
23 Hydrobates pelagicus	European Storm-Petrel Storm Petrel	—	—

PELECANIFORMES

PELICANS: PELECANIIDAE

24 Pelecanus crispus P. philippensis	Dalmatian Pelican	1	8
25 P. onocrotalus	Eastern White Pelican White Pelican	1	8

CORMORANTS: PHALACROCORACIDAE

26 Phalacrocorax carbo	Great Cormorant Black Cormorant Large Cormorant Cormorant	1	9
27 P. capillatus P. filamentosus	Temminck's Cormorant Japanese Cormorant	1	9
28 P. pelagicus	Pelagic Cormorant	1	10
29 P. urile	Red-faced Cormorant	1	10
30 P. aristotelis	European Shag Shag	1	11
31 P. pygmeus	Pygmy Cormorant	1	11

BOOBIES: SULIDAE

32 Sula bassana Morus bassanus	Northern Gannet North Atlantic Gannet Gannet	1	—
33 S. sula	Red-footed Booby	—	—

FRIGATEBIRDS: FREGATIDAE

34 Fregata minor	Great Frigatebird	—	—

CICONIIFORMES

HERONS: ARDEIDAE

35 Ardea cinerea	Gray Heron Heron	6	12
36 A. purpurea	Purple Heron	6	12

37 Egretta alba
    Ardea alba
    Casmerodius albus
	Great Egret
	Common Egret
	Great White Egret
	Large Egret
	American Egret
	White Heron
		6	13

38 E. garzetta	Little Egret	6	13
39 E. eulophotes	Chinese Egret Swinhoe's Egret	—	—
40 E. intermedia	Short-billed Egret Intermediate Egret Plumed Egret Yellow-billed Egret Median Egret	—	—

41 Bubulcus ibis
    Ardeola ibis
    Egretta ibis
	Cattle Egret
	Cattle Heron
	Buff-backed Heron
		6	14

42 Ardeola ralloides	Squacco Pond-Heron Squacco Heron	6	14
43 A. bacchus	Chinese Pond-Heron	—	14
44 Butorides striatus Ardeola striata	Little Heron Green Heron Green-winged Heron Green backed Heron Striated Heron Mangrove Bittern	6	15

		Plate	Range Map
45 Nycticorax nycticorax	Black-crowned Night-Heron Night Heron	6	15
46 Ixobrychus minutus	Little Bittern Eurasian Little-Bittern	6	16
47 I. eurythmus	Schrenck's Bittern Von Schrenck's Little-Bittern	6	16
48 I. sinensis	Yellow Bittern Chinese Little-Bittern	6	15
49 Botaurus stellaris	Eurasian Bittern Great Bittern Bittern	6	17
50 Gorsachius goisagi	Japanese Night-Heron	—	—

IBISES: THRESKIORNITHIDAE

		Plate	Range Map
51 Platalea leucorodia	Eurasian Spoonbill Spoonbill White Spoonbill Royal Spoonbill Black-faced Spoonbill	6	18
52 Plegadis falcinellus	Glossy Ibis	6	19
53 Nipponia nippon	Japanese Crested Ibis Crested Ibis	6	19
54 Threskiornis aethiopicus	Sacred Ibis Black-headed Ibis	—	—

STORKS: CICONIIDAE

		Plate	Range Map

55 Ciconia ciconia
    C. boyciana
	White Stork
	    Oriental Stork
		7	20

56 C. nigra	Black Stork	7	20

PHOENICOPTERIFORMES

FLAMINGOS: PHOENICOPTERIDAE

		Plate	Range Map
57 Phoenicopterus ruber P. roseus	Greater Flamingo Flamingo	7	20

ANSERIFORMES

DUCKS: ANATIDAE

		Plate	Range Map
58 Cygnus cygnus Olor cygnus	Whooper Swan	2	21

59 C. bewickii
    C. columbianus
    (if merged with 61)
	Bewick's Swan	2	22

60 C. olor	Mute Swan	2	22
61 C. columbianus	Whistling Swan	—	—
62 Anser cygnoides	Swan Goose	2	23
63 A. canagicus	Emperor Goose	2	23
64 A. indicus	Bar-headed Goose	2	24
65 A. caerulescens	Snow Goose (includes Blue Goose)	2	24

66	A. anser	Greylag Goose	2	25
67	A. albifrons	Greater White-fronted Goose White-fronted Goose	2	25
68	A. erythropus	Lesser White-fronted Goose	2	26
69	A. fabalis	Bean Goose	2	27
70	Branta bernicla	Brent Goose Brant (includes Black Brant)	2	28
71	B. leucopsis	Barnacle Goose	2	29
72	B. ruficollis Rufibranta ruficollis	Red-breasted Goose	2	29
73	B. canadensis	Canada Goose	2	—
74	Tadorna tadorna	Red-billed Shelduck Northern Shelduck Shelduck	4	—
75	T. ferruginea	Ruddy Shelduck	4	28
76	T. cristata	Crested Shelduck	4	—
77	Anas platyrhynchos	Mallard	3	30
78	A. poecilorhyncha	Spot-billed Duck Spotbill Duck	3	30
79	A. crecca A. carolinensis	Green-winged Teal Teal Common Teal	3	31
80	A. formosa	Baikal Teal Formosa Teal	3	32
81	A. falcata	Falcated Duck Falcated Teal	3	32
82	A. strepera	Gadwall	3	33
83	A. penelope	Eurasian Wigeon Wigeon	3	—
84	A. acuta	Northern Pintail Pintail	3	31
85	A. angustirostris	Marbled Duck Marbled Teal	3	34
86	A. querquedula	Garganey Garganey Teal	3	34
87	A. clypeata	Northern Shoveler Shoveler Shoveller	3	35
88	A. americana	American Wigeon	—	—
89	Aix galericulata	Mandarin Duck	3	36
90	Somateria mollissima	Common Eider Eider	5	36
91	S. spectabilis	King Eider	5	37
92	S. fischeri	Spectacled Eider	5	38
93	S. stelleri Polysticta stelleri	Steller's Eider	5	38
94	Netta rufina	Red-crested Pochard	4	35
95	Aythya ferina	Northern Pochard Eurasian Pochard Pochard	4	35
96	A. nyroca	Ferruginous Pochard Ferruginous Duck White-eyed Pochard	3	39

		Plate	Range Map
97 A. baeri	Baer's Pochard	4	39
98 A. fuligula	Tufted Pochard Tufted Duck	4	40
99 A. marila	Greater Scaup Northern Scaup Scaup	4	40
100 Melanitta fusca M. deglandi	White-winged Scoter Velvet Scoter	4	41
101 M. nigra	Black Scoter Common Scoter	4	41
102 M. perspicillata	Surf Scoter	4	—
103 Histrionicus histrionicus	Harlequin Duck	5	42
104 Clangula hyemalis	Long-tailed Duck Oldsquaw	4	42
105 Bucephala clangula	Common Goldeneye Green-headed Goldeneye Goldeneye	4	43
106 B. islandica	Barrow's Goldeneye	4	—
107 B. albeola	Bufflehead	4	—
108 Mergus albellus	Smew	5	44
109 M. serrator	Red-breasted Merganser	5	45
110 M. squamatus	Chinese Merganser Scaly-sided Merganser	5	45
111 M. merganser	Common Merganser Goosander Great Merganser	5	44
112 Oxyura leucocephala	White-headed Duck	5	43

ACCIPITRIFORMES

OSPREY: PANDIONIDAE

113 Pandion haliaetus	Osprey	9	46

HAWKS: ACCIPITRIDAE

114 Pernis apivorus	Eurasian Honey-Buzzard Eurasian Honey-Kite Honey Buzzard	9	47
115 P. ptilorhynchus P. apivorus	Crested Honey-Buzzard Crested Honey-Kite	9	47
116 Milvus migrans M. korschun	Black Kite Brown Kite Pariah Kite Black-eared Kite Fork-tailed Kite	9	48
117 M. milvus	Red Kite	9	48
118 Haliaeetus albicilla	White-tailed Sea-Eagle	8	49
119 H. leucoryphus	Pallas's Sea-Eagle	8	50
120 H. pelagicus	Steller's Sea-Eagle	8	50
121 Accipiter gentilis	Northern Goshawk Goshawk	10	—

122	A. badius	Shikra Levant Sparrowhawk Little Banded Goshawk	10	52
123	A. virgatus	Besra Sparrowhawk	10	52
124	A. nisus	Eurasian Sparrowhawk Sparrowhawk	10	51
125	Buteo buteo	Common Buzzard Buzzard Steppe Buzzard	9	53
126	B. lagopus	Rough-legged Buzzard Rough-legged Hawk	9	53
127	B. hemilasius	Upland Buzzard	9	54
128	B. rufinus	Long-legged Buzzard	9	54
129	Butastur indicus	Gray-faced Buzzard Gray-faced Buzzard-Eagle	9	55
130	Aquila chrysaetos	Golden Eagle	8	56
131	A. heliaca	Imperial Eagle	8	56
132	A. rapax A. nipalensis	Steppe Eagle Tawny Eagle	8	57
133	A. clanga	Greater Spotted Eagle Spotted Eagle	8	58
134	A. pomarina	Lesser Spotted Eagle	8	58
135	Hieraaetus fasciatus	Bonelli's Eagle	8	57
136	Hieraaetus pennatus	Booted Eagle	9	57
137	Neophron percnopterus	Egyptian Vulture White Griffon	8	59
138	Gypaetus barbatus	Lammergeier Lammergeyer Bearded Vulture	8	59
139	Aegypius monachus	Cinereous Vulture Cinereous Griffon Black Vulture	8	60
140	Gyps fulvus	Eurasian Griffon Griffon Vulture	8	60
141	G. himalayensis	Himalayan Griffon	—	60
142	G. bengalensis Pseudogyps bengalensis	Indian White-rumped Vulture White-backed Griffon	—	—
143	Circaetus gallicus	Short-toed Snake-Eagle Short-toed Eagle	9	55
144	Circus cyaneus	Northern Harrier Hen Harrier Marsh Hawk	10	61
145	C. pygargus	Montagu's Harrier	10	62
146	C. macrourus	Pallid Harrier Pale Harrier	10	62
147	C. melanoleucus	Pied Harrier	10	61
148	C. aeruginosus	Marsh Harrier Eurasian Marsh Harrier	10	63
149	Elanus caeruleus	Black-shouldered Kite Black-winged Kite White-tailed Kite	—	—

			Range
Falcons: Falconidae		Plate	Map

150 Falco peregrinus
    F. pelegrinoides
	Peregrine Falcon
	    Peregrine
	    Shaheen Falcon
		11	64

151 F. cherrug	Saker Falcon	11	64
152 F. biarmicus	Lanner Falcon	11	—
153 F. rusticolus F. gyrfalco	Gyrfalcon	11	65

154 F. subbuteo	Northern Hobby
	    Eurasian Hobby
	    Hobby
		11	65

155 F. columbarius	Merlin	11	66

156 F. vespertinus
    F. amurensis
	Red-footed Falcon
	    Red-footed Kestrel
	    Amur Falcon
	    Eastern Red-footed Falcon
		11	66

157 F. tinnunculus	Common Kestrel
	    Eurasian Kestrel
	    Kestrel
		11	67

158 F. naumanni	Lesser Kestrel	11	67
159 F. jugger	Laggar Falcon	—	—

GALLIFORMES

		Plate	Range Map
Grouse: Tetraonidae			
160 Lagopus lagopus	Willow Ptarmigan Red Grouse	15	68
161 L. mutus	Rock Ptarmigan	15	68

162 Lyrurus tetrix
    Tetrao tetrix
	Northern Black Grouse
	    Black Grouse
		14	69

163 L. mlokosiewiczi Tetrao mlokosiewiczi	Caucasian Black Grouse	14	69
164 Tetrao urogallus	Western Capercaillie Capercaillie	14	70
165 T. urogalloides	Black-billed Capercaillie	14	70
166 Falcipennis falcipennis	Siberian Spruce Grouse	15	71
167 Tetrastes bonasia	Northern Hazelhen Hazel Hen	15	71
Partridges: Phasianidae			

168 Coturnix coturnix
    C. japonicus
	Common Quail
	    Quail
	    Japanese Quail
		15	72

169 Ammoperdix griseogularis	See-see Partridge	15	72

170 Alectoris chukar
    A. kakelik
    A. graeca
	Chukar Partridge
	    Chukar
		15	73

171 Perdix perdix	Gray Partridge
	    Partridge
	    Hungarian Partridge
		15	74

172 P. dauuricae	Daurian Partridge	15	74
173 Francolinus francolinus	Black Francolin Black Partridge	15	73

174	Tetraogallus caucasicus	Caucasian Snowcock	14	75
175	T. caspius	Caspian Snowcock	14	75
176	T. himalayensis	Himalayan Snowcock	14	75
177	T. altaicus	Altai Snowcock	14	75
178	T. tibetanus	Tibetan Snowcock	14	75
179	Phasianus colchicus	Common Pheasant Ring-necked Pheasant	14	76

GRUIFORMES

CRANES: GRUIDAE

180	Grus grus	Common Crane Eurasian Crane Gray Crane Crane	7	77
181	G. canadensis	Sandhill Crane	7	77
182	G. vipio	White-naped Crane	7	77
183	G. monachus	Hooded Crane	7	78
184	G. leucogeranus	Siberian White Crane	7	78
185	G. japonensis	Japanese Crane Red-crowned Crane Manchurian Crane	7	79
186	G. rubricundus	Brolga Crane Australian Crane	—	—
187	Anthropoides virgo	Demoiselle Crane	7	79

BUSTARDS: OTIDIDAE

188	Otis tarda	Great Bustard	7	80
189	Chlamydotis undulata Otis undulata	Houbara Bustard Houbara	7	78
190	Tetrax tetrax Otis tetrax	Little Bustard	7	80

RAILS: RALLIDAE

191	Fulica atra	Common Coot Black Coot Coot	16	81
192	Porphyrio porphyrio P. poliocephalus P. madagascariensis	Purple Swamphen Purple Gallinule King Reedhen Purple Coot	16	81
193	Gallinula chloropus	Common Gallinule Moorhen	16	81
194	Rallus aquaticus	Water Rail	16	82
195	Crex crex	Corn Crake Corncrake	16	82
196	Porzana porzana	Spotted Crake	16	83
197	P. parva	Little Crake	16	84
198	P. pusilla	Baillon's Crake	16	83
199	P. exquisita Coturnicops exquisita	Swinhoe's Yellow Crake Swinhoe's Yellow Rail	—	83

		Plate	Range Map
200 P. paykullii Rallina paykullii	Band-bellied Crake	16	84
201 Gallicrex cinereus	Watercock	16	—

BUTTONQUAIL: TURNICIDAE

| 202 Turnix tanki | Yellow-legged Buttonquail | 15 | 80 |

CHARADRIIFORMES

THICK-KNEES: BURHINIDAE

| 203 Burhinus oedicnemus | Stone Thick-knee
Stone Dikkop
Stonecurlew | 17 | 85 |

COURSERS: GLAREOLIDAE

204 Cursorius cursur	Cream-colored Courser	17	85
205 Glareola pratincola	European Pratincole Pratincole	18	86
206 G. nordmanni	Black-winged Pratincole	18	86
207 G. maldivarum G. pratincola	Oriental Pratincole Eastern Pratincole	18	86

PLOVERS: CHARADRIIDAE

208 Pluvialis squatarola Squatarola squatarola	Gray Plover Black-bellied Plover Silver Plover	18	87
209 P. apricaria	Greater Golden Plover European Golden Plover Golden Plover	18	88
210 P. dominica	Lesser Golden Plover American Golden Plover Golden Plover	18	88
211 Charadrius hiaticula	Greater Ringed Plover Ringed Plover	18	89
212 C. dubius	Little Ringed Plover	18	90
213 C. placidus	Long-billed Plover	—	90
214 C. alexandrinus	Kentish Plover Salt Plover Snowy Plover	18	91
215 C. mongolus	Mongolian Plover Lesser Sand Dotterel Lesser Sand Plover	18	91
216 C. leschenaultii	Sand Plover Great Sand Plover Great Sand Dotterel	18	92
217 C. asiaticus	Caspian Plover	18	92
218 C. veredus	Oriental Plover Oriental Dotterel	—	92
219 C. morinellus (Eudromias)	Eurasian Dotterel	18	89
220 Vanellus vanellus	Northern Lapwing Lapwing	17	93

221 Chettusia gregaria Vanellus gregarius	Sociable Lapwing Sociable Plover	17	94
222 C. leucuria Vanellus leucurus	White-tailed Lapwing White-tailed Plover	17	94
223 Lobivanellus indicus Hoplopterus indicus Vanellus indicus	Red-wattled Lapwing Red-wattled Plover	17	93
224 Hoplopterus spinosus Vanellus spinosus	Spur-winged Lapwing Spur-winged Plover	—	—
225 Microsarcopus cinerea Vanellus cinereus	Gray-headed Lapwing Gray-headed Plover	—	—

SANDPIPERS: SCOLOPACIDAE

226 Arenaria interpres	Ruddy Turnstone Turnstone	18	94
227 A. melanocephala	Black Turnstone	18	—
228 Calidris ferruginea C. testacea	Curlew Sandpiper	19	95
229 C. alpina	Dunlin	19	95
230 C. minuta	Little Stint	19	96
231 C. ruficollis	Rufous-necked Stint Red-necked Stint Rufous-necked Sandpiper	19	96
232 C. subminuta	Long-toed Stint	19	97
233 C. temmincki	Temminck's Stint	19	98
234 C. mauri	Western Sandpiper Western Stint	19	99
235 C. bairdii	Baird's Sandpiper	19	98
236 C. melanotos	Pectoral Sandpiper	19	97
237 C. acuminata	Sharp-tailed Sandpiper	19	97
238 C. alba Crocethia alba	Sanderling	19	100
239 C. canutus	Red Knot Knot	19	98
240 C. tenuirostris	Great Knot Long-billed Knot Eastern Knot	19	101
241 C. maritima	Purple Sandpiper	19	101
242 C. fuscicollis	White-rumped Sandpiper	—	—
243 Tryngites subruficollis	Buff-breasted Sandpiper	19	99
244 Philomachus pugnax	Ruff	20	99
245 Limicola falcinellus	Broad-billed Sandpiper	19	100
246 Eurynorhynchus pygmaeus	Spoon-billed Sandpiper	19	100
247 Limnodromus scolopaceus	Long-billed Dowitcher	20	102
248 L. semipalmatus	Asian Dowitcher Asiatic Dowitcher	20	102
249 Tringa ochropus	Green Sandpiper	20	103
250 T. glareola	Wood Sandpiper	20	104
251 T. nebularia	Greater Greenshank Common Greenshank Greenshank	20	105

		Plate	Range Map
252 T. totanus	Common Redshank Lesser Redshank Redshank	20	106
253 T. erythropus	Spotted Redshank Greater Redshank	20	106
254 T. stagnatilis	Marsh Sandpiper Little Greenshank	20	103
255 T. guttifer Pseudototanus guttifer	Spotted Greenshank Nordmann's Greenshank Armstrong's Sandpiper	20	105
256 T. brevipes Heteroscelus brevipes	Gray-tailed Tattler Polynesian Tattler	20	104
257 T. incana Heteroscelus incanus	Wandering Tattler	—	105
258 Actitis hypoleucos Tringa hypoleucos	Common Sandpiper	20	107
259 Xenus cinereus Terekia cinerea	Terek Sandpiper	20	107
260 Limosa limosa	Black-tailed Godwit	17	108
261 L. lapponica	Bar-tailed Godwit	17	108
262 Numenius arquata	Eurasian Curlew Northern Curlew Curlew	17	109
263 N. phaeopus	Whimbrel	17	110
264 N. madagascariensis	Eastern Curlew Far Eastern Curlew	—	109
265 N. tenuirostris	Slender-billed Curlew	17	110
266 N. minutus	Little Curlew Little Whimbrel	17	110
267 N. borealis	Eskimo Curlew	—	—
268 Phalaropus lobatus Lobipes lobatus	Red-necked Phalarope Little Phalarope Northern Phalarope	18	111
269 P. fulicarius	Red Phalarope Gray Phalarope	18	111

STILTS: RECURVIROSTRIDAE

		Plate	Range Map
270 Himantopus himantopus	Black-winged Stilt Common Stilt	17	112
271 Recurvirostra avosetta	Black-capped Avocet Avocet	17	112
272 Scolopax rusticola	Eurasian Woodcock Woodcock	20	113
273 Gallinago gallinago Capella gallinago	Common Snipe Fantail Snipe Snipe	20	114
274 G. media Capella media	Great Snipe	20	115
275 G. megala Capella megala	Swinhoe's Snipe Chinese Snipe	—	115
276 G. stenura Capella stenura	Pin-tailed Snipe Pintail Snipe	20	114

277	G. solitaria Capella solitaria	Solitary Snipe	20	116
278	G. hardwickii Capella hardwickii	Latham's Snipe Japanese Snipe Australian Snipe	—	—
279	Lymnocryptes minimus Gallinago minima	Jack Snipe Jacksnipe	20	116

IBISBILL: IBIDORHYNCHIDAE

| 280 | Ibidorhyncha struthersi | Ibisbill | 17 | 117 |

OYSTERCATCHERS: HAEMATOPODIDAE

| 281 | Haematopus ostralegus | Common Oystercatcher
Eurasian Oystercatcher
Oystercatcher | 17 | 117 |

PAINTED-SNIPE: ROSTRATULIDAE

| 282 | Rostratula benghalensis | Painted-snipe
Greater Painted-snipe
Painted Snipe | — | — |

SKUAS: STERCORARIIDAE

283	Stercorarius parasiticus	Parasitic Jaeger Arctic Skua	21	118
284	S. longicaudus	Long-tailed Jaeger Long-tailed Skua	21	118
285	S. pomarinus	Pomarine Jaeger Pomarine Skua	21	119
286	Catharacta skua Stercorarius skua	Great Skua Brown Skua	21	—

GULLS: LARIDAE

287	Pagophila eburnea Larus alba	Ivory Gull	22	119
288	Rissa tridactyla Larus tridactylus	Black-legged Kittiwake Kittiwake	22	120
289	R. brevirostris Larus brevirostris	Red-legged Kittiwake	22	120
290	Rhodostethia rosea Larus roseus	Ross's Gull Ross' Gull	22	120
291	Xema sabini Larus sabini	Sabine's Gull	22	121
292	Larus marinus	Great Black-backed Gull	21	119
293	L. schistisagus	Slaty-backed Gull	21	—
294	L. crassirostris	Black-tailed Gull	21	122
295	L. fuscus	Lesser Black-backed Gull	21	120
296	L. argentatus	Herring Gull	22	122
297	L. canus L. kamtschatschensis	Mew Gull Common Gull Kamchatka Gull	22	123
298	L. hyperboreus	Glaucous Gull	21	123

		Plate	Range Map
299 L. glaucescens	Glaucous-winged Gull	—	—
300 L. ichthyaetus	Great Black-headed Gull	21	124
301 L. ridibundus	Black-headed Gull	22	124
302 L. brunnicephalus	Brown-headed Gull	—	—
303 L. relictus	Relict Gull	22	303
304 L. melanocephalus	Mediterranean Gull	22	125
305 L. minutus	Little Gull	22	125
306 L. genei	Slender-billed Gull	22	125
307 L. glaucoides	Iceland Gull	—	—
308 L. saundersi	Saunder's Gull	—	—

TERNS: STERNIDAE

		Plate	Range Map
309 Chlidonias niger Sterna nigra	Black Tern Black Marsh-Tern	23	126
310 C. leucopterus Sterna leucoptera	White-winged Tern White-winged Marsh-Tern	23	126
311 C. hybrida Sterna hybrida	Whiskered Tern Whiskered Marsh-Tern	23	127
312 Sterna hirundo	Common Tern	23	128
313 S. paradisea	Arctic Tern	23	129
314 S. aleutica	Aleutian Tern	23	129
315 S. albifrons	Little Tern Least Tern	23	130
316 S. sandvicensis	Sandwich Tern	23	130
317 S. nilotica Gelochelidon nilotica	Gull-billed Tern	23	127
318 S. caspia Hydroprogne tschegrava	Caspian Tern	23	128

ALCIDS: ALCIDAE

		Plate	Range Map
319 Cepphus grylle	Black Guillemot	24	131
320 C. carbo	Spectacled Guillemot	24	131
321 Alca torda	Razorbill Razor-billed Auk	24	132
322 Alle alle Plautus alle	Dovekie Little Auk Arctic Auklet	24	132
323 Uria aalge	Thin-billed Murre Common Murre Guillemot	24	133
324 U. lomvia	Thick-billed Murre Brunnich's Guillemot	24	133
325 Brachyramphus marmoratus	Marbled Murrelet	24	134
326 B. brevirostris	Kittlitz's Murrelet	24	134
327 Synthliboramphus antiquus	Ancient Murrelet	24	135
328 S. wumizusume	Japanese Murrelet	—	—
329 Aethia cristatella	Crested Auklet	24	135
330 A. pygmaea	Whiskered Auklet	24	136
331 A. pusilla	Least Auklet	24	136
332 Cyclorrhynchus psittacula	Parakeet Auklet	24	136

333	Cerorhinca monocerata	Rhinoceros Auklet	24	137
334	Fratercula arctica	Atlantic Puffin Puffin	24	137
335	F. corniculata	Horned Puffin	24	138
336	Lunda cirrhata	Tufted Puffin	24	138

PTEROCLIDIFORMES

SANDGROUSE: PTEROCLIDIDAE

337	Pterocles orientalis	Black-bellied Sandgrouse Imperial Sandgrouse	25	139
338	P. alchata	Pin-tailed Sandgrouse	25	139
339	Syrrhaptes paradoxus	Pallas's Sandgrouse	25	140
340	S. tibetanus	Tibetan Sandgrouse	25	140

COLUMBIFORMES

DOVES: COLUMBIDAE

341	Columba livia	Rock Pigeon Rock Dove Domestic Pigeon	25	141
342	C. rupestris	Hill Pigeon Blue Hill Pigeon Eastern Rock Dove	25	141
343	C. leuconota	Snow Pigeon	25	142
344	C. eversmanni	Eastern Stock Pigeon Yellow-eyed Stock Dove	25	143
345	C. oenas	Western Stock Pigeon Stock Dove	25	142
346	C. palumbus	Wood Pigeon European Wood Pigeon	25	143
347	Streptopelia turtur	European Turtle-Dove Turtle Dove	25	144
348	S. orientalis	Oriental Turtle-Dove Rufous Turtle-Dove	25	145
349	S. decaocto	Collared Turtle-Dove Collared Dove	25	145
350	S. senegalensis	Laughing Turtle-Dove Palm Dove	25	144
351	S. tranquebarica	Red Turtle-Dove	—	—
352	Treron sieboldii Sphenurus sieboldii	Japanese Green-Pigeon White-bellied Green-Pigeon	—	—

CUCULIFORMES

CUCKOOS: CUCULIDAE

353	Cuculus canorus	Eurasian Cuckoo Common Cuckoo Clock Cuckoo Cuckoo	26	146
354	C. saturatus	Oriental Cuckoo	—	146

		Plate	Range Map
355 C. poliocephalus	Lesser Cuckoo Little Cuckoo	26	147
356 C. micropterus	Indian Cuckoo Short-winged Cuckoo	26	147
357 C. fugax	Hodgson's Hawk-Cuckoo Fugitive Hawk-Cuckoo	26	147
358 Clamator glandarius	Great Spotted Cuckoo	—	—

STRIGIFORMES

Owls: Strigidae

359 Nyctea scandiaca	Snowy Owl	12	148
360 Bubo bubo	Northern Eagle-Owl Eagle Owl Eurasian Horned-Owl	12	149
361 Ketupa blakistoni	Blakiston's Fish-Owl	12	148
362 Otus scops	Eurasian Scops-Owl Scops Owl	13	150
363 O. bakkamoena	Collared Scops-Owl	13	151
364 O. brucei	Striated Scops-Owl	13	151
365 O. sunia	Eastern Scops-Owl Indian Scops-Owl	13	150
366 Asio otus	Long-eared Owl Northern Long-eared Owl	13	149
367 A. flammeus	Short-eared Owl	13	151
368 Ninox scutulata	Brown Hawk-Owl	13	152
369 Aegolius funereus	Boreal Owl Tengmalm's Owl	13	152
370 Athene noctua	Little Owl	13	153
371 Glaucidium passerinum	Eurasian Pygmy-Owl Pygmy Owl	13	153
372 Surnia ulula	Northern Hawk-Owl Long-tailed Owl Hawk Owl	13	154
373 Strix aluco	Tawny Owl	12	154
374 S. uralensis	Ural Owl	12	155
375 S. nebulosa	Great Gray Owl	12	155

Barn Owl: Tytonidae

376 Tyto alba	Barn Owl	13	155

CAPRIMULGIFORMES

Nightjars: Caprimulgidae

377 Caprimulgus europaeus	European Nightjar Nightjar	26	156
378 C. aegyptius	Egyptian Nightjar	26	156
379 C. indicus	Gray Nightjar Indian Nightjar	26	156
380 C. inornatus	Plain Nightjar	—	—

APODIFORMES

SWIFTS: APODIDAE

381 Apus apus	Northern Swift Common Swift Swift	28	157
382 A. melba	Alpine Swift	28	157
383 A. pacificus	Pacific Swift Fork-tailed Swift White-rumped Swift	28	158
384 A. affinis	House Swift Little Swift White-rumped Swift	28	158
385 Hirundapus caudacutus	White-throated Needletail Needle-tailed Swift	28	158

CORACIIFORMES

ROLLERS: CORACIIDAE

386 Coracias garrulus	Eurasian Roller Roller	26	159
387 Eurystomus orientalis	Broad-billed Roller Dollar Roller Dollarbird Eastern Broad-billed Roller	26	159

KINGFISHERS: ALCEDINIDAE

388 Alcedo atthis	Eurasian Kingfisher River Kingfisher Common Kingfisher Kingfisher	26	160
389 Halcyon smyrensis	White-throated Kingfisher White-breasted Kingfisher	—	—
390 H. pileata	Black-capped Kingfisher	26	—
391 Ceryle rudis	Pied Kingfisher Lesser Pied Kingfisher	26	—
392 C. lugubris	Crested Kingfisher Great Pied Kingfisher	—	—

BEE-EATERS: MEROPIDAE

393 Merops apiaster	European Bee-eater Bee-eater	26	161
394 M. superciliosus M. persicus	Blue-cheeked Bee-eater	26	161

HOOPOE: UPUPIDAE

395 Upupa epops	Hoopoe	26	160

PICIFORMES

WOODPECKERS: PICIDAE

396 Dryocopus martius	Black Woodpecker	27	162
397 Picus viridus	Eurasian Green Woodpecker Green Woodpecker	27	163

		Plate	Range Map
398 P. canus	Gray-headed Green Woodpecker Gray-headed Woodpecker	27	163
399 P. squamatus	Scaly-bellied Green Woodpecker Scaly-bellied Woodpecker	27	163
400 Picoides tridactylus	Northern Three-toed Woodpecker Three-toed Woodpecker	27	162
401 Dendrocopos major Picoides major	Great Spotted Woodpecker	27	164
402 D. leucopterus Picoides leucopterus	White-winged Spotted Woodpecker	—	164
403 D. syriacus Picoides syriacus	Syrian Woodpecker	27	165
404 D. leucotos Picoides leucotos	White-backed Woodpecker	27	165
405 D. medius Picoides medius	Middle Spotted Woodpecker	27	166
406 D. minor Picoides minor	Lesser Spotted Woodpecker	27	166
407 D. kizuki Yungipicus kizuki	Japanese Pygmy Woodpecker	27	167
408 D. nanus Yungipicus canicapillus	Gray-headed Pygmy Woodpecker	27	167
409 Jynx torquilla	Eurasian Wryneck Wryneck	27	167

PASSERIFORMES

LARKS: ALAUDIDAE

410 Alauda arvensis	Northern Skylark Skylark	29	168
411 A. gulgula	Oriental Skylark Lesser Skylark Small Skylark	—	168
412 Lullula arborea	Wood Lark Woodlark	29	169
413 Galerida cristata	Crested Lark	29	169
414 Calandrella leucophaea C. rufescens	Lesser Short-toed Lark	29	170
415 C. pispoletta C. rufescens	Gray Lark Lesser Short-toed Lark	29	170
416 C. cinerea	Greater Short-toed Lark Short-toed Lark	29	171
417 C. acutirostris	Hume's Short-toed Lark	29	171
418 Melanocorypha yeltoniensis	Black Lark	29	172
419 M. leucoptera	White-winged Lark	29	172
420 M. mongolica	Mongolian Lark	29	173
421 M. calandra	Calandra Lark	29	173
422 M. bimaculata	Bimaculated Lark Eastern Calandra Lark White-tipped Lark	29	174
423 Ammomanes deserti	Desert Lark	29	174

424 Eremophila alpestris	Horned Lark Shore Lark	29	175

SWALLOWS: HIRUNDINIDAE

425 Hirundo rustica	Barn Swallow Field Swallow Swallow	28	176
426 H. daurica	Red-rumped Swallow Striated Swallow	—	176
427 H. smithii	Wire-tailed Swallow	28	177
428 Delichon urbica	Northern House Martin House Martin	28	177
429 Riparia riparia	Sand Martin Bank Swallow	28	178
430 R. paludicola	Plain Martin Brown-throated Sand Martin African Sand Martin	—	178
431 Ptyonoprogne rupestris Hirundo rupestris	Crag Martin Northern Crag Martin	28	178
432 Petrochelidon albifrons	Cliff Swallow Cliff Martin Capistrano Martin	—	—
433 Iridoprocne bicolor Tachycineta bicolor	Tree Swallow	—	—

PIPITS: MOTACILLIDAE

434 Anthus richardi A. novaeseelandiae	Richard's Pipit Australian Pipit	30	179
435 A. campestris A. godlewskii	Tawny Pipit Godlewski's Pipit	30	179
436 A. trivialis	Tree Pipit Brown Tree Pipit	30	180
437 A. hodgsoni	Olive-backed Pipit Olive Tree Pipit	30	180
438 A. gustavi	Petchora Pipit Pechora Pipit	30	181
439 A. pratensis	Meadow Pipit	30	181
440 A. cervinus	Red-throated Pipit	30	182
441 A. spinoletta	Water Pipit Rock Pipit	30	182
442 Dendronanthus indicus	Forest Wagtail	30	183
443 Motacilla flava	Yellow Wagtail Blue-headed Wagtail	30	183
444 M. lutea M. flava	Yellow-backed Wagtail Yellow Wagtail	30	184
445 M. citreola	Citrine Wagtail Yellow-headed Wagtail	30	184
446 M. cinerea	Gray Wagtail	30	185
447 M. alba	White Wagtail Pied Wagtail	30	185
448 M. grandis	Japanese Wagtail	—	—

		Plate	Range Map

MINIVET: CAMPEPHAGIDAE
| 449 Pericrocotus divaricatus | Ashy Minivet | 31 | 186 |

BULBULS: PYCNONOTIDAE
450 Microscelis amaurotis	Brown-eared Bulbul	—	—
Hypsipetes amaurotis			
451 Pycnonotus leucogenys	White-cheeked Bulbul	—	—

SHRIKES: LANIIDAE
452 Lanius excubitor	Great Gray Shrike	31	186
	Northern Shrike		
453 L. sphenocercus	Chinese Gray Shrike	31	187
454 L. minor	Lesser Gray Shrike	31	187
455 L. bucephalus	Bull-headed Shrike	31	188
456 L. schach	Long-tailed Shrike	31	188
	Schach's Shrike		
	Black-headed Shrike		
	Rufous-backed Shrike		
	Variable Shrike		
457 L. senator	Woodchat Shrike	31	189
458 L. tigrinus	Tiger Shrike	31	189
	Thick-billed Shrike		
459 L. cristatus	Brown Shrike	31	190
L. collurio	Red-backed Shrike		
L. isabellinus	Central Asian Shrike		
L. phoenicuroides	Red-tailed Shrike		
460 L. vittatus	Bay-backed Shrike	31	190
461 L. nubicus	Masked Shrike	—	—

WAXWINGS: BOMBYCILLIDAE
462 Bombycilla garrulus	Bohemian Waxwing	31	191
	Waxwing		
463 B. japonica	Japanese Waxwing	31	191
464 Hypocolius ampelinus	Hypocolius	31	303

DIPPERS: CINCLIDAE
465 Cinclus cinclus	Eurasian Dipper	40	192
	Dipper		
466 C. pallasii	Brown Dipper	40	192
	Asian Dipper		

WRENS: TROGLODYTIDAE
467 Troglodytes troglodytes	Northern Wren	41	192
	Winter Wren		
	Wren		

THRUSHES: TURDIDAE
468 Turdus dauma	Scaly Thrush	32	193
Zoothera dauma	Tiger Thrush		
	White's Thrush		
469 T. sibiricus	Siberian Thrush	32	194
Zoothera sibiricus			

470 T. pilaris	Fieldfare	32	194
471 T. viscivorus	Mistle Thrush	32	193
472 T. philomelos	Song Thrush	32	195

473 T. iliacus
    T. musicus
	Red-winged Thrush
	    Redwing
		32	195

474 T. naumanni
    T. eunous
	Naumann's Thrush
	    Dusky Thrush
		32	196

475 T. ruficollis	Dark-throated Thrush
	    Black-throated Thrush
	    Red-throated Thrush
		32	196

476 T. hortulorum	Gray-backed Thrush	32	197

477 T. pallidus
    T. obscurus
    T. chrysolaus
	Pale Thrush
	    Eye-browed Thrush
	    Gray-headed Thrush
	    Red-bellied Thrush
	    Red-billed Thrush
	    Brown-headed Thrush
	    Japanese Thrush
	    Brown Thrush
		32	197

478 T. torquatus	Ring Thrush Ring Ouzel	33	198

479 T. merula	Eurasian Blackbird
	    Eurasian Black Thrush
	    Black Thrush
	    Blackbird
		33	198

480 Catharus minimus Turdus minimus	Gray-cheeked Thrush	32	199

481 Turdus cardis	Gray Thrush
	    Japanese Thrush
	    Japanese Gray Thrush
		32	—

482 Catharus ustulatus	Swainson's Thrush	—	—
483 Myophonus caeruleus	Blue Whistling-Thrush	33	199
484 Monticola saxatilis	White-backed Rock-Thrush Rock Thrush	33	200
485 M. solitarius	Blue Rock-Thrush	33	200
486 M. gularis	White-throated Rock-Thrush	33	200
487 Oenanthe oenanthe	Northern Wheatear Wheatear	34	201
488 O. deserti	Desert Wheatear	34	201

489 O. hispanica
    O. pleschanka
	Black-eared Wheatear
	    Pied Wheatear
		34	202

490 O. lugens	Finsch's Wheatear Arabian Wheatear	34	202
491 O. isabellina	Isabelline Wheatear	34	203
492 O. xanthopryma	Red-tailed Wheatear	34	203
493 O. picata	Variable Wheatear Eastern Pied Wheatear	34	203
494 Saxicola rubetra	Whinchat Marsh Bushchat	34	204
495 S. torquata	Stonechat Stone Bushchat	34	204
496 S. caprata	Pied Bushchat Pied Stonechat	34	205

		Plate	Range Map
497 S. insignis	Hodgson's Bushchat Hodgson's Stonechat	—	—
498 Tarsiger cyanurus	Orange-flanked Bush-Robin Red-flanked Bluetail	35	206
499 Chaimarrornis leucocephala	White-capped River Chat White-capped Redstart Water Redstart	35	206
500 Phoenicurus phoenicurus	Eurasian Redstart White-fronted Redstart Redstart	35	207
501 P. ochruros	Black Redstart	35	207
502 P. erythronotus	Eversmann's Redstart Rufous-backed Redstart	35	208
503 P. auroreus	Daurian Redstart	35	208
504 P. erythrogaster	Guldenstadt's Redstart Great White-winged Redstart	35	209
505 P. caeruleocephalus	Blue-headed Redstart	35	209
506 Rhyacornis fuliginosus	Plumbeous Water Redstart	—	—
507 Luscinia megarhynchos Erithacus megarhynchos	Nightingale Southern Nightingale	36	210
508 L. luscinia Erithacus luscinia	Thrush-Nightingale Northern Nightingale Sprosser	36	210
509 L. calliope Erithacus calliope	Siberian Rubythroat	36	211
510 L. pectoralis Erithacus pectoralis	Himalayan Rubythroat	36	211
511 L. sibilans Erithacus sibilans	Rufous-tailed Robin Swinhoe's Robin Whistling Nightingale	36	212
512 L. cyane Erithacus cyane	Siberian Blue Robin	35	212
513 L. svecica Erithacus svecicus	Bluethroat	36	213
514 Erithacus rubecula	European Robin Robin	35	213
515 E. akahige	Japanese Robin	35	214
516 Irania gutturalis	Persian Robin White-throated Robin Irania	36	214
517 Enicurus scouleri	Little Forktail	40	215
518 Erythropygia galactotes Cercotrichas galactotes	Rufous Scrub-Robin Rufous Bush Robin Rufous Bush Chat Rufous Robin Rufous Warbler	36	215

BABBLERS: TIMALIIDAE

519 Garrulax lineatus	Streaked Laughing-thrush	33	216
520 Panurus biarmicus	Bearded Reedling Bearded Tit	41	216

521 Suthora webbiana	Vinous-throated Parrotbill	41	217
522 Paradoxornis heudei	Reed Parrotbill Yangtze Parrotbill	—	303

LONG-TAILED TITS: AEGITHALIDAE

523 Aegithalos caudatus	Long-tailed Tit Common Long-tailed Tit	41	217

WARBLERS: SYLVIIDAE

524 Phylloscopus trochilus	Willow Warbler Willow Leaf-Warbler	37	218
525 P. collybitus P. collybita	Chiffchaff Chiffchaff Leaf-Warbler Brown Leaf-Warbler	37	218
526 P. sibilatrix P. sibilator	Wood Warbler Wood Leaf-Warbler	37	219
527 P. borealis	Arctic Warbler Arctic Leaf-Warbler	37	219
528 P. trochiloides P. nitidus	Greenish Warbler Greenish Leaf-Warbler Dull-green Leaf-Warbler	37	220
529 P. tenellipes	Pale-legged Leaf-Warbler	37	220
530 P. occipitalis	Western Crowned Warbler Western Crowned Leaf-Warbler Large Crowned Leaf-Warbler	37	221
531 P. coronatus	Eastern Crowned Warbler Eastern Crowned Leaf-Warbler	37	221
532 P. inornatus	Yellow-browed Warbler Yellow-browed Leaf-Warbler Inornate Leaf-Warbler Plain Leaf-Warbler		
533 P. proregulus	Pallas's Warbler Pallas's Leaf-Warbler Yellow-rumped Leaf-Warbler	37	222
534 P. neglectus P. collybita	Plain Leaf-Warbler Plain Chiffchaff Plain Willow-Warbler	37	223
535 P. griseolus	Olivaceous Leaf-Warbler Sulphur-bellied Warbler	37	223
536 P. fuscatus	Dusky Leaf-Warbler Dusky Warbler	37	223
537 P. bonelli	Bonelli's Warbler Bonelli's Leaf-Warbler	—	—
538 P. subviridis	Brook's Leaf-Warbler Brook's Willow-Warbler	—	—
539 Herbivocula schwarzi Phylloscopus schwarzi	Radde's Warbler Thick-billed Leaf-Warbler Radde's Willow-Warbler	37	222
540 Cettia squameiceps	Stub-tailed Bush-Warbler Short-tailed Bush-Warbler Scaly-headed Bush-Warbler	37	224
541 C. diphone	Japanese Bush-Warbler Manchurian Bush-Warbler Bush Warbler	37	224
542 C. cetti	Cetti's Bush-Warbler Cetti's Warbler	37	224

		Plate	Range Map
543 Bradypterus thoracicus	Spotted Bush-Warbler	38	225
544 B. taczanowskia	Chinese Bush-Warbler	—	225
545 B. major	Large-billed Bush-Warbler	—	—
546 Acrocephalus melanopogon	Moustached Warbler Moustached Grasshopper-Warbler	38	225
547 Locustella fasciolata	Gray's Grasshopper-Warbler	38	226
548 L. fluviatilis	River Warbler River Grasshopper-Warbler	38	226
549 L. luscinioides	Savi's Warbler Savi's Grasshopper-Warbler	38	226
550 L. certhiola	Pallas's Grasshopper-Warbler	38	227
551 L. ochotensis	Middendorff's Grasshopper-Warbler	38	227
552 L. naevia	European Grasshopper-Warbler Grasshopper Warbler	38	228
553 L. lanceolata	Lanceolated Warbler Lanceolated Grasshopper-Warbler	38	228
554 Acrocephalus aedon	Thick-billed Reed-Warbler	38	229
555 A. arundinaceus	Great Reed-Warbler	38	229
556 A. scirpaceus	European Reed-Warbler Reed Warbler	38	230
557 A. palustris	Marsh Warbler Mimic Reed-Warbler	38	230
558 A. dumetorum	Blyth's Reed-Warbler	38	231
559 A. agricola	Paddyfield Warbler Paddy Reed-Warbler	38	232
560 A. bistrigiceps	Black-browed Reed-Warbler	38	232
561 A. schoenobaenus	Sedge Warbler	38	233
562 A. paludicola	Aquatic Warbler	38	233
563 Hippolais icterina	Icterine Warbler	37	234
564 H. languida	Upcher's Warbler	37	234
565 H. caligata	Booted Warbler	37	235
566 H. pallida	Olivaceous Warbler	37	235
567 H. olivetorum	Olive-tree Warbler	37	—
568 Sylvia hortensis	Orphean Warbler	36	236
569 S. borin	Garden Warbler	36	236
570 S. nisoria	Barred Warbler	36	237
571 S. atricapilla	Blackcap Black-capped Warbler	36	237
572 S. communis	Greater Whitethroat Whitethroat	36	238
573 S. curruca	Lesser Whitethroat	36	238
574 S. nana	Desert Warbler	36	239
575 S. mystacea	Ménétries's Warbler	36	240
576 S. melanocephala	Sardinian Warbler	—	—
577 Scotocerca inquieta	Streaked Scrub Warbler Scrub Warbler	36	240
578 Regulus regulus	Goldcrest	41	241
579 R. ignicapillus	Firecrest	41	241
580 Leptopoecile sophiae	Severtzov's Tit-Warbler	41	241

Flycatchers: Muscicapidae

581 Muscicapa striata	Spotted Flycatcher Brown-streaked Flycatcher	39	242
582 M. sibirica	Dark-sided Flycatcher Sooty Flycatcher	39	242
583 M. griseisticta	Gray-streaked Flycatcher	39	243
584 M. latirostris	Asian Brown Flycatcher Brown Flycatcher	39	243
585 M. ruficauda	Rufous-tailed Flycatcher	39	243
586 M. hypoleuca Ficedula hypoleuca	Pied Flycatcher	39	244
587 M. albicollis Ficedula albicollis	Collared Flycatcher	39	244
588 M. parva Ficedula parva	Red-throated Flycatcher Red-breasted Flycatcher	39	245
589 M. mugimaki Ficedula mugimaki	Mugimaki Flycatcher	39	245
590 M. narcissina Ficedula narcissina	Narcissus Flycatcher	39	246
591 M. cyanomelana Cyanoptila cyanomelana	Blue-and-white Flycatcher	39	246
592 Terpsiphone paradisi	Asian Paradise-Flycatcher Paradise Flycatcher	39	246
593 T. atrocaudata	Japanese Paradise-Flycatcher	—	—

Tits: Paradidae

594 Parus major	Great Tit	40	247
595 P. cyanus	Azure Tit	40	248
596 P. caeruleus	Blue Tit	40	248
597 P. varius	Varied Tit	40	247
598 P. ater	Coal Tit	40	249
599 P. rufonuchalis	Rufous-naped Tit Simla Crested Tit	40	249
600 P. cristatus	Crested Tit Northern Crested Tit	40	249
601 P. palustris	Marsh Tit	40	250
602 P. montanus	Willow Tit	40	250
603 P. cinctus	Siberian Tit Gray-headed Chickadee	40	251
604 P. lugubris	Sombre Tit	40	251
605 Remiz pendulinus	Eurasian Penduline-Tit Penduline Tit	41	251

Nuthatches: Sittidae

606 Sitta europaea	Eurasian Nuthatch Nuthatch	41	252
607 S. kruperi S. canadensis	Kruper's Nuthatch	41	252
608 S. tephronota	Greater Rock Nuthatch Eastern Rock Nuthatch	41	253
609 S. neumayer	Lesser Rock Nuthatch Western Rock Nuthatch Neumayer's Nuthatch	41	253

		Plate	Range Map
WALLCREEPER: TICHODROMA			
610 Tichodroma muraria	Wallcreeper	41	254
TREECREEPERS: CERTHIIDAE			
611 Certhia familiaris	Northern Treecreeper Tree Creeper Brown Creeper	41	255
612 C. brachydactyla	Short-toed Treecreeper	41	255
613 C. himalayana	Himalayan Treecreeper	41	255
WHITE-EYE: ZOSTEROPIDAE			
614 Zosterops erythropleura	Chestnut-flanked White-eye	37	254
ACCENTORS: PRUNELLIDAE			
615 Prunella modularis	Dunnock Hedge Accentor Hedge Sparrow	33	256
616 P. rubida	Japanese Accentor	33	256
617 P. atrogularis	Black-throated Accentor	33	256
618 P. montanella	Siberian Accentor	33	257
619 P. fulvescens	Brown Accentor	33	257
620 P. ocularis	Radde's Accentor	—	258
621 P. collaris	Alpine Accentor	33	258
622 P. himalayana	Himalayan Accentor	33	258
BUNTINGS: EMBERIZIDAE			
623 Emberiza calandra	Corn Bunting	42	259
624 E. citrinella	Yellowhammer	42	259
625 E. leucocephala	Pine Bunting	43	260
626 E. melanocephala	Black-headed Bunting	42	260
627 E. bruniceps	Red-headed Bunting	42	261
628 E. rutila	Chestnut Bunting	42	261
629 E. aureola	Yellow-breasted Bunting	42	262
630 E. elegans	Yellow-throated Bunting	42	262
631 E. chrysophrys	Yellow-browed Bunting	42	263
632 E. spodocephala	Black-faced Bunting	42	264
633 E. stewarti	White-capped Bunting	43	264
634 E. hortulana	Ortolan Bunting	42	265
635 E. buchanani	Gray-necked Bunting	42	265
636 E. cia	Rock Bunting	43	266
637 E. cioides	Meadow Bunting	43	266
638 E. jankowskii	Jankowski's Bunting	43	267
639 E. fucata	Chestnut-eared Bunting Gray-headed Bunting	43	267
640 E. rustica	Rustic Bunting	43	268
641 E. pusilla	Little Bunting	43	268
642 E. tristrami	Tristram's Bunting	43	263
643 E. yessoensis	Japanese Reed Bunting	43	269
644 E. schoeniclus	Northern Reed Bunting Reed Bunting	43	270

645 E. pallasi	Pallas's Reed Bunting	43	269
646 E. variabilis	Japanese Gray Bunting	42	270
647 E. cirlus	Cirl Bunting	42	—
648 E. caesia	Cretzschmar's Bunting	42	—
649 Calcarius lapponicus Emberiza lapponica	Lapland Longspur Lapland Bunting	43	271
650 Plectrophenax nivalis	Snow Bunting	29	271
651 Junco hyemalis	Northern Junco Dark-eyed Junco Slate-colored Junco Oregon Junco	43	—
652 Pipilo fuscus P. hyperboreus	Brown Towhee	—	—
653 Zonotrichia atricapilla	Golden-crowned Sparrow	—	—
654 Passerculus sandwichensis	Savannah Sparrow	—	—
655 Spizella arborea	Winter Sparrow American Tree Sparrow Tree Sparrow	—	—
656 Zonotrichia iliaca Passerella iliaca	Fox Sparrow	—	—

Parulas: Parulidae

657 Dendroica coronata	Yellow-rumped Warbler Yellow-rumped Parula Myrtle Warbler Audubon's Warbler	—	—
658 Seiurus noveboracensis	Northern Waterthrush	—	—

Finches: Fringillidae

659 Coccothraustes coccothraustes	Hawfinch Short-tailed Hawfinch	47	272
660 Mycerobas carnipes	White-winged Grosbeak White-winged Hawfinch	47	272
661 Eophona personata Coccothraustes personatus	Japanese Grosbeak Japanese Hawfinch	47	273
662 E. migratoria Coccothraustes migratorius	Yellow-billed Grosbeak Black-tailed Hawfinch	47	273
663 Chloris chloris Carduelis chloris	European Greenfinch Greenfinch	44	274
664 C. sinica Carduelis sinica	Oriental Greenfinch	44	274
665 Carduelis carduelis C. caniceps	Eurasian Goldfinch Goldfinch Gray-headed Goldfinch	44	275
666 Spinus spinus Carduelis spinus	Eurasian Siskin Siskin	44	275
667 Acanthis cannabina Carduelis cannabina	Linnet Northern Linnet	44	276
668 A. flavirostris Carduelis flavirostris	Twite	44	276
669 A. flammea Carduelis flammea	Common Redpoll Lesser Redpoll Redpoll	44	277

		Plate	Range Map
670 A. hornemannii Carduelis hornemannii C. flammea	Hoary Redpoll Arctic Redpoll	44	277
671 Serinus pusillus	Red-fronted Serin Gold-fronted Serin	44	278
672 S. serinus S. canaria	European Serin Serin	44	278
673 Uragus sibiricus	Long-tailed Rosefinch	45	279
674 Rhodopechys githagineus Bucanetes githagineus	Trumpeter Finch Trumpeter Desert-Finch Trumpeter Bullfinch	46	279
675 R. sanguinea	Crimson-winged Finch Crimson-winged Desert-Finch	46	280
676 Rhodospiza obsoleta	Black-billed Desert-Finch Desert Finch	46	280
677 Pyrrhula pyrrhula	Northern Bullfinch Bullfinch	45	280
678 Carpodacus rubicilla	Great Rosefinch Spot-crowned Rosefinch	45	281
679 C. rhodochlamys	Red-mantled Rosefinch	45	281
680 C. roseus	Pallas's Rosefinch Siberian Rosefinch	45	282
681 C. erythrinus	Scarlet Rosefinch Scarlet Grosbeak	45	282
682 C. puniceus	Red-breasted Rosefinch	45	283
683 Pinicola enucleator	Pine Rosefinch Pine Grosbeak	45	283
684 Loxia leucoptera	White-winged Crossbill Two-barred Crossbill	45	284
685 L. curvirostra	Red Crossbill Fir Crossbill Scottish Crossbill Crossbill	45	284
686 L. pytyopsittacus	Parrot Crossbill Pine Crossbill	45	284
687 Fringilla coelebs	Chaffinch Common Chaffinch	44	285
688 F. montifringilla	Brambling	44	285
689 Leucosticte nemoricola	Hodgson's Rosy-Finch	46	286
690 L. brandti	Brandt's Rosy-Finch	46	286
691 L. arctoa	Arctic Rosy-Finch Gray-crowned Rosy-Finch	46	287

WEAVERS: PLOCEIDAE

		Plate	Range Map
692 Montifringilla nivalis	White-winged Snow-Finch Snow Finch	46	287
693 Pyrgilauda davidiana Montifringilla davidiana	Pere David's Snow-Finch Lesser Snow-Finch	46	288
694 P. theresae Montifringilla theresae	Theresa's Snow-Finch Bar-tailed Snow-Finch	46	—
695 Petronia petronia	Rock Petronia Rock Sparrow	46	288

696 P. brachydactyla	Pale Petronia Pale Rock Sparrow	46	288
697 Passer domesticus	House Sparrow English Sparrow	46	289
698 P. hispaniolensis	Spanish Sparrow Black-striped Sparrow	46	289
699 P. ammodendri	Saxaul Sparrow	46	290
700 P. montanus	Tree Sparrow Eurasian Tree Sparrow	46	291
701 P. rutilans	Cinnamon Sparrow	46	290
702 P. simplex	Desert Sparrow	46	291

STARLINGS: STURNIDAE

703 Sturnus vulgaris	Northern Starling Eurasian Starling Common Starling Starling	47	292
704 S. roseus Pastor roseus	Rose-colored Starling Rosy Pastor	47	292
705 Spodiopsar cineraceus Sturnus cineraceus	White-cheeked Starling Gray Starling	47	293
706 Acridotheres tristis	Indian Myna Common Mynah	47	293
707 Sturnia sturnina Sturnus sturnininus	Daurian Starling Purple-backed Starling	47	294
708 S. philippensis Sturnus philippensis	Red-cheeked Starling	47	294
709 Temenuchus pagodarum Sturnus pagodarum	Brahminy Myna Black-crowned Starling	—	—

TROUPIALS: ICTERIDAE

710 Euphagus carolinus	Rusty Blackbird	—	—

ORIOLES: ORIOLIDAE

711 Oriolus oriolus	European Golden Oriole Golden Oriole	47	295
712 O. chinensis	Black-naped Oriole	47	295

DRONGOS: DICRURIDAE

713 Dicrurus macrocercus	Black Drongo Asian Farm Drongo	47	—
714 Chibia hottentotta Dicrurus Hottentottus	Spangled Drongo Hair-crested Drongo	47	—

CORVIDS: CORVIDAE

715 Corvus corax	Northern Raven Raven Common Raven	48	296
716 C. corone C. cornix	Eurasian Crow Hooded Crow Carrion Crow	48	297
717 C. macrorhynchos	Large-billed Crow Jungle Crow	48	296

		Plate	Range Map
718 C. frugilegus	Eurasian Rook Rook	48	298
719 Coloeus monedula Corvus monedula C. dauricus	Jackdaw Daurian Jackdaw	48	298
720 Pyrrhocorax pyrrhocorax	Red-billed Chough Long-billed Chough Chough	48	299
721 P. graculus	Alpine Chough Short-billed Chough	48	299
722 Nucifraga caryocatactes	Spotted Nutcracker Eurasian Nutcracker Nutcracker	48	300
723 Podoces panderi	Pander's Ground-Jay	47	300
724 P. hendersoni	Henderson's Ground-Jay	47	301
725 Pica pica	Black-billed Magpie Magpie	48	302
726 Cyanopica cyana	Azure-winged Magpie	48	302
727 Garrulus glandarius	Eurasian Jay White-rumped Jay Jay	48	301
728 Cractes infausus Perisoreus infaustus	Siberian Jay	48	301

INDEX OF GENERA

THIS is an index of each genus of bird found in the U.S.S.R. The genus is the first of the two names in binomial nomenclature. For example, the Alpine Swift's scientific name is *Apus melba*. In this index *Apus* is followed by the numbers 381-384. These numbers refer to numbers used in the Cross-Reference List, and to the same numbers used preceding each species account in the text. The Alpine Swift is number 382.

Acanthis 667-670
Accipiter 121-124
Acridotheres 706
Acrocephalus 546, 554-562
Actitis 258
Aegithalos 523
Aegolius 369
Aegypius 139
Aethia 329-331
Aix 89
Alauda 410-411
Alca 321
Alcedo 388
Alectoris 170
Alle 322
Ammomanes 423
Ammoperdix 169
Anas 77-88
Anser 62-69
Anthropoides 187
Anthus 434-441
Apus 381-384
Aquila 130-134
Ardea 35-37
Ardeola 41-44
Arenaria 226-227
Asio 366-367
Athene 370
Aythya 95-99

Bombycilla 462-463
Bonasa 167
Botaurus 49
Brachyramphus 325
Bradypterus 543-545
Branta 70-73
Bubo 360
Bubulcus 41
Bucanetes 674
Bucephala 105-107
Burhinus 203
Butastur 129
Buteo 125-128
Butorides 44

Calandrella 414-417
Calcarius 649
Calidris 228-242
Capella 273-278

Caprimulgus 377-380
Carduelis 663-670
Carpodacus 678-682
Casmerodius 37
Catharacta 286
Catharus 480, 482
Cepphus 319-320
Cercotrichas 518
Cerorhinca 333
Certhia 611-613
Ceryle 391-392
Cettia 541-542
Chaimarrornis
Charadrius 211-219
Chettusia 221-222
Chibia 714
Chlamydotis 189
Chlidonias 309-311
Chloris 663-664
Ciconia 55-56
Cinclus 465-466
Circaetus 143
Circus 144-148
Clamator 358
Clangula 104
Coccothraustes 659, 661-662
Coloeus 719
Columba 341-346
Coracias 386
Corvus 715-719
Coturnicops 199
Coturnix 168
Cractes 728
Crex 195
Crocethia 238
Cuculus 353-357
Cursorius 204
Cyanopica 726
Cyanoptila 591
Cyclorrhynchus 332
Cygnus 58-61

Delichon 428
Dendrocopos 401-408
Dendroica 657
Dendronanthus 442
Dicrurus 713-714
Diomedea 14-16
Dryocopus 396

Egretta 37-41
Elanus 149
Emberiza 623-649
Enicurus 517
Eophona 661-662
Eremophila 424
Erithacus 507-515
Erythropygia 518
Euphagus 710
Eurynorhynchus 246
Eurystomus 387

Falcipennis 166
Falco 150-159
Ficedula 586-590
Francolinus 173
Fratercula 334-335
Fregata 34
Fringilla 687-688
Fulica 191
Fulmarus 10

Galerida 413
Gallicrex 201
Gallinago 273-279
Gallinula 193
Gallulax 519
Garrulus 727
Gavia 1-4
Gelochelidon 317
Glareola 205-207
Glaucidium 371
Gorsachius 50
Grus 180-186
Gypaetus 138
Gyps 140-142

Haematopus 281
Halcyon 389-390
Haliaeetus 118-120
Herbivocula 539
Heteroscelus 257
Hieraaetus 135-136
Himantopus 270
Hippolais 563-567
Hirandapus 385
Hirundo 425-427, 431
Histrionicus 103
Hoplopterus 223-224
Hydrobates 23
Hydroprocne 318
Hypocolius 464
Hypsipetes 450

Ibidorhyncha
Irania 516

Iridoprocne 433
Ixobrychus 46-48

Junco 651
Jynx 407

Ketupa 361

Lagopus 160-161
Lanius 452-461
Larus 287-308
Leptopoecile 580
Leucosticte 689-691
Limicola 245
Limnodromus 247-248
Limosa 260-261
Lobipes 268
Lobivanellus 223
Locustella 547-553
Loxia 684-686
Lullula 412
Lunda 336
Luscinia 507-513
Lymnocryptes 279
Lyrurus 162-163

Melanitta 100-102
Melanocorypha 418-422
Mergus 108-111
Merops 393-394
Microsarcops 225
Microscelis 450
Milvus 116-117
Monticola 484-486
Montifringilla 692-694
Motacilla 443-448
Muscicapa 581-591
Mycerobas 660
Myophoneus 483

Neophron 137
Netta 94
Ninox 368
Nipponia 53
Nucifraga 722
Numenius 262-267
Nyctea 359
Nycticorax 45

Oceanodroma 11-13
Oenanthe 487-493
Olor 58
Oriolus 711-712
Otis 188-190
Otus 362-365
Oxyura 112

Pagophila 287
Pandion 113
Panurus 520
Paradoxornis 522
Parus 594-604

Passer 697-702
Passerculus 654
Passerella 656
Pastor 704
Pelecanus 24-25
Perdix 171-172
Pericrocotus 449
Perisoreus 728
Pernis 114-115
Petrochelidon 432
Petronia 695-696
Phalacrocorax 26-31
Phalaropus 268-269
Phasianus 179
Philomachus 244
Phoenicopterus 57
Phoenicurus 500-505
Phylloscopus 524-539
Pica 724-725
Picoides 400-406
Picus 397-399
Pinicola 683
Pipilo 652
Platalea 51
Plautus 322
Plectrophenax 650
Plegadis 52
Pluvialis 208-210
Podiceps 5-9
Podoces 723-724
Polysticta 93
Porphyrio 192
Porzana 196-200
Procellaria 21
Prunella 615-622
Pseudogyps 142
Pseudototanus 255
Pterocles 337-338
Pterodroma 22
Ptyonoprogne 431
Puffinus 17-21
Pycnonotus 451
Pyrgilauda 693-694
Pyrrhocorax 720-721
Pyrrhula 677

Rallina 200
Rallus 194
Recurvirostra 271
Regulus 578-579
Remiz 605
Rhodopechys 674-675
Rhodospiza 676
Rhodostethia 290
Rhyacornis 506
Riparia 429-430
Rissa 288-289
Rostratula 282
Rufibranta 72

Saxicola 494-497
Scolopax 272
Scotocerca 577
Seiurus 658
Serinus 671-672
Sitta 606-609
Somateria 90-93
Sphenurus 352
Spinus 666
Spizella 655
Spodiopsar 705
Squatarola 208
Stercorarius 283-286
Sterna 309-318
Streptopelia 347-351
Strix 373-375
Sturnia 707-708
Sturnus 704-709
Sula 32-33
Surnia 372
Suthora 521
Sylvia 568-576
Synthliboramphus 327-328
Syrrhaptes 339-340

Tachybaptus 9
Tachycineta 433
Tadorna 74-76
Tarsiger 498
Temenuchus 709
Terekia 259
Terpsiphone 592-593
Tetrao 164-165
Tetraogallus 174-178
Tetrastes 167
Tetrax 190
Threskiornis 54
Tichodroma 610
Treron 352
Tringa 249-257
Troglodytes 467
Tryngites 243
Turdus 468-481
Turnix 202
Tyto 376

Upupa 395
Uragus 673
Uria 323-324

Vanellus 220-225

Xema 291
Xenus 259

Yungipicus 407-408

Zonotrichia 653, 656
Zoothera 468-469
Zosterops 614

INDEX OF RUSSIAN NAMES

Aleutskaya Krachka 314
Alpiyskaya Galka 721
Alpiyskaya Zavirushka 621
Altaysky Ular 177
Amerikansky Bekasovidny Veretennik 247
Amerikansky Pepelny Ulit 257
Amursky Sviristel 463
Amursky Volchok 47
Archyovy Dubonos 660
Avdotka 203
Aziatsky Bekas 276
Aziatsky Bekasovidny Veretennik 248

Baloban 151
Begunok 204
Bekas 273
Belaya Chayka 287
Belaya Kuropatka 160
Belaya Lazorevka 595
Belaya Sova 359
Belaya Tryasoguzka 447
Belobrovik 473
Belobryukhy Ryabok 338
Belobryukhy Strizh 382
Belobryushka 332
Beloglazka 614
Beloglazy Nyrok 96
Belogolovy Sip 140
Belogrudy Golub 343
Belokhvostaya Pigalitsa 222
Belokhvosty Pesochnik 233
Beloklyuvaya Gagara 3
Belokrylaya Krachka 310
Belokrylaya Tsaplya 43
Belokryly Dyatel 402
Belokryly Klyost 684
Belokryly Pogonysh 199
Belokryly Zhavoronok 419
Beloloby Gus 67
Belonozhka 517
Beloplechy Orlan 120
Belopoyasnichny Strizh 383
Beloschokaya Kazarka 71
Beloschokaya Krachka 311
Beloshapochnaya Gorikhvostka 499
Beloshapochnaya Ovsyanka 625
Beloshey 63
Belospinny Dyatel 404
Belousaya Slavka 575
Belozoby Drozd 478
Bely Aist 55
Bely Gus 65
Berdov Pesochnik 235

Beregovushka 429
Beringov Baklan 28
Berkut 130
Berov Nyrok 97
Blednaya Peresmeshka 566
Blednaya Zavirushka 619
Blednonogaya Penochka 529
Bledny Drozd 477
Bolotnaya Kamyshovka 557
Bolotnaya Sova 367
Bolotny Lun 148
Bolshaya Belaya Tsaplya 37
Bolshaya Chechevitsa 678
Bolshaya Gorlitsa 348
Bolshaya Konyuga 329
Bolshaya Sinitsa 594
Bolsheklyuvaya Vorona 717
Bolshoy Baklan 26
Bolshoy Chernogolovy Dubonos 661
Bolshoy Kozodoy 379
Bolshoy Krokhal 111
Bolshoy Kronshnep 262
Bolshoy Ostrokryly Dyatel 408
Bolshoy Pesochnik 240
Bolshoy Podorlik 133
Bolshoy Pogonysh 200
Bolshoy Skalisty Popolzen 608
Bolshoy Ulit 251
Bolshoy Veretennik 260
Bormotushka 565
Borodach 138
Borodataya Neyasyt 375
Bulanaya Sovka 364
Bulany Kozodoy 378
Bulany Vyurok 676
Buraya Olyapka 466
Buraya Penochka 536
Burgomistr 298
Burogolovaya Chayka 302
Burogolovaya Gaichka 602
Burokrylaya Rzhanka 210
Bury Golub 344

Chaykonosaya Krachka 317
Cheglok 154
Chegrava 318
Cheornosheynaya Poganka 8
Chernobryukhy Ryabok 337
Chernogolovaya Chayka 304
Chernogolovaya Gaichka 601
Chernogolovaya Ivolga 712
Chernogolovaya Ovsyanka 626
Chernogolovy Chekan 495
Chernogolovy Khokhotun 300

Chernogolovy Popolzen 607
Chernogorlaya Zavirushka 617
Chernogrudaya Krasnosheyka 510
Chernogrudy Vorobey 698
Chernokhvostaya Chayka 294
Chernoloby Sorokoput 454
Chernosheynaya Kamenka 490
Chernozobaya Gagara 2
Chernozobik 229
Chernysh 249
Cheshuychaty Dyatel 399
Cheshuychaty Krokhal 110
Chibis 220
Chirok-svistunok 79
Chirok-treskunok 86
Chistik 319
Chizh 666
Chomga 5
Chyornaya Kamenka 493
Chyornaya Kazarka 70
Chyornaya Krachka 309
Chyornaya Kryakva 78
Chyorny Aist 56
Chyorny Chekan 496
Chyorny Drozd 479
Chyorny Grif 139
Chyorny Korshun 116
Chyorny Strizh 381
Chyorny Zhavoronok 418
Chyorny Zhuravl 183

Dalnevostochny Kronshnep 264
Daursky Zhuravl 182
Derbnik 155
Derevenskaya Lastochka 425
Deryaba 471
Dikusha 166
Dlinnokhvostaya Neyasyt 374
Dlinnokhvostaya Sinitsa 523
Dlinnokhvosty Pomornik 284
Dlinnokhvosty Snegir 673
Dlinnokhvosty Sorokoput 456
Dlinnoklyuvy Pyzhik 325
Dlinnonosy Krokhal 109
Dlinnopaly Pesochnik 232
Domovoy Sych 370
Domovoy Vorobey 697
Drevesnaya Tryasoguzka 442
Drofa 188
Drozd Naumanna 474
Drozdovidnaya Kamyshovka 555
Dubrovnik 629
Dupel 274
Dutysh 236
Dvupyatnisty Zhavoronok 422

Fazan 179
Fifi 250

Filin 360
Flamingo 57

Gaga-grebyonushka 91
Gagarka 321
Galka 719
Galstuchnik 211
Garshnep 279
Gimalayskaya Pishchukha 613
Gimalayskaya Zavirushka 622
Gimalaysky Ular 176
Gimalaysky Vyurok 689
Glukhar 164
Glukhaya Kukushka 354
Glupysh 10
Gogol 105
Golubaya Soroka 727
Gorikhvostka-chernushka 501
Gornaya Chechetka 668
Gornaya Ovsyanka 636
Gornaya Tryasoguzka 446
Gorny Dupel 277
Gorny Gus 64
Gorny Konyok 441
Gorodskaya Lastochka 428
Grach 718
Gryazovik 245
Gumennik 69

Iglokhvosty Strizh 385
Iglonogaya Sova 368
Indiyskaya Kamyshovka 559
Indiyskaya Kukushka 356
Indiyskaya Penochka 534
Indiysky Zhulan 460
Ipatka 335
Iranskaya Penochka 534
Islandsky Pesochnik 239
Ivolga 711

Kamenka-plyasunya 491
Kamenny Glukhar 165
Kamenny Vorobey 695
Kamenushka 103
Kamnesharka 226
Kamyshnitsa 193
Kamyshovaya Ovsyanka 644
Kamyshovka-barsuchok 561
Kanadsky Zhuravl 181
Kanareechny Vyurok 672
Kanyuk 125
Karavayka 52
Kasatka 81
Kaspiysky Ular 175
Kaspiysky Zuyok 217
Kavkazky Teterev 163
Kavkazky Ular 174
Kedrovka 722
Keklik 170

Khodulochnik 270
Khokhlataya Chernet 98
Khokhlataya Sinitsa 600
Khokhlaty Baklan 30
Khokhlaty Zhavoronok 413
Khoklaty Osoed 115
Khrustan 219
Kitayskaya Zelenushka 664
Kitaysky Volchok 48
Klinokhvosty Sorokoput 453
Klintukh 345
Kloktun 80
Klusha 295
Klushitsa 720
Klyost-sosnovik 686
Klyost-yelovik 685
Kolchataya Gorlitsa 349
Kolpitsa 51
Konoplyanka 667
Konyuga-kroshka 331
Korolevsky Vyurok 671
Korolkovaya Penochka 533
Korostel 195
Korotkokhvostka 540
Korotkokhvosty Pomornik 283
Korotkoklyuvy Pyzhik 326
Korotkokrylaya Shirokokhvostka 541
Korotkopalaya Pishchukha 612
Korotkopaly Vorobey 696
Krapivnik 457
Krasavka 187
Krasnobryukhaya Gorikhvostka 504
Krasnogolovy Korolyok 579
Krasnogolovy Nyrok 95
Krasnogolovy Sorokoput 457
Krasnokryly Chechevichnik 675
Krasnolitsy Baklan 29
Krasnonogaya Govorushka 289
Krasnonogy Ibis 53
Krasnonosy Nyrok 94
Krasnosheynaya Poganka 7
Krasnospinnaya Gorikhvostka 502
Krasnoukhaya Ovsyanka 637
Krasnozobaya Gagara 1
Krasnozobaya Kazarka 72
Krasnozobik 228
Krasnozoby Konyok 440
Krasny Korshun 117
Krasny Vyurok 682
Krechet 153
Krechetka 221
Kronshnep-malyutka 266
Kruglonosy Plavunchik 268
Kryakva 77
Kudryavy Pelikan 24
Kuksha 728
Kulik-lopaten 246
Kulik-soroka 281
Kulik-vorobey 230

Kumay 141
Kurgannik 128
Kvakva 45

Laplandsky Podorozhnik 649
Lazorevka 596
Lebed-klikun 58
Lebed-shipun 60
Lesnaya Zavirushka 615
Lesnoy Dupel 275
Lesnoy Kamenny Drozd 486
Lesnoy Konyok 436
Lugovaya Tirkushka 205
Lugovoy Chekan 494
Lugovoy Konyok 439
Lugovoy Lun 145
Lutok 108
Lysukha 191
Lyurik 322

Malaya Belaya Tsaplya 38
Malaya Chayka 305
Malaya Gorlitsa 350
Malaya Konyuga 330
Malaya Krachka 315
Malaya Kukushka 355
Malaya Lastochka 430
Malaya Mukholovka 588
Malaya Pestrogrudka 543
Malaya Poganka 9
Maly Baklan 31
Maly Chernogolovy Dubonos 662
Maly Drozd 480
Maly Lebed 59
Maly Ostrokryly Dyatel 407
Maly Perepelyatnik 123
Maly Podorlik 134
Maly Pogonysh 197
Maly Polevoy Zhavoronok 411
Maly Pyostry Dyatel 406
Maly Skalisty Popolzen 609
Maly Skvorets 707
Maly Strizh 384
Maly Veretennik 261
Maly Zhavoronok 416
Maly Zuyok 212
Mandarinka 89
Mayna 706
Moevka 288
Mogilnik 131
Mokhnonogy Kurgannik 127
Mokhnonogy Sych 369
Mongolskaya Saksaulnaya Soyka 724
Mongolsky Zemlyanoy Vorobey 693
Mongolsky Zhavoronok 420
Mongolsky Zuyok 215
Morodunka 259
Morskaya Chayka 292
Morskaya Chernet 99

Morskoy Golubok 306
Morskoy Pesochnik 241
Morskoy Zuyok 214
Moryanka 104
Moskovka 598
Mramorny Chirok 85
Mukholovka-belosheyka 587
Mukholovka-kasatka 582
Mukholovka-pestrushka 586

Nitekhvostaya Lastochka 427

Obyknovennaya Chechetka 669
Obyknovennaya Chechevitsa 681
Obyknovennaya Gaga 90
Obyknovennaya Gorikhvostka 500
Obyknovennaya Gorlitsa 347
Obyknovennaya Kamenka 487
Obyknovennaya Kukushka 353
Obyknovennaya Ovsyanka 624
Obyknovennaya Pishchukha 611
Obyknovenny Dubonos 659
Obyknovenny Kozodoy 377
Obyknovenny Popolzen 606
Obyknovenny Skvorets 703
Obyknovenny Solovey 508
Obyknovenny Sverchok 552
Obyknovenny Zimorodok 388
Ochkovaya Gaga 92
Ochkovy Chistik 320
Ogar 75
Okhotsky Sverchok 551
Okhotsky Ulit 255
Olyapka 465
Orlan-belokhvost 118
Orlan-dolgokhvost 119
Oryol-karlik 136
Osheynikovaya Sovka 363
Osheynikovaya Ovsyanka 639
Osoed 114
Ostrokhvosty Pesochnik 237
Ovsyanka Kroshka 641
Ovsyanka Remez 640
Ovsyanka Styuarta 633.
Ovsyanka Yankovskovo 638
Ozernaya Chayka 301

Pastushok 194
Peganka 74
Pegy Lun 147
Penochka-talovka 527
Penochka-tenkovka 525
Penochka-treshchotka 526
Penochka-vesnichka 524
Penochka-zarnichka 532
Perepel 168
Perepelyatnik 124
Pereponchatopaly Pesochnik 234
Perevozchik 258

Peschanka 238
Pesochnik-krasnosheyka 231
Pestrogolovaya Kamyshovka 560
Pestrogrudaya Mukholovka 583
Pestrogrudaya Zavirushka 620
Pestronosaya Krachka 316
Pevchaya Slavka 568
Pevchy Drozd 472
Pevchy Sverchok 550
Piskulka 68
Pleshanka 489
Ploskonosy Plavunchik 269
Pogonysh 196
Pogonysh-kroshka 198
Polarnaya Ovsyanka 645
Polevoy Konyok 435
Polevoy Lun 144
Polevoy Vorobey 700
Polevoy Zhavoronok 410
Polosataya Timeliya 519
Porucheynik 254
Prosyanka 623
Punochka 650
Pustynnaya Kamenka 488
Pustynnaya Kuropatka 169
Pustynnaya Peresmeshka 564
Pustynnaya Slavka 574
Pustynny Snegir 674
Pustynny Vorobey 702
Pustynny Zhavoronok 423
Pyatnisty Konyok 437
Pyatnisty Sverchok 553
Pyostry Drozd 468
Pyostry Dyatel 401
Pyostry Kamenny Drozd 484

Raspisnaya Sinichka 580
Rayskaya Mukholovka 592
Rechnaya Krachka 312
Rechnoy Sverchok 548
Reliktovaya Chayka 303
Remez 605
Rogaty Zhavoronok 424
Rozovaya Chayka 290
Rozovaya Chechevitsa 679
Rozovy Pelikan 25
Rozovy Skvorets 704
Ryabchik 167
Ryabinnik 470
Rybny Filin 361
Ryzhaya Ovsyanka 628
Ryzhaya Tsaplya 36
Ryzhekhvostaya Mukholovka 585
Ryzhepoyasnichnaya Lastochka 426
Ryzhesheynaya Ovsyanka 643
Ryzhesheynaya Sinitsa 599
Ryzhy Vorobey 701

Sadovaya Kamyshovka 558

Sadovaya Ovsyanka 634
Sadovaya Slavka 569
Sadzha 339
Saksaulnaya Soyka 723
Saksaulny Vorobey 699
Sapsan 150
Savka 112
Sedogolovaya Gorikhvostka 505
Sedogolovaya Ovsyanka 632
Sedoy Dyatel 398
Seraya Kuropatka 171
Seraya Mukholovka 581
Seraya Neyasyt 373
Seraya Slavka 572
Seraya Tsaplya 35
Seraya Utka 82
Serebristaya Chayka 296
Serogolovaya Gaichka 603
Serokrylaya Chayka 299
Seroshchyokaya Poganka 6
Serpoklyuv 280
Sery Gus 66
Sery Lichinkoed 449
Sery Skvorets 705
Sery Sorokoput 452
Sery Zhavoronok 415
Sery Zhuravl 180
Severnaya Kachurka 11
Shchegól 665
Shchur 683
Shchyógol 253
Shilokhvost 84
Shiloklyuvka 271
Shirokoklyuvaya Mukholovka 584
Shirokokrylaya Kukushka 357
Shirokonoska 87
Shirokorot 387
Sibirskaya Chechevitsa 680
Sibirskaya Gaga 93
Sibirskaya Gorikhvostka 503
Sibirskaya Pestrogrudka 544
Sibirskaya Zavirushka 618
Sibirsky Drozd 469
Sibirsky Konyok 438
Sibirsky Pepelny Ulit 256
Sibirsky Vyurok 691
Sinaya Mukholovka 591
Sinaya Ptitsa 483
Sinekhvostka 498
Singa 101
Siny Kamenny Drozd 485
Siny Solovey 512
Sipukha 376
Siriysky Dyatel 403
Sizaya Chayka 297
Sizaya Kachurka 13
Sizovoronka 386
Sizy Drozd 476
Sizy Golub 341

Skalistaya Lastochka 431
Skalistaya Ovsyanka 635
Skopa 113
Skototserka 577
Slavka-chernogolovka 571
Slavka-melnichek 573
Snegir 677
Snezhny Vyurok 692
Solonchakovy Zhavoronok 414
Solovey-belosheyka 516
Solovey-krasnosheyka 509
Solovey-svistun 511
Solovinaya Shirokokhvostka 542
Soloviny Sverchok 549
Soroka 725
Soyka 727
Splyushka 362
Sredizemnomorskaya Gaichka 604
Sredizemnomorsky Sokol 152
Sredny Kronshnep 263
Sredny Pomornik 285
Sredny Pyostry Dyatel 405
Starik 327
Stenolaz 610
Stepnaya Pustelga 158
Stepnaya Tirkushka 206
Stepnoy Konyok 434
Stepnoy Lun 146
Stepnoy Oryol 132
Stepnoy Zhavoronok 421
Sterkh 184
Stervyatnik 137
Strepet 190
Sukhonos 62
Sultanka 192
Sutora 521
Svetlogolovaya Penochka 531
Sviristel 462
Sviristelevy Sorokoput 464
Sviyaz 83
Sych-vorobey 371

Taezhnaya Mukholovka 589
Taezhnaya Ovsyanka 642
Taezhny Sverchok 547
Temnozoby Drozd 475
Teterev 162
Teterevyatnik 121
Tibetskaya Sadzha 340
Tibetsky Ular 178
Tigrovy Sorokoput 458
Tikhookeanskaya Chayka 293
Tolstoklyuvaya Kayra 324
Tolstoklyuvaya Kamyshovka 554
Tolstoklyuvaya Penochka 539
Tolstoklyuvy Zuyok 216
Tonkoklyuvaya Kamyshovka 546
Tonkoklyuvaya Kayra 323
Tonkoklyuvy Kronshnep 265

Tonkoklyuvy Zhavoronok 417
Toporik 336
Travnik 252
Trostnikovaya Kamyshovka 556
Trostnikovaya Sutora 522
Tryokhpaly Dyatel 400
Tryokhpyorstka 202
Tugayny Solovey 518
Tuless 208
Tundryanaya Chechetka 670
Tundryanaya Kuropatka 161
Tupik 334
Tupik-nosorog 333
Turach 173
Turpan 100
Turukhtan 244
Tyuvik 122

Udod 395
Ukrashenny Chibis 223
Usataya Sinitsa 520
Ushastaya Sova 366
Ussuriyskaya Sovka 365
Ussuriysky Baklan 27
Ussuriysky Zuyok 213

Valdshnep 272
Varakushka 513
Vertisheyka 409
Vertlyavaya Kamyshovka 562
Vilokhvostaya Chayka 291
Vilokhvostaya Kachurka 12
Volchok 46
Voron 715
Vorona 716
Vostochnaya Tirkushka 207
Vostochny Zuyok 218
Vyakhir 346
Vyurok 688
Vyp 49

Yaponskaya Ovsyanka 646

Yaponskaya Sinitsa 597
Yaponskaya Zaryanka 515
Yaponskaya Zavirushka 616
Yaponsky Skvorets 708
Yaponsky Sorokoput 455
Yaponsky Zhuravl 185
Yastrebinaya Slavka 570
Yastrebinaya Sova 372
Yastrebny Oryol 135
Yastrebny Sarych 129
Yegipetskaya Tsaplya 41
Yula 412
Yuzhny Solovey 507

Zaryanka 514
Zelenokrylaya Penochka 530
Zelenushka 663
Zelyonaya Kvakva 44
Zelyonaya Penochka 528
Zelyonaya Peresmeshka 563
Zelyonaya Shchurka 394
Zelyony Dyatel 397
Zhelna 396
Zheltobrovaya Ovsyanka 631
Zheltogolovaya Tryasoguzka 445
Zheltogolovy Korolyok 578
Zheltogorlaya Ovsyanka 630
Zheltospinnaya Mukholovka 590
Zheltospinnaya Tryasoguzka 444
Zheltozobik 243
Zhemchuzhny Vyurok 690
Zholchnaya Ovsyanka 627
Zholtaya Tryasoguzka 443
Zholtaya Tsaplya 42
Zhulan 459
Zimnyak 126
Zlatoguzaya Kamenka 492
Zmeeyad 143
Zolotistaya Rzhanka 209
Zolotistaya Shchurka 393
Zyablik 687

Library of Congress Cataloging in Publication Data

Ptit͡sy SSSR. English.
A Field guide to birds of the USSR.

Translation of Ptit͡sy SSSR.
Bibliography: p.   Includes indexes.
1. Birds—Soviet Union—Identification.   I. Flint,
Vladimir Evgen'evich.   II. Title.   III. Title: Birds
of the USSR.   IV. Title: Birds of the U.S.S.R.
QL690.S65P7513   1983   598.2947   83-42558
ISBN 0-691-08244-8